Genetics of Industrial Microorganisms

Second International Symposium

President Professor G. PONTECORVO, FRS

Vice-President Professor J. A. ROPER

ORGANIZING COMMITTEE
Chairman   C. T. CALAM

Secretaries   A. FLEMING
K. SARGEANT

Treasurer   N. J. BUTLER

Editor-in-Chief   K. D. MACDONALD

Members   R. S. C. AYTOUN
C. BALL
J. D. BU'LOCK
D. J. COVE
J. P. R. HERRMANN
G. HOLT
D. A. HOPWOOD
J. S. HOUGH
M. D. LILLY
D. II. SHARP

Ladies Committee   Mrs D. ROPER

GIM 74

Second International Symposium on the Genetics of Industrial Microorganisms

Proceedings of a Symposium organized by the
Society of Chemical Industry, London, in
association with the Society for General
Microbiology and the Genetical Society, and in
cooperation with the International Committee
on Economic and Applied Microbiology of the
International Association of Microbiological
Societies. This Symposium was held in Sheffield,
25–31 August 1974.

edited by

K. D. MACDONALD
Microbiological Research Establishment
Porton Down, Salisbury, Wiltshire, England

1976

ACADEMIC PRESS

LONDON   NEW YORK   SAN FRANCISCO

A Subsidiary of Harcourt Brace Jovanovich, Publishers

Academic Press Inc. (London) Ltd
24–28 Oval Road
London NW1

US edition published by
Academic Press Inc.
111 Fifth Avenue,
New York, New York 10003

Library of Congress Catalog Card Number: 75–19659
ISBN: 0–12–464350–7

Printed in Great Britain by
Page Bros (Norwich) Ltd, Norwich

Contributors

E. P. ABRAHAM, *Sir William Dunn School of Pathology, University of Oxford, Oxford, England*

M. ALAČEVIĆ, *Institute of Biotechnology, Faculty of Technology, University of Zagreb, Yugoslavia*

S. I. ALIKHANIAN, *Institute of Genetics and Selection of Industrial Micro-organisms, Moscow, USSR*

K. ARAKI, *Tokyo Research Laboratory, Kyowa Hakko Kogyo Co., Ltd, Tokyo, Japan*

P. R. AVNER, *Department de Biologie Cellulaire, L'Institut Pasteur, 25 rue du Docteur Roux, Paris XV ^{eme} France*

J. L. AZEVEDO, *Institute of Genetics, University of São Paulo, Piracicaba, Brazil*

B. W. BAINBRIDGE, *Department of Microbiology, Queen Elizabeth College, London, England*

C. BALL, *Glaxo Laboratories Ltd, Ulverston, Cumbria, England*

R. BAUMANN, *Société d'Assistance Technique pour Produits, Nestlé SA, 1350 Orbe, Switzerland*

S. BAUMBERG, *Department of Genetics, University of Leeds, Leeds LS2 9JT, England*

V. BĚHAL, *Institute of Microbiology, Czechoslovak Academy of Sciences, Prague, Czechoslovakia*

M. BLUMAUEROVÁ, *Institute of Microbiology, Czechoslovak Academy of Sciences, Prague, Czechoslovakia*

K. F. BOTT, *Department of Bacteriology and Immunology, University of North Carolina, Chapel Hill, 27514, USA*

W. J. BRAMMAR, *Department of Molecular Biology, University of Edinburgh, King's Buildings, Edinburgh EH9 3JR, Scotland*

B. A. BRIDGES, *MRC Cell Mutation Unit, University of Sussex, Falmer, Brighton BN1 9QG, England*

J. D. BU'LOCK, *Microbial Chemistry Laboratory, Department of Chemistry, The University, Manchester, England*

C. T. CALAM, *Department of Biology, Liverpool Polytechnic, Byrom Street, Liverpool L3 3AF, England*

A. CARERE, *Istituto Superiore di Sanità, Roma, Italy*

J. ČÁSLAVSKÁ, *Institute of Microbiology, Czechoslovak Academy of Sciences, Prague, Czechoslovakia*

v

C. E. CATEN, *Department of Genetics, University of Birmingham, Birmingham B15 2TT, England*

K. F. CHATER, *Department of Genetics, John Innes Institute, Colney Lane, Norwich NR4 7UH, England*

PATRICIA H. CLARKE, *Department of Biochemistry, University College, London, England*

J. H. COATS, *The Upjohn Research Laboratories, Kalamazoo, Michigan, USA*

J. F. COLLINS, *Department of Molecular Biology, University of Edinburgh, Edinburgh, Scotland*

C. J. CORUM, *Antibiotic Manufacturing and Development Division, Eli Lilly and Company, Indianapolis, Indiana 46206, USA*

D. J. COVE, *Department of Genetics, University of Cambridge, Cambridge, England*

IAN CRAIG, *Genetics Laboratory, Department of Biochemistry, University of Oxford, Oxford, England*

J. CUDLÍN, *Institute of Microbiology, Czechoslovak Academy of Sciences, Prague, Czechoslovakia*

E. ČURDOVÁ, *Institute of Microbiology, Czechoslovak Academy of Sciences, Prague, Czechoslovakia*

L. BARBARA DAGLISH, *Fermentation Products Department, ICI Ltd, Pharmaceuticals Division, Trafford Park Works, Westinghouse Road, Manchester 17, England*

V. N. DANILENKO, *Institute of Genetics and Selection of Industrial Microorganisms, Moscow, USSR*

A. L. DEMAIN, *Department of Nutrition and Food Science, Massachusetts Institute of Technology, USA*

H. DeVALERIA, *Antibiotic Manufacturing and Development Division, Eli Lilly and Company, Indianapolis, Indiana 46206, USA*

P. DITCHBURN, *Glaxo Laboratories Ltd, Ulverston, Cumbria, England*

E. L. DUBOIS, *Institut de Recherches, CERIA, and Laboratoire de Microbiologie, Université Libre de Bruxelles, 1070 Brussels, Belgium*

G. F. ST L. EDWARDS, *Sir William Dunn School of Pathology, University of Oxford, South Parks Road, Oxford OX1 3RE, England*

V. N. EGOROVA, *Department of Genetics and Selection, Leningrad State University, USSR*

R. P. ELANDER, *Smith Kline and French Laboratories, Philadelphia, Pennsylvania 19101, USA*

PATRICIA A. FAWCETT, *Sir William Dunn School of Pathology, University of Oxford, Oxford, England*

H. HAGINO, *Tokyo Research Laboratory, Kyowa Hakko Kogyo Co., Ltd, Tokyo, Japan*

A. HINNEN, *Research Department, Pharmaceutical Division, Ciba-Geigy Ltd, Basel, Switzerland*

G. HOLT, *Bio-Organic Research Group, Polytechnic of Central London, 115 New Cavendish Street, London W1M 8JS, England*

D. A. HOPWOOD, *Department of Genetics, John Innes Institute, Colney Lane, Norwich NR4 7UH, England*

Z. HOŠŤÁLEK, *Institute of Microbiology, Czechoslovak Academy of Sciences, Prague, Czechoslovakia*

S. G. INGE-VECHTOMOV, *Department of Genetics and Selection, Leningrad State University, USSR*

V. JECHOVÁ, *Institute of Microbiology, Czechoslovak Academy of Sciences, Prague, Czechoslovakia*

J. C. JEFFRIES, *Department of Botany, University of Edinburgh, The King's Buildings, Mayfield Road, Edinburgh EH9 3JH, Scotland*

J. L. JINKS, *Department of Genetics, University of Birmingham, Birmingham B15 2TT, England*

J. R. JOHNSTON, *Department of Applied Microbiology, University of Strathclyde, Glasgow G1 1XW, Scotland*

H. KASE, *Tokyo Research Laboratory, Kyowa Hakko Kogyo Co., Ltd, Tokyo, Japan*

H. P. KOCHER, *Microbiology Department, Swiss Federal Institute of Technology, Zürich, Switzerland*

I. KOMERSOVÁ, *Institute of Microbiology, Czechoslovak Academy of Sciences, Prague, Czechoslovakia*

G. C. LANCINI, *Research Laboratories, Gruppo Lepetit SpA, Via Durando, 38, Milan, Italy*

P. A. LEMKE, *Mellon Institute of Science, Carnegie-Mellon University, Pittsburgh, USA*

C. W. LEWIS, *Department of Applied Microbiology, University of Strathclyde, Glasgow G1 1XW, Scotland*

M. LIERSCH, *Research Department, Pharmaceutical Division, Ciba-Geigy Ltd, Basel, Switzerland*

N. D. LOMOVSKAYA, *Institute of Genetics and Selection of Industrial Microorganisms, Moscow, USSR*

J. LUDVÍK, *Institute of Microbiology, Czechoslovak Academy of Sciences, Prague, Czechoslovakia*

K. D. MACDONALD, *Microbiological Research Establishment, Porton Down, Salisbury, Wiltshire, England*

J. MATĚJŮ, *Institute of Microbiology, Czechoslovak Academy of Sciences, Prague, Czechoslovakia*

B. P. MATSELYUKH, *D. K. Zabolotny Institute of Microbiology and Virology, Academy of Sciences of the Ukrainian SSR, Kiev, USSR*

E. P. McCANN, *Fermentation Products Department, ICI Ltd, Pharmaceuticals Division, Trafford Park Works, Westinghouse Road, Manchester 17, England*

M. J. MERRICK, *Department of Genetics, John Innes Institute, Colney Lane, Norwich NR4 7UH, England*

K. NAKAYAMA, *Tokyo Research Laboratory, Kyowa Hakko Kogyo Co., Ltd, Tokyo, Japan*

C. H. NASH, *Antibiotic Development Department, Eli Lilly and Company, Indianapolis, USA*

J. NÜESCH. *Research Department, Pharmaceutical Division, Ciba-Geigy Ltd, Basel, Switzerland*

G. PONTECORVO, *Imperial Cancer Research Fund, London WC2, England*

A. M. PUGLIA, *Istituto di Genetica, University of Palermo, Palermo, Italy*

E. G. RABINOWITZ, *Department of Genetics and Selection, Leningrad State University, USSR*

R. RANDAZZO, *Istituto di Genetica, Università, Palermo, Italy*

K. N. SAKSENA, *Mellon Institute of Science, Carnegie-Mellon University, Pittsburgh, USA*

JOHN SCAIFE, *Department of Molecular Biology, University of Edinburgh, Edinburgh, Scotland*

T. SCHUPP, *Ciba-Geigy AG, Basel, Switzerland*

G. SERMONTI, *Istituto di Istologia, via Elce di Sotto, The University, Perugia, Italy*

T. R. SOIDLA, *Department of Genetics and Selection, Leningrad State University, USSR*

J. O. SOOM, *Department of Genetics and Selection, Leningrad State University, USSR*

K. STAJNER, *Institute of Microbiology, Czechoslovak Academy of Sciences, Prague, Czechoslovakia*

N. STEINEROVÁ, *Institute of Microbiology, Czechoslovak Academy of Sciences, Prague, Czechoslovakia*

J. TAX, *Institute of Microbiology, Czechoslovak Academy of Sciences, Prague, Czechoslovakia*

H. J. TREICHLER, *Research Department, Pharmaceutical Division, Ciba-Geigy Ltd, Basel, Switzerland*

J. J. USHER, *Sir William Dunn School of Pathology, University of Oxford, Oxford, England*

Z. VANĚK, *Institute of Microbiology, Czechoslovak Academy of Sciences, Prague, Czechoslovakia*

D. I. C. WANG, *Department of Nutrition and Food Science, Massachusetts Institute of Technology, USA*

R. J. WHITE, *Research Laboratories, Gruppo Lepetit SpA, Via Durando, 38, Milan, Italy*

J. M. WIAME, *Institut de Recherches, CERIA, and Laboratoire de Microbiologie, Université Libre de Bruxelles, 1070 Brussels, Belgium*

R. M. WILGUS, *Antibiotic Manufacturing and Development Division, Eli Lilly and Company, Indianapolis, Indiana 46206, USA*

E. WILLIAMS, *Department of Microbiology, University of Edinburgh, Edinburgh, Scotland*

H. M. WRIGHT, *Department of Genetics, John Innes Institute, Colney Lane, Norwich NR4 7UH, England*

H. YOSHIDA, *Tokyo Research Laboratory, Kyowa Hakko Kogyo Co., Ltd, Tokyo, Japan*

Preface

The papers published in this book were presented by invited lecturers at the Second International Symposium on the Genetics of Industrial Micro-organisms (GIM 74) held during August 1974 in Sheffield, UK.

They are printed here in the order in which they were presented and open with the stimulating Presidential Address by Professor G. Pontecorvo, FRS, whose research in the field of microbial genetics served as a model for so much work which was to come.

Five scientific sessions were organized for the presentation of invited papers at GIM 74. The first was devoted to reviews of work in different areas of genetics; the subjects covered included mutation induction, mutant isolation, gene expression and amplification, organelle, cultured cell and quantitative genetics. Experts were invited to discuss recent findings in these various fields and to highlight those of potential benefit to industry.

It was pointed out that most mutagens do not cause mutations directly but produce a specific damage which is misrepaired by the organism. The concept that it is usually the cell and not the mutagen which makes the mutation is of interest to the industrial microbiologist. Rather than try a number of different mutagens on a refractory microbe, he might be better advised to use a different strain. For improvements in the industrial production of enzymes it can be expected that increasing use will be made of microbial regulatory mutants differing from their parents in producing enzymes constitutively rather than by induction, in synthesizing enzymes with altered specificities for both inducer and substrate, as well as mutants resistant to catabolite repression or with altered permeability characteristics. Also, although industrial scientists may be wary of the more elaborate prophecies of workers in pure science, reviews of studies on gene expression and gene amplification indicated that genetic engineering is reaching the stage where practical benefits can be expected. The use of restriction enzymes to yield fragments of DNA which can be fused into foreign DNA leads to the possibility, for example, of incorporating DNA from a eukaryote into the genome of a prokaryote. It is conceivable therefore that a fragment of animal DNA bearing information for the synthesis of a useful product could be multiplied in a bacterial system. The industrial possibilities are immense but they remain to be determined and will doubtless be discussed at future symposia on the genetics of industrial microorganisms.

In the second scientific session under the title, "Stretegy of Strain Improvement", a number of papers were given on the genetic regulation of the synthesis and overproduction of antibiotics. Work on identifying individual genes concerned with increased yield was described and the relevance of biometrical genetics to yield improvement discussed. In this session there were also reports of recent work on the biosynthesis of antibiotics, including the use of mutant strains with specific blockages to elucidate pathways of commercial significance, and a report on extracellular antibiotic production with enzymatic extracts.

The third session comprised papers on genetic aspects of microbes synthesizing fermentation products other than antibiotics and included those on yeasts and on the viruses of industrial fungi. The fourth session was given over to papers on recent work concerning the genetic regulation of microbial metabolism indicating how the yields of useful metabolites such as amino acids can be raised as a consequence of our widening knowledge of genetic regulation.

The final session was devoted to papers on the genetics of actinomycetes, an important group of bacteria many species of which are used in industrial fermentation processes, notably for the production of antibiotics. Well developed genetic maps are now available for several species of *Streptomyces* which should aid attempts to derive practical advantage from genetic recombination in actinomycetes. The phenomenon of co-mutation described in these microbes provides a method of obtaining a high rate of mutation in a restricted and defined region of the chromosome. Also, the occurrence of plasmids leads to the hope that suitable genes could be transferred between unrelated strains of these microorganisms to give novel and useful industrial strains.

In the space available it has been possible to mention only a very little of the great deal of interesting and important work which was presented at GIM 74 and which will be found in these Proceedings but to end by looking to the future development of industrial processes which at present depend on the microbial production of a useful compound, there appear to be at least two directions which can be taken neither of which is mutually exclusive. The first, by methods of genetic engineering, could lead to organisms tailor-made for their industrial function. For this to be possible a much more detailed knowledge of the formal genetics of industrial microorganisms will be required than is at present available. The message is clear for fermentation industries— invest in microbial genetics. The second direction could lead to the syntheses of useful microbial compounds, *in vitro*. Not *de novo* complete syntheses by the organic chemist, which are almost always much too expensive to contemplate for the more complex microbial metabolites, but syntheses using isolated enzyme fractions. The likelihood of exercising better control over synthetic processes in this way is obvious. The microbial geneticist would be required here to breed microorganisms with suitable enzyme yields and elaborating enzymes with suitable substrate affinities.

It is a great pleasure to acknowledge the help given by members of the Editorial Subcommittee of GIM 74 in the preparation of this book. I am deeply grateful to the following members of this subcommittee for their editorial assistance: Dr R. S. C. Aytoun, Dr C. Ball, Dr J. D. Bu'Lock, Dr C. T. Calam, Dr D. J. Cove, Dr J. P. R. Herrmann, Dr G. Holt, Professor D. A. Hopwood and Dr M. D. Lilly.

On behalf of the Editorial Subcommittee of GIM 74 I would also like to express sincere thanks to Mrs D. Sharp of Academic Press for her unfailing courtesy and generous help while these Proceedings were being prepared for the printers.

All of us who were concerned with the organization of GIM 74 are now looking forward to the Third International Symposium on the Genetics of Industrial Microorganisms (GIM 78) which is due to be held in the USA in 1978.

August 1975   K. D. MACDONALD

Contents

Contributors   v

Preface   xi

G. Pontecorvo   Presidential address   .   .   .   1

Perspectives in Genetics

B. A. Bridges   Mutation induction   .   .   .   7

Patricia H. Clarke   Mutant isolation   .   .   .   15

J. Scaife   Some observations on gene expression   .   29

J. F. Collins   Gene amplification in bacterial systems   .   41

P. R. Avner   Organelle genetics in *Saccharomyces cerevisiae*   59

I. Craig   Cultured cell genetics   73

C. E. Caten and J. L. Jinks   Quantitative genetics   .   .   93

Strategy of Strain Improvement
I Biosynthesis of Antibiotics

A. L. Demain and D. I. C. Wang   Enzymatic synthesis of gramicidin S   115

Patricia A. Fawcett, J. J. Usher and E. P. Abraham   Aspects of cephalosporin and penicillin biosynthesis.   .   .   129

G. C. Lancini and R. J. White   Rifamycin biosynthesis   .   139

Z. Hošťálek, M. Blumauerová, J. Ludvík, V. Jechová, V. Běhal, J. Čáslavská and E. Čurdová   The role of the genome in secondary biosynthesis in *Streptomyces aureofaciens*   .   155

M. Liersch, J. Nüesch and H. J. Treichler   Final steps in the biosynthesis of cephalosporin C   .   .   .   179

Strategy of Strain Improvement
II Mutation and Recombination in Antibiotic-producing Organisms

G. Holt, G. F. St. L. Edwards and K. D. Macdonald   The genetics of mutants impaired in the biosynthesis of penicillin   199

P. Ditchburn, G. Holt and K. D. Macdonald   The genetic location of mutations increasing penicillin yield in *Aspergillus nidulans* 213

M. J. Merrick   Hybridization and selection for penicillin production in *Aspergillus nidulans*—a biometrical approach to strain improvement 229

C. Ball and J. L. Azevedo   Genetic instability in parasexual fungi 243

R. P. Elander, C. J. Corum, H. DeValeria and R. M. Wilgus   Ultraviolet mutagenesis and cephalosporin synthesis in strains of *Cephalosporium acremonium* . . . 253

C. T. Calam, L. Barbara Daglish and E. P. McCann   Penicillin: tactics in strain improvement 273

Genetic Aspects of Nonantibiotic Fermentation Products

W. J. Brammar   Genetic approaches to the stimulation of bacterial protein synthesis 291

J. C. Jeffries   Genetic aspects of asparaginase-2 production in *Escherichia coli*. 301

E. Williams and B. W. Bainbridge   Mutation, repair mechanisms and transformation in the methane-utilizing bacterium, *Methylococcus capsulatus* 313

P. A. Lemke, K. N. Saksena and C. H. Nash   Viruses of industrial fungi 323

J. R. Johnston and C. W. Lewis   Genetic analysis of flocculation in *Saccharomyces cerevisiae* and tetrad analysis of commercial brewing and baking yeasts . . . 339

S. G. Inge-Vechtomov, E. G. Rabinowitz, V. N. Egorova, J. O. Soom and T. R. Soidla   Mutants of *Saccharomyces cerevisiae* utilizing hydrocarbons 357

Regulation of Metabolism

S. Baumberg   Genetic control of arginine metabolism in prokaryotes. 369

J. M. Wiame and E. L. Dubois   The regulation of enzyme synthesis in arginine metabolism of *Saccharomyces cerevisiae* 391

D. J. Cove   The control of catabolism in *Aspergillus nidulans* 407

K. F. Bott   Regulation of bacterial sporulation . . 419

K. Nakayama, K. Araki, H. Hagino, H. Kase and H. Yoshida
Amino acid fermentations using regulatory mutants of
Corynebacterium glutamicum 437

J. Nüesch, A. Hinnen, M. Liersch and H. J. Treichler   A
biochemical and genetical approach to the biosynthesis of
cephalosporin C 451

Z. Vaněk, J. Tax, J. Cudlín, M. Blumauerová, N. Steinerova, J.
Matějů, I. Komersová and K. Stajner   Biogenesis of
linear tri- and tetracyclic oligoketides and their glycosides   473

J. D. Bu'Lock   Cascade expression of the mating-type locus
in Mucorales 497

Genetics of Actinomycetes

M. Alacěvić   Recent advances in *Streptomyces rimosus*
genetics 513

J. H. Coats   Genetic recombination in *Streptomyces
achromogenes* var. *rubradiris* 521

T. Schupp   Genetic analysis in *Nocardia mediterranei* . 531

R. Baumann and H. P. Kocher   Genetics of *Streptomyces
glaucescens* and regulation of melanin production . . 535

B. P. Matselyukh   Structure and function of the *Actinomyces olivaceus* genome 553

G. Sermonti and A. M. Puglia   Progressive fertilization in
Streptomyces coelicolor 565

A. Carere and R. Randazzo   Co-mutation in *Streptomyces* . 573

K. F. Chater and M. J. Merrick   Approaches to the study of
differentiation in *Streptomyces coelicolor* A3(2) . . 583

S. I. Alikhanian, N. D. Lomovskaya and V. N. Danilenko
Suppressor-sensitive mutations of *Streptomyces coelicolor* A3(2) and actinophage ϕC31 595

D. A. Hopwood and H. M. Wright   Interactions of the plasmid SCPI with the chromosome of *Streptomyces coelicolor* A3(2) 607

Subject Index 621

Presidential address

G. PONTECORVO
Imperial Cancer Research Fund, London WC2, England

It is a pleasure to welcome the many participants to this Symposium. Surely the quality of your deliberations will match quantity. It is a great honour for me that your Committee chose me to preside. I am afraid they could not have chosen a less qualified person. My only incursion into the genetics of industrial microorganisms was in the early 50s when with my colleagues in Glasgow—foremost our present host, Professor J. A. Roper—Mr E. C. Forbes, the late Elizabeth Tarr Gloor and, later, Professor G. Sermonti, we elucidated the parasexual cycle in moulds.

This led to microbio-legal history. The National Research Development Corporation took a patent for the production of improved industrial strains by means of the parasexual cycle. A biological patent of this kind was quite a novelty. The patent was granted in most countries of the world, with one notable exception: Denmark. There my good friend and colleague Professor O. Maaloe, who was advising the Danish Patent Office, argued that one could not patent the parasexual cycle, no more than one could patent sexual reproduction. The argument, of course, was very weak: the patent was not on the process, which is natural, but on its use in synthesizing improved strains. However, it was an amusing story. Incidentally, the patent, which I believe has now lapsed, did not lead to any world-shaking applications, and this will lead me to the main subject of my talk.

Apart from that early experience, I never again did any work related to industrial microorganisms. What became an exciting challenge was the application of the principles of segregation and recombination in vegetative cells—emerged from the work on parasexuality—to the genetics of higher organisms, including man, by means of somatic cells in culture. This application has led, after a lag phase of about 10 years, to very fruitful advances.

1

I should say spectacular. The formal genetics of man has made more progress in the last 5 years, by means of approaches like those worked out with the parasexual cycle in fungi, than in the previous 70 years.

Having made it clear that I have very few, if any, qualifications for talking at this Symposium, let alone for being its President, I shall be rash enough to make some general remarks as an outsider on the progress of genetics as applied to industrial microorganisms. As a justification for omissions and misinterpretations there is the fact that, being otherwise engaged, I have not followed the literature on the subject for at least 15 years.

One thing is clear to the outsider: the advances in the applications of genetics to the improvement of strains of industrial microorganisms are trifles compared to the advances in the fundamental genetics of micro-organisms. Suffice it to recall the Berg's report which proposes a voluntary moratorium on certain types of research in microbial genetics because of their possible risks to humans and other living organisms. The knowledge and technical know-how in microbial genetics have so vastly outstripped those in the relevant fields of pathology, epidemiology and ecology—human or other—that there is no way of estimating the size of those risks.

With a general basis of knowledge and techniques as formidable as that in microbial genetics it is very disappointing to see how far behind are the applications to the improvement of industrial microorganisms.

The main technique used is still a prehistoric one: mutation and selection. In 1944, independently Demerec in the USA and myself in Scotland proposed this technique only as a war-time emergency measure for improving penicillin yields. Penicillin was desperately needed then and even an approach intellectually crude and, *a priori*, not very likely to be successful was worth a trial. The success was so unexpectedly good that, unfortunately, since then most industrial laboratories have been contented with its *exclusive* use.

Nature, in its remarkable ways of coping with the improvement of living organisms—what we call evolution—has given up the exclusive use of mutation and selection at least one billion years ago. It has supplemented mutation and selection with a wonderful variety of mechanisms for the transfer of genetic information. Sexual reproduction, combined with diploidy, is the most highly elaborate of these mechanisms. It is at least 25 years since Muller showed in a simple graphic way why mutation and selection *by themselves* are so much less effective than in combination with processes of genetic information transfer.

In this Symposium we shall hear of some research—notably from the Laboratories of Alikhanian on *Streptomyces*, of Macdonald on *Penicillium* and *Aspergillus* and of Jinks on *Aspergillus*—aiming at the production of more desirable strains by means of the transfer of genetic information.

The work of all three of these groups comes from Government supported laboratories. If industrial laboratories were doing successfully something along these lines, we would not hear of it. Most of them use secrecy to hide what they do not know. My guess is that there is little work of the right calibre using genetic information transfer as a means towards strain improvement.

Why this enormous gap between basic knowledge and its applications? Two reasons are clear to the outsider: fragmentation of effort and predominance of chemical outlook in the microbiological industries. Let me deal with this second point first.

Most of the fermentation industries are offshoots of the chemical and, more particularly, pharmaceutical industries. Naturally in these mother industries the predominant outlook was that of the organic chemist. This was carried over into the fermentation industries, later only partially infiltrated by biochemistry. There is no more unsuitable approach to handling living things than that of the organic chemist unless, of course, he makes the big effort to become utterly converted to a biological outlook. There are a few examples of such successful conversion, and our host Professor Roper is one of them. Clearly, a microbiological industry run by organic chemists recruits geneticists as tools and treats them accordingly. Imaginative first class geneticists are difficult to attract. The idea that genetics is as tough a science as chemistry is only beginning to dawn.

The second reason for the disappointing state of the application of genetics to the improvement of industrial microorganisms is the fragmentation of effort. Every industrial concern has his own mini-team working in secrecy and trying to produce more desirable strains. How absurd is this situation can be illustrated by an analogy. Agriculture in Great Britain is a highly fragmented, privately run industry vastly more important than all the microbiological industries taken together. Yet, the improvement of varieties of crop plants, which was mainly an individual concern up to a century ago, is now concentrated in three main plant breeding stations. They are quite successful and the farming community seems to be happy about them. No farmer in his senses, no matter how large his farm, would dream of breeding his own varieties of crop plant and, in addition, keep them jealously for himself. Recruitment of first class geneticists to the plant breeding stations is no problem at all. The charge that academic geneticists are reluctant to turn to full-time applied work, quite correct in the case of the microbiological industries, is wrong in the case of agriculture.

What plagues genetic progress in the fermentation industries is the combination of fragmentation, secrecy and unattractive outlook. It makes the average quality of recruitment very poor and prevents the free pooling of know-how. Strangely enough, from the little that transpires, these limitations occur also in countries where the microbiological industry is entirely in public ownership.

What should we do about all this? The problem is how to have industrial plant and know-how directly connected with teams of first class geneticists working on strain improvement. In analogy to plant breeding, this improvement can be carried out efficiently only in a few highly specialized centres. I understand that in California and in Japan there are currently attempts at a solution on the part of two specialized firms making contracts with the fermentation industries. The adverse effects on recruitment of secrecy and private use of improved strains are still there, but at least these attempts are encouraging. For this country, I would prefer centralization of strain improvement in two or three publicly owned plants. The results of the work, both know-how and strains, should be public and available to all, just as in the case of plant breeding stations.

I realize that I have dropped a few huge bricks, but I hope they will lead to a serious reappraisal of the situation.

PERSPECTIVES IN GENETICS

Mutation induction

B. A. BRIDGES

MRC Cell Mutation Unit, University of Sussex,
Falmer, Brighton BN1 9QG, England

Summary

The effect of strong mutagens on microorganisms is determined very largely by the activity of various repair systems capable of acting on single strand gaps formed in the DNA either directly or indirectly. Two such systems, excision repair and post-replication repair, and their effects are described on the basis of work with *Escherichia coli*. A third system of largely unknown mechanism is error prone and appears to operate as a minor alternative pathway simultaneously with the two major pathways. Ultraviolet and ionizing radiations, most alkylating agents, DNA strand-breaking agents and cross-linking agents cause mutations by misrepair through this pathway. Of these agents, ultraviolet light is preferred as a practical mutagen on various grounds.

Some microorganisms do not possess such an error-prone repair system and may therefore be essentially immutable by these agents. In these organisms a mutagen must be used that operates by causing replication errors rather than repair errors; the best is probably ethyl methanesulphonate. The other main alternative, "nitrosoguanidine", has severe disadvantages and its use should be regarded as constituting a laboratory hazard.

Introduction

The availability of mutations is fundamental to the whole of genetical research whether pure or applied. To read many textbooks one might be led to think that the way in which mutations arise is essentially understood, whereas nothing could be further from the truth. Early work on base analogues (e.g. 2-aminopurine and 5-bromouracil) was elegant and very credible (for a review see Drake, 1970). These substances masquerade as nucleic acid pre-cursors and deceive the organism into incorporating them into its DNA. Their true nature is then revealed as they fail to pair consistently with the "right" complementary base and mistakes (seen as mutations) arise with a certain probability.

Base analogues are, however, usually weak mutagens and are atypical in that most mutagens act in quite different ways which are not well understood. Moreover, it now seems that even the classic base analogue, 5-bromouracil, acts in an indirect way through an error-prone pathway to be described below (Pietrzykowska, 1973). Although some alkylating agents produce types of damage (for example, alkylations at the 0–6 position of guanine) which miscode during subsequent replications, most mutagens produce chemical damage to DNA which triggers off cellular repair enzymes. An understanding of DNA repair is therefore necessary for an understanding of the mode of action of many mutagens. Repair of DNA is the way in which the cell attempts to conserve the integrity of its genetic material. When it fails completely the result is death; when it makes a mistake the result may be mutation. For a more detailed review of repair see Howard-Flanders (1973).

In this presentation I shall be concerned solely with base-pair substitution mutations. These are usually mis-sense mutations which are the type most likely to be of use to the industrial microbiologist. Where nonleaky mutations leading to inactivation of a gene function are desired, nonsense mutations arising from base-pair substitutions are to be preferred to frameshift muta-tions at the present time, since the latter offer no advantages over the former and specific frameshift mutagens are not widely available nor is their mecha-nism of action well studied.

Results and discussion

Most of the information to be described has been obtained with *Escherichia coli*, and most of the mutation induction experiments refer to base-pair substitution mutations induced by ultraviolet light (uv). Ultraviolet light is the ideal mutagen for studying mechanisms of mutagenesis because the cyclobutane pyrimidine dimer is known to be the photoproduct involved in the production of most mutations. Most organisms possess an enzyme capable of monomerizing pyrimidine dimers in the presence of light, a process known as photoreactivation. The pyrimidine dimer can in this way be induced in and removed from DNA at will, a property not possessed by any other premutational lesion and one which has proved to be extremely useful in analysing the pathway that ultimately leads to the production of a mutation.

EXCISION REPAIR

The term "excision repair" describes a process whereby a lesion in one strand of the DNA duplex can be cut out and the resulting gap filled in by a DNA polymerase using the other undamaged strand as a template (Fig. 1). Good progress has been made in identifying the enzymes involved in this process in several species of bacteria. There are rather specific endonucleases which

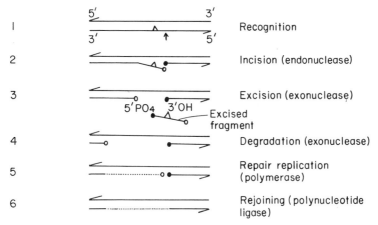

FIG. 1. A model for excision-repair. The parallel lines represent the DNA duplex and △ represents a uv photoproduct.

make a nick to one side of the damaged base but which do not attack un-damaged DNA at all. A second nuclease then breaks a sugar phosphate bond on the other side of the lesion. In some species there is a specific nuclease to do this (e.g. *Micrococcus luteus*), in others the exonuclease activity of DNA polymerase I is probably used (e.g. *Escherichia coli*). The resulting gap may sometimes be enlarged by nonspecific nuclease activity. The filling of the gap in *E. coli* involves DNA polymerase I (Kornberg polymerase) and, possibly to a limited extent, DNA polymerases II and III. The final joining of the newly synthesized region to the rest of the DNA is believed to be effected by a polynucleotide ligase. Despite the enzymological progress, it is still not known how the process is organized, whether attachment to a membrane is involved, and how repolymerization is permitted to supplant exonuclease action at the gap.

Excision repair is important in influencing the action of many chemical mutagens because a lesion that is excised is much less likely to give rise to a mutation than one that is not. This can be seen from the fact that strains of bacteria that cannot perform excision are up to twenty times more mutable by the action of ultraviolet light and some chemical mutagens than excision-proficient bacteria. A similar increase in sensitivity (although less dramatic) is obtained if chemicals that inhibit excision (e.g. caffeine, acriflavine, 8-methoxypsoralen) are added to the bacteria after irradiation. When excision is absent or inhibited, large numbers of mutants may be obtained following very low doses of mutagen. Unfortunately, the increase in sensitivity to cell killing is comparable to that for mutation induction in many cases, and after high doses of mutagen the mutant yield at a given level of survival does not usually differ greatly in the presence or absence of excision repair. Moreover, the effectiveness of chemical inhibitors is greatest at low uv doses and falls off at higher (and perhaps more practical) doses.

POST-REPLICATION REPAIR

When excision repair is absent mutations arise as a consequence of DNA replication and the chief process that is known to occur then has been called post-replication or "recombination" repair (Fig. 2).

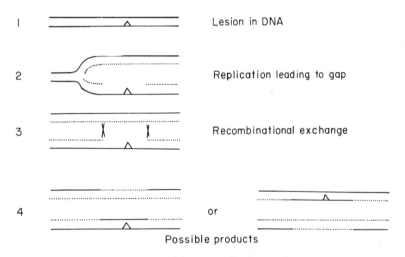

FIG. 2. A model for post-replication repair.

When DNA containing uv-photoproducts is replicated in *E. coli* the new daughter strands laid down have gaps ($\sim 10^3$ nucleotides long) opposite the photoproducts in the parental strands. The majority of these gaps are filled in over a period of 15 to 30 minutes by a process that involves recombination between the two daughter chromosomes (for review see Howard-Flanders, 1973). During this process pieces of parental DNA about the same size as the gaps become associated covalently with the newly synthesized strands (Rupp et al., 1971) including pieces containing photoproducts (Ganesan, 1974) so that the photoproducts are not inherited lineally, as might have been expected, but are diluted out among all the progeny chromosomes formed after irradiation.

ERROR-PRONE REPAIR

It was natural to assume that since mutations in excision-deficient bacteria arise as a consequence of DNA replication, they might arise during post-replication repair rather than as mistakes during replication itself (Bridges, 1969; Witkin, 1969). It is, however, only recently that experiments establishing this have been carried out (Eyfjord, Green and Bridges, in preparation). The fact that bacteria deficient at the recA gene and unable to carry out genetic recombination are also unable to fill daughter-strand gaps and are nonmutable by uv (Miura and Tomizawa, 1968; Witkin, 1969; Kondo et al., 1970) is the only piece of evidence that mutations arise during genetic exchanges. There is, however, another gene, exr A, a deficiency in which blocks uv mutagenesis much more specifically than recA (Witkin, 1967; Sedgwick and Bridges, 1972) and which has little or no effect on recombination or on daughter-strand gap-filling (except after quite high doses of uv: Bridges and Sedgwick, 1974).

There are, in fact, two general possibilities which have not yet been convincingly distinguished. Either mutations arise as errors during genetic exchanges requiring the $exrA^+$ gene, or the $exrA^+$ gene is necessary for the operation of a minor but distinct method of gap filling, which is not recombinational.

We know that most exchanges are error free (Bridges et al., 1967) so that even if they are involved the probability that a mutation will arise is still low (< 5 per cent). There are many situations known where daughter-strand gaps are filled with no detectable mutation induction, e.g. in exrA bacteria (Sedgwick and Bridges, 1972), in $exrA^+$ bacteria in buffer, or during the first 20 minutes after irradiation (Eyfjord, Green and Bridges, in preparation).

Because excision repair so obviously led to a reduction in mutant yield, it has tended to be thought of as an error-free repair process. While the vast majority of excision repair events are accurate there is evidence that a small minority are error-prone and can lead to mutations (Nishioka and Doudney, 1969, 1970; Bridges and Mottershead, 1971). A number of agents appear to give rise to mutations by a variant of this $exr A^+$- and $rec A^+$-dependent excision-repair pathway. The difference from uv lies in the fact that the specific uv-endonuclease appears not to be required, the sugar-phosphate backbone of DNA being broken by other means directly, for example, by ionizing radiation, or via an unstable apurinic site following spontaneous depurination, for example possibly after N-7 methylation by methyl methanesulphonate. It is not yet clear how much of the total mutagenesis involves this excision-repair pathway in wild-type E. coli. It has been generally assumed that mutations (after uv irradiation, for example) largely originate from a minority of DNA photoproducts that fail to be excised for one reason or another. However there is remarkably little evidence to support this hypothesis except for ochre suppressor mutations which appear to arise during DNA replication *after* excision is complete (Nishioka and Doudney, 1970). It is quite possible that, in many organisms possessing the ability to carry out excision repair, a good proportion of mutations at many loci may arise during a very small fraction of excision repair events.

I have, elsewhere, discussed the possible mechanisms of error-prone repair in greater detail (Bridges, 1975). In general, the data seem to me to be most consistent with the idea that the $exrA^+$-dependent mutational pathway is an independent error-prone pathway capable of repairing single-strand DNA gaps. The larger the gap and the longer it persists, the more likely it is to be repaired by this pathway. Such a large and persisting gap may also, of course, be more likely to initiate a recombinational exchange.

The arguments against the necessary involvement of recombination are telling but not conclusive. There are two situations where mutations do arise under conditions where recombinational exchanges appear to be excluded. The first is where they arise following excision in *E. coli* bacteria grown in a chemostat such that they nearly all have a single chromosome (Bridges and Mottershead, 1971). The second is in the single-stranded phage ØX174 where uv mutagenesis is *recA*-dependent and where it can occur at multiplicities of infection less than 1 (Tessman and Ozaki, 1960; Bleichrodt, personal communication). Recently it has been suggested that the $exrA^+$ mutation pathway is inducible, i.e. that uv not only produces premutational lesions in DNA but also stimulates the activities of the metabolic process necessary to enable them to give rise to stable mutations (Defais *et al.*, 1971; Witkin and George, 1973). This suggestion is still controversial because we do not know what this "induction" might mean at the molecular level. Indeed, we know almost nothing about either the molecular steps or the enzymes involved in the $exrA^+$-dependent mutation pathway.

WHICH MUTAGEN TO USE?

I have emphasized the importance of the $exrA^+$- and $recA^+$-dependent mutational pathway because its use is so widespread among agents capable of mutagenizing *E. coli*. In addition to uv and ionizing radiations and thymine starvation, most alkylating and cross-linking agents mutate only $exrA^+$ $recA^+$ strains, e.g. methyl methanesulphonate, 7-bromomethyl benzanthracene, nitrogen mustard, mitomycin C, captan (the fungicide), dichlorvos (the insecticide), a number of nitrofurans, nitroquinoline-1-oxide, psoralens in the presence of 360 nm light, and probably many others.

Of all these agents, uv is to be generally preferred as a practical mutagen on three grounds: (i) the ratio of mutation induction to lethal effect is usually high; (ii) all known types of molecular change can be induced (including frameshifts as well as base-pair substitutions); and (iii) it is one of the few mutagens that can be contained and directed solely to the experimental material—it cannot enter the body and constitute a hazard to the laboratory worker. Having stated this, it must be pointed out that an increasing number of strains are being reported that are nonmutable by uv and appear not to have a functional $exr\,A^+$-dependent pathway (or its equivalent). Examples include some *Haemophilus* spp., *Proteus* spp., and *Micrococcus radiodurans* (Moseley, personal communication). In addition, at this meeting Williams and Bainbridge report nonmutability by uv in *Methylococcus capsulatus,* and a number of other methane-oxidizing bacteria including *Methylococcus* sp., *Methylobacter* sp., *Methylomonas* sp., *Methylocystis* sp., and *Methylosinus* sp. appear to be similar (Shimmin and Bainbridge, personal communication).

If one is working with an organism that is refractory to uv, what other mutagen should one try as a substitute? In *E. coli* there are two potent chemicals that act even on *exrA* and *recA* strains; ethyl methanesulphonate (EMS) and *N*-methyl-*N'*-nitro-*N*-nitrosoguanidine (MNNG). Strains nonmutable by uv are, however, usually rather sensitive to the lethal action of these agents. EMS is to be preferred on the grounds of safety. It appears to produce changes from guanine:cytosine to adenine:thymine base pairs rather specifically and this has been correlated with the ethylation of guanine at the 0–6 position. This ethylated base appears to pair with thymine and not cytosine at replication. It is, of course, always possible that this change may not be able to produce the desired mutational phenotype but in most cases it will be the preferred alternative to uv. I know of only two instances of organisms not mutated by EMS: one is the *rad-6* uv-sensitive mutant of *Saccharomyces cerevisiae* (Lawrence, personal communication), the other is the methane oxidizing group, but this could well be due to the extreme sensitivity of these bacteria to EMS (Williams, personal communication).

MNNG has been widely used as a mutagen in recent years, mainly because of its generally high mutation to lethality ratio. Its mechanism of action is still somewhat obscure but it is clear that there is a preferential action at the DNA replication point. Like EMS, MNNG also produces 0–6 alkylations of guanine and it has been shown that these are specifically excised in contrast to the main alkylation product at the N-7 position of guanine (Lawley and Orr, 1970).

MNNG would normally be my last choice as a potent mutagen for three reasons. Firstly, it is known that MNNG produces clusters of closely linked mutations. It is thus almost impossible with MNNG, even at low doses, to avoid putting other unwanted mutations into the genome. Of course, this may sometimes be useful, particularly where the desired phenotype requires more than one mutation in the same cistron or operon.

The other two reasons are concerned with safety. MNNG is a known carcinogen and must be considered particularly hazardous in the dry micro-crystalline state. The risk of inhaling small crystals of such a potent mutagen into the lung could be substantial if appropriate precautions are not taken. MNNG is also liable to explode when heated. At least one instance has come to the attention of the author of a major incident in which an imperfectly cooled platinum loop inserted into a jar of MNNG caused it to explode and scatter the mutagen among a room in which several dozen students were working.

It should never be forgotten that all mutagenic agents are potential carcino-gens; the stronger the mutagen, the more likely it is to be carcinogenic. Whether a given agent can produce cancer in man will depend upon many factors, including its solubility, size, route of entry, the metabolic activity of gut flora and of various organs within the body, the repair capacity of cells in various parts of the body, the presence of latent oncogenic viruses, and the occurrence of possible synergistic treatments such as cigarette smoking. Many of these factors are imponderables and it is surely sensible to treat all mutagens as deadly poisons and handle them accordingly.

References

Bridges, B. A. (1969). *A. Rev. nucl. Sci.* **19**, 139.
Bridges, B. A. (1975). *Proc. Int. Congr. Rad. Res.* In press.
Bridges, B. A., Dennis, R. E. and Munson, R. J. (1967). *Genetics,* **57**, 897.
Bridges, B. A. and Mottershead, R. P. (1971). *Mutation Res.* **13**, 1.
Bridges, B. A. and Sedgwick, S. G. (1974). *J. Bact.* **117**, 1077.
Defais, M., Fauquet, P., Radman, M. and Errera, M. (1971). *Virology,* **43**, 495.
Drake, J. W. (1970). "The Molecular Basis of Mutation". Holden-Day, San Francisco.
Ganesan, A. K. (1974). *J. molec. Biol.* **87**, 103.
Howard-Flanders, P. (1973). *Br. med. Bull.* **29**, 226.
Kondo, S., Ichikawa, H., Iwo, K. and Kato, T. (1970). *Genetics,* **66**, 187.
Lawley, P. D. and Orr, D. J. (1970). *Chem.-Biol. Interactions,* **2**, 154.
Miura, A. and Tomizawa, J. (1968). *Molec. gen. Genet.* **103**, 1.
Nishioka, H. and Doudney, C. O. (1969). *Mutation Res.* **8**, 215.
Nishioka, H. and Doudney, C. O. (1970). *Mutation Res.* **9**, 349.
Pietrzykowska, I. (1973). *Mutation Res.* **19**, 1.
Rupp, W. D., Wilde, C. E., Reno, D. L. and Howard-Flanders, P. (1971). *J. molec. Biol.* **61**, 25.
Sedgwick, S. G. and Bridges, B. A. (1972). *Molec. gen. Genet.* **119**, 93.
Tessman, E. S. and Ozaki, T. (1960). *Virology,* **12**, 431.
Witkin, E. M. (1967). *Brookhaven Symp. Biol.* **20**, 17.
Witkin, E. M. (1969). *A. Rev. Microbiol.* **23**, 487.
Witkin, E. M. and George, D. L. (1973). *Genetics Suppl.* **73**, 91.

Mutant isolation

PATRICIA H. CLARKE

Department of Biochemistry, University College, London, England

Summary

Selective methods for the isolation of mutants are based on differences between the growth rates of the required mutants and their parent strains. Continuous culture may allow the complete replacement of the parent strain by the mutant. For biosynthetic pathways it may be possible to inhibit the parent strain by metabolic analogues and to select resistant mutants from plate media. Sensitivity to analogue inhibition is greater with bradytrophic mutants or with a carbon source which limits the metabolic pool of precursors of the pathway. These methods select feedback inhibition-resistant mutants and derepressed mutants which may overproduce end products or intermediates of the pathway.

Regulatory and structural gene mutants for catabolic pathways can be selected from media containing analogues of normal growth substrates. These include constitutive mutants, mutants with altered inducer specificities, mutants resistant to catabolic repression, mutants with altered permeability characteristics and mutants producing enzymes with altered substrate specificities.

Selection pressures may be increased by buffering the growth medium at pH values away from the growth optimum or by incubation at elevated temperatures. Several successive steps may be needed to obtain mutants giving high enzyme yields or high rates of synthesis of particular products.

Introduction

All methods for the isolation of mutants may be considered as variations on the problem of finding the needle in the haystack. The simplest method of all, and the most tedious, is to test a very large number of independent clones with the hope of finding at least one which shows some improvement over the parent

B

strain. Screening in this way is a time-honoured method and without doubt has yielded strains of considerable importance for production processes. It may be the only possible method for selecting useful variants of some of the industrially important microorganisms. However, it is worth considering whether any of the methods employed in mutant selection for laboratory studies of genetic structure, and for the regulation of enzyme synthesis and activity, are of more general application to species other than those in which they have been developed. The underlying assumption in this approach is that for a production process the improved strain is expected either to produce more of a particular end product, intermediate or secondary metabolite, or to produce more of the macromolecular components of the cell. All these involve mutations which alter the metabolic balance of the organisms. There are no instant answers to these problems and each case needs detailed analysis directed towards the specific problems presented but it is not necessary to wait until a classical genetic system has been identified and explored in detail. Some of the methods known for the isolation of derepressed mutants, or mutants with particular metabolic derangements, are of very general application. The following discussion will be concerned with some examples of methods described for the isolation of stable mutants with robust growth characteristics which might reasonably be used for cultivation on the industrial scale.

The chance of finding the desired mutant may be improved by increasing the mutational frequency by any of the standard mutagenic treatments. Then it may also be possible to increase the ratio of the number of potentially valuable mutants to the total population by enrichment procedures which allow the mutants to grow faster than the parent strain. Such methods include alternate subculture in selective and nonselective media and continuous culture.

Selection methods which can identify individual mutant colonies by colour reactions which are not given by the parent strain are obviously very useful and need not be restricted to methods based on the presence of indicator compounds in the growth medium. The use of replica plates allows the master plate to be treated with reagents which may reveal the presence of high concentrations of end products or intermediates and it may be possible to carry out enzyme assays on the plate itself.

A positive selection method, using media which restrict the growth of the parent strain and allow the growth of particular classes of mutants, is probably the most useful method of all. Examples will be discussed of various ways in which the sensitivity of cultures to particular metabolic analogues may be enhanced by varying the growth medium or the growth condition of the inoculum. Selection for growth on novel substrates may demand a critical balance of nutrients to restrict the growth of the parent and yet allow the mutants to reach a threshold growth rate.

Sometimes it is appropriate to use a roundabout method and to start by selecting for mutants which have special properties which make them more likely to give rise to mutants of the desired type. A leaky auxotroph may be more sensitive to growth inhibition by metabolic analogues and this may be the only possible route to derepressed mutants for some biosynthetic pathways. Similarly, it may be essential to start by making constitutive mutants for catabolic enzymes, thus releasing the system from the constraints of inducer specificity, before selecting for mutants producing altered enzymes.

Finally, it may not be necessary to produce an all-weather mutant. Provided that the necessary conditions are not too stringent it may be most useful to produce a leaky, or partially derepressed mutant which can be controlled by varying the composition of the medium at some stage of growth. For example, a bradytrophic mutant can be grown with a suboptimal amount of the end product of the pathway and, as this becomes limiting, intermediates may start to accumulate as early enzymes become derepressed. This method of exploiting differences in regulatory patterns (or altering the medium) at different stages of growth, is of course common practice in the production of antibiotics. Applied to a leaky mutant it can allow the culture to reach an appreciable growth yield and then enable the metabolic activities to be diverted to produce the required compounds.

Results and discussion

CONTINUOUS CULTURE OR PLATE SELECTION?

The theoretical basis of using continuous culture for mutant isolation is that mutants producing *more* enzyme, *better* enzyme or capable of taking up the growth-limiting compound more efficiently will have a growth advantage and outgrow the parent strain. Only relatively small differences in growth rate should be necessary and cultures are grown in the chemostat for as many generations as are required to enable the mutant to take over. The steady-state biomass of the culture and the concentration of metabolites in the effluent medium can be monitored for this.

Horiuchi *et al.* (1962) isolated mutants of *Escherichia coli* which produced β-galactosidase constitutively by growing an inducible strain in a chemostat with limiting lactose for about 10 generations. Since lactose is not effective as an inducer at low concentrations (it is converted *in vivo* to the actual inducer molecule) any constitutive mutants which arise have a growth advantage over the inducible wild type. This method has been successful for other inducible enzymes; for example, Hegeman (1966) obtained mutants of *Pseudomonas putida* which were constitutive for the mandelate enzymes in this way. Constitutive mutants are able to compete with inducible strains by producing more enzyme and, if the selection process is prolonged, a further increase in the amount of enzyme may result from gene amplification. Horiuchi *et al.* (1962) found that after about 100 generations of continuous culture in lactose-limited medium, strains appeared which had several gene copies and produced β-galactosidase in amounts which constituted up to 25 per cent of the total cell protein. These "hyper-strains" were very unstable when removed from the chemostat.

More recently, Hartley *et al.* (1972) and Hartley (1974) selected mutant strains of *Klebsiella aerogenes* which grew faster in chemostat cultures limited by xylitol. The parent strain was constitutive for ribitol dehydrogenase which has low activity for xylitol and some of the mutants, producing 20 per cent of their total protein as ribitol dehydrogenase, were thought to have acquired additional gene copies. Chemostat selection following mutagenesis with nitrosoguanidine led to the production of mutant strains which produced a ribitol dehydrogenase with a lowered K_m for xylitol and an increased xylitol to ribitol activity ratio.

A combination of direct selection pressure and continuous culture was used by Francis and Hansche (1972) to select for an altered acid phosphatase in *Saccharomyces cerevisiae*. In this case, growth was limited by providing β-glycerophosphate as the phosphate source and the culture was maintained at a pH higher than the optimum for the enzyme. After 400 generations they obtained a mutant which produced an acid phosphatase with a higher pH optimum.

Results of studies of this sort would suggest that selection by continuous culture is of limited application and is most likely to select regulatory mutants and mutants with gene amplification but can be extended to select altered enzyme mutants.

Selection of mutants from plate media also depends on differences in growth rates between parent and mutant strains but here the differences must be great enough to identify colonies of the mutants. The ideal selection medium allows the growth of the mutant strain but not the parent but it is quite sufficient if the mutant produces recognizable colonies among a background growth. Many selection media have been devised to intensify growth rate differences and these are based on the particular characteristics of the enzyme system concerned.

THE ISOLATION OF MUTANTS FOR BIOSYNTHETIC PATHWAYS

Mutants of several biosynthetic pathways have been used for the biosynthesis of the normal end product or intermediates or for the production of one or more of the enzymes of the pathway. Certain mutations of biosynthetic pathways are associated with increased synthesis of secondary metabolites (Demain, 1973).

Methods for the isolation of auxotrophic mutants are of very general application but the isolation of regulatory mutants presents more difficulties.

Metabolic analogues inhibit growth by competing with normal cell metabolite for an essential binding site and by selecting for analogue-resistance a very large range of mutants can be isolated. Mutants of *Escherichia coli*, derepressed for the tryptophan biosynthetic enzymes, were isolated by Cohen and Monod (1959) as mutants resistant to growth inhibition by 5-methyltryptophan. Since then many amino acid analogues have been used for the isolation of derepressed and feedback inhibition-resistant mutants.

The histidine biosynthetic enzymes of *Salmonella typhimurium* are almost fully repressed in the wild-type strain grown in minimal medium and this strain is insensitive to repression by histidine analogues. Cultures can be made sensitive to growth inhibition by 1,2,4-triazole-3-alanine either by introducing a leaky mutation in the pathway or by partial inhibition of imidazole glycerol phosphate dehydrase by another analogue, 3-amino-1,2,4-triazole. When the rate of functioning of the pathway is restricted the culture requires fully derepressed levels of the enzymes in order to grow and then 1,2,4-triazole-3-alanine inhibits growth by analogue repression. Mutants resistant to this analogue were found to be derepressed for the enzymes of the histidine operon (Roth *et al.*, 1966). The regulation of the histidine operon is complex but the complexity of the control system is no bar to using metabolic analogues and by presenting more potential sites for analogue interaction may make it easier to select regulatory mutants.

A comprehensive list of metabolic analogues which have been used in studies with *Escherichia coli* and *Salmonella typhimurium* will be found in a recent review by Umbarger (1971) on the use of these compounds as genetic and biochemical tools.

It is frequently reported that other microbial species are less sensitive than *E. coli* to growth inhibition by metabolic analogues. This is due partly to differences in specificities of the proteins concerned and also to differences in the regulatory controls. Waltho and Holloway (1966) and Kay and Gronlund (1969) tested a large number of amino acid analogues and found that very few inhibited the growth of *Pseudomonas aeruginosa*. However, by extending the range of analogues tested and by altering growth conditions, several workers have obtained mutants of *Pseudomonas* species which are derepressed or resistant to feedback inhibition. Maurer and Crawford (1971) isolated mutants of *P. putida* resistant to 5-fluorotryptophan (or other tryptophan analogues) which were derepressed for the early enzymes of the pathway and excreted anthranilate. In *P. putida* the first few enzymes of the pathway are repressible by tryptophan; phosphoribosyl anthranilate isomerase (*trpC*) is constitutive; tryptophan synthetase is induced by indole glycerol phosphate. Although the same type of gene structure and regulation operates in *P. aeruginosa*, Calhoun

et al. (1973) found that 5-fluorotryptophan-resistant mutants excreted tryptophan and not anthranilate. These differences occur between two wild-type
strains but it might be possible to obtain mutants of *P. aeruginosa* which excrete
anthranilate by a mutation in the *trpC* gene determining the phosphoribosyl
anthranilate isomerase. This is put forward as an example of how a double
mutant might be developed to overproduce a metabolic intermediate.

One factor which affects the sensitivity of cultures to a metabolic analogue
is the physiological state of the culture and the growth medium. It has long
been understood that a culture would be sensitive to growth inhibition by an
amino acid analogue in a minimal medium when the activity of the biosynthetic enzyme was required for growth but not in a complex medium.
However, as we have seen, the extent of repression or derepression of biosynthetic enzymes in minimal media varies widely among different species.
Calhoun and Jensen (1972) found that β-thienylalanine inhibited growth of
P. aeruginosa with fructose as the carbon source but not with glucose. Phenylalanine relieved the growth inhibition and they suggest that this effect of fructose in enhancing the sensitivity of the organism to an aromatic amino acid
analogue is due to restriction of the size of the metabolic pool of precursors of
this pathway. The manipulation of metabolic pools by providing particular
carbon compounds as growth substrates is most interesting and could be
applied to the isolation of other analogue-resistant mutants for biosynthetic
pathways.

Studies on the regulation of the branched pathways for amino acid biosynthesis illustrate ways in which metabolites may be channelled into a
particular branch of the pathway. This has some relevance to a consideration
of the metabolic flow into a secondary metabolic pathway (Demain, 1973).
The branched pathway for the biosynthesis of the aromatic amino acids in
P. aeruginosa provides a direct example of this. The pigment pyocyanine is
synthesized from chorismate at a branch point of the pathway (Calhoun *et al.*,
1972). It is synthesized during growth but behaves as a typical secondary
metabolite in that it is synthesized in high yield by stationary cultures deprived
of inorganic phosphate (Ingeldew and Campbell, 1969). This could be a useful
model system for the genetic analysis of the regulation of the synthesis of a
secondary metabolite and methods for isolation of pyocyanine mutants have
been described by Carson and Jensen (1974).

THE ISOLATION OF MUTANTS FOR CATABOLIC ENZYMES

Many of the methods for the isolation of mutants for catabolic enzymes are
also based on the use of analogues for selective media. Jacob and Monod
(1970) pointed out that one of the main reasons for choosing lactose utilization
by *Escherichia coli*, rather than another inducible system, for the detailed
investigation of enzyme induction, was that it was possible to prepare galacto-

side analogues to investigate inducer and substrate specificities. It was already known that several media could be used to differentiate between lactose-positive and lactose-negative strains by including an indicator to show the presence or absence of acid production. Lac indicator plates include Mac-Conkey agar, eosin-methylene blue lactose agar, and lactose-tetrazolium agar and lactose-bromothymol blue agar.

The chromogenic substrate 5-bromo-4-chloro-3-indolyl-β-D-galactoside (XG) (Horwitz *et al.*, 1964) is used to distinguish between inducible and constitutive colonies on plates; the noninducing substrate phenyl-β-D-galactoside can be used to select constitutive mutants; the weak substrate lactobionic acid can be used to select constitutive mutants and mutants which produce high levels of β-galactosidase (Langridge, 1969). Other galactosides such as isopropyl-β-D-galactoside (IPTG) are nonsubstrate inducers; 2-nitrophenyl-β-D-fucoside (ONPF) competes with inducing galactosides and inhibits induction and also represses synthesis in some constitutive strains. Orthonitrophenyl-β-D-thiogalactoside (TONG) is transported by the *lac* permease and inhibits growth and Müller-Hill *et al.* (1968) used this compound to select mutants producing increased amounts of the *lac* repressor by selecting mutants with an inducible phenotype at 43 °C from a temperature-sensitive constitutive mutant. The constitutive parent strain was unable to grow at 43 °C in the presence of TONG and, by including in the medium lactose and IPTG, those mutants which became resistant to TONG by the loss of the *lac* permease were also eliminated. The surviving mutants produced more of the *i* gene product and were thought to be promoter mutants.

The galactoside analogues have been used primarily for biochemical and genetic studies on the *lac* operon as a model system for understanding the regulation of gene expression. However, by investigating the effects of galactoside analogues on the system it was possible to develop extremely elegant methods for mutant selection. Analogues have also been used to isolate mutants for other sugar-utilizing enzyme systems. For example, Buttin (1963) obtained constitutive *gal* mutants by growing *E. coli* in a medium containing galactose as the carbon source in the presence of methyl-β-D-thiogalactoside (TMG) which inhibits the induction of the *gal* operon. Engelsberg *et al.* (1965) isolated mutants which were constitutive for the arabinose enzymes by selecting from a medium with L-arabinose as the carbon source in the presence of L-fucose which prevents the induction of the *ara* operon.

With *Pseudomonas aeruginosa*, media containing various different amides have been used to select regulatory and structural gene mutants of the aliphatic amidase (Betz *et al.*, 1974; Clarke, 1974). Minimal medium containing succinate as carbon source and formamide (a poor inducer and a poor substrate) as nitrogen source, is used to select constitutive mutants and also mutants which are more readily induced by formamide. Butyramide is a very poor substrate and inhibits induction in the wild-type strain and can be used to select a class of constitutive mutants which are resistant to repression by butyramide. However, among the constitutive mutants selected from the succinate + for-mamide medium are some which are very sensitive to butyramide repression and these were used to select a class of butyramide-utilizing mutants producing altered enzymes. These butyramide-utilizing mutants produce a mutant B amidase with a higher V_{max} and a lower K_m for butyramide. Valeramide-utilizing mutants, producing V amidases were isolated from a mutant pro-ducing B amidase (Brown et al., 1969). Phenylacetamide as nitrogen source with succinate as carbon source was used to select mutants producing phenylacetamidases using several different constitutive mutants as parental strains (Betz and Clarke, 1972). A very derepressed mutant producing wild-type A amidase was used to obtain a mutant producing an enzyme which hydrolyses acetanilide (N-phenylacetamide) (Brown and Clarke, 1972).

Another amide which has been used for the selection of negative rather than positive mutants is fluoroacetamide. The noninduced wild type is relatively insensitive to this compound which exerts its effect only after hydrolysis and incorporation into fluorocitrate by the condensing enzyme, i.e. by lethal synthesis. By starting with a constitutive strain grown with a nonrepressing carbon source, or with a catabolite repression-resistant strain, or with a fully induced wild type, it is possible to isolate amidase-negative mutants from plates containing fluoroacetamide together with pyruvate and ammonium salts. This positive selection method enables large numbers of amidase-negative mutants to be isolated which are useful for developing further mutations as well as for genetic analysis in their own right. (Clarke and Tata, 1973).

Few enzymes have absolute specificity and studies with several other systems have confirmed that the most usual mutation leading to a new growth phenotype, by the utilization of a novel substrate, is a regulatory mutation. If an organism already has a structural gene for an enzyme with low activity for the novel substrate then a constitutive mutation may enable sufficient of the enzyme to be produced for growth to occur. Selection for growth on poor substrates which are not inducers thus provides a straight-forward method for the selection of constitutive strains. Mutants of Klebsiella aerogenes selected for the ability to grow on D-arabinose were found to produce fucose isomerase constitutively (Camyre and Mortlock 1965). Further mutations in the genes for this enzyme resulted in the production of a fucose isomerase with a higher relative activity for D-arabinose and a lower K_m for both sugars (Oliver and Mortlock, 1971).

The key to selecting constitutive mutants, or mutants with altered inducer response, lies in exploiting the differences between inducer and substrate specificities. In those cases in which altered enzyme mutants were selected it was essential that the new strain should also have a regulatory mutation which allowed expression of the structural gene in the presence of the novel substrate.

MUTANTS RESISTANT TO CATABOLITE REPRESSION

Most inducible enzymes and a few biosynthetic enzymes are known to be produced at much lower rates when certain potential growth substrates or metabolites are present in the growth medium. Repression of this sort is rather loosely referred to as catabolite repression although this term is used in a much more specific sense to refer to the repression exerted by glucose on some of the well-known catabolic enzymes of *Escherichia coli*. For the *lac* operon of *E. coli* transcription of the *lac* genes requires an activator protein (CRP), in combination with cyclic adenosine monophosphate (cAMP), which binds to the promoter and facilitates transcription by RNA polymerase (Silverstone *et al.*, 1969). Pastan and Perlman (1968) showed that glucose repression of β-galactosidase synthesis could be relieved by cAMP and it was later shown that a cAMP binding protein was essential for both *in vivo* and *in vitro* transcription of the *lac* and *ara* operons (Emmer *et al.*, 1970; Zubay *et al.*, 1970; Crombrugghe *et al.*, 1971). A mutation in the promoter region may confer resistance to catabolite repression and mutants of this class may produce high enzyme levels. Other mutations affecting catabolite repression may be in the gene for the CRP protein or for the gene determining adenyl cyclase and mutations of this type may have pleiotropic effects on several operons for catabolic enzymes. Mutations for genes determining the rates of functioning of central metabolic pathways can affect indirectly the extent of catabolite repression and many catabolic repression-resistant mutants isolated are of this ill-defined class. Permeability mutations may also affect catabolite repression either by excluding the potential repressing compound or by altering any effect it might have on the transport of an inducer into the cell. As an encouragement to those who wish to isolate catabolite repression-resistant mutants it should be said that for most systems it is far easier to isolate such mutants than to be certain of the genetic lesion that has occurred. From the practical point of view, the value of these mutants is that if an enzyme is not appreciably affected by the carbon source used for growth it might be possible to choose a cheaper growth substrate and to achieve high growth yields without sacrificing specific activity.

For the *lac* operon the promoter mutants exhibiting resistance to catabolite repression were isolated as revertants from a class of lactose-negative mutants which could be induced by IPTG to synthesize β-galactosidase at about 5 per cent of the rate of the inducible parent strain. Some of the promoter mutants with these very low rates of β-galactosidase synthesis were themselves more or less insensitive to glucose repression (Silverstone *et al.*, 1969). The lactose-positive revertants produced β-galactosidase at a high rate and, for some, the rate of synthesis was the same whether they were induced in media containing glycerol, glucose or glucose-6-phosphate (Arditti *et al.*, 1968; Magasanik, 1970). The earlier catabolite repression-resistant mutants for β-galactosidase were selected on a medium containing *N*-acetyl-lactosamine as the nitrogen source with IPTG as inducer and glucose as the carbon source and catabolite repressor (Loomis and Magasanik, 1965). It was later shown that these mutants were not specific for the *lac* operon and probably carried defects in glucose metabolism (Rickenberg *et al.*, 1968).

Pseudomonas aeruginosa is very sensitive to catabolite repression by succinate or malate and less sensitive to repression by glucose or lactate. Catabolite repression-resistant mutants which appear to have promoter mutations were isolated by Smyth and Clarke (1972). These were selected as revertants from a class of mutants which grew poorly on acetamide and the catabolite repression-resistant mutation was shown to be very closely linked to the amidase structural gene. Other classes of catabolite repression-resistant mutants have been isolated from media containing lactamide (a poor substrate but a good inducer) as a nitrogen source and succinate as the carbon source. This method selects stable mutants which produce high enzyme levels. Some have lower growth rates in succinate medium but others grow as well as the wild type and their defects are not known. These stable mutants are particularly useful for routine enzyme production and have also been used as parental strains for the isolation of altered enzyme mutants.

A medium containing glucose as the carbon source and proline as the nitrogen source was used to isolate mutants of *Salmonella typhimurium* which were resistant to catabolite repression by glucose of two of the enzymes of the proline degradative pathway (Newell and Brill, 1972).

The two different ways in which catabolite repression-resistant mutants have been isolated for the enzymes discussed above are: (1) selection of revertants from mutants with very slow rates of enzyme synthesis; (2) selection of mutants from plates containing a known catabolite repressor as the carbon source and a nitrogen-containing substrate as the nitrogen source for growth. Both these methods are potentially of general application.

ISOLATION OF MUTANTS FOR THE HISTIDINE DEGRADATIVE PATHWAY OF
PSEUDOMONAS AERUGINOSA

The pathway for histidine degradation by *Pseudomonas aeruginosa* is shown in Fig. 1. The enzymes of the pathway are induced by urocanate, the product of the first enzyme, and subject to catabolite repression by succinate (Lessie and Neidhardt, 1967). We have recently isolated various classes of mutants and some of this work will be discussed as a case history in mutant isolation.

P. aeruginosa, strain PAC1, unlike most strains of this species, cannot utilize histidine as the sole carbon source for growth although it can utilize it as a nitrogen source. The defect is in the histidine permease and not in any of the enzymes of the pathway. Histidine can be transported at a rate sufficient to satisfy the requirements of a histidine auxotroph and sufficient to induce histidase and permit rather poor growth on a medium containing histidine and succinate (Potts and Clarke, 1974). This naturally occurring defect provided an unexpected advantage. Mutants selected for better growth on a medium containing succinate and histidine were found to include some which

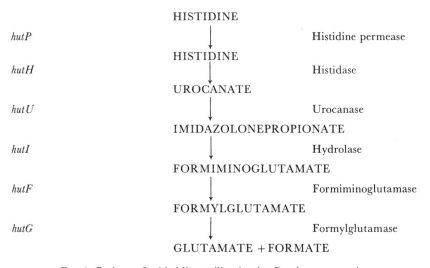

FIG. 1. Pathway for histidine utilization by *Pseudomonas aeruginosa*.

produce histidase and urocanase constitutively. This selection of regulatory mutants depended on differences in growth rates of inducible and constitutive strains both carrying permeability defects. In the constitutive strain, histidine is converted fairly rapidly to urocanate so that it is removed from the internal pool and the entry of histidine from the external medium is thereby facilitated. The background growth of the inducible strain could be reduced by incubation at 43 °C instead of 37 °C, and the same effect was obtained when the succinate concentration was increased from 1 to 2 per cent. These nonspecific minor modifications increased the selection pressure and made it easier to identify and isolate the constitutive mutants. These findings suggested that constitutive mutants for other pathways might be isolated via permease-defective mutants but for the histidine degradative pathway an important, and perhaps an essential, element was that the inducer was not the substrate but the product of the first enzyme.

Selection for growth on media in which histidine provided both carbon and nitrogen gave rise to inducible histidine-positive strains from the wild-type PAC1 and constitutive histidine-positive strains from the constitutive mutants previously selected for better growth on succinate + histidine medium. The histidine-positive (hut^+) mutants were compared with the inducible and constitutive histidine-negative strains (hut^-) and it was shown that growth on histidine could be related to the rates of histidine uptake by these strains. The concentration of histidine used in the selection medium was important in determining the class of mutants selected. The mutants which grew faster on histidine had higher rates of histidine uptake and were selected from plates containing 0.1 per cent histidine whereas the slower-growing mutants were selected from plates containing higher concentrations. With this system variations in the composition of the medium allowed the selection of mutants with varying capacities for transporting a potential growth substrate into the cell. This was not pursued further but does suggest that it should be possible to select from a mutant with a very severe defect in a transport system a range of mutants with different transport capacities for the compound used for selection. This could be very useful for further mutant isolation since such permeability mutants might have different concentrations of meta-bolites in their metabolic pools which would make them more or less suscept-ible to selection pressures.

Catabolite repression of the enzymes for histidine and proline degradation by *Klebsiella aerogenes* requires an adequate supply of nitrogen (Prival and Magasanik, 1971). This is also the case for *P. aeruginosa hut* enzymes and while the addition of succinate to a culture growing exponentially in pyruvate + ammonium salts medium results in very severe repression of histidase and uro-canase synthesis, it has no effect on the rates of synthesis of these enzymes by strain PAC1 growing in pyruvate medium with histidine as the nitrogen source. Since there is no catabolite repression by succinate under conditions of nitrogen limitation, it was not possible to select catabolite repression-resistant mutants from succinate + histidine plates. It had been hoped that this method would have been applicable since it had been possible to select catabolite repression-resistant mutants for amidase from succinate + lactamide plates. However, it was found that growth of the inducible and constitutive mutants, and the wild-type PAC1, on succinate + histidine plates was inhibited in the presence of methyl ammonium chloride. The mutants that appeared were resistant to catabolite repression by succinate and produced high levels of histidase and urocanase during exponential growth in succinate + ammonium salts medium. Methyl ammonium chloride appears to be acting as an ammonia analogue in this selective medium although its exact role is not certain. Tyler et al. (1974) have implicated the ammonia assimilation system involving glutamine synthetase in the regulation of transcription of the *hut* enzymes of *S. typhimurium* but we have no evidence to show whether or not this might also be the case for *P. aeruginosa*.

Mutants with defects in one or more of the enzymes of the pathway were isolated by a negative selection method from *P. aeruginosa*, strain PAC1 and also from the histidine-positive strain PAO1 (Potts, 1974). From strain PAO1 constitutive mutants were also isolated. Conjugational and transductional mapping showed that the *hut* genes belonged to at least two linkage groups although in *P. putida* they appear to be all in the same gene cluster (Leidigh and Wheelis, 1973). We have not explored the possibility of using any of the constitutive mutants with defects in the early enzymes of the pathway for preparing any intermediates of the pathway, but it would be predicted that this would be possible. We have also as yet left unexplored the possibility of isolating mutants which can utilize histidine or urocanate analogues.

We were interested in the histidine degradative pathway as a slightly more complex model system than amidase for exploring methods of isolating mutants. We found it possible to isolate both constitutive and catabolite repression-resistant mutants as well as defective enzyme mutants. The methods used, which were based on the general methods of mutant isolation which were discussed earlier, were successful because they made use of the special properties of the enzyme system and of the strains themselves. This is the main conclusion which can be drawn from all these studies on mutant isolation. The best results are obtained by exploiting the system itself and the more information that is available on the properties of the enzymes and their regulation, the more elegant will be the selection methods.

References

Arditti, R. R., Scaife, J. G. and Beckwith, J. R. (1968). *J. molec. Biol.* **38**, 421.
Betz, J. L., Brown, P. R., Smyth, M. J. and Clarke, P. H. (1974). *Nature, Lond.* **247**, 261.
Betz, J. L. and Clarke, P. H. (1972). *J. gen. Microbiol.* **73**, 161.
Brown, J. E., Brown, P. R. and Clarke, P. H. (1969). *J. gen. Microbiol.* **57**, 273.
Brown, P. R. and Clarke, P. H. (1972). *J. gen. Microbiol.* **70**, 287.
Buttin, G. (1963). *J. molec. Biol.* **7**, 164.
Calhoun, D. H., Carson, M. and Jensen, R. A. (1972). *J. gen. Microbiol.* **72**, 581.
Calhoun, D. H. and Jensen, R. A. (1972). *J. Bact.* **109**, 365.
Calhoun, D. H., Pierson, D. L. and Jensen, R. A. (1973). *Molec. gen. Genet.* **121**, 117.
Camyre, K. P. and Mortlock, R. P. (1965). *J. Bact.* **90**, 1157.
Carson, M. and Jensen, R. P. (1974). *J. Bact.* **117**, 312.
Clarke, P. H. (1974). *In* "Evolution in the Microbial World" (Ed. M. J. Carlile and J. J. Skehel) p. 183. Soc. gen. Microbiol., Symposium 24. Cambridge University Press, London.
Clarke, P. H. and Tata, R. (1973). *J. gen. Microbiol.* **75**, 287.
Cohen, G. and Monod, J. (1959). *C.r. hebd. Séanc. Acad. Sci. Paris*, **248**, 3490.

Crombrugghe, B. De, Chen, B. Anderson, W., Nissley, P., Gottesman, M., Pastan, I. and Perlman, R. (1971). *Nature, New Biol.* **231**, 139.

Demain, A. (1973). *Adv. appl. Microbiol.* **16**, 177.

Emmer, M., Crombrugghe, B. De, Pastan, I. and Perlman, R. (1970). *Proc. natn. Acad. Sci. U.S.A.* **66**, 480

Englesberg, E., Irr, J., Power, J. and Lee, N. (1965). *J. Bact,* **90**, 946.

Francis, J. C. and Hansche, P. E. (1972). *Genetics,* **70**, 50.

Hartley, B. S. (1974). *In* "Evolution in the Microbial World" (Ed. M. J. Carlile and J. J. Skehel), p. 151. Soc. gen. Microbiol. Cambridge University Press, London.

Hartley, B. S., Burleigh, B. D., Midwinter, G. G., Moore, C. H., Morris, H. R., Rigby, P. W. J., Smith, M. J. and Taylor, S. S. (1972). "Enzymes: Structure and Function" (Ed. J. Dreuth, R. A. Oosterbaan and C. Veegar), vol. 29, p. 151, 8th FEBS meeting. North Holland, Amsterdam.

Hegeman, G. (1966). *J. Bact.* **91**, 1161.

Horiuchi, T., Tomizawa, J. and Novick, A. (1962). *Biochim. biophys. Acta,* **55**, 152.

Horwitz, J. P., Chua, J., Curby, R. J., Tomson, A. J., DaRooge, M. A., Fisher, B. E., Mauricio, J. and Klunot, I. (1964). *J. med. Chem.* **7**, 574.

Ingledew, W. M. and Campbell, J. J. R. (1969). *Can. J. Microbiol.* **15**, 535.

Jacob, F. and Monod, J. (1970). *In* "The Lactose Operon" (Eds J. R. Beckwith and D. Zipser), p. 2. Cold Spring Harbor Laboratory, New York.

Kay, W. W. and Gronlund, A. F. (1969). *J. Bact.* **98**. 116.

Langridge, J. (1969). *Molec. gen. Genet.* **105**, 74.

Leidigh, B. J. and Wheelis, M. (1973). *Molec. gen. Genet.* **120**, 201.

Lessie, T. G. and Neidhardt, F. C. (1967). *J. Bact.* **93**, 1800.

Loomis, W. F. and Magasanik, B. (1965). *Biochem. biophys. Res. Commun.* **20**, 230.

Magasanik, B. (1970). *In* "The Lactose Operon" (Eds J. R. Beckwith and D. Zipser), p. 189. Cold Spring Harbor Laboratory, New York.

Maurer, R. and Crawford, I. P. (1971). *J. Bact.* **106**, 331.

Müller-Hill, B., Crapo, L. and Gilbert. W. (1968). *Proc. natn. Acad. Sci. U.S.A.* **59**, 1259.

Newell, S. L. and Brill, W. J. (1972). *J. Bract.* **111**, 375.

Oliver, E. J. and Mortlock, R. P. (1971). *J. Bact.* **108**, 293.

Pastan, I. and Perlman, R. L. (1968). *Proc. natn. Acad. Sci. U.S.A.* **61**, 1336.

Potts, J. R. (1975) Ph.D. Thesis, University of London.

Potts, J. R. and Clarke, P. H. (1974). *Proc. Soc. gen. Microbiol.* **1**, 63

Prival, M. and Magasanik, B. (1971). *J. biol. Chem.* **246**, 6288.

Rickenberg, H. V., Hsie, A. W. and Janeček J. (1968). *Biochem. biophys. Res. Commun.* **31**, 603.

Roth, J. R., Anton, M. J. and Hartman, P. E. (1966). *J. molec. Biol.* **22**, 305.

Silverstone, A. E., Magasanik, B., Reznikoff, W. S., Miller, J. H. and Beckwith, J. R. (1969). *Nature, Lond.* **221**, 1012.

Smyth, P. F. and Clarke, P. H. (1972). *J. gen. Microbiol.* **73**, ix.

Tyler, B., Deleo, A. B. and Magasanik, B. (1974). *Proc. natn. Acad. Sci. U.S.A.* **71**, 225.

Umbarger, H. E. (1971). *Adv. Genet.* **16**, 119.

Waltho, J. A. and Holloway, B. W. (1966). *J. Bact.* **92**, 35.

Zubay, G., Schwartz, D. and Beckwith, J. (1970). *Proc. natn. Acad. Sci. U.S.A.* **66**, 104

Some observations on gene expression

JOHN SCAIFE

Department of Molecular Biology, University of Edinburgh, Edinburgh, Scotland

Summary

Recent advances in our understanding of gene regulation mechanisms at the physiological and genetic levels are presented and discussed in relation to improvement of product yield and genetic engineering.

Introduction

Most people define a gene in terms either of its product or, less directly, of product function. This attitude, deeply enshrined in our systems of nomenclature, derives from our dependence in genetic studies on mutant organisms which have suffered a change or total loss of an easily recognized property. From this point of view the most striking feature of the gene is the primary information it contains: the sequence of RNA or DNA bases or base pairs in the genetic material which serves to define the structure of a gene's product, be it RNA or protein.

Now that we understand in principle and to some extent in practice how that information is transcribed into RNA (Losick, 1972) and can subsequently be translated into protein (Haselkorn and Rothman-Denes, 1973) our focus of interest is moving to the mechanisms by which transcription and translation are initiated and terminated. The nature of the stop and start signals which delineate a gene or group of genes from its chromosomal neighbours is a fascinating problem whose elucidation is a challenge to molecular and cell biologists alike.

Results and discussion

BIOLOGICAL SIGNALS

The flexibility of living organisms is very striking. It is dependent upon signal systems which ensure that functions of a cell, organ or organism appear when they are needed. These systems can be divided into two general classes. Firstly, there are signals operating on the function of "nongenetic" molecules already present in the cell. They play an important role in communication between cells and can elicit a variety of responses ranging from alteration of cell metabolism to cell migration. Secondly, the synthesis of gene products may itself be controlled by signals which no doubt also vary both in mechanism and response. However, we can distinguish a class of these which act directly either on the chromosome or the product RNA. It is such systems which form the context of the present discussion.

The agent initially activating control systems of many genes is extra-cellular in origin. In bacteria such control systems are very familiar to us. The *ara* (arabinose) genes of *Escherichia coli* are induced when arabinose is present in the growth medium (Zubay *et al.*, 1971). Similarly, the *lac* (lactose) system is normally induced in lactose medium (Beckwith and Zipser, 1970). This does not mean, of course, that the agent is chemically conserved through the chain of events leading to induction. On the contrary, when lactose enters the cell it is probably converted to allolactose by a transgalactosidation activity vested in one of the *lac* gene products: β-galactosidase. This conclusion is drawn from the finding that *lacZ* mutants, with no functional β-galactosidase, are not induced by lactose, and from *lac*-inducer studies *in vitro* (Jobe and Bourgeois, 1972). Likewise, the regulation of genes for amino acid biosynthesis often involves the charging of the cognate tRNA (Umbarger, 1969).

In fact, a signal may be passed between entirely different chemical species. The separate regulatory circuits of catabolic pathways in bacteria are often dramatically modified when glucose or a related sugar is added to the growth medium (Magasanik, 1970). Physiological and genetic studies on several bacteria, including *Escherichia coli* and its mutants, strongly indicate that the cell translates the glucose signal by modulating its intracellular concentration of 3′–5′ cyclic AMP (cAMP) which acts as the effector in gene regulation (Pastan and Perlman, 1970).

In discussing signals of extracellular origin we should remember an important fact. Since a chemical signal must have direct access to its target, a cell may regulate its response by denying access to the signal, either by degrading or excluding the signal molecule. Inducer exclusion in the *lac* system of *E. coli* is well documented (Magasanik, 1970). It is tempting to suppose that similar controls exist in more complex organisms.

CONTROL MECHANISMS FOR GENE EXPRESSION

Once inside the cell how does the signal reach its target? Since this is an article about gene expression, the ultimate target of interest to us is a nucleic acid: either DNA or RNA. In the (prokaryotic) systems we understand best, the target is a short nucleic acid sequence (a regulatory site less than 100 bases long) with specific control over transcription or translation of a few adjacent genes (Murray and Old, 1974). However, it is possible that, particularly in eukaryotic cells whose chromosomes have a more complex structure, some signals act by causing gross structural changes in extensive regions of the chromosome.

Implicit in our thinking so far is the idea that signal molecules (effectors) are small, be they metabolites or hormones. Many such molecules would be unlikely to have chemical properties suitable to permit binding to a specific nucleic acid sequence. It is therefore not surprising to find in the systems we can study at the molecular level that the effector binds to a protein which in turn interacts with the regulatory site. This concept originates in the operon model of Jacob and Monod (1961) and has been put to extensive experimental test. In its original form the model was applied to gene regulation in *E. coli* and its temperate phage λ. It was proposed that such systems respond to a repressor, the product of a regulatory gene which can prevent the expression of the (structural) genes under its control. Several repressors have now been isolated from bacteria (see Scaife, 1973) and their properties are under intensive investigation. In addition it has been possible to define chemically the regulatory site (operator) with which two of them interact (Gilbert and Maxam, 1973; Maizels, 1973; Maniatis and Ptashne, 1973a; Maurer *et al.*, 1974).

Further studies on phage λ (Thomas, 1971) and, amongst others, the *E. coli ara* (arabinose) and *mal* (maltose) genes (Zubay *et al.*, 1971; Hofnung and Schwartz, 1971) lead to the conclusion that the product of a regulatory gene may act in a positive way, being *required* for full structural gene expression. This idea has been elaborated and applied to eukaryotic systems (Davidson and Britten, 1973).

a. *Negative control by the lac and λ repressors*

The *lac* and λ repressors both bind tightly to operator DNA (Gilbert and Müller-Hill, 1970; Ptashne, 1971) and specifically prevent transcription of the appropriate templates by *E. coli* RNA polymerase *in vitro* (de Crombrugghe *et al.*, 1971; Eron and Block, 1971). Since the operators precede the genes under their control, we conclude that these repressors block initiation of transcription. How do they do this?

In attempting to answer this question we must recall that RNA polymerase binds to defined sites, promoters (Scaife and Beckwith, 1966; see Brammar, this Symposium), in order to initiate a RNA transcript. In phage λ, *lac* and other systems (Brammar, this Symposium) these sites are, at least in part, functionally distinct from the operator, since mutations in the promoter region affecting the maximum level of operon expression do not automatically affect repression, and *vice versa* (Miller, 1970; Maurer *et al.*, 1974). The *lac* promoter region contains both the polymerase binding site and a sequence probably recognized by an additional regulatory protein CRP, CAP or CGA, the protein potentiated by cAMP, whose action is common to many catabolic systems (Pastan and Perlman, 1970; Beckwith *et al.*, 1972). It is separated from the first structural gene by the operator as it is genetically defined. The λ operator regions which are also known in some detail are discussed below.

As a first step to understanding how repressors act two groups have sequenced the *lac* regulatory region (Gilbert and Maxam, 1973; Maizels, 1973; Barnes, Reznikoff, Dickson and Abelson, personal communication). *Lac* operator fragments can be protected from DNAase by bound repressor. RNA transcripts from the protected material have been analysed (Gilbert and Maxam, 1973). The following features emerge. They have been independently confirmed by Barnes and co-workers. The *lac* repressor, a stable tetramer of identical subunits (MW 150 000 daltons) protects a unique operator fragment about 27 base-pairs long. The fragment has, towards one end, a sequence of six base pairs symmetrically orientated with respect to six at the other. The 9-base sequence between them, which also shows a degree of symmetry, separates the two stretches by what would normally be a single turn of the DNA double helix. Similar features are associated with a site on λDNA recognized by the *ter* enzyme(s) which cuts λDNA circles to give linear genomes (see Murray and Old, 1974), and may therefore be common to many proteins interacting with DNA.

The repressor may be assumed to interact with certain groups contained in the operator fragment. The identification of these groups, which would allow a precise definition of the true *lac* promoter, awaits further investigation. For the moment we can speculate that the true operator includes the symmetric sequences. Such sequences could allow the operator DNA to take up a cruciform structure (Gierer, 1966; Sobell, 1973) detectable by a protein molecule. However, this hypothesis is rendered unlikely by X-ray crystallographic and electron micrographic studies on the repressor tetramer (Steitz *et al.*, 1974). Nor can it explain the properties of phage λ operator fragments (Maniatis and Ptashne, 1973b). A hypothesis which is more likely on current evidence is that the symmetric sequences determine features in one of the grooves of the DNA double helix able to accommodate opposing subunits of the repressor tetramer which itself has two-fold rotational symmetry (Gilbert *et al.*, 1973). The studies of Steiz *et al.* (1974) show that the tetramer has steric properties fully compatible with this proposal.

The *lac* operator is already genetically defined by O^c (operator constitutive) mutations which lead to a loss of repression. Interestingly, most of the O^c mutations analysed biochemically have base changes *between* the symmetric sequences (Gilbert, Maxam and Majors, personal communication). We can interpret this result in at least two ways. The true operator may not include the entire symmetric sequence. Alternatively, the relevant O^c mutations may have slipped through the selective net. For example, some mutations inside *lac* operator may diminish or eliminate *lac* expression altogether. They would not be recovered in a typical search for lac^+ constitutive mutants.

How does the *lac* repressor stop transcription? Two hypotheses have been tested experimentally (Reznikoff *et al.*, 1969; de Crombrugghe *et al.*, 1971; Eron and Block, 1971). The repressor could block RNA polymerase binding or subsequent step in transcript initiation. The *lac* operator studies (Maizels, 1973) show that *lac* transcription is probably initated just inside the *lac* DNA sequence protected by the repressor. Thus the binding sites for repressor and RNA polymerase could overlap, on which basis our first hypothesis is rendered more likely.

Parallel studies are under way on the interaction between the λ repressor and its operators (O_L and O_R). The phage protein appears to interact with operator quite differently from the *lac* repressor. The λ repressor, at least *in vitro*, has monomers, dimers and tetramers in equilibrium (Ptashne, 1971). Moreover, studies on λDNA fragments suggest that the operators have multiple, nonidentical binding sites which are loaded sequentially (Maniatis and Ptashne, 1973b). The first site, which binds repressor more tightly and is nearest to the first structural gene, is deduced from endonuclease studies to be about 30 base-pairs long and has a base-sequence with three axes of two-fold symmetry (Maniatis, Ptashne, Bennett and Donelson, personal communication). Subsequent sites are about half that size. (A dimer could cover 30 base pairs). An operator constitutive mutation is located in the first site of O_L confirming the biological significance of the *in vitro* studies (Maniatis and Ptashne, 1973a). In addition, promoter mutations have been mapped in the operator region (Allet *et al.*, 1974; Maurer *et al.*, 1974).

The studies which lead to this conclusion employ an experimental approach which proves to be both powerful and widely applicable (Murray and Old, 1974). A class of DNA restriction enzymes commonly encountered in the bacterial world cut DNA molecules exclusively at specific sequences. These are symmetric and occur sufficiently rarely to allow, for example, virus genomes to be broken into a few fragments. It is often possible by using fragment size and other criteria to pinpoint the location of the endonucleolytic cut precisely on the genome. A restriction endonuclease from *Haemophilus influenzae* attacks λ sites protected by the repressor (Maniatis and Ptashne, 1973). In addition, not only does RNA polymerase protect these sites but also genetically defined promoter mutations remove their susceptibility to attack (Allet *et al.*, 1974; Maurer *et al.*, 1974). These mutations map within O_L and O_R. Thus there is very strong evidence that the operators and promoters of λ overlap. Consequently we have good reason to suppose that, although their primary interaction with operator DNA may be different, both *lac* and λ repressors prevent transcription by blocking polymerase binding.

b. *Positive control systems*

The position is less clear when we turn to positive control factors which regulate transcription. Do they bind to DNA, rendering a promoter more able to bind polymerase or initiate a transcript? Genetic arguments (Beckwith *et al.*, 1972) lead us to believe that the *lac* promoter region contains a CRP binding site, although attempts to demonstrate gene-specific DNA binding by purified CRP factor have yielded negative results (Riggs *et al.*, 1971). Symmetric sequences do occur in the proposed CRP binding site (Barnes, Reznikoff, Dickson and Abelson, personal communication). The N gene product of phage λ on the other hand may interact primarily with RNA polymerase, since bacterial mutations blocking N function alter the host enzyme (Georgopoulos, 1971). It probably acts, not by stimulating polymerase binding or initiation, but by reversing a host stop signal, thus permitting a transcript to be extended into previously unread genes (Roberts, 1970). Nevertheless, recent studies suggest that its primary interaction occurs when the enzyme is upstream at the operator–promoter region (Friedman *et al.*, 1973).

The regulatory mechanisms I have discussed refer to the few bacterial systems we are beginning to understand at the molecular level. We can already see that the cell's regulatory options are quite diverse. In addition, we now know that RNA transcripts may be subject to further processing, e.g. endonucleolytic breaks, polyadenylation (see Davidson and Britten, 1973), which could themselves be controlled. Finally the regulation of some phage systems is known to operate at the translation level, a mechanism which host cells may use to control expression of some of their own genes (Hazelkorn and Rothman-Denes, 1973).

THE PURPOSE OF GENE CONTROL SYSTEMS

During the course of evolution, it is fair to assume living organisms have developed control systems which optimize their biosynthetic potential. At the level of gene expression this objective can be attained in more than one way. We can suppose that some genes are best controlled by simple on-off switches. For example the structural genes of the temperate bacteriophages are either completely shut down (lysogenic response) or fully operational (lytic response). To achieve this end both phage λ and the *Salmonella* phage P22 have apparently evolved controls (*cro* and *immI* respectively) to supplement the primary repressor (see Davison, 1973).

On the other hand, the operation of genes supplying enzymes for individual biochemical pathways can be set at different levels, which we presume are appropriate to the cell's immediate requirements and determine limits within which regulation of enzyme *function* may provide fine-level control (Ennis and Gorini, 1961; McFall and Maas, 1967). The setting is determined, at least in part, by the affinities of the regulatory macromolecule for its target and for the effector molecule, whose intracellular concentration serves to monitor the cell's needs. A particular pathway may be subject to other controls, integrating it into the overall metabolic pattern of the cell. For example, the CRP factor, required for full expression of genes determining catabolic enzymes, is dependent on cAMP which monitors the availability of a "preferable" carbon source (e.g. glucose). Analogous overriding controls may determine choice between nitrogen sources (Prival and Magasanik, 1971).

The cell may have other more subtle requirements calling for gene control. It may need to buffer its responsiveness to a call for more enzyme. It may also need to coordinate the synthesis of a gene product with cell growth. Such requirements may be satisfied by autogenous control systems (Goldberger, 1974).

Autogenous control systems have recently received a good deal of attention. The feature they have in common is structural gene product able to control its synthesis by interacting with its own operator. The first enzyme of the biosynthetic pathway for histidine, a hexamer coded by the first gene (*hisG*) of the *his* operon of *Salmonella typhimurium* (Ames and Hartman, 1963), represses *his* expression *in vitro* (Blasi *et al.*, 1973). This evidence corroborates studies showing that a *his* constitutive mutant is altered in *hisG* (Kovach *et al.*, 1968; Rothman-Denes and Martin, 1971). Other *his* constitutives have mutations affecting the synthesis and utilization of tRNA[His] which, when charged, is the presumed effector in *his* control, or operator mutations. Despite intensive search no gene coding for a regulatory macromolecule has been identified outside the operon (see Goldberger, 1974). These combined studies suggest that the *his* operon is regulated by the *his* product which interacts with charged tRNA[His] and the operator. Thus a paucity of histidine in the cell will lead to a decrease in the concentration of charged tRNA[His], and a consequent reduction in the amount of *hisG* product bound to the operator, causing derepression of the operon. However, this sequence of events will automatically lead to a rise in the concentration of the regulatory macromolecule available to shut the system down as histidine, and consequently charged tRNA[His] begin to accumulate. Other candidates for autogenous control, recently reviewed by Goldberger (1974), can be found in bacteriophages, fungi, mouse and man.

Sompayrac and Maaløe (1973) have argued that autogenous control mechanisms could provide a way for cells to maintain a constant amount of a gene product throughout the growth cycle and have suggested that it may operate in the regulation of DNA synthesis. Synthesis of RNA could depend at least in part on the autogenous control of RNA polymerase synthesis. In

Escherichia coli this enzyme has four "core" subunits β, β' and α_2 (Burgess, 1971). Recent studies from our laboratory indicate that the genes for at least two of these subunits β and β' map together and share a common promoter (Errington *et al.*, 1974). We also know that their synthesis parallels total protein synthesis over a wide range of growth conditions, and, in synchronized cultures, bears out a prediction we would make if they were under autogenous control (Matzura *et al.*, 1973). It has not been possible to detect a doubling in the rate of synthesis of the β and β' subunits at any stage of the growth cycle in such cultures. If RNA polymerase synthesis were unregulated, its subunits should be made at twice the rate following replication of their genes. On the other hand, if one or more polymerase subunits were able to repress their own synthesis, we could suppose that following gene duplication there would be a brief burst of subunit synthesis (not detected in the synchrony experiments) after which expression of these genes would be restored to its initial rate by the subunits made in excess. This hypothesis could also explain why the rate of synthesis of the β and β' subunits increases several-fold as polymerase molecules are inactivated by rifampicin (Hayward *et al.*, 1973). Finally we would expect, and observe, that a cell containing many (more than 100) copies of the β and β' genes, carried on an induced λd*rif* transducing phage, synthesizes only marginally more of these subunits than normal (Kirschbaum, 1973; Kirschbaum and Scaife, 1974).

We have recently developed a system to test for autogenous RNA polymerase control by the β' subunit and possibly others (Errington *et al.*, 1974). We have fused the β (*rif*) gene to the nearby *argCBH* operon by deleting the intervening DNA. Our deletion leaves the β' gene intact but removes its promoter, shared with the *rif* gene. It puts the β' gene under *arg* control, because it is read in the same direction as *argCBH*. The fused operon is on a transmissible F' factor, KLF10. In a genetically derepressed strain (*argR*⁻) it causes β' to be synthesized at a rate much higher (2.5-fold) than normal. In a repressed (*argR*⁺) strain it makes no detectable contribution to synthesis of this subunit.

In addition to the episomal polymerase genes these strains retain their chromosomal copy of the β-β' operon, together with any target sites for regulation. Their only intact copy of the β gene is on the chromosome under normal regulation. If the β' subunit alone (or products of other operon genes not removed by the deletion) regulated polymerase synthesis our *argR*⁻ strain should synthesize β at a different rate from the *argR*⁺. We can detect no difference between them, implying that either other polymerase subunits, or an as yet undefined mechanism, regulate synthesis of the enzyme.

CONTROL SYSTEMS AND THE YIELD OF GENE PRODUCTS

The recent studies on gene regulation which I have described have interesting implications for the industrial microbiologist, since they have a bearing on the strategy adopted to improve the yield of a gene product.

Firstly to ensure maximum gene expression it may be necessary to circumvent more than one regulatory barrier either genetically or physiologically.

Secondly, inactivation of a regulatory gene in a haploid organism, e.g. *E. coli argR⁻*, commonly leads to a more massive gene derepression than deprivation for the effector molecule, viz arginine (Jacoby, 1972). On this basis we could argue that constitutive mutants should give a higher yield. On the other hand those diploid organisms with functional regulatory genes represented twice per nucleus should not yield constitutive derivatives as a result of a single mutation in one of their regulatory gene copies. Only (*cis*-dominant) mutations with an altered regulatory *site* would yield the desired phenotype. However analysis of the *lac* and λ operators indicates that these sites may overlap with initiation sites for transcription. Thus a direct selection for operator constitutive mutants could favour those derivatives with functionally intact promoters, a population which may be skewed towards a low degree of constitutivity. This is a characteristic of the classical *lac*O^c mutations.

Equally it may prove difficult to improve product yields for a gene under autogenous control. If a gene product with an activity of industrial importance is also a repressor acting on its own operator, many apparently desirable mutations eliminating repression would in fact reduce or destroy the required activity.

Thus we can expect that, thanks to the control systems acting on their expression, some genes will be refractory to the conventional methods of mutation and direct selection for improved product yields. It may be preferable to separate such genes from their own controls and fuse them to a more amenable genetic system. This strategy is rapidly becoming more feasible thanks to the growing armoury of specific endonucleases to which I have already referred and to developments in gene transfer technique (Brammar; Collins; these Proceedings). Otherwise, it may be preferable initially to isolate (constitutive) mutants with *reduced* activity and subsequently select for improved yield from them (see Collins, these Proceedings).

GENETIC ENGINEERING

Techniques are now being developed which permit a gene to be transferred to an alien cell (Brammar; Collins; these Proceedings). The success of these techniques depends on whether the gene can be expressed in the new cytoplasm. Our experience from plasmid transfer *in vivo* between different bacterial species encourages us to view the latter problem optimistically (Datta and Hedges, 1972). Even regulatory proteins may function on alien genes, at least in related species (Chater, 1970), and perhaps more strikingly, *Salmonella typhimurium* can put the β subunit of the *E. coli* RNA polymerase to general use. This conclusion is drawn from the behaviour of *Salmonella typhimurium* derivatives carrying the β- and, probably, the β'-genes of *E. coli* (Scaife and Flynn, unpublished).

Admittedly I have given examples of heterospecific gene expression in fairly closely related bacterial species and it would be unwise to underestimate the problems which could arise as genes are moved over greater taxonomic distances. Some of them can already be anticipated. Genes using specific transcription or translation factors may not be expressed in a foreign cytoplasm. Equally, some genes could respond to foreign repressors or termination factors (acting prematurely and thereby truncating the gene product). Others could impair vector functions thus preventing their own transfer or maintenance. We shall better be able to take the measure of these limitations as our experience grows.

Acknowledgement

I should like to thank Drs Gilbert, Ptashne and Reznikoff for providing data in advance of publication.

References

Allet, B., Roberts, R. J., Gesteland, R. F. and Solem, R. (1974). *Nature, Lond.* **249**, 217.
Ames, B. N. and Hartman, P. E. (1963). *Cold Spring Harb. Symp. quant. Biol.* **28**, 349.
Beckwith, J. R., Grodzicker, T. and Arditti, R. R. (1972). *J. molec. Biol.* **69**, 155.
Beckwith, J. and Zipser, D. (1970). *In* "The Lactose Operon" (Eds J. R. Beckwith and D. Zipser). Cold Spring Harbor Laboratory, New York.
Blasi, F., Bruni, C. B., Avitabile, A., Deeley, R. G., Goldberger, R. F. and Meyers, M. F. (1973). *Proc. natn. Acad. Sci. U.S.A.* **70**, 2692.
Burgess, R. (1971). *A. Rev. Biochem.* **40**, 711.
Chater, K. F. (1970). *J. gen. Microbiol.* **63**, 95.
de Crombrugghe, B., Chen, B., Anderson, W., Nissley, P., Gottesman, M., Pastan, I. and Perlman, R. (1971). *Nature, New Biol.* **231**, 139.
Datta, N. and Hedges, R. W. (1972). *J. gen. Microbiol.* **70**, 453.
Davidson, E. H. and Britten, R. J. (1973). *Q. Rev. Biol.* **48**, 565.
Davison, J. (1973). *Br. med. Bull.* **29**, No. 3, 208.
Ennis, H. L. and Gorini, L. (1961). *J. molec. Biol.* **3**, 439.
Eron, L. and Block, R. (1971). *Proc. natn. Acad. Sci. U.S.A.* **68**, 1828.
Errington, L., Glass, R. E., Hayward, R. H. and Scaife, J. G. (1974). *Nature, Lond.* **249**, 519.
Friedman, D. I., Wilgus, G. S. and Mural, R. J. (1973). *J. molec. Biol.* **81**, 505.
Georgopoulos, C. P. (1971). *Proc. natn. Acad. Sci. U.S.A.* **68**, 2977.
Gierer, A. (1966) *Nature, Lond.* **212**, 1480.
Gilbert, W., Maizels, N. and Maxam, A. (1973). *Cold Spring Harb. Symp. quant. Biol.* **38**, 845.
Gilbert, W. and Maxam, A. (1973). *Proc. natn. Acad. Sci. U.S.A.* **70**, 3581.
Gilbert, W. and Müller-Hill, B. (1970). *In* "The Lactose Operon" (Eds J. R. Beckwith and D. Zipser). Cold Spring Harbor Laboratory, New York.

Goldberger, R. F. (1974). *Science* (*Wash.*) **183**, 810.
Hayward, R. S., Tittawella, I. P. B. and Scaife, J. G. (1973). *Nature, New Biol.* **243**, 6.
Hazelkorn, R. and Rothman-Denes, L. B. (1973). *A. Rev. Biochem.* **42**, 397.
Hofnung, M. and Schartz, M. (1971). *Molec. gen. Genet.* **112**, 117.
Jacob, F. and Monod, J. (1961). *Cold Spring Harb. Symp. quant. Biol.* **26**, 193.
Jacoby, G. A. (1972). *Molec. gen. Genet.* **117**, 337.
Jobe, A. and Bourgeois, S. (1972). *J. molec. Biol.* **69**, 397.
Kirschbaum, J. B. (1973). *Proc. natn. Acad. Sci. U.S.A.* **70**, 2651.
Kirschbaum, J. and Scaife, J. G. (1974). *Molec. gen. Genet.* In press.
Kovach, J. S., Berberich, M. A., Venetianer, P. and Goldberger, R. F. (1968). *J. Bact.* **97**, 1283.
Losick, R. (1972). *A. Rev. Biochem.* **41**, 409.
Magasanik, B. (1970). *In* "The Lactose Operon" (Eds J. R. Beckwith and D. Zipser). Cold Spring Harbor Laboratory, New York.
Maizels, N. (1973). *Proc. natn. Acad. Sci. U.S.A.* **70**, 3585.
McFall, E. and Maas, W. K. (1967). *In* "Molecular Genetics II" (Ed. J. H. Taylor). Academic Press, New York and London.
Maniatis, T. and Ptashne, M. (1973a). *Nature, Lond.* **246**, 133.
Maniatis, T. and Ptashne, M. (1973b). *Proc. natn. Acad. Sci. U.S.A.* **70**, 1531.
Matzura, H., Hansen, B. S. and Zeuthen, J. (1973). *J. molec. Biol.* **74**, 9
Maurer, R., Maniatis, T. and Ptashne, M. (1974). *Nature, Lond.* **249**, 221.
Miller, J. H. (1970). *In* "The Lactose Operon" (Eds J. R. Beckwith and D. Zipser). Cold Spring Harbor Laboratory, New York.
Murray, K. and Old, R. W. (1974). *Prog. Nuc. Acid Res. and Mol. Biol.* **14**, 117.
Pastan, I. and Perlman, R. (1970). *Science.,* **169**, 339.
Prival, M. J. and Magasanik, B. (1971). *J. biol. Chem.* **246**, 6288.
Ptashne, M. (1971). *In* "The Bacteriophage λ (Ed. A. D. Hershey). Cold Spring Harbor Laboratory, New York.
Reznikoff, W. S., Miller, J. H., Scaife, J. G. and Beckwith, J. R. (1969). *J. molec. Biol.* **43**, 201.
Riggs, A. D., Reiness, G. and Zubay, G. (1971). *Proc. natn. Acad. Sci. U.S.A.* **68**, 1222.
Roberts, J. W. (1970). *Nature, Lond.* **224**, 1168.
Rothman-Denes, L. and Martin, R. G. (1971). *J. Bact.* **106**, 227.
Scaife, J. G. (1973). *Br. med. Bull.* **29**, No. 3, 214.
Scaife, J. G. and Beckwith, J. R. (1966). *Cold Spring Harb. Symp. quant. Biol.* **31**, 403.
Sobell, H. M. (1973). *Prog. Nucl. Acid Res.* **13**, 153.
Sompyrac, L. and Maaløe, O. (1973). *Nature, New Biol.* **241**, 133.
Steitz, T. A., Richmond, T. J., Wise, D. and Engelman, D. (1974). *Proc. natn. Acad. Sci. U.S.A.* **71**, 593.
Thomas, R. (1971). *In* "The Bacteriophage" (Ed. A. D. Hershey). Cold Harbor Laboratory, New York.
Umbarger, H. E. (1969). *Curr. Top. Cell Reg.* **1**, 57.
Zubay, G., Gielow, L. and Englesberg, E. (1971). *Nature, New Biol.* **233**, 164.

Gene amplification in bacterial systems

J. F. COLLINS

Department of Molecular Biology, University of Edinburgh, Edinburgh, Scotland

Summary

Gene amplification covers both the physiological and genetic means of enhancing gene expression and gene dosage in an organism. Chromosome replication produces a gradient of gene dosage which can be varied over a limited range; pathological states can favour those genes replicated early, still further. Simple gene transpositions or duplication offer some improvement, but movement of genes into different genetic environments, and onto plasmids and prophage structures can give large increases in effective gene dosage.

The use of the mutator phage, and of the restriction enzymes that produce staggered double-stranded breaks, offer the most interesting possibilities for genetic engineering. Hybrid plasmids have been produced with both prokaryotic and eukaryotic DNA and the prospects for gene amplification seem very bright.

Introduction

The relationship between the genetic constitution of an organism and the yield of a specific product is unfortunately rarely simple to explain, even though considerable information may be available about the structural and regulatory genes concerned. Even in the best cases we have only a working description of a very limited part of the set of integrated processes that make up a living cell. Genetic amplification, indeed any form of strain improvement, has been carried out mainly from experience and only partly by rational design based on genetic analysis of the system.

The primary process of strain improvement usually entails cycles of muta-

41

tion and selection (or screening) for enhanced production. The starting organism chosen probably gave a better yield than other organisms in a preliminary screening. The initial improvements stem trom regulatory mutations in regions such as the operator or promoter as well as loss of catabolite repression (see articles by Scaife, and by Clarke, this Symposium). Many mutant strains improve for unknown reasons, perhaps connected with the physiological state of the cells during the productive phase of growth. The next phase is essentially gene amplification, adapting the strain or the growth conditions to raise the effective dosage of the desired genes as high as possible. It has been shown that translation of messenger RNA into polypeptides is equally efficient at different growth rates, and that the limitation on the expression of many genes is the rate of transcription (Kjelgaard and Kurland, 1963; Maaløe and Kjelgaard, 1966). An increase in gene dosage will normally be accompanied by increased formation of the gene product.

Recent developments in bacterial physiology and genetic engineering indicate that rational design in the production of improved strains may become a key factor in the future. The production of hybrid strains, expressing genes from any source in a bacterial environment, is becoming a focal point for both research and public debate.

In this review, I will discuss both physiological control and the amplification afforded by genetic manipulation, including some aspects of genetic engineering.

Gene dosage may be influenced by physiological conditions; though these effects are of relatively small magnitude compared to the improvements often produced by mutation, they can amplify the yield from the best mutant strain with considerable net gain. Physiological control need not depend on prior genetic knowledge or manipulation, and must be exploited in organisms where only a limited genetic background is available.

The remaining aspects of gene amplification involve genetic manipulation to increase gene dosage. The optimum configuration for the individual structural gene, for example, combined with a promoter region that is expressed at a high rate, may be difficult to achieve, but there are a variety of different approaches that are generally applicable.

Results and discussion

PHYSIOLOGICAL CONTROL

The practical aspects of the optimization of an industrial fermentation process need no emphasis here. Part of this process is undoubtedly an exercise in increasing gene dosage, particularly where the product required is the first stable product from the gene, that is, either a stable species of RNA or a polypeptide. The conditions for protein production differ from those needed for a secondary metabolite fermentation. While secondary metabolites can be formed by the enzymes present in the cell, provided the supply of direct precursors and energy lasts, the production of proteins requires the synthesis of the many precursors of protein and RNA synthesis together with a continuing supply of energy—virtually the conditions of normal growth. Within the range of normal growth conditions it is possible to vary the relative gene dosage over a limited range by exploiting the way in which the bacterial chromosome is replicated.

The model for replication of the bacterial chromosome reviewed by Sueoka *et al.* (1973) has been modified only in one major detail recently, bidirectional replication, documented in *E. coli, Bacillus subtilis* and *Salmonella typhimurium* (Nishioka and Eisenstark, 1970; Masters and Broda, 1971; McKenna and Masters, 1972; Bird *et al.*, 1972; Wake, 1972; Gyurasits and Wake, 1973). Replication of the circular DNA molecule starts from a fixed point (the origin), and proceeds through two replication complexes in opposite directions round the molecule till the complexes meet and two completed chromosomes are formed. In *E. coli* each replication complex takes about 40 minutes to traverse half the chromosome. This transit time is independent of the growth rate, and, during the cell cycle, genes replicated early predominate (Fig. 1). Initiations of rounds of DNA replication occur at intervals equal to the doubling time for the cells; when growth is so fast that initiations occur faster than the replication complexes can traverse the chromosome, the number of active replication complexes increases and the chromosome assumes a branched structure which futher raises the gradient of effective gene dosage. Painter's re-analysis (1974) suggests that the transit time may be as short as 28 minutes; this does not modify the basic model, but lowers the expected gradient somewhat. Fast growth favours genes replicated early; slow growth aids the expression of genes replicated late, provided that expression of the gene is effectively unregulated.

More highly branched chromosomes have been discovered by Pritchard (1974) and his co-workers during a study of replication in *E. coli* strains auxotrophic for thymine. Cells with limited thymine grew almost as fast as cells supplied with abundant thymine, and in spite of the low pool of thymidine triphosphate continued to initiate rounds of replication at the normal frequency. As each replication complex now synthesized DNA slower than normal, the chromosome acquired a highly branched structure, with a further 2–4-fold enhancement of the gene dosage for early genes. Strains prototrophic for thymine maintain pool levels of the triphosphates that saturate the polymerase system, which thus takes a constant time to replicate the chromosome in such strains.

It may not be practical to control levels of thymine during a fermentation using a thymine auxotroph; however, the same physiological state may exist in prototrophs in at least three classes of mutants (Fig. 2).

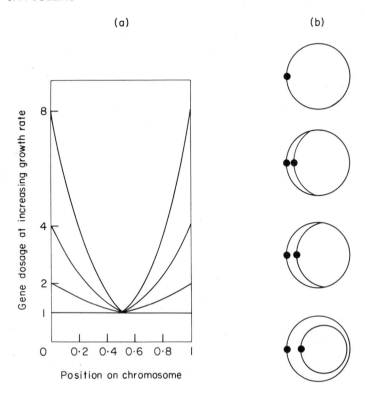

Fig. 1. (a) Gene dosage at increasing growth rates in bidirectionally replicating chromosome. Gene position runs from 0, at origin, back to origin at 1. (b) Diagrammatic scheme for bidirectional replication. Origin at dot.

CLASS 1 Mutants able to synthesize thymidine triphosphate only at a reduced rate. These might be found amongst revertants of thymine auxotrophs which show evidence of abnormality, such as a return of the thymine requirement at high growth temperatures.

$$
\begin{array}{l}
\qquad\qquad 2 \\
\text{Ribonucleotides} \rightarrow \text{Deoxyribonucleotides} \rightarrow \text{Deoxyribonucleotide} \\
\qquad\qquad\qquad\qquad\qquad\qquad\qquad\qquad\qquad \text{triphosphates} \\
\qquad\qquad 1 \\
\text{Uridine-deoxyribose-} \rightarrow \text{Thymidylate} \rightarrow \text{Thymidine} \\
\text{phosphate} \qquad\qquad\qquad\qquad\qquad \text{triphosphate}
\end{array}
\left.\begin{array}{l} \\ \\ \\ \\ \\ \end{array}\right\} \begin{array}{l} 3 \\ \rightarrow \text{DNA} \end{array}
$$

Fig. 2. Patterns of DNA synthesis. Stages at which mutations might lead to slow DNA synthesis per replicating complex, and hence increase branching of the replicating chromosome. 1, reduced thymidylate synthetase activity; 2, reduced ribonucleotide reductase activity; 3, DNA polymerase with lowered affinity for triphosphates.

CLASS 2 Mutants with lowered ribonucleotide reductase activity. Temperature-sensitive mutants of *E. coli* in the *dnaF* class are defective in this activity (Gross, 1972).

CLASS 3 Mutants with modified polymerase enzymes, specifically with lowered affinity for the normal DNA precursors.

Mutants in class 3 may have been obtained already in *Bacillus subtilis* among mutants containing modified DNA polymerases resistant to the joint action of 6-(*p*-hydroxyphenylazo)-uracil and 6-(*p*-hydroxyphenylazo)-iso-ocytosine (Gass *et al.*, 1973). These inhibitors, unlike many others (Goldberg and Friedman, 1971), work on the polymerase itself, and the joint use of both antimetabolites selects strongly for mutants with modified DNA polymerase, possibly with a lowered affinity for both the normal substrate and the analogue.

Mutants with these properties should be screened for possible enhanced levels of expression of suitable early genes.

These methods of physiological control benefit an early gene; genes replicated late cannot be amplified by this method. In addition, the effect is not specific to a single gene, but must apply to genes over a considerable region of the chromosome. The output of the cellular systems is diluted over a range of products which may be of no interest and high level expression of the target gene is therefore very important. Transposition of gene order may improve the lot of genes normally replicated late, but usually cannot be forced. Transposition of the origin of replication could change the gene dosage just as moving the target gene closer to the origin would do, but the degree of organization in the chromosome that would be disturbed by this transposition is unknown. It is interesting to note that *dnaA* mutants of *E. coli*, thermosensitive for initiation of DNA replication, can grow at the restrictive temperature if a plasmid such as F is present (Nishimura *et al.*, 1971). In these strains the F genome is often integrated near the normal origin of replication; the strains are somewhat sick, though it is not possible to say whether this is due to the presence of two potential sites of initiation, or from a disturbance to the chromosomal organization. Changes in gene order might be secondary in importance to changes leading to modified gene regulation and expression.

There are usually some genes that can be expressed at high levels, even under the natural regulation systems. For instance, the control of asparaginase-2 synthesis is complex, but in the stationary phase when asparaginase is synthesized the enzyme forms about 25 per cent of all soluble protein made during this period (Jeffries, these Proceedings). Similarly, in Bacilli, a number of hydrolytic enzymes are formed at high levels after the main phase of growth. Another example is the formation of the parasporal protein by *Bacillus thuringiensis*, produced in such large quantities that it forms crystals inside sporulating cells (Hannay and FitzJames, 1955). The regulation of the genes concerned with sporulation functions in general could be exploited. During sporulation, the expression of many genes required for normal exponential growth is diminished, and other groups of genes become active at different stages of the sporulation process. The control of these genes is not understood; in *Bacillus subtilis* they are not grouped together, but must be regulated by cytoplasmic signals (Szulmajster, 1973). Current theories favour some change in the RNA polymerase (Sonenshein and Losick, 1970) or a new initiation factor to promote the transcription of a distinct class of genes (Dube and Rudland, 1970). If the high efficiency of expression of genes controlled in any of these ways could be extended to a target gene, considerable gene amplification might result.

For gene amplification to be successful, increased gene dosage should be reflected in proportionally higher yields. This fact is sometimes regarded as evidence for the constitutive expression of genes; for example, in strains of *Saccharomyces cerevisiae*, haploid, diploid and tetraploid for tryptophan synthetase genes, the yield per gene copy is constant (Ciferri *et al.*, 1969). However, the expression of so-called constitutive genes may be subject to metabolic regulation (Clarke and Lilly, 1969; see Clarke, these Proceedings). On the other hand, amplification may fail for unknown reasons: the presence of two independent plasmids each carrying a constitutive gene for penicillinase synthesis (not known to be affected by catabolite repression) in *Staphylococcus aureus* does not give the expected additive yield of the enzyme (Richmond, 1968).

Gene dosage will not be reflected in product yield in autoregulatory systems, in which the protein coded by a gene plays a direct and negative regulatory role in the expression of the gene (see Scaife, these Proceedings). If the gene cannot be transferred to the control of an independent promoter region, it may be possible that some separation of the control function and the desirable property (such as enzymic activity) of the protein can be obtained. Any mutant that has lost its autoregulation, no matter how much activity has been lost in the process, can be mutated further in an attempt to restore the activity without restoring the regulation at the same time. There is no guarantee that this will be possible, of course.

CHROMOSOMAL GENE DUPLICATIONS

Amongst the earliest examples of deliberate gene amplification are the hyper strains, in which regions of the chromosome have been duplicated. In *E. coli*, such overproducers of β-galactosidase were produced by Novick and Horiuchi (1961) by maintaining cultures on very low levels of lactose in a chemostat. From an inducible parental strain, constitutive β-galactosidase producers were first obtained. Hyper strains were then isolated which had spontaneously duplicated the *lac* region into a tandem genetic sequence. Cultured without the limiting lactose, such strains segregate at a frequency of 1 in 1000 per generation (Horiuchi *et al.*, 1963). The β-galactosidase formed 24 per cent of the soluble protein in batch culture, and up to 36 per cent in a lactose-limited chemostat.

Selective pressure of this type is not generally available, and more diploids have been produced accidentally. Curtiss (1964) found that an unstable strain originating from an Hfr cross in *E. coli* carried as much as 9 per cent of the chromosome as a duplication, though the genetic structure of the strain was not clear. Amongst unstable *E. coli* strains selected for suppressor mutations, the gene for a glycyl-tRNA function was found to be duplicated, and both the wild-type and mutant alleles were retained. The region duplicated included the markers *metB*, *argH* and *thi*, flanking the suppressor gene (Hill *et al.*, 1969a, 1969b; Folk and Berg, 1971). Russell *et al.* (1970) have shown that the su$_{\overline{III}}$ gene, coding for a tyrosyl-tRNA function, is duplicated in normal strains of *E. coli*. Mutants to the su$_{III}^{+}$ state were heterozygous and unstable; recombination led to triploids for this gene which were even less stable. The reason why the diploid state is maintained normally is not known.

Gene duplication can also restore the expresssion of genes affected by a polar mutation. Cunin *et al.* (1970) studied an arginine auxotroph of *E. coli* which contained a strong polar mutation abolishing expression of all genes in the *arg* operon. One class of revertants able to utilize ornithine expressed the *argH* gene in a duplicate *arg* operon whose messenger did not appear to include the original polar mutation.

Gene duplication was found by Zavada and Calef (1969) to explain the loss of prophage inducibility in a lambda-cryptic strain. Part of the prophage had been deleted, and a segment (5 per cent of the chromosome) inserted between the remainder of the prophage genes.

Most classes of gene duplications, selected on some other ground than overproduction of a particular product, seem unlikely to be of great promise. Prokaryotic organisms seem inherently unstable with duplicated sequences of DNA; recombination-deficient strains can overcome this limitation, but in general they show less favourable growth characteristics.

GENE AMPLIFICATION WITH PLASMID-BORNE GENES

Additional copies of genes may be introduced by using unusual recombinations between any plasmid and the chromosome; strains carrying such modified plasmids are partially diploid for the region of the chromosome carried in the plasmid. The independent replication of the plasmid, though controlled by the chromosome, lends stability to the diploid state, though recombination involving the gene of interest on the chromosome and on the plasmid can result in loss of the extra copy.

c

The best known factors are the F factor in *E. coli*, the wide range of transmissible R factors and *col* factors. These plasmids are usually present as a single copy per genome (Silver and Falkow, 1970a, 1970b; Cohen and Miller, 1969, 1970). This ratio is determined by the interaction between the host and the plasmid, and varies in different host strains. For instance, the plasmid R100 is present in a 1:1 ratio with the genome in *E. coli*, but when the plasmid is transferred into *Proteus mirabilis* the proportion of plasmid DNA increases ten-fold. Even higher ratios have been observed: 20–60 copies per genome, rising as the culture enters the stationary phase to 200 copies per cell (Rownd, 1969; Meynell, 1972). Strains of *Proteus* carrying many copies of an R factor show a tendency to lyse, possibly due to osmotic fragility (Falkow *et al.*, 1969). There is evidence that the level of expression rises in proportion to the number of plasmid copies present (Kontomichalou *et al.*, 1970). The genes were not expressed at a very high level per plasmid, and the practical limits of such amplification are not know. Falkow *et al.* (1969) noted a rise of 300 per cent and 260 per cent in the content of chloramphenicol acetylase and penicillinase from plasmid-borne genes in *Proteus* cultures as they entered the stationary phase, presumably following the rise in plasmid content at this time. The R factors do not readily recombine with the chromosome, and are not well developed agents for producing diploid strains for chromosomal genes.

F factors, by contrast, interact readily with the chromosome, and F′ factors carrying almost any region of the *E. coli* chromosome are known. Low (1972) has compiled a useful catalogue of these derivatives. The properties of *E. coli* diploids carrying F′ factors are well known (Jacob and Monod, 1961). The manipulations with the F′ factors carrying the *lac* region can be repeated in principle with any chromosomal region. There is, however, little knowledge about the stability of F′ diploid strains under the conditions or over the time of a large-scale fermentation. The diploid state can be maintained if survival of the strain depends on expression of a gene on the episome; for example, Fowler (1972) studied *E. coli* strains diploid for the *lac* region, and maintained the F′ *lac* episome through the *pro*$^+$ allele it carried. The strains were:

Strain A324/4 *lac* I$^-$Z$^+$Y$^+$A$^+$ *pro*$^-$/F′*lac* I$^+$Z$^+$Y$^+$A$^+$ *pro*$^+$

Strain A324/5 *lac* I$^-$Z$^+$Y$^+$A$^+$ *pro*$^-$/F′*lac* I$^-$Z$^+$Y$^+$A$^+$ *pro*$^+$

Such strains can produce up to 25 per cent of their soluble protein as β-galactosidase (strain A324/4 must be induced first, of course).

Transmissible plasmids can not only transfer themselves, but can mobilize chromosomal and other plasmid genes. Since the regulation of many genes depends on cytoplasmic factors, transfer can itself lead to enhanced gene expression. Transfer can occur between different species and even different genera; for example, genes can be mobilized between *Escherichia, Shigella,*

Salmonella, Pasteurella, Serratia, Vibrio and *Proteus* (Richmond, 1973). Transfer can also occur between the pseudomonads and enteric bacteria (Sykes and Richmond, 1970; Datta and Hedges, 1972; Ingram *et al.*, 1972). Dixon and Postgate (1972) have transferred the nitrogen-fixation genes, *nif*, from *Klebsiella* into *Escherichia*, and Dunican and Kierney (1974) have transferred the *nif* genes from *Rhizobium trifolii* into *Klebsiella aerogenes*. Further development will exploit known interspecies and intergeneric relationships (Jones and Sneath, 1970).

Hybrid strains are therefore relatively easy to make, and the genes introduced function without corruption of their information content.

SPECIALIZED TRANSDUCING PHAGE

Specialized transducing phage can be exploited for gene amplification. The temperate coliphages, lambda, and $\phi80$, for instance, give specialized transducing phages by the integration of bacterial genes into the phage genome. When such phages lysogenize a host cell, the bacterial genes are carried as part of the prophage into the host chromosome, forming a partial diploid strain. When the prophage in such a strain is induced, it is excised and replicated to give about 50 copies of the phage genome, including the bacterial genes in the prophage, per cell. These genes can be expressed till the cell lyses.

Since the temperate phages tend to have highly specific and, in most cases, unique attachment sites at which the homology between chromosomal DNA and phage DNA strongly favours recombination, only a very limited number of genes lie close enough to the prophage to be incorporated into transducing particles, formed by a rare recombination between regions of DNA that are not perfectly homologous. The isolation of transducing particles is easy if a technique is available to detect transfer of the gene into a suitable recipient strain. Progeny give a high frequency transducing lysate on induction if a specialized transducing phage has been formed.

There are several methods to bring distant bacterial genes close to the prophage attachment site. One makes use of the fact that the gene determining sensitivity to the virulent phage T_1 lies adjacent to the $\phi80$ attachment site on the genetic map of *E. coli*. The gene of interest is first picked up onto an episome which carries a mutation making it unable to survive at high growth temperatures. By selecting for the continuing function of the target gene at high temperatures simultaneously with resistance to phage T_1, strains are obtained in which the gene has been integrated with some of the episome into the T_1-sensitivity gene, rendering it inoperative. The gene is then close enough to be picked up into transducing phage derived from phage $\phi80$ (Beckwith *et al.*, 1966). Extensions of this technique have been used by Miller *et al.* (1970), Ippen *et al.* (1971) and more recently by Davison *et al.* (1974).

In the latter case, the prophage carrying the *trp* genes was heat-inducible and carried a further mutation delaying lysis of the host cell (see Brammar, these Proceedings). On induction, many more copies of the phage genome can be formed than usual, and over the course of 5 hours the enzymes specified by the *trp* genes increase to about 75 per cent of the total protein. The *trp* genes are transcribed very efficiently from the N gene promoter of phage lambda, rather than the original bacterial *trp* promoter.

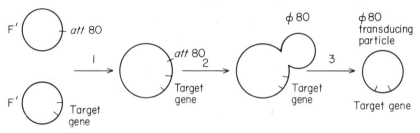

Fɪɢ. 3. Fusion of two F′ factors, and formation of φ80 transducing particle (Press *et al.*, 1971). 1, selection for characters on both plasmids gives survivors with fused F factors; 2, challenge by φ80 phage, integrating at the *att*80 site; 3, faulty excision leading to desired transducing particle carrying target gene.

When there is a strongly favoured attachment site in the chromosome, integration at other sites can rarely be detected. Integration at less usual sites, widening the range of genes that can be picked up in transducing particles, can occur in strains lacking the normal attachment site. Shimada *et al.* (1972) selected survivors at 41 C of an *E. coli* strain carrying a thermoinducible lambda prophage, and characterized some that had lost the *gal, bio* and *uvr* genes. These strains contained deletions of the region of the chromosome around the lambda attachment site. Such strains integrated lambda poorly, but formed lysogens at a variety of new sites on the chromosome. The chances of producing a transducing particle carrying a specified gene can be raised if the prophage can be detected in the neighbourhood of the target gene, for example, by selection at one and the same time for immunity from phage infection and loss of function of a gene close to the target gene.

Maas and his co-workers have demonstrated another method for bringing the target gene close to a phage attachment site (Press *et al.*, 1971). A cell carrying an F′ factor which includes the region of the chromosome containing the φ80 attachment site is infected with another F′ factor carrying the chromosomal region with the target gene. Two F factors do not propagate freely in the same cell; usually one or other is rapidly eliminated. By selecting the functions from both episomes, strains are obtained in which a rare recombination has occurred between the F factors to produce a hybrid episome (Fig. 3). The population of cells is challenged by φ80 phage. This integrates at its attachment site in the episome; when it excises, it can capture the target gene where it was closely linked to the *att* gene. Transduction with selection for the target gene completes the isolation of the specialized transducing particle which was desired.

USES OF THE MUTATOR PHAGE

A further tool for the mobilization of specific genes in *E. coli* and other organisms is the mutator phage, Mu1. Taylor (1963) showed that this phage induced a high rate of mutation during lysogenization because the prophage

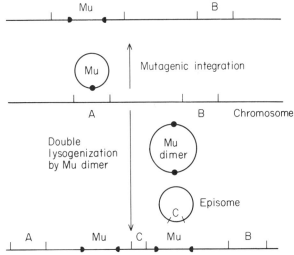

Fig. 4. A, Mutagenic integration of Mu prophage into gene A on chromosome; B, Mu-promoted integration of episome into chromosome, involving a Mu dimer, and leading to a double Mu lysogen (Toussaint and Faelen, 1973). Specific recombination region in Mu genome indicated by dot.

integrated into the mutated gene. Bukhari and Zipser (1972) found that the integration of Mu1 into the *lacZ* gene in *E. coli* occurred at so many distinguishable sites that the recombination could not rely on homology of the phage genome and the chromosome over any extensive region. The Mu prophage is always inserted by recombination at a unique site in its own genome, and this occurs independently of the host cell recombination functions. van der Putte and Gruijthuijsen (1972) showed that infection of a *recA* strain carrying an F′ factor leads to Mu lysogens with stable Hfr-like properties. A Mu dimer undergoes a double recombination event with the F′ factor and the chromosome, and a double Mu lysogen is in fact formed (Fig. 4; Toussaint and Faelen, 1973).

The potential of Mu looks very considerable. de Graaff *et al.* (1973) obtained Mu lysogens in mutants of *Citrobacter freundii* defective in restriction functions. When such strains carrying F′ factors were lysogenized with Mu, strains with Hfr properties were obtained. The insertion of the Mu prophage at a selected site can also provide a region of homology for recombination by normal systems, say, with an incoming episome already carrying a Mu prophage. This phage offers a unique means of producing unusual recombinant structures in any strain into which the Mu genome can be introduced. The *in vitro* properties of such a recombination system and the nucleic acid sequence involved are of considerable laboratory interest.

RESTRICTION SYSTEMS

The restriction and modification systems present in a wide variety of organisms present a barrier to the transmission of DNA between different strains. However, mutants can usually be obtained which are deficient in restriction or in both restriction and modification, and genetic manipulations are then possible. But the *in vitro* characterization of the restriction enzymes represents a major advance in nucleic acid technology, leading to the construction of biologically active hybrid DNA molecules. Restriction enzymes that produce staggered double-stranded breaks leave fragments with complementary regions of single-stranded DNA at the ends (Fig. 5; Murray and Old, 1974). When these fragments pair together (in any order, since the ends are common to all fragments produced by the same restriction enzyme), they can be covalently linked by polynucleotide ligase (Mertz and Davis, 1972) to produce novel DNA sequences.

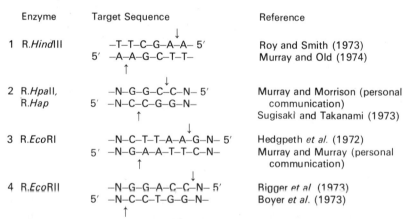

Enzyme	Target Sequence	Reference
1 R.*Hind*III	↓ –T–T–C–G–A–A– 5′ 5′ –A–A–G–C–T–T– ↑	Roy and Smith (1973) Murray and Old (1974)
2 R.*Hpa*II, R.*Hap*	↓ –N–G–G–C–C–N– 5′ 5′ –N–C–C–G–G–N– ↑	Murray and Morrison (personal communication) Sugisaki and Takanami (1973)
3 R.*Eco*RI	↓ –N–C–T–T–A–A–G–N– 5′ 5′ –N–G–A–A–T–T–C–N– ↑	Hedgpeth *et al.* (1972) Murray and Murray (personal communication)
4 R.*Eco*RII	↓ –N–G–G–A–C–C–N– 5′ 5′ –N–C–C–T–G–G–N– ↑	Bigger *et al.* (1973) Boyer *et al.* (1973)

FIG. 5. Taget sequences for restriction enzymes producing staggered double-stranded breaks. Note bilateral symmetry in cases 1, 2 and 3; in case 4, symmetry extends either side of the central A:T base pair.

GENETIC MANIPULATIONS WITH ESCHERICHIA COLI

The manipulations stem from two developments: the use of the restriction enzymes *in vitro*, and the development of a transformation system in *E. coli*. Mandel and Higa (1970) obtained reproducible transfection with phage DNA by adding calcium ions to the medium, though the frequency of infection was only 1 in 10^6. Cohen *et al.* (1972) applied this technique very successfully with R factor DNA; up to 1 in 10^3 cells could be recovered carrying the R factor. The DNA had recyclized inside the cell, and replication and

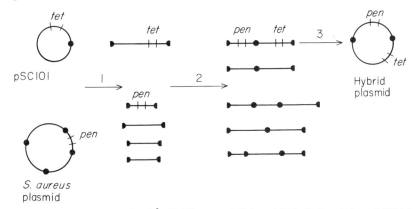

FIG. 6. Construction of hybrid plasmid (Chang and Cohen, 1974). 1, Restriction of DNA by R.*Eco*RI enzyme. 2, Aggregation of fragments, followed by polynucleotide ligase treatment, leading to mixed composite molecules. 3, Transformation of DNA into *E. coli*, followed by joint selection for tetracycline and penicillin resistance. Progeny carry hybrid plasmid.

expression of the plasmid appeared normal. This ability to recyclize may protect the R factor DNA from cellular enzymes which would otherwise destroy it, and probably explains why the frequency of transformation for a chromosomal marker, carried on linear fragments of DNA which do not cyclize, is so much lower. Cosloy and Oishi (1973) have recently described how transformation for chromosomal markers can be improved by the use of recipient strains deficient in an ATP-dependent nuclease (*recB recC*) and in exonuclease I (sbcB), presumably because the linear DNA molecules survive long enough to undergo recombination.

Cohen and Chang (1973), using sheared DNA from an R factor derivative produced a plasmid, pSC101, carrying a determinant for tetracycline resistance but no other resistance marker from the original factor. It contained only 10 per cent of the original plasmid DNA, including the genes for replication but not those needed for transfer. Hybrid plasmids have been constructed in the following way (Chang and Cohen, 1974) (Fig. 6). DNA from the plasmid pSC101 and from a plasmid conferring penicillin resistance in *Staphylococcus aureus* was treated with the R.*Eco*RI restriction enzyme. The mixed fragments were treated with polynucleotide ligase to join any paired fragments. Transformation of *E. coli* with this mixture followed by selection for both tetracycline and penicillin resistance gave progeny carrying a new hybrid plasmid, formed from both the original plasmids.

The pSC101 plasmid is particularly suitable for these techniques since it contains only a single target for the restriction enzyme R.*Eco*RI. The genes for replication and tetracycline resistance are always associated in the single fragment formed with the restriction enzyme. The hybrid is formed by the inclusion of another DNA fragment generated by the same restriction enzyme. Cohen *et al.* (1973) have shown that it is not necessary to join the DNA fragments by ligase treatment prior to transformation, though the treatment does not raise the frequency of formation of hybrid plasmids. The cohesive ends must pair within the cell, and the ligase in the cell joins the fragments before the new plasmid can be replicated. Fusion of eukaryotic DNA into this plasmid has been reported (Morrow *et al.*, 1974). DNA carrying information for the ribosomal RNA from *Xenopus laevis* was combined with pSC101 DNA, and the hybrid plasmid showed evidence of some ability to express the *Xenopus* genes, although at a low level.

N. E. Murray and K. Murray (Department of Molecular Biology, Edinburgh) have used similar techniques to generate hybrid derivatives of phage lambda. This phage usually had 5 restriction targets for the R.*Eco*RI enzyme; by genetic manipulation the number of target sequences can be reduced to one or two. Fragments of DNA derived from different variants by R.*Eco*RI treatment can be rejoined into functional genomes detected by plaque forming ability on transfection into sensitive *E. coli*. Chromosomal genes have also been introduced from a lambda derivative carrying the *trp* operon (Brammar, Murray and Winton, in press), and hybrids with eukaryotic DNA have also been formed.

If restricted fragments of DNA can recyclize within the bacterial cell, use of the mutator phage may give a general method of integrating such DNA molecules into the chromosome, without the intervention of any plasmid at all.

A more complex method of generating hybrid phage DNA by adding specific complementary sequences to DNA fragments has been used by Jackson *et al.* (1972, 1973), who have linked lambda DNA to SV40 DNA. This method is probably more limited in scope than the other methods described, since fairly pure preparations of DNA are needed.

Conclusions

Bacterial fermentations can be quick and convenient processes for the production of individual proteins in quantity, but the quality of the organism can be critical to the success of the operation. A higher specific yield of a protein pays dividends not just in the output from the fermenter, but the extraction and purification processes also become more efficient. The decision to undertake gene amplification should be made early, ideally once the demand for a suitable product has been assessed and a source organism found. A programme for developing improved strains does not need heavy capital investment, but needs hands, time and the appropriate genetic tools. As I have attempted to illustrate, these can range from the simple to the most sophisticated in concept, and each has a general field of application. Some of the questions that need to be considered are: what cell forms a suitable host for the target gene, from the standpoint of safety, possible genetic manipulation, ease of handling and product isolation? What organism should provide the initial genetic structure coding for the desired product?

The choice of the starting organism is no longer so important as it used to be. It is not obvious that the best source is necessarily the organism whose initial yield is highest; the initial yield may be less important than the desirable structural features of the protein and the potential to carry out different types of genetic manipulation (including mutation). In an ideal state, each structural gene should be coupled to a highly efficient promoter (such as that for the N gene in phage lambda: see Brammar, these Proceedings; Davison et al., 1974).

Safety and ease of handling are important considerations. A basic reason for moving a gene from one organism to another can be the economy of using an organism whose growth characteristics are well documented. The gene should be moved before the expression of the gene has been optimized in the parental organism, since secondary mutations enhancing yield may not be transferred with the target gene. Similarly, an early decision should be made if the gene is to be moved from a pathogenic organism into one normally regarded as nonpathogenic, so that the product may more readily be accepted by any relevant government agency.

The application of genetic engineering to specific problems has only just begun. Unlike many other forms of human endeavour, genetic manipulation need succeed only once for the goal to be reached. The use of restriction enzymes to generate DNA fragments which can be fused together with surprising ease may have the most far-reaching consequences. As the range of restriction enzymes increases, and different DNA sequences form the targets at which staggered breaks can be induced, it becomes possible to think of choosing the enzyme to isolate fragments with integral sequences of target genes.

The potential to create molecules which will be propagated indefinitely in a natural host should be regarded with some awe and caution. Where eukaryotic DNA is fused into prokaryotic structures, there will inevitably be controversy and concern; where that eukaryotic material is viral, the wisdom of the operation is in serious doubt. A full public debate is in progress and guidelines have been proposed for such work in the future. It is not an attractive prospect to add to all the other problems we face the problem of genetic pollution!

References

Beckwith, J. R., Singer, E. R. and Epstein, W. (1966). *Cold Spring Harb. Symp. quant. Biol.* **31,** 393.
Bird, R. E., Louarn, J., Martuscelli, J. and Caro, L. (1972). *J. Molec. Biol.* **70,** 549.
Bigger, C. H., Murray, K. and Murray, N. E. (1973). *Nature, New Biol.* **244,** 7.
Boyer, H. W., Chow, L. T., Dugaiczyk, A., Hedgpeth, J. and Goodman, H. M. (1973). *Nature, New Biol.* **244,** 40.
Bukhari, A. I. and Zipser, D. (1972). *Nature, New Biol.* **236,** 240.
Chang, A. C. Y. and Cohen, S. N. (1974). *Proc. natn. Acad. Sci. U.S.A.* **71,** 1030.
Ciferri, O., Sora, S. and Tiboni, O. (1969). *Genetics,* **61,** 567.
Clarke, P. H. and Lilly, M. D. (1969). *Symp. Soc. gen. Microbiol.* **19,** 113.
Cohen, S. N. and Chang, A. C. Y. (1973). *Proc. natn. Acad. Sci., U.S.A.* **70,** 84.
Cohen, S. N., Chang, A. C. Y., Boyer, H. W. and Helling, R. B. (1973). *Proc. natn. Acad. Sci. U.S.A.* **70,** 3240.
Cohen, S. N., Chang, A. C. Y. and Hsu, L. (1972). *Proc. natn. Acad. Sci. U.S.A.* **69,** 2110.
Cohen, S. N. and Miller, C. A. (1969). *Nature,* **224,** 1273.
Cohen, S. N. and Miller, C. A. (1970). *J. molec. Biol.* **50,** 671.
Cosloy, S. D. and Oishi, M. (1973). *Proc. natn. Acad. Sci. U.S.A.* **70,** 84.
Cunin, R., Elseviers, D. and Glansdorff, N. (1970). *Molec. gen. Genet.* **108,** 154.
Curtiss, R. (1964). *Genetics,* **50,** 679.
Datta, N. and Hedges, R. W. (1972). *J. gen. Microbiol.* **70,** 453.
Davison, J., Brammar, W. J. and Brunel, F. (1974). *Molec. gen. Genet.* **130,** 9.
Dixon, R. A. and Postgate, J. R. (1972). *Nature,* **237,** 102.
Dube, S. K. and Rudland, P. S. (1970). *Nature,* **226,** 820.
Dunican, L. K. and Tierney, A. B. (1974). *Biochem. biophys. Res. Commun.* **57,** 62.
Falkow, S., Hääpala, D. K. and Silver, R. P. (1969). *In* "Bacterial Episomes and Plasmids" (Eds G. W. E. Wolstenholme and M. O'Connor), p. 136. CIBA Symposium. Churchill, London.
Folk, W. R. and Berg, P. (1971). *J. molec. Biol.* **58,** 595
Fowler, A. V. (1972). *J. Bact.* **112,** 856.
Gass, K. B., Low, R. L. and Cozzarelli, N. (1973). *Proc. natn. Acad. Sci. U.S.A.* **70,** 103.
Goldberg, I. H. and Friedman, P. A. (1971). *A. Rev. Biochem.* **40,** 775.
Graaff, J. de, Kreuning, P. C. and Putte, P. van der. (1973). *Molec. gen. Genet.* **123,** 283.
Gross, J. (1972). *Current Topics in Microbiology and Immunology,* **57,** 39.
Gyurasits, E. B. and Wake, R. G. (1973). *J. molec. Biol.* **73,** 55.
Hannay, C. L. and FitzJames, P. (1955). *Can. J. Biochem.* **1,** 694.
Hedgpeth, J., Goodman, H. M. and Boyer, H. W. (1972). *Proc. natn. Acad. Sci. U.S.A.* **69,** 3448.
Hill, C. W., Foulds, J., Soll, L. and Berg, P. (1969a). *J. molec. Biol.* **39,** 563.
Hill, C. W., Shiffer, D. and Berg, P. (1969b). *J. Bact.* **99,** 274.
Horiuchi, T., Horiuchi, S. and Novick, A. (1963). *Genetics,* **48,** 157.

Ingram, L., Sykes, R. B., Grinsted, J., Saunders, J. R. and Richmond, M. H. (1972). *J. gen. Microbiol.* **72**, 269.
Ippen, K., Shapiro, J. A. and Beckwith, J. R. (1971). *J. Bact.* **108**, 5.
Jackson, D. A. Symons, R. H. and Berg, P. (1972). *Proc. natn. Acad. Sci. U.S.A.* **69**, 2904.
Jackson, D. A., Symons, R. H. and Berg, P. (1973). *Colloq. Intern. CNRS*, **212**, 385.
Jacob, F. and Monod, J. (1961). *Cold Spring Harb. Symp. quant. Biol.* **26**, 193.
Jones, D. and Sneath, P. H. A. (1970). *Bact. Rev.* **34**, 40.
Kjelgaard, N. O. and Kurland, G. C. (1963). *J. molec. Biol.* **6**, 341.
Kontomichalou, P., Mitani, M. and Clowes, R. C. (1970). *J. Bact.* **104**, 34.
Low, K. B. (1972). *Bact. Rev.* **36**, 587.
Maaløe, O. and Kjelgaard, N. O. (1966). "Control of Macromolecular Synthesis". Benjamin, New York.
Mandel, M. and Higa, A. (1970). *J. molec. Biol.* **53**, 159.
Masters, M. and Broda, P. (1971). *Nature, New Biol.* **232**, 137.
McKenna, W. G. and Masters, M. (1972). *Nature*, **240**, 536.
Mertz, J. E. and Davis, R. W. (1972). *Proc. natn. Acad. Sci. U.S.A.* **69**, 3370.
Meynell, G. G. (1972). "Bacterial Plasmids". Macmillan, London.
Miller, J. H., Reznikoff, W. S., Silverstone, A. E., Ippen, K., Signer, E. R. and Beckwith, J. (1970). *J. Bact.* **104**, 1273.
Morrow, J. F., Cohen, S. N., Chang, A. C. Y., Boyer, H. W., Goodman, H. M. and Helling, R. B. (1974). *Proc. natn. Acad. Sci. U.S.A.* **71**, 1743.
Murray, K. and Old, R. W. (1974). "Progress in Nucleic Acid Research and Molecular Biology" (Ed. W. E. Cohn), vol. 14, p. 117. Academic Press, New York and London.
Nishimura, Y., Caro, L., Berg, C. M. and Hirota, Y. (1971). *J. molec. Biol.* **55**, 441.
Nishioka, Y. and Eisenstark, A. (1970). *J. Bact.* **102**, 320.
Novick, A. and Horiuchi, T. (1961). *Cold Spring Harb. Symp. quant. Biol.* **26**, 239.
Painter, P. R. (1974). *Genetics*, **76**, 401.
Press, B., Glandsorff, N., Miner, P., de Vries, J., Kadner, R. and Maas, W. K. (1971). *Proc. natn. Acad. Sci. U.S.A.* **68**, 795.
Pritchard, R. H. (1974). *Phil. Trans. R. Soc. Ser. B*, **267**, 303.
Putte, P. van der and Gruijthuijsen, M. (1972). *Molec. gen. Genet.* **118**, 173.
Richmond, M. H. (1968). *In* "Recent Advances in Microbial Physiology" (Eds A. H. Rose and J. F. Wilkinson), vol. 2, p. 43. Academic Press, New York and London.
Richmond, M. H. (1973). *In* "Progress in Nucleic Acid Research and Molecular Biology" (Ed. W. E. Cohn), vol. 13, p. 191. Academic Press, New York and London.
Rownd, R. (1969). *J. molec. Biol.* **44**, 387.
Roy, P. and Smith, H. O. (1973). *J. molec. Biol.* **81**, 445.
Russell, R. L., Abelson, J. N., Landy, A., Gefter, M. L., Brenner, S. and Smith, J. D. (1970). *J. molec. Biol.* **47**, 1.
Shimada, K., Weisberg, R. A. and Gottesman, M. E. (1972). *J. molec. Biol.* **63**, 483.
Silver, R. P. and Falkow, S. (1970a). *J. Bact.* **104**, 331.
Silver, R. P. and Falkow, S. (1970b). *J. Bact.* **104**, 340.
Sonenshein, A. L. and Losick, R. (1970). *Nature, Lond.* **227**, 906.
Sueoka, N., Bishop, J. R., Harford, N., Kennett, R. H., O'Sullivan, A. and Quinn, W. G. (1973). *In* "Genetics of Industrial Microorganisms: Bacteria" (Eds Z. Vaněk, Z. Hošťálek and J. Cudlín), p. 73. Academia, Prague.

Sugisaki, H. and Takanami, M. (1973). *Nature, New Biol.* **246,** 138.
Sykes, R. B. and Richmond, M. H. (1970). *Nature, Lond.* **226,** 952.
Szulmajster, J. (1973). *Symp. Soc. gen. Microbiol.* **23,** 45.
Taylor, A. L. (1963). *Proc. natn. Acad. Sci. U.S.A.* **50,** 1043.
Toussaint, A. and Faelen, M. (1973). *Nature, New Biol.* **242,** 1.
Wake, R. G. (1972). *J. molec. Biol.* **68,** 501.
Zavada, V. and Calef, E. (1969). *Genetics,* **61,** 9.

Organelle genetics in *Saccharomyces cerevisiae*

P. R. AVNER*

Centre de Génétique Moleculaire, Centre Nationale de la Recherche Scientifique, Gif-sur-Yvette, France

Summary

The isolation of new cytoplasmically inherited antibiotic resistance mutations in *Saccharomyces cerevisiae* has led to an explosion in both the number of studies into, and understanding of, the mitochondrial genetic system. This progress has also been aided in no small measure by the use of the ρ^- mutation for mapping studies and a much improved though still incomplete understanding of the nature of this mutation. This article reviews some of the progress made towards a complete understanding of the mitochondrial genetic system of *S. cerevisiae*.

Introduction

It is now clear that the formation of organelles such as the mitochondrion and the chloroplast are the result of complex interactions between the nuclear and organelle genomes and the cytoplasmic and organelle protein synthesizing systems. This interrelationship not only manifests itself, in the mitochondrion for instance, by the presence of both nuclear and mitochondrial mutants causing lesions in mitochondrial metabolism (Ephrussi, 1953; Sherman and Slonimski, 1964; Sherman *et al.*, 1966; Beck *et al.*, 1971) and by the mitochondrion being composed of a mixture of mitochondrially and cytoplasmically synthesized proteins, but also at the level of the individual enzyme complex where it is now well documented that some subunits of both the oligomycin sensitive ATPase complex and the cytochrome oxidase assembly

---

* Present address: Department de Biologie Cellulaire, L'Institut Pasteur, 25 rue du Docteur Roux, Paris XVème, France.

are synthesized in the mitochondrion itself, and others on the cytoplasmic ribosomes (Tzagaloff et al., 1973). Although there is so far no concrete evidence that the mitochondrially *synthesized* subunits are mitochondrially *coded* this seems highly probable, particularly in view of the isolation of mitochondrially coded oligomycin resistant mutants whose oligomycin sensitive ATPase complex still expresses its resistance after initial purification and separation from the mitochondrial inner membrane (Griffiths et al., 1972; Griffiths, D. E. personal communication).

This article will be restricted to a discussion of the recent advances in our understanding of the behaviour of mutations affecting mitochondrial function which are due to changes in the mitochondrial genome. The use of the expression "mitochondrial" mutations or mutants is made with this restriction in mind. Space limitations have not permitted a discussion of parallel advances in chloroplast genetics in *Chlamydomonas reinhardi* for which the reader is referred to the monograph of Sager (1972) and the reviews of Preer (1971, Gillham (1975) and Gillham et al. (1974).

Results and discussion

GENERAL CHARACTERISTICS OF *S. cerevisiae*

This yeast is a facultative anaerobe able to grow with or without functional mitochondria if supplied with, as an energy source, either glucose or a similar sugar metabolizable in the absence of oxygen via the glycolysis pathway to ethanol. It can also grow on nonfermentable substrates such as glycerol, ethanol or lactate but oxygen and functional mitochondria then become obligatory.

S. cerevisiae can exist and grow stably in either the haplophase or the diplophase, fusion of two haploid cells to give a diploid depending on the cell lines possessing the alternative nuclear mating types a and α. Diploids can be easily recovered by plating haploid strains having complementary auxotrophic requirements on minimal media. During diploidization cell fusion is complete and there is no apparent sexual specialization. Under suitable conditions (sporulation) meiosis in such diploids occurs to produce 4 meiotic products which are all retained together within a single tetrad.

ISOLATION AND CHARACTERIZATION OF MITOCHONDRIAL MUTATIONS

a. *Isolation and characterization of petite mutants*

If *S. cerevisiae* is plated on to media containing limited amounts of a fermentable carbon source such as glucose, a variable but sizeable proportion (0.1 — >20 per cent) of the colonies that grow are small ("petite") and also are often whiter than the usual creamy coloured yeast colonies observed. Such colonies when tested by replica plating fail to grow on nonfermentable carbon sources such as ethanol or glycerol and are normally respiration deficient. Amongst petite mutants two classes can be distinguished on the basis of their mode of inheritance.

i. *Genic or nuclear petites.* Such petites arise spontaneously at frequencies that are typical of those shown by other nuclear gene mutations (10^{-6}–10^{-8}) and can be induced by mutagens such as MNNG, X-rays and uv but not euflavine, which, however, is a very effective mutagen for the second class of petites (see also Sager, 1972). They are characterized by a 2:2 Mendelian segregation when diploids from crosses with the wild type are sporulated, and by a measurable reversion rate back to the wild type. A large series of such mutants have been isolated, falling into a number of complementation groups, the majority showing marked but variable lesions in their cytochrome contents (Beck *et al.*, 1971; Chen *et al.*, 1950).

ii. *Cytoplasmic or ρ^- petites.* The vast majority of spontaneous petites isolated are of this type, which arise at frequencies ranging from 0.1 to >20 per cent depending on the strain and the growth conditions. They are all characterized by the pleiotropic loss of cytochromes b, c_1 and a + a_3 (Sager, 1972). Such petites can be induced by an enormous variety of compounds many of which have no known mutational or carcinogenic properties in other systems (Nagai *et al.*, 1961) and by a wide variety of mutagens, notably polynuclear aromatic dyes such as euflavine and ethidium bromide, which in growing cultures can induce 100 per cent petite formation (Slonimski *et al.*, 1968). No petite of this class has ever been observed to revert to wild type.

Cytoplasmic petites in their turn can be subdivided into 2 subclasses, neutral and suppressive, on the basis of their behaviour on crossing to a wild type (ρ^+) strain. In a cross of a neutral petite by a ρ^+ wild-type strain essentially only ρ^+ diploid progeny are obtained. (The frequency of ρ^- diploids is no higher than that observed in the homologous $\rho^+ \times \rho^+$ cross; this will not normally be zero due to the presence of spontaneous ρ^- mutants.) Sporulation of these diploids gives 4:0 segregation ratios for the ρ^+ versus ρ^- phenotype. Backcrosses of these F_1 meiotic progeny to the original petite mutant have shown that the observed segregation ratio is not due to a series of recessive nuclear genes since at least twenty unlinked genes would be needed to explain the observed results (Ephrussi *et al.*, 1949). These ρ^- mutants are postulated to have lost a cytoplasmic particle ρ present in the wild-type strain.

Suppressive ρ^- petites when crossed to a ρ^+ tester strain give both ρ^- and ρ^+ diploids. The proportion of ρ^- diploids may vary from near 0 per cent to 100 per cent and is a measure of the suppressiveness of the ρ^- haploid strain. Sporulation of the ρ^+ diploids obtained gives 4:0 ratios for wild type versus petite phenotype. The ρ^- diploids cannot normally be induced to sporulate other than by sporulating them almost immediately after zygotic fusion when a $0:4$ $\rho^+:\rho^-$ segregation ratio is observed, all the progeny being suppressive petites (Ephrussi et al., 1955).

Examination of the DNA extracted from ρ^- petites has allowed the correlation of the ρ factor with mitochondrial DNA (mitDNA) as p^- strains normally show either a complete absence of mitDNA or, alternatively, gross changes in both its base composition and nucleotide sequence (see reviews by Mounolou et al., 1966; Bernardi et al., 1968; Borst, 1972). Moreover, neutral petites lack mitDNA completely and therefore mitochondrial informational content, and are now frequently referred to as ρ^0 petites (Michaelis et al., 1971; Nagley and Linnane, 1970, 1972). Ethidium bromide, which causes 100 per cent ρ^- petite induction, has been shown to act specifically to cause the degradation and breakdown of mitDNA (Slonimski et al., 1968; Goldring et al., 1970).

b. *Isolation and characterization of mitochondrial drug-resistant mutants*

Certain drugs are toxic to the growth of *S. cerevisiae* when growing on non-fermentable substrates such as glycerol which are either nontoxic when glucose is the carbon source or only toxic at considerably higher concentrations (Griffiths et al., 1972; Avner and Griffiths, 1973a; Rank and Bech-Hansen, 1973). This has been shown in some cases to be due to a selective toxicity against mitochondrial metabolism and assumed to be in others (Linnane and Haslam, 1970). By growing cells on nonfermentable substrates in the presence of such drugs, strains resistant to a variety of inhibitors have been isolated, three main groups of inhibitors having been used successfully until now: (1) ribosomal inhibitors active against the 50s subunit of the 70s ribosome such as chloramphenicol, spiramycin and erythromycin (Coen et al., 1970; Kleese et al., 1972); (2) ribosomal inhibitors directed against the 30s subunit of the 70s ribosome such as paromomycin (Wolf et al., 1973; Kutzleb et al., 1973); (3) inhibitors of mitochondrial oxidative phosphorylation such as oligomycin, rutamycin, venturicidin and triethyltin (Lancashire and Griffiths, 1971; Griffiths et al., 1972; Avner and Griffiths, 1973a, 1973b; Avner et al., 1973; Wakabayashi and Kamei, 1973; Lancashire et al., 1974).

Accepting that the target of these drugs is the mitochondrion in the cell itself, the resistance observed could theoretically be conferred by: (a) changes in cellular permeability; (b) cytoplasmic detoxifying mechanisms; (c) changes in mitochondrial permeability; (d) changes in the site of action of the drug within the mitochondrion. It is self-evident that only resistance changes of types (c) and (d) are likely to be due to mitochondrial mutations. Even changes at the true site of action of the drug within the mitochondrion may, given the now well-established fact that mitochondria are only semi-autonomous organelles, be due to either mutations in the mitochondrial or nuclear genomes. Two preliminary screens can eliminate mutants resistant due to mechanisms (a) and (b), which are obviously unlikely to be mitochondrially coded. Firstly, where the drug is toxic on both glycerol and glucose media, mutants of types (a) and (b) can be screened out since such mutants should show a simultaneously increased resistance on both media (Lancashire and Griffiths, 1971). Secondly, mutants of types (a) and (c) but not (d) may show collateral resistance to inhibitors with diverse sites of action in cases where the permeability change is nonspecific. Thus screening with a variety of inhibitors should enrich for type (d). Such a procedure may well remove most of type (c) mutants, but no mutant showing widespread collateral resistance has so far been shown unambiguously to be mitochondrially coded (Avner and Griffiths, 1973a, 1973b; Rank and Bech-Hansen, 1973).

The ratio of mitochondrially coded to nuclear coded resistant mutants may also be improved by using a diploid strain as starting material if the nuclear coded resistance found is frequently due to recessive mutations, or by the careful choice of mutagens. Work with *Chlamydomonas reinhardi* has shown that chloroplast and nuclear DNAs are replicated independently, so that by the use of synchronized cultures and a mutagen such as MNNG, which seems to act preferentially on replicating DNA, selective mutation of the chloroplast DNA can be obtained (Cerdà-Olmedo *et al.*, 1968; Lee and Jones, 1973).

Several criteria have been established for the identification of mito-chondrial mutants: criteria based firstly on the observation of non-Mendelian inheritance as expressed by an instability or mitotic segregation during vegetative divisions following the fusion of two pure haploid strains and the failure to observe classical meiotic segregation during the subsequent meiosis; and secondly on the association of the mutation with mitDNA.

(1) In crosses of the prospective antibiotic resistant (Ant^r) ρ^+ strain to an antibiotic sensitive (Ant^s) ρ^+ tester the resulting diploid cells should show mitotic segregation for Ant^r and Ant^s colonies. (2) The meiotic progeny of the Ant^r diploids should show $4:0$ segregation for resistance versus sensitivity whilst Ant^s diploids should show $0:4$ segregation. (3) Crosses of the pro-spective Ant^r ρ^+ strain to a ρ^0 tester strain should give rise to Ant^r diploids only, which on sporulation should show $4:0$ segregation for resistance versus sensitivity. (4) The majority of ρ^- petites recovered from Ant^r ρ^+ strains after petite induction with high levels of ethidium bromide or euflavine should have lost their antibiotic resistance.

Loss of an antibiotic resistance marker cannot be demonstrated directly since by definition the Ant^r and Ant^s phenotypes are expressed only on a nonfermentable carbon source, on which petite mutants themselves cannot grow. It can, however, be tested indirectly by crossing the petite isolated from the original ρ^+ stock containing the Ant allele to a ρ^+ tester stock and examining the diploid progeny. In the case of an original $Ant^r \rho^+$ strain which has been converted to ρ^- and then crossed with a $Ant^s \rho^+$ tester strain, four types of progeny could theoretically be expected. (1) If they are all $Ant^s \rho^+$ then the petite parent must have been $Ant^0 \rho^0$, that is both ρ and the Ant marker have been simultaneously lost. (2) If they contain a mixture of ρ^- and ρ^+ progeny all of which are Ant^s, then the ρ^- petite parent must have been $Ant^0 \rho^-$, that is the mutation from ρ^+ to ρ^- has been accompanied by the functional loss of the Ant^r marker. (3) If they include petite and respiration sufficient progeny, some of which are Ant^s and some Ant^r, then the petite parent must have been $Ant^r \rho^-$, that is the Ant^r allele was retained in the petite parent though it could not be expressed. (4) If they are all respiration sufficient but include both Ant^r and Ant^s diploids, then the petite must have been $Ant^r \rho^0$. This last type of ρ^- petite has never been found for any of the well characterized mitochondrial mutations, a result to be expected if the Ant markers lie within the ρ factor, as all the current evidence indicates (Deutsch et al., 1974).

It should be emphasized that the observation of mitotic (vegetative) segregation is not alone sufficient to establish the cytoplasmic, let alone the mitochondrial nature of a mutation, several situations interpreted in terms of cytoplasmic genes having been shown later not to be cytoplasmic, or to represent complex situations of apparent joint nuclear and cytoplasmic inheritance (Mitchell et al., 1972; Avner and Griffiths, 1973b; Howell et al., 1974).

So far unambiguous evidence for mitochondrial inheritance has probably only been presented for mutants resistant to chloramphenicol, erythromycin, spiramycin, paromomycin, oligomycin (and its associated rutamycin resistance) and venturicidin (Coen et al., 1970; Wolf et al., 1973; Avner et al., 1973; Howell et al., 1973; Suda and Uchida, 1974). Mutants resistant to triethyltin and ethidium bromide have also been isolated and may represent mitochondrial mutants but the evidence is less certain (Lancashire and Griffiths, 1971; Griffiths et al., 1972; Gouhier and Mounolou, 1973).

The group working at Gif have been able to classify their mutants and others from collaborating laboratories as follows: all chloramphenicol resistant mutants (C^r) are allelic and map at a locus denoted as R_1; all mutants resistant to erythromycin and/or spiramycin (E^r) form two major allelic groups denoted as R_{II} and R_{III}; all oligomycin mutants (O^r) fall into two allelic groups known as O_I and O_{II}; all paromomycin (P^r) mutants are allelic and map together at a locus denoted as P. There is no definite information as to the type of genetic change giving rise to these antibiotic-resistant mutants but the working hypothesis is that unlike most ρ^- petites, they represent point mutations.

Although the number of mitochondria in haploid and diploid yeast strains is uncertain, estimates of 5–30 and 15–50 probably cover the range of recorded values although occasional reports of a single highly branched mitochondrion have also been published (Avers *et al.*, 1965; Cottrell and Avers, 1971; Avner, 1973). The mechanism by which pure homogeneous mitochondrial antibiotic-resistant strains arise is thus of considerable interest. Recent evidence suggests that mitochondrial mutants do not arise by direct induction of mutations by the antibiotic, but by intracellular selection for pre-existing resistant mitochondria. The presence of the drug stops the division and growth of sensitive mitochondria but not of the resistant ones, leading eventually, presumably by dilution, to a homogeneous population of mitochondria containing the mutant mitDNA (Birky, 1973). A gradual intracellular selection similar to that proposed by Birky has been elegantly demonstrated amongst the diploid ex-conjugant progeny of *Paramecium aurelia* obtained by crossing an erythromycin-sensitive strain by an erythromycin-resistant one, where on selective media an originally sensitive ex-conjugant which had received some resistant mitochondria from its mating partner during conjugation could be seen to turn resistant, in the sense that it changed colour, improved its aspect, changed its mitochondrial morphology and increased its fission rate over a number of days (Adoutte and Beisson, 1970; Parasso and Adoutte, 1974).

Three methods have been used to study the segregation and recombination of mitochondrial genes in yeast. These are: pedigree analysis of diploid buds produced by individual zygotes and their progeny; analysis of the genotypic composition of the diploid progeny of a population of individual zygotic clones after many generations of vegetative growth; analysis of the genotypic composition of the diploid progeny of a population of zygotes, irrespective of their lineage, after some 20 mitotic divisions (Coen *et al.*, 1970). The methodology used by the Gif group in respect of studies of the third type has been widely adopted and has been termed the "Standard Cross". In this procedure the purified haploid strains are mass mated to give about 1000 zygotic clones which are allowed to grow for about 20 generations, when the progeny are collected and analysed. This is done either by respreading on nonselective media to allow the formation of individual colonies which are analysed by replica plating on to drug media, or occasionally by aliquot plating in parallel on nonselective and selective media.

GENERAL FEATURES OF THE BEHAVIOUR OF MITOCHONDRIAL GENES DURING
MITOTIC CELL DIVISION AS STUDIED BY PEDIGREE AND ZYGOTIC CLONAL ANALYSIS

When individual zygotic clones from a cross of two mitochondrially pure
strains as in a Ant^r × Ant^s cross are examined, it is apparent that they may
behave quite differently from each other in respect to both the types and
proportions of the mitochondrial genotypes they contain (Coen *et al.*, 1970).
Moreover pedigree analysis has shown that not only is this clonal variation
present from the earliest stages of budding but also the order in which the
genotypes appear may vary even amongst clones containing the same genotypes (Lukins *et al.*, 1973; Wilkie and Thomas, 1973; Waxman *et al.*, 1973).
The simplest interpretation of these results is that mitochondrial DNA
molecules are sorted out between the mother cell and the bud at each cell
division, such segregation eventually leading to the formation of pure breeding
cells homozygous for mitochondrial genes. Most of the rules governing this
segregation are unknown except that in the vast majority of cases it proceeds
rapidly (Coen *et al.*, 1970; Dujon *et al.*, 1974) and that mitochondrial recombination is probably not restricted to the zygote but can occur in the
early buds as well (Lukins *et al.*, 1973; Wilkie and Thomas, 1973). Preliminary
data suggest that each bud may receive only a few molecules of mitDNA, but
if this is true then a rapidly acting mechanism must exist to increase the
number of copies to that compatible with the normal number of mitochondria
in the cell (Dujon *et al.*, 1974).

GENERAL FEATURES OF THE BEHAVIOUR OF MITOCHONDRIAL GENES DURING
MITOTIC CELL DIVISION AS OBSERVED USING THE STANDARD CROSS TECHNIQUE

a. *Recombination, segregation and the ω locus*

Reassortment of mitochondrial genes was first shown in yeast by Thomas and
Wilkie (1968). This was later shown unambiguously to be due to genetic
recombination by an analysis of post-meiotic stability involving the back-
crossing of the postulated recombinants (Coen *et al.*, 1970; Bolotin *et al.*, 1971).
Michaelis *et al.* (1973) have shown that such genetic recombination is accompanied by a physical recombinational event at the level of the mitDNA
molecules.

    A certain number of basic rules have become apparent regarding mito-
chondrial crosses. In crosses, involving the C^r (chloramphenicol resistant)
mutations at the R$_1$ locus, the ratio of the reciprocal recombinants (e.g. in
a C^{r}E^r × C^{s}E^s cross, the C^{r}E^s and C^{s}E^r recombinants) may either be extremely biased, one of the recombinants being up to 100 times more frequent
than the other, or else they may be present in equal proportions. Crosses of
the former type are called heterosexual crosses and of the latter, homosexual

crosses. In the original heterosexual crosses the strain donating the R_I marker present in the majority recombinant was arbitrarily called the ω^+ strain and its partner the ω^-. Homosexual crosses have been shown to be either $\omega^+ \times \omega^+$ or $\omega^- \times \omega^-$. Whether a strain is ω^+ or ω^- can be easily tested by crossing to several known tester strains. So far amongst all the strains examined, only the two allelic forms ω^+ and ω^- have been found.

The bias in the frequencies of the reciprocal recombinants is accompanied by a parallel polarity in the transmission frequencies of the individual alleles of loci R_I and R_{III}. This polarity of transmission is greater for the R_I locus than for R_{II} which, in turn, is greater than for R_{III}, whilst the O_I, O_{II} and P loci show no polarity of transmission in heterosexual crosses. Thus, in summary, crosses that are heterosexual in showing polarity for the recombinant pairs involving the R_I locus also show polarity of transmission for the R_I, R_{II} and R_{III} loci which can therefore be regarded as constituting a polar region, whilst within the same cross the O_I, O_{II} and P loci do not show polarity of transmission and are regarded as forming a nonpolar region.

Crosses showing strong polarity of recombination always show a strong polarity of transmission for at least one of the genes involved in the polar recombinant pair. The converse is not necessarily true. Some crosses show bias in transmission frequencies without any bias in recombination frequencies and this has proved to be due to the action of various nuclear genes. The ω factor is quite distinct from such nuclear genes in its action, and in showing cytoplasmic inheritance being closely linked to those mitochondrial genes constituting the ribosomal segment of the genome R_I, R_{II} and R_{III}. For this reason ω has been called the mitochondrial sex factor. It is completely independent of the cellular mating types "α" and "a". In both types of homosexual crosses, $\omega^+ \times \omega^+$ and $\omega^- \times \omega^-$, the mitochondrial sex of the progeny corresponds to that of the parent strains, but in heterosexual crosses all the recombinant progeny are ω^+.

The observed polarity of transmission of a marker depends on its distance from the ω locus and the polarity of recombination depends on the distance of the proximal gene of the recombinant pair from ω rather than on the distance between the genes. Since the polarity of recombination is greater for recombinants containing R_I than R_{II} which is in turn greater than R_{III}, the gene order is ω–R_I–R_{II}–R_{III}. The nonpolar region containing the three loci O_I, O_{II}, and P must lie outside the ω–R_I–R_{II}–R_{III} segment and distal from ω.

Recombination frequencies in heterosexual crosses also support such an ordering of the ribosomal segment although the recombination frequencies are not strictly additive. The maximal recombination frequency in heterosexual crosses is found in the polar region where it approximates to 50 per cent, whilst recombination between the nonpolar markers reaches only 20–25 per cent.

Recombination frequencies in homosexual crosses are never greater than 25 per cent. The recombination frequencies observed suggest again that the R_I, R_{II} and R_{III} loci are linked, with recombination frequencies of around 10 per cent but unlinked from the other loci, with which they show recombinant frequencies of about 25 per cent, as do O_I, O_{II} and P with each other. By using petites for a type of deletion mapping (see below), a gene order of ω–R_I–R_{II}–R_{III}–O_I–O_{II} has been tentatively established with P also lying somewhere in the nonpolar region.

Dujon *et al.* (1974) proposed a detailed model for the behaviour of genes during crossing which, although too complicated to discuss in detail here, suggests that both heterosexual and homosexual crosses are analogous to bacteriophage crosses. They assume a panmictic pool of mitDNA molecules in the yeast zygote, an assumption supported to some extent by electron microscopy of zygotes which appears to show a breakdown of mitochondrial membranes during the early stages after fusion, which would permit the mixing of the mitDNAs from the parents (Smith *et al.*, 1972). Pairings are postulated to occur between both identical and nonidentical DNA molecules in proportion to the number of molecules of each type, this being postulated to be determined by the proportion of molecules derived from each parent. Several, random in time, rounds of mating may occur in the panmictic pool. In the proposed model the elementary act of recombination is assumed to be nonreciprocal, each act generating one recombinant and one parental genotype. The equal frequencies of reciprocal recombinants seen for all genes in homosexual crosses and nonpolar genes in heterosexual crosses is thus a statistical result of the occurrence of two recombinational events which are each fundamentally nonreciprocal. The polarity of recombination seen in heterosexual crosses for the R_I, R_{II} and R_{III} genes is explained on this hypothesis by there being an obligatory recombinational event every time that an ω^- molecule pairs with an ω^+ molecule, the process being initiated at the ω^+ locus and there being a conversion event, the probability of conversion of an allele carried by the ω^- to that carried by the ω^+ parent decreasing as one proceeds from ω to R_{III}. Thus all recombinants in heterosexual crosses should be ω^+ and the polarity should be, as found, $R_I > R_{II} > R_{III}$.

This model has also been adopted as the basis for a model of chloroplast inheritance in *Chlamydomonas reinhardi* by Gillham (1974, 1975).

DELETION MAPPING WITH CHARACTERIZED ρ^- PETITES

Although both extensive euflavine and ethidium bromide treatments at high doses on growing ρ^+ cultures lead only very occasionally to clones retaining an Ant marker due to the tendency under these conditions for all the petites to be ρ^0, special treatment with lower doses for shorter periods and especially the use of ethidium bromide for short periods on nongrowing cultures can result in a sizeable fraction of the ρ^- petite population having retained their Ant markers, and this provides an additional mapping technique that is extremely powerful. Deutsch *et al.* (1974) carried out a quantitative study of the recovery frequencies of the various petite types from a $\rho^+ C^R E^R O^R$ strain after mild treatment with ethidium bromide and performed a target analysis on the data obtained. The data suggest that the ρ^- phenotype can result from a mutational event at any of a number of sites within the mitDNA, so that a particular ρ^- mutation may be limited to a part of the genome not including a particular Ant marker. Amongst the ρ^- petites recovered, the C^r and E^r genes tended to be lost together whilst the correlation of the loss of these markers with that of O^r was less strong. This result agrees well with those obtained by recombination analysis where the R_I and R_{III} genes were found to be linked to each other but unlinked to the O_I and O_{II} loci.

Although freshly isolated ρ^- petites are normally unstable, tending to lose their resistance markers, stable petites can be obtained after repeated sub-cloning. Slonimski's group has obtained such petites carrying markers in the majority of possible configurations; for instance $C^0 E^r$, $C^r E^r$ and $C^0 E^0$ ρ^- petites from a $C^r E^r \rho^+$ strain. Such petites have been used for deletion mapping. If we consider the example of the oligomycin resistant loci, from recombination mapping and polarity studies, the two loci, O_I and O_{II}, could either have been arranged in the order R_I–R_{II}–R_{III}–O_I–O_{II} or R_I–R_{II}–R_{III}–O_{II}–O_I. Using a ρ^- petite whose full genotype was known to be $R_I^0 R_{III}^r O_I^s O_{II}^0$ if we assume that the retained sequences are adjacent and contiguous then the O_{II} locus cannot lie between R_{III} and O_I, and the order must be R_I–R_{II}–R_{III}–O_I–O_{II}, though if the genome is circular a circular permutation of this order cannot be formally excluded (Avner *et al.*, 1973).

NATURE OF THE MOLECULAR CHANGES OCCURRING IN ρ^- PETITES

The loss of mitochondrial genes, the results of DNA/DNA and RNA/DNA hybridization, and the decrease in kinetic complexity of the ρ^- DNA suggest that the phenotype of the ρ^- petites results from large deletions in the wild-type mitDNA. These deletions are compensated for, since the quantity of mitDNA is not reduced in nonneutral ρ^- petites, by the periodic intra-molecular reiteration of the nondeleted sequences of the wild-type mitDNA, leading to gene redundancy. Apparently any segment of the genome may be lost or retained. With the help of genetic markers one can select stable ρ^- mutants in which parts of the mitDNA are repeated and amplified in various combinations, often up to 100 times the level of the wild type. Thus selective purification of different tRNA, rRNA and mRNA genes can be achieved (Faye *et al.*, 1973).

If it proves possible in the future to introduce limited regions of such petite mitDNA into ρ^+ strains which are not carrying compensatory gene deletions the alteration in gene dosage may be profoundly important as a means of strain improvement or at least of generating new deversity within *S. cerevisiae*.

References

Adoutte, A. and Beisson, J. (1970). *Molec. gen. Genet.* **108**, 70.

Avers, C. J., Rancourt, M. W. and Lin, F. H. (1965). *Proc. natn. Acad. Sci. U.S.A.* **54**,

Avner, P. R. (1973). Ph.D. thesis, University of Warwick, England.

Avner, P. R., Coen, D., Dujon, B. and Slonimski, P. P. (1973). *Molec. gen. Genet.* **125**, 9.

Avner, P. R. and Griffiths, D. E. (1973a). *Europ. J. Biochem.* **32**, 301.

Avner, P. R. and Griffiths, D. E. (1973b). *Europ. J. Biochem.* **32**, 312.

Beck, J. C., Parker, J. H., Balcavage, N. X. and Mattoon, J. R. (1971). *In* "The Autonomy and Biogenesis of Mitochondria and Chloroplasts" (Eds N. K. Boardman, A. W. Linnane and R. M. Smillie). Aust. Acad. Sci. symposium. North Holland, Amsterdam.

Bernardi, G., Carnevali, F., Nicolaieff, A., Piperno, G. and Tecce, G. (1968). *J. molec. Biol.* **37**, 493.

Birky, C. J. (1973). *Genetics,* **74**, 421.

Bolotin, M., Coen, D., Deutsch, J., Dujon, B., Netter, P., Petrochilo, E. and Slonimski, P. P. (1971). *Bull. Inst. Pasteur,* **69**, 215.

Borst, P. (1972). *A. Rev. Biochem.* **41**, 333.

Cerdà-Olmedo, E., Hanawalt, P. C. and Guerola, N. (1968). *J. molec. Biol.* **33**, 705.

Chen, S. Y., Ephrussi, B. and Hottinguer, H. (1950). *Heredity,* **4**, 337.

Coen, D., Deutsch, J., Netter, P., Petrochilo, E. and Slonimski, P. P. (1970). *Symp. Soc. exp. Biol.* XXIV. Cambridge University Press, London.

Cottrell, S. F. and Avers, C. J. (1971). *In* "The Autonomy and Biogenesis of Mitochondria and Chloroplasts" (Eds N. K. Boardman, A. W. Linnane and R. M. Smillie). Aust. Acad. Sci. Symposium. North Holland, Amsterdam.

Deutsch, J., Dujon, B., Netter, P., Petrochilo, E., Slonimski, P. P., Bolotin-Fukuhara, M. and Coen, D. (1974). *Genetics,* **76**, 195.

Dujon, B., Slonimski, P. P. and Weill, L. (1974). Proc. XIII International Congress of Genetics. *Genetics,* **78**, 415.

Ephrussi, B. (1953). "Nucleo-Cytoplasmic Relationships in Micro-organisms". Clarendon Press, Oxford.

Ephrussi, B., Le Heritier, P. and Hottinguer, H. (1949). *Anns Inst. Pasteur, Paris,* **77**, 64.

Ephrussi, B., Margaret Hottinguer, H. de and Roman, H. (1955). *Proc. natn. Acad. Sci., U.S.A.* **41**, 1065.

Faye, G., Fukuhara, H., Grandchamp, C., Lazowska, J., Michel, F., Casey, J., Getz, G., Locker, J., Rabinowitz, M., Bolotin–Fukuhara, M., Coen, D., Deutsch, J., Dujon, B., Netter, P. and Slonimski, P. P. (1973). *Biochimie,* **55**, 779.

Gillham, N. W. (1975). *Ann. Rev. Genetics,* **9**, In press.

Gillham, N. W., Boynton, J. E. and Lee, R. W. (1974). Proc. XIII International Congress of Genetics. *Genetics,* **78**, 439.

Goldring, E. S., Grossman, L. I., Krupnick, D., Cryer, D. R. and Marmur, J. (1970). *J. molec. Biol.* **52**, 323.

Gouhier, M. and Mounolou, J. C. (1973). *Mol. gen. Genet.* **122**, 149.

Griffiths, D. E., Avner, P. R., Lancashire, W. E. and Turner, J. R. (1972). *In* "The Biochemistry and Biophysics of Mitochondrial Membranes" (Eds E. Carafoli, A. L. Lehninger and N. Siliprandi). p. 505. Academic Press, New York and London.

Howell, N., Molley, P. L., Linnane, A. W. and Lukins, H. B. (1974). *Molec. gen. Genet.* **128**, 43.

Howell, N., Trembath, M. K., Linnane, A. W. and Lukins, H. B. (1973). *Molec. gen. Genet.* **127**, 37.

Kleese, R. A., Grotbeck, R. C. and Snyder, J. R. (1972). *J. Bact.* **112**, 1025.

Kutzleb, R., Schweyer, R. J. and Kaudewitz, F. (1973). *Molec. gen. Genet.* **125**, 91.

Lancashire, W. E. and Griffiths, D. E. (1971). *FEBS Letters,* **17**, 209.

Lancashire, W. E., Houghton, R. L. and Griffiths, D. E. (1974). *Biochem. Soc. Trans.* **2**, 213.

Lee, R. W. and Jones, R. F. (1973). *Molec. gen. Genet.* **121**, 99.

Linnane, A. W. and Haslam, J. M. (1970). *In* "Current Topics in Cellular Regulation" (Eds Bernard L. Horecker and Earl R. Stadman), vol. 2, p. 102. Academic Press, New York and London.

Lukins, H. B., Tate, J. R., Saunders, G. W. and Linnane, A. W. (1973). *Molec. gen. Genet.* **120**, 17.

Michaelis, G., Douglass, S., Tsai, M. J. and Criddle, R. S. (1971). *Biochem. Genetics,* **5**, 437.

Michaelis, G., Petrochilo, E. and Slonimski, P. P. (1973). *Molec. gen. Genet.* **123**, 51.

Mitchell, C. H., Bunn, C. L., Lukins, H. B. and Linnane, A. W. (1972). *Bioenergetics,* **4**, 24.

Mounolou, J. C., Jakob, H. and Slonimski, P. (1966). *Biochem. biophys. Res. Commun.* **24**, 218.

Nagai, S., Yanagiushima, N. and Nagai, H. (1961). *Bact. Rev.* **25**, 404.

Nagley, P. and Linnane, A. W. (1970). *Biochem. biophys. Res. Commun.* **39**, 989.

Nagley, P. and Linnane, A. W. (1972). *J. molec. Biol.* **66**, 181.

Parasso, R. and Adoutte, A. (1974). *J. Cell. Sci.* **14**, 475.

Preer, J. R. Jr (1971). *A. Rev. Genetics,* **5**, 361.

Rank, G. H. and Bech-Hansen, N. T. (1973). *Molec. gen. Genet.* **126**, 93.

Sager, R. (1972). "Cytoplasmic Genes and Organelles". Academic Press, New York and London.

Sherman, F. and Slonimski, P. P. (1964). *Biochim. biophys. Acta,* **90**, 1.

Sherman, F., Stewart, J. W., Margoliash, E., Parker, J. H. and Campbell, W. (1966). *Proc. natn. Acad. Sci., U.S.A.* **55**, 1498.

Slonimski, P. P., Perodin, G. and Crofts, J. H. (1968). *Biochem. biophys. Res. Commun.* **30**, 232.

Smith, D. G., Wilkie, D. and Srivastrava, K. C. (1972). *Microbios,* **6**, 231.

Suda, K. and Uchida, A. (1974). *Molec. gen. Genet.* **128**, 331.

Thomas, D. Y. and Wilkie, D. (1968). *Biochem. biophys. Res. Commun.* **30**, 368.

Tzagaloff, A., Rubin, M. S. and Sierra, M. F. (1973). *Biochim. biophys. Acta,* **301**, 71.

Waxman, M. F., Eaton, N. and Wilkie, D. (1973). *Molec. gen. Genet.* **127**, 277.

Wakabayashi, K. and Kamei, S. (1973). *FEBS Letters,* **33**, 263.

Wilkie, D. and Thomas, D. Y. (1973). *Genetics,* **73**, 367.

Wolf, K., Dujon, B. and Slonimski, P. P. (1973). *Molec. gen. Genet.* **125**, 53.

Cultured cell genetics

IAN CRAIG

Genetics Laboratory, Department of Biochemistry, University of Oxford, Oxford, England

Summary

Cultured cells provide convenient source material for genetic studies on higher organisms. They can be employed in some experimental approaches which would be difficult or inappropriate if applied to whole animals or plants.

The selection of various types of mutants in tissue culture has facilitated investigations into the genetics and biochemistry of specific cellular processes. Although some difficulties exist, a wide variety of mutants have been isolated including drug-resistant, auxotrophic and temperature-sensitive classes. The availability of biochemically "marked" cell lines, together with the advent of techniques for the fusion of cultured cells to form inter- and intraspecific hybrids has provided a powerful approach to the genetic analysis of cellular processes. Cell hybrids, particularly those from inter-specific crosses, frequently segregate chromosomes during passage in culture. This has enabled important advances to be made in such areas as the assignment of genes to chromosomes, studies on differentiation, malignancy or mitochondrial biogenesis and genetics.

Attempts to manipulate the genotype of animal cells in culture by incubation with nucleic acids or by viral infection have provided conflicting results. The validity of several claims for success in this field has yet to be confirmed.

Major advances have also been made in the development of techniques for genetic analysis and manipulation of plant cells in culture. It is now possible to obtain mature plants from the fusion product of protoplasts from two species of tobacco.

Introduction

When it became possible to grow cells of higher organisms routinely in tissue culture, a new dimension to their genetic study was made available. Experiments and manipulation could now be carried out at the level of the individual cells rather than with whole organisms.

A great advantage of work with microorganisms is the enormous number of individuals which can be subjected to a particular set of experimental conditions. In the case of animal or plant cells in tissue culture, while obviously not able to compete with bacteria in this respect, extremely large numbers of cells can be handled. Thus the same techniques and approaches which have been the traditional prerogative of the microbial geneticist can be put to good use by those interested in studying the genetics of higher organisms.

More recently, the development of techniques for the fusion of somatic cells and for the biochemical and cytological analysis of the products has led to a spectacular increase in the number of laboratories which have turned their attention toward cultured cell genetics. As somatic cell hybridization acts as a focus for genetic studies on cultured cells, I will consider this aspect in some detail together with its potential applications in the fields of gene assignment, linkage analysis, the control of differentiation, malignancy and organelle biogenesis.

Results and discussion

CELL FUSION–HYBRIDIZATION

The first step in establishing a hybrid between cells in culture is to achieve fusion. Cell fusion of course occurs regularly between gametes of opposite mating types in animals and plants with sexual life cycles. The production of multinucleate cells by fusion of somatic cells has also been observed in nature, sometimes occurring spontaneously and sometimes as a result of infection by a viral pathogen. However, genetic studies on the hybrid products of some somatic animal cells in tissue culture have been facilitated by advances in two directions: (a) use of uv-inactivated Sendai virus to increase the yield of hybrid products; (b) availability of selective techniques to recover hybrid cells from a mixed population of hybrid and parental cells. Although cells in tissue culture have been observed to fuse spontaneously at very low frequencies (Barski *et al.*, 1960; Ephrussi *et al.*, 1964), the yield of hybrid cells can be increased dramatically by treatment with inactivated Sendai virus. The experimental procedure employed today stems from Okada's (1962) observation that mouse ascites tumour cells *in vitro* fused to form giant polynuclear aggregates after incubation at 37°C in presence of the virus. Harris and Watkins (1965) adapted this basic procedure and, using virus inactivated with uv light, showed that artificial heterokaryons containing both mouse and human cell nuclei could be obtained by mixing mouse ascites tumour cells and cells from a permanently established human tissue culture line (Hela) with virus

Since this time, Sendai virus-mediated fusion has been successfully applied to a wide variety of cell types from many different species.

The first products of the fusion process are homo- or heterokaryons depending on whether the two, or more, nuclei of the aggregate cell are of one, or both parental types. Heterokaryons with only one or two nuclei of each parental type survive for several days and can be used to study the interaction between the nuclei and cytoplasm of cells from different species, or stages of activity. In addition, if the nuclei within the heterokaryon undergo synchronous division a viable mononucleate cell may be produced which contains chromosomes of both parental cell types. Unfortunately, even in virus mediated fusions, the proportion of hybrid cells capable of continued division and growth is rather low (1 per 10^3–10^4 parental cells). Thus one of the main problems in studying them is the selection of hybrids from parental classes of cells.

There have been a number of ingenious approaches; some depend on particular growth characteristics of one, or both, parental cell type. However, one of the most successful and widely applied approaches depends on the availability of biochemically marked (enzyme deficient) cells. Parental cells having different enzyme deficiencies can be selected against, under appropriate conditions; the hybrid cell should survive if each parent supplies to it the enzyme lacking in the other. The approach is best illustrated by Littlefield's procedure in which hybrids are selected from fusions between thymidine kinase deficient (TK$^-$) and hypoxanthine guanine phosphoribosyl transferase deficient (HGPRT$^-$) parental cell types (see section on the isolation of mutants, p. 76).

Cells lacking either of these enzymes can survive in normal culture medium. However, in the presence of aminopterin, enzyme-deficient cells are selected against. Synthesis of thymidine and purines is inhibited in normal cells by aminopterin, but they can still survive by utilizing exogenous thymidine or hypoxanthine. This aminopterin-independent, alternative supply of DNA precursors is denied to TK$^-$ or HGPRT$^-$ cell lines.

Fusion between cell lines carrying one or other of the deficiencies can result in a hybrid containing both enzymes and capable of growth in medium containing aminopterin, exogenous thymidine and hypoxanthine (HAT medium). Littlefield (1964a, 1964b) employed this selection procedure to demonstrate the spontaneous production of mouse fibroblast hybrids at a frequency of 10^{-5}–10^{-6} cells. Obviously, success of such a procedure depends on stability of the biochemical deficiences. Later, other techniques for promoting fusion have been developed including treatment with lysolecithin (Lucy, 1970) or by micromanipulation (Diakumakos, 1973) and alternative selection procedures have made use of some of the other biochemical markers available (see section on the isolation of mutants, p. 76).

One further property of hybrid cells which is fundamental to their wide potential for genetic analysis is that of chromosome segregation. Many of the early observations were on hybrid cells resulting from fusions between different mouse lines (Barski *et al.*, 1960; Littlefield, 1964a). Karyotype analysis suggested that both parental sets of chromosomes were present in the nucleus. It later became apparent that hybrids resulting from interspecific crosses, e.g. rat × mouse and hamster × mouse, although retaining many chromosomes and phenotypic properties from both parents, did lose some chromosomes, particularly during the early stages of culture (Ephrussi and Weiss, 1965; Davidson *et al.*, 1966). A more extreme case of chromosome segregation was reported by Weiss and Green (1967). They observed that in human–mouse "crosses" many human chromosomes were eliminated soon after formation of the hybrids. Eventually, different clones could be established which exhibited fairly stable karyotypes retaining the normal mouse complement plus a few (2–15) human chromosomes.

Usually, preferential loss of one parental type of chromosomes occurs and segregation is more frequently observed in hybrids formed between more distantly related species. However, extensive chromosome loss can also occur in intraspecific crosses, e.g. between human diploid fibroblasts and the heteroploid line D98 (Kennet *et al.*, 1974). In selective medium (HAT) the human chromosome necessary to make good the enzyme deficiency of the mouse parent must be retained for the hybrid to survive. However, removal from HAT selective medium and re-exposure to the appropriate analogue (8-azaguanine, or BUdR) selects for hybrids which have lost the chromosome necessary for the expression of HGPRT, or TK (see Weiss and Green, 1967).

Once a system has been established in which chromosome segregation can be obtained, and to a very limited extent controlled, assignment of specific functions to the segregating chromosomes can be made. This approach depends on the availability of the necessary techniques to detect the presence or loss of a particular function (e.g. human) against the background of cellular functions, controlled by the remaining chromosomes of the other parental cell. Some of the more notable successes of genetic analysis applied to somatic cell hybrids are discussed in the section on the applications of cell fusion, p. 81.

THE ISOLATION OF MUTANTS

Mutants of cultured cells are of obvious importance both as a basis for selection of hybrid cells from parental types and for the study of other aspects of cellular function.

One source of cells carrying specific biochemical markers, or enzyme deficiencies, are animals known to have inherited the particular trait in question. However, most of this discussion is concerned with attempts to isolate various classes of mutant cells in culture.

Apart from a few notable exceptions, cells in tissue culture are diploid, or originally derived from diploid cells. They may therefore be expected to contain at least two copies of each autosome. Expression of a mutant phenotype is likely to occur only if the mutant gene is dominant, or present in homozygous (or hemizygous) condition. This consideration suggests that selection of cell lines with enzyme deficiencies would be difficult, at least two mutations being necessary (if structural genes are involved). Furthermore, pretreatment with mutagens should improve recovery of selected mutants. However, the isolation of variants from cultured cells does not always conform to these expectations.

Thompson and Baker (1973) have provided a detailed discussion of the problems involved in the isolation of mutants of which three are particularly worthy of mention.

Harris (1971) compared mutation rates for diploid, tetraploid and octaploid Chinese hamster cells to heat resistance, or to 8-azaguanine resistance. Although variants arise in a manner expected for mutations (by the criterion of the Luria and Delbruck (1943) fluctuation test), the "mutation" rate did not alter dramatically with the degree of ploidy. Mezger-Freed (1971) found that the frequency of resistance colonies obtained after selection of haploid or pseudodiploid frog lines in puromycin was apparently independent of ploidy and mutagen pretreatment. Thus it is important to bear in mind the possibility that some tissue culture variants may not have a simple genetic basis.

A second problem in the isolation of drug-resistant mutants is that the sensitivity of cells to drugs may vary with cell density. A ten-fold increase in cell density was found to change the phenotype of cells from puromycin sensitivity to resistance (Cass, 1972). Finally, it should be borne in mind that a complex character such as cell permeability is probably determined by many genes. In highly heteroploid lines it would be reasonable to expect some variation in the character to be generated by the fluctuating chromosome content (Terzi, 1973).

Nevertheless, although these complications should be borne in mind, they have clearly not prevented the isolation of a variety of cell lines whose properties suggest that they result from true mutations and which can form the basis for investigations into the genetic control of cellular processes.

Some selected examples of mutant isolation and characterization are presented below (see also Table 1).

a. *Resistant mutants*

i. *Resistance to purine analogues: 6-thioguanine, 8-azaguanine.* Pioneering studies by Szybalski (1958), Brockman *et al.* (1961), Szybalski *et al.* (1962) and Littlefield (1963) indicated that stable, resistant clones could be recovered after

TABLE 1
"Mutants" of cultured animal cells

Biochemically recognized modifications possibly associated with drug resistant or auxotrophic phenotypes are parenthesized.

MUTATION RESISTANCE TO BASE ANALOGUES

1-β-D Arabinofuranosyl cytosine	(deficient in deoxycytidine kinase)	a
8-Azaguanine	(deficient in hypoxanthine guanine phosphoribosyl transferase)	
2-Bromodeoxyuridine/³H-thymidine	(deficient in thymidine kinase transport)	
2,6-Diaminopurine	(deficient in adenine phosphoribosyl transferase)	b
2-Fluoroadenine	(deficient in adenine phosphoribosyl transferase)	
5-Fluorouridine/³H-uridine	(deficient in uridine kinase)	c
6-Thioguanine	(deficient hypoxanthine guanine phosphoribosyl transferase)	
(2-Bromodeoxyuridine dependence)		d

RESISTANCE TO OTHER COMPOUNDS

Actinomycin D		
α-Amanitin	(altered RNA polymerase II)	
Amethopterin	(increased activity of	
Aminopterin	dihydrofolate reductase)	
Chloramphenicol	(modification of mitochondrial protein synthesis?)	
Colchicine		
Concanavalin A		
2-Deoxyglucose		
Ouabain	(modification of ATPase?)	
Puromycin		

AUXOTROPHS

Requirements for, e.g.	(deficient formyl glycinamide	
adenine(AdeB⁺)	ribotideamido transferase)	e
Glycine (GlyA⁺)	(deficient in serine hydroxymethylase)	f
Inositol		
Proline		
Thymidine		

TEMPERATURE SENSITIVE

Modifications recognized:
expression of transformation by tumour virus; processing of ribosomal RNA precursor; defective leucyl tRNA synthetase; defective cyclic AMP metabolism; defect in cytokinesis   g

References and more detailed information are provided in the text, or in the review by Thompson and Baker (1973).
a. Robert de Saint-Vincent and Buttin (1973); b. Lieberman and Ove (1960); c. Medrano and Green (1974); d. Davidson and Bick (1973); e. New Haven Conference (1973); f. Kao et al. (1969); g. Renger and Basilico (1972).

growth in 8-azaguanine and that sequential exposure to increasing drug concentrations, or to different analogues, could result in highly resistant strains. It was found that resistance could be correlated with a loss of HGPRT activity; indeed Littlefield (1963) demonstrated a direct relationship between the extent of resistance and the drop in enzyme activity (measured in extracts). Beaudet *et al.* (1973) isolated several 8-azaguanine resistant Chinese hamster cell lines after mutagen pretreatment. Some of these had no detectable HGPRT activity but contained protein which cross-reacted with antibody prepared against the normal enzyme. Resistance was therefore thought to result from mutations in the enzyme structural gene. Other clones possessed neither detectable enzyme activity *in vitro*, nor material which cross-reacted with the enzyme specific antisera. These could have resulted from mutations resulting in extensive alterations to enzyme structure, or from control gene mutants. (Revertants from both phenotypic classes were obtained.) Mouse L cells selected for 8-azaguanine and 6-thioguanine resistance following mutagenesis (Sharp *et al.*, 1973) were found to possess enzymes with altered kinetic properties or heat sensitivity. Thus it would appear that at least in some cases, a change in the phenotype of cultures cells can result from mutations affecting specific structural genes.

ii. *Resistance to bromodeoxyuridine (BUdR).* The lethal effect of BUdR probably results from its incorporation into DNA in place of thymidine. Drug resistance can be acquired stepwise (as in the case of 8-azaguanine resistance) and can result from an alteration in the thymidine uptake mechanism of the cell (Mezger-Freed, 1972) and/or from decreased activity of thymidine kinase (Kit *et al.*, 1963; Littlefield, 1964b). Clayton and Teplitz (1972) showed that the mouse L cell line, Clone 1D with very low levels of thymidine kinase, nevertheless incorporated BUdR into mitochondrial DNA, thus suggesting the existence of a separate form of the enzyme localized within the organelle. Further studies have confirmed the presence of a mitochondrial form of the enzyme in both mouse and human BUdR-resistant cell lines (Berk and Clayton, 1973; Kit *et al.*, 1973; Kit and Leung, 1974a). Kit and Leung (1974b) have presented evidence from studies with human–mouse somatic cell hybrids that the two enzymes are coded by genes on different chromosomes.

iii. *Resistance to aminopterin.* Cell lines resistant to this inhibitor of dihydrofolate reductase have been isolated, resistance being correlated with profound increases in the intracellular levels of the enzyme (Fischer, 1961; Hakala *et al.*, 1961; Perkins *et al.*, 1967; Littlefield, 1969).

iv. *Resistance to chloramphenicol.* Chloramphenicol is a potent inhibitor of bacterial protein synthesis. Resistance in bacteria can result from altered

D

ribosome binding, or from an enzyme-mediated inactivation (Osawa *et al.*, 1973; Shaw, 1967). The sensitivity of eukaryotic cells to this antibiotic probably results from its inhibitory action on protein synthesis of organelles. The pattern of inheritance in yeast has suggested that resistance to chloramphenicol can result from mutation of the mitochondrial DNA (Coen *et al.*, 1970).

Several attempts have been made to select for similar mutants in mammalian cells to provide a basis for studies of the mitochondrial genome. Spolsky and Eisenstadt (1972) have reported the isolation of human cell lines capable of growing at the normally toxic concentration of 25 and 50 µg cm^{-3} chloramphenicol. The protein synthetic activity of isolated mitochondria was also partially resistant to the antibiotic when compared with preparations from the parental cell type. We have isolated and characterized several chloramphenicol-resistant human cell lines (Siegel *et al.*, 1974). Mitochondrial protein synthesis of these cells assayed *in vivo* or *in vitro* is unaffected by 100 µg cm^{-3} of the drug. Studies with labelled chloramphenicol showed that the permeability of the cells to the drug is not affected. Nor have modification or detoxification mechanisms been detected.

v. *Resistance to α amanitin.* This toxin, obtained from mushrooms, specificially inhibits one of the nuclear localized DNA-dependent RNA polymerases of eukaryotes. Chan *et al.* (1972) isolated resistant clones from a Chinese hamster cell line. The RNA polymerase II of some of these showed increased resistance *in vitro*. A change in the properties of the enzyme was also suggested by its altered elution profile from a DEAE cellulose column.

vi. *Resistance to ouabain.* The Na/K ATPase of mammalian cell plasma membranes is specifically inactivated by this steroid. Baker *et al.* (1974) report the isolation of clones up to 100-fold more resistant than the hamster parental cell line. Resistance was associated with decreased sensitivity of the Na/K ATPase activity of isolated plasma membranes.

vii. *Resistance to colchicine.* Minor (1973) and Till *et al.* (1973) have obtained mammalian cells resistant to this microtubule binding inhibitor. In both cases it was suggested that resistance resulted from an alteration in cell permeability, as no alteration in the binding of colchicine by microtubule containing extracts was detected.

These examples demonstrate the wide variety of drugs to which resistance has been obtained in cultured mammalian cells, the resistance in many cases being associated with an alteration in a specific cellular function.

h   *Auxotrophs and temperature-sensitive mutants*

A major difficulty in isolating nutritional mutants, unable to grow without a particular supplement, is elimination of wild-type parental cells. Kao and Puck (1968) succeeded in isolating nutritionally deficient mutants from Chinese hamster cells and developed a now widely used procedure for their selection (Puck and Kao, 1967). Complementation analysis of those isolated has implicated mutations in 15 different genes associated with requirements for nutrients such as glycine, proline, adenine, inositol and thymidine (Kao and Puck, 1974).

Selection of nutritionally defective cells is based on growth of mutagen-treated cell populations in the absence of a particular supplement but in the presence of BUdR. Only nondefective parental cells will replicate their DNA and incorporate the base analogue; subsequent exposure to uv near visible light kills them. Specific mutant classes can then be grown by replacing the nonpermissive medium with one containing known additional nutrients.

This approach can be adapted in several ways, for example to select temperature-sensitive mutants (see Thompson and Baker, 1973). Two such mutants, recently isolated, have defects in functions associated with protein synthesis. Toniolo *et al.* (1973) isolated a temperature-sensitive hamster line with an apparent defect in the processing of ribosomal RNA precursors. The defect in a temperature-sensitive Chinese hamster cell line isolated by Thompson *et al.* (1973) was identified as an altered leucyl-tRNA synthetase which showed *in vitro* temperature sensitivity. Willingham *et al.* (1973) described a temperature sensitive mouse line apparently defective in cyclic AMP metabolism at the nonpermissive temperature.

Mutations are the stock-in-trade of the geneticist and are invaluable for the study of specific cell processes as well as in the selection and analysis of somatic cell hybrids and in aiding the assignment of particular genes to chromosomes. It is therefore extremely encouraging for the future prospects of cultured cell genetics that a wide variety of drug resistant, nutritional and temperature-sensitive mutants can be obtained.

APPLICATIONS OF CELL FUSION

The most widely reported application of somatic cell hybridization is in the assignment of genes for the expression of various enzymes and antigens to a particular chromosome, or linkage group. However, more complex aspects of cellular function are also amenable to study by this technique, and selected examples are discussed here.

a. *Heterokaryons—interactions between nuclei and cytoplasm*

The discovery of Sendai virus mediated fusion has facilitated study of the interaction in heterokaryons between nuclei and cytoplasm from cells of various genetic compositions and stages of activity. One of the most striking observations (Harris, 1965; Harris *et al.*, 1966) was that the inactive nuclei of chicken erythrocytes (inactive in that no DNA or RNA synthesis can be detected by radioautography) can be activated in heterokaryons between Hela cells (a permanently established human tissue culture line) and chicken erythrocytes. Autoradiography showed that not only did the Hela nuclei incorporate DNA and RNA precursors, but also the erythrocyte nuclei began to show signs of doing so. The reactivated chicken nuclei in the heterokaryons were later shown to direct the synthesis of chick-specific proteins (Cook, 1970). During the early stages of this reactivation, macromolecules specified by the mammalian nuclei are thought to migrate into the chick nuclei. This conjecture is based on immunofluorescent studies with antisera which react with human nuclei; reactivation is associated with the appearance of mammalian antigens in the chick nucleus. As yet the nature of the molecule(s) involved is uncertain (Ringertz *et al.*, 1971; Appels *et al.*, 1974).

b. *Assignment of genes to linkage groups and chromosomes*

The main emphasis in the assignment of genes to chromosomes and mapping employing somatic cell hybrids has been directed towards the human genome (Nabholz, 1971; Ruddle, 1973; Ruddle and Kucherlapati, 1974).

Hamster–human and mouse–human hybrids usually retain a "parental set" of rodent chromosomes and a variable but reduced number of human ones. Fairly stable hybrid cell lines can be obtained and examined for the presence of human functions such as enzymes or antigens. Any detected must result from the expression of genes on the retained human chromosomes. The least equivocal assignments can be obtained in the case of human functions which are expressed in a hybrid line retaining a single identifiable human chromosome. A possible complication is the presence of human chromosome fragments that escape identification in the karyotype analysis.

One of the first examples of an assignment was that of thymidine kinase. Hybrids between human cells and TK-deficient mouse cells must retain the human genetic information for expression of TK in order to survive in HAT medium (Weiss and Green, 1967); Migeon and Miller (1968) obtained a hybrid clone capable of survival which retained a single human chromosome. This was identified on the basis of quinacrine fluorescent banding pattern to be chromosome 17 (Miller *et al.*, 1971).

Assignment of genes coding for, or controlling, a particular function can also be made even if the segregation of human chromosomes is not so extensive. In this case a large number of independent hybrid lines (preferably from a variety of parental types) are characterized for chromosome content and expression of human enzymes, etc. Data thus accumulated can be analysed for associations between functions and chromosomes. If a particular enzyme and chromosome are consistently retained, or lost, together in a large number of hybrids a tentative assignment can be made. Evidence supporting the association can be obtained from the analysis of segregant subclones derived from a hybrid retaining both enzyme and chromosome.

Similarly, co-segregation of two marker enzymes, or antigens, suggests that the genes necessary for their expression are linked. The first autosomal linkage detected in this way was that between lactate dehydrogenase B and peptidase B (Santachiara *et al.*, 1970; Ruddle *et al.*, 1970), the linkage group being subsequently assigned to chromosome 12 (see Ruddle, 1973).

The most likely complications in this type of analysis are heterogeneity of some hybrid cell populations and the possible occurrence of chromosomal rearrangements which could confuse the detection of human genetic material. Partly resulting from these problems, eventual acceptance of a gene assignment is now based on the confirmation of an original observation by an independent laboratory working with different hybrid lines (New Haven Conference 1973).

c. *The control of differentiation*

Genetic analysis by somatic cell hybridization offers the possibility of examining the factors concerned in the control of differentiation. To this end several hybridizations have been made between cells which do and cells which do not express well characterized differentiated functions (Davidson, 1971; Ephrussi, 1972; Davis and Adelberg, 1973). The main conclusion is that some differentiated functions (e.g. dihydroxyphenylalanine oxidase which is necessary for the production of melanin) disappear after fusion of hamster melanoma cells with mouse fibroblasts, whereas basic functions from both cell types continue to be expressed. A wide variety of other differentiated traits, ranging from the production of immunoglobulins (Periman, 1970; Coffino *et al.*, 1971) to that of growth hormone by a line derived from pituitary cells (Sonnenschein *et al.*, 1968) also appear to be "extinguished" after inter- or intraspecific hybridization. However, more complicated patterns of expression/extinction have been observed. Furthermore, although in most cases (particularly in intraspecific crosses) extensive chromosome segregation was not observed, the possibility that extinction of differentiated function results from loss of the appropriate chromosomes from the differentiated parent has not always been excluded.

Although extremely interesting, the above observations do not alone solve the problem of how differentiation is controlled. However, further analysis with hybrid cells has provided a clue to how "extinction" is effected. A suggestion that the nondifferentiated parent produces a repressor which "switches off" the differentiated functions of the other parent was supported by studies on the expression of a kidney-specific esterase (Es-2) in hybrids between a mouse renal adeno-carcinoma line and human fibroblasts. One of the clones examined 2 months after fusion had no detectable enzyme; thus either the mouse chromosome(s) necessary for expression had been lost, or the function was suppressed by products from human chromosomes. When further subclones were made from the Es-2 negative hybrid, some were found to remain negative, some were weakly positive and some showed full re-expression of the enzyme. Es-2 producing hybrids always retained their phenotype after subcloning. Karyotype analysis indicated that re-expression of the differentiated function was associated with loss of *human* chromosomes (Klebe *et al.*, 1970). At first, a specific association was suspected, chromosome 10 being tentatively identified as the site for the esterase "regulator". Ruddle (unpublished data) has more recently indicated that the basis for extinction/re-expression may be more complex.

In some cases, for example, fusions between rat hepatomas and nonliver derived cell lines, differential traits (albumin production) of both parental types may be expressed (Peterson and Weiss, 1972; Darlington *et al.*, 1973; Malawista and Weiss, 1974) in hybrids possessing twice the normal input of chromosomes from the differentiated parents, or after extensive chromosome segregation.

Clearly, analysis of such situations provides enormous possibilities for arriving at some understanding of cellular control processes. Whether such mechanisms are the same as those involved in activating or maintaining the differentiated state has yet to be established, nor in many cases is it certain that the observed regulation acts at the transcriptional rather than the translational level. One of the main difficulties lies in the establishment of hybrids (beyond the heterokaryon stage) with normal diploid differentiated cells as opposed to the tumour derived lines which have been largely employed so far.

d. *Malignancy*

The malignancy of cultured cells can be tested by injection into suitable histocompatible and/or immune suppressed animals and examining the resulting incidence of tumours. The mechanism underlying the expression of malignancy is thus amenable to study by somatic cell genetics. Many investigations have examined the malignancy of hybrids derived from combinations between high and low malignant types of parental classes (see Harris, 1970; Ephrussi, 1972). Several early studies suggested malignancy to be dominant. Subsequently, Harris *et al.* (1969) observed that the highly malignant phenotype of a variety of mouse tumours was suppressed after hybridization to a cell line of low malignancy (A9) derived from mouse fibroblasts.

Both the derived hybrids and the mouse fibroblast line also gave rise to tumours but at very low frequency. However, cells recovered from those tumours which did develop following injection of the hybrids were found to have regained the highly malignant phenotype of the parental tumour cells and furthermore had undergone a variable but frequently extensive chromosome segregation (particularly of the bi-armed chromosomes characteristic of the mouse fibroblast line parent). This pattern of loss followed by reappearance of the differentiated highly malignant phenotype is reminiscent of the extinction and re-expression of differentiated functions and perhaps to this extent the basis for malignancy could be considered in the same context as the control activating a particular set of differentiated functions (Ephrussi, 1972). However, the data are also consistent with the malignant phenotype being controlled by one (or more) recessive lesions which would require the alteration or loss of the equivalent normal allele by mutation or chromosome segregation before being expressed (Wiener et al., 1971).

e. *Organelle biogenesis*

Mitochondria result from a cooperation between the nuclear genome and DNA of the organelle itself (mitDNA) (see Avner, these Proceedings). In principle, interspecific hybrids may segregate mitDNA and/or chromosomes of either species. They thus provide a means of examining the interaction between the organelle DNA of one species and the nuclear coded mitochondrial components provided by the other. In addition the existence of controls acting on the mitDNA, or on the production of the nuclear coded organelle components, could be recognized and examined. Human–mouse hybrids which, as we have seen, in general lose substantial numbers of chromosomes, apparently retain only mouse mitDNA (Clayton et al., 1971; Attardi and Attardi, 1971). This suggested that human chromosomal genes are required for the replication of human mitDNA, or that human mitDNA replicates less efficiently in the hybrid cell environment, or even that mouse cells produce an inhibitor of human mitDNA replication. However, the latter two possibilities are less likely in light of the observations of Coon et al. (1973) that hybrids obtained between rodent embryonic cells and human cells may retain either, or both types of mitDNA depending on the extent and nature of chromosome loss.

We have examined the production of human nuclear coded mitochondrial components in hybrids which have lost human mitDNA by developing a variety of electrophoretic and immunological procedures to detect the presence of human mit components (Craig, 1973; van Heyningen et al., 1973). Many human–mouse hybrids and subclones were screened for the production of four mitochondrially located, but nuclearly coded enzymes. Each of the human enzymes was found in at least one hybrid. As human mitDNA was not detected in a representative selection from these cell lines, its presence is apparently not required for the expression of nuclear genes for human mitochondrial enzymes. Either mitDNA has no control over the nuclear coded components, or else the control is not species specific.

The four mitochondrial enzymes (three of which act consecutively in the citric acid cycle) segregate independently and the genes necessary for the expression of all but one have been provisionally assigned to chromosomes (van Heyningen *et al.*, 1973, 1974a, 1974b; Craig *et al.*, 1974; van Someren *et al.*, 1974). The mitochondrial form of superoxide dismutase has been provisionally assigned to chromosome 6 (Tischfield *et al.*, 1974) which also segregates independently of the other mitochondrial markers examined in this laboratory (preliminary unpublished observations).

Recent reports suggest that in some types of hybrid either, or both, parental types of mitDNA may be retained (Coon *et al.*, 1973; Eliceiri, 1973) and may recombine (Horak *et al.*, 1974). We have developed procedures to resolve the proteins made in the mitochondria which are thought to be coded by the organelle DNA (Jeffreys and Craig, 1974). None of the human–mouse hybrids analysed so far produce human mitochondrial proteins. Nevertheless, the procedure has potential interest as a probe for investigating hybrids which have recombinant mitDNA.

f. *"Genetic improvement" of cell lines*

The problem of employing cell fusion to this end is not so much in achieving input of additional genetic information but in restricting the retention to the minimum requirement, thus eliminating additional and potentially undesirable changes.

There are examples of hybridization between evolutionarily widely separated species, e.g. mouse fibroblast line × chick erythrocytes, in which almost complete elimination of the genetic input of one species occurs (Schwartz *et al.*, 1971). Although the hybrid expressed chicken HGPRT, necessary for survival of the hybrid in HAT medium, only mouse chromosomes could be recognized in the karyotype. Similar dramatic elimination of chicken genetic information (except the selected marker) occurred in a fusion between an HGPRT⁻ hamster line and chicken erythrocytes (Boyd and Harris, 1973). In human–mouse hybrids loss of the human genome is generally neither so rapid nor so extensive. Nevertheless, hybrids obtained after prolonged propagation retained a selected human enzyme (TK) but had lost all identifiable human chromosomes including number 17, to which it had been assigned (Migeon and Miller, 1968).

Somatic cells in culture are also a convenient starting point to examine whether other mechanisms, normally thought of in the context of bacterial genetics, such as transduction and transformation, could be used to obtain specific genetic alterations. Many of the more spectacular claims in this field have been made with plant material. However, transformation of mammalian cells in tissue culture has been attempted on several occasions. Szybalski and Szybalska (1962) made use of their HGPRT-deficient line as a recipient for

DNA prepared from normal cells. Their initial results were encouraging but the involvement of transformation in the production of HGPRT⁻ cells has been questioned. Since this time, there have been a number of claims and counter claims for the uptake and expression of exogenous mammalian (or even bacterial) DNA by transformation, or transduction-like mechanisms (Merril et al., 1971; Raspe, 1972).

Few experiments have been reported in which the postulated gene products of the input DNA have been unambiguously characterized. McBride and Ozer (1973) obtained "correction" of HGPRT-deficient mouse cells with metaphase chromosomes isolated from Chinese hamster fibroblasts. Cells surviving selection were found to express hamster HGPRT rather than the mouse form of the enzyme.

There are well-established examples of genes carried by viruses altering the biochemical properties of infected recipient cells. For example, Munyon et al. (1971) demonstrated the ability of uv-inactivated Herpes simplex to restore (by expression of the viral enzyme) a TK positive phenotype to mouse cells originally TK⁻.

CULTURED PLANT CELL GENETICS

In the space available it is impossible to cover more than one or two aspects of the parallel developments in cultured plant cell genetics. Surely one of the most exciting aspects, and one in which plant systems have an advantage over mammalian cells, is the possibility of returning to the whole organism from cultured cells.

There are three major aspects of plant cultured cell genetics: (1) normal *in vitro* culture (including haploid culture from anthers); (2) meristem culture; (3) isolation and culture of protoplasts. Although the first two have wide interest and application to the propagation of plants, or to increasing genetic variability, it is the third aspect which has the broadest potential in terms of genetic research and manipulation. (See reviews by Cocking, 1970, 1972; Morel and Tempe, 1972; Smith, 1974.)

Removal of the plant cell wall during the preparation of protoplasts allows application of the techniques and approaches of somatic cell hybridization (Power et al., 1970) and raises the possibility of achieving plant hybridization in the test tube. Preliminary success in this direction (Carlson, 1973) involved fusions between two *Nicotiana* species. Hybrid selection was based on the ability to grow without hormone supplement. Karyotypes and isozyme patterns of hybrid clones suggested that they retained a complete genetic complement of both parents.

Additional experiments by Carlson have investigated nuclear–cytoplasmic interactions. Wild-type chloroplasts supplied to protoplasts of an albino mutant of *Nicotiana tabacum* were taken up and maintained by the cells in culture. Whole plants could be eventually derived from these, their original deficiency having now been corrected. The above procedures illustrate the additional flexibility that protoplasts provide. They can of course be used (as can normal *in vitro* cultures of plant cells) as a basis for mutant selection.

Attempts have also been made to induce genetic alterations by treating cultured plant cells with DNA, or virus. For example, Doy *et al.* (1973) reported that treatment with *E. coli* transducing phage carrying lactose genes can "convert" carrot cells to lactose utilization and that the β-galactosidase produced by the cells is immunologically identical with that of the bacteria. Similar results have been achieved by incubating λ plac bacteriophage with sycamore cells in culture but in this case the identity of the expressed enzyme could not be established immunologically (Johnson *et al.*, 1973).

Controversy still surrounds the interpretation of many experiments designed to investigate the uptake and integration of exogenous DNA supplied to animal or plant cells in culture. Perhaps the most important evidence (which is, unfortunately, rarely provided) is the demonstration that the presumptive product of the input DNA is identical with that expected. Otherwise, it is difficult to exclude the possibility that "masked" genes of the recipient genome are being activated. Furthermore, rigorous controls must be established to check for contamination.

However, it is clear that genetic manipulation of cells in culture by mutation, fusion or perhaps by a DNA mediated, transformation-like process is potentially of great value in providing increased genetic variability and for studying many basic problems in cell biology.

Some of the work described has been supported by grants from the Cancer Research Campaign, NATO and from The Medical Research Council.

References

Appels, R., Bolund, L., Goto, S. and Ringertz, N. R. (1974). *Expl Cell Res.* **85**, 182.

Attardi, B. and Attardi, G. (1971). *Proc. natn. Acad. Sci. U.S.A.* **69**, 129.

Baker, R. M., Brunette, D. M., Mankovitz, R., Thompson, L. H., Whitmore, G. F., Siminovitch, L. and Till, J. E. (1974). *Cell*, **1**, 1.

Barski, G., Sorieul, S. and Cornefert, F. (1960). *Compt. Rend.* **251**, 1825.

Beaudet, A. L., Roufa, D. J. and Caskey, C. T. (1973). *Proc. natn. Acad. Sci. U.S.A.* **70**, 320.

Berk, A. J. and Clayton, D. A. (1973). *J. biol. Chem.* **248**, 2722.

Boyd, Y. L. and Harris, H. (1973). *J. Cell Sci.* **13**, 841.

Brockman, R. W., Kelley, G. G., Stutts, P. and Copeland, V. (1961). *Nature, Lond.* **191**, 469.

Carlson, P. S. (1973). *Proc. natn. Acad. Sci. U.S.A.* **70**, 598.

Cass, C. E. (1972). *J. Cell. Comp. Physiol.* **79**, 139.

Chan, V. L., Whitmore, G. F. and Siminovitch, L. (1972). *Proc. natn. Acad. Sci. U.S.A.* **69**, 3119.

Clayton, D. A. and Teplitz, R. I. (1972). *J. Cell Sci.* **10**, 487.

Clayton, D. A., Teplitz, R. L., Nabholz, M., Dovey, H. and Bodmer, W. F. (1971). *Nature, Lond.* **234**, 560.

Coffino, P., Knowles, B., Natheson, S. G. and Scharff, D. (1971). *Nature, New Biol.* **231**, 87.

Cocking, E. C. (1970). *Int. Rev. Cytol.* **28**, 89.

Cocking, E. C. (1972). *A. Rev. Plant Physiol.* **23**, 29.

Coen, D., Deutsch, J., Netter, P., Petrochilo, E. and Slonimski, P. P. (1970). *Symp. Soc. exp. Biol.* **24**, 449.

Cook, P. R. (1970). *J. Cell Sci.* **7**, 1.

Coon, H. G., Horak, I. and David, I. B. (1973). *J. molec. Biol.* **81**, 285.

Craig, I. W. (1973). *Biochem. Genet.* **9**, 351.

Craig, I. W., van Heyningen, V., Finnegan, D. and Bodmer, W. F. (1974). 1st Int. Workshop on Human Gene Mapping Birth Defects: Original Articles Series *X* 3, p. 76. National Foundation. New York.

Darlington, G. J., Bernhard, H. P. and Ruddle, F. H. (1973). *In vitro*, **8**, 444.

Davidson, R. L. (1971). *In vitro*, **6**, 411.

Davidson, R. L. and Bick, M. D. (1973). *Proc. natn. Acad. Sci. U.S.A.* **70**, 138.

Davidson, R. L., Ephrussi, B. and Yamamoto, K. (1966). *Proc. natn. Acad. Sci. U.S.A.* **56**, 1437.

Davis, F. M. and Adelberg, E. A. (1973). *Bact. Rev.* **37**, 197.

Diacumakos, E. G. (1973). *Proc. natn. Acad. Sci. U.S.A.* **70**, 3382.

Doy, C. H., Gresshoff, P. M. and Rolfe, B. G. (1973). *Proc. natn. Acad. Sci. U.S.A.* **70**, 723.

Ephrussi, B. (1972). "Hybridization of Somatic Cells". Princeton University Press, Princeton.

Ephrussi, B., Scaletta, L. J., Stenchever, M. A. and Yoshida, M. C. (1964). *Intern. Soc. for Cell Biol. on Cytogenetics of Cells in Culture*, **3**, 13. Academic Press, New York and London.

Ephrussi, B. and Weiss, M. C. (1965). *Proc. natn. Acad. Sci. U.S.A.* **53**, 1040.

Eliceiri, G. L. (1973). *Nature, New Biol.* **241**, 233.

Fischer, G. A. (1961). *Biochem. Pharmac.* **7**, 75.

Hakala, M. T., Zakrzewski, S. F. and Nichol, C. A. (1961). *J. biol. Chem.* **236**, 952.

Harris, H. (1970). "Cell Fusion". Harvard University Press, Cambridge, Mass.

Harris, H., Miller, O. J., Klein, G., Worst, P. and Tachibana, T. (1969). *Nature, Lond.* **223**, 363.

Harris, H. and Watkins, J. F. (1965). *Nature, Lond.* **205**, 640.

Harris, H., Watkins, J. F., Ford, C. E. and Schoefl, G. I. (1966). *J. Cell Sci.* **1**, 1.

Harris, M., (1971). *J. cell. comp. Physiol.* **78**, 177.

Horak, I., Coon, H. and David, I. B. (1974). *Proc. natn. Acad. Sci. U.S.A.* **71**, 1828.

Jeffreys, A. and Craig, I. W. (1974). *Biochem. J.* **144**, 161.

Johnson, C. B., Grierson, D. and Smith, H. (1973). *Nature, New Biol.* **244**, 105.

Kao, F. T. and Puck, T. T. (1968). *Proc. natn. Acad. Sci. U.S.A.* **60**, 1275.

Kao, F. T. and Puck, T. T. (1974). "Methods in Cell Physiology" (Ed. D. M. Prescott), vol. 8. Academic Press, New York and London.

Kao, F. T., Chasin, L. A. and Puck, T. T. (1969). *Proc. natn. Acad. Sci. U.S.A.* **64**, 1284.

Kennet, R., Bengtsson, B. and Bodmer, W. F. (1974). *Tissue Antigens*. In press.

Kit, S., Dubbs, D. R., Piekarski, L. J. and Hsu, T. C. (1963). *Expl Cell Res.* **31**, 297.

Kit, S., Leung, W.-C. and Trkula (1973). *Biochem. biophys. Res. Commun.* **54**, 455.

Kit, S. and Leung, W.-C. (1974a). *Biochem. Genet.* **11**, 231.

Kit, S. and Leung, W.-C. (1974b). *J. Cell Biol.* **61**, 35.

90   IAN CRAIG

Klebe, R. J., Chen, T. and Ruddle, F. H. (1970). *Proc. natn. Acad. Sci. U.S.A.* **66**, 1220.
Lieberman, I. and Ove, J. (1960). *J. biol. Chem.* **235**, 1765.
Littlefield, J. (1963). *Proc. natn. Acad. Sci. U.S.A.* **50**, 568.
Littlefield, J. W. (1964a). *Science,* **145**, 709.
Littlefield, J. W. (1964b). *Cold Spring Harb. Symp. quant. Biol.* **29**, 161.
Littlefield, J. W. (1969). *Proc. natn. Acad. Sci. U.S.A.* **62**, 88.
Luria, S. E. and Delbruck, M. (1943). *Genetics,* **28**, 491.
Lucy, J. A. (1970). *Nature, Lond.* **227**, 815.
Malawista, S. E. and Weiss, M. C. (1974). *Proc. natn. Acad. Sci. U.S.A.* **71**, 927.
Medrano, L. and Green, H. (1974). *Cell,* **1**, 23.
Mezger-Freed, L. (1971). *J. Cell Biol.* **51**, 742.
Mezger-Freed, L. (1972). *Nature, New Biol.* **235**, 245.
Merrill, C. R., Geier, M. R. and Petricciani, J. C. (1971). *Nature, Lond.* **233**, 398.
Migeon, B. R. and Miller, C. S. (1968). *Science,* **162**, 1105.
Miller, O. J., Allderdice, P. W., Miller, D. A., Breg, W. R. and Migeon, B. R. (1971). *Science,* **173**, 244.
Minor, P. (1973). Ph.D. thesis, University of London.
Morel, G. and Tempe, J. (eds) (1972). Proc. 1st Int. Symp. on Plant Protoplasts.
Munyon, W., Kraiselburd, E., Davis, D. and Mann, J. (1971). *J. Virol.* **7**, 813.
McBride, O. W. and Ozer, H. L. (1973). *Proc. natn. Acad. Sci. U.S.A.* **70**, 1258.
Nabholz, M. (1971). Proc. IX Can. Cancer Res. Conf. (Ed. P. G. Scholefield), p. 76.
New Haven Conference (1973). 1st Int. Workshop on Human Gene Mapping. Birth Defects: Original Article Series X, 3. 1974. The National Foundation, New York.
Okada, Y. (1962). *Exp. Cell Res.* **26**, 98.
Osawa, S., Takata, R., Tanaka, K. and Tamaki, M. (1973). *Molec. gen. Genet.* **127**, 163.
Periman, P. (1970). *Nature, Lond.* **228**, 1086.
Perkins, J. P., Hillcoat, B. L. and Bertino, J. R. (1967). *J. biol. Chem.* **242**, 4771.
Peterson, J. A. and Weiss, M. C. (1972). *Proc. natn. Acad. Sci. U.S.A.* **69**, 571.
Power, J. B., Cummins, S. E. and Cocking, E. C. (1970). *Nature, Lond.* **225**, 1016.
Puck, T. T. and Kao, F. T. (1967). *Proc. natn. Acad. Sci. U.S.A.* **58**, 1227.
Raspe, G. (ed.) (1972). "Advances in the Biosciences", vol. 8. Pergamon Press, Vieweg.
Renger, H. C. and Basilico, C. (1972). *Proc. natn. Acad. Sci. U.S.A.* **69**, 109.
Ringertz, N. R., Carlsson, S.-A., Ege, T. and Bolund, L. (1971). *Proc. natn. Acad. Sci. U.S.A.* **68**, 3228.
Robert de Saint-Vincent, B. and Buttin, G. (1973). *Eur. J. Biochem.* **37**, 481.
Ruddle, F. H. (1973). *Nature, Lond.* **242**, 165.
Ruddle, F. H. and Kucherlapati, R. S. (1974). *Scientific American,* **231**, 36.
Ruddle, F. H., Chapman, V. M., Chen, T. R. and Klebe, R. J. (1970). *Nature, Lond.* **227**, 251.
Santachiara, A. S., Nabholz, M., Miggiano, V., Darlington, A. J. and Bodmer, W. F. (1970). *Nature, Lond.* **227**, 248.
Schwartz, A., Cook, P. R. and Harris, H. (1971). *Nature, New Biol.* **230**, 5.
Sharp, J. D., Capecchi, N. E. and Capecchi, M. R. (1973). *Proc. natn. Acad. Sci. U.S.A.* **70**, 3145.
Shaw, W. V. (1967). *J. biol. Chem.* **242**, 687.
Siegel, L., Sly, W. and Craig, I. W. (1974). Manuscript in preparation.
Smith, H. H. (1974). *Bioscience,* **24**, 269.
Sonnenschien, C., Tashjian, A. and Richardson, V. I. (1968). *Genetics,* **60**, 227.
Spolsky, C. M. and Eisenstadt, J. M. (1972) *FEBS letters,* **25**, 319.

CULTURED CELL GENETICS   91

Szybalski, W. (1958). *Microb. Genetics Bull.* **16**, 30.
Szybalski, W. and Szybalska, E. H. (1962). *Univ. Michigan Med. Bull.* **28**, 277.
Szybalski, W., Szybalska, E. H. and Ragni, G. (1962). *Natn. Inst. Canc. Monograph*, **7**, 75.
Terzi, M. (1973). *Genetics*, **74**, S274.
Thompson, L. H. and Baker, R. M. (1973). "Methods in Cell Biology", vol. 6, chapter 7, p. 209.
Thompson, L. H., Harkins, J. L. and Stanners, C. P. (1973). *Proc. natn. Acad. Sci. U.S.A.* **70**, 3094.
Till, J. E., Baker, R. M., Brunette, D. M., Ling, V., Thompson, L. H. and Wright, J. A. (1973). *Fedn. Proc. Fedn. Am. Socs. exp. Biol.* **32**, 29.
Tischfield, J. A., Creagan, R. P., Rucciuti, F. and Ruddle, F. H. (1974). First International Workshop on Human Gene Mapping. Birth Defects: Original Article series X, p. 164. National Foundation, New York.
Toniolo, D., Meiss, H. K. and Basilico, C. (1973). *Proc. natn. Acad. Sci. U.S.A.* **70**, 1273.
van Heyningen, V., Craig, I. W. and Bodmer, W. F. (1973). *Nature, Lond.* **242**, 509.
van Heyningen, V., Bobrow, M., Bodmer, W. F., Povey, S., Gardiner, S. E. and Hopkinson, D. A. (1974a). Second International Congress Human Gene Mapping, Rotterdam. In press.
van Heyningen, V., Craig, I. W. and Bodmer, W. F. (1974b). *In* "Biogenesis of Mitochondria" (Eds A. M. Kroon and Saccone). Academic Press, New York and London.
van Someren, H., van Henegouwen, H. B., Westerweld, A. and Bootsma, D. (1974). Humangenetik.
Wiener, F., Klein, G. and Harris, H. (1971). *J. Cell Sci.* **8**, 681.
Weiss, M. C. and Green, H. (1967). *Proc. natn. Acad. Sci. U.S.A.* **58**, 1104.
Willingham, M. C., Carchman, R. A. and Pastan, I. H. (1973). *Proc. natn. Acad. Sci. U.S.A.* **70**, 2906.

Quantitative genetics

C. E. CATEN and J. L. JINKS

Department of Genetics, University of Birmingham, Birmingham B15 2TT, England

Summary

Many characters of economic importance in higher organisms and micro-organisms vary in a continuous manner. Such quantitative variation is determined by many chromosomal genes whose individual effect cannot be discerned against the background of environmental variation. In higher organisms, where "strain" improvement has depended upon the exploitation of natural quantitative differences, biometrical methods, based on comparisons of generation means and variances, have been developed for measuring the variation and interpreting it in Mendelian terms. These methodologies can be readily adapted to microorganisms possessing meiotic recombination systems and provide information concerning the heritability of the character, the number of factors involved and their mode of action and chromosomal location. Genotypes giving extreme expressions can be produced by repeated cycles of hybridization and selection, and significant strain improvement may be obtained in this way.

The extension of quantitative genetics to nonmeiotic recombination systems is complicated by the selective nature of these systems which restricts the use of the biometrical methods. However, marked regions of the genome can be assayed for alleles determining the character in question, thereby making possible the construction of strains incorporating desirable genome segments from several sources. Markers frequently affect quantitative characters and it may be necessary to adopt balanced experimental designs to overcome this complication.

Quantitative genetics provides information on the evolutionary processes occurring in nature, while its application to strain improvement helps in the choice of optimum experimental procedure and allows the outcome of selection to be predicted.

Introduction

Genetics is concerned with the inheritance of differences, be these between individual plants and animals or strains of microorganisms. The differences of classical, Mendelian genetics are discrete and any individual can be unambiguously assigned to a particular class. Such differences constitute qualitative or discontinuous variation. However, where the individuals are sampled from a natural population or separated by many mutational steps, they frequently form a continuous gradient of types and discrete classes cannot be recognized. Such differences constitute quantitative or continuous variation and it is with their inheritance that quantitative genetics is concerned. Qualitative or quantitative variation are not properties of particular characters, but depend upon the complexity of the underlying genetic situation in each case. The same character may be inherited in a discontinuous manner in one cross-lineage and in a continuous way in another.

Microbial genetics has, with few exceptions, been concerned with discrete character differences whose transmission through meiotic or nonmeiotic systems could be unambiguously followed in a qualitative manner. The complications of quantitative variation have been excluded by: (1) concentrating on characters close to the primary action of the genes; (2) working only with closely related strains; (3) discarding strains which were difficult to classify. This approach has been highly successful in determining the location, structure, mode of functioning and regulation of individual genes. The industrial microbial geneticist, like all applied geneticists, however, can neither choose his character and organism nor ignore variation because it is in unrelated strains or insufficiently discrete. Furthermore, the characters of interest are frequently sensitive to environmental variables and difficult to measure so that even where the underlying genetic determination is simple, the inherent discontinuities may be hidden by this environmental blurring. Quantitative genetics therefore has a part to play in strain improvement, along with the more widely recognized techniques of mutagenesis, hybridization and biochemical genetics.

Plant and animal breeders, for the same reasons, have long been faced with the problem of continuous variation, and a branch of genetics, quantitative or biometrical genetics, has been developed to determine the kinds of gene action and interaction involved, and to predict the outcome of future generations and the consequences of selection (Mather, 1949; Falconer, 1960; Mather and Jinks, 1971). It is a direct development of Mendelian genetics, seeking to interpret continuous variation in these terms, and is in no way a conflicting or even an alternative approach. As Mather (1971) states, "The biometrical approach is from a different direction starting with the character rather than the individual determinant".

Results and discussion

THE NATURE AND ANALYSIS OF QUANTITATIVE VARIATION

a. *The genetic determination of quantitative variation*

That continuous variation could be accounted for by genes inherited in the Mendelian fashion was initially appreciated by Nilsson-Ehle (1909) and East (1915), and the basis of present-day analyses was laid down by Fisher (1918). Their conclusion was that continuously varying characters are controlled by many chromosomal genes of similar and supplementary action but with individual effects so small in relation to the total phenotypic variation as to be indiscernible. The smoothing effect of the simultaneous segregation of many allelic pairs in this polygenic system is further enhanced by nonheritable factors. In this way continuous variation of the phenotype can arise from discontinuous variation of the genotype.

Evidence for this multiple factor hypothesis comes from demonstrations that the genes in polygenic systems segregate in a Mendelian manner and are linked to known chromosomal gene markers. Linkage is revealed by differences in the means of the various marker genotypes, provided that the markers do not themselves affect the character. However, with free recombination this technique is unlikely to reveal linkage unless individual genes of relatively large effect are present or many genes are concentrated in short chromosome regions. To overcome this difficulty, systems have been devised in *Drosophila melanogaster* (Mather, 1942; Mather and Harrison, 1949) and wheat (Law, 1967) by which the contribution of all genes on a particular chromosome or chromosome segment can be determined. Using these chromosome assay techniques, Mather and Harrison (1949) were able to show that the three large chromosomes of *D. melanogaster* accounted for 85 per cent of the genetic variation for number of abdominal chaetae among 12 lines. This dissection of a polygenic system has, in certain cases, been followed to the point of locating individual genes or polygenic blocks along the chromosomes (Breese and Mather, 1957; Thoday, 1961). Breese and Mather (1957) split chromosome III of *D. melanogaster* into six segments and found that each was active in determining the difference in chaetae number between selected high and low lines. From a comparison of the average phenotypic expression of marker genotypes the actual location of a gene between flanking markers can be estimated (Mather and Jinks, 1971).

At this level of resolution quantitative genetics merges with Mendelian genetics. However, it is only achieved by fractionating the polygenic system and by rigorous control of the environment; once the system is put together again and normal environmental variability reintroduced, as it must be in applied situations, the original complexity reappears. Nevertheless these studies have clearly shown that continuous variation is mediated through chromosomal genes, while the detection of activity in most chromosome regions tested is consistent with the notion of many genes distributed throughout the genome. Together the assays of Mather and Harrison (1949) and Breese and Mather (1957) have identified 11 chromosome regions affecting abdominal chaetae number in *D. melanogaster*. Taking into account evidence from other studies, the actual number of genes involved must be considerably larger than this (Mather and Jinks, 1971).

The individual factors of a polygenic system are interspersed along the chromosome among the marker genes of major effect. They also overlap in the magnitude of their phenotypic effects, some of the factors having a sufficiently large effect for their segregation to be followed qualitatively. In many instances, it would seem likely that the same genes are involved and that individual factors in a polygenic system are allelic variants with only a minor, quantitative effect on the activity of the gene product. Electrophoretic surveys of enzymes have shown that allelic variation of this type is widespread within natural populations (Harris and Hopkinson, 1972). Even where a given allelic difference has a major effect it may also contribute to polygenic variation through pleiotropic effects on a second character (Penrose, 1951). In addition, certain chromosomes or chromosome regions which are heterochromatic may have polygenic activity in the absence of demonstrable major genes (Mather, 1944). These relationships between the genes determining continuous and discontinuous variation have been discussed in detail by Mather (1954) and Mather and Jinks (1971).

b. *The aims and methods of quantitative genetics*

The aims of quantitative genetics are the same as those of Mendelian genetics, namely, to understand the genetic determination of a character difference in sufficient detail that useful predictions can be made concerning the genotype(s) and phenotype(s) of future generations. To achieve this we need to know the number of genes, their location, how they act and interact, and how they are influenced by the environment. Where quantitative genetics differs is in the analytical methods that can be used. Every generation is composed of a continuous gradation of phenotypes and the properties of any generation and the relationships between generations can only be described in statistical terms, that is, by means and variances and by correlations and covariances respectively. These statistics represent the working units of the quantitative geneticist and are the direct counterpart of the segregation ratios of Mendelian genetics. From the expected relationships between generations, the observed means and correlations (first-degree statistics) and variances and covariances (second-degree statistics) can be interpreted in terms of, and partitioned into, effects due to additive gene action, dominance, epistasis, linkage, environment and genotype × environment interactions. An important distinction should be drawn between the information provided by first- and second-degree statistics. With multiple factors the estimates of additive, dominance, epistatic effects, etc. are the sums over all factors. Where the direction of action of individual factors may be opposing, as with dominance and epistasis, there is a balancing out of such effects in their contribution to means but not to variances. Thus, unless contributions from all factors have the same sign, comparisons of generation means lead to underestimates of the contribution of these nonadditive gene effects.

For detailed treatments of the history and methodology of quantitative genetics in higher organisms the reader is referred to Falconer (1960), Mather (1971) and Mather and Jinks (1971). The remainder of this paper is devoted to studies of the inheritance of quantitative variation in microorganisms.

QUANTITATIVE GENETICS OF MICROORGANISMS

Few studies of the inheritance of quantitative variation have been carried out in microorganisms despite the fact that many of their technical advantages for genetic studies apply equally to quantitative genetics (Simchen and Jinks, 1964; Fripp and Caten, 1971). This deficiency can be attributed to the fact that, because of its historical development, quantitative genetics is closely associated with plant and animal breeding and its methods are firmly based in meiotic genetic systems. Indeed, the biometrical models for generation means and variances assume complete diploid formation, unbiased segregation and the recovery of all possible genotypes in the proportions determined by their linkage relationships. Clearly, many microbial genetic systems do not satisfy these assumptions and require the development of new techniques of quantitative analysis. Eukaryotic microorganisms, however, possess meiotic systems and to these the available methods of quantitative genetics can be readily applied. That the predominant phase of the life cycle is, in many instances, haploid rather than diploid, simplifies the analysis since the complications of dominance do not arise.

a. *Meiotic systems in fungi*

Collections of wild isolates of fungal species exhibit continuous variation for a range of characters (Brasier, 1970; Butcher *et al.*, 1972). An example is shown in Fig. 1. We will illustrate how and what information can be obtained about the inheritance of this variation by considering a cross between two strains of *Aspergillus amstelodami*. The character is colony radial growth rate and the two strains (2 and 37), although isolated from different continents, are very similar in general morphology and rate of growth. A sample of 76 single asco-spore progeny from the cross was grown with the parents in a randomized and replicated experiment and the rate of increase in colony diameter measured.

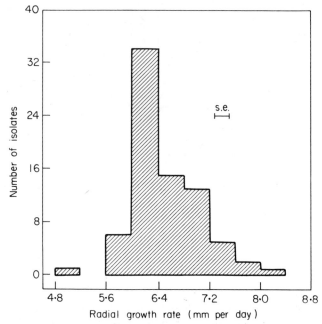

FIG. 1. Frequency distribution for radial growth rate at 25 °C among 77 dikaryons of *Schizophyllum commune* isolated from a natural population (by courtesy of Dr C. M. Brasier).

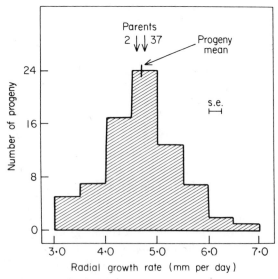

FIG. 2. Frequency distribution for radial growth rate among the progeny of *Aspergillus amstelodami* cross 2 × 37.

The F_1 progeny vary continuously with the extreme phenotypes lying outside the parental range (Fig. 2). There is no indication of discrete classes as would be produced by the segregation of alleles with a major effect. From the kind of data summarized in Fig. 2 information can be obtained concerning: (1) the contribution of genotype and environment to the observed phenotypic variation; (2) the number of effective factors segregating; (3) the location of the effective factors; (4) the mode of gene action. The methods used to deduce this information will be illustrated by referring to this cross. The corresponding results obtained from other crosses involving the same or different characters and species will then be tabulated and any general conclusions drawn.

i. *The contribution of genotype and environment.* Continuously varying characters are notoriously sensitive to environmental modification and we cannot immediately attribute the observed variation to the segregation of alleles controlling growth rate, even though great care was taken to control the environment. It is first necessary to carry out a test of significance to show that the observed variation is greater than expected purely from environmental influences. Such a test is possible because clonal replication provides a measure of the environmental effects, and the total phenotypic variation can be partitioned by the analysis of variance into that between replicates within progeny, which equals the environmental component (σ_E^2), and that between the individual progeny, which equals the genetic (σ_G^2) plus environmental components (Table 1). Since the between progeny item is significantly greater than the within progeny, the variation contains a genetic component. Estimation of σ_G^2 and σ_E^2 enables the former to be expressed as a proportion of the total phenotypic variation (Table 1). This ratio, which is referred to as a heritability,

TABLE 1

Analysis of variance for colony radial growth rate among 76 progeny from cross 2×37 in *Aspergillus amstelodami*

Source of variation	df	MS	VR	Expected mean square
Between progeny	75	1.08	8.23*	$\sigma_E^2 + 2\sigma_G^2$
Within progeny	75	0.13		σ_E^2

	Component	Estimate	% of total variation
	Genetic (σ_G^2)	0.48	78
	Environmental (σ_E^2)	0.13	22

* $P < 0.001$

TABLE 2

Proportion of crosses showing significant genetic variation and estimates of heritability for quantitative characters in fungi

Character	Species	Number of crosses Total	$\hat{\sigma}_G^2$ significant	Heritability (%) Mean	Range	Reference*
Radial growth rate	Aspergillus amstelodami	8	7	47	0–78	a
	A. nidulans	7	6	66	17–94	b, c
	Schizophyllum commune	6	6	69	40–89	d
	Collybia velutipes	7	7	92	83–96	e
	Cochliobolus carbonum	4	4	75	66–86	f
	Neurospora crassa	7	7	47†	30–60†	g
Penicillin titre	A. nidulans	7	4	33	0–77	h
Growth yield	A. nidulans	2	1	44	22–65	c

* a. Caten, unpublished; b. Jinks et al. (1966); c. Caten and Lawrence (unpublished); d. Simchen (1966b); e. Croft and Simchen (1965); f. MacKenzie et al. (1971); g. Papa et al. (1966); h. Merrick (1975).

† Realized heritabilities

indicates the proportion of the total observed variation which could be fixed by selection. The proportion of crosses showing segregation and the mean and range of the heritability estimates for a number of characters in several species are shown in Table 2. Genetic variation was detected for each character in each species, although not in all crosses. In most cases the heritability estimates are greater than 50 per cent, although they vary from character to character as a result of differences in the amount of genetic variation present and/or in environmental sensitivities. They also vary markedly from cross to cross for the same character within the same species, reflecting the extent of genetic differences between the parental strains.

This method of estimating the genetic and environmental components of variation is applicable to any population of strains, whether it be the progeny of a cross, a collection of wild isolates, or the survivors of a mutagenic treatment.

ii. *The number of effective factors.* Where only a single gene is segregating both the difference between the extreme genotypes, the range $(P_H - P_L)$, and the genetic variance (σ_G^2) are determined solely by the magnitude of the gene effect(d). Where many genes are concerned the expectations of these two parameters contain a coefficient, k, which is the number of effective factors segregating. Both the range and genetic variance can be estimated and a solution for k found as $k = (P_H - P_L)/4\sigma_G^2$ (Croft and Simchen, 1965). In a finite progeny population each effective factor corresponds to a chromosome segment and may carry just one or several closely linked genes affecting the character.

The data for *A. amstelodami* 2 × 37 indicate a minimum of seven factors, with an average effect of 0.27 mm per day. Further estimates for other characters and species are given in Table 3. This method leads to a minimal estimate of the number of genes affecting a quantitative character for several reasons which include (1) a statistical limit set by the progeny sample size, (2) the fact that only those factors for which the parents carry different alleles are detected and (3) the likely compound nature of the individual effective factors. Despite these limitations the estimates in Table 3 support the multiple gene theory in indicating the involvement of several factors each of relatively small effect.

iii. *The location of the effective factors.* Information on the location of genes mediating quantitative variation can be obtained from crosses in which they are segregating along with chromosome markers. The *A. amstelodami* cross (2 × 37) was segregating not only for radial growth rate, but also for two conidial colour markers, *whi* (white) and *brw* (brown), which have no pleiotropic effects on growth rate. If the growth rate genes are unlinked to those for conidial colour there should be no differences in mean growth rate between the colour classes in the progeny. This was the case with the white marker

TABLE 3

Estimates of number of effective factors and their average effect for crosses between wild isolates of fungi

Character	Species	Number of crosses*	Number of effective factors (k)		Average effect (d)†		Reference‡
			Mean	Range	Mean	Range	
Radial growth rate	A. amstelodami	7	9	4–18	0.13	0.04–0.27	a
	A. nidulans	6	9	3–17	0.19	0.04–0.31	b, c
	S. commune	6	9	8–12	1.70	1.10–2.07	d
	C. velutipes	7	6	3–11	4.62	2.50–10.18	e
Penicillin titre	A. nidulans	4	8	5–15	1.22	0.51–1.63	h
Growth yield	A. nidulans	1	5	—	0.19	0.19	c

* Only crosses showing significant genetic variation included.
† Units are the same as initially used to assess the character.
‡ a. Caten, unpublished; b. Jinks et al. (1966); c. Caten and Lawrence (unpublished); d. Simchen (1966b); e. Croft and Simchen (1965); f. MacKenzie et al. (1971); g. Papa et al. (1966); h. Merrick (1975).

($whi = 4.69$ mm per day, $whi^+ = 4.69$ mm per day). However, among the nonwhite progeny, brown spored strains grew significantly faster than green ($brw = 5.01$ mm per day, $brw^+ = 4.47$ mm per day), indicating a factor for high growth rate linked to the brw allele introduced from isolate 2. This factor accounts for 20 per cent of the genetic variation and has been detected only in crosses involving isolate 2. This parent must therefore carry an allele(s) for high growth rate on the brw chromosome (linkage group I) while all other isolates examined carry a low growth rate allele(s) at this locus. Linkage of members of polygenic systems to known chromosomal markers has similarly been demonstrated in *Schizophyllum commune* (Connolly and Simchen, 1968) and *Neurospora crassa* (Papa, 1971).

iv. *The mode of gene action.* Where more than a single gene is responsible for a particular character two major patterns of gene action can be distinguished, depending upon whether the various alleles are independent (additive) or interdependent (nonadditive) in their action. In haploid organisms, nonindependent gene action can only arise through epistasis.

In any haploid cross the progeny segregate $1:1$ for the alleles at each locus for which the parents differ. Hence the additive contributions at each locus to the progeny mean will cancel and, in the absence of any nonadditive variation, the progeny should be symmetrically distributed about a mean equal to the mean of the two parents (Fig. 2). The presence of epistatic effects with a directional element, however, will lead to skewness of the distribution and

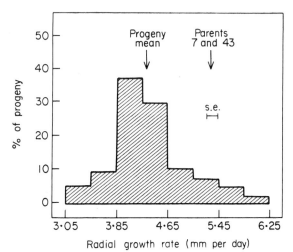

Fig. 3. Frequency distribution for radial growth rate among the progeny of *Aspergillus nidulans* cross 7 × 43 (Jinks *et al.*, 1966). Compare the skewness of the distribution and the relationship between the parental and progeny means with those for the progeny in Fig. 2.

TABLE 4

Contribution of additive ($\hat{\sigma}^2_A$), nonadditive ($\hat{\sigma}^2_I$) and environmental ($\hat{\sigma}^2_E$) effects to the total phenotypic variation for dikaryotic characters in *Schizophyllum commune* and *Collybia velutipes*

Character	Species	Origin	% Phenotypic variation			Sufficiency of model†	Reference‡
			$\hat{\sigma}^2_A$*	$\hat{\sigma}^2_I$*	$\hat{\sigma}^2_E$		
Radial growth rate	*S. commune*	dikaryon 1	47	12	41	✓	a
		dikaryon 6	36	14	50	✓	b
	C. velutipes	wild dikaryon	71	21	8	✓	c
Fruiting time	*S. commune*	dikaryon 1	50	29	21	—	b
		dikaryon 6	60	24	16	✓	b
	C. velutipes	wild dikaryon	48	31	21	✓	c
Fruit weight	*S. commune*	dikaryon 1	43	27	30	—	b
		dikaryon 6	41	27	32	✓	b
Number of sporophores	*C. velutipes*	wild dikaryon	48	31	21	—	c

* All significantly different from zero.
† Sufficiency of a model involving additive and dominance effects only.
‡ a. Simchen and Jinks (1964); b. Simchen (1966a); c. Simchen (1965).

deviation of the progeny mean from the parental mean (Fig. 3). Comparison of these two means provides a simple test for the occurrence of epistasis (Mather and Jinks, 1971). For the *A. nidulans* cross 7 × 43 (Fig. 3) the progeny mean is significantly less than the parental mean, indicating epistatic interactions giving a high growth rate in the parental isolates. The contributions of additive and epistatic effects on the means and, where backcross generations are also available, on the variances can be readily estimated (Mather and Jinks, 1971).

On the basis of the simple comparison of generation means examples of characters showing predominantly additive gene action—e.g. penicillin titre in *A. nidulans* (Merrick, 1975), radial growth rate in *A. amstelodami* (Caten, unpublished)—or a combination of additive and nonadditive gene action—e.g. radial growth rate in *A. nidulans* (Butcher, 1969) and *Neurospora crassa* (Papa, 1970)—have been found.

More complex types of gene action involving both dominance and epistasis occur in fungi with a stable heterokaryotic or diploid phase. To investigate the genetic determination of a quantitative character in dikaryons of *Schizophyllum commune*, Simchen and Jinks (1964) used a multiple mating programme which allowed tests of significance for, and estimation of, the additive genetic, nonadditive genetic and environmental effects. Furthermore, by examining the relationship between the variances and covariances of members of half sib families, the sufficiency of a model involving only additive and dominance variation could be tested. Simchen (1965, 1966a, 1967) applied this method to dikaryotic characters of *S. commune* and *Collybia velutipes* and some of his results are summarized in Table 4. In all cases significant additive and nonadditive genetic effects were detected. The former were always the larger, although there was a suggestion that nonadditive variation was more important for the fruiting characters. Whereas a model involving additive and dominance effects only was generally sufficient for growth rate, the genetic architecture of the fruiting characters appeared to be more complex.

b. *Nonmeiotic systems*

Selective techniques are used in all nonmeiotic genetic systems to separate those individuals which have undergone segregation and recombination from the majority of parental cells which have not taken part in mating. All the progeny therefore carry the particular chromosome(s) or chromosome segment(s) on which the selective markers are located and are not a random sample of genotypes. In these circumstances, expectations of the relationships between generations cannot be derived and the biometrical approach based on the comparison of means and variances is not applicable. Estimation of the genetic component of variation may be misleading since only part of the genome is segregating. One way round this difficulty would be to use two or more independent selective systems and to reconstitute a sample of all possible genotypes from the resulting progenies.

Croft (unpublished) has compared the segregation of polygenic systems occurring during the sexual and parasexual cycles in *A. nidulans*. Pairs of strains were crossed both sexually and parasexually and the radial growth rates of samples of single ascospore and haploid segregants determined. While the results clearly demonstrated the segregation and reassociation of alleles

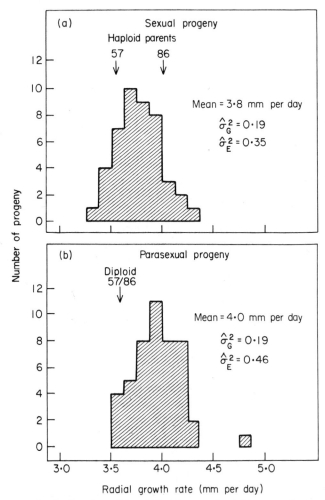

Fig. 4. Frequency distributions for radial growth rate among haploid progeny from strains 57 and 86 of *Aspergillus nidulans* crossed (a) sexually and (b) parasexually (by courtesy of Dr J. Croft). The two progeny means are significantly different.

affecting a quantitative character during the parasexual cycle, differences between the two types of progeny sample were frequently observed. For example, for the strains 57 and 86, the variance components of the two distributions agree closely, but the mean of the parasexual segregants is significantly higher than that of the sexual (Fig. 4). In other examples the variances but not the means differed. These discrepancies could have arisen through the presence of growth rate genes on chromosome I which carried the selective markers, through the reduced level of intrachromosomal recombination in the parasexual cycle, or through nonrandom chromosome segregation during haploidization.

Although nonmeiotic systems are not immediately amenable to biometrical treatments they have a number of advantages for chromosome assay techniques and development of this "quasi-mendelian" analysis is likely to be the most rewarding approach to the investigation of quantitative variation in these systems. In essence, chromosome assay involves substituting a marked chromosome or chromosome region from a selected strain into a tester strain, or vice versa, while the rest of the genome is either held constant or allowed to vary in a random manner. If the substitution produces a significant effect then it can be concluded that a gene or genes affecting the character are located within the region in question (Mather, 1942). Only gene differences between the selected strain and the tester are detected and the results are therefore dependent upon the particular tester used. More complex assay systems can be devised in which the genomes of the selected and tester strains are divided into a number of marked regions (the individual chromosomes in eukaryotes) and strains carrying all possible combinations of these are synthesized. If these strains are then compared in a randomized and replicated trial and the quantitative character in question assessed, the between strains item in an analysis of variance can be partitioned into orthogonal components which test for and estimate the contribution of each marked region as well as the interactions between them (Mather and Harrison, 1949).

Chromosome assay techniques of necessity involve markers, and a thorough knowledge of the linkage map and a series of suitable markers are essential for their use. Interpretation of the results may be complicated if the markers themselves influence the quantitative character. A way round this difficulty is to compare the effect of chromosome substitution from two strains with contrasting phenotypes into the tester. Then, the difference between strains carying high and low substitutions of the same chromosome region is independent of markers in the tester and provides a direct test for allelic differences on the chromosome region (Mather and Harrison, 1949). In this case the marked tester is an intermediary and its genotype is important only in as much as it may interact differentially with the substituted genes.

The flexibility of nonmeiotic systems and their amenability to techniques

selective for the substitution of particular segments of the genome lend themselves to the dissection of polygenic systems in this way. For example, the low
frequency of mitotic crossing-over in the parasexual cycle (Käfer, 1961) means
that whole chromosomes can be assayed through haploidization analysis
without the complication of intrachromosomal recombination. To our
knowledge, however, this possibility has yet to be exploited. The heterokaryon incompatibility of unrelated isolates of *Aspergillus* spp. (Caten and
Jinks, 1966) has prevented its use in the investigation of natural quantitative
variation in these fungi. Likewise, an early attempt to investigate the polygenic nature of multi-step resistance to chloramphenicol in *Escherichia coli*
(Cavalli and Maccacaro, 1952) has not been followed up now that the genetic
system of this bacterium is much better understood.

c. *Selection*

Genotypes showing the extreme expressions of a continuously varying trait can
be obtained by a classical selection experiment in which the phenotypically
highest or lowest progeny from a cross are mated amongst themselves and this
process repeated through a number of cycles. Theoretical considerations and
experience with higher organisms suggest that a cumulative response should
be obtained over several generations until all useful variation is fixed and the
response reaches a plateau. Accompanying the change in mean performance
is a progressive decline in the genetic variation (Lerner, 1958; Falconer, 1960).
This decline should occur more rapidly in haploids where there is no masking
of variation through dominance.

In fungi, selection has been carried out for radial growth rate in *Schizophyllum commune* (Simchen, 1966b; Connolly and Simchen, 1973), *Neurospora
crassa* (Papa *et al.*, 1966) and *A. nidulans* (Caten and Lawrence, unpublished)
and for penicillin titre in *A. nidulans* (Merrick, 1975). Similar results have been
obtained in all studies and Fig. 5 shows an example from the data of Caten and
Lawrence. These studies have confirmed that considerable phenotypic and
genotypic modification of a quantitative character can be achieved through
repeated hybridization and selection. The associated genotypes produced
offer useful experimental material for further dissection of the character
through chromosome assay or physiological studies.

d. *Applications of quantitative genetics*

Hybridization and selection have been used successfully for many years in the
improvement of yeast strains for brewing and baking (Winge and Laustsen,
1939) and in future may find a wider application in industrial microbiology
(Ball, 1973). Knowledge of the genetics of the character provides a rational
basis from which to choose the most efficient experimental procedure. The first
step is the choice of the initial parent strains. The response to selection depends

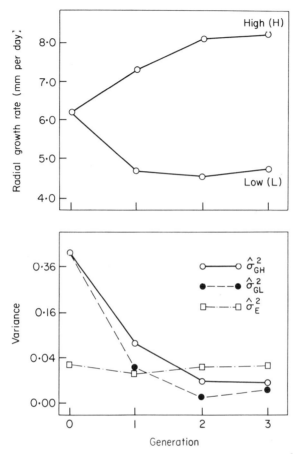

Fig. 5. The changes in the progeny mean radial growth rate and the genetic (σ_G^2) and environmental (σ_E^2) variance components during three generations of high and low selection among the progeny of *Aspergillus nidulans* cross 43 × 184.

upon the phenotypic variance and the heritability, while additive variation is easier to fix than epistatic. It follows that those crosses which show the highest phenotypic variances and heritabilities and where mainly additive gene action is involved offer the best prospect for a large and rapid response. Once the parents have been chosen, the crossing scheme has to be decided and one of the most important factors to be considered is the nature of the gene action. With mainly additive effects, improvement is simply a matter of combining the maximum number of increasing alleles into a single genotype and it does not matter how or in what order this is accomplished. It can be most readily achieved by a programme of line selection in which a number of independent lines are carried forward until response ceases. Crosses are then made between them to incorporate the increasing alleles into one population and allow further advance (Merrick, 1975). If, on the other hand, epistasis is important there is no guarantee that crossing between selection lines will lead to further advance (Papa, 1970). In these circumstances, opportunity should be provided from the outset for free recombination between alleles by maintaining a single breeding population on which selection is practised. The value of information on the location of genes affecting quantitative characters is more direct, since it makes possible the deliberate construction of strains incorporating desirable genome segments from several sources.

Not only can information from quantitative genetics help in the design of selection programmes, but it also enables prediction of the expected response. From estimates of the phenotypic standard deviation and heritability for a population, the mean of the next generation can be predicted for any given intensity of selection (Falconer, 1960). Provided that these parameters remain unchanged, predictions can be extrapolated over several generations.

Finally, a possible indirect benefit of quantitative genetics to industrial microbiology through familiarization with the handling of quantitative variation should not be overlooked. The principles of experimental design, of valid tests of significance and of estimation of parameters, that play such an important role in quantitative genetics, are equally applicable wherever quantitative variation is involved.

Conclusion

Through combination of a suitable crossing programme and experimental design, it is possible to conduct genetic analyses of continuous variation in microorganisms and provide answers to the same questions as are posed for the inheritance of discrete characters. The answers obtained are, of course, less precise, but this is inevitable in any move from a simple to a more complex situation. Despite this loss of precision, the information obtained is of value since it relates to characters of direct ecological or economic significance. From it, conclusions can be drawn about the genetic and evolutionary processes occurring in nature, while its application to strain improvement through selection helps in the choice of optimum experimental procedure and allows the outcome of selection to be predicted.

Acknowledgements

We thank Dr J. Croft for permission to use his unpublished data and Dr Jean Lawrence for her excellent technical assistance. The previously unpublished work on growth yield and selection for radial growth rate in *Aspergillus nidulans* was supported by a grant from the Science Research Council.

References

Ball, C. (1973). "Progress in Industrial Microbiology" (Ed. D. J. D. Hockenhull), vol. 12, p. 47. Churchill Livingstone, Edinburgh and London.
Brasier, C. M. (1970). *Am. Nat.* **104**, 191.
Breese, E. L. and Mather, K. (1957). *Heredity, Lond.* **11**, 373
Butcher, A. C. (1969). *Heredity, Lond.* **24**, 621
Butcher, A. C., Croft, J. and Grindle, M. (1972). *Heredity, Lond.* **29**, 263.
Caten, C. E. and Jinks, J. L. (1966). *Trans. Br. mycol. Soc.* **49**, 81.
Cavalli, L. L. and Maccacaro, G. A. (1952). *Heredity, Lond.* **6**, 311.
Connolly, V. and Simchen, G. (1968). *Heredity, Lond.* **23**, 387.
Connolly, V. and Simchen, G. (1973). *Genet. Res.* **22**, 25.
Croft, J. H. and Simchen, G. (1965). *Am. Nat.* **99**, 453.
East, E. M. (1915). *Genetics, Princeton.* **1**, 164.
Falconer, D. S. (1960). "Quantitative Genetics". Oliver and Boyd, Edinburgh and London.
Fisher, R. A. (1918). *Trans. R. Soc. Edinb.* **52**, 399.
Fripp, Y. J. and Caten, C. E. (1971). *Heredity, Lond.* **27**, 393.
Harris, H. and Hopkinson, D. A. (1972). *Ann. hum. Genet.* **36**, 9.
Jinks, J. L., Caten, C. E., Simchen, G. and Croft, J. H. (1966). *Heredity, Lond.* **21**, 227.
Käfer, E. (1961). *Genetics, Princeton,* **46**, 1581.
Law, C. N. (1967). *Genetics, Princeton,* **56**, 445.
Lerner, M. I. (1958). "The Genetic Basis of Selection". John Wiley, New York.
MacKenzie, D. R., Nelson, R. R. and Cole, H. (1971). *Phytopathology,* **61**, 471.
Mather, K. (1942). *J. Genet.* **43**, 309.
Mather, K. (1944). *Proc. R. Soc. B.* **132**, 308.
Mather, K. (1949). "Biometrical Genetics" (1st ed.). Methuen, London.
Mather, K. (1954). *Proc. IXth Int. Cong. Genetics, Caryologia, Vol. suppl.* p. 106.
Mather. K. (1971). *Heredity, Lond.* **26**, 349.
Mather, K. and Harrison, B. J. (1949). *Heredity, Lond.* **3**, 1.
Mather, K. and Jinks, J. L. (1971). "Biometrical Genetics" (2nd ed.). Chapman and Hall, London.
Merrick, M. J. (1975). p. 229 These Proceedings.
Nilsson-Ehle, H. (1909). "Kreuzunguntersuchungen an Hafer und Weizen". Lund.
Papa, K. E. (1970). *Can. J. Genet. Cytol.* **12**, 1.
Papa, K. E. (1971). *Genetica,* **42**, 181.
Papa, K. E., Srb, A. M. and Federer, W. T. (1966). *Heredity, Lond.* **21**, 595.
Penrose, L. S. (1951). *Ann. Eugen.* **16**, 134.
Simchen, G. (1965). *Genetics, Princeton,* **51**, 709.
Simchen, G. (1966a). *Genetics, Princeton,* **53**, 1151.
Simchen, G. (1966b). *Heredity, Lond.* **21**, 241.
Simchen, G. (1967). *Evolution, Lancaster, Pa.* **21**, 310.
Simchen, G. and Jinks, J. L. (1964). *Heredity, Lond.* **19**, 629.
Thoday, J. M. (1961). *Nature, Lond.* **191**, 368.
Winge, O. and Laustsen, P. (1939). *C.r. Trav. Lab. Carlsberg,* **22**, 337.

E

STRATEGY OF STRAIN IMPROVEMENT
I BIOSYNTHESIS OF ANTIBIOTICS

Enzymatic synthesis of gramicidin S

A. L. DEMAIN and D. I. C. WANG
Department of Nutrition and Food Science,
Massachusetts Institute of Technology, USA

Summary

Although the biochemistry of gramicidin S (GS) formation by *Bacillus brevis* is fairly well understood, the use of cell-free extracts has been limited to incorporation of isotopic tracers into the antibiotic. Our goal is the repeated use of GS synthetases for large-scale enzymatic production of this decapeptide antibiotic.

Complex and chemically defined media were developed which support rapid and extensive growth and a high degree of synthesis of GS and its two synthetases. Of the five constituent amino acids of GS, only phenylalanine (in the L form) stimulates GS synthesis. Since it fails to stimulate formation of synthetases I and II, it probably acts as the limiting precursor of the antibiotic. The synthetases are formed toward the end of the logarithmic growth phase and then rapidly disappear. The rate of disappearance is slower in complex medium which is one of the reasons for the more extensive GS production in this medium.

Using partially purified extracts of *B. brevis* grown in complex medium, GS was enzymatically produced in a one-litre reactor. The product was isolated, subjected to biological, chemical and physical tests and found to be identical to authentic GS.

Attempts are now being made to isolate mutants capable of overproducing the GS synthetases. In other laboratories, mutants incapable of producing GS have been obtained. These have been shown to be affected in either GS synthetase I or II or in both.

Introduction

THE SYNTHESIS OF USEFUL PRODUCTS BY ENZYMES

Past developments in enzyme technology have been mainly limited to degradative enzymes or enzymes which interconvert similar types of molecules. These reactions are simpler than synthetic reactions and do not generally require organic co-factors nor coupling to energy-yielding reactions. The reluctance to exploit the potential of enzyme-catalysed synthesis has severely limited the development of enzyme technology.

In 1972, the MIT Interdisciplinary Enzyme Group was formed to explore the potential of synthesis by cell-free enzymes. Because of the high degree of bioactivity exhibited by peptides and the medical importance of antibiotics, we chose as our model system the enzymatic synthesis of gramicidin S (GS). We take the view that successful cell-free synthesis of this antibacterial peptide could lead the way to two important developments, namely an improvement over traditional means of microbial biosynthesis (i.e. fermentation) and new drug discovery.

Fermentations today are conducted in essentially the same manner as they were twenty years ago. There have been no major innovations introduced. Despite the impressive increases in total productivity per fermenter achieved mainly by mutation, the fermentation process is still relatively slow and inefficient. One of our hopes is to radically change the method of preparing antibiotics, i.e. to shift from cellular synthesis to enzymatic synthesis to achieve rapid and efficient manufacture of these useful drugs.

The traditional antibiotic fermentation process is slow and inefficient. Several weeks are needed to bring the culture to the production stage. In the production fermenter, one or more days is usually devoted to "non-productive" growth of the cells since antibiotic synthetases are usually repressed during vegetative growth. Once all the antibiotic synthetases are formed, it would be desirable to maintain linear production for as long as possible but the enzymes are inactivated and the process soon comes to a halt. The inefficiency of the fermentation in terms of conversion of sugar to product is presumably the result of sugar usage for growth, for maintenance of the cells in the nongrowing state and for side-reactions catalysed by the hundreds of unrelated enzymes in the intact cells. Slow rates of antibiotic formation are probably caused by the lack of optimal levels of the substrates of each enzyme. Since the product is a secondary metabolite, having no apparent function in the growth of the cell, evolution cannot select for better producers of the antibiotic. Indeed the reverse is true and causes one of the major problems of fermentation, strain degradation, i.e. the selection of poorly producing strains which are faster growers.

In the area of drug discovery, we feel that enzymatic synthesis can play an important role in directed biosynthesis of new antibiotics. Since secondary metabolites are usually produced as a family of closely related structures and since it is possible to direct synthesis towards one or the other product of the group by nutritional modifications, "directed biosynthesis" has been used to make antibiotic analogues with intact cells. However, the value of this technique is limited by the permeability of the precursor, by its toxicity to the cell, and by its susceptibility to degradation or incorporation into macromolecules. A potential benefit of an enzymatic technique of antibiotic formation is that such "nonutilizable" precursors could be utilized for cell-free production of new antibiotic molecules. Evidence already exists that enzymatic systems are capable of producing new antibiotics. For example, although intact *B. brevis* ATCC 8185 can synthesize four tyrocidines by substituting L-tryptophan for L-phenylalanine and D-tryptophan for D-phenylalanine, cell-free extracts can produce 3 additional tyrocidines by substituting L-phenylalanine for L-tyrosine, L-lysine for L-ornithine, and L-isoleucine for L-leucine (Fujikawa *et al.*, 1968). Similarly, a new echinomycin has been produced in a cell-free enzymatic system from *Streptomyces* strain X-63 (Arif *et al.*, 1970).

A second approach used for production of new antibiotics has been the chemical modification of conventional antibiotics. This technique is receiving much industrial attention now and has yielded some excellent new antibiotics. Despite these successes, there is still need for better antibiotic agents; and, although attempts at chemical modification will continue, the chemist is limited by the nature of the structure produced by the organism. Enzyme systems, in contrast, would permit production of biosynthetic intermediates as starting materials for chemical conversion into new antibiotics. By omitting certain enzymes from the system, intermediates could be accumulated which have never before been available to the chemist for molecular modification.

IMPORTANCE OF MICROBIAL PEPTIDES

Microbially produced peptides are among the most biologically active and important groups of compounds known to man. In this group are included molecules consisting solely of amino acids as well as complex molecules which contain moieties other than amino acids. Among the microbial peptides, the peptide antibiotics are currently the most important compounds, over 200 having been described. Excellent discussions of these compounds and their biosyntheses can be found in the papers of Katz (1971) and Bodanzsky and Perlman (1964).

The modes of action of peptide antibiotics cover a wide spectrum of biological activities. Some inhibit protein synthesis, some RNA synthesis, and some DNA synthesis. Other vital microbial activities inhibited by particular peptides are cell wall synthesis, membrane integrity, oxidative phosphorylation and cation transport. Peptide antibiotics are of medical and nutritional importance and are manufactured commercially (Bodanszky and Perlman, 1969). They are used for parenteral, oral and topical therapy against Gram-positive and Gram-negative bacterial infections, for antitumour therapy, against bovine mastitis and against plant pathogens; some are important veterinary antibiotics and growth promotants for animals. Their extensive biological activities allow us to predict that many new applications, especially those of pharmacological nature, are yet to be discovered.

CELL-FREE SYNTHESIS OF PEPTIDE ANTIBIOTICS

A number of systems have been described in which cell-free extracts of microorganisms are capable of incorporating a radioactive precursor into a peptide antibiotic. These antibiotics include GS, tyrocidine, linear grami-cidin, edeine, malformin, bacitracin, colistin and echinomycin. At the start of our work, large-scale net synthesis of antibiotic had not been demonstrated in any of these systems. Doubts concerning such a possibility were derived from a consideration of the following potential problems: (a) harshness of cell disruption techniques; (b) lability of biosynthetic enzymes; (c) dilution of enzymes and co-factors during disruption; (d) dissociation of multi-enzyme complexes; (e) disturbance of spatial arrangement of enzymes in cell compartments or in cell organelles; (f) competing reactions for the substrate and competition for the energy supply. Despite the potential difficulties involved, it was felt that an attempt to produce an antibiotic enzymatically should be made. From the list of possible antibiotics, the enzymatic synthesis of GS was chosen as the model system. Some of the reasons for this selection were: (a) the synthetases involved were better characterized than those for any other antibiotic; (b) more was known about the biosynthesis of GS than of any other antibiotic; (c) biosynthesis involved only two synthetases (or synthetase complexes); (d) the structure of the antibiotic was among the simplest of the peptide antibiotics; (e) the only organic co-factor required (4' phosphopantetheine) was tightly bound to one of the synthetases; (f) production by a unicellular bacterium would facilitate genetic manipulation to improve enzyme biosynthesis.

MECHANISM OF GS BIOSYNTHESIS

GS is a cyclic decapeptide containing two identical pentapeptides (Dphe-pro-val-orn-leu) as shown in Fig. 1. It is produced by *Bacillus brevis* by a nonribosomal polypeptide synthesizing system. The biochemical mechanism of GS formation has been reviewed by Kurahashi *et al.* (1969), Saito *et al.* (1970), Lipmann (1973) and Laland and Zimmer (1973) and is summarized in the next few paragraphs.

The process involves two enzymes. Synthetase II, the light enzyme of 100 000 molecular weight, is responsible for activating and thioesterifying L-phenylalanine and racemizing it to the D-isomer. The activation involves a reaction with ATP to produce amino acyl-AMP which is attached, but not covalently bound, to synthetase II. The reaction requires Mg^{2+} and liberates pyrophosphate. The ATP-activated L-phenylalanine is then transferred to a sulphhydryl group on the enzyme in a covalent thioester linkage. Racemization occurs at this SH site. In a similar manner but without racemization, the heavy enzyme (synthetase I, 280 000 molecular weight) activates proline, valine, ornithine and leucine and transfers each to their specific SH sites.

Polymerization begins when the light synthetase II transfers D-phenyl-alanine to proline on the heavy enzyme. Elongation occurs by transfer of phe-pro to valine attached to its SH site. Finally, the heavy enzyme is charged with the pentapeptide phe-pro-val-orn-leu attached to the leucine SH site. 4'-Phosphopantetheine, bound to the heavy synthetase I, is the co-factor of GS biosynthesis. It apparently acts by mediating the transfer of phe-pro to val, i.e. the dipeptide is transferred from the pro thiol site to the SH group of phosphopantetheine. The phosphopantetheine then appears to swing to the val site and brings the activated pro carboxyl group in contact with the free

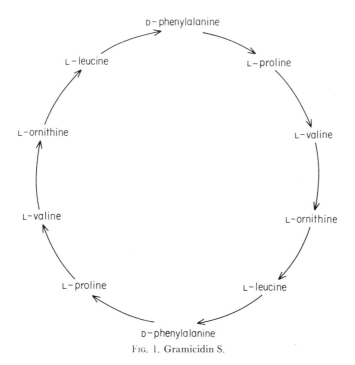

Fig. 1. Gramicidin S.

val amino group forming the tripeptide. Phosphopantetheine similarly acts in the formation of the tetra- and then the pentapeptide. Rapidly, two such pentapeptides on the same synthetase I molecule cyclize by reaction of the active carboxyls of two thioester-linked leucines with the free amino groups of two chain-terminal phenylalanines, and GS is released from the heavy enzyme.

Results and discussion

NUTRITIONAL STUDIES

There are three strains of *Bacillus brevis* known to produce GS: the Nagano strain used in Japan, strain GB in the USSR, and ATCC 9999 in the rest of the world. No nutritional studies have been reported on the Nagano strain and only complex media have been described for its growth. In such media, production of only 0.3 g GS dm^{-3} has been observed (Yamada and Kurahashi, 1968). On the other hand, the strain in which GS was discovered (Gause and Bhazhnikova, 1944), i.e. *B. brevis* GB, has been the subject of considerable nutritional research in the USSR (Korshunov and Egorov, 1962; Zharikova, 1965; Udalova and Fedorova, 1965) and potencies as high as 5 g GS dm^{-3} have been reported (Kupletskaya *et al.*, 1969). At the start of our own work with ATCC 9999, the literature indicated that this culture had not been investigated nutritionally. Various complex and chemically defined media had been used for production of GS and its synthetases apparently without prior investigation. As a result, no more than 0.25 g GS dm^{-3} had been reported. When we later found that ATCC 9999 was apparently derived from strain GB (Consden *et al.*, 1947; American Type Culture Collection, Catalogue of Strains, 9th edition, 1970), we attempted to use one of the better media developed in the USSR. This medium contained glycerol, ammonium oxalate, NaCl, K$_2$HPO$_4$, MgSO$_4$ and a crude material described as "nutrient lactic acid" and "digested lactic acid". The crude component is apparently an extract of malt sprouts and sugar-containing substrates which has been fermented by lactic acid bacteria. We substituted pure lactic acid for the crude component but growth was sporadic and GS titres never exceeded 0.25 g dm^{-3}. We then examined other media formulations and found that a modification of the original Gause and Bhazhnikova (1944) medium was the best for GS production. In our modification (YPG), which contains 5 per cent yeast extract, 5 per cent peptone and 0.5 per cent glucose, growth was rapid ($\mu = 1.2$ h^{-1}) and extensive (12.5 g DCW dm^{-3}) and GS production was remarkably high (2.5 g dm^{-3}; 0.25 g g^{-1} DCW). The optimum temperature was found to be 37°C. The GS fermentation required less than one day. The yeast extract and peptone components were synergistic for GS production, elimination of either decreasing antibiotic production by about 90 per cent.

The sugar was found to be unnecessary. Replacement of glucose by glycerol appears to be beneficial in recent experiments.

Since chemically defined media are necessary for nutritional studies, we began by devising a simple medium which contained 0.5 per cent glycerol, 0.2 per cent ammonium sulphate and mineral salts. When inoculated with exponentially growing vegetative cells, we observed a specific growth rate of $0.35 \ \mathrm{h}^{-1}$, a total crop of $1.5 \ \mathrm{g} \ \mathrm{DCW} \ \mathrm{dm}^{-3}$ and GS production amounting to $0.05 \ \mathrm{g} \ \mathrm{dm}^{-3}$ and $0.03 \ \mathrm{g} \ \mathrm{g}^{-1} \ \mathrm{DCW}$. The medium was not satisfactory since the above values were low and stationary phase inocula suffered an extended lag phase, often as long as 24 h. Spores failed to germinate and grow out in this medium. A series of improvements involving an increase in the concentrations of glycerol and ammonium sulphate and addition of 0.1 M tris (hydroxymethyl)-aminomethane buffer resulted in medium G2T which was much improved, i.e. we obtained a specific growth rate of $0.46 \ \mathrm{h}^{-1}$, a final cell mass of $6 \ \mathrm{g} \ \mathrm{dm}^{-3}$, and GS production of $0.23 \ \mathrm{g} \ \mathrm{dm}^{-3}$; specific GS productivity remained low, however, at $0.04 \ \mathrm{g} \ \mathrm{g}^{-1} \ \mathrm{DCW}$. Medium G2T is suitable for proposed chemostat studies in which the effect of carbon, nitrogen and phosphorus limitation on GS production will be examined since it contains single sources of these three elements. Growth lags using stationary phase inocula are much reduced in G2T.

Further nutritional experiments revealed that *B. brevis* ATCC 9999 cannot produce amino acids fast enough in medium G2T to support the rapid and extensive growth observed in complex medium. The most important amino acids were found to be glutamine, methionine, proline, arginine, and histidine. An optimum mixture of these amino acids when added to G2T resulted in an enriched defined medium (G2T5) which supported a growth rate of $0.75 \ \mathrm{h}^{-1}$, a total crop of $10 \ \mathrm{g} \ \mathrm{DCW} \ \mathrm{dm}^{-3}$ and GS production of $0.43 \ \mathrm{g} \ \mathrm{dm}^{-3}$ and $0.04 \ \mathrm{g} \ \mathrm{g}^{-1} \ \mathrm{DCW}$. The last figure shows that the increased growth obtained upon amino acid supplementation has no specific effect on GS formation. A benefit of medium G2T5 is the short lag phase (*c.* 2 h) when inoculated with stationary phase inocula and its ability to support spore germination and outgrowth.

The above studies indicated that yeast extract and peptone contain additional factors which are nutritionally beneficial to ATCC 9999, i.e. complex medium supports greater growth and especially GS production than the enriched chemically defined medium.

LABORATORY STUDIES ON GS SYNTHETASES

As is the case with many secondary metabolites, GS is not produced until late in the cell cycle. This is explained by the lack of formation of both GS synthetases until after the midpoint of the logarithmic growth phase (Tomino *et al.*, 1967; Spaeren *et al.*, 1967; Yamada and Kurahashi, 1968; Otani *et al.*, 1969).

After reaching their peak specific activities, the enzymes rapidly disappear as the cells proceed into the stationary growth phase. We observed similar kinetics of appearance and disappearance of GS synthetases I and II and the overall activity incorporating amino acids into GS in both complex and defined media (Matteo *et al.*, 1974; Tzeng *et al.*, 1974). Excellent GS synthetase production was obtained in complex medium (Fig. 2) but enzyme production was poor in G medium. However defined medium G2T supported much greater synthesis of GS synthetases I and II than did the G medium.

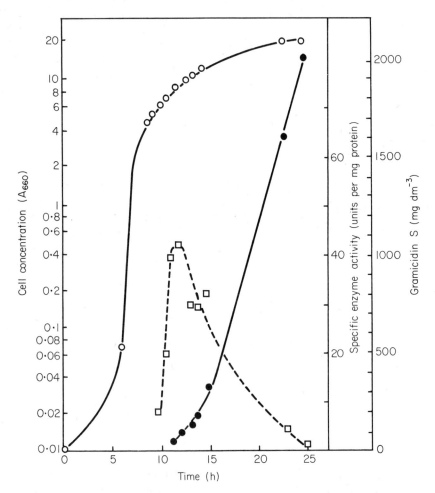

FIG. 2. Growth (○) of *Bacillus brevis* ATCC 9999 in shake flasks containing complex (YPG) medium and production of gramicidin S (●) and gramicidin S synthetase I (□). An A_{660} of 2.5 is equivalent to 1 g DCW dm^{-3}.

In fact, GS synthetase I in medium G2T reached specific activities as high as in complex medium. This was puzzling in view of the much greater ability of complex medium to support GS production. This does not appear to be simply a function of growth rate since addition of amino acids (either the five growth stimulatory amino acids mentioned above or a mixture of 21 amino acids) increased growth rates but reduced GS synthetase I specific activities. Furthermore, the specific production of GS (g GS g^{-1} DCW) was the same in amino acid-enriched medium G2T5 and in G2T despite the lower peak synthetase I specific activity in the former medium. At present, the following suggestions can be made concerning the discrepancies observed between *in vivo* antibiotic formation and *in vitro* peak specific activities of GS synthetases:

a. The amount of GS produced per volume of broth is a function of both the specific activity of the synthetases and the cell density. Since cell density is higher in complex medium, the *total* synthetase activity will be higher in complex medium.

b. The amount of GS produced per volume of broth or per gram of cells is affected by the rate of synthetase disappearance after the peak specific activity is reached. We find the rate of GS synthetase I disappearance to be higher in defined medium G2T than in complex medium.

c. Assay of GS synthetase I and II is done by measuring the activation of an amino acid, i.e. ornithine-dependent ATP-pyrophosphate exchange and phenylalanine-dependent ATP-pyrophosphate exchange respectively. Since these are complex enzymes, it is dangerous to extrapolate from values of *in vitro* amino acid activation to *in vivo* antibiotic biosynthesis. Laland *et al.* (1972) has pointed out that GS synthetase I carries out 18 to 19 catalytic functions. Merely measuring one of these functions does not allow us to conclude that the entire enzyme complex is fully matured or functional.

d. Complex medium may contain factors which are beneficial for antibiotic synthesis. As will be discussed in the next section, phenylalanine is one such factor.

EFFECT OF PRECURSOR AMINO ACIDS

Barry and Ichihara (1958) reported a stimulation of GS formation by phenylalanine. This was also noted by Zharikova *et al.* (1963) and Zharikova (1965). We were interested in confirming the phenylalanine effect and determining whether the action of phenylalanine involved synthetase induction. We found a mixture of the five precursor amino acids to double the specific production of GS and L-phenylalanine to be responsible for the stimulation. The optimum concentration of phenylalanine was 0.1 per cent. Figure 3 shows the marked effect of phenylalanine on GS synthesis but the very slight effect on formation

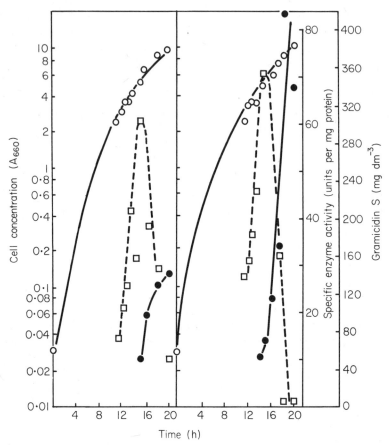

FIG. 3. Effect of phenylalanine on growth (○), production of gramicidin S (●) and gramicidin S synthetase I (□) in shaken flasks. Left graph, no phenylalanine. Right graph, 0.1 per cent L-phenylalanine. Medium was chemically defined medium G2T. An A_{660} of 2.5. is equivalent to 1 g DCW dm^{-3}.

of GS synthetase I. Our conclusion from several experiments is that phenylalanine has no effect on synthetase formation or disappearance but nevertheless stimulates antibiotic formation. The effect on GS production is probably due to a precursor role.

DISAPPEARANCE OF GS SYNTHETASES

In recent years, many microbial enzymes have been shown to be rapidly destroyed or inactivated after production (Thurston, 1972). In some cases, the enzyme is inactivated by chemical modification or by binding to a macromolecule; in others, proteolysis destroys the enzyme.

The rapid destruction or inactivation of GS synthetases after reaching their peak specific activity is a major problem for both research on synthetase regulation and development of enzyme technology. Virtually nothing has been reported on the mechanism involved. Kleinkauf and Gevers (1969) reported that incubation of GS synthetase I at 37°C in pH 7.3 buffer containing triethanolamine·HCl, $MgCl_2$, dithiothreitol and EDTA for 1 hour resulted in an 80 per cent loss of GS synthesizing activity without a concomitant loss in amino acid activating activity. Although no further work has been reported on this *in vitro* loss of GS-synthesizing activity, the Lipmann group has carried out related studies on the tyrocidine-synthesizing system from *B. brevis*, ATCC 8185 (Lee *et al.*, 1973; Lipmann, 1973). Incubation of crude extracts at 37°C led to disaggregation of the heavy and intermediate weight enzymes into subunits of 70 000–75 000 molecular weight which still carry out amino acid activation and thioesterification but not polymerization. It is thought that a disaggregating enzyme is present in the crude extract.

LARGE-SCALE PRODUCTION OF GS SYNTHETASES

The production of GS synthetases in medium YPG has been scaled up to a 14 litre bench-scale fermentation. Aeration and agitation rates were controlled to maintain dissolved oxygen concentrations above 20 per cent saturation. The appearance and disappearance of GS synthetases I and II were found to follow closely the overall enzymatic activity responsible for amino acid incorporation into GS.

Based on our 14-litre fermenter studies, we scaled up the YPG fermentation to the pilot scale of 180 litres. To allow sufficient oxygen transfer capability, the fermentation was performed at an elevated overall fermenter pressure (10 psig) using pure oxygen to enrich the air stream. The objective was to maintain dissolved oxygen and concentration above 20 per cent saturation with respect to air at one atmosphere. Cell growth was excellent and corresponded very closely to that achieved in the 14-litre fermenter. From this 180 litre fermentation, approximately 1 kg of cells (dry weight) was recovered. Crude enzyme prepared from these cells had an amino acid incorporation activity of 7.0 mg GS g^{-1} h^{-1}.

PRODUCTION OF GS BY ENZYMATIC SYNTHESIS

Using GS synthetases purified from cells grown in the 14-litre fermenter, the enzyme reaction was conducted using a litre of reaction mixture (Table 1). The time course of GS synthesis as measured by the incorporation of labelled leucine, the limiting amino acid, was linear for the six-hour duration of the experiment. In the absence of any one of the four other amino acids (phe, pro, val, or orn), no product synthesis occurred. We have also used other

TABLE 1

Quantities charged for enzymatic synthesis of gramicidin S in one-litre reaction*
volume

Material	Amount	Concentration mM
L-Leucine	52.45 mg (limiting)	0.4
^{14}C-L-Leucine	51.5 μCi	—
L-Ornithine	1.0 g	8.5
L-Valine	1.0 g	8.6
L-Proline	1.0 g	8.7
L-Phenylalanine	1.0 g	6.1
Dithiothreitol	1.5 g	10
ATP	6.0 g	14
Triethanolomine	9.4 g	50
MgCl$_2$	0.94 g	10
Enzyme preparation	2.2 g	—

* Conditions: pH 7.6 (controlled), 37°C.

^{14}C-labelled amino acids (orn, L-phe) to study GS synthesis, and the molar incorporation of the various labelled amino acids in these experiments has always been close to one to one.

In order to prepare enough product for purification, isolation, and authentication, another one-litre reaction was performed. ^{14}C-Labelled leucine containing a total activity of 10^8 cpm was added as marker in order to quantitatively estimate conversion. The synthesized product was assayed using the radiochemical technique. The time course of the overall reaction is shown in Fig. 4. The reaction was linear as expected for about three hours and then continued at slower rates up to five hours. In many other studies that we have performed at lower reactant and product concentrations, constant and linear rates up to ten hours have been observed. It is possible that the results shown in Fig. 4 with respect to decreases in the rate with time were caused by product inhibition and/or ATP hydrolysis. In any case, based on ^{14}C-leucine incorporation, we calculated the degree of conversion of the limiting amino acid to GS to be 80 per cent of the theoretical maximum.

In another reaction, product from the reactor was isolated using extraction and crystallization operations modified from Gause and Brazhnikova (1944). The amount of GS synthesized, as determined by radiochemical assay, was 507 mg. The amount of product recovered in solid form after extraction and crystallization operations was 430 mg. Thin-layer chromatography, ir spectroscopy, and bioassay all yielded results showing that the recovered product was virtually pure GS (Hamilton et al., 1974).

STUDIES WITH MUTANTS

A series of mutants incapable of producing GS have been obtained in two

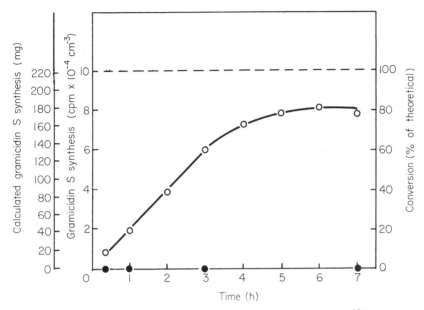

FIG. 4. Preparative scale synthesis of gramicidin S (○) in one-litre reactor using ^{14}C-L-leucine as limiting amino acid. A control (●) was included without the other four amino acids of gramicidin S. The dashed line represents the theoretical maximum for leucine incorporation into gramicidin S.

laboratories (Shimura *et al.*, 1974; Kambe *et al.*, 1974). Most of these mutants are deficient either in GS synthetase I or GS synthetase II or in both as judged by amino acid activation studies. With respect to GS synthetase I, some of the mutants are deficient in activating activity for all four amino acids whereas some are deficient in only a single activating activity, i.e. pro, val or leu. In five mutants (Shimura *et al.*, 1974), activation activities are present but an alteration in the particular synthetase can be seen by tests on GS synthesis with combinations of GS synthetases from different mutants, i.e. enzyme complementation tests. These latter mutants could be affected in their thiol ester binding sites, in their phenylalanine racemizing activity or in other functions of these complex synthetases. In our laboratory, various mutants have been isolated which will be examined for increased synthetase production. These have been altered morphologically, in pigmentation, in colonial growth rate, in nutritional requirements (i.e. auxotrophy) and in degree of GS excretion by colonies.

Acknowledgements

We gratefully acknowledge the support of the National Science Foundation for Grant GI-34284.

This paper is Contribution No. 2476 from the Department of Nutrition and Food Science, Massachusetts Institute of Technology, Cambridge, Massachusetts 02139, USA.

References

Arif, A. J., Singh, C., Bhaduri, A. P., Gupta, C. M., Khan, A. W. and Dhar, M. M. (1970). *Indian J. Biochem.* **7**, 193.
Barry, J. M. and Ichihara, E. (1958). *Nature, Lond.* **181**, 1274.
Bodanszky, M. and Perlman, D. (1964). *Nature, Lond.* **204**, 840.
Bodanszky, M. and Perlman, D. (1969). *Science*, **163**, 352.
Consden, R., Gordon, A. H., Martin, A. J. P. and Synge, R. L. M. (1947). *Biochem. J.* **41**, 596.
Fujikawa, K., Sakamoto, Y., Suzuki, T. and Kurahashi, K. (1968). *Biochim. biophys. Acta*, **169**, 520.
Gause, G. F. and Bhazhnikova, M. G. (1944). *Lancet*, **247**, 715.
Hamilton, B. K., Montgomery, J. P. and Wang, D. I. C. (1974). *In* "Enzyme Engineering II" (Eds L. B. Wingard and E. K. Pye). Plenum Press, New York.
Kambe, M., Imae, Y. and Kurahashi, K. (1974). *J. Biochem.* **75**, 481.
Katz, E. (1971). *Pure Appl. Chem.* **28**, 551.
Kleinkauf, H. and Gevers, W. (1969). *Cold Spring Harb. Symp. quant. Biol.* **34**, 805.
Korshunov, V. V. and Egorov, N. S. (1962). *Mikrobiologiya*, **31**, 515.
Kupletskaya, M. B., Maksimov, V. N. and Kasatkina, T. B. (1969). *Prikl. Biokhim. Mikrobiol.* **5**, 541.
Kurahashi, K., Yamada, M., Mori, K., Fujikawa, K., Kambe, M., Imae, Y., Sato, E., Takahashi, H. and Sakamoto, Y. (1969). *Cold Spring Harb. Symp. quant. Biol.* **34**, 815.
Laland, S. G., Frøyshov, Ø., Gilhuus-Moe, C. and Zimmer, T.-L. (1972). *Nature, Lond.* **239**, 43.
Laland, S. G. and Zimmer, T.-L. (1973). "Essays in Biochemistry" (Eds P. N. Campbell and G. D. Greville), vol. 9, p. 31, Academic Press, New York and London.
Lee, S. G., Roskoski, R., Bauer, K. and Lipmann, F. (1973). *Biochemistry*, **12**, 398.
Lipmann, F. (1973). *Accts. Chem. Res.* **6**, 361.
Matteo, C. C., Glade, M., Tanaka, A., Piret, J. and Demain, A. L. (1974). Submitted for publication.
Otani, S., Yamanoi, T. and Saito, Y. (1969). *J. Biochem.* **66**, 445.
Saito, Y., Otani, S. and Otani, S. (1970). *Adv. Enzymol.* **33**, 337.
Shimura, K., Iwaki, M., Kanda, M., Hori, K., Kaji, E., Hagesawa, S. and Saito, Y. (1974). *Biochim. biophys. Acta*, **338**, 577.
Spaeren, U., Froholm, L. O. and Laland, S. G. (1967). *Biochem. J.* **102**, 592.
Thurston, C. F. (1972). *Proc. Biochem.* **7**(8), 18.
Tomino, S., Yamada, M., Itoh, H. and Kurahashi, K. (1967). *Biochemistry*, **6**, 2552.
Tzeng, C. H., Thrasher, K. D., Montgomery, J. P., Hamilton, B. K. and Wang, D. I. C. (1974). Submitted for publication.
Udalova, T. P. and Federova, R. I. (1965). *Mikrobiologiya*, **34**, 631.
Yamada, M. and Kurahashi, K. (1968). *J. Biochem.* **63**, 59.
Zharikova, G. G. (1965). *Prikl. Biokhim. Mikrobiol.* **1**, 83.
Zharikova, G. G., Silaev, A. B. and Sushkova, I. V. (1963). *Antibiotiki*, **8**, 425.

Aspects of cephalosporin and penicillin biosynthesis

PATRICIA A. FAWCETT, J. J. USHER and E. P. ABRAHAM

Sir William Dunn School of Pathology, University of Oxford, Oxford, England

Summary

Strains of *Cephalosporium acremonium* and of certain species of the prokaryotic *Streptomyces* produce cephalosporins and 7-methoxycephalosporins, respectively, and also penicillin N. All these β-lactam antibiotics have a D-α-aminoadipyl side-chain.

The tripeptide δ-(L-α-aminoadipyl)-L-cysteinyl-D-valine has been isolated in small amount from the mycelium of *C. acremonium*. The same (LLD) peptide has been synthesized with a tritium label in the methyl groups or α-hydrogen of its valine residue and the corresponding methyl-labelled all-L-peptide has also been synthesized. Tritium was incorporated into penicillin N from both LLD tripeptides by a cell-free system from protoplasts of *C. acremonium* but not from the all-L-tripeptide.

Analysis by nuclear magnetic resonance and mass spectroscopy of cephalosporin C and penicillin N produced by *C. acremonium* in the presence of valine labelled asymmetrically with carbon-13 and deuterium in the methyl groups has shown that the chiral isopropyl group is incorporated stereospecifically into the antibiotics.

These findings are relevant to hypotheses concerned with the mechanisms of ring closure in the biosynthesis of β-lactam antibiotics.

Introduction

The theme of this Symposium is the genetics of industrial microorganisms and it is clear that microbial geneticists have now begun to make significant contributions to our knowledge of the biosynthesis of penicillins and cephalo-

129

sporins. Some of these contributions will be described in papers given at the present meeting. In this contribution, however, it is proposed to review briefly some of the problems relating to the pathways and mechanisms of biosynthesis of these antibiotics and to discuss attempts we have made to solve them, by use of isotopically labelled intermediates, with whole cells or cell extracts of such relatively low yielding strains of organisms as have been available to us.

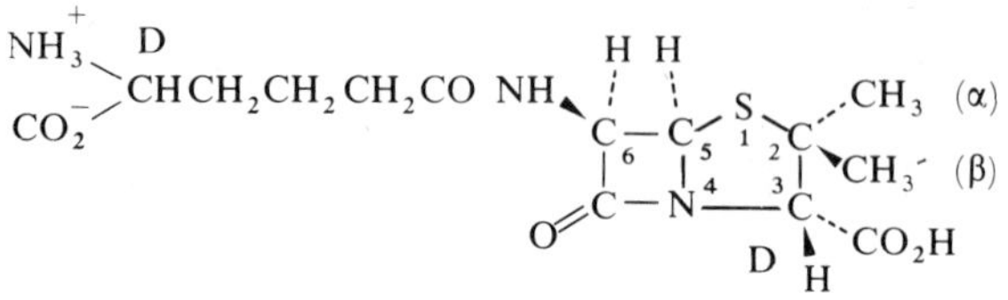

(1)

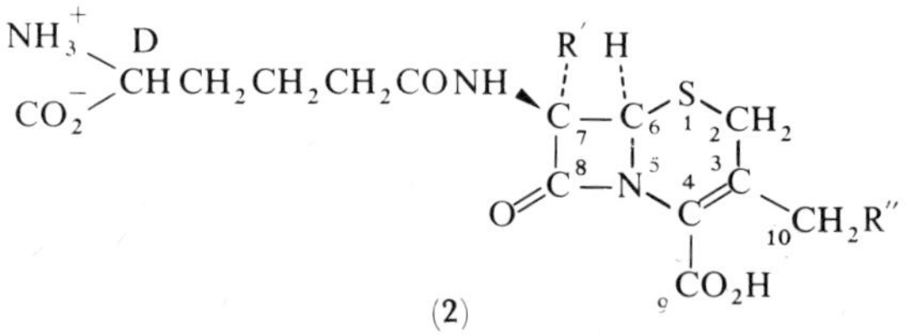

(2)

Two of the main types of β-lactam antibiotics have structures (1) and (2). *Cephalosporium acremonium* has long been known to produce only one penicillin, penicillin N (1), with a D-α-aminoadipyl side chain, and also cephalosporin C (2, R'=H, R''=OCOCH$_3$) with the same side chain but a different nucleus. Recent work with mutants of this eukaryotic organism, carried out in the USA, Switzerland and Japan, has now shown that deacetylcephalosporin C (2, R'=H, R''=OH) and deacetoxycephalosporin C (2, R'=H, R''=H) must be added to the compounds mentioned above (Fujisawa *et al.*, 1973); Queener and Capone, 1974); Liersch *et al.*, 1974). In addition, certain strains of the prokaryotic *Streptomyces* have been shown to produce 7-methoxycephalosporins, again with a D-α-aminoadipyl side chain, but with a methoxy group attached to carbon-7 of the β-lactam ring (2, R'=OCH$_3$, R''=OCONH$_2$). In contrast, *Penicillium chrysogenum* produces isopenicillin N, with an L-α-aminoadipyl side chain, some 6-aminopenicillanic acid, and a variety of penicillins with nonpolar side chains whose nature depends on the side chain precursor added to the fermentation medium.

Dissection of these structures suggests that they are all built up from cysteine, valine and α-aminoadipic acid or other side-chain precursors. By the use of amino acids labelled with carbon-14 or tritium it has been easy to show that this is in fact the case, since these amino acids are readily incorporated into the antibiotics when added to suspensions of mycelium. However, it became clear that L-valine was the precursor of the D-penicillamine fragment of the penicillins and that L-α-aminoadipic acid was the precursor of the D-α-aminoadipyl side chain of pencillin N and the cephalosporins.

Against the background of these facts several obvious problems arise. For example, what intermediates exist between the amino acids and the complated antibiotic molecules and at what stage does the inversion of the optical configuration of the α-aminoadipic acid and valine residues respectively occur? How far does the biosynthesis of the penicillin and cephalosporin molecule proceed along a common pathway? And what are the mechanisms of formation of the two bicyclic ring systems?

Results and discussion

The first substance to be found with a structure which made it a candidate for consideration as an intermediate was δ-(α-aminoadipyl)cysteinylvaline. This was obtained in minute amounts from the mycelium of *P. chrysogenum* by Arnstein and Morris (1960), but the optical configurations of its amino acid residues were not determined. Subsequently Loder and Abraham (1971a) isolated a tripeptide from the mycelium of *C. acremonium* and showed that it was δ-(L-α-aminoadipyl)-L-cysteinyl-D-valine (3).

$$
\overset{+}{NH_3}\diagdown \overset{L}{}\qquad\qquad\qquad \overset{L}{}\qquad \diagup SH
$$

NH₃⁺, L: CHCH₂CH₂CH₂CONHCH—CH₂, SH   CH(CH₃)₂
CO₂⁻ | |
                        CO—NH————CHCO₂H
                                        D

(3)

They also obtained two related tetrapeptides from the mycelium, both containing an additional glycine residue and one containing a residue of β-hydroxyvaline in place of the valine. More recently, we have found that the same or very similar peptides are present in the mycelium of *Streptomyces clavuligerus* which produces a 7-methoxycephalosporin.

A certain amount of circumstantial evidence was obtained for the view that the tripeptide from the *Cephalosporium* species was in fact a precursor of penicillin N and cephalosporin C. This tripeptide began to be rapidly labelled from ^{14}C-valine, and turned over rapidly, at about the same time in the fermentation as that at which rapid antibiotic production was first observed (Warren *et al.*, 1967). Lemke and Nash (1972) found that neither the tripeptide nor the antibiotics were synthesized by a mutant of the *Cephalosporium* which was auxotrophic for lysine when this organism was grown in the presence of lysine, but that both the tripeptide and the antibiotics were formed on addition of α-aminoadipic acid. Further mutants which did not produce an antibiotic fell into two classes. Those in one class appeared to synthesise the tripeptide while those in the other did not. This suggested that the former were blocked at a stage on the pathway after peptide formation and that the latter were blocked earlier.

With a view to obtaining more direct information about the possible role of a tripeptide in penicillin N and cephalosporin C biosynthesis we have synthesized the LLD isomer of δ-(α-aminoadipyl)cysteinylvaline labelled with tritium in the methyl groups of its valine residue and also labelled only with tritium in the α-hydrogen of its valine residue. We have also synthesized the corresponding all-L-tripeptide labelled with tritium in the methyl groups of its valine residue. The role of such peptides cannot be studied with intact mycelium, because they do not enter the cell. Attempts to use grinding with sand, or ultrasonic treatment to produce extracts of the *Cephalosporium* which showed a detectable ability to synthesize the antibiotics were unsuccessful. However, the use of protoplasts for the production of a cell-free system gave results which were more promising. Protoplasts of the *Cephalosporium* species were obtained by Fawcett *et al.* (1973) by treatment of the mycelium harvested at an early stage of antibiotic production with a mixture of lytic enzymes from *Cytophaga* in the presence of sodium chloride as an osmotic stabilizer. Aerated suspensions of these protoplasts produced penicillin N and cephalosporin C. Protoplasts were lysed by the addition of the minimum amount of dilute tris-HCl buffer, pH 7.0 to pellets obtained by centrifugation. The resulting preparations were then used as test systems after the addition of an energy-generating system, comprising ATP, phosphoenolpyruvate and pyruvate kinase together with magnesium and potassium ions. For some experiments they were separated into particulate and supernatant fractions by centrifugation at 50000 g.

This system differed from those obtained by methods used earlier (Loder and Abraham, 1971b) in that it could synthesize labelled tripeptide from ^{14}C-labelled α-aminoadipic acid, cysteine and valine and did not require the addition of preformed δ-(L-α-aminoadipyl)-L-cysteine. It was also able to incorporate traces of labelled valine into penicillin N. For several studies with the labelled isomers of δ-(α-aminoadipyl)cysteinylvaline (ACV) the latter were added to the cell-free preparations in the concentrations shown in Tables 1 and 2. After incubation for 2 hours at 28°C the reaction mixtures were centrifuged and the supernatants were freeze-dried. In most cases the resulting solids were then treated with performic acid to oxidize thiol-containing peptides to their sulphonic acids and to degrade penicillin N to, *inter alia*, penicillaminic acid. The products of oxidation were analysed by electrophoresis on paper at pH 1.8 and by chromatography on paper in

TABLE 1

Incorporation of tritium from labelled isomers of δ-(L α-aminoadipyl)-L-cysteinylvaline into penicillin N

The whole cell extract used $(0.5cm^3)$ contained about 146 μg of DNA. The energy-generating system added consisted of ATP, phosphoenolpyruvate and pyruvate kinase. In each case the total radioactivity of the tripeptide added was 4.8 μCi. Labelling in the methyl group of the valine residue is denoted by (γ) and that at the α-position by (α). The specific radioactivities of the methyl-labelled peptides were 20 μCi μmol^{-1} and that of the α-labelled peptide was 10 μCi μmol^{-1}. The radioactivity in penicillin N has been taken to be that found in the penicillaminic acid spot on paper after oxidation, minus that formed in the same position in control experiments to which no cell extract was added (4 nCi).

Experimental enzyme system	Tritium-labelled tripeptide	Radioactivity (nCi) in penicillaminic acid
1 Whole extract	LLL(γ)	0
1 Whole extract	LLD(γ)	8
2 Whole extract	LLD(γ)	12
2 Whole extract	LLD(α)	16

butan-1-ol:acetic acid:water (4:1:4 by volume). The locations of the ACV sulphonic acid and penicillaminic acid on the paper were established by addition of authentic samples of these compounds to the extracts and spraying the paper with ninhydrin. The radioactivities in these positions and in adjoining areas were then determined and parallel control experiments were carried out with solutions of the tripeptides containing no protoplast extract. In some cases the radioactivity in penicillin N itself was determined by two-dimensional paper electrophoresis and chromatography after extraction of the antibiotic from freeze-dried unoxidized extracts. Determinations were also made of the loss of radioactivity in the position corresponding to penicillin N and the gain in the position corresponding to its penicilloate after treatment of the extracts with penicillinase and electrophoresis at pH 7.0.

The results shown in Table 1 indicated that tritium was incorporated by the extract into the penicillaminic acid-yielding moiety of penicillin N from the LLD form of ACV labelled in the methyl groups of its valine residue, but not from the corresponding all-L-tripeptide. The results in Table 2 indicated that the incorporation was catalysed by enzymes in the supernatant fraction of the cell-free extract. Incorporation of tritium from the LLD isomer labelled in the α-position of its valine residue was similar to that with the same isomer labelled in its valine methyl groups. Since incorporation of tritium from labelled free valine of the same specific radioactivity was too low to be detectable under the conditions used, it appeared that the results obtained with the LLD-tripeptide could not be attributed to hydrolysis of the latter.

TABLE 2

Incorporation of tritium from methyl-labelled δ-(L-α-aminoadipyl)-L-cysteinyl-D-valine into penicillin N

The conditions are those given in Table 1 except that the amount of radioactivity added in each experiment was 2.4 µCi and the total DNA in the whole extract was 25 µg. The particulate and supernatant fractions of the extract were obtained by centrifugation at 50 000 g.

Enzyme system	Tritium-labelled tripeptide	Radioactivity (nCi) in penicillaminic acid
Whole extract	LLD(γ)	30
Particulate fraction	LLD(γ)	1
Supernatant fraction	LLD(γ)	11

In an experiment in which 30 µCi of the methyl-labelled LLD-tripeptide was used there was a gain in radioactivity of 20 nCi in the location of penicillin N penicilloate after treatment with penicillinase. With the same cell extract 84 nCi was found, after oxidation, in penicillaminic acid. In a further experiment in which 4.8 µCi of the same labelled tripeptide was used 30 nCi was found in the location of penicillin N.

These findings are consistent with the hypothesis that the LLD tripeptide is converted to penicillin N with optical inversion of its L-α-aminoadipic acid residue, but without the involvement of an intermediate in which the asymmetry of the D-valine residue is lost. If this tripeptide is indeed a precursor of penicillin N and the cephalosporins in the mycelial cell, the D-configuration of the δ-(α-aminoadipyl) side chain of these antibiotics must arise at a late stage. This may be during ring formation, because no evidence has been obtained for the production by the *Cephalosporium* sp. of antibiotics which contain an L-α-aminoadipic acid residue. The D-configuration was found by Loder and Abraham to be present in the small amount of cell-bound cephalosporin C that is detectable (Abraham, 1974) and it is also present in the deacetoxycephalosporin C and deacetylcephalosporin C which are produced by certain mutants and are possible cephalosporin C precursors.

Although a cell-free system was required to study the ability of the tripeptide to function as an antibiotic precursor, certain aspects of the mechanisms of ring closure could be investigated with intact mycelium. This became possible with the interpretation of the pmr and ^{13}C nmr spectra of penicillin N and cephalosporin C and the finding that fragmentation of derivatives of the penicillins and cephalosporins in the mass spectrometer yielded ions of relatively high abundance derived from the ring systems, such as (4) and (5) (Demarco and Nagarajan, 1972). For example, with these techniques the two methyl groups of the penicillin molecule could be distinguished from each other, as could C-2 and the exocyclic methylene carbon (C-10) of cephalosporin C (2); and the number and location of deuterium atoms incorporated into the antibiotics from a deuterated valine precursor could be determined. It followed that, if valine could be prepared which was labelled asymmetrically in one of its two methyl groups, the fate of each methyl group during ring closure could be determined.

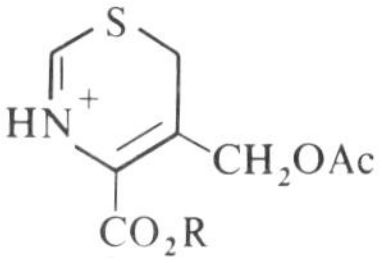

(4)

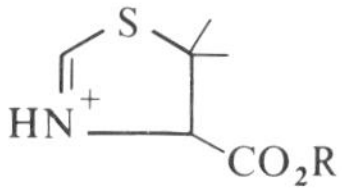

(5)

Kluender *et al.* (1973) synthesized $2S(3S)$-[4-^{13}C]valine (6) by a process in which the labelled chiral isopropyl group (^{13}C being denoted by *C in (6)) was generated during an enzymic reaction. By a similar procedure they later synthesized $(2S)$ $(3S)$-[4,4,4-$D3$] valine and $(2S)$ $(3R)$-[4,4,4-^{2}H$_3$] valine, in which the different methyl groups were labelled with deuterium instead of with ^{13}C, and, by another route, a hexadeuterated valine in which both methyl groups were labelled (Kluender *et al.*, 1974). Baldwin *et al.* (1973) synthesized $(2RS)(3R)$-[4-^{13}C]valine (7) by a process involving a stereospecific reduction of a cyclopropane ring.

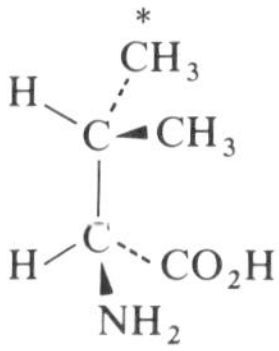

(6)

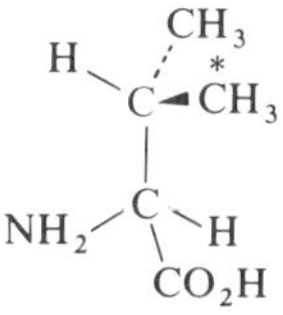

(7)

The ^{13}C of (6) was incorporated by an aerated mycelial suspension of *C. acremonium* exclusively into the exocyclic methylene carbon of cephalosporin C (2) and into the α-methyl group of penicillin N (1). The ^{13}C of (7) was incorporated by *C. acremonium* exclusively into C-2 of cephalosporin C (2) and by *P. chrysogenum* exclusively into the β-methyl group of phenoxymethylpenicillin (Neuss *et al.*, 1973).

These complementary results showed that the incorporation of the carbon atoms of the valine isopropyl group into penicillin and cephalosporin C was stereospecific and that the incorporation into the penicillin ring system occurred with retention of configuration at C-3.

The three deuterated valines were incorporated into penicillin N without loss of deuterium. It thus followed that the methyl groups remained intact during the formation of the pencillin ring system and that no β,γ-unsaturated valine derivative was an intermediate, or in equilibrium with an intermediate, in penicillin biosynthesis. With the 3S-deuterated valine (in which 3D were attached to *C of 6) two deuterium atoms were incorporated into the exo-cyclic methylene group of cephalosporin C and with the 3R-deuterated valine (with 3D attached to *C of 7) two deuterium atoms were incorporated into the C-2 position in the ring. Hence, closure of the dihydrothiazine ring of cephalosporin C does not involve the oxidation of a valine methyl group to a state of oxidation (such as to the level of an aldehyde) which is higher than that formally necessary.

The results of these experiments with ^{13}C- and deuterium-labelled valine are consistent in themselves with the hypothesis that the dehydrovaline, derivative (8) is the immediate precursor of penicillin N and that oxidation of the methyl group in (8) that becomes the β-methyl of the penicillin is followed by the formation of the cephalosporin C ring system, as shown in (9). It is stated that ring closure of (8) will lead to a D-configuration at C-3 (Birch and Smith, 1958; Wolfe et al., 1969). However, this hypothesis is not established by the results available and it could only be reconciled with the assumption that δ-(L-α-aminoadipyl)-L-cysteinyl-D-valine yields penicillin N without loss of the α-hydrogen of its valine residue if the dehydrovaline derivative were enzyme bound and regained the same hydrogen atom during ring closure as that which it lost during its formation. It remains an open question whether an immediate precursor of the penicillin ring system con-tains a derivative of a D-β-hydroxyvaline residue, and whether the first cyclic product is a derivative of "cyclic cysteinylvaline (10)", rather than one containing the β-lactam ring such as (8).

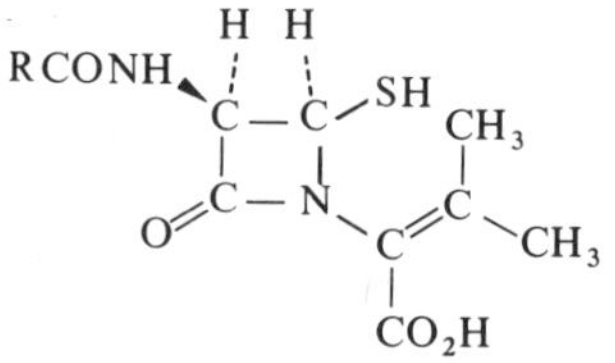

8

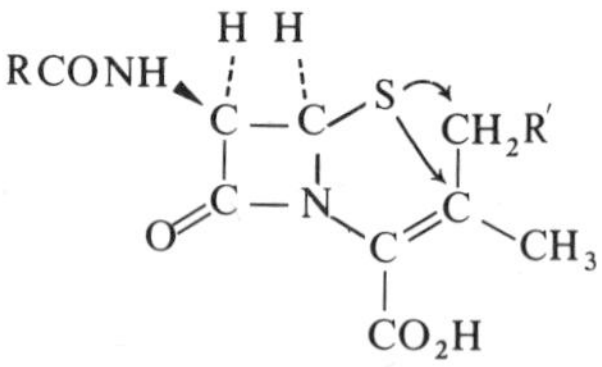

9

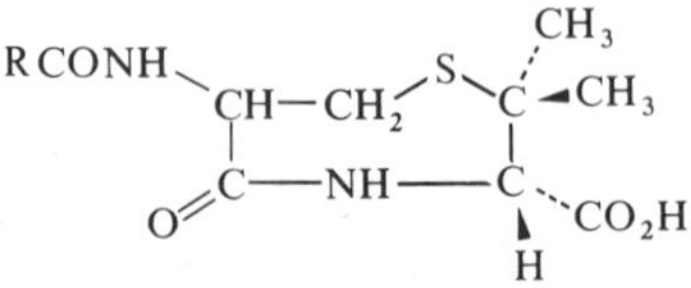

10

The structural relationship of penicillin N and cephalosporin C and the indication that the formation of a cephalosporin is always accompanied by that of penicillin N strongly suggest that some stage in the biosynthesis of the two-ring systems is reached by a common pathway. Moreover, reduction in the efficiency of aeration of suspensions of washed mycelium of *C. acremonium* results in a decrease in the production of cephalosporin C but an increase in that of penicillin N (Smith *et al.*, 1967). A similar effect is observed on addition to such suspension of methionine (Smith *et al.*, 1967), or the structurally related carboxymethyl-L-cysteine (Stevens, 1974), and is clearly different from the stimulatory effect produced on the formation of both antibiotics by addition of methionine to fermentations, in which mycelial growth and the rapid synthesis of enzymes involved in antibiotic production takes place. But whether penicillin N itself is a precursor of deacetoxycephalosporin C and of cephalosporin C, or whether the pathways to the two-ring systems diverge at an earlier stage, is still an open question. Although tritium-labelled penicillin N and deacetoxycephalosporin C have now been synthesized, the production of a cell-free system of increased efficiency may be necessary before the question whether one or both of these substances function as intermediates can be finally answered.

Acknowledgements

We are grateful to the Medical Research Council and the National Research Development Corporation for financial support and to Mrs Sheila Francis for technical assistance.

References

Abraham, E. P. (1974). "Biosynthesis and Enzymic Hydrolysis of Penicillins and Cephalosporins", p. 17. University of Tokyo Press, Tokyo.

Arnstein, H. R. V. and Morris, D. (1960). *Biochem. J.* **76**, 357.

Baldwin, J. E., Löliger, J., Rastetter, W., Neuss, N., Huckstep, L. L. and De La Higuera, N. (1973). *J. Am. chem. Soc.* **95**, 3796, 6511.

Birch, A. J. and Smith, H. (1958). "Amino Acids and Peptides with Antimetabolite Activity" (Ciba Foundation Symposium), p. 247. Churchill, London.

Demarco, P. V. and Nagarajan, R. (1972). "Cephalosporins and Penicillins, Chemistry and Biology" (Ed. E. H. Flynn), p. 311. Academic Press, New York and London.

Fawcett, P. A., Loder, P. B., Duncan, M. J., Beesley, T. J. and Abraham, E. P. (1973). *J. gen. Microbiol.* **79**, 293.

Fujisawa, Y., Shirafuji, H., Kida, M., Nara, K., Yoneda, M. and Kanzaki, T. (1973). *Nature, New Biol.* **246**, 154.

Kluender, H., Bradley, C. H., Sih, C. J., Fawcett, P. and Abraham, E. P. (1973). *J. Am. chem. Soc.* **95**, 6149.

Kluender, H., Huang, F., Fritzberg, A., Schnoes, H., Sih, C. J., Fawcett, P. and Abraham, E. P. (1974). *J. Am. chem. Soc.* In press.

Lemke, P. A. and Nash, C. H. (1972). *Can. J. Microbiol.* **18,** 255.

Liersch, M., Nüesch, J. and Treichler, H. J. (1974). Abstracts, p. 48. 2nd Int. Symp. Genetics of Industrial Microorganisms, Sheffield, England.

Loder, P. B. and Abraham, E. P. (1971a). *Biochem. J.* **123,** 471.

Loder, P. B. and Abraham, E. P. (1971b). *Biochem. J.* **123,** 477.

Neuss, N., Nash, C. H., Baldwin, J. E., Lemke, P. A. and Grutzner, J. B. (1973). *J. Am. chem. Soc.* **95,** 3797, 6511.

Queener, S. W. and Capone, J. J. (1974). Abstracts, p. 33, 2nd Int. Symp. Genetics of Industrial Microorganisms, Sheffield, England.

Smith, B., Warren, S. C., Newton, G. G. F. and Abraham, E. P. (1967). *Biochem. J.* **103,** 877.

Stevens, C. (1974). Unpublished experiments.

Warren, S. C., Newton, G. G. F. and Abraham, E. P. (1967). *Biochem. J.* **103,** 902.

Wolfe, S., Bassett, R. N., Caldwell, S. M. and Nasson, F. (1969). *J. Am. chem. Soc.* **91,** 7205.

Rifamycin biosynthesis

G. C. LANCINI and R. J. WHITE

Research Laboratories, Gruppo Lepetit SpA, Via Durando, 38, Milan, Italy

Summary

Studies utilizing precursors labelled with ^{3}H, ^{14}C and ^{13}C have established the origin of thirty of the thirty-seven carbon atoms present in rifamycin S. The results of ^{13}C incorporation, studied by nuclear magnetic resonance, suggest a biogenetic scheme in which a seven-carbon amino moiety initiates a single polyketide chain composed of eight *propionate* and two *acetate* units. Two unusual features of this scheme are the loss of a propionate-derived methyl and the introduction of an ether linkage between two carbons of the same *propionate* unit. Structural considerations coupled with the results of ^{14}C-methyl malonate and 2-^{13}C-malonate incorporation suggest that all propionate incorporation occurs via methyl malonate and acetate incorporation via malonate. Substitution of the aliphatic bridge occurs after completion of the polyketide chain; the acetoxyl on C-25 deriving from acetate and the methoxyl on C-27 from methionine. The incorporation pattern of 1-^{14}C-glycerate, 3,4-^{14}C-glucose and 1-^{13}C-glucose is in agreement with formation of the seven-carbon amino moiety from an early intermediate of aromatic amino acid biosynthesis. The scheme for rifamycin biogenesis has been confirmed by the isolation of a novel ansamycin, rifamycin W, that possesses the structural features of the hypothetical rifamycin progenitor. This compound is the precursor of rifamycin S which plays a key role in the formation of other members of this family of antibiotics giving rise to rifamycins B, O, Y, G and complex.

The rifamycin biogenetic scheme appears applicable to ansamycins in general, and in particular it seems that all naphthalenic ansamycins (rifamycins, tolypomycins, and streptovaricins) could derive from a common progenitor.

Introduction

Nocardia mediterranei was first isolated in 1957 at the Lepetit Research Laboratories (Sensi *et al.*, 1959a). Although initially considered to belong to the genus *Streptomyces* subsequent analysis of the diaminopimelic acid in its cell wall showed that only the *meso* isomer was present and thus the strain was reclassified as a *Nocardia* (Thiemann *et al.*, 1969). Fermentation broths of *N. mediterranei* contain a mixture of at least five related compounds possessing antimicrobial activity and these have been collectively referred to as the rifamycin complex. The different members of this family of antibiotics were designated rifamycins A–E on the basis of their mobility on paper chromatography (Sensi *et al.*, 1959b). Due to its strongly acidic character rifamycin B proved rather easy to separate from the other members of this complex. Production and isolation of rifamycin B was further facilitated by adding sodium diethyl barbiturate to fermentation media which caused an almost exclusive synthesis of this component (Margalith and Pagani, 1961). Rifamycin B can be degraded by a simple series of chemical reactions (oxidation and hydrolysis) into rifamycin S. This process of oxidation and hydrolysis also occurs spontaneously and is responsible for the increase in activity of aqueous solutions of rifamycin B on "ageing"; rifamycin B is inactive *per se* on intact bacteria but gives rise to the highly active rifamycin S. This latter compound has served as an important starting point for the production of large numbers of semi-synthetic variants, the most noteworthy being rifampicin [3-(4-methyl-1-piperazinyl)imino methyl rifamycin SV], a broad spectrum antibiotic of primary importance in the treatment of tuberculosis. The structure of rifamycins B, O, S and SV (see Fig. 1) was solved independently by two groups: one using chemical degradation experiments and spectroscopic techniques (Oppolzer *et al.*, 1964; Oppolzer and Prelog, 1973) and the other X-ray crystallography (Brufani *et al.*, 1964).

The rifamycins were the first examples of a new class of secondary metabolites which Prelog has denominated the ansamycins (Prelog and Oppolzer, 1973), characterized by the possession of an aliphatic chain bridging an aromatic moiety, which for convenience are referred to as ansa chain and chromophore.

KNOWN NATURAL RIFAMYCINS

In Fig. 1 are shown the structural formulae of all known natural rifamycins. Rifamycin Y is produced in small quantities together with rifamycin B, the major product, in the industrial fermentation of *Nocardia mediterranei* (Leitich *et al.*, 1967; Brufani *et al.*, 1967). Rifamycin O besides being an oxidation product of rifamycin B has been isolated from fermentation broths of *Streptomyces* 4107 A2 (Sugawara *et al.*, 1964). Rifamycin S was first obtained chemicaally by hydrolysis of rifamycin O but subsequently mutants of *N. mediterranei* (Lancini and Hengeller, 1969) were isolated that produced rifamycin S directly; rifamycins S and SV are readily interconvertible by oxidizing and reducing agents, being a quinone-hydroquinone pair. More recently a *Nocardia* isolated in Australia, strain NT19, has been shown to produce rifamycin S (Birner *et al.*, 1972). Rifamycin L has only been found as a transformation product during experiments in which rifamycin S was incubated with washed mycelium (Lancini *et al.*, 1969); it has never been isolated from a fermentation. Demethyl rifamycin SV was isolated from the fermentation broth of a mutant of *N. mediterranei* together with smaller quantities of 25-deacetyl, demethyl rifamycin SV and demethyl rifamycin B (Lancini *et al.*, 1970). Rifamycin G is an inactive component of the rifamycin complex and has been obtained from fermentations of *N. mediterranei* in media lacking barbiturate (Lancini *et al.*, 1974). Rifamycin W is the major fermentation product of a morphological variant of *N. mediterranei* (White *et al.*, 1974).

Results and discussion

ORIGIN OF THE RIFAMYCIN CARBON SKELETON

Once the structure of the rifamycins was established it became evident that the carbon skeleton of the ansa chain bore a close resemblance to macrolide antibiotics of the erythromycin type (Corcoran and Chick, 1966). Two proposals have been made for the biogenesis of macrolides: Woodward (1956 and 1957) postulated that they derived from mixed condensations of *acetate* and *propionate*, the C-methyls all coming from C-3 of propionate; Birch (1957), on the other hand, suggested that a polyketide chain was first formed from *acetate* and subsequently methylated, methionine being the source of the C-methyls in this case. Preliminary experiments soon showed that $[3\text{-}^{14}\text{C}]$-propionate was a good precursor of rifamycin B and incorporations of more than 10 per cent were achieved. On Kuhn–Roth oxidation of the labelled antibiotic, 85.5 per cent of the radioactivity was recovered as acetic acid, whilst in a similar degradation of the rifamycin labelled with $[1\text{-}^{14}\text{C}]$-propionate only 2 per cent of the radioactivity was recovered in this fraction. This indicated that most, if not all, of the C-methyls derived from C-3 of propionate (Brufani *et al.*, 1973). Further support for this came from the results of $[^{14}\text{CH}_3]$-methionine incorporation; this precursor labelled exclusively the methoxyl carbon on C-27. Thus it appeared that not only the C-methyls of the ansa chain, but also those of the chromophore derived from C-3 of propionate (Brufani *et al.*, 1973). A more detailed analysis of the $[^{14}\text{C}]$-propionate incorporation was performed by subjecting the labelled antibiotic to systematic chemical degradation. The distribution of radio-

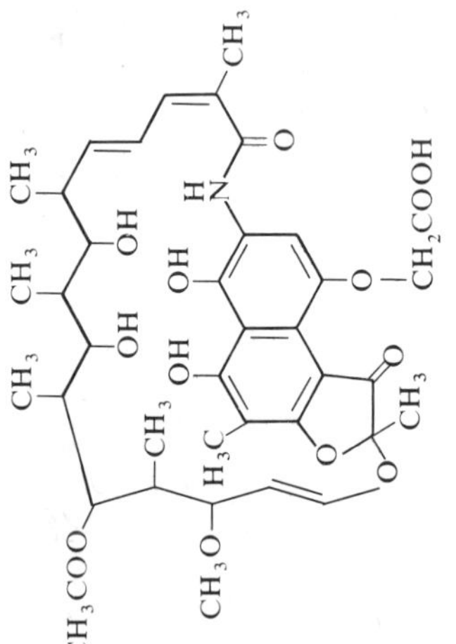

Rifamycin O

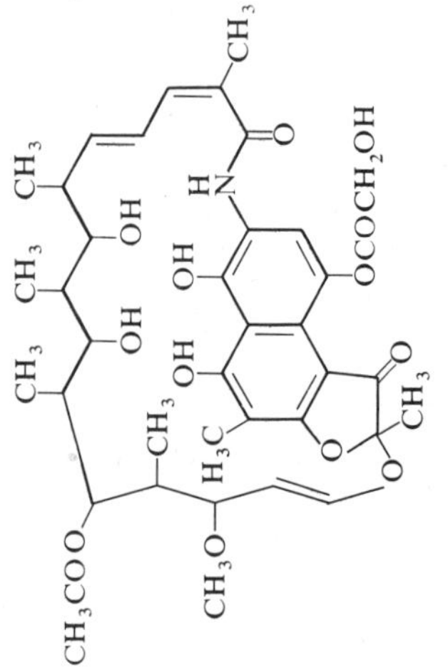

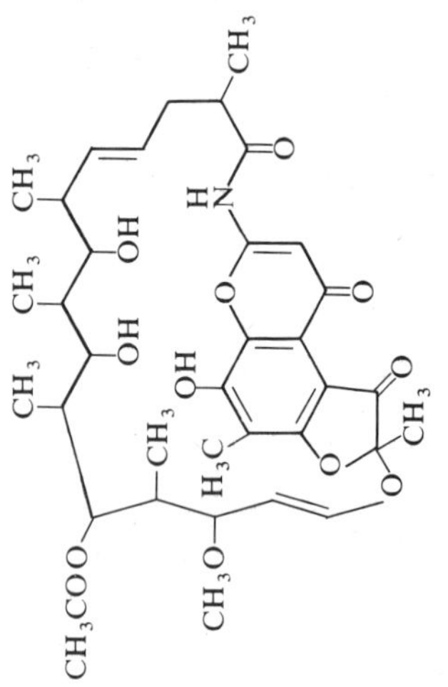

Rifamycin G

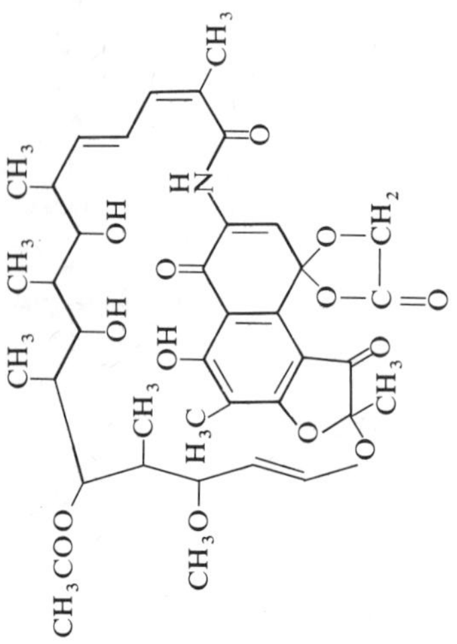

Rifamycin Y

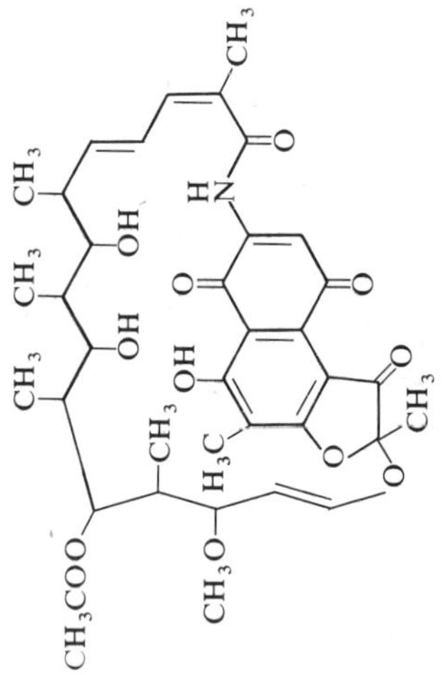

Rifamycin S

Rifamycin B

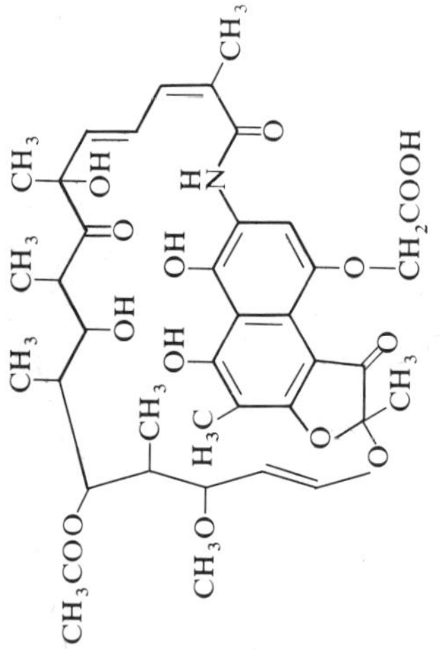

Rifamycin L

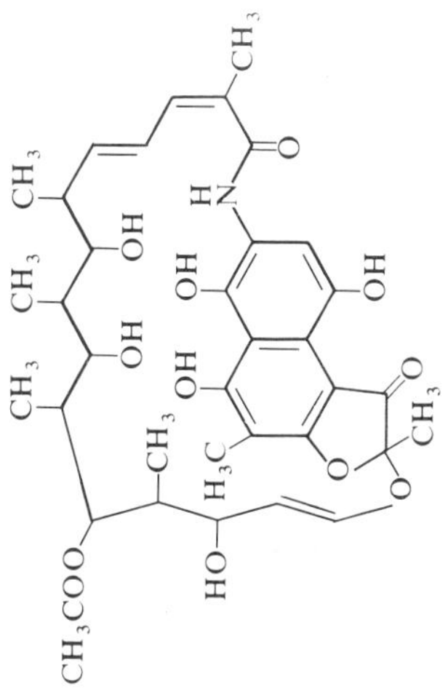

FIG. 1. Structures of known natural rifamycins.

Rifamycin W

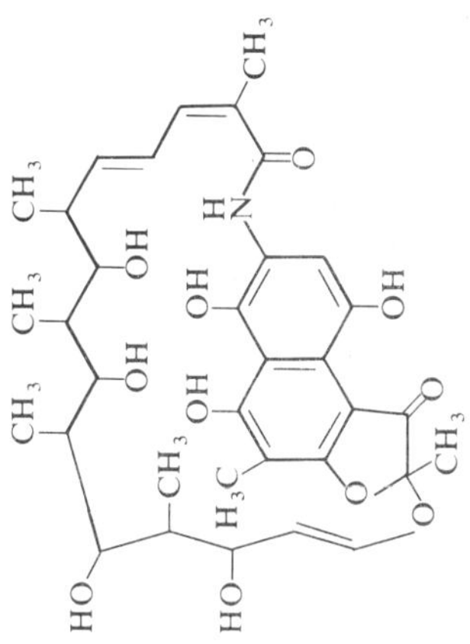

25-Deacetyl, demethyl rifamycin SV

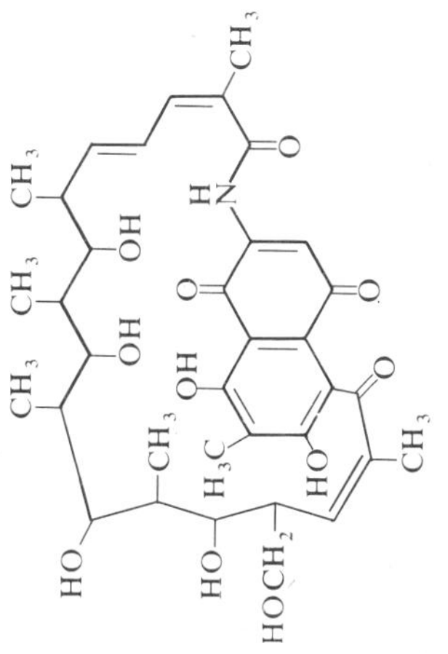

Demethyl rifamycin SV

F

activity between the different fragments indicated that all seven C-methyls present in rifamycin S were equally labelled by [3-^{14}C]-propionate and so presumably there were seven molecules of propionate altogether, two in the chromophore and five in the ansa chain.

However, when the same degradation scheme was performed on rifamycin S labelled with [1-^{14}C]-propionate a somewhat different picture emerged as the ratio of labelling of chromophore to ansa chain was less than 1:5 instead

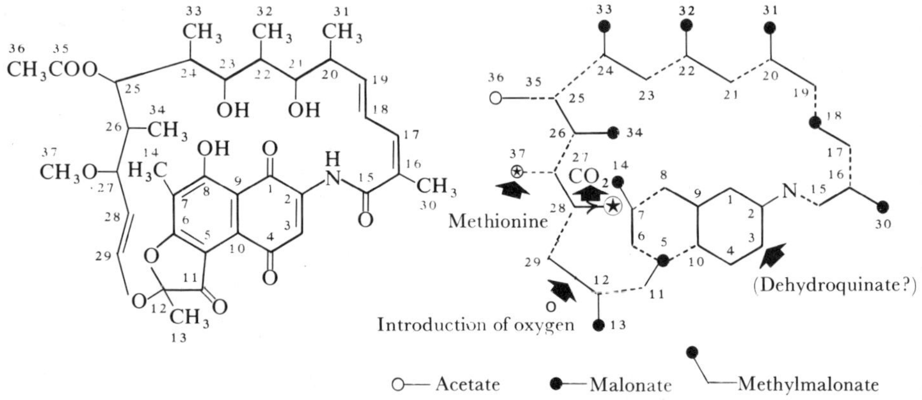

FIG. 2. Biogenetic scheme for rifamycin S. (After White *et al.*, 1973, and Karlsson *et al.*, 1974.)

of the 2:5 observed with [3-^{14}C]-propionate. Thus, in spite of the elegant chemical dissection of ^{14}C-labelled rifamycin S carried out in Prelog's laboratory, the information provided on isotope distribution was insufficient to permit an unambiguous interpretation of the results. This problem was eventually solved by studying the incorporation of ^{13}C-enriched precursors with carbon magnetic resonance (cmr) spectroscopy (White *et al.*, 1973). Application of this technique requires the prior assignment of the resonances on the cmr spectrum to the various carbons of the molecule. This was achieved by a combination of techniques (Martinelli *et al.*, 1973; Furher, 1973; Martinelli *et al.*, 1974a) and the combined results of ^{13}C-propionate and ^{13}C-acetate incorporation permitted the biogenetic scheme shown in Fig. 2 to be proposed. The ^{14}C data of Brufani *et al.* (1973) are in perfect agreement with such a proposal but the unusual biogenetic scheme operating in this case had hampered their interpretation. Until the studies with ^{13}C, it had been assumed that the chromophore and the ansa chain were biogenetically two different entities, separately synthesized and then joined together. According to the ^{13}C findings the entire molecule derives from a single polyketide chain obtained by condensation, in the appropriate order, of eight *propionates* and two *acetates*, initiated by a seven-carbon compound. The second ring of the chromophore derives, in part, from the polyketide chain (C-14, C-7, C-6 and C-5). Two surprising features of this biogenetic scheme are loss of a methyl group from C-28 and introduction of an ether linkage between C-12 and C-29, which derive from the same *propionate* unit.

ORIGIN OF THE POLYKETIDE CHAIN

In analogy with fatty acid synthesis it has been proposed that acetate and propionate incorporation in chain elongation occurs via the intermediate formation of the chemically more reactive malonyl CoA and methyl malonyl CoA (Lynen and Tada, 1961). The biogenetic scheme for rifamycin S shows that none of the *propionate* units is in a chain initiating situation. This fact, coupled with the results of [^{14}CH$_3$]-methyl malonate incorporation (Karlsson *et al.*, 1974), which gave the same distribution of isotope as [3-^{14}C]-propionate, was interpreted as meaning that all propionate incorporation occurs via methyl malonyl coenzyme A. The results of [^{13}C]-acetate incorporation (White *et al.*, 1973) were complicated by an indirect incorporation resulting from the metabolic conversion of *acetate* to *propionate*, but by disregarding the carbons already known to derive from *propionate* the presence of two *acetate* units in the primary skeleton was established. Comparison of the intensity of labelling of these units in respect to that of the acetoxy group at C-25 suggested a different origin. This was confirmed by the results of [2-^{13}C]-malonate incorporation (Karlsson *et al.*, 1974); this precursor enriched C-18 and C-5 without significantly affecting C-36. Thus it was concluded that in all probability the two *acetate* units in the polyketide chain involve malonyl coenzyme A as an intermediate and that the acetoxyl substitution on C-25 comes directly from acetyl coenzyme A. This result also means that acetyl coenzyme A is readily converted to malonyl coenzyme A but the reverse occurs poorly, if at all. Although a ready transformation of propionyl coenzyme A to methyl malonyl CoA is assumed to take place, no information about the reverse process is available. In this respect it is of interest to note that labelled succinate gave a distribution of incorporated isotope very similar to propionate suggesting that succinyl CoA is the source of methyl malonyl CoA (Karlsson *et al.*, 1974).

ORIGIN OF AROMATIC RING

The experiments described this far with labelled precursors have established the origin of thirty out of the thirty seven carbon atoms of rifamycin S. The remaining seven carbon atoms appear to constitute the compound initiating the polyketide chain. Studies with ^{14}C-labelled shikimate and aromatic amino acids failed to reveal a specific incorporation into the chromophore, indicating that the normal aromatic pathway was probably not the source of this moiety (Karlsson *et al.*, 1974). The only ^{14}C precursors that specifically labelled this part of the molecule were [3,4-^{14}C]-glucose and [1-^{14}C]-glycerate. However, the pattern of [1-^{13}C]-glucose incorporation (Karlsson *et al.*, 1974) was reminiscent of that established for shikimate labelled with [1-^{14}C]-glucose (Srinivasan *et al.*, 1956). These apparent contradictions would be reconciled if the first aromatic ring derived from an intermediate of the normal aromatic pathway before the level of shikimate, i.e. 5-dehydro-shikimate of 5-dehydroquinate. More recent data with [1-^{13}C]-glucose and [1-^{13}C]-glycerate fully support a shikimate-type origin and establish the orientation of the seven carbon with C-1 of rifamycin deriving from C-2 of shikimate (White and Martinelli, 1974).

BIOSYNTHETIC INTERRELATIONSHIPS

Rifamycin W, the missing link

Studies with ^{13}C-enriched precursors resulted in the proposal of a biogenetic scheme in which the carbon skeleton of rifamycin S was made up of eight methyl malonates, two malonates and a seven-carbon amino moiety. The primary product resulting from these condensations would have an extra methyl and lack the ether linkage characteristic of the other rifamycins. In this respect the rifamycin progenitor would have fundamentally the same carbon skeleton as the streptovaricins (Rinehart, 1972), another family of ansamycin antibiotics.

During recent studies at the Lepetit Research Laboratories a novel ansa-mycin, rifamycin W, was isolated from a mutant of *N. mediterranei* (White *et al.*, 1974). Physicochemical studies have established the structure of this compound (see Fig. 1) and it bears a close resemblance to the hypothetical progenitor molecule (Martinelli *et al.*, 1974b), the only difference being the presence of a primary alcohol group (C-34a) in place of a methyl; this not only confirmed the proposed biogenetic scheme but also indicated that methyl loss occurs via the normal oxidative route. Incorporation of ^{13}C precursor in rifamycin W was exactly as predicted from the biogenetic scheme proposed for rifamycin S (White *et al.*, 1974). It is thought that rifamycin W is a normal intermediate in the formation of the other rifamycins as its addition to washed mycelium (500 µg dm^{-3} ^{14}C-rifamycin W) gave rise to rifamycin B (85 µg dm^{-3} ^{14}C-rifamycin B formed in 24 h). Thus rifamycin W represents the link in the biogenesis of naphthalenic ansamycins. The biogenesis of streptovaricin D (Milavetz *et al.*, 1973) has now been shown to follow the scheme proposed for it on the basis of the rifamycin results (White *et al.*, 1973).

Relationship of rifamycin SV to rifamycins B and O

Structural and biosynthetic considerations suggested that rifamycin S, first obtained by the chemical degradation of rifamycin B, might be the biological precursor of rifamycin B. The only difference between these compounds being the glycolic acid moiety attached via ether linkage to carbon 4 of the chromophore. This hypothesis was checked by adding chemically derived rifamycin S to washed mycelium of the producer organism *N. mediterranei.* Under these conditions there is very little endogenous synthesis of antibiotic but the mycelium is still capable of carrying out an efficient metabolic transformation of exogenous substrates. In experiments of this type either rifamycin S or rifamycin SV could be used as this quinone–hydroquinone pair of rifamycins are readily interconvertible. Up to 50 per cent of rifamycin SV (or S) added was transformed to rifamycin B by washed mycelium. Similarly [^{14}C]-rifamycin SV could be added to normal fermentations and about 35 per cent of the radioactivity was converted into rifamycin B (Lancini and Sensi, 1967). A confirmation of the precursor–product relationship was sought by looking for blocked mutants that produced rifamycin SV directly, instead of rifamycin B, i.e. mutants unable to transform SV into B. This search was facilitated by the fact that rifamycin SV is a much more active antibacterial agent than rifamycin B and with a judicious choice of test organism (*Pseudomonas reptilivora*) and the use of a medium which prevented the spontaneous degradation of B into S (slightly alkaline pH), an effective screen was derived which yielded several rifamycin SV-producing mutants (Lancini and Hengeller, 1969). In addition a mutant was isolated that produced a mixture of new compounds, the predominant one being very similar to rifamycin SV. Physicochemical studies on the purified compound revealed that it was 27-demethoxy, 27-hydroxy rifamycin SV (Lancini *et al.*, 1970). Evidently this mutant has an altered methylation enzyme and the 27-demethoxy, 27-hydroxy rifamycin SV accumulates because of the poor conversion of this compound to 27-demethoxy, 27-hydroxy rifamycin B, which is only found in small quantities.

It has already been mentioned that rifamycin W is transformed to rifa-mycin B; having now established that rifamycin SV is a precursor of rifamycin B this must mean that rifamycin SV is an intermediate in the conversion of rifamycin W to B.

The relationship of rifamycin O to rifamycins SV and B is uncertain. An organism has been isolated that produces rifamycin O directly and not rifamycin B (Sugawara *et al.*, 1964). However, as this pair of rifamycins are readily interconvertible, the one found depends simply on the oxygen tension at the end of the fermentation. It has been suggested that rifamycin O is an obligatory intermediate in rifamycin B formation (Lancini *et al.*, 1969).

Origin of glycolic acid moiety

The biosynthetic studies so far described have been mostly concerned with rifamycin S. Both rifamycins B and O contain two carbons more than rifamycin S. The origin of this two-carbon fragment has been studied with ^{14}C-labelled precursors (Lancini *et al.*, 1969). With [1-^{14}C]-glucose 90 per cent of the radioactivity was found in the methylene carbon and an almost identical result was obtained with [6-^{14}C]-glucose. None of the two carbon compounds tested as precursors labelled the glycolate moiety. No definite conclusions can at present be made as to the exact origin of these two carbons but the results with ^{14}C-glucose suggest that a three-carbon glycolytic fragment could be involved.

During the studies on transformation of rifamycin SV into rifamycin B two additional products were noted: rifamycins L and G.

Rifamycin L. The structure of rifamycin L is shown in Fig. 1: this compound has never been isolated from normal fermentations and is perhaps best considered as a transformation artefact. Its structural relationship to rifamycins B and O is interesting and led to the suggestion mentioned previously that rifamycin O is an obligatory intermediate in the formation of rifamycins B and L, which are obtained simply by opening the spiro-lactone ring one way or the other leaving the glycolic moiety attached in ether or ester linkage (Lancini *et al.*, 1969).

Rifamycin G. This compound is produced together with the rifamycin complex, i.e. no barbiturate present in fermentation medium, but escaped notice as a result of its total lack of antibacterial activity. The subsequent finding that it was also a transformation product of rifamycin SV (as much as 38 per cent of rifamycin S added to washed mycelium at 200 µg cm^{-3} was transformed into rifamycin G—Lancini *et al.*, 1974) gave important support to the proposed structure shown in Fig. 1.

Carbon 1 of the chromophore has presumably been lost as CO_2 via intermediate ring opening and formation of a carboxyl group. The only other difference in comparison with rifamycin S is the double bond C-16:C-17 which has been hydrogenated.

Rifamycin Y. During the first industrial fermentation small amounts of a second product, rifamycin Y, were noticed in addition to rifamycin B. This compound was very similar to rifamycin B but devoid of antibacterial activity. Its structure (see Fig. 1) was solved both by classical chemical techniques (Leitich *et al.*, 1967) and X-ray crystallography (Brufani *et al.*, 1967). The pattern of oxygen substitution on its ansa chain suggested that it derived from rifamycin B rather than vice versa; there is no oxygen function on C-20 in the original polyketide chain. This hypothesis was confirmed by demonstrating a 22 per cent conversion of ^{14}C-rifamycin B added to a fermentation into ^{14}C-rifamycin Y (Lancini et al., 1967). The relative amounts of rifamycins B and Y produced in fermentation are influenced by the inorganic phosphate concentration, and by diminishing the amount of this compound in culture media it is possible to limit the formation of rifamycin Y (Lancini et al., 1967).

Origin of rifamycin complex and role of barbiturates

The studies with mutant strains and the transformation experiments using washed mycelium reported so far have highlighted an important role for rifamycin SV in the formation of rifamycins O, B, Y, L and G.

In media lacking barbiturate the rifamycin complex is produced comprising rifamycin A, B, C, D, E, G and Y. Even though the structures of rifamycins A, C, D, and E are not known it now seems that they also derive from rifamycin SV. Co-synthesis experiments in which a rifamycin SV producing mutant and a nonproducing mutant are fermented together have shown that the fate of the rifamycin SV produced by one mutant depends on the presence of barbiturate in the medium. In its presence the non-producer converts the rifamycin SV into rifamycin B, but in its absence the rifamycin complex is formed (Lancini et al., 1974). The mechanism of the barbiturate effect is not clear but it is not a precursor of rifamycins and none of the metabolites formed from it elicit the same effect as the parent compound if added back to a fermentation (Kluepfel et al., 1965). The structural requirements are quite rigid and of the many derivatives tested diethyl barbituric acid was the most effective in stimulating the formation of rifamycin B (Margalith and Pagani, 1961). It has been suggested that the increase in rifamycin B synthesis is correlated with a prolonged logarithmic phase of growth (Ruczaj et al., 1972).

Thus it seems that rifamycin SV plays a central role in the biosynthesis of the other rifamycins and that barbiturates can decide its fate by stimulating transformation into rifamycin B.

Generalized scheme of ansamycin biogenesis

The biogenetic scheme established for rifamycin S seems applicable to ansamycins in general. In addition to the rifamycins and streptovaricins a third family of naphthalenic ansamycins is known: the tolypomycins (Kishi et al., 1969). Several ansamycins have now been described that contain a benzenic chromophore, e.g. geldanamycin (De Boer et al., 1970) and maytansine (Kupchan et al., 1972). Examination of their structure discloses that they too could be constructed from a single polyketide chain initiated by a seven carbon amino compound. If the proposed origin of this chromophore moiety

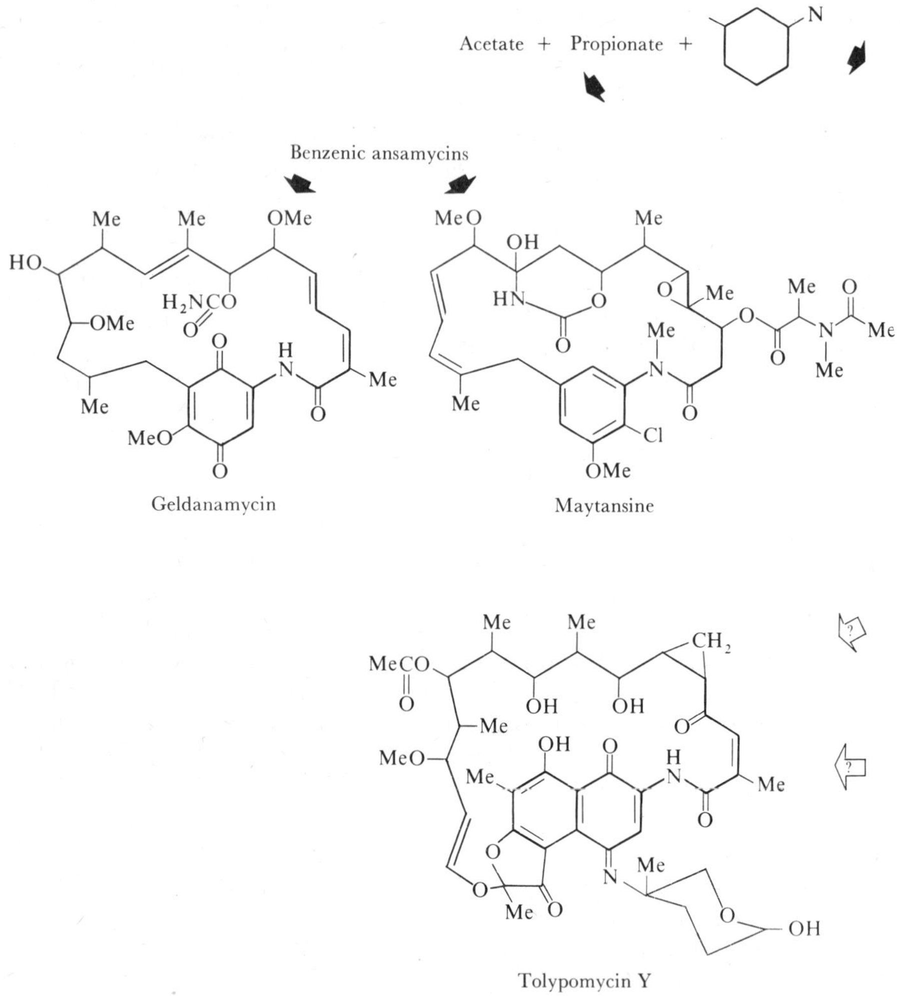

Acetate + Propionate +

Benzenic ansamycins

Geldanamycin

Maytansine

Tolypomycin Y

FIG. 3. General scheme of ansamycin biogenesis with special reference to the rifamycins. (After White *et al.*, 1974.)

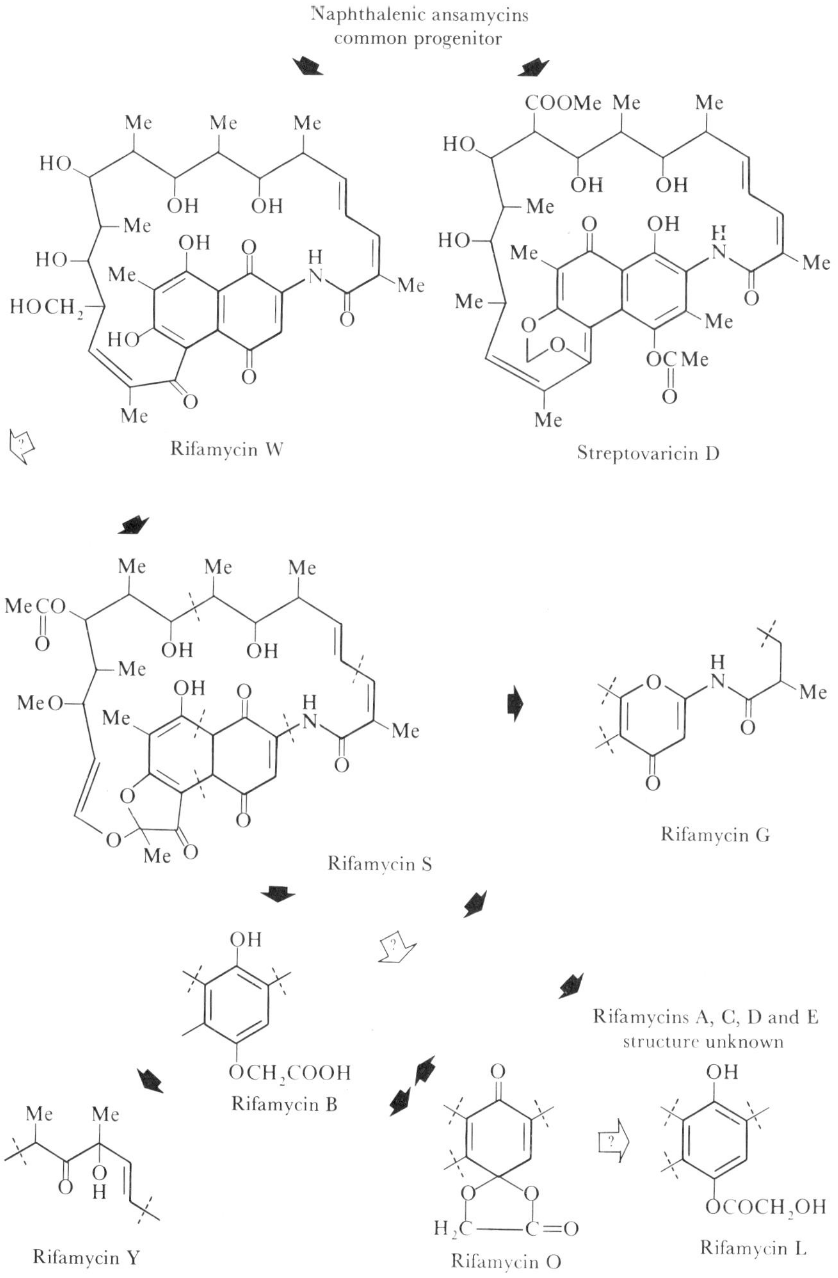

Naphthalenic ansamycins
common progenitor

Rifamycin W

Streptovaricin D

Rifamycin S

Rifamycin G

Rifamycin B

Rifamycins A, C, D and E
structure unknown

Rifamycin Y

Rifamycin O

Rifamycin L

is correct, the oxygen function required for closure of the second ring when naphthalenic ansamycins are formed is of a secondary nature (there is no oxygen on carbon 2 of 5-dehydroquinic acid). A generalized scheme of ansamycin biogenesis with special reference to the rifamycins is presented in Fig. 3.

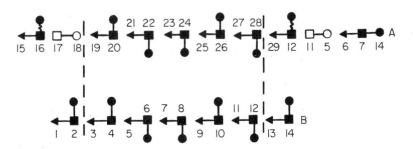

FIG. 4. Scheme illustrating the configuration of the C-methyl groups on the ansa chain of rifa-mycins, tolypomycins and streptovaricins (A) in comparison with Celmer's macrolide model (B) (Celmer, 1971). (From Brufani *et al.*, 1973.)

Relationship of ansamycins to the macrolides

The structural similarity of the rifamycins to the macrolide antibiotics has already been mentioned. Prelog has recently pointed out a remarkable similarity in the configuration of the C-methyl groups in these two classes of compounds (Brufani *et al.*, 1973). Previously Celmer (1971) had proposed a common configurational model for macrolide biogenesis which fits known members of this class very well. The ansa chains of the rifamycins, strepto-varicins and tolypomycins conform remarkably well to Celmer's model (see Fig. 4) indicating that the macrolides and ansamycins are formed according to the same biogenetic pattern and have presumably evolved from a common enzyme system.

References

Birch, A. J. (1957). *Fortschr. Chem. Org. Naturstoffe*, **14**, 186.
Birner, J., Hodgson, P. R., Lane, W. R. and Baxter, E. H. (1972). *J. Antibiotics*, **25**, 356.
Brufani, M., Fedeli, W., Giacomello, G. and Vaciago, A. (1964). *Experientia*, **20**, 339.
Brufani, M., Fedeli, W., Giacomello, E. and Vaciago, A. (1967). *Experientia*, **23**, 508.
Brufani, M., Kluepfel, D., Lancini, G. C., Leitich, J., Mesentsev, A. S., Prelog, V., Schmook, F. P. and Sensi, P. (1973). *Helv. Chim. Acta*, **56**, 2315.
Celmer, W. D. (1971). *Pure Appl. Chem.* **28**, 413.
Corcorran, J. W. and Chick, M. (1966). "Biosynthesis of Antibiotics" (Ed. J. F. Snell), vol. 1, p. 159. Academic Press, New York and London.

De Boer, C., Meulman, P. A., Wnuk, R. J. and Peterson, D. H. (1970). *J. Antibiotics*, **23**, 442.

Fulmer, H. (1973). *Helv. chim. Acta*, **56**, 2377.

Karlsson, A., Sartori, G. and White, R. J. (1974). *Eur. J. Biochem.* Accepted for publication.

Kishi, T., Asai, M., Muroi, M., Harada, S., Mizuta, E., Terao, S., Miki, T. and Mizuno, K. (1969). *Tetrahedron Letters*, 91.

Kleupfel, D., Lancini, G. C. and Sartori, G. (1965). *Appl. Microbiol.* **13**, 600.

Kupchan, S. M., Komoda, Y., Court, W. A., Thomas, G. J., Smith, R. M., Karim, A., Gilmore, C. J., Haltiwanger, R. C. and Boyan, R. F. (1972). *J. Am. chem. Soc.* **94**, 1354.

Lancini, G. C. and Sensi, P. (1967). "Proceeding 5th International Congress for Chemotherapy" (Eds K. H. Spitzy and H. Haschek), vol. 1, p. 47. Verlag der Wiener Medizinischen Akademie, Vienna.

Lancini, G. C., Thiemann, J. E., Sartori, G. and Sensi, P. (1967). *Experientia*, **23**, 899.

Lancini, G. C., Gallo, G. G., Sartori, G. and Sensi, P. (1969). *J. Antibiotics*, **22**, 369.

Lancini, G. C. and Hengeller, C. (1969). *J. Antibiotics*, **22**, 637.

Lancini, G. C., Hengeller, C. and Sensi, P. (1970). "Progress in Antimicrobial and Anticancer Chemotherapy", vol. 1, p. 1166. University of Tokyo Press, Tokyo.

Lancini, G. C., Sartori, G., Gallo, G. G. and White, R. J. (1974). Manuscript in preparation.

Leitich, J., Prelog, V. and Sensi, P. (1967). *Experientia*, **23**, 505.

Lynen, F. and Tada, M. (1961). *Angew. Chem.* **73**, 513.

Margalith, P. and Pagani, H. (1961). *Appl. Microbiol.* **9**, 325.

Martinelli, E., White, R. J., Gallo, G. G. and Beynon, P. (1973). *Tetrahedron*, **29**, 3441.

Martinelli, E., White, R. J., Gallo, G. G. and Beynon, P. (1974a). *Tetrahedron Letters*, 1367.

Martinelli, E., Gallo, G. G., Antonini, P. and White, R. J. (1974b). *Tetrahedron*. In press.

Milavetz, B., Kakinuma, L., Rinehart, K. L. Jr., Roles, J. P. and Haak, W. J. (1973). *J. Am. chem. Soc.* **93**, 5793.

Oppolzer, W. and Prelog, V. (1973). *Helv. chim Acta*, **56**, 2287.

Oppolzer, W., Prelog, V. and Sensi, P. (1964). *Experientia*, **20**, 336.

Prelog, V. and Oppolzer, V. (1973). *Helv. chim . Acta*, **56**, 2279.

Rinehart, K. L. (1972). *Accounts Chem. Res.* **5**, 57.

Ruczaj, Z., Ostrowska-Kryscak, B., Sawnor-Kotszynska, D. and Raczynska-Bojan- owska, K. (1972). *Acta microbiol. polon.* **4**, 201.

Sensi, P., Margalith, P. and Timbal, M. T. (1959a). *Il Farmaco* (Ed. Sc.), **14**, 146.

Sensi, P., Greco, A. M. and Ballotta, R. (1959b). *Antibiotics A.* 262.

Srinivasan, P. R., Shigeura, H. T., Sprecher, M., Sprinson, D. B. and Davis, B. D. (1956). *J. biol. Chem.* **220**, 5477.

Sugawara, S., Karasawa, K., Watanabe, M. and Hidaka, T. (1964). *J. Antibiotics*, **17**, 29.

Thiemann, J. E., Zucco, G. and Pelizza, G. (1969). *Arch. Mikrobiol.* **67**, 147.

White, R. J., Martinelli, E., Gallo, G. G., Lancini, G. and Beynon, P. (1973). *Nature, Lond.* **243**, 273.

White, R. J., Martinelli, E. and Lancini, G. (1974). *Proc. natn. Acad. Sci. U.S.A.* **71**, 3260.

White, R. J. and Martinelli, E. (1974). *FEBS Letters*, **49**, 233.

Woodward, R. B. (1956). *Angew. Chem.* **68**, 19.

Woodward, R. B. (1957). *Angew. Chem.* **69**, 50.

The role of the genome in secondary biosynthesis in *Streptomyces aureofaciens*

Z. HOŠŤÁLEK, M. BLUMAUEROVÁ, J. LUDVÍK, V. JECHOVÁ, V. BĚHAL,
J. ČÁSLAVSKÁ and E. ČURDOVÁ

*Institute of Microbiology, Czechoslovak Academy of Sciences, Prague,
Czechoslovakia*

Summary

The biological properties and the biochemical activities of a low-production strain of *Streptomyces aureofaciens* resembling the standard type were compared with those of variants with altered biosynthetic activities obtained by mutagenic treatment. A strain with an increased production of tetracyclines was obtained by uv irradiation; variants with qualitative changes in the spectrum of secondary metabolites produced were induced by uv irradiation and treatment with N-methyl-N'-nitro-N-nitrosoguanidine.

Comparison of the biochemical activities of strains with varying production capacity, synthesizing metabolites of the standard type (chlortetracycline, tetracycline) confirmed the low activity of energy metabolism in the high-production variant. A study of variants blocked in the tetracycline biosynthesis pathway, producing so-called mutant metabolites, showed that a change in biosynthetic activity is accompanied by a series of changes in mutability, culture morphology and cell ultrastructure, by changes in growth rate and in the viability of strains. These are linked with further biochemical changes including those in sensitivity to their own metabolites.

The results obtained indicate that excessive biosynthesis of chlortetracycline in high-production variants is subject to a number of genetic changes in primary metabolic pathways, competing with secondary biosynthesis. In these strains probably no changes in the actual secondary biosynthetic pathway occur but the activity of specific enzyme systems yielding biosynthetic intermediates is intensified. Changes accompanying the genetic block in the secondary biosynthetic pathway, resulting in a qualitative shift of the spectrum of metabolites produced, cannot be interpreted as a pleiotropic effect of a single point mutation but are probably due to multi-site mutations affecting simultaneously a series of biochemical functions in the cell.

Introduction

Mutagenic treatment of industrial strains producing antibiotics may result in three fundamental types of variants, differing in their production characteristics from the standard parent strain.

Firstly, strains where the spectrum of metabolites produced is identical but where the quantitative parameters of their formation are altered: secondly, mutants in which the synthesis of one or more of the metabolites produced by the parent is completely suppressed. Frequently, a genetic block may lead to the formation of novel compounds, usually intermediates of a biosynthetic pathway or their derivatives formed by a metabolic bypass. The third category is comprised of partly blocked, so-called leaky mutants. In addition to the typical mutant metabolites, these strains also produce certain amounts of substances characteristic for the parent strain.

In *Streptomyces aureofaciens* which produces chlortetracycline (CTC), the eleven postulated steps of biosynthesis (from condensation of acetate units to the hypothetical nonaketide precursor to the final product) give the possibility of synthesizing numerous metabolites of a tetracycline type. These may arise by a single or multiple genetic blocks in the biosynthetic pathway. So far, 26 such compounds have been described, 45 remaining undiscovered (Vaněk *et al.*, 1971).

A number of results indicate that the genetic basis underlying the altered (increased) productivity of CTC (in contrast with mutants of the second and third categories) is not a genetic block of the biosynthetic pathway proper but hereditary changes in metabolic pathways, competing with secondary biosynthesis (Hošťálek and Vaněk, 1973). Mutants of the second category producing, in place of CTC, other mutant metabolites were characterized by McCormick (1969) as point-blocked, i.e. as intact strains with the exception of the loss of any single intermediate reaction on the way to CTC.

In previous work with the CTC producer *S. aureofaciens* we obtained a series of strains belonging to each of the three above categories (Blumauerová *et al.*, 1969, 1973). In the present contribution we have attempted to analyse the genetic changes in the biosynthetic capacity of these mutants not only from the point of view of the spectrum of the metabolites produced but above all as a general investigation of their biological properties and biochemical activities.

Results

ORIGIN OF STRAINS AND THEIR PRODUCTION PROPERTIES

Mutants used were derived from one common ancestor, *S. aureofaciens* Bg. Several selection steps led from this strain to the production variant 84/25. The blocked mutants were prepared by mutagenic treatment of both strains. These strains differed markedly in their biosynthetic activity from the parent strains as well as from each other. Their origin is shown in Fig. 1. The characteristics of agar cultures of these mutants as well as of the parent strains are shown in Table 1.

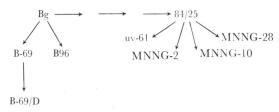

FIG. 1. Interrelationships among the standard strains of *S. aureofaciens* and their blocked mutants. Strains 84/25, B-69, B-96 and uv-61 were isolated after uv irradiation. Strain B-69/D is a spontaneous variant of B-69. The remaining mutants (MNNG-2, MNNG-10 and MNNG-28) were obtained after treatment with *N*-methyl-*N'*-nitro-*N*-nitrosoguanidine.

a. *Biosynthetic activity*

Both parent strains, the low-production Bg and the high-production 84/25, form three major metabolites, typical of all the standard strains of *S. aureofaciens*: CTC, tetracycline (TCN), and the structurally related, antibiotically inactive, aureovocin (4,6-dihydroxy-6-methylpretramid glucoside; Vokoun *et al.*, 1973). The yields of aureovocin in both strains are proportional to the rate of tetracycline biosynthesis. In addition to these metabolites, the strains were found to contain a minor component, B.

The B-96 mutant lost its ability to produce CTC and TCN, probably as a consequence of a block in the oxidation of ring A (Vaněk *et al.*, 1971), with simultaneous increased production of aureovocin and component B. The MNNG-28 mutant is also blocked in the biosynthesis of tetracyclines; it forms aureovocin in lower yield than the B-96 mutant and does not produce component B.

The B-69 mutant does not form aureovocin but has retained the ability to produce CTC and TCN; the original culture of this mutant produced as little as a quarter of the levels of the two antibiotics yielded by the parent strain Bg. In strain B-69/D, a spontaneous variant of B-69, the yields increased by 50 per cent compared with those of the parent strain Bg. Preliminary

TABLE 1

Characteristics of two standard strains of S. *aureofaciens* and their blocked mutants after 14 days of cultivation on agar medium*

Strain† Standard parent	Mutant derivative	Colour of substrate mycelium	Diffusible pigment	Sporulation
Bg	—	yellow-orange to light yellow-brown	yellow	good, grey
—	B-96	dark brown	orange	abundant, dark grey
—	B-69/D	brown	yellow	sparse, light grey
84/25	—	brown-orange to yellow-brown	yellow	good, grey
—	MNNG-28	orange-brown	light orange	abundant, grey-brown
—	uv-61	cream (colourless)	none	none‡
—	MNNG-2	dark red-brown to dark red-violet	red-brown	abundant, dark grey
—	MNNG-10	brown-green	dark brown	good, grey-brown

* Sporulation medium with sucrose and dextrin (Herold et al., 1956); all cultivations were performed at 28 C.
† For the origin of strains see Fig. 1.
‡ No aerial mycelium is formed.

in vivo and *in vitro* experiments showed that both variants of the B-69 strain possess (in contrast with other mutants blocked in aureovocin biosynthesis) a completely inactive glucosidase, transforming aureovocidine (a glucone of aureovocin) to aureovocin (Matějů, unpublished results).

The uv-61 mutant does not produce tetracycline, aureovocin or the B component.

The remaining two metabolic types are characterized by the production of qualitatively different metabolites which do not occur in the standard strains. The MNNG-2 mutant, blocked in the 6-methylation step of the tetra-cycline skeleton, gives rise to demethyltetracyclines, the demethyl analogue of aureovocin (compound F) and compound G. The MNNG-10 mutant belongs to a category of leaky mutants producing, together with mutant metabolites, small amounts of tetracyclines.

It may be seen from Table 2 that the strains differ also in the production of pigments in submerged cultures.

b.   *Effect of chlortetracycline*

The strains compared also differed in their reaction to the concentration of CTC in the medium. Addition of CTC to sporulation medium inhibited the growth of all strains. The degree of resistance did not correspond to the actual production of CTC attained during submerged cultivation but was generally related to the potential ability to produce tetracycline antibiotics during cosynthesis. The uv-61 strain was most sensitive to the presence of CTC (inhibition at 100 μg CTC cm^{-3}). The 84/25 strain was able to grow at relatively high concentrations of the antibiotic (above 1000 μg cm^{-3}).

c.   *Stability*

Mutants MNNG-2, MNNG-10, MNNG-28 and B-69/D are relatively stable and retain their qualitative spectra of metabolites for prolonged periods of transfers on an agar medium. The B-96 mutant loses the ability to produce a green pigment under submerged conditions (without alteration in the produc-tion of aureovocin) in the third sporulation generation. In the uv-61 mutant, prolonged transfers result in the appearance of traces of aureovocin. None of the mutants reverted completely to the parent type.

d. *Viability and growth ability*

Spores of parent strains Bg and 84/25 and of mutants MNNG-2, MNNG-10 and MNNG-28 retain their viability for about 1–2 years, those of B-96 for 2–3 years and those of B-69/D for about 1 year. The nonsporulating mutant uv-61 survives for about 1 month at 4°C and for about 3 months at room temperature. Under submerged conditions (Herold *et al.*, 1956), the highest

TABLE 2

Biosynthetic characteristics of two standard strains of S. *aureofaciens* and their blocked mutants*

| Strain | | Mutant group† | Production of tetracyclines (μg cm^{-3}) | Type of metabolites produced‡ | | | | | | | | | Pigment§ |
| Standard parent | Mutant derivative | | | Standard | | | | Mutant | | | | | |
				CTC, TCN	AVC§	B	C	DCT, DTC	F	G	J	K	
Bg	—	—	400	+	+	+	+						brown-orange
—	B-96	IIa	0	—	+	+	+	—	—	—	—	—	dark green
—	B-69/D	IV	600	+	—	—	+	—	—	—	—	—	light brown
84/25	—	—	2000	+	+	+	+						brown
—	MNNG-28	IIb	0	—	+	—	+	—	—	—	—	—	light brown
—	uv-61	V	0	—	—	—	+	—	—	+	—	—	cream
—	MNNG-2	VI	100	—	—	—	+	+	+	—	—	—	red-violet
—	MNNG-10	IX	150	+	—	—	+	—	—	—	+	+	brown-green-black

* Cultivation under submerged conditions according to Herold *et al.* (1956).

† See Blumauerová *et al.* (1969).

‡ Abbreviations: CTC, chlortetracycline; TCN, tetracycline; AVC, aureovocin; DCT, demethylchlortetracycline; DTC, demethyltetracycline. The structures of the other substances (B, C, F, G, J and K) have not yet been established; for their preliminary characterization see Blumauerová *et al.* (1969).

§ In submerged culture after 96 hours of cultivation.

rate of growth and greatest amount of mycelial growth is exhibited by strain B-96. Yields lower than those of the parent strains are obtained with mutants MNNG-2, MNNG-10 and, usually, MNNG-28.

GENETICS

a. *Mutability*

During isolation of genetically labelled (auxotrophic or streptomycin-resistant) mutants for recombination studies, differences in the response to mutagenic agents were observed, both between the two parent strains and between their blocked mutant descendants (Table 3). Comparison of the total auxotroph yields showed no correlation between strain origin and the type of mutagenic treatment. For instance, in strain B-96 obtained from strain Bg after uv irradiation, auxotrophic mutations were induced with an approximately identical (relatively low) frequency both by uv irradiation and by N-methyl-N'-nitro-N-nitrosoguanidine (MNNG). On the other hand, strain B-69/D derived from the same parent yielded 4 times as many auxotrophs as strain B-96 after treatment with MNNG. The high mutability of strain B-69/D was apparent also in the yields of spontaneous mutants. Similar differences in total mutability were observed in strain MNNG-28 as compared with MNNG-2 and MNNG-10.

Most auxotrophs isolated from standard strains as well as from their mutants required arginine. The frequency of *arg* mutants, similarly to the spectrum of other growth requirements, was characteristic for each of the strains irrespective of their origin. Hence it has not been generally possible to isolate identical type of auxotrophs from individual strains representing different metabolic types from the point of view of secondary metabolites. Spectra of auxotrophic mutations remained usually similar or identical even in second-step auxotrophs isolated from the first-step ones by further mutagenic treatment (Blumauerová *et al.*, 1973).

In strain 84/25 obtained by several selection steps from strain Bg, the increase in biosynthetic activity seems to be accompanied by changes in the genome which influence total mutability. In comparison with strain Bg, strain 84/25 yielded more than 4 times as many unidentified auxotrophs. On the other hand the yield of auxotrophs from strain 84/25, requiring other factors than arginine, was the lowest of all strains tested and was restricted to lysine mutants only which were isolated neither from strain Bg nor from other blocked mutants. In contrast to strain Bg, strain 84/25 also gave rise to spontaneous mutants all of which required arginine.

Mutants resistant to higher levels of streptomycin ($100-1000 \, \mu g \, cm^{-3}$) were isolated only from strains Bg, MNNG-28, MNNG-2 and MNNG-10. The extreme sensitivity of strains 84/25, B-69/D and B-96 to streptomycin obviously

TABLE 3

Comparison of mutability of two standard strains of S. *aureofaciens* and their blocked mutants referring to the isolation of auxotrophic and streptomycin-resistant mutants

| Strain | Total yield of auxotrophs (%)* | | | Total yield of *arg* mutants (%)§ | Mutants requiring factors other than arginine | | Unidentified (%)§ | Total yield of uv-induced *str* mutants‖ (%) |
	Spontaneous	Induced with uv	MNNG†		Total yield (%)§	Spectrum of requirements‖		
Bg	0	3.75	1.11	90.2	7.1	Gly/Ser; Met; Tyr	2.7	0.00001
B-96	0	0.48	0.53	92.6	5.0	Ile + Val	2.4	0
B-69D	0.55	0.84	2.18	80.0	14.5	Cis; Gly/Ser; Ade	5.5	0
84/25	0.39	1.70	0.70	86.9	0.2	Lys	11.9	0
MNNG-28	0	0.63	0.53	79.5	17.1	Met; Gly/Ser; Trp + Tyr; Ade/Gua	3.4	0.00004
uv-61	non-sporulating strain, not very suitable for genetic manipulation							
MNNG-2	0	0.79	1.35	65.0	21.4	Cys; Gly/Ser; Ile + Val; Met; Tyr; Ade/Gua; Ura	13.6	0.0001
MNNG-10	0	0.49	1.46	84.4	11.2	Gly/Ser; Ade/Gua	4.4	0.00004

* Summarized frequencies found both by the total isolation and the delayed enrichment method (Blumauerová *et al.*, 1973), expressed as percentages of surviving populations.

† *N*-methyl-*N'*-nitro-*N*-nitrosoguanidine (1 mg or 3 mg cm⁻³) applied at pH 9.0 for 30, 60 and 120 min.

§ Percentage of the total number of mutants isolated.

‖ Requirements: +, simultaneous; /, alternative.

¶ Only stable mutants resistant to high levels of streptomycin (100–1000 μg cm⁻³) are included here. Such mutants did not occur either spontaneously or after treatment with MNNG. For the method of isolation see Blumauerová *et al.* (1972).

correlates with their increased resistance towards their own metabolites (tetracyclines and aureovocin, respectively).

b. *Sexual behaviour*

When crossing auxotrophic mutants derived from standard parent strains as well as from their blocked mutants, no pronounced sexuality was observed. Irrespective of their origin, the *arg* mutants were always recipients. Mutants with other growth requirements were either recipients or donors, depending on the sexuality of the complementary partner even if they were derived from the same parent. In crosses where one of the partners was a mutant derived from B-69/D, a relatively high frequency of recombinations (10^{-1}–10^{-2}) was observed in comparison with the frequency of recombinants in other types of crosses (10^{-4}–10^{-7}).

ULTRASTRUCTURE

When studying the ultrastructure of submerged cultures of both standard strains and their blocked mutants structures were found that are characteristic of the genus *Streptomyces* (Williams *et al.*, 1973). Mesosomes of all three types (lamellar, tubular and vesicular) are shown in Fig. 2, (a), (b), (c). On the other hand, the fibrous sheath as a differentiated component of the mycelium could not be identified. The fibrous sheath is not an organic structural component, its presence probably characterizing aerial mycelium. It is subject to phenotypic influence.

Comparison of both strains of the standard metabolic type showed a relatively uniform ultrastructure in strain Bg throughout cultivation. Simple, morphologically undifferentiated filamentous cells were found to contain homogeneous cytoplasm without apparent vacuolization and to survive in the culture up to 72 h (Fig. 2, (d), (e), (f)). On the other hand, from the very beginning of cultivation the cells of strain 84/25 show different densities of cytoplasm and contain a relatively large number of mesosomes (Fig. 3, (a), (b)). Beginning at the 12th hour, vacuolization sets in, accompanied by a multiplication of membraneous, multi-lamellar bodies. After 72 h, the progressive vacuolization of cytoplasm approaches total cell lysis (Fig. 3, (c), (d)). In contrast with strain Bg, strain 84/25 is characterized by a high incidence of electron-dense ribosomeless bodies in cytoplasm which survive in cells together with remnants of the membrane system, even after autolysis of the surrounding cytoplasm. Ribosomes appear after 48 h in aggregating clusters. Strain 84/25 is characterized by extreme polymorphism but was never found to contain forms described by Kurylowicz and Malinowski (1972), viz. bulges extruded on the mycelial surface and considered to represent organelles in which antibiotic synthesis takes place.

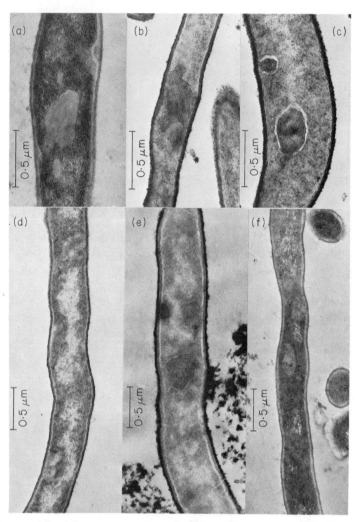

FIG. 2. Ultra-thin sections of cells from submerged cultures of *S. aureofaciens*. (a) Lamellar meso-some in strain B-69/D. (b) Tubular mesosome in strain B-96. (c) Vesicular mesosome in strain B-96. (d) Strain Bg after 12 hours' cultivation. (e) Strain Bg after 48 hours' cultivation. (f) Strain Bg after 72 hours' cultivation. For cultivation conditions see Hošťálek *et al.* (1969a). All samples were fixed in 6 per cent glutaraldehyde in 0.1 M cacodylate buffer pH 6.1 and in 1 per cent osmium tetroxide in phosphate buffer pH 6.1.

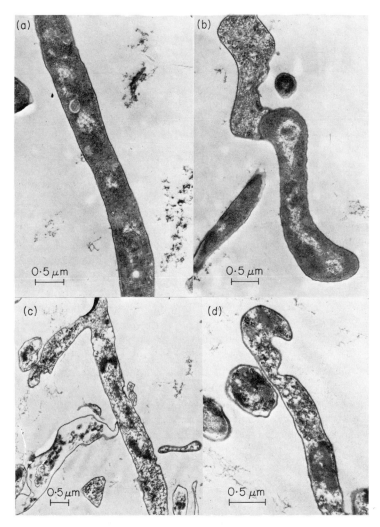

FIG. 3. Ultra-thin sections of cells from submerged culture of *S. aureofaciens*. (a) Strain 84/25 after 12 hours' cultivation. (b) Strain 84/25 after 12 hours' cultivation. (c) Strain 84/25 after 72 hours' cultivation. (d) Strain 84/25 after 72 hours' cultivation. For experimental conditions see Fig. 2.

Mutants derived from *S. aureofaciens* strain Bg differered markedly in ultrastructure from the parent strain. A characteristic feature of strain B-69/D is the formation of extracellular material. Likewise, typical progressive vacuolization of cytoplasm and irregularities in cell wall thickness at later hours of cultivation were observed (Fig. 4, (a), (b)). Numerous membraneous structures were found to occur in the periplasmic space between the cell wall and the plasma membrane.

Strain B-96 is characterized by a high incidence of large mesosomes in a relatively homogeneous cytoplasm (Fig. 4, (c)). Mesosomes decreased in number with age. The hyphae contain abundant membrane bodies in the periplasmic space (Fig. 4, (d)). The mycelium forms long hyphae without septa containing more nucleoids. The cell wall contains irregular thickened areas, mainly towards the end of cultivation (Fig. 4, (e)).

Most strains derived from *S. aureofaciens* strain 84/25 (MNNG-2, MNNG-10, MNNG-28), are characterized, like the parent strain, by progressive vacuolization, formation of electron-dense ribosome-less bodies and by irregularities in the membrane system. In addition, strains MNNG-2 and MNNG-28 are characterized by an overproduction of wall material probably to do with a disturbance in cell division which results in differences in the size and shape of cells and in an irregular distribution of wall material. In strain MNNG-2, the wall material often invaginates into the cell space (Fig. 5, (a), (b)). Strain MNNG-28 accumulates large layers of wall material mainly after 48 h of cultivation which results in extreme local thickenings of the cell wall (Fig. 5, (d)). Strain MNNG-28 is also characterized by the formation of extracellular material of meshed structure toward the end of cultivation (Fig. 5, (c)).

Strain MNNG-10 forms long unbranched filaments containing very few septa and is also characterized by anomalies in cell division reflected mainly during the second phase in the occurrence of membraneous bodies surrounded by wall material. The wall material probably penetrates into the cell interior and surrounds the membraneous bodies which lay originally in the periplasmic space (Fig. 6, (a), (b), (c), (d)). This strain is further defined by the production of extracellular material (Fig. 6, (d)).

The uv-61 mutant differs in its ultrastructure from other strains derived from *S. aureofaciens* 84/25. The cytoplasm is relatively homogeneous but there are apparent differences in its density in individual cells throughout cultivation. Besides cells with electron-transparent cytoplasm cells with homogenous electron-dense cytoplasm also occur. This mutant is characterized by anomalies in cell division—the cells branch imperfectly with indications of budding at various sites without actual division (Fig. 7, (a)). After 48 h, a pronounced multiplication of membranes may be observed in the periplasmic space, the cytoplasm bounded by the plasma membrane being pushed

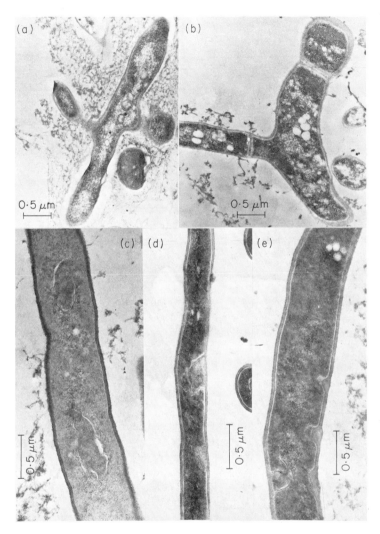

FIG. 4. Ultra-thin sections of cells from submerged culture of *S. aureofaciens.* (a) Strain B-69/D after 72 hours' cultivation. (b) Strain B-69/D after 48 hours' cultivation. (c) Strain B-96 after 48 hours' cultivation. (d) Strain B-96 after 72 hours' cultivation. (e) Strain B-96 after 72 hours' cultivation. For experimental conditions see Fig. 2.

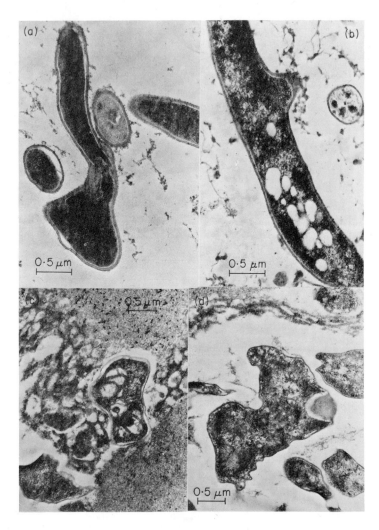

FIG. 5. Ultra-thin sections of cells from submerged culture of *S. aureofaciens*. (a) Strain MNNG-2 after 12 hours' cultivation. (b) Strain MNNG-2 after 72 hours' cultivation. (c) Strain MNNG-28 after 72 hours' cultivation. (d) Strain MNNG-28 after 72 hours' cultivation. For experimental conditions see Fig. 2.

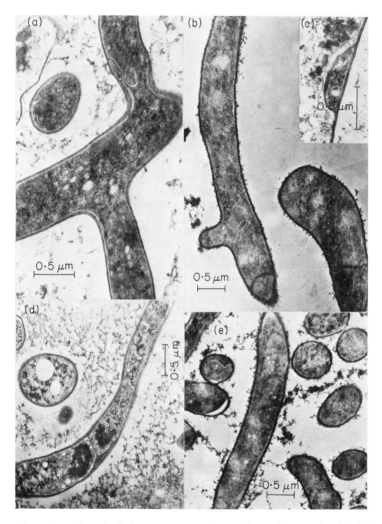

FIG. 6. Ultra-thin sections of cells from submerged culture of *S. aureofaciens*. (a) Strain MNNG-10 after 48 hours' cultivation. (b) Strain MNNG-10 after 12 hours' cultivation. (c) Strain MNNG-10 after 72 hours' cultivation. (d) Strain MNNG-10 after 72 hours' cultivation. (e) Strain MNNG-10 after 12 hours' cultivation. For experimental conditions see Fig. 2.

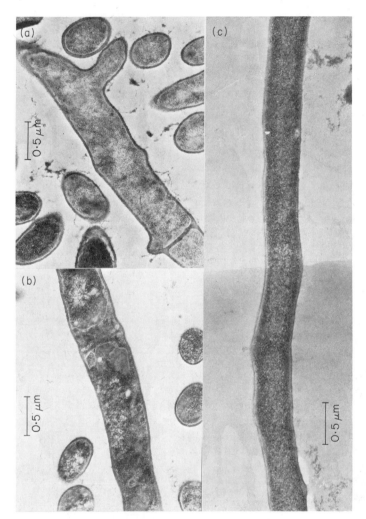

FIG. 7. Ultra-thin sections of cells from submerged culture of *S. aureofaciens*. (a) Strain uv-61 after 12 hours' cultivation. (b) Strain uv-61 after 48 hours' cultivation. (c) Strain uv-61 after 72 hours' cultivation. For experimental conditions see Fig. 2.

toward the cell interior (Fig. 7, (b)). After 72 h, the culture contains non-dividing, budding long filaments which still contain homogenous cytoplasm (Fig. 7, (c)).

All strains derived from the two parents are characterized by a relatively uniform appearance of their ultrastructure at the beginning of cultivation which differentiates with advancing age of the culture. Differences in the ultrastructure of individual strains are most pronounced towards the end of cultivation.

The activities of several enzymes holding key positions in the formation or in further metabolism of the building units of CTC, acetyl-CoA and malonyl-CoA, respectively were examined. Assays of pyruvate kinase and phospho-enolpyruvate carboxylase provided information on the possible meta-bolic fate of phosphoenolpyruvate; estimations of activity of citrate synthase and malate dehydrogenase supplied data on the activity of the tricarboxylic acid cycle; activities of acetyl-CoA carboxylase and malate dehydrogenase (de-carboxylating) indicated the role of lipogenesis in the metabolism of the strains examined (Table 4).

Comparison of the two strains with standard biosynthetic activities (Bg and 84/25) clearly shows differences in the activity of the tricarboxylic acid cycle. The enzyme activity in the low-production strain after 48 h (in the second, catabolic, phase of cultivation) attains values twice those of strain 84/25. No substantial differences were found in the activities of acetyl-CoA carboxylase and malate dehydrogenase (decarboxylating), both enzymes being most active during the first, anabolic, phase of cultivation. Significant differences were found in the activities of pyruvate kinase and phosphoenol-pyruvate carboxylase. Strain Bg showed two clear maxima during the anabolic as well as during the catabolic phase of cultivation. The highest activity of phosphoenolpyruvate carboxylase was reached during the ana-bolic phase, the enzyme having here a typical anaplerotic function in generat-ing the oxaloacetate required for the activity of the tricarboxylic acid cycle. During the catabolic phase the enzyme activity is lower. In Strain 84/25, the activity of pyruvate kinase in the catabolic phase sharply decreases, falling to its lowest value during the period of optimum antibiotic synthesis. As the rate of CTC formation increases, the activity of phosphoenolpyruvate carboxylase rises (at low activities of citrate synthase and malate dehydro-genase). This indicates increased formation of malonyl-CoA for tetracycline biosynthesis via decarboxylation of oxaloacetate (Běhal, unpublished results).

Fundamental differences in the activities of enzymes studied have been found in mutants derived from both parent strains. Mutant B-69/D has relatively low activities of tricarboxylic acid cycle enzymes during the ana-

TABLE 4

Activities of enzymes of two standard strains of *S. aureofaciens* and their blocked mutants during submerged cultivation*

Strain	Enzyme	Specific activity								
		12 h	18 h	24 h	36 h	48 h	60 h	72 h	84 h	96 h
Bg	Pyruvate kinase†	183	138	171	92	81	131	152	29	15
	PEP carboxylase‡	345 571	483 265	572 041	687 565	194 622	501 383	434 989	329 232	201 887
	AcetylCoA carboxylase§	124	209	144	126	68	0	0	0	0
	Malic enzyme‖	106	103	140	31	34	68	71	34	40
	Citrate synthase¶	293	269	261	175	164	250	318	443	473
	Malate dehydrogenase**	3 654	2 523	3 325	4 410	4 092	5 038	5 976	8 256	8 797
B-69/D	Pyruvate kinase	4	11	38	123	108	156	132	126	136
	PEP carboxylase	655 782	602 703	283 058	515 402	596 409	672 895	540 238	540 312	803 739
	Acetyl-CoA carboxylase	111	337	252	170	98	127	0	0	0
	Malic enzyme	17	43	88	158	57	64	54	43	49
	Citrate synthase	153	124	230	268	279	297	317	405	365
	Malate dehydrogenase	2 982	2 756	2 912	3 355	3 916	5 096	5 212	6 386	6 521
B-96	Pyruvate kinase	60	204	241	176	136	89	23	22	10
	PEP carboxylase	454 453	626 502	361 194	323 473	223 064	567 055	393 089	258 583	187 149
	Acetyl-CoA carboxylase	66	141	94	31	0	0	0	0	0
	Malic enzyme	174	136	191	102	52	34	20	52	15
	Citrate synthase	127	254	377	417	290	358	353	521	213
	Malate dehydrogenase	2 621	2 792	4 766	6 374	5 794	6 061	4 517	7 036	6 048
84/25	Pyruvate kinase	150	152	100	264	163	72	31	25	0
	PEP carboxylase	560 188	366 495	143 230	128 320	500 393	782 435	479 460	163 580	77 365
	Acetyl-CoA carboxylase	66	128	797	823	286	203	180	102	75
	Malic enzyme	12	25	17	11	7	2	0	0	0
	Citrate synthase	138	215	189	151	142	208	286	221	206
	Malate dehydrogenase	2 770	4 256	3 946	3 280	3 128	4 120	4 920	4 615	4 270

Strain	Enzyme	1	2	3	4	5	6	7	8	9
MNNG-28	Pyruvate kinase	31	21	8	6	3	3	0	0	0
	PEP carboxylase	182 925	136 326	162 035	269 805	59 001	53 289	27 492	36 902	30 398
	Acetyl-CoA carboxylase	105	165	197	145	10	0	0	0	0
	Malic enzyme	14	13	7	10	10	8	9	4	11
	Citrate synthase	203	218	211	145	262	254	199	225	212
	Malate dehydrogenase	3 376	3 144	1 971	3 187	1 900	1 946	2 538	3 365	2 679
uv-61	Pyruvate kinase	10	104	95	138	160	160	171	196	41
	PEP carboxylase	362 677	322 566	365 977	214 059	172 856	117 069	678 306	733 252	111 508
	Acetyl-CoA carboxylase	166	163	154	108	123	0	0	0	0
	Malic enzyme	4	9	7	4	10	9	6	8	6
	Citrate synthase	225	294	394	300	331	327	477	426	386
	Malate dehydrogenase	2 559	3 083	2 894	5 171	4 675	4 616	8 170	7 848	5 080
MNNG-2	Pyruvate kinase	64	156	177	266	154	189	121	99	30
	PEP carboxylase	700 060	308 425	546 766	871 600	304 529	501 955	357 991	526 150	108 905
	Acetyl-CoA carboxylase	189	349	212	45	10	8	6	0	0
	Malic enzyme	81	84	116	177	180	354	255	283	350
	Citrate synthase	195	206	240	331	331	354	255	283	350
	Malate dehydrogenase	2 520	2 320	3 291	3 868	4 676	4 613	5 470	4 432	4 421
MNNG-10	Pyruvate kinase	31	79	93	112	107	55	61	49	28
	PEP carboxylase	68 152	106 489	112 155	295 736	324 666	146 756	151 166	238 343	268 879
	Acetyl-CoA carboxylase	0	0	109	30	0	0	0	0	0
	Malic enzyme	10	13	16	12	9	6	7	6	6
	Citrate synthase	190	266	252	298	342	173	252	421	201
	Malate deyhydrgenase	2 823	2 791	2 266	5 041	3 793	2 871	3 046	3 401	3 215

* Enzyme activities were measured in cell-free extracts of mycelia. For cultivation conditions and experimental techniques see Hošťálek et al. (1969a).
† ATP: pyruvate phosphotransferase (E.C. 2.1.7.40). Activity in nmol NAD formed per min per mg protein (Bücher and Pfleiderer, 1955.)
‡ Orthophosphate: oxaloacetate carboxylyase (phosphorylating) (E.C.4.1.1.31). Activity in d.p.m. per mg protein. (Voříšek et al., 1969.)
§ Acetyl-CoA: Coligase (ADP) (E.C.6.4.1.2). Activity in d.p.m. per mg protein. (Běhal and Vaněk, 1970.)
‖ L-malate: NADP oxidoreductase (decarboxylating) (E.C.1.1.1.40.). Activity in nmol NADP formed per min per mg protein. (Jechová et al., 1969.)
¶ Citrate oxaloacetatelyase (CoA-acetylating) (E.C.4.1.3.7.). Activity in nmol CoASH liberated per min per mg protein. (Hošťálek et al., 1963b.)
** L-malate: NAD oxidoreductase (E.C.1.1.1.37). Activity in nmol NAD formed per min per mg protein (Hošťálek et al., 1969a.)

bolic phase. Strain B-96 has much higher activities of enzymes of the tricarboxylic acid cycle than the parent strain Bg.

In contrast with the parent strain 84/25 the MNNG-2 mutant showed higher maxima of pyruvate kinase, PEP carboxylase and citrate synthase during the first 36 hours of cultivation. In the MNNG-10 mutant, relatively low activities of PEP carboxylase and malate dehydrogenase (decarboxylating) were observed throughout the cultivation period. Strain MNNG-28 differs from the other strains in having a very low activity of pyruvate kinase and PEP carboxylase and in showing a decrease of most enzyme activities after 36 hours' cultivation. The uv-61 mutant is characterized by very high activity of phosphoenolpyruvate carboxylase, pyruvate kinase and citrate synthase compared with those found in the parent strain. The activities of acetyl-CoA carboxylase and malate dehydrogenase (decarboxylating) in all the strains indicate that in no case is a metabolic block connected with changes in the utilization of acetyl-CoA or malonyl-CoA in lipid metabolism (Table 4).

The sequence of enzyme activities, in the standard Bg strain, suggests a typical biphasic character of culture development under the given experimental conditions. On the other hand, mutant strains showed many anomalies indicating major changes in the general metabolic pattern.

Determinations of cytochrome activities confirmed differences in activities of energy metabolism in the various mutants. From estimations of the differential spectra of the cytochromes one may conclude that the amount of cytochrome a and b in the mycelium of the tested strains was relatively low. On the other hand, the pronounced absorption in the gamma region indicates substantial differences in the concentration of cytochrome c. We found relatively high activity of cytochrome c in strains Bg and 84/25 at the beginning of cultivation. Strain 84/25 was characterized by a rapid drop of activity in submerged cultivation after 24 h. A relatively high activity of cytochrome was detected in strains B-69/D and uv-61, all other mutants displaying only minute activities.

Discussion

The results obtained represent only a fragmentary list of some of the properties of several strains of a broad set of blocked mutants isolated after mutagenic treatment. However some conclusions can be drawn on the role of the genome in secondary biosynthesis in S. aureofaciens.

Comparison of the metabolic activity of the low-production parent strain (Bg) with the production descendant (84/25) confirmed that increased antibiotic production is due to the concerted action of many biochemical changes which are accompanied by changes in mutability, ultrastructure and other properties, including resistance towards a strain's own metabolite. The basis of high productivity lies in changes in metabolic pathways and control systems which permit the production organism (in contrast with the wild parent) to express that fraction of the genome which in the standard strain usually remains unexpressed. (Its expression is possible only under certain conditions of nutritional limitation, e.g. at a low concentration of inorganic phosphate in the medium—Hošťálek and Vaněk, 1973.)

The results obtained also showed that hereditary changes in the biosynthetic pathway proper which lead to the formation of mutant metabolites do not exist alone but are closely linked to other changes in cell metabolism. The data available on the properties of blocked mutants are insufficient to draw conclusions on the relationship between the various reactions of the biosynthetic pathway and the general metabolism of the producer but they do indicate that the individual steps of tetracycline biosynthesis are tightly coupled with seemingly remote processes.

In strains blocked in oxidation of the ring A of the tetracycline skeleton which produce aureovocin (B-96, MNNG-28) changes were found in ultrastructure, activities of enzymes of the tricarboxylic acid cycle and associated reactions and in cytochrome spectra. Likewise, a block in the biosynthesis of aureovocin B-69/D), or in the methylation of the tetracycline skeleton (MNNG-2) is accompanied by changes in the character of the cell wall and in the activities of the enzymes examined. Pronounced changes in ultrastructure as well as in general metabolism were found in mutants obtained from the production strain 84/25 (the MNNG-10 mutant with a markedly depressed production activity and suppressed ability to form aureovocin, and the uv-61 mutant which is completely blocked in overall tetracycline biosynthesis). Both mutants are characterized by very low activity of malate dehydrogenase (decarboxylating) throughout cultivation. In all the mutants studied, apparent point mutation (McCormick, 1969) is accompanied by changes in various biological phenomena.

A special position among the mutants examined·is held by strain MNNG-28. This mutant is probably double-blocked, both in the oxidation of ring A (it produces aureovocin) and in control mechanisms of the glycolytic pathway. After termination of the first, anabolic phase of cultivation, growth ceases and biochemical activity decreases. The new synthesis of pyruvate kinase and phosphoenolpyruvate carboxylase and the new increase in metabolic activity do not occur. In contrast with all the strains studied, this metabolic block prevents the onset of the second, catabolic phase of cultivation.

When assessing the metabolic phases and the conditions under which a secondary metabolite is synthesized, one must bear in mind the important fact that we are following the life expressions of an organism under practically nonphysiological conditions of carbohydrate and nitrogen overfeeding. The cause of the biphasic character of culture development under these condi-

G

tions lies apparently in the necessity to switch on the end of the vegetative cycle (anabolic phase) to the qualitatively new type of physiological state characterized in low-production standard strains by catabolic processes. Under given experimental conditions a high level of nutrients induces, after 48 h of cultivation, the synthesis of enzymes de novo (Ramadan, unpublished results). A rapid degradation of carbohydrates sets in while growth and antibiotic synthesis comes to a stop.

The biochemical basis of productivity must be sought in changes in the genome leading to leaky mutations in catabolic processes. In contrast with the wild type, production variants are seen to form CTC in quantity during the second phase of cultivation. The "tetracycline" part of the genome is expressed, an amphibolic type of metabolism ensues and intermediates formed during dissimilation of the sugar are not drawn into energy-producing metabolism but rather are exploited for secondary biosynthesis. In this process one may see a certain detoxicating mechanism whereby the accumulating intermediates are drained by the energetically nondemanding process of formation of the ketide polymer. However, only those mutants are viable where the specific changes in cell metabolism are accompanied by an increased resistance to their own metabolite.

Acknowledgement

This work was supported by the International Atomic Energy Agency under research contract No. 845/RB.

References

Běhal, V. and Vaněk, Z. (1970). Folia microbiol., Praha, 15, 354.
Blumauerová, M., Mraček, M., Vondráčková, J. Podojil, M., Hošťálek, Z. and Vaněk, Z. (1969). Folia microbiol, Praha, 14, 215.
Blumauerová, M., Hošťálek, Z. and Vaněk, Z. (1972). "Fermentation Technology Today" (Ed. G. Terui), p. 223. Society of Fermentation Technology, Japan, Osaka.
Blumauerová, M. Hošťálek, Z. and Vaněk, Z. (1973). Studia Biophys. 36/37, 311.
Bücher, T. and Pfleiderer, G. (1955). "Methods in Enzymology" (Eds S. P. Colowick and N. O. Kaplan), vol. 1, p. 435. Academic Press, New York.
Herold, M., Bělík, E. and Doskočil, J. (1956). Giorn. Microbiol. 2, 302.
Hošťálek, Z. and Vaněk, Z. (1973). "Genetics of Industrial Microorganisms. Actinomycetes and Fungi" (Eds Z. Vaněk, Z. Hošťálek and J. Cudlín), p. 353. Academia, Prague.
Hošťálek, Z., Tintěrová, M. Jechová, V. Blumauerová, M., Suchý, J. and Vaněk, Z. (1969a). Biotechnol. Bioeng. 11, 539.
Hošťálek, Z., Ryabushko, T. A., Cudlín, J. and Vaněk, Z. (1969b). Folia Microbiol. 14, 121.
Jechová, V., Hošťálek, Z. and Vaněk, Z. (1969). Folia Microbiol. 14, 128.

Kurylowicz, W. and Malinowski, K. (1972). *Post. Hig. Med. Dosw.* **26**, 563.

McCormick, J. R. D. (1969). "Genetics and Breeding of Streptomyces" (Eds G. Sermonti and M. Alačević), p. 163. Yugoslav Acad. Sci. and Arts, Zagreb.

Vaněk, Z., Cudlín, J., Blumauerová, M. and Hošťálek, Z. (1971). *Folia Microbiol.* **16**, 227.

Vokoun, J., Vaněk, Z. Podojil, M., Blumauerová, M., Vondráček, M. and Benda, A. (1973). *Czech. Pat.* 153, 722.

Vořišek, J., Powell, A. J. and Vaněk, Z. (1969). *Folia Microbiol.* **14**, 398.

Williams, S. T., Sharples, G. P. and Bradshaw, R. M. (1973). "Actinomycetales: Characteristics and Practical Importance" (Eds G. Sykes and F. A. Skinner), p. 113. Academic Press, New York and London.

Final steps in the biosynthesis of cephalosporin C

M. LIERSCH, J. NÜESCH and H. J. TREICHLER

Research Department, Pharmaceutical Division, Ciba-Geigy Ltd, Basel, Switzerland

Summary

Besides cephalosporin C, some tripeptides, penicillin N, and deacetyl-cephalosporin C are formed during the growth cycle of *Cephalosporium* species (Lemke and Brannon, 1972; Fujisawa *et al.*, 1973).

In addition we were able to isolate and characterize another fermentation product from *Cephalosporium acremonium* cultures: deacetoxycephalosporin C (Liersch *et al.*, 1973b; Nüesch *et al.*, 1975).

Mutants of *Cephalosporium acremonium* which produce deacetoxycephalo-sporin C alone and deacetoxycephalosporin C together with deacetyl-cephalosporin C have been isolated. By disrupting mycelium we were able to detect two enzymes, one of which catalyses the hydroxylation of deacetoxy-cephalosporin C at the 3-CH$_3$-group, and the other the acetylation of deacetylcephalosporin C to cephalosporin C. We conclude that deacetoxy-cephalosporin C and deacetylcephalosporin C are late intermediates in the biosynthesis of cephalosporin C.

Some properties of the above enzymes are presented.

Introduction

In 1963, Demain published a hypothetical unified pathway for the bio-synthesis of the antibiotic cephalosporin C in *Cephalosporium* sp. (Demain, 1963). According to this scheme the synthesis proceeds through intermediate formation of a deacetoxycephalosporin C and a deacetylcephalosporin C, both compounds containing α-aminoadipic acid in the L-configuration. Similar pathways were outlined by Abraham and Newton (1961, 1965, 1967).

We have tried to find out whether deacetoxycephalosporin C and deacetyl-cephalosporin C are true intermediates in the biosynthetic pathway. By disrupting mycelium of the fungus *Cephalosporium acremonium* we were able to detect and isolate two enzyme systems catalysing the hydroxylation of deacetoxycephalosporin C and the acetylation of deacetylcephalosporin C, respectively.

Materials and methods

MATERIALS

The different cephalosporins (Na salts) were provided by Ciba–Geigy Ltd, Basel (Switzerland); all other chemicals used were purchased from commercial sources. Deacetoxycephalosporin C produced by a mutant strain $(8650\text{-}S^-\text{-}M26\text{-}I27a/\overset{.}{2})$ of *C. acremonium* was isolated as described by Liersch *et al.*, (1973b). Acetyl Coenzyme A Li_3 trihydrate, 85 per cent A grade, and *O*-acetyl-L-serine, A grade were purchased from Calbiochem (Lucerne, Switzerland). *O*-acetyl-DL-homoserine was prepared as described by Nagai and Flavin (1967). (Acetyl-1-C-14)-coenzyme A $(59\ mCi\ mmol^{-1})$ was obtained from the Radiochemical Centre, Amersham. Sephadex G-200 was received from Pharmacia (Uppsala, Sweden). D-amino acid oxidase (EC 1.4.3.3) from hog kidney, oxidized and reduced nicotinamide adenine dinucleotide phosphates (NAD^+, NADH) and the corresponding trinucleotide phosphates ($NADP^+$, NADPH) were purchased from Boehringer Mannheim GmbH (Mannheim, Germany).

SEPARATION AND ANALYSIS

Thin-layer chromatography was carried out on cellulose precoated plates (E. Merck AG, Darmstadt, Germany) as described before (Benz *et al.*, 1971) with the following solvent systems. Solvent A, isopropanol–formic acid–water (77:4:19, by volume); solvent B, *n*-butanol–acetone–diethylamine–water (37:37:8:18, by volume); solvent C, *n*-butanol–acetic acid–pyridine–water (37.5:7.5:25:30, by volume); solvent D, *n*-butanol–ethanol–water–acetic acid (50:15:20:15, by volume); solvent E, 66 per cent acetonitrile; solvent F, 80 per cent phenol; solvent G, *n*-butanol–formic acid–water (4:1:4, by volume, upper phase); solvent H, *n*-butanol–acetic acid–water (11:3:7, by volume, upper phase); solvent I, 70 per cent *n*-propanol.

Separation of the cephalosporins was performed on a Technicon TS M 1 amino acid autoanalyser (Technicon Corporation, Tarryton, NY, USA) as described by Arx *et al.* (1974). Analysis of the cephalosporins by high-pressure liquid chromatography was done according to Konecny *et al.* (1973).

For the polarographic measurement of the oxygen uptake an oxygen electrode (Model YSI Biological Oxygen Monitor, Yellow Springs Instrument Co., Yellow Springs, Ohio, USA) was used.

CULTURAL CONDITIONS AND ENZYME PREPARATIONS

A mutant strain $(8650\text{-}S^-\text{-}M26)$ of *C. acremonium* was grown and used for preparing the crude cell-free extract as described previously (Benz *et al.*, 1971). The crude extract from 72 hours grown mycelium in 0.05 M tris-HCl buffer pH 7.2 (protein concentration *c.* 20 mg cm^{-3}) was used as enzyme preparation for the hydroxylation of deacetoxycephalosporin C. During use it was kept under argon.

Purification of the deacetylcephalosporin C O-acetyltransferase enzyme was done with a cell free extract from 96 hours old cells in 0.06 M phosphate buffer pH 7. The crude extract was fractionated with solid $(NH_4)_2SO_4$, the transacetylase activity precipitating between 0 per cent and 33 per cent $(NH_4)_2SO_4$ saturation. This fraction was dissolved in 0.06 M phosphate buffer, pH 7, and fractionated again with solid $(NH_4)_2SO_4$. The enzyme activity precipitated between 25 per cent and 33 per cent $(NH_4)_2SO_4$ saturation. This fraction was dissolved in buffer as above and 1.5 cm^3 was applied to a Sephadex G-200 column (0.9 × 60 cm) equilibrated with the same buffer. Fractions of 1.7 cm^3 were collected and the main activity of the enzyme was received in fractions 10 to 13.

The acetone powder of the acetyl hydrolase from *Bacillus subtilis* ATCC 6633 was prepared as described before (Nüesch *et al.*, 1967).

Mutant strains which show no deacetoxycephalosporin C hydroxylase activity $(8650\text{-}S^-\text{-}M26\text{-}I27a/2)$ and no deacetylcephalosporin C O-acetyltransferase activity $(8650\text{-}S^-\text{-}M26\text{-}CP52c)$ have been isolated as described by Nüesch *et al.* (1975). The two mutant strains have been grown and treated under the same conditions as the parental strain, $8650\text{-}S^-\text{-}M26$, of *C. acremonium*.

ENZYME ASSAYS

The assay for hydroxylation of deacetoxycephalosporin C was done as a linked enzymatic assay (assay A). The incubation mixture contained 20 μmol of tris-HCl-buffer pH 7.2, 100 mμmol of deacetoxycephalosporin C, 50 mμmol of NADH, 0.1 mμmol of $MnCl_2$, 1 mg of protein and in addition trans-acetylase enzyme (40 μg of protein of fraction No. 12 of Sephadex G-200 gelfiltrate, see above) and 50 mμmol of (acetyl-1-C-14)-coenzyme A (5.6 ×

10° cpm μmol^{-1}). The reaction mixture (total volume 0.25 cm^3) was incubated for four hours at 23°C with shaking with air as gas phase. The reaction was stopped by heating for 30 seconds at 100°C. Aliquots of the reaction mixture were then applied to thin-layer chromatography together with 20 mμmol of cephalosporin C and developed with solvent system A. The cephalosporin C spots ($R_F = 0.25$) were detected under uv light (254 nm), scraped off the plates and counted in a toluene scintillator.

Oxygen consumption during the hydroxylation of deacetoxycephalosporin C was followed by an oxygen electrode at 30°C for 10 minutes. The reaction mixture (assay B) in a total volume of 3 cm^3 contained tris-HCl buffer pH 8 (100 μmol), deacetoxycephalosporin C (20 μmol), NADH (10 μmol), MnCl$_2$ (2 μmol) and the enzyme (6 mg). Assay of deacetylcephalosporin C O-acetyltransferase was done as follows. The incubation mixture (assay C) containing 20 μmol of phosphate buffer pH 7.5, 100 mμmol of deacetylcephalosporin C, 50 mμmol of (acetyl-1-C-14)-coenzyme A (5.6 × 10^5 cpm μmol^{-1}) and 20 μg of protein in a total volume of 0.25 cm^3 was incubated at 23°C for 30 minutes. At the end of this period the reaction mixture was stopped by heating and analysed by thin-layer chromatography as described in assay A. One unit of the enzyme was defined as the amount required to form 1 mμmol of cephalosporin C per hour under the experimental conditions. If other deacetylcephalosporin C derivatives or hydroxyamino acids were used as substrates instead of deacetylcephalosporin C, the analysis by thin-layer chromatography was done in the presence of the corresponding O-acetyl derivatives instead of cephalosporin C. The zones of the O-acetylcephalosporins were detected under uv light, those of the O-acetyl amino acids by spraying with 0.1 per cent ninhydrin solution in alcohol.

The oxidative deamination experiments with different cephalosporin derivatives were performed as already described (Benz et al., 1971); 0.15 mg of D-amino acid oxidase (EC 1.4.3.3) was used as enzyme (Mazzeo and Romeo, 1972) in the test assay.

For treatment of the radioactive cephalosporin C with acetyl hydrolase, 2 mg of acetone powder were added to the reaction mixtures of assay A and C after the reaction has been stopped. After one hour of enzymatic treatment at 23°C the reaction mixtures were analysed by thin-layer chromatography as described above. During all enzymatic assays, controls without substrates and without enzymes were incubated and the values obtained were subtracted as blanks.

Results

During our studies of the biosynthesis of cephalosporin C we were able to isolate and characterize deacetoxycephalosporin C for the first time in a culture filtrate of *C. acremonium* mutant 8650-S⁻-M26-127a/2 (Liersch *et al.*, 1973). The antibiotic was recovered and purified in the normal way, and the identification was made by uv, nmr and ir spectra, thin-layer, paper and high-pressure liquid chromatography, amino acid and polarometric analysis. The isolated product behaved identically with chemically synthesized deacetoxycephalosporin C and some analytical data are reported in Tables 1 to 4 and Figs 1 and 2.

The oxidative deamination experiments (Table 5) show that deacetoxy-cephalosporin C isolated from a culture filtrate contains the D-α-aminoadipyl side chain. Acid hydrolysis of the compound with 6 N HCl in a sealed tube at

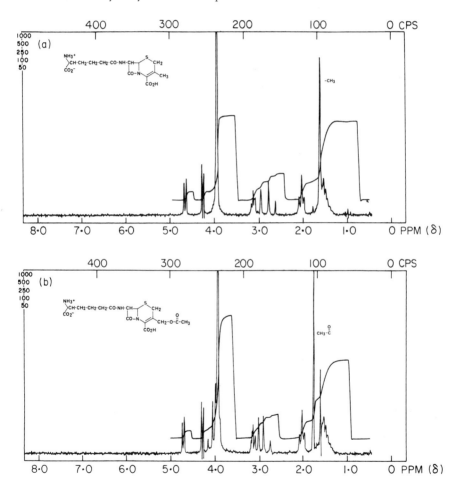

Fig. 1. Nuclear magnetic resonance of 0.3 M deacetoxycephalosporin C (*a*) and 0.3 M cephalosporin C (*b*); Na salts in D₂O (100 Mc).

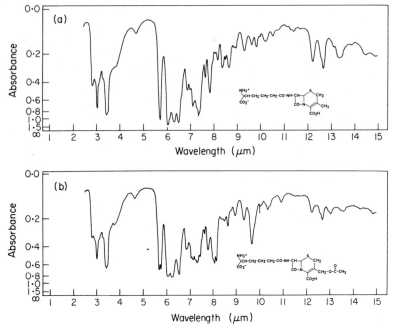

F$_{IG}$. 2. Infrared spectrum of deacetoxycephalosporin C (*a*) and cephalosporin C (*b*); Na salts in Nujol paste.

120°C for 24 hours resulted in the formation of D-α-aminoadipic acid besides other degradation products. The amino acid was detected by thin-layer chromatography (see Table 1) and separated from other amino acids by an amino acid analyser (see Table 3).

In addition we could transform deacetoxycephalosporin C with a crude enzyme preparation of *C. acremonium* (8650-S⁻-M26, parental strain) into cephalosporin C via deacetylcephalosporin C. As can be seen in Fig. 3 the hydroxylation is linear with protein concentration. Table 6 shows the requirements for this hydroxylation reaction at the 3-CH$_3$-group with deacetoxycephalosporin C as substrate. The radioactive product formed was identified as cephalosporin C by chromatographic comparison with an authentic reference sample in different solvent systems (Table 1). In addition the radioactive cephalosporin C was treated with an acetyl hydrolase from *Bacillus subtilis*. Afterwards no radioactivity could be detected in the cephalosporin C region or in the deacetylcephalosporin C formed. These results indicate that *C. acremonium* contains an enzyme system which transforms deacetoxycephalosporin C into its corresponding C-10-hydroxy derivative. The oxygen requirement for the hydroxylation of deacetoxycephalosporin C (tested under the conditions of assay A) is shown in Table 7. Without oxygen in the gas phase

TABLE 1

Thin-layer chromatography of cephalosporins and some amino acids. 20 mμmol of each compound were applied to the chromatograms. The (C-14) products were formed according to assay A or C respectively

Compound	R_F values in solvent system								
	A	B	C	D	E	F	G	H	I
7-Aminocephalosporanic acid (7-ACA)	0.23	0.40	0.18	0.00	0.57	0.82	—	—	—
7-Aminodeacetylcephalosporanic acid (7-ADCA)	0.18	0.26	0.18	0.19	0.46	0.67	—	—	—
Cephalosporin C	0.25	0.00	0.27	0.22	0.38	0.72	0.29	0.44	0.33
Deacetylcephalosporin C	0.16	0.00	0.17	0.14	0.25	0.52	0.25	0.36	0.16
Deacetylcephalosporin C lactone	0.20	0.00	0.37	0.17	0.45	0.90	—	0.47	—
Deacetoxycephalosporin C	0.21	0.18	0.20	0.33	0.27	0.62	0.33	0.49	0.22
Deacetoxycephalosporin C (from strain 8650-S⁻-M26-127a/2)	0.21	0.18	0.20	0.33	0.27	0.62	0.33	0.49	0.22
Cephacetrile (Ba-36278)	0.71	0.43	0.70	0.55	0.77	0.65	—	—	—
Deacetylcephacetrile (Ba-40161)	0.53	0.39	0.56	0.39	0.68	0.50	—	—	—
Cephaloram (Ba-38671)	0.90	0.75	0.91	0.83	0.90	0.93	—	—	—
Deacetylcephaloram (Ba-49419)	0.80	0.67	0.82	0.74	0.83	0.83	—	—	—
O-Acetyl-L-serine	0.45	—	0.40	—	—	0.50	—	—	—
O-Acetyl-DL-homoserine	0.74	0.34	0.46	—	—	0.78	—	—	—
D-α-Aminoadipic acid	0.38	0.07	—	0.33	0.27	0.21	—	—	0.24
(C-14) product formed from:									
7-ADCA	0.23	0.40	0.18	0.00	0.57	0.82	—	—	—
Deacetylcephalosporin C	0.25	0.00	0.27	0.22	0.38	0.72	0.29	0.44	0.33
Deacetoxycephalosporin C	0.25	0.00	0.27	0.22	0.38	0.72	0.29	0.44	0.33
Deacetylcephacetrile (Ba-40161)	0.71	0.43	0.70	0.55	0.77	0.65	—	—	—
Deacetylcephaloram (Ba-49419)	0.90	0.75	0.91	0.83	0.90	0.93	—	—	—

TABLE 2

Separation of cephalosporins by high-pressure liquid chromatography

Compound	Retention time min
Deacetylcephalosporin C lactone	5.5
Deacetylcephalosporin C	10.0
Deacetoxycephalosporin C	11.0
Cephalosporin C	12.4
Deacetoxycephalosporin C (from strain 8650-S⁻-M26-I27a/2)	11.0

TABLE 3

Separation of cephalosporins by an amino acid analyser. 20 µl samples of 5×10^{-3} M solutions of each compound in 0.2 M sodium citrate buffer pH 2 were applied to the column

Compound	Retention time min
Cephalosporin C	54
Deacetoxycephalosporin C	59
Deacetylcephalosporin C	93
Deacetylcephalosporin C lactone	93
Deacetoxycephalosporin C (from strain 8650-S⁻-M26-I27a/2)	59
DL-α-Aminoadipic acid	74
DL-α-Aminoadipic acid (from acid hydrolysis of deacetoxycephalo-sporin C from strain 8650-S⁻-M26-I27a/2)	74

TABLE 4

Specific rotation of cephalosporins in water

Compound	Specific rotation $[\alpha]_D^{20}$	Concentration %w/v
Deacetoxycephalosporin C	$+139° \pm 1°$	1.0
Deacetoxycephalosporin C (from strain 8650-S⁻-M26-I27a/2)	$+139° \pm 1°$	1.0
Deacetylcephalosporin C*	$+107° \pm 1°$	1.4
Deacetylcephalosporin C lactone†	$+139° \pm 1°$	1.25
Cephalosporin C‡	$+104° \pm 1°$	2.2
Cephalexin‡	$+153° \pm 1°$	1.0

* Jeffery et al. (1961).
† Abraham and Newton (1961).
‡ Patterson et al. (1964).

TABLE 5
Oxidative deamination of cephalosporins. The experimental conditions are
described in the section on materials and methods

Compound*	Oxygen consumption μmol h^{-1}
Deacetoxycephalosporin C	5.9
Deacetoxycephalosporin C (from strain 8650-S$^-$-M26-127a/2)	5.9
Deacetylcephalosporin C	2.9
Cephalosporin C	7.1
DL-α-Aminoadipic acid	0.0
D-Methionine	12.4

* 50 μmol of cephalosporin derivatives and 25 μmol of the D-amino acids were used in the experiments.

TABLE 6
Hydroxylation of deacetoxycephalosporin C with an enzyme preparation
from *C. acremonium*. Incubations were carried out according to assay A

Reaction mixture	Cephalosporin C mμmol
Complete + crude extract	1.5
Complete + heat inactivated crude extract	0.0
Complete + crude extract + acetyl hydrolase	0.0
Complete + crude extract:	
— deacetoxycephalosporin C	0.3
— deacetoxycephalosporin C + cephalosporin C	0.3
— deacetylcephalosporin C O-acetyltransferase	0.0

TABLE 7
Requirement for molecular oxygen in the hydroxylation of deacetoxycephalosporin C.
The experimental conditions were those of assay A

Conditions	Strain	Cephalosporin C mμmol
Incubation in air		1.5
Flushed with argon, incubated in air	8650-S$^-$-M26	1.4
Flushed with argon, incubated in argon		0.0
Incubation in air		0.0
Flushed with argon, incubated in air	8650-S$^-$-M26-127a/2	0.0
Flushed with argon, incubated in argon		0.0

neither cephalosporin C nor deacetylcephalosporin C were formed. The amount of oxygen consumed during the hydroxylation was determined polarographically with an oxygen electrode. Table 8 shows that when deacetoxycephalosporin C is incubated with the crude extract there is an uptake of oxygen. The hydroxylation reaction depends strongly on NADH and to a lesser extent on NADPH as co-factors and clearly shows dependence

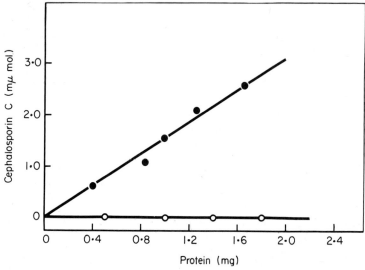

Fig. 3. Linearity of the deacetoxycephalosporin C hydroxylase of *C. acremonium* with protein concentration. The procedure reported in the section on materials and methods (assay A) was followed. ●, *C. acremonium*, strain 8650-S⁻-M26; ○, *C. acremonium*, strain 8650-S⁻-M26-I27a/2.

on manganese ions. Neither cephalosporin C or deacetylcephalosporin C could be used as substrates instead of deacetoxycephalosporin C, while 7-aminodeacetoxycephalosporanic acid had about 50 per cent activity under these conditions. The oxygen uptake with deacetoxycephalosporin C as substrate as a function of the concentration is shown in Fig. 5. The K_m value was found to be 3 mM. The enzyme turned out to be very labile and had to be prepared freshly each day. Purification of the enzyme has not yet been successful. We could detect no enzymatic activity in the crude extract of a mutant strain (8650-S⁻-M26-127a/2) (see Fig. 3 and Table 7). These findings indicate that this enzyme of the biosynthetic pathway is blocked in the mutant and explains the presence of deacetoxycephalosporin C in culture filtrates (Nüesch *et al.*, 1975). As reported before by many authors, deacetylcephalosporin C is also present in culture filtrates of *Cephalosporium* species (Lemke and Brannon, 1972). The question of whether it is an inter-

TABLE 8

Oxygen consumption by deacetoxycephalosporin C hydroxylase. Incubations were carried out according to assay B. 20 μmol of the compounds indicated below were used

Reaction mixture		Oxygen uptake μmol h^{-1}
Lacking	Added	
—	—	4.3
NADH	—	0.4
NADH	NAD$^+$	0.4
NADH	NADPH	1.8
MnCl$_2$	—	2.0
—	0.001 M EDTA	0.0
Deacetoxycephalosporin C	Cephalosporin C	0.0
Deacetoxycephalosporin C	Deacetylcephalosporin C	0.0
Deacetoxycephalosporin C	7-Aminodeacetoxycephalosporanic acid	1.6
Deacetoxycephalosporin C	DL-α-Aminoadipic acid	0.0
Enzyme	Heat inactivated crude extract	0.0

mediate product or formed from cephalosporin C by degradation is still open. During the preparation of this manuscript Fujisawa and co-workers published experiments which support the suggestion that deacetylcephalo-sporin C is an intermediate in the biosynthetic pathway (Fujisawa et al., 1973). Independently we obtained the same results and isolated and purified an enzyme, which can transform deacetylcephalosporin C, in the presence of acetyl-coenzyme A, into cephalosporin C. The acetylation of deacetyl-cephalosporin C is enzyme-dependent and linear with protein concentration (Fig. 4). Table 9 shows the requirements for the deacetyl cephalosporin C

TABLE 9

Requirements for deacetylcephalosporin C O-acetyl transferase activity. The experimental conditions are described in the section on materials and methods (assay C)

Reaction mixture		Cephalosporin C mμmol h^{-1}
Lacking	Added	
—	—	13.4
—	Acetyl hydroxylase	0.0
Deacetylcephalosporin C	—	0.0
Deacetylcephalosporin C	Cephalosporin C	0.0
(Acetyl-1-C-14)-coenzyme A	—	0.0
(Acetyl-1-C-14)-coenzyme A	Acetate-1-C-14	0.0
(Acetyl-1-C-14)-coenzyme A	Acetate-1-C-14 + coenzyme A	0.0
Enzyme	—	0.0
Enzyme	Denatured enzyme	0.0

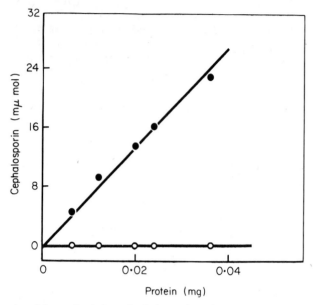

Fig. 4. Linearity of deacetylcephalosporin C *O*-acetyltransferase of *C. acremonium* with protein concentration. The procedure reported in the section on materials and methods was followed (assay C). ●, *C. acremonium*, strain 8650-S⁻-M26; ○, *C. acremonium*, strain 8650-S⁻-M26-CP52c.

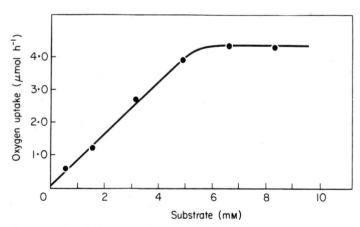

Fig. 5. Oxygen uptake of deacetoxycephalosporin C hydroxylase of *C. acremonium* as a function of the substrate concentration. The incubations were carried out under standard incubation conditions (assay B), except that the substrate was varied.

TABLE 10

Purification of C. acremonium deacetylcephalosporin C O-acetyl transferase. For details see experimental section

Fraction	Strain 8650-S⁻-M26					Strain 8650-S⁻-M26-CP52c		
	Volume cm³	Total protein mg	Total activity units	Specific activity units mg^{-1}	Degree of purification -fold	Volume cm³	Total protein mg	Total activity units
Crude extract	190	4 260	17 466	4.1	1.0	250	7 020	0
0–33% (NH$_4$)$_2$SO$_4$	40	2 360	16 284	6.8	1.7	30	640	0
25–33% (NH$_4$)$_2$SO$_4$	1.5	32	1 709	53.4	13.0	1.5	15	0
Eluate, Sephadex G-200, fraction 12	1.7	0.48	204	425.0	104.0	—	—	—

O-acetyltransferase activity and Table 10 presents the results of the purification procedure. The substrate specificity of the purified enzyme is given in
Table 11. As can be seen, only 3-hydroxymethyl-3-cephem compounds can
be acetylated. DL-Serine or DL-homoserine could not be used as substrates.
The fact that 7-ADCA, deacetylcephacetrile and deacetylcephaloram act as
substrates for the enzyme proves that no acetylation occurs at the α-aminoadipyl moiety of deacetylcephalosporin C. According to the recommendations of the International Commission of Enzymes (Enzyme Nomenclature,

TABLE 11

Substrate specificity of *C. acremonium* deacetylcephalosporin C O-acetyltransferase.
The experiments were performed according to assay C. 100 mµmol of the substrates
indicated below were used

Substrate	Corresponding O-acetyl-derivative formed mµmol h^{-1}
7-Aminodeacetylcephalosporanic acid (7-ADCA)	15.4
Deacetylcephalosporin C	13.4
Deacetylcephalosporin C lactone	0.0
Deacetoxycephalosporin C	0.0
Cephalosporin C	0.0
Deacetylcephaloram (Ba-49419)	13.6
Deacetylcephacetrile (Ba-40161)	12.6
D-,L-Homoserine	0.0
D-,L-Serine	0.0

1973) we propose the following systematic name for this enzyme: Acetyl–
CoA: deacetylcephalosporin C O-acetyltransferase (E.C. 2.3.1.?.)

After mutagenic treatment of *C. acremonium* with uv light we isolated a
mutant strain (8650-S$^-$-M26-CP-52c), which excreted only deacetylcephalosporin C into the culture medium (Nüesch *et al.*, 1975). In a cell-free extract
of this mutant, as well as in 0–33 per cent $(NH_4)_2SO_4-$, 25–33 per cent
$(NH_4)_2SO_4$ fractions (see Table 10 and Fig. 4) no transacetylase activity
with deacetylcephalosporin C as substrate could be detected.

We also tested the influence of some other β-lactam antibiotics on the
transacetylase (Table 12). 3-Acetoxycephalosporins inhibited the enzyme
completely, while deacetoxycephalosporin C and penicillin N showed 60 per
cent and 25 per cent inhibition respectively at 0.005 M. Because of the relative
strong inhibitory effect of deacetoxycephalosporin C and tris-HCl buffer
(Liersch, 1974) on the transacetylase, we had to incubate assay A for a longer
time than assay C, in order to make it possible to follow the hydroxylation of
deacetoxycephalosporin C by the linked enzymatic assay.

TABLE 12

Effect of β-lactam antibiotics on the deacetylcephalosporin C
O-acetyltransferase activity. The same assay conditions were
used as described in the section on materials and methods
(assay C)

Lactam antibiotic	Concentration mM	Inhibition %
Deacetoxycephalosporin C	5	60
Cephalosporin C	5	100
Penicillin N	5	25
Cephacetrile	5	100
Cephaloram	5	100

Discussion

Hydroxylation of methyl groups is a well-known reaction performed by
fungi and other microorganisms (Fonken and Johnson, 1972; Boyd and
Smellie, 1972). Very often the introduction of a hydroxyl group is an intermediate step in the biosynthesis of certain metabolic products. Both hydroxylation and acetylation reactions play an important role in fungi and bacteria,
utilizing different chemicals as a carbon source or inactivating toxic substances, e.g. antibiotics (Fonken and Johnson, 1972; Benveniste and Davies,
1973; Bod et al., 1973; Kieslich et al., 1973; Walker and Cooney, 1973).

From our results with C. acremonium, we conclude that the hydroxylation
of the 3-CH_3-group of deacetoxycephalosporin C is an intermediate step in
the biosynthesis of the antibiotic cephalosporin C. The oxygen consumption,
the dependence on NAD(P)H as co-factors and the necessity of manganese
ions for the oxygenation of deacetoxycephalosporin C indicate an enzyme of
the class-1 oxido-reductases (E.C. 1.?). In a final, separate enzymatic reaction
the intermediate deacetylcephalosporin C is converted into the end product
cephalosporin C, which is released into the culture medium in a much higher
amount than its precursors.

Our data support the conclusion that deacetoxycephalosporin C and
deacetylcephalosporin C are direct precursors of the antibiotic cephalosporin
C. The pathway indicated in Fig. 6 is proposed for the final steps in the
biosynthesis of cephalosporin C in C. acremonium. Our experimental results
are supported by the fact that deacetoxycephalosporin C is synthesized by
other Cephalosporium species and other penicillin N producers (Higgens et al.,
1974.).

A more detailed investigation of the properties of the above mentioned
enzyme systems is in progress. Undoubtedly it will give an answer to the

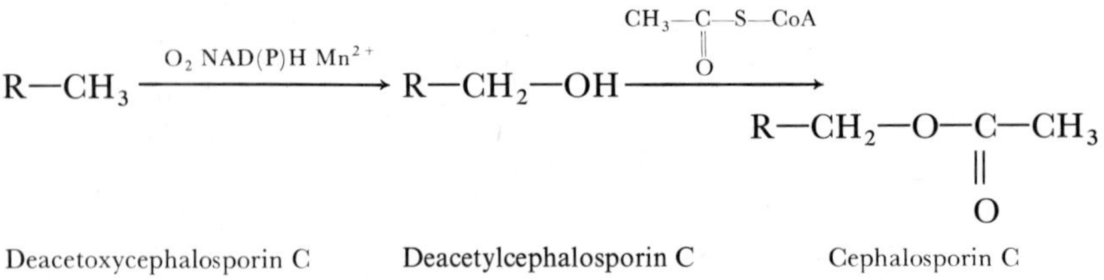

$$R-CH_3 \xrightarrow{O_2\ NAD(P)H\ Mn^{2+}} R-CH_2-OH \xrightarrow{\overset{\displaystyle CH_3-C-S-CoA}{\underset{\displaystyle O}{\|}}}$$

$$R-CH_2-O-\underset{\displaystyle O}{\overset{\displaystyle \|}{C}}-CH_3$$

Deacetoxycephalosporin C   Deacetylcephalosporin C   Cephalosporin C

FIG. 6. Pathway proposed for the final steps in the biosynthesis of cephalosporin C.

question, how these two steps in antibiotic production by *C. acremonium* are regulated.

Acknowledgements

We are very grateful to Mr E. von Arx and to Mr A. Linder for the analyses with the amino acid analyser, to Dr H. Peter and Dr W. Voser for the preparation of some cephalosporins and to Dr J. Urech for a sample of deacetylcephalosporin C. We also thank Mrs B. Hauss and Mrs H. Bachmann for technical assistance.

References

Abraham, E. P. and Newton, G. G. F. (1961). *Biochem. J.* **79**, 377
Abraham, E. P. and Newton, G. G. F. (1965). "Advances in Chemotherapy" (Eds A. Goldin, F. Hawking and R. J. Schnitzer), vol. 2, p. 23. Academic Press, New York and London.
Abraham, E. P. and Newton, G. G. F. (1967). *In* "Antibiotics" (Eds D. Gottlieb and P. D. Shaw), vol. 2, pp. 1–16. Springer Verlag, New York.
Arx, E. von, Brugger, M., Liersch, M. and Linder, A. (1974). 6th Technicon Symposium, Frankfurt aM., Germany. Paper in press.
Benveniste, R. and Davies, J. (1973). *A. Rev. Biochem.* **42**, 471.
Benz, F. Liersch, M., Nüesch, J. and Treichler, H. J. (1971). *Eur. J. Biochem.* **20**, 81.
Bod, P., Szarka, E., Gyimesi, J., Horvath, I., Vanjna-Mehesfalvi, Z. and Horvath, I. (1973). *J. Antibiotics,* **26**, 101.
Boyd, G. S. and Smellie, R. M. S. (1972). "Biological Hydroxylation Mechanisms". Academic Press, New York and London.
Demain, A. L. (1963). *Trans. N.Y. Acad. Sci.* II, **25**, 731.
Enzyme Nomenclature, Recommendations (1973) of the IUP and AC and IUB, Elsevier, Amsterdam.
Fonken, G. S. and Johnson, R. A. (1972). "Chemical Oxidations with Micro-organisms". Academic Press, New York and London.
Fujisawa, Y., Shirafuji, H., Kida, M., Nara, K., Yoneda, M. and Kanzaki, T. (1973). *Nature, New Biol.* **246**, 154.

Higgens, C. E., Hamill, R. L., Sands, T. H., Hoehn, N. M., Davis, N. E., Nagarajan, R. and Boeck, L. D. (1974). *J. Antibiotics*, **27**, 298.

Jeffery, J. D'A,, Abraham, E. P. and Newton, G. G. F. (1961). *Biochem. J.* **81**, 591.

Kieslich, K., Wieglepp, H., Hoyer, G–A. and Rosenberg, D. (1973). *Chem. Ber.* **106**, 2636.

Konecny, J., Felber, E. and Gruner, J. (1973). *J. Antibiotics*, **26**, 135.

Lemke, P. A. and Brannon, D. R. (1972). "Cephalosporins and Penicillins" (Ed. E. H. Flynn), pp. 370–437. Academic Press, New York and London.

Liersch, M., Treichler, H. J., Voser, W. and Nüesch, J. (1973). Patent application filed.

Liersch, M. (1974). Unpublished observations.

Mazzeo, P. and Romeo, A. (1972). *J. chem. Soc. Perkin I*, 2532.

Nagai, S. and Flavin, M. (1967). *J. biol. Chem.* **242**, 3884.

Nüesch, J., Gruner, J. Knüsel, F. and Triechler, H. J. (1967). *Path. Microbiol.* **30**, 880.

Nüesch, J., Hinnen, A., Liersch, M. and Treichler, H. J. (1975). These Proceedings.

Patterson, E. L., Meter, J. C. van and Bohonos, N. (1964). *J. med. Chem.* **7**, 689.

Walker, J. D. and Cooney, J. J. (1973). *J. Bact.* **115**, 635.

STRATEGY OF STRAIN IMPROVEMENT

II

MUTATION AND RECOMBINATION IN
ANTIBIOTIC-PRODUCING ORGANISMS

The genetics of mutants impaired in the biosynthesis of penicillin

G. HOLT, G. F. ST L. EDWARDS* and K. D. MACDONALD†

*Bio-Organic Research Group, The Polytechnic of Central London,
115 New Cavendish Street, London W1M 8JS, England*

Summary

As part of a study of the genetic control of penicillin production in fungi, mutants of *Aspergillus nidulans* and *Penicillium chrysogenum* impaired in the synthesis of β-lactam antibiotics were investigated. Mutants were classified as "penicillinless" when they gave penicillin titres of 10 per cent or less than that of their parents. The gene symbol *npe* has been assigned to this type of mutation.

Of various chemical and physical mutagens tested, gamma irradiation from a ^{60}Co source produced the highest frequency of *npe* mutants in *Aspergillus nidulans*. Studies with heterokaryons and diploids showed that the *npe* mutations tested were all nuclear in origin and recessive. Diploid complementation tests have established that twenty of the twenty-eight *npe* mutants isolated from *A. nidulans* belonged to a single complementation group, designated *npeA*. The remaining eight were representatives of at least three other complementation groups. Diploids were synthesized between "master strains" genetically labelled on all eight chromosomes and strains carrying a mutation at the *npeA* locus. Haploidization analysis of these diploids assigned *npeA* to chromosome VI. Meiotic data showed that *npeA* was loosely linked to the *sbA* locus and the latter to the *sB* mutation while an analysis of mitotic recombinants revealed that *npeA* was distal to the *sB* locus.

In *Penicillium chrysogenum* diploid complementation tests with five penicillinless mutants demonstrated the existence of four complementation groups.

* Present address: Sir William Dunn School of Pathology, University of Oxford, South Parks Road, Oxford OXI 3RE, England.
† Microbiological Research Establishment, Porton Down, Salisbury, Wiltshire, England.

Introduction

There are several ways in which mutants impaired in a biosynthetic pathway may be used to investigate properties of that pathway. Co-fermentation experiments, in which the biosynthetic capabilities of two mutants grown together are examined, can demonstrate the formation by one of an intermediate of the pathway which can be utilized as a precursor by the other. The success of this technique depends on the ability of such intermediates to pass from the site of biosynthesis in one strain to that in the other. Another method involves the chemical identification of intermediates accumulated by mutants and the ability of such mutants to perform conversions of postulated precursors into others or into the final product of the pathway. Genetic techniques can also be employed to give information on the number of loci concerned in the pathway and the existence of regulatory mechanisms. Genetic complementation tests can define, with more certainty than co-fermentation experiments, the biochemical reaction of a step controlled by a single gene and are not restricted by the necessity for intermediates to be readily diffusible.

Bonner (1947) was unable to observe the synthesis of penicillin in co-fermentation experiments using fifty-five penicillinless mutants of *Penicillium notatum* induced by X-irradiation. Penicillin production could not be restored by feeding certain compounds which had been suggested as possible intermediates in the pathway.

The discovery of the parasexual cycle in *Penicillium chrysogenum* (Pontecorvo and Sermonti, 1953) led to Caglioti and Sermonti (1956) using heterokaryon and diploid complementation tests to investigate mutants of this mould blocked in penicillin biosynthesis. Eight penicillinless mutants were found to belong to a single complementation group; a ninth, with a penicillin titre of about one tenth that of the parental strain complemented in both heterokaryons and diploids with a member of the first group (Sermonti, 1956). The paucity of genetic information available in *P. chrysogenum* as well as the relatively sparse background knowledge of the biosynthesis of penicillin available at that time seemed to have discouraged further investigation.

The work of Holt and Macdonald (1968a, 1968b) and Macdonald *et al.* (1972) with the fungus *Aspergillus nidulans* has established a useful model system for the genetic study of penicillin production. In this mould, although penicillin yields are low (Holt and Macdonald, 1968a), the genetic interpretation is easier than in *Penicillium chrysogenum* since the genetics of the former has been investigated extensively (Pontecorvo *et al.*, 1953; Clutterbuck and Cove, 1974). Work was therefore undertaken to produce mutants of *A. nidulans* impaired in penicillin biosynthesis. To reduce possible effects of mutagen specificity a variety of physical and chemical mutagens were

employed. Complementation analyses have been made and selected mutations have been mapped genetically.

Recent information on the biosynthesis of β-lactam antibiotics (Lemke and
Brannon, 1972) has increased the likelihood of successful biochemical investigations with blocked mutants. Accumulation of possible intermediates has been
investigated in mutants of *Cephalosporium acremonium* by Lemke and Nash (1972)
and Fujisawa *et al.* (1973). Studies have therefore been initiated in our laboratory using *Penicillium chrysogenum*, strain NRRL 1951, as starting material. Preliminary complementation analyses of some penicillinless mutants from this
strain have been made with a view to using them in subsequent biochemical
work.

Materials and methods

ORGANISMS

a. Strains derived from the "Glasgow" wild-type isolate of *Aspergillus
nidulans*, NRRL 194 (Pontecorvo *et al.*, 1953), were kindly supplied by Dr A. J.
Clutterbuck and Mr E. C. Forbes of the University of Glasgow.

b. *Penicillium chrysogenum* All the strains used were derived from strain
NRRL 1951 (Raper and Alexander, 1945).

Domestic codes, penicillin yields and genotypes of all parental strains used
are given in Table 1. The gene symbols and nomenclature are those in common
use (Clutterbuck, 1973; Clutterbuck and Cove, 1974).

SYMBOLS EMPLOYED

Genes determining: inability to utilize a specific sugar as sole carbon source—
fac = acetate, *gal* = galactose, *lac* = lactose, *sb* = sorbitol; nutritional requirements—*ad* = adenine, *an* = aneurin, *arg* = arginine, *bi* = biotin, *cho* =
choline, *ino* = inositol, *lys* = lysine, *meth* = methionine, *nic* = nicotinic acid,
paba = *p*-aminobenzoic acid, *pro* = proline, *pyro* = pyridoxin, *ribo* = riboflavin, *s* = reduced sulphur, *tryp* = tryptophan; ability to suppress nutritional
requirement—*suAadE20* = suppressor of adenine auxotrophy at the *adE*
locus; inability to utilize specific nitrogen compounds as sole nitrogen source—
cnx = nitrate and hypoxanthine, *nia* = nitrate, *ua* = uric acid; resistance—
acr = acriflavine, *act* = actidione, *apl* = allopurinol, *fan* = fluoroacetate,
mol = molybdate; mutant spore colour—*bw* = brown, *fw* = fawn, *w* =
white, *y* = yellow; others—*aps* = anucleate primary sterigmata, *npe* = penicillinless, *pac* = lacks the enzyme acid phosphatase, *ts* = temperature sensitivity (inability to grow at 37°C).

MEDIA

Minimal medium (MM) and complete medium (CM) were based on those

TABLE 1

Domestic codes, penicillin yields and genotypes of strains of *Aspergillus nidulans* and *Penicillium chrysogenum* in which penicillinless mutations were induced

	Domestic code	Penicillin yield (μg cm^{-3})	Genotype
Aspergillus nidulans	G5	3.0	*biA1*
	G26	3.0	*biA1; w-010*
	G30	2.0	*suAadE20 yA2 adE20; acr A1; galA1; pyroA4; facA303; sB3; nicB8; riboB2*
	G31*	2.0	*galA1; pyroA4; facA303; sB3; nicB8; riboB2*
	GH8	2.5	*biA1; fwA1*
	GH11	3.0	*yA2; pyroA4; cnxA5*
	GH13	2.0	*biA1; niaD17*
	GH26	2.0	*biA1; methGl; w-005*
Penicillium chrysogenum	HP15	27.0	*an-004 choA001*
	HP16	24.0	*an-004 inoA001*
	HP20	20.0	*an-004 proA001*
	HP41	30.0	*an-004 pyroA001 bw-005*

* May also bear *suAadE20 adE20*

Penicillin titres of the ancestral strains NRRL 194 of *Aspergillus nidulans* and NRRL 1951 of *Penicillium chrysogenum* were 3.0 and 30.0 μg cm^{-3} respectively.

described by Pontecorvo *et al.* (1953). The fermentation medium (FM) for penicillin production was that used by Holt and Macdonald (1968a).

INCUBATION

This was at 37°C for *Aspergillus nidulans* and 25°C for *Penicillium chrysogenum* unless otherwise stated.

PRODUCTION OF MUTANTS

Details of mutagenic treatments have been given by Edwards *et al.* (1974). Mutagen abbreviations were as follows: fuv = far ultraviolet light (254 nm), MNNG = *N*-methyl-*N'*-nitro-N-nitrosoguanidine, EMS = ethylmethane sulphonate, GC = gamma rays from a ^{60}Co source, 8MOP = near ultraviolet light (365 nm), in the presence of 8-methoxypsoralen, NA = nitrous acid.

A RAPID SCREENING METHOD FOR THE ISOLATION OF MUTANTS IMPAIRED IN PENICILLIN SYNTHESIS

This was based on a surface culture method (Edwards *et al.*, 1974). All mutants were subsequently grown in submerged shaken culture and their penicillin yields assayed accurately (Holt and Macdonald, 1968a). Mutant isolates were classified as "penicillinless" when they gave titres of 10 per cent or less that of the strains from which they were derived.

GENETIC METHODS

Basic methods are those in general use with *Aspergillus nidulans* (Pontecorvo *et al.*, 1953; McCully and Forbes, 1965) and *Penicillium chrysogenum* (Macdonald *et al.*, 1963a, 1963b).

Results

STUDIES WITH ASPERGILLUS NIDULANS

Penicillinless mutants

The frequency of mutants selected after different mutagenic treatments was given by Edwards *et al.* (1974) and is shown in Table 2.

TABLE 2
Frequency of penicillinless mutants induced in strains of *Aspergillus nidulans* by different mutagens

Strain	Mutagen	Number of isolates screened	Number of isolates selected	Percentage of penicillinless mutants
G5	fuv	500	1 ⎫	
G30	fuv	1000	2 ⎬	0.19
G31	fuv	1200	2 ⎭	
G26	MNNG	4100	3	0.07
GH8	EMS	4900	5	0.10
GH11	GC	1600	10	0.63
GH13	8MOP	5200	4	0.08
GH26	NA	1400	1	0.07
		Total 19900	Total 28	Mean 0.14

Some mutants were phenotypically different from their parents. Eleven of the twenty-eight had appreciably lower radial colony growth rates than their parents on surface culture. Heavier mycelial pigmentation occurred in five and a lightening of spore colour in three. Mutants which were similar to the parental strain in growth rate, pigmentation and spore colour were classed as morphologically normal. None of the mutants had additional auxotrophic requirements.

Heterokaryon tests Two heterokaryons were synthesized between a penicillinless strain with white conidia, G23 (*biA1 w-08 npeA01*), and a master strain with yellow conidia, G30 genetically labelled on all eight chromosomes and yielding approximately 2 μg penicillin cm^{-3}. Strain G23 was a white sporing derivative of an *npe* mutant obtained from strain G5 following fuv irradiation. When conidia were plated on CM agar from the first heterokaryon the ratio of yellow to white conidia was 50 to 1 as established by the numbers of white and yellow colonies which grew. In the second heterokaryon this ratio was 1 to 1. Two hundred single colony isolates were made following each plating. In both cases all penicillin producers had the genotype of strain G30 and all nonproducers that of strain G23. The other *npe* mutations tested behaved similarly and demonstrated that the ability to suppress penicillin yield was under nuclear control.

Dominance tests All of the *npe* mutations tested were recessive in diploids.

Diploid complementation tests The first three penicillinless mutants isolated failed to show complementation in diploids in any possible pairing. These mutations were assigned to locus *npeA*. Further *npe* mutants were first tested against a strain carrying a mutation at this locus (*npeA03*). Twenty of the twenty-eight *npe* mutants, including all those with normal morphology were assigned to this locus. Further tests have been made with these mutations in a preliminary search for intracistronic complementation. All twenty failed to complement with at least two other *npeA* alleles and no intracistronic complementation has been found. Results of complementation with the remaining eight mutations are incomplete but three of the eight, designated *npeB006*, *npeC007* and *npeD0045*, complemented with *npeA03* and with each other in all possible pairs. Therefore the *npe* mutations studied were representatives of at least four complementation groups.

Genetic mapping of the npeA locus A heterozygous diploid was synthesized between strains G21 (*biA1; npeA01*) and the yellow-spored master strain, G30 (*suAadE20 yA2 adE20; acrA1; galA1; pyroA4; facA303; sB3; nicB8; riboB2*) with a titre of 2 μg penicillin cm^{-3}. Haploidization of this green diploid on CM containing *p*-fluorophenylalanine (McCully and Forbes, 1965) gave rise to yellow and green haploid segregants. After purification, 64 were assayed for penicillin and gave an allele ratio for *npeA*$^-$:*npeA*$^+$ of 27:37. These 64 isolates were tested for joint segregation of markers in all possible pairs. Table 3 shows this segregation in full. As no recombinants were obtained between *npeA01* and *sB3* (known to be on chromosome VI) it was concluded that *npeA01* was situated on chromosome VI. A control for these results was provided by the absence of recombination between *biA1* and *yA2* both located on chromosome I. Four separate alleles at the *npeA* locus have since been assigned to chromosome VI by parasexual haploidization analysis.

A sexual cross was then made between strain G53 (*yA2*; *facA303*; *sB3* *npeA01*; *riboB2*) and G44 (*biA1*; *acrA1 wA3*; *nicC10*). Meiotic analysis was carried out using green spored recombinants. Strain G44 bore *nicC10* and strain G53, *sB3*, both on linkage group VI (Dorn, 1967; Clutterbuck and

TABLE 3

Distribution of genetic markers in 64 haploid segregants isolated from a diploid of the following genotype:

$$\frac{suAadE20\ yA2\ adE20\ +\ acrA1\ galA1\ pyroA4\ facA303}{+\ \ \ \ +\ \ \ \ +\ \ \ biA1\ +\ \ \ +\ \ \ +\ \ \ +}$$

$$\frac{sB3\ \ (+)\ \ nicB8\ riboB2}{+\ (npeA01)\ +\ \ \ +}$$

− represents the mutant allele and + the wild-type allele

Joint segregation of markers (*cis*)*	Parental		Recombinant		Recombination fraction
	− −	+ +	+ −	− +	
yA2 and *acrA1*	20	15	11	18	29/64
yA2 and *galA1*	17	17	9	21	30/64
yA2 and *pyroA4*	20	13	13	18	31/64
yA2 and *facA303*	20	15	11	18	29/64
yA2 and *sB3*	20	9	17	18	35/64
yA2 and *nicB8*	17	13	13	21	34/64
yA2 and *riboB2*	16	17	9	22	31/64
acrA1 and *galA1*	13	20	13	18	31/64
acrA1 and *pyroA4*	18	18	15	13	28/64
acrA1 and *facA303*	15	17	16	16	32/64
acrA1 and *sB3*	18	14	19	13	32/64
acrA1 and *nicB8*	13	16	17	18	35/64
acrA1 and *riboB2*	9	17	16	22	38/64
galA1 and *pyroA4*	14	19	19	12	31/64
galA1 and *facA303*	11	18	20	15	35/64
galA1 and *sB3*	20	21	17	6	23/64
galA1 and *nicB8*	10	18	20	16	36/64
galA1 and *riboB2*	10	23	15	16	31/64
pyroA4 and *facA303*	14	14	17	19	36/64
pyroA4 and *sB3*	19	13	18	14	32/64
pyroA4 and *nicB8*	16	17	14	17	31/64
pyroA4 and *riboB2*	12	18	13	21	34/64
facA303 and *sB3*	16	11	21	16	37/64
facA303 and *nicB8*	17	20	13	14	27/64
facA303 and *riboB2*	13	21	12	18	30/64
sB3 and *nicB8*	13	10	17	24	41/64
sB3 and *riboB2*	15	17	10	22	32/64
nicB8 and *riboB2*	10	19	15	20	35/64
biA1 and *npeA1*	9	20	18	17	35/64

TABLE 3—*cont.*

Joint segregation of markers (*trans*)*	Parental + −	− +	Recombinant − −	+ +	Recombination fraction
biA1 and *yA2*	38	26	0	0	0/64
biA1 and *acrA1*	20	15	11	18	29/64
biA1 and *galA1*	17	17	9	21	30/64
biA1 and *pyroA4*	20	13	13	18	31/64
biA1 and *facA303*	20	15	11	18	29/64
biA1 and *sB3*	20	9	17	18	35/64
biA1 and *nicB8*	17	13	13	21	34/64
biA1 and *riboB2*	16	17	9	22	31/64
npeA01 and *yA2*	20	9	18	17	35/64
npeA01 and *acrA1*	18	14	13	19	32/64
npeA01 and *galA1*	18	19	8	19	27/64
npeA01 and *pyroA4*	19	13	14	18	32/64
npeA01 and *facA303*	16	12	15	21	36/64
npeA01 and *sB3*	37	27	0	0	0/64
npeA01 and *nicB8*	13	10	17	24	41/64
npeA01 and *riboB2*	16	18	9	21	30/64

Allele ratios:

$$\frac{yA2}{+}\frac{38}{26}; \frac{acrA1}{+}\frac{31}{33}; \frac{galA1}{+}\frac{26}{38}; \frac{pyroA4}{+}\frac{33}{31}$$

$$\frac{facA303}{+}\frac{31}{33}; \frac{sB3}{+}\frac{37}{27}; \frac{nicB8}{+}\frac{30}{34}; \frac{riboB2}{+}\frac{25}{39}$$

$$\frac{biA1}{+}\frac{26}{38}; \frac{npeAO1}{+}\frac{27}{37}$$

* The terms *cis* and *trans* in relation to two markers are used for short to indicate parental origins. *cis*, both markers from the same haploid strain; *trans*, one marker from each of the haploid strains.

Cove, 1974). Table 4 gives the results of this cross and it can be seen that there is no evidence of close linkage between *sB3*, *nicC10* or *npeA01*. In addition further meiotic analyses demonstrated that *npeA* was not closely linked to any of the following markers located on chromosome VI: *aplA7, apsB8, argA1. cnxG4, lacA1, lysA1, methB, molA33, pacC5,tsB, trypE17* and *uaX1*. However, a cross set up between GH28 (*biA1; wA3; sbA3*) and G39 (*suAadE20 yA2 adE20; acrA1; galA1; pyroA4; facA303; sB3 npeA03; nicB8; riboB2*) gave results indicating loose linkage of *npeA* to *sbA* (36 per cent recombinants) and possible linkage of *sbA* to *sB* (43 per cent recombinants). The details are presented in Table 5.

It was shown by Arst (1968) that mutants at the *sB* locus were resistant to selenate. Two diploids were synthesized in the hope of using selenate to select mitotic recombinants homozygous for the *sB3* mutant allele. The genotypes of the diploids were as follows:

DIPLOID 1
$$\frac{suAadE20\ yA2\ +\ adE20}{+\ \ +\ \ hiA1\ \ +}\ ;\ \frac{acrA1}{+}\ ;\ \frac{galA1}{+}\ ;\ \frac{pyroA4}{1}\ ;\ \frac{facA303}{+}\ ;$$

$$\frac{sB3\ npeA03\ +}{+\ \ +\ \ argA1}\ ;\ \frac{nicB8}{+}\ ;\ \frac{riboB2}{+}$$

DIPLOID 2
$$\frac{suAadE20\ yA2\ +\ adE20}{+\ \ +\ \ hiA1\ adE20}\ ;\ \frac{acrA1\ +}{+\ wA1}\ ;\ \frac{galA1}{+}\ ;\ \frac{pyroA4}{+}\ ;\ \frac{facA303}{+}\ ;$$

$$\frac{+\ \ sB3\ npeA03}{lysA1\ +\ \ +}\ ;\ \frac{nicB8}{+}\ ;\ \frac{riboB2}{+}$$

Eleven diploid mitotic recombinants resistant to selenate (at a final concentration of 1 mM in agar) were selected from Diploid 1 and seven from Diploid 2. In addition to being homozygous for the *sB3* mutant allele, all were shown to be nonproducers of penicillin and hence homozygous for *npeA* which suggested that the *npeA* locus was distal to the *sB* locus. These results, together with those of Jansen (personal communication) for the location of *sB3*, suggested the following gene order for that part of chromosome VI bearing the mutation *npeA*: *nicC lacA sB sbA npeA*. The centromere is either between *nicC* and *lacA* or on the other side of *nicC*.

TABLE 4

Segregation of chromosome VI markers among 95 haploid progeny from a cross between G53 (*yA2; facA303; sB3 npeA01; riboB2*) and G44 (*biA1; acrA1; wA3; nicC10*). The number of parental and recombinant strains for each pair of markers on chromosome VI is presented; − represents the mutant allele, + represents the wild-type allele

	$npeA^+$	$npeA^-$
sB^+	36	16
sB^-	26	17

Recombination fraction 42/95 (44%)
2×2 contingency $\chi^2 = 0.8\ P > 10\%$

	$npeA^+$	$npeA^-$
$nicC^+$	45	19
$nicC^-$	17	14

Recombination fraction 59/95 (62%)
2×2 contingency $\chi^2 = 2.2\ P > 10\%$

	sB^+	sB^-
$nicC^+$	36	28
$nicC^-$	16	15

Recombination fraction 51/95 (54%)
2×2 contingency $\chi^2 = 0.2\ P > 10\%$

H

TABLE 5

Distribution of genetic markers on chromosome VI in 149 haploid progeny isolated from a cross between GH28 (*biA1; wA3; sbA3*) and G39 (*suAadE20 yA2 adE20; acrA1; galA1; pyroA4; facA303; sB3 npeA03 nicB8; ribob2*). − Represents the mutant allele and +, the wild-type allele

	npeA+	*npeA*−
sbA+	28	43
sbA−	53	25

Recombination fraction 53/149 (36%)
2 × 2 contingency $\chi^2 = 12.2.P < 1\%$

	npeA+	*npeA*−
sB+	47	35
sB−	34	33

Recombination fraction 69/149 (46%)
2 × 2 contingency $\chi^2 = 0.6. P > 10\%$

	sbA+	*sbA*−
sB+	34	48
sB−	37	30

Recombination fraction 64/149 (43%)
2 × 2 contingency $\chi^2 = 2.85\% < P < 10\%$

STUDIES WITH PENICILLIUM CHRYSOGENUM

This is a preliminary report of complementation analyses, using penicillinless mutants, undertaken in our laboratories by Mr I. D. Normansell and Mrs P. J. M. Gore. Eighty of these mutants have so far been produced from genetically labelled derivatives of *Penicillium chrysogenum*, strain NRRL 1951. However, experiments with only five of these have demonstrated the existence of four complementation groups. Three strains with mutations, *npe-0052* (induced by 8MOP in strain HP16), *npe-0066* (induced by fuv in strain HP15) and *npe-0067* (induced by EMS in strain HP20) gave negligible penicillin titres and were examined initially. Two others, with mutations *npe-006* (induced by fuv in strain HP41) and *npe-0010* (also induced by fuv in strain HP41) gave penicillin yields one-tenth that of their parents. All five mutants were morphologically similar to their parents including the production of the pigment, chrysogenin. Many strains were isolated as penicillinless but did not exude this pigment. Some pigmentless strains were shown to complement in that diploids synthesized between certain pairs of these strains produced chrysogenin. Pigmentless strains have not been employed in the present complementation studies of which results are presented below.

Complementary auxotrophic and spore colour mutations were used to facilitate the selection of diploids. All the *npe* mutations tested behaved as recessives in diploids. The mutation *npe-006* complemented in diploids with each of the mutant alleles *npe-0052*, *npe-0066* and *npe-0067*, whereas *npe-0010* complemented with *npe-0066* and *npe-0067* but not with *npe-0052*. In addition *npe-0066* complemented with *npe-0067*. These results suggested that at least four separate loci were involved in the biosynthesis of penicillin.

Discussion

Although penicillinless mutations were induced in different strains and hence in different genetic backgrounds, of those tested, ^{60}Co gamma-irradiation appeared to be the most effective mutagen for the production of *npe* mutations in *Aspergillus nidulans*. Das and Nandi (1972) have compared the mutagens, nitrogen mustard, colchicine, far ultraviolet light and gamma-irradiation for their efficiency in producing mutants of *Aspergillus niger* with increased or decreased citric acid production. The most effective mutagen for inducing either type of mutation was gamma-irradiation.

Gamma-irradiation has been shown to induce a high frequency of chromosomal aberrations in *Aspergillus nidulans* (Kafer and Chen, 1964). However, only one chromosomal aberration has so far been revealed in a penicillinless mutant; this was a translocation in a mutant induced by far ultraviolet light but not involving the linkage group on which the *npe* allele was carried (Edwards and Holt, unpublished data).

Diploid complementation tests, made between selected pairs of mutants, have established that twenty of the twenty eight penicillinless mutants selected belonged to a single complementation group and that the remaining eight were representatives of at least three other complementation groups. All *npe* mutants with normal morphology were members of the complementation group which was assigned to the locus *npeA* and at which most *npe* mutations were located. Evidence suggested that this locus was on chromosome VI and distal to the *sB3* mutation. The morphological abnormalities may be pleiotropic effects of the *npe* allele or may result from separate mutations. Certainly in one cross involving *npeCOO7*, not reported here, the pigmentation and loss of titre appeared to result from a single mutation.

The results of the experiments with selenate suggested the possibility of obtaining auxotrophs unable to utilize sulphate by isolating colonies resistant to selenate. We have recently selected mutants of *Penicillium chrysogenum* strain NRRL 1951 which were resistant to selenate (Roberts and Holt, unpublished data). Some of these were, indeed, auxotrophic, growing only in the presence of a reduced sulphur compound such as thiosulphate. The work of Cove (1972) and Arst and Cove (1973) suggests that it might be possible to obtain, in a similar way, mutants unable to utilize nitrate, by selection for resistance to chlorate. A further example of the association of auxotrophy with resistance to a toxic chemical was reported by Sing and Sherman (1974). Mutant strains of *Saccharamyces cerevisiae* resistant to methyl mercury chloride were found to be methionine auxotrophs.

Such techniques might prove important for selecting auxotrophic mutations in an organism when the use of mutagenic agents is thought undesirable.

Bonner (1947) found that certain lysine auxotrophs of *Penicillium notatum* yielded no penicillin. Therefore, it might be expected that lysine auxotrophs would be among mutants selected for loss of penicillin titre. However, tests with lysine auxotrophs of *Aspergillus nidulans* (kindly supplied by Dr H. N. Arst) showed that additional lysine had to be added to the fermentation medium before they would grow (Edwards and Holt, unpublished data). Such mutants would, therefore, not have been selected with the screening method employed.

Sermonti (1959) suggested several explanations for the notable absence of complementation among penicillinless mutants in *Penicillium chrysogenum*: a single locus controlling the condensation of the three components of penicillin, cysteine, valine and α-aminoadipic acid; an exceedingly high mutation rate of one among several loci controlling penicillin biosynthesis; antibiotic activity of some precursor of penicillin, which would not have allowed a mutant producing it to be detected among "inactive" mutants; alternative pathways to penicillin biosynthesis, except for one obligatory step which alone could suppress completely penicillin production.

However, in the present study four complementation groups have been demonstrated in *Penicillium chrysogenum* as a result of complementation analysis on five morphologically normal penicillinless mutants. Fourteen mutants have so far been examined and it appeared that one group had about four times as many members as any of the others (Normansell, Gore and Holt, unpublished data).

Mutants of both *Aspergillus nidulans* and *Penicillium chrysogenum* representative of different complementation groups are currently under biochemical investigation in the hope of elucidating aspects of penicillin biosynthesis. The presence of a trophophase (growth phase) followed by an idiophase (production phase) in antibiotic fermentations is indicative that control mechanisms occur. It is possible, therefore, that some of the penicillinless loci may not be structural genes coding for enzymes of the pathway, or genes altering permeability so that penicillin is not excreted, but may have regulatory functions.

Acknowledgements

We are pleased to acknowledge a research studentship from Glaxo Laboratories Ltd to Mrs Pamela Gore. We are also grateful to Miss Fiona Stirrup for results from her undergraduate project at the Polytechnic of Central London, demonstrating the selection of mitotic recombinants using selenate. We gratefully acknowledge the technical assistance of Mr T. J. Roberts.

References

Arst, H. N., Jr. (1968). *Nature, Lond.* **219**, 268.
Arst, H. N., Jr. and Cove, D. J. (1973). *Molec. gen. Genet.* **126**, 111.
Bonner, D. (1947). *Arch. Biochem.* **13**, 1.
Caglioti, M. T. and Sermonti, G. (1956). *J. gen. Microbiol.* **14**, 38.
Clutterbuck, A. J. (1973). *Genet. Res.* **21**, 291.
Clutterbuck, A. J. and Cove, D. J. (1974). "Handbook of Microbiology". The Chemical Rubber Company, Cleveland, Ohio.
Cove, D. J. (1972). *Biochem. J.* **127**, 19P.
Das, A. and Nandi, P. (1972). *Folia microbiol., Praha*, **17**, 248.
Dorn, G. L. (1967). *Genetics*, **56**, 619.
Edwards, G. F. St L., Holt, G. and Macdonald, K. D. (1974). *J. gen. Microbiol.* **84**, 420.
Fujisawa, Y., Shirafugi, H., Kida, M., Nara, K., Yoneda, M. and Kanzaki, T. (1973). *Nature New Biol.* **246**, 154.
Holt, G. and Macdonald, K. D. (1968a). *Antonie van Leeuwenhoek*, **34**, 409.
Holt, G. and Macdonald, K. D. (1968b). *Nature, Lond.* **219**, 636.
Kafer, E. and Chen, T. L. (1964). *Can. J. Genet. Cytol.* **6**, 249.
Lemke, P. A. and Brannon, D. R. (1972). "Cephalosporins and Penicillins" (Ed. E. H. Flynn), p. 370. Academic Press, New York and London.
Lemke, P. A. and Nash, C. H. (1972). *Can. J. Microbiol.* **18**, 255.
Macdonald, K. D., Holt, G. and Ditchburn, P. (1972). "Fermentation Technology Today" (Ed. Terui, G.), p. 251. Society of Fermentation Technology, Japan.
Macdonald, K. D., Hutchinson, J. M. and Gillett, W. A. (1963a). *J. gen. Microbiol.* **33**, 375.
Macdonald, K. D., Hutchinson, J. M. and Gillett, W. A. (1963b). *J. gen. Microbiol.* **33**, 385.
McCully, K. S. and Forbes, E. (1965). *Genet. Res.* **6**, 352.
Pontecorvo, G., Roper, J. A., Hemmons, L. M., Macdonald, K. D. and Bufton, A. W. J. (1953). "Advances in Gentics" (Ed. M. Deremec) vol. 5, p. 141. Academic Press, New York and London.
Pontecorvo, G. and Sermonti, G. (1953). *Nature, Lond.* **172**, 126.
Raper, K. B. and Alexander, D. F. (1945). *J. Elisha Mitchell scient. Soc.* **61**, 74.
Sermonti, G. (1956). *J. gen. Microbiol.* **15**, 599.
Sermonti, G. (1959). *Ann. N.Y. Acad. Sci.* **81**, 950.
Singh, A. and Sherman, F. (1974). *Nature, Lond.* **247**, 227.

The genetic location of mutations increasing penicillin yield in *Aspergillus nidulans*

P. DITCHBURN*, G. HOLT† and K. D. MACDONALD

*Microbiological Research Establishment,
Porton Down, Salisbury, Wiltshire, England*

Summary

Since strains of *Aspergillus nidulans* yield penicillin and the genetics of this fungus has been investigated in considerable depth, it seemed a suitable choice of organism in which to study the formal genetics of penicillin production. Single mutants with raised penicillin yields were isolated from derivatives of the Glasgow wild-type strain NRRL 194 following ultraviolet light treatment. Penicillin production was shown to be under nuclear control.

Using parasexual haploidization analysis, three mutations designated *penA1*, *penB2* and *penC3* were assigned to chromosomes VIII, III and IV, respectively. Subsequently, cleistothecial analysis allowed each mutation to be positioned in relation to other loci on these chromosomes. Strains bearing *penB2* were morphologically abnormal with poorly formed and sparse conidial heads. This was possibly a pleiotropic expression of the *penB2* mutation. Strains carrying *penA1* produced fewer cleistothecia than usual and those with *penC3* no cleistothecia so there may have been physiological changes associated with these mutations additional to those determining increased antibiotic titre. When each was combined with its wild-type allele in a heterozygous diploid, *penA1* behaved as a recessive, *penB2* as a dominant and *penC3* as a semi-dominant mutation. Haploid recombinants bearing pairs of these nonallelic mutations which increased penicillin yield were selected.

Present addresses:
  * Glaxo Laboratories Ltd., Ulverston, Cumbria, England.
  † Bio-Organic Research Group, Polytechnic of Central London, 115 New Cavendish Street, London W1M 8JS, England.

Preliminary investigations indicated that *penA1* was epistatic to *penB2* and *penC3*, and that *penC3* was epistatic to *penB2*.

Introduction

Studies on the genetics of penicillin production in *Penicillium chrysogenum* have been hampered by an insufficient knowledge of the formal genetics of this fungus. However when penicillin first began to be manufactured on a large scale, a survey of fungi indicated that strains of *Aspergillus nidulans* yielded a substance similar to penicillin (Foster and Karow, 1945). Since then, this fungus, although it is homothallic, has been shown to be amenable to genetic analysis via its sexual cycle by methods devised by Pontecorvo (1948). It has also been found to possess a parasexual cycle (Pontecorvo *et al.*, 1953); a genetic analysis utilizing the latter mechanism complements one through the sexual cycle by facilitating the positioning of centromeres and the assignment of genetic markers to specific linkage groups. Genetic analyses using both sexual and parasexual systems have led to the development of a detailed chromosome map (Pontecorvo and Käfer, 1958; Dorn, 1967; Clutterbuck and Cove, 1974).

The great majority of mutants of *A. nidulans* used in genetic studies were derived from the wild-type strain, NRRL 194. After appropriate analytical tests, Holt and Macdonald (1968a) showed that this strain, and a number of derivatives, elaborated a metabolite indistinguishable from penicillin; they also found that antibiotic production as in *P. chrysogenum* was under nuclear control. The way was thus opened for an examination of the quantitative inheritance of antibiotic production in an organism whose genetics was well understood.

From derivatives of strain NRRL 194, single mutants with raised penicillin titres were isolated after mutagenic treatments and, following parasexual haploidization analyses (McCully and Forbes, 1965), each of three such mutations was assigned to one of the eight chromosomes of *A. nidulans*. Attempts were then made to position these mutations relative to other loci on the chromosomes which bore them. The present paper reviews and extends previous results on the genetic location of these mutations (Macdonald *et al.*, 1972) and describes the outcome of experiments designed to isolate individual recombinants bearing different nonallelic mutations increasing penicillin titre.

Materials and methods

Organisms. All strains were derived from the Glasgow wild-type strain of *A. nidulans*, NRRL 194.

Media. Minimal medium was as described by Pontecorvo *et al.* (1953). Details of complete medium, fermentation medium and penicillin bioassay medium can be found in the publication by Ditchburn *et al.* (1974).

Incubation temperature. Cultures were incubated at 37°C apart from shake flask cultures which were grown at 25°C which is about optimum for penicillin production.

Production and assay of penicillin. The techniques are given by Ditchburn *et al.* (1974).

Mutagenic treatment. A conidial suspension, containing 10^7 conidia in 10 cm^3 of distilled water, was irradiated with ultraviolet light (uv) from a Hanovia type 11 lamp for 8 min to give a survival level of 1 to 5 per cent. The suspension was rocked mechanically 30 cm underneath the uv source in an uncovered glass Petri dish of 9 cm diameter.

Methods of genetic analysis. These were as described for *Aspergillus nidulans* by Pontecorvo *et al.* (1953) and McCully and Forbes (1965).

Explanation of genetic symbols. acr, resistance to acriflavine; *bi,* requirement for biotin; *cha,* chatreuse coloured conidia; *fac,* inability to use acetate as sole carbon source; *gal,* inability to use a galactose as sole carbon source; *mo,* abnormal morphology; *nic,* requirement for nicotinamide; *nir,* requirement for more reduced form of inorganic nitrogen than nitrate; *orn,* requirement for ornithine; *pen,* increased penicillin titre; *pyro,* requirement for pyridoxin; *pal,* reduced alkaline phosphatase activity; *ribo,* requirement for riboflavin; *s,* requirement for more reduced form of inorganic sulphur than sulphate, *sgp,* slow growth and no cleistothecial production; *w,* white (colourless) conidia; *y,* yellow coloured conidia.

In the text, a capital letter after a symbol indicates its locus. Different capital letters after one symbol indicate different genetic loci and different numbers indicate independent isolates of the same phenotype.

Results

THE ISOLATION OF MUTANTS WITH INCREASED PENICILLIN TITRE

Three mutants with increased penicillin titres were found among 2800 colonies isolated after uv irradiation of conidia from two strains, in separate mutation programmes. These were coded *penA1, penB2* and *penC3* and details are given in Table 1.

THE ASSIGNMENT OF *penA1*, *penB2* AND *penC3* TO SPECIFIC LINKAGE GROUPS
FOLLOWING PARASEXUAL HAPLOIDIZATION ANALYSIS

Each mutation was positioned on one of the eight haploidization groups of
A. nidulans using the method of parasexual haploidization analysis devised by
McCully and Forbes (1965). In this technique, a heterozygous diploid is
synthesized between a strain carrying the genetic marker whose linkage group
is to be determined, and a tester strain genetically labelled on all chromosomes. Diploid conidia are plated on complete medium containing *para*-
fluorophenylalanine (PFP) to induce haploidization. Haploids arise as
vigorously growing sectors on the surface of poorly growing diploid colonies.

TABLE 1

Mutants with raised penicillin yields and their chromosomal location

Parents		Mutants		Chromosomal assignment following parasexual haploidization analysis
Phenotype	Penicillin titre $u\,cm^{-3}$	Phenotype	Penicillin titre $u\,cm^{-3}$	
biA	6	*biA penA1*	20	VIII
biA w-010	6	*biA w-010 penB2*	12	III
biA w-010	6	*biA w-010 penC3*	20	IV

Free recombination of whole chromosomes occurs during haploidization so
that the unlocated marker recombines freely with all the genetic markers
from the tester strain except that marker on the homologue of the chromosome
bearing the unpositioned marker. The latter can thus be assigned to a
specific linkage group.

To position a mutation increasing penicillin yield, a heterozygous diploid
was made between the mutant with raised penicillin titre and a tester strain
labelled on all eight chromosomes. More than 100 haploid segregants were
isolated following PFP treatment of conidia from each diploid synthesized;
their phenotypes were characterized, and penicillin yields estimated following
the growth of each segregant in duplicate shake-flask cultures. Because of
biological variation an accurate estimation of the penicillin titre of a single
haploid segregant would have required an unacceptable degree of replication
considering the number to be tested. Therefore it was not always possible to
decide whether individual segregants bore the mutation raising penicillin titre
or its wild-type allele. However, as explained below, an estimation of linkage
was obtained by comparing the mean penicillin titres of segregants carrying a

particular mutant allele from the tester strain with the mean titre of segregants with the mutant's wild-type allele.

If a mutant allele introduced from the tester strain segregated independently from the mutation for increased antibiotic titre then the mean penicillin titre of haploid segregants with the mutant allele should be similar to that of haploid segregants with the mutant's wild-type allele. Half of the haploids with the mutant allele from the tester strain should carry the mutation raising penicillin yield and half the wild-type allele of this mutation. Similarly, half the haploid segregants with the wild-type allele of the mutant from the tester strain should carry the mutation raising yield and half its wild-type allele. On the other hand, when a mutant allele from the tester strain was located on the homologue of the chromosome carrying the mutation for increased titre, the mean titre of haploid segregants with the mutant allele from the tester strain should be significantly less than the mean titre of those with this mutant's wild-type allele. On these criteria, the mutants, *penA1*, *penB2* and *penC3*, have been assigned to specific linkage groups as reported previously (Macdonald *et al.*, 1972) and the results are summarized in Table 1.

THE POSITIONING OF THE MUTATION *penA1* RELATIVE TO OTHER LOCI ON CHROMOSOME VIII USING CLEISTOTHECIAL ANALYSIS

Two sexual crosses were made between a strain carrying *penA1*, first with a strain carrying *ornB* and the second with a strain carrying *riboB*. These auxotrophic markers were situated about 140 units apart on the right arm of chromosome VIII and it was hoped, by performing these crosses, to scan a wide region of this chromosome for the location of *penA1*.

Following the methods of Pontecorvo *et al.* (1953), a single hybrid cleistothecium was isolated from each cross and ascospores spread onto complete medium agar. Individual colonies which grew were tested for the presence or absence of a requirement for ornithine (or riboflavin) and their penicillin yields assessed. Because of biological variation, as discussed previously, the normal 2 × 2 tables could not be used to assess linkage between *penA1* and *ornB* or *riboB*. However, an estimate of linkage was made by comparing the mean penicillin titres of segregants bearing *ornB* or *riboB* with the mean titres of segregants bearing the wild-type alleles of *ornB* or *riboB*.

In the cross involving *ornB*, if this marker were 50 or more map units distant from *penA1* then half of the segregants carrying *ornB* would carry *penA1* (determining a penicillin titre of 20 units per cm^3) and half the wild-type allele, *penA1$^+$* (determining a penicillin titre of 6 units per cm^3). Similarly half the recombinants with *ornB$^+$* would bear *penA1* and half, *penA1$^+$*. It followed that the ratio of the mean penicillin titres of segregants bearing *ornB$^+$* to that of those with *ornB* would approximate to unity, unless the *ornB* marker modified antibiotic titre. However, if *ornB* were linked to *penA1* at a distance of less than 50 map units then more than 50 per cent of the segregants carrying *ornB* would carry *penA1*[+] and more than 50 per cent of the segregants with *ornB*[+] would carry *penA1*. The ratio of the mean penicillin titre of segregants bearing *ornB*[+] to that of those bearing *ornB* would therefore be greater than unity and the closer the linkage distance the higher this value would be up to a theoretical limit of 3.33. The results of the crosses involving *ornB* and *riboB* have been reported previously (Macdonald *et al.*, 1972). In each case the ratios of mean penicillin titres approximates to unity suggesting that *penA1* was 50 or more map units distant from *ornB* or *riboB*.

In subsequent crosses another section of chromosome VIII was scanned for the presence of *penA1* in the region of the marker *chaA* and *nirA* which are at the distal end of the right arm of this chromosome. Eight crosses were performed in which *chaA* was introduced in the *cis* position with *penA1*, and with *nirA* in both *cis* and *trans* positions.

When the penicillin yields of strains bearing *penA1* and *chaA* or *chaA*[+] were compared there was no evidence that the *chaA* mutation affected penicillin titre. The results of crosses 1 to 5, illustrated in Table 2, gave information on linkage between *penA1* and *chaA*. Among segregants from all 5 crosses the mean penicillin titres of those bearing *chaA*, introduced with *penA1*, and the mean penicillin titres of those bearing *chaA*[+], introduced with *penA1*[+], were calculated. The ratios of these means are shown in the final column of Table 2. These are consistently greater than unity and, as discussed earlier, indicated linkage between *penA1* and *chaA*.

The results of crosses 6 to 8 in Table 2 suggested linkage between *penA1* and *nirA*. In this series of crosses *penA1* and *nirA* were introduced in both *cis* and *trans* configurations to observe if the latter affected penicillin yield. In cross 6, where the two mutations were introduced in *trans*, a figure of 1.45 was obtained as the ratio of the mean penicillin yield between haploids bearing *nirA*[+] to that of those carrying *nirA*. In crosses 7 and 8 where the mutations were introduced in *cis* the average ratio was 1.64 when the mean yields of segregants bearing *nirA* was divided by the mean of those bearing *nirA*[+] in both crosses (Table 2). The mutation *nirA* had therefore no obvious effect on penicillin yield.

A map distance of 25 units has been reported between *nirA* and *chaA* (Clutterbuck and Cove, 1974) and confirmed in our laboratory. The present results indicate that *penA1* is located between *chaA* and *nirA*. If *penA1* were located outside this region the titre ratios as calculated would be expected to reveal this. Since the average of these ratios for crosses 1 to 5, 1.54, is similar to the average for crosses 6 to 8, 1.58 (see final column in Table 2), *penA1* can be tentatively positioned about equidistant between *chaA* and *nirA*.

TABLE 2

Summary of data from crosses made in an attempt to position penA1 relative to chaA and nirA on chromosome VIII

Cross	Phenotype of parents	Allele introduced with penA1	Number of segregants bearing this allele	Mean penicillin titre u cm^{-3}	Allele introduced with penA1$^+$	Number of segregants bearing this allele	Mean penicillin titre u cm^{-3}	Mean penicillin titre ratios Alleles	Ratios
1	a. chaA penA1 b. yA	chaA	81	13.1	chaA$^+$	76	10.0	chaA:chaA$^+$	1.31
2	a. chaA penA1 b. yA nirA	chaA	67	15.6	chaA$^+$	63	10.8	chaA:chaA$^+$	1.44
3*	a. chaA penA1 b. yA biA palB	chaA	64	11.8	chaA$^+$	6	7.2	chaA:chaA$^+$	1.64
4*	a. chaA nirA penA1 b. y-013 biA palB	chaA	95	12.4	chaA$^+$	9	9.3	chaA:chaA$^+$	1.33
5	as for Cross 4	chaA	166	16.8	chaA$^+$	24	8.5	chaA:chaA$^+$	1.96
6	a. chaA penA1 b. yA nirA	nirA$^+$	59	16.0	nirA	71	11.0	nirA$^+$:nirA	1.45
7	a. chaA nirA penA1 b. y-013 biA palB	nirA	55	14.8	nirA$^+$	49	8.4	nirA:nirA$^+$	1.76
8	as for Cross 7	nirA	109	18.4	nirA$^+$	81	12.1	nirA:nirA$^+$	1.52

* Only those segregants bearing palB$^+$ included in the data as evidence suggested that palB reduced penicillin titre.

THE POSITIONING OF THE MUTATION $penB2$ RELATIVE TO OTHER LOCI ON CHROMOSOME III USING CLEISTOTHECIAL ANALYSIS

Strains bearing $penB2$ are morphologically abnormal and have poorly formed and sparse conidial heads. The genetic locus of this morphological trait, designated mo-01, was positioned on the same chromosome as $penB2$ and was located at a point 13 map units from moC and 17 units from sA. Since mo-01 and $penB2$ were induced during the same mutagenic treatment, the possibility existed that they were different manifestations of the same genetic lesion. The results of genetic analysis were not inconsistent with mo-01 and $penB2$ being identical or very closely linked (Macdonald et al., 1972).

THE POSITIONING OF THE MUTATION $penC3$ RELATIVE TO OTHER LOCI ON CHROMOSOME IV USING CLEISTOTHECIAL ANALYSIS

The mutant bearing $penC3$ appeared to be infertile but several crosses were set up in the hope that hybrid cleistothecia would be formed between this strain and others with genetic markers on chromosome IV and that $penC3$ could then be located relative to other loci on this chromosome. However, although several hundred cleistothecia were isolated none proved to be hybrid. Attempts to induce fertility in the mutant after growth on either minimal medium or complete medium, at a variety of incubation temperatures, were unsuccessful.

Houghton (1970) has described mutations, designated sgp, which reduce growth rate and cause infertility. While crosses between strains bearing allelic sgp mutations were sexually sterile, those between strains bearing nonallelic sgp mutations were fertile and all the cleistothecia which arose were hybrid. In the hope that the mutant with $penC3$ might in some way mimic the behaviour of those with sgp mutations, since both types of mutations lead to a lack of fertility, a cross was made between a strain bearing $penC3$ and $pyroA$, isolated after parasexual haploidization segregation, and a strain bearing $sgpC$. From this cross, hybrid cleistothecia were isolated with ease and one was chosen for genetical analysis with the results shown in Table 3. The marker, $pyroA$, is

TABLE 3

Comparison of penicillin yields of segregants bearing mutant and wild-type alleles of $pyroA$ from a cross between strains of phenotype w-010, $pyroA$, $penC3$ and $sgpC$

Number of segregants bearing $pyroA$	Mean penicillin titre u cm^{-3}	Number of segregants bearing $pyroA^+$	Mean penicillin titre u cm^{-3}	Mean penicillin titre ratio $pyroA:pyroA^+$
86	20.7	76	12.2	1.70

situated on the right arm of chromosome IV and differences between the mean antibiotic titre of haploids bearing the mutant and those bearing the wild-type allele of *pyroA* suggest linkage between this marker and *penC3* of less than 50 map units. In this cross the mutant allele, *pyroA*, was introduced in *cis* with *penC3*. There was no indication from the behaviour of parental cultures that the possession of *pyroA* affected penicillin yield but if it did, deleteriously, the effect would be to lower the mean penicillin yield of segregants bearing *pyroA* and thus reduce the ratio of the mean penicillin titre of segregants bearing *pyroA* to that of those bearing *pyroA⁺*. Since this ratio is substantially in excess of unity the possibility that the marker *pyroA* might reduce titre did not affect the conclusion that *pyroA* and *penC3* were closer than 50 map units (Table 3).

THE PENICILLIN TITRES OF HETEROZYGOUS DIPLOIDS CARRYING MUTATIONS
FOR INCREASED PENICILLIN YIELD

In *Penicillium chrysogenum*, the performance of the heterozygous diploids synthesized between haploid parents with relatively high penicillin titres indicated that mutations responsible for increasing antibiotic productivity were recessive to their wild-type alleles (Macdonald *et al.*, 1964).

Heterozygous diploids were made between three strains of *A. nidulans* bearing *penA1*, *penB2* or *penC3* and a strain bearing the wild-type allele of these mutations. The penicillin yields of the three diploids and their haploid parents are shown in Table 4 where the results for each strain are the mean of 10 separate fermentations in shake-flask cultures. The results suggested that *penA1* is recessive, *penB2* dominant and *penC3* semi-dominant to their respective wild-type alleles.

TABLE 4

The penicillin titres of heterozygous diploids bearing a mutation for increased penicillin yield and its wild type allele

	Haploid parents	Heterozygous diploids
Phenotype	Penicillin titre u cm⁻³	Penicillin titre u cm⁻³
a. *biA penA1* b. tester strain*	20.0 5.5	5.3
a. *biA w-010 penB2 mo-01* b. tester strain*	14.0 5.5	12.9
a. *biA w-010 penC3* b. tester strain*	19.7 5.5	11.3

* The tester strain carried the following genetic markers on chromosomes I to VIII respectively: *yA*; *acrA*; *galA*; *pyroA*; *facA*; *sB*; *nicB*; *riboB*.

Two heterozygous diploids were then synthesized between haploid parents each carrying a different mutation for increased antibiotic titre as illustrated in Table 5 where the titres given for each strain are the mean of 10 fermentations. The penicillin yields in this experiment were higher than normal but comparable with each other. When the titre of the diploid bearing *penA1* and *penB2* in the *trans* arrangement is compared with those of the parental haploids, the results support the findings that *penA1* is recessive and *penB2* dominant.

TABLE 5

The penicillin titres of heterozygous diploids carrying nonallelic mutations for increased penicillin yield

Haploid parents		Heterozygous diploids	
Phenotype	Penicillin titre u cm^{-3}	Combination of mutations for increased penicillin titre	Penicillin titre u cm^{-3}
a. *chaA yA biA penA1* b. *yA riboB pyroA penB2*	39.1 16.8	*penA1 penB2*	18.3
a. *w-010 pyroA penC3* b. *yA riboB mo-01 penB2*	35.2 16.2	*penB2 penC3*	16.1

In the second diploid *penB2* and *penC3* were introduced in the *trans* configuration and its yield was similar to that of the haploid parent bearing *penB2* and less than that carrying *penC3*. From Table 4 it can be seen that diploids with *penB2* or *penC3* in the heterozygous condition have similar titres so the semi-dominance of *penC3* does not raise titre to a level beyond that of the dominant *penB2*. There is no additive effect of the semi-dominant *penC3* and the dominant *penB2* when present in *trans* in the same diploid (Table 5) which supports findings to be discussed later that *penC3* is epistatic to *penB2*.

The diploid heterozygous for *penB2* had normal morphology, when grown on complete medium or fermentation medium solidified with agar, although haploids bearing *penB2* had abnormal morphology (designated *mo-01*). As discussed earlier, the phenotypic characteristics determined by *penB2* and *mo-01* could be pleiotropic effects of a single mutational event. If so, while one ramification of the genetic lesion, an increase in penicillin yield, was dominant, the other, abnormal morphology, was recessive.

HAPLOID RECOMBINANTS CARRYING TWO NONALLELIC MUTATIONS DETERMINING INCREASED PENICILLIN TITRE

Since *penA1*, *penB2* and *penC3* were located on different chromosomes it was possible to consider isolating individual haploid recombinants bearing two or three of these mutant alleles. Parasexual crosses were made between haploid parent strains shown in Table 6 in an attempt to select haploid recombinants with the following combinations of markers; *penA1, penB2*; *penA1, penC3*; *penB2, penC3*; *penA1, penB2, penC3*. After their synthesis, diploids were treated with *p*-fluorophenylalanine and selection made for haploids carrying the marker mutations as shown in Table 6. All those sought were isolated apart

TABLE 6

The penicillin titres of haploid segregants bearing two nonallelic mutations for increased penicillin yield

Cross	Haploid parents		Haploid segregants		
	Phenotype	Penicillin titre u cm^{-3}	Markers selected*	Number	Mean penicillin titre u cm^{-3}
1	a. *chaA nirA penA1*	33.1	*chaA nirA* (VIII, *penA1*)	3	27.5
	b. *biA w-010 pyroA*		*mo-01*, (III, *penB2*)		
	mo-01 penB2	17·8			
2	a. *yA w-010 pyroA penC3*	28.6	*pyroA* (IV, *penC3*) *mo-01* (III, *penB2*)	2	25.0
	b. *yA riboB mo-01 penB2*	16.1			
3	a. *pyroA riboB mo-01 penB2 penC3*	17.5	*pyroA* (IV, *penC3*) *chaA nirA riboB* (VIII, *penA1*)	24	26.8
	b. *chaA nirA penA1*	29.4			

* The chromosome on which each allele is borne is given in parentheses together with the *pen* mutations carried on these chromosomes.

from recombinants bearing all three *pen* mutations. In no case was a recombinant found which had a titre greater than the higher yielding parent (Table 6). Recombinants of type *penA1, penB2* had titres closer to that of the parent bearing *penA1*. Segregants of type *penA1, penC3* and *penB2, penC3* had penicillin yields similar to those of their respective higher yielding parents. From these results, it can be tentatively suggested that *penA1* is epistatic to *penB2* and *penC3* and that *penC3* is epistatic to *penB2*.

Discussion

A genetic analysis of quantitative characters presents problems not associated with that concerned with qualitative characters. Our estimates of the degree of linkage between *pen* mutations and other markers were based on concepts which at this stage did not allow distances to be calculated in map units although they could be, and in some cases were, used to position *pen* mutations relative to other loci on specific linkage groups.

Auxotrophic and other genetic markers can affect penicillin yield (Macdonald *et al.*, 1963) and mutations of this sort were avoided as far as possible, as markers in crossing experiments. However, even when marker interference is present from one parent, an estimate of linkage can be obtained, following meiotic segregation, by comparing recombinant and parental classes not carrying the interfering marker.

Assuming no marker interference, then, in a cross designed to estimate linkage between a mutation increasing penicillin yield and a marker mutation, it is possible to devise a theoretical nonlinear relationship between their map distance and the ratio of the mean penicillin titre of meiotic segregants bearing the marker's mutant allele to that of those bearing the marker's wild-type allele, as illustrated in Table 7 and Fig. 1. If the mutant's penicillin titre were increased over the parent's by a factor of 4 then a mean titre ratio of 4 would indicate that the marker and *pen* mutations were located at the same locus; as the value of this ratio reduced so would map distance increase up to 50 or more map units when the ratio became unity. In the illustration the *pen* and marker mutations were introduced in the *cis* arrangement but it is possible to construct a similar relationship for *trans* configurations. Clearly, the accuracy

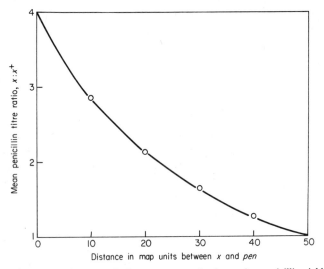

Fig. 1. Estimate of linkage in map units between a mutation increasing penicillin yield from 5 to 20 u cm^{-3} and a genetic marker x, introduced in *cis* configuration, based on the ratio of the mean penicillin yield of meiotic segregants bearing x to that of segregants bearing x^+ (see Table 7). Parental genotypes and their penicillin yields: $x\ pen$ (20 u cm^{-3}); $x^+\ pen^+$ (5 u cm^{-3}).

TABLE 7

Theoretical relationship between mean penicillin yield ratio of $x:x^+$ and map distance between marker x and *pen* marker introduced in *cis* configuration, examining 100 products of meiosis and where the parent of phenotype x has a titre of 20 u cm^{-3} and that of phenotype x^+ a titre of 5 u cm^{-3}

Map unit distance between x and *pen*	Segregant type	Phenotype	Number	Penicillin yield of individual segregants u cm^{-3}	Mean penicillin yield ratio $x:x^+$
0	parental	x	50	20	4.00
	parental	x^+	50	5	
10	parental	x	45	20	
	parental	x^+	45	5	2.85
	recombinant	x^+	5	20	
	recombinant	x	5	5	
20	parental	x	40	20	
	parental	x^+	40	5	2.13
	recombinant	x^+	10	20	
	recombinant	x	10	5	
30	parental	x	35	20	
	parental	x^+	35	5	1.63
	recombinant	x^+	15	20	
	recombinant	x	15	5	
40	parental	x	30	20	
	parental	x^+	30	5	1.27
	recombinant	x^+	20	20	
	recombinant	x	20	5	
50 or more	parental	x	25	20	
	parental	x^+	25	5	1.00
	recombinant	x^+	25	20	
	recombinant	x	25	5	

of such an estimation would be determined by the number of segregants tested, the level of replication and the increase in penicillin yield of the mutant relative to its parent. Other factors of possible consequence would be the behaviour of mutations increasing penicillin yield, in novel genetic backgrounds following recombination, and also possible interactions between different genetic markers introduced from separate parents.

All three mutants with raised penicillin yields were isolated after single mutagenic treatments and each had concomitant morphological changes. The strain bearing *penA1* had a slight reduction in the length of its conidial heads and produced fewer cleistothecia than normal, that with *penB2* had poorly formed and sparse conidial heads and that carrying *penC3* was infertile. It is possible that these morphological abnormalities are pleiotropic effects of the *pen* mutations. The evidence for this is compelling in the case of *penB2* where it has been found impossible to separate the locus of *penB2* from that of its associated morphological trait, *mo-01*, following meiotic segregation (Macdonald *et al.*, 1972).

In *Penicillium chryogenum*, after repeated cycles of mutation and selection, isolates with high penicillin yields have been found to be macroscopically different from their ancestral strains, growing considerably slower on surface culture and often sporing less well. However, detailed evidence on the association of single step *pen* mutations with morphological abnormalities is lacking in this fungus.

The results presented here suggest that in *A. nidulans* mutations increasing antibiotic production may also produce pleiotropic and visually recognizable changes and that some could be used as qualitative genetic markers for antibiotic yield like the one associated with *penB2* and possibly, less easily, the one associated with *penC3*. If so, genetic analysis would become less tedious than it is now when individual segregants have to be tested for penicillin yield.

One of the mutations examined, *penB2*, behaved as a dominant and the existence of such mutations, contrary to earlier findings in *P. chrysogenum* (Macdonald *et al.*, 1964), suggests a short-cut way of breeding for increased penicillin titre dependent only on the isolation of a heterozygous diploid rather than recombinants from sexual or parasexual crosses. If different mutations of this sort with additive effects were isolated in *P. chrysogenum*, diploids heterozygous for two or more could be used as plant strains in industrial fermentations since ways of preserving the stability of heterozygous diploids and avoiding the consequences of breakdown due to parasexual segregation have been proposed (Macdonald, 1964; Azevedo and Roper, 1967).

Individual haploid recombinants bearing two mutations increasing antibiotic yield have been isolated from heterozygous diploids but none had better yields than the higher yielding haploid parent carrying one *pen* mutation. It has been proposed that epistasis could account for these effects. When further mutations are examined it will be interesting to discover if different reaction patterns emerge in recombinants carrying more than one *pen* mutation. Additive effects on penicillin yield have already been found in recombinants from hybrids between natural isolates of *A. nidulans* (Holt and Macdonald, 1968b; Merrick, 1975) and in recombinants from a cross between a natural isolate and a strain bearing *penA1* (Holt and Macdonald, 1968b).

Acknowledgements

We are grateful to Mr E. Forbes of the University of Glasgow for the gift of a number of strains used in this investigation and to Dr J. A. Houghton of University College, Galway, for the gift of strains bearing *sgp* mutations. We are indebted to Mrs T. M. Tessier for expert technical assistance.

References

Azevedo, J. L. and Roper, J. A. (1967). *J. gen. Microbiol.* **49**, 149.
Clutterbuck, A. J. and Cove, D. J. (1974). The genetic loci of *Aspergillus nidulans.* Handbook of Microbiology, The Chemical Rubber Company, Cleveland, Ohio.
Ditchburn, P., Giddings, B. and Macdonald, K. D. (1974). *J. appl. Bact.* **37**, 515.
Dorn, G. (1967). *Genetics,* **56**, 619.
Foster, J. W. and Karow, E. O. (1945). *J. Bact.* **49**, 19.
Holt, G. and Macdonald, K. D. (1968a). *Antonie van Leeuwenhoek,* **34**, 409.
Holt, G. and Macdonald, K. D. (1968b). *Nature, Lond.,* **219**, 636.
Houghton, J. A. (1970). *Genet. Res. Camb.,* **16**, 285.
McCully, K. S. and Forbes, E. (1965). *Genet. Res. Camb.* **6**, 352.
Macdonald, K. D. (1964). *Nature, Lond.* **204**, 404.
Macdonald, K. D., Holt, G. and Ditchburn, P. (1972). "Fermentation Technology Today". Proceedings of the Fourth International Fermentation Symposium (Ed. G. Terui), p. 251. Society of Fermentation Technology, Japan.
Macdonald, K. D., Hutchinson, J. M. and Gillett, W. A. (1963). *J. gen. Microbiol.* **33**, 365.
Macdonald, K. D., Hutchinson, J. M. and Gillett, W. A. (1964). *Antonie van Leeuwenhoek,* **30**, 209.
Merrick, M. J. (1975). These Proceedings.
Pontecorvo, G. (1948). Proceedings of the Eighth International Congress of Genetics, *Heriditas* supplement, p. 642.
Pontecorvo, G., Roper, J. A., Hemmons, L. M., Macdonald, K. D. and Bufton, A. W. J. (1953). "Advances in Genetics" (Ed. M. Demerec), vol. 5, p. 141. Academic Press, New York and London.
Pontecorvo, G. and Käfer, E. (1958). "Advances in Genetics" (Ed. M. Demerec), vol. 9, p. 71. Academic Press, New York and London.

Hybridization and selection for penicillin production in *Aspergillus nidulans*—a biometrical approach to strain improvement

M. J. MERRICK*

Department of Genetics, University of Birmingham, Birmingham B15 2TT, England

Summary

The use, in recent years, of the fungus *Aspergillus nidulans* for studies of the genetics of penicillin production (Holt and Macdonald, 1968a, 1968b) prompted an investigation of the quantitative inheritance of this character. A comparison of fifty-two wild isolates revealed significant variation in productivity with a continuous range of titres from 0 to 14 u cm^{-3}. Analysis of the titres of progeny from sexual crosses indicated that differences between isolates were under genetic control. Segregation of genes controlling titre was detected in four out of seven crosses and heritabilities ranged from 0 to 77%. Progeny distributions were continuous in all cases and no segregation of major genes affecting titre was observed. In nearly all crosses examined during this study genes controlling titre were acting in an additive manner.

A selection programme was initiated to investigate the extent of natural variation and the genetic architecture of "high-titre" strains. Four independent selection lines were set up and in each line the mean penicillin titre was approximately doubled after four or five generations. At this point the response tended to reach a plateau and genetic variation within lines had been exhausted. Crosses between "improved" strains from the selection lines showed as much genetic variation as crosses between wild isolates, indicating that different genes had been fixed in each line. These genes recombined in

Present address: Department of Genetics, John Innes Institute, Colney Lane, Norwich NR4 7UH, England.

an additive manner, making further selection possible. In this way mean titre has been increased by a factor of three in seven generations. This study demonstrates the importance of biometrical analysis when dealing with a quantitative character such as antibiotic yield, and the increase in productivity obtained indicates that hybridization may be a valuable method of producing improved strains.

Introduction

It is now twenty years since a parasexual cycle was first described in *Penicillium chrysogenum* (Pontecorvo and Sermonti, 1953) and genetic analysis of peni-cillin production became feasible. In the last two decades genetic studies of *P. chrysogenum* have been carried out by a number of workers (see Sermonti, 1969, and Ball, 1973b, for reviews) in order to examine the possibilities of using hybridization and recombination in strain improvement. The quanti-tative nature of a character such as penicillin production has, however, rarely been discussed. The problems of sensitivity of the character to the environ-ment and of the interactions between different genotypes and different environments have been mentioned by a number of authors including Sermonti (1959) and Ball (1973a) but there has been very little reference to the fact that these problems are characteristic of metrical traits and that biometrical and statistical methods have been specifically designed (Mather and Jinks, 1971) to analyse such characters. Thus, although penicillin production is undoubtedly a quantitative character, in many previous studies analysis of the results has been largely qualitative.

A study of the quantitative genetics of penicillin production has never been carried out despite the fact that the information derived from such a study could be of considerable value in planning a breeding programme to increase titre. A biometrical investigation could reveal the type of gene action en-countered in high-titre strains and the amount of genetic variation available in different selection lines. However, at the present time, there are un-fortunately a number of factors which could make such a programme in *P. chrysogenum* considerably more difficult than it appears in theory.

　　i. *The parasexual cycle.* The use of this cycle is obligatory in genetic analysis of *P. chrysogenum* and many of the assumptions upon which the theory of biometrical genetics is based, e.g. that progeny samples from a cross are a true sample of all possible recombinant types from that cross, may not always be valid in samples from a parasexual cross. Parasexual analysis of metrical characters is, however, perfectly feasible and in crosses between strains of *Aspergillus nidulans* Croft (personal communication) has shown that, for radial growth rate, the means and variances of progeny samples from sexual and parasexual crosses are very similar.

ii. *Linkage data.* Whilst a knowledge of the linkage map of an organism is not essential for quantitative genetic analysis, when using the parasexual cycle a map is of great value in assessing whether there is any selection against particular chromosomes during haploidization, and in allowing selective markers on different chromosomes to be used. Although there is no available linkage map for wild-type strains of *P. chrysogenum* a haploidization map of a high-titre strain has been published (Ball, 1971).

iii. *Parental genome segregation.* The low frequency of recombinants amongst segregants from a heterozygous diploid, which has been encountered by nearly all authors who have worked with *P. chrysogenum* (Sermonti, 1961; Macdonald *et al.*, 1964; Elander, 1967) presents a serious problem in any genetic analysis.

The work of Ball (1971, 1973a) suggests that these problems may nevertheless be soluble and that in some strains of *P. chrysogenum* detailed genetic analysis might be a practical proposition. The foundations for a quantitative investigation of penicillin production in a different species have in the meantime been laid by Holt and Macdonald (1968a, 1968b) working with *Aspergillus nidulans*. Genetic analysis is possible by both the sexual and parasexual cycles in this organism and a number of metrical characters in the species have already been analysed genetically. For these reasons it has been chosen as a model organism in which to examine the application of biometrical genetics to antibiotic production.

Materials and methods

Strains. The isolates of *A. nidulans* used were from a collection of wild isolates at the Department of Genetics, University of Birmingham.

Media. Czapek agar was used as the basic medium for routine transfers and crossing. 2 per cent (w/v) malt extract agar was used as a conidiation medium and spore suspensions were prepared in a solution of 0.02 per cent (w/v) "calsolene" oil (ICI Ltd). The fermentation medium was that given by Macdonald *et al.* (1963).

Crossing techniques. All crosses were carried out by single perithecium analysis (Pontecorvo *et al.*, 1953) using, as parents, a green-spored prototroph and either a yellow- or a white-spored prototroph. (Spore colour mutations were induced by ultraviolet irradiation.) The crossing technique was essentially that of Butcher (1968). When a hybrid perithecium had been selected a sample of progeny was taken at random for antibiotic yield testing.

Yield testing. Fermentation flasks (250 cm^3 Erlenmeyer conicals +40 cm^3

medium) were incubated on a rotary shaker for 5 days at 26°C. Shake-flask broths were filtered, diluted if necessary, and assayed using a large-plate microbiological assay (Lees and Tootill, 1955). The indicator organism used was *Bacillus subtilis* strain ATCC 6633.

Results

PRIMARY SCREEN

In order to assess the amount of naturally occurring variation for penicillin production among wild isolates of *A. nidulans* a random sample of 52 isolates was tested for penicillin yield. Each isolate was tested on two occasions, single-flask replication being used in each experiment. The productivity of the isolates (Fig. 1) ranged from $0.0\,\mathrm{u\,cm}^{-3}$ to $14.4\,\mathrm{u\,cm}^{-3}$ with a mean of $8.0 \pm 0.4\,\mathrm{u\,cm}^{-3}$. An analysis of variance (Table 1) shows that the differences

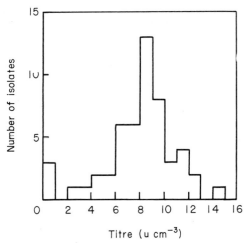

FIG. 1. Penicillin yields of fifty-two wild isolates of *Aspergillus nidulans*.

TABLE 1

Analysis of variance of penicillin titre, on two occasions, for a random sample of 52 wild isolates of *A. nidulans*

Item	df	MS	VR
Between isolates	51	17.51	4.14***
Between occasions	1	244.00	57.97***
Isolates × occasions	51	4.21	

*** Significant at $P = 0.001$.

between isolates are highly significant. These significant differences suggest that there are genetic differences between the isolates and the normal frequency distribution (Fig. 1) indicates that penicillin production is a continuously varying character.

In *A. nidulans* heterokaryon formation between pairs of isolates is restricted to members of a single heterokaryon-compatibility (h-c) group (Grindle, 1963) but sexual outcrossing is possible between all wild isolates to a greater or lesser extent regardless of heterokaryon-compatibility (Butcher, 1968).

TABLE 2

Analysis of variance of penicillin titre for those isolates in known heterokaryon-compatibility groups

Item	df	MS	VR
Between h–c groups	9	36.40	4.19**
Within h–c groups	21	8.68	2.26*
Occasions	1	179.86	46.73***
Isolates × occasions	30	3.85	

*** $P < 0.001$ ** $P = 0.01–0.001$ * $P = 0.05–0.01$

Thirty-one of the isolates tested have been allocated to h-c groups and an analysis of variance (Table 2) of the yields of these isolates indicated that 67% of the variation between isolates was due to differences between h-c groups.

CROSSES BETWEEN WILD ISOLATES

In order to confirm that the observed differences between isolates were genetically controlled and, if so, to determine the nature of this control, sexual crosses were carried out between pairs of isolates and the titres of progeny samples were examined. When testing the strains for their penicillin yield, two or more replicate flasks of each strain were always employed to obtain an estimate of the amount of environmental variation present.

Crosses were made between pairs of "high-titre" isolates and pairs of "low-titre" isolates classified according to their performance in the primary screen. The effect of heterokaryon-compatibility was investigated by making crosses between compatible isolates and between incompatible isolates. In all cases the frequency distributions for the progeny were continuous and approximately normal. No indication of segregation of major genes affecting titre was found. The progeny titres were analysed using a standard form of analysis of variance (Table 3).

TABLE 3

Standard analysis for variation in titre among samples of progeny from a single cross

Item		df*	EMS
Between progeny	Between spore colours	1	$\sigma_E^2 + p\sigma_G^2 + pn_0^\dagger\sigma_C^2$
	Within spore colours	s-2	$\sigma_E^2 + p\sigma_G^2$
Between plates		p-1	$\sigma_E^2 + s\sigma_P^2$
Plates × progeny		(s-1) (p-1)	σ_E^2
TOTAL		sp-1	

* s, number of progeny strains; p, number of replicate assay plates.

† n_0 was calculated from $n_0 = 1/(a-1)[N - (\Sigma n_i^2)/N]$ (Snedecor and Cochran, 1967).
σ_E^2 is a measure of the environmental variation and includes all items which contribute to variation between replicate flasks of the same strain, except differences between assay plates.
σ_P^2 is a measure of the variation between assay plates.
σ_C^2 is a measure of the variation attributable to the spore colour marker.
σ_G^2 is a measure of the variation due to segregation of natural allelic differences affecting penicillin titre.

Analysis of the titres of progeny from these crosses provides information on a number of aspects of the inheritance of penicillin production:

a. *Is the phenotypic variation genetically determined?* The analysis of variance partitions the total phenotypic variation into that between replicates which equals the environmental component and that between the individual progeny which equals the genetic plus environmental components. If the "between-progeny" item is significantly greater than the "flasks within progeny" item, the phenotypic variation contains a genetic component. By estimating each of the components of variation (Table 3) the proportion of the total variation which is genetically determined may be calculated as:

$$h_n^2 = \frac{\sigma_G^2}{\sigma_G^2 + \sigma_P^2 + \sigma_E^2}$$

This ratio is known as the "narrow heritability" (Mather and Jinks, 1971) and is an indication of the proportion of the phenotypic variation which could be fixed by selection. The variation (σ_C^2) attributable to the spore colour marker has been ignored in this calculation since, although it is genetic and could be fixed, it was not present in the original isolates. Variance estimates and values of h_n^2 for the eight crosses examined are given in Table 4.

Cross M42 was a sample of ascospores from a selfed perithecium and is therefore a control in which no genetic variation is expected. Of the remaining seven crosses four showed segregation for natural allelic differences affecting penicillin titre and three of these four crosses were between heterokaryon-

TABLE 4

Components of variation and heritability estimates for crosses between wild isolates of *A. nidulans*

Type of cross†	Parents $P_1 \times P_2$	Cross number	$\widehat{\sigma_G^2}$	$\widehat{\sigma_C^2}$	$\widehat{\sigma_E^2}$	h_n^2
HC	109/1 × 65	M1	10.02	0.00	11.45	0.47*
	111 × 65/1	M2	0.27	0.84*	5.38	0.05
HI	159 × 131/1	M3	0.23	0.82*	3.38	0.06
	183 × 189/1	M4	3.84	2.22*	6.36	0.38*
	139 × 82/1	M5	15.43	0.0	11.15	0.58*
LC	134 × 176/1	M40	0.00	0.96*	1.98	0.00
LI	154 × 176/1	M41	11.37	0.60	3.47	0.77*
S	65 × 65	M42	0.78	—	14.38	0.05

* Significantly different from zero.

† H and L indicate "high" and "low" titre respectively. C and I indicate heterokaryon compatible and incompatible parents respectively. S, sample of ascospores from a selfed perithecium.

incompatible isolates. Of the three compatible crosses only one showed segregation. These results are consistent with those obtained in the primary screen where comparatively little variation in titre was found within h-c groups suggesting that members of an h-c group are genotypically quite similar and that incompatible isolates are genotypically dissimilar. The data are in general agreement with those obtained by Jinks *et al.* (1966) for radial growth rate in wild isolates of *A. nidulans*.

b. *How are the genes arranged on the chromosome?* When a cross is segregating for one or more marker genes the data can be tested for linkage of a gene or group of genes affecting penicillin production to a particular marker. In the present case each cross was segregating for yellow conidial colour and the analysis of variance (Table 3) was used to extract, from the "between-progeny" item, an item which tests whether there is a difference between the mean titre of "green" and "yellow" progeny. If such a difference is found this may be attributable to linkage of genes affecting titre to the gene for conidial colour or alternatively to a pleiotropic effect of the marker gene. In all crosses the mean titre of the "yellow" progeny was less than that of the "green" progeny and in four cases this difference was significant. However, further experiments indicated that this was attributable to a pleiotropic effect of the *y* allele and not to linkage.

c. *How do the genes act?* Where the actions of a number of genes contribute to a single phenotype the pattern of gene action depends upon whether the various alleles are independent or nonindependent in their action. In a diploid organism nonindependent gene action can be due to dominance or epistasis or a combination of the two, but in haploids epistasis (nonallelic interaction) is the only possible cause. In a quantitative analysis independent gene action will appear as statistical additivity and nonindependence as statistical nonadditivity. Hence in an F_1 progeny sample the progeny mean

TABLE 5

Estimates of [i] (the contribution of non-additive gene effects to the mean phenotype) in eight crosses between wild isolates of *A. nidulans*

Cross number†	$\overline{P_1}$ u cm^{-3}	$\overline{P_2}$ u cm^{-3}	$\overline{F_1}$ u cm^{-3}	[i]
M1	11.8	10.4	14.6	−3.47*
M2	12.6	11.8	13.9	−1.77*
M3	7.9	5.3	6.7	−0.13
M4	10.3	9.5	11.1	−1.23
M5	9.6	4.2	6.1	0.75
M40	4.8	3.8	4.3	−0.02
M41	5.1	4.9	3.9	1.08
M42	14.3	13.5	13.9	−0.07

* Significantly different from zero.
† For parent strains see Table 4.

will be equal to the parental mean in the absence of epistasis (Butcher, 1969) but in the presence of any epistatic effects with a directional element the progeny distribution will be skewed and the progeny mean will deviate from the parental mean. Tests for epistasis were carried out in the present crosses and estimates of the contribution of gene interaction effects [i] to the mean phenotype were calculated (Table 5). Epistatic variation was detected in only one of the four segregating crosses, suggesting that the natural allelic differences affecting penicillin production act in a predominantly additive manner.

SELECTION FOR INCREASED TITRE

In order to investigate the extent of naturally occurring variation for penicillin production and to examine the genetic architecture of strains with increased titres, a programme to obtain "high-titre" strains by successive generations of hybridization and selection was carried out. As the gene action in crosses had been found to be predominantly additive, titre improvement was simply a matter of combining the maximum number of "increasing" alleles into a single genotype. The method used and the order in which these alleles are recombined is not important and therefore a simple line selection programme was chosen. A number of independent lines were set up and these were carried forward until response ceased at which time crosses were made between lines to incorporate the increasing alleles into one population and allow further advance.

Eight "high-titre" wild isolates were chosen and in order to ensure that these were as genetically diverse as possible they were selected such that each was a member of a different h-c group. The eight isolates were crossed in pairs to initiate four selection lines. In each generation 44 progeny were tested and the highest green-spored and highest yellow-spored progeny were

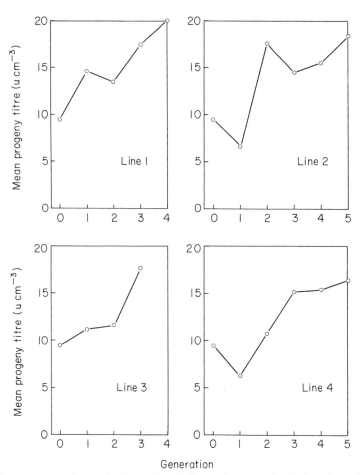

Generation

Fig. 2. Response to selection for increased penicillin production in four independent selection lines. Mean progeny titre (u cm^{-3}) in each generation.

chosen. These then became the parents of the next generation. In this way repeated mutagenesis to introduce new colour markers was avoided and hence any induction of chromosome aberrations by irradiation was kept to a minimum.

In each generation the progeny mean titre and the components of variation σ_G^2 and σ_E^2 were estimated (Figs 2 and 3). After four or five generations of selection a 60–100 per cent increase in titre had been obtained in each line and in at least two lines a reduction in the rate of increase in titre was apparent.

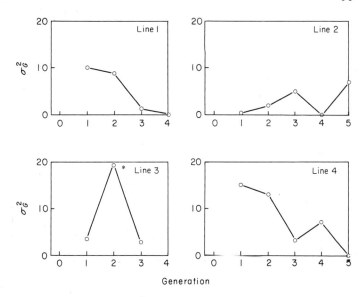

Fig. 3. Changes in genetic variance (σ_G^2) associated with selection for increased titre in the four selection lines. * Faulty fermentation.

Examination of the associated changes in the amount of genetic variation present showed a clear reduction in σ_G^2 as selection progressed and by the fifth generation it had been reduced to zero in lines 1 and 4. When using a haploid organism and a selection scheme with a fairly high degree of inbreeding (as in the present work) one expects the value of σ_G^2 to drop quite rapidly, even if no selection for high titre is being imposed, and therefore these observations are quite consistent with theoretical expectations.

CROSSES BETWEEN SELECTED LINES

The increases in titre obtained in lines 1 to 4 could have been obtained by selection of the same genes in each line. If this were so crosses between "high-titre" strains from different lines should release no (or relatively little) genetic variation. Crosses were therefore carried out in all combinations between three of the four lines (line 3 was terminated after the 3rd generation as hybrid perithecia could not be obtained). In each of the three "between-line" crosses considerable segregation was found (Table 6) and the values of σ_G^2 were as high or higher than those for crosses between wild isolates. It would appear, therefore, that different genes for increased titre had been selected in each of the lines. Furthermore, tests for epistasis indicated that in each of the "between-line" crosses the gene action was additive (Table 6).

TABLE 6

Data from analyses of crosses between "high-titre" selection lines

Selection lines	Cross number	σ_G^2	σ_E^2	h_n^2	$[i]$
1 × 2	M60	12.02	26.51	0.31*	1.49 ± 1.88
1 × 4	M70	16.51	25.77	0.39*	1.13 ± 1.58
2 × 4	M50	12.26	15.69	0.44*	−2.17 ± 2.51

* Significantly different from zero, $P < 0.001$.

RENEWED SELECTION FOR INCREASED TITRE

The generation of new genetic variation in the between-line crosses meant that it should be possible to achieve new increases in titre by a further round of selection until such time as this new variation was in turn exhausted.

The highest-titre green-spored and highest-titre yellow-spored strains were selected from the progeny of the cross between lines 2 and 4 (M50) and these two strains were used to initiate a second cycle of hybridization and selection. The procedure used was identical to that employed previously. Only two generations of selection were carried out but the mean progeny titre was raised from $16.1\,\text{u cm}^{-3}$ to $28.5\,\text{u cm}^{-3}$ (Fig. 4), an increase of 77%. During these two generations the value of σ_G^2 remained stable. The total selection response in lines 2 and 4 is shown in Fig. 4 and the association between the changes in mean titre and changes in σ_G^2 can be clearly seen. Although the second cycle of selection was not continued beyond two generations there were a number of indications that, had further selection been carried out, the level of genetic variation would have dropped considerably in the next generation.

Discussion

These studies have demonstrated that strains with increased penicillin titre may be obtained by hybridization and recombination in *A. nidulans* and that

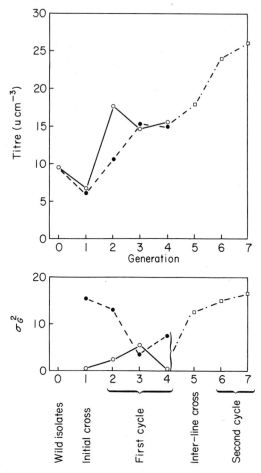

FIG. 4. Response to selection for increased titre in lines 2 and 4 and renewed selection from a cross between the lines. O———O, line 2; ●------●, line 4; □ – . –□ line 2 × 4.

this could be a valuable method for producing improved strains of micro-organisms. The results obtained indicate that penicillin production in *A. nidulans* is controlled by a large number of genes and that the biometrical techniques which have been designed to analyse quantitative characters in fungi may be applied in exactly the same way whether the character under investigation is radial growth rate or production of a secondary metabolite such as penicillin.

The importance of background genetic knowledge and of preliminary genetic studies before commencing a selection programme deserve particular emphasis and are exemplified in the present study, e.g. the use of heterokaryon incompatible isolates as the initial strains in order to obtain a genetically diverse base population from which to select. Likewise the type of gene action found in crosses between isolates has a number of implications, in particular: (i) in determining the type of crossing scheme which is most suitable when a selection programme is being designed; (2) in estimating the number of progeny from a cross which should be tested in order that there may be a significant probability of picking strains with increased titres.

While the mean penicillin titre has been raised almost three-fold in seven generations of selection, when viewed against the productivity of current commercial *Penicillium* strains both the mean titre and the response appear trivial. It must be stressed, however, that this response has been obtained solely by recombination of naturally occurring variation. The methods of analysis which have been used could equally well be applied to variation produced by mutagenesis, and the combination of hybridization and muta-genesis is now clearly both possible and desirable. Examination of the application of this approach to mutagenically induced variation in *A. nidulans* is currently being undertaken and will hopefully provide further useful guide lines for strain improvement in microorganisms.

Acknowledgements

I am very grateful to Dr C. E. Caten for his advice and encouragement throughout this work. I thank Glaxo Research Laboratories Ltd, Sefton Park, for the provision of equipment and materials and the Glaxo Staff for their continued support. A Science Research Council CAPS Studentship is gratefully acknowledged.

References

Ball, C. (1971). *J. gen. Microbiol.* **66**, 63.
Ball, C. (1973a). "Genetics of Industrial Microorganisms, Actinomyces and Fungi" (Ed. Z. Vaněk, Z. Hošťálek and J. Cudlín). p. 227. Academia, Prague.
Ball, C. (1973b). *Prog. ind. Microbiol.* **12**, 47.
Butcher, A. C. (1968). *Heredity, Lond.* **23**, 443.
Butcher, A. C. (1969). *Heredity, Lond.* **24**, 621.
Elander, R. P. (1967). *Abh. dt. Akad. Wiss. Berl.* 403.
Grindle, M. (1963). *Heredity, Lond.* **18**, 397.
Holt, G. and Macdonald, K. D. (1968a). *Antonie van Leeuwenhoek,* **34**, 409.
Holt, G. and Macdonald, K. D. (1968b). *Nature, Lond.* **219**, 636.
Jinks, J. L., Caten, C. E., Simchen, G. and Croft, J. H. (1966). *Heredity, Lond.* **21**, 227.
Lees, K. A. and Tootill, J. P. R. (1955). *Analyst, Lond.* **80**, 95.
Macdonald, K. D., Hutchinson, J. M. and Gillett, W. A. (1963). *J. gen. Microbiol.* **33**, 365.
Macdonald, K. D., Hutchinson, J. M. and Gillett, W. A. (1964). *Antonie van Leeuwen-hoek,* **30**, 209.

Mather, K. and Jinks, J. L. (1971). "Biometrical Genetics". Chapman and Hall Ltd, London.

Pontecorvo, G., Roper, J. A., Hemmons, L. M., Macdonald, K. D. and Bufton, A, (1953). *Adv. Genet.* **5**, 141.

Pontecorvo, G. and Sermonti, G. (1953). *Nature, Lond.* **172**, 126.

Sermonti, G. (1959). *Ann. N.Y. Acad. Sci.* **81**, 950.

Sermonti, G. (1961). *Sci. Repts. Ist Super. Sanita.* **1**, 462.

Sermonti, G. (1969). "Genetics of Antibiotic Producing Microorganisms". Wiley-Interscience, London.

Snedecor, G. W. and Cochran, W. G. (1967). "Statistical Methods", p. 258. Iowa State University Press, Ames, Iowa, USA.

Genetic instability in parasexual fungi

C. BALL* and J. L. AZEVEDO†

*Glaxo Laboratories Ltd. Ulverston, Cumbria, England
† Institute of Genetics, University of São Paulo, Piracicaba, Brazil

Summary

The significance of nuclear genetic instability in a variety of parasexual fungi is stressed. Studies in this field are relevant both to yield improvement and to prevention of yield degeneration in commercially important fungi in which the parasexual cycle is the only means of gene reassortment. Segregation in this cycle is the result of diploid instability, giving rise to strains that are genetically either stable or unstable. The very unstable segregants are mainly aneuploids or carry partial chromosome duplications, depending on the treatment of the diploid and its component parental strains. Strains may often be stabilized by genetic change or by control of the growth environment and thus, in appropriate cases, yield degeneration may be prevented.

Introduction

An understanding of genetic instability can result in commercial gains for the fermentation industry, both by improvement of yield and by prevention of yield degeneration. This paper intends to stress that reported work on nuclear genetic instability in a variety of parasexual fungi has significance that can be given practical application. In many ways the fact that so much work has been carried out with *Aspergillus nidulans* rather than with commercially important fungi is regrettable. Nevertheless, these studies have provided a background of information for more detailed work on organisms such as *Penicillium chrysogenum* and *Aspergillus niger* from the latter group.

243

Results and discussion

DEFINITION OF GENETIC INSTABILITY

Spontaneous instability is an inherent characteristic of genetic material but, in most situations, instability is so low that it is neither of significant use to generate useful variation nor is it usually a serious challenge to the desired genetic stability of a strain. Nevertheless, it is difficult to define genetic instability strictly. Such a definition must be relative, implying a greater frequency of occurrence of spontaneous genetically determined variation in a dividing population than could reasonably be attributed to conventional point mutation. This variation, to meet our strict definition of genetic instability, has to be the product of a high rate of genetic change (i.e. mutation or recombination) or the product of genetic change plus selection for certain genotypes in a population. Of particular importance is the need to establish that such variation is due to genetic causes and not microenvironmental differences. If the phenotypic change observed is retained on subculture, a genetic basis may be suspected.

YIELD IMPROVEMENT BY ENHANCING INSTABILITY

The parasexual cycle is genetically an unstable process in that segregants can be obtained from a diploid in high frequencies (Roper, 1966). Two general types of segregant can be produced, one being chromosomally balanced and the other chromosomally unbalanced. Both types have many stages in common during production but, for discussion purposes, these will be treated separately as follows.

Production of balanced genomes

i. *Mitotic interchromosomal exchange.* Haploidization and nondisjunction are the two related processes involved when whole chromosomes segregate in the parasexual cycle (i.e. when there is interchromosomal exchange). The key feature of recombination of these methods is that all genes on the same chromosome segregate together, thus facilitating not only the ready allocation of genes to linkage groups but also genetic engineering of whole chromosome exchange between closely related strains (McCully and Forbes, 1965). This is a clear advantage of the parasexual over the sexual cycle in the controlled breeding of strains that have improved yield. Such methods have been used to increase the penicillin yield of *P. chrysogenum* (Ball, 1973a, and Table 1) and also to allocate penicillin yield increasing mutations unequivocally to linkage groups in *A. nidulans* (Macdonald *et al.*, 1972).

The initial events involved in the spontaneous haploidization process have been analysed by Käfer (1961) for *A. nidulans*. Initial nondisjunction or chromosome loss gives rise to balanced segregant genomes that can be either haploid

TABLE 1

Titres* of ancestors, parents and segregants relative to diploidization br_1 $(t2)$; rib_1 × bg_1 an_1; nic_1 $(t5)$

	Haploid genotypes‡	Yield groups†												
		D	E	F	G	H	I	J	K	L	M	N	O	P
Ancestors	$br_1 nic_1$	—	—	3	3	—	—	—	—	—	—	—	—	—
	$br_1(t2); nic_1$	—	—	—	—	—	—	—	2	17	18	—	—	—
	$br_1; nic_1(t5)$	1	2	—	—	2	9	5	—	—	—	—	—	—
	$bg_1 an_1$	—	—	4	4	1	—	—	—	—	—	—	—	—
Parents	$bg_1 an_1; nic_1(t5)$	—	—	1	6	—	—	—	—	—	—	—	—	—
	$br_1(t2); rib_1$	—	—	—	—	2	—	—	—	—	—	—	—	—
Segregant Categories§	$br_1(t2); nic_1(t5)$	—	—	—	—	—	1	—	1	—	1	1	6	4
	$br_1(t2); rib_1$	—	—	—	—	3	—	2	—	—	—	—	—	—
	$bg_1 an_1; rib_1$	1	2	5	2	—	—	—	—	—	—	—	—	—
	$bg_1 an_1; nic_1(t5)$	1	—	1	3	—	—	—	—	—	—	—	—	—

* Data discussed by Ball (1973a).

† Each yield group covers 500 units of penicillin G.

‡ br, brown spore colour; bg, bright green spore colour; rib, inability to use ribose as sole carbon source; an, nic, requirement for aneurin and nicotinamide respectively; t_2, t_5, mutations increasing penicillin yield.

§ Numbers refer to strains in each yield group.

or diploid. Induction of haploidization by *para*fluorophenylalanine (PFA) has been described independently by Morpurgo (1961) and by Lhoas (1961). Other agents will also induce haploidization (Sermonti, 1969) but, as with PFA, the exact mechanism is often unknown.

The above well-documented processes in *A. nidulans* have been inferred for *P. chrysogenum* (Sermonti, 1969) and in principle confirmed in both this organism (Ball, 1971) and *A. niger* (Lhoas, 1967).

ii. *Mitotic intrachromosomal exchange.* Mitotic crossing-over and gene conversion are the only means whereby exchange of parts of chromosomes can take place. The spontaneous frequencies vary in different organisms being about 4 per cent for the whole genome of *P. chrysogenum* (Ball, 1971) which is about 20 times more than that found for *A. nidulans* (Pontecorvo and Käfer, 1958) and about 5 times less than found for *A. niger* (Lhoas, 1967). The significance of these processes in the parasexual breeding of strains for improved yield is that certain barriers to recombination by haploidization, such as reciprocal chromosome translocation, can be overcome. In certain cases a double or multiple cross-over event might be required. For this reason, work carried out with agents known to increase the frequency of mitotic crossing-over or conversion in various fungi is very important. These processes have been inferred in *P. chrysogenum* (Macdonald *et al.*, 1965; Macdonald, 1971) and recently unequivocal studies have been carried out on induction of mitotic intrachromosomal exchange (see Table 2).

TABLE 2
Frequencies of mitotic crossing-over in *P. chrysogenum**

Treatment	Colonies observed	Brown prototrophic diploid sectors	Frequency of mitotic crossing-over[†] (%)	Frequency ratio (*treated/control*)
1 Control	640	3	0.47	
uv light	3 600	6	0.17	0.36
2 Control	1 604	1	0.06	
Ethyleneimine	502	6	1.19	19.83‡
3 Control	3 957	0	0	
Nitrous Acid	10 255	10	0.10	∞
4 Control	3 612	5	0.14	
5-fluorouracil	11 803	263	2.23	15.93‡

* Data of Morrison and Ball.
† In a green spored diploid, heterozygous for a mutation determining brown spore colour and a proximally linked lysine auxotrophic marker.
‡ Significantly different from 1.0 (Chi-squared test).

iii. *Sequential mitotic intra- and interchromosomal exchange.* In parasexual breeding for yield improvement, the recovery of recombinant haploid products is desirable. Steps to increase the sequential occurrence of the processes just now described should be taken. One way is to select initially the products of mitotic crossing-over by the use of recessive selective markers in the parent strains, such as drug resistance or spore colour. Selection of homozygotes for such markers from a heterozygous diploid population will, if followed by induced haploidization, give recombinant haploid genomes.

Alternatively, more empirical methods may be tried such as sequential treatment with agents known to increase respectively intra- and interchromosomal exchange. Such methods are of greater importance when the location of genes that limit penicillin yield are unknown (Ball, 1973b). In addition, the production of slow-growing mutants through induction of semi-dominant lethals can give rise to parental and recombinant haploids as well as to diploid strains (arising by mitotic crossing-over or nondisjunction as faster growing sectors from slow growing centres).

In *A. nidulans* the processes of mitotic recombination have been well documented following uv (Käfer, 1969) and γ-ray (Käfer, 1963) treatment.

Possibly other agents such as nitrogen mustard act in similar ways. Several such agents have been used by Sermonti (1961 and 1969) and Macdonald *et al.* (1965) in studies with *P. chrysogenum* but without success in improvement of penicillin yield. One reason for this lack of success could be that the parents of the diploidization were insufficiently divergent in mutation lineage rather than, as is often supposed, too divergent and so possessing barriers to recombination through chromosome aberration.

Production of unbalanced genomes

Unbalanced genomes may be of use in yield improvement if limiting genes can be duplicated. In most organisms, unbalanced genomes are characterized by abnormal effects on the morphology of the organism. The most common cause of imbalance is whole chromosome duplication, i.e. aneuploidy, and partial chromosome duplication. In *A. nidulans,* such types are characterized by phenotypic instability whereby faster growing sectors come from colonies with abnormal slow growing centres. The details are as follows.

i. *Aneuploids.* As already stated aneuploids are intermediates in the haploidization process. Upshall (1971) and Käfer and Upshall (1973), following the earlier work of Käfer (1961), have shown that each of the eight chromosomes of *A. nidulans* has a specific effect on morphology when duplicated in $n + 1$ genotypes and therefore aneuploids can be typed on a morphological basis.

There are several problems in exploiting aneuploids of filamentous fungi for yield improvement. Firstly, these aneuploids are unstable. For example, Ball and Roper (1967) showed that an $n + $ IV aneuploid of *A. nidulans* only rarely survived to pass through meiosis, probably because of selection against it during heterokaryon formation and growth. Secondly, while aneuploids may have duplicated useful genes for yield improvement, they also may have duplicated deleterious genes, giving a net decreasing effect on yield. These are hypotheses however: no experiments to test them have been reported.

ii. *Partial chromosomes duplications.* The problems previously discussed might be less severe with partial chromosome duplications, giving unbalanced genomes some possible advantages over aneuploids. Another advantage is that a greater variety of genotypes can be derived.

Although the production of partially duplicated types is not achieved as readily as are aneuploids, appropriate methods for doing this are available (Bainbridge and Roper, 1966; Nga and Roper, 1968). Some of the essential features of partially duplicated strains of *A. nidulans* and their behaviour are:

Strains with a chromosome segment in excess of the standard haploid genome are unstable at mitosis (Bainbridge and Roper, 1966; Nga and

Roper, 1968; Roper, 1973). All duplicated strains so far analysed have a similar pattern of instability; they have a characteristic "crinkled" morphology and a reduced growth rate. Moreover they produce sectors whose varying degrees of phenotypic improvement arise from nuclei that have lost, by an intra-chromosomal process, a variable part of one or other duplicate segment. Stability, and a quantitatively haploid or near-haploid genome, are achieved either by one large deletion or by a series of independent, smaller deletions. Besides such improved sectors, duplication strains produce sectors with deterioriated morphology, some of which have modified, sometimes greatly enhanced, instability (Nga and Roper, 1968). Azevedo and Roper (1973) suggested that deterioriation and increased instability result from tandem duplications in either duplicate segment; transposing these to nonduplicated regions reduces instability.

iii. *Aneuploidy plus partial chromosome duplication.* Analysis of survivors from diploids treated with γ-rays or uv leads to the conclusion that in addition to other changes, semi-dominant lethal mutations can be induced (see also section on yield preservation by reducing instability). If these mutations are deletions of genetic material, diploid genotypes will be produced that are chromosomally unbalanced. Relatively stable abnormal types have been obtained, certain of which could be due to balanced lethals (see page 249). It is not surprising therefore that, following empirical studies, Alikhanian and Kameneva (1961) and Alikhanian (1962) advocated routine mutagenesis of diploids as an aid to yield improvement. The degree of novelty among genotypes that can be treated is not likely to occur by conventional mutation of haploids. Furthermore Calam (this symposium) describes the investigation of selection lines to increase penicillin yield, starting with a heterozygous diploid. For yield improvement by recombination the heterozygozity may have been exploited making recessive genes homozygous or by deletion of dominant genes enabling such recessives to be expressed.

YIELD PRESERVATION BY REDUCING INSTABILITY

The manifestation of instability in certain commercial strains and the instability of the genotypes previously discussed might be reduced by control of environment or by genetic methods.

Reducing instability by environmental control

Certain commercially useful strains may show an instability pattern due to low-yielding derivatives in populations of stored spores. However, the empirical skills of the fermentation technologist are geared to prevent the latter types from becoming established in a fermentation. This is achieved in part by putting emphasis on culture preservation methods. Indeed, the work of Macdonald (1968) with *P. chrysogenum* supports this attitude. In addition, propagating strains on media containing certain metal ions has reduced instability in *A. nidulans* (Burr, 1973), and $MnCl_2$ reduced instability in *P. chrysogenum* (Morpurgo and Sermonti, 1959). In the latter case, the stabilization was not due to selection against the faster-growing types. In other cases such selection pressures have enabled an exposed duplicated strain to survive, e.g. an unstable strain of *A. nidulans* that was methionine independent was kept on minimal media on which faster growing methionine-requiring derivatives could not grow (Ball, 1967).

Thus, in the fermentation industry, tests of the relative growth abilities of high- and low-yielding strains in carefully selected media may yield commercial gains by preventing yield degeneration.

Reducing instability by genetic methods

i. *Balanced lethals.* The method of balanced lethals is perhaps the most favoured method for reducing the instability that results from duplication of the whole chromosome type (such as diploidy and aneuploidy) or from partial chromosome duplications. Balanced lethals can be produced in a controlled way as suggested by Macdonald (1964), Azevedo and Roper (1967) and Ball (1973b) or they can be produced empirically by mutagen treatment as claimed by Ball (1973a) in *P. chrysogenum*, and by Azevedo (1970) in *A. nidulans.* The essential feature of the balanced lethals condition is that recessive mutations, preventing growth in fermentation medium, are introduced onto homologous chromosome regions. These mutations include certain types of auxotrophs, chromosome rearrangements or mutations affecting unknown functions. A case of strain stabilization in *P. chrysogenum* by direct selection for morphological stability (Ball, 1971) could have been due to spontaneous balanced lethality because chromosomal change was shown. Balanced lethality could also explain the diploid of *P. chrysogenum* with a reduced rate of segregation described by Elander (1967).

ii. *Nonbalanced lethals.* Synthesis of a homozygous diploid from a high-yielding strain might protect against degeneration if low-yielding mutations are recessive. Such a diploid would have to be synthesized in a controlled way, because it would be unlikely to arise at high frequency following mutagenic treatment of the haploid. A stable diploid described by Elander *et al.* (1973) could have arisen for the above reasons. Additional methods of stabilization have been highlighted by recent work with *A. nidulans.* Azevedo (1973) showed that from a duplicated strain which produced an average of 3.2 variants per colony, a uv-induced derivative was isolated that was more stable, giving only 0.9 variants. Genetic analysis showed that this more stable derivative had a determinant of stability which behaved as a single gene

TABLE 3

Classification* of 20 crinkled segregants from a diploidization between a stabilized crinkled strain and strain MSE

Linkage groups		I	II‡	III	IV	V	VI	VII	VIII§
Marker alleles†		+ −	+ −	+ −	+ −	+ −	+ −	+ −	+ −
Stability of crinkled phenotype	Unstable	6 4	10 0	4 6	3 7	5 5	7 3	6 4	0 10
	Stable	6 4	10 0	6 4	2 8	6 4	5 5	6 4	10 0

* Data presented by Azevedo (1973).

† All linkage groups were marked. The parent crinkled strain had markers *proA1* and *pabaA6* on group I and the MSE strain had markers *wA3* on II, *galA1* on III, *pyroA4* on IV, *facA303* on V, *sB3* on VI, *nicB8* on VII and *riboB2* on VIII.

‡ All crinkled segregants carried the positive allele of *wA3* since a I–II duplication determined the crinkled phenotype.

§ All stable crinkled segregants carried the positive allele of *riboB2*. Therefore the mutation-determining stability is located on group VIII.

mutation located in a linkage group not involved in the duplication (see Table 3).

Conclusions

Genetic instability is important to the fermentation industry not merely as an undesirable factor in yield degeneration but also as a useful means of yield improvement. Recent knowledge about genetic instability in *A. nidulans* must substantially moderate many of the earlier pessimistic models that attempted to explain segregation of genes influencing penicillin titres. This now encourages our belief that parasexual breeding has a large part to play in yield improvement, particularly among the high-yielding strains where mutational improvements may be restricted. Furthermore, we hope that the preceding discussion has added fresh perspective to the uses of diploidization.

Acknowledgements

The authors wish to thank their respective employers for permission to publish this paper, and also the British Council, England, and the Research Council of the State of São Paulo, Brazil, for their support during preparation of the manuscript. The suggestions of Professor J. A. Roper and Mr K. B. Morrison are also acknowledged.

References

Azevedo, J. L. (1970). *Mut. Res.* **10**, 11.
Azevedo, J. L. (1973). Proceedings of the 13th International Congress of Genetics. *Genetics, N.Y.*, **74**, supp. S14.
Azevedo, J. L. and Roper, J. A. (1967). *J. gen. Microbiol.* **49**, 149.
Azevedo, J. L. and Roper, J. A. (1973). *Genet. Res.* **16**, 79.
Alikhanian, S. I. (1962). *Adv. appl. Microbiol.* **4**, 1.
Alikhanian, S. I. and Kamaneva, S. V. (1961). *Sci. Rept. 1st. Super. Sanita*, **1**, 441.
Bainbridge, B. W. and Roper, J. A. (1966). *J. gen. Microbiol.* **42**, 417.
Ball, C. (1967). *Genet. Res.* **10**, 173.
Ball, C. (1971). *J. gen. Microbiol.* **66**, 63.
Ball, C. (1973a). "Genetics of Industrial Micro-organisms—Actinomycetes and Fungi" (Eds Z. Vaněk, Z. Hošťálek and J. Cudlin), p. 227. Academia, Prague and Elsevier.
Ball, C. (1973b). "Progress in Industrial Microbiology" (Ed. D. J. D. Hockenhull), vol. **12**, p. 47. Churchill Livingstone, Edinburgh and London.
Ball, C. and Roper, J. A. (1967). *Genet. Res.* **7**, 207.
Burr, K. W. (1973). Ph.D. Thesis. University of Sheffield, England.
Elander, R. P. (1967). *Abh. dt. Akad. Wiss. Berl.* **2**, 403.
Elander, R. P., Espenshade, M. A., Pathak, S. G. and Pan, C. H. (1973). "Genetics of Industrial Micro-organisms—Actinomycetes and Fungi" (Eds Z. Vaněk, Z. Hošťálek and J. Cudlin), p. 239. Academia, Prague and Elsevier.
Käfer, E. (1961). *Genetics, N.Y.* **46**, 1581.
Käfer, E. (1963). *Genetics, N.Y.* **48**, 27.
Käfer, E. (1969). *Genetics, N.Y.* **63**, 821.
Käfer, E. and Upshall, A. (1973). *J. Hered.* **64**, 35.
Lhoas, P. (1961). *Nature, Lond.* **190**, 734.
Lhoas, P. (1967). *Genet. Res.* **10**, 45.
Macdonald, K. D. (1964). *Nature, Lond.* **204**, 404.
Macdonald, K. D. (1968). *Nature, Lond.* **218**, 371.
Macdonald, K. D. (1971). *J. gen. Microbiol.* **67**, 247.
Macdonald, K. D., Hutchinson, J. M. and Gillett W. A. (1965). *Genetica*, **36**, 378.
Macdonald, K. D., Holt, G. and Ditchburn, P. (1972). "Fermentation Technology Today" (Ed. G. Terui), p. 251. Society of Fermentation Technology, Japan.
McCully, K. S. and Forbes, E. (1965). *Genet. Res.* **6**, 352.
Morpurgo, G. (1961). *Aspergillus Newsletter*, **2**, 10.
Morpurgo, G. and Sermonti, G. (1959). *Genetics, N.Y.* **44**, 1371.
Nga, B. H. and Roper, J. A. (1968). *Genetics, N.Y.* **58**, 193.
Pontecorvo, G. and Käfer, E. (1958). "Advances in Genetics" (Ed. M. Demerec), vol. 9, p. 71. Academic Press, New York and London.
Roper, J. A. (1966). "The Fungi" (Eds G. C. Ainsworth and A. S. Sussmann), vol. 2, p. 589. Academic Press, New York.
Roper, J. A. (1973). "Genetics of Industrial Micro-organisms—Actinomycetes and Fungi" (Eds Z. Vaněk, Z. Hošťálek and J. Cudlin), p. 81. Academia, Prague and Elsevier.
Sermonti, G. (1961). *Sci. Rep. 1st. Super. Sanita.* **1**, 441.
Sermonti, G. (1969). "Genetics of Antibiotic-producing Micro-organisms", p. 175. Wiley-Interscience, New York.
Upshall, A. (1971). *Genet. Res.* **18**, 167.

Ultraviolet mutagenesis and cephalosporin synthesis in strains of *Cephalosporium acremonium*

R. P. ELANDER,* C. J. CORUM, H. DE VALERIA and R. M. WILGUS

Antibiotic Manufacturing and Development Division, Eli Lilly and Company, Indianapolis, Indiana 46206, USA

Summary

An intensive mutation and selection programme using *Cephalosporium acremonium* resulted in the step-wise selection of a series of strains with enhanced cephalosporin formation. Ultraviolet radiation (253 nm) was an effective mutagen. Colony populations resulting from survivor spores exhibited a decrease in relative antibiotic potency and increased variability in antibiotic potencies with increasing ultraviolet treatment. The maximum number of morphological and biochemical variants, expressed as a percentage of original viable spores, occurred at intermediate dose levels. The probability for enhanced antibiotic formation was highest at intermediate dose levels when strains of wild-type colony morphology were selected. Biochemical and morphological variants were poor cephalosporin producers, and non was found to elaborate modified cephalosporin or penicillin antibiotics, to accept side-chain precursor compounds, or to synthesize free penicillin nucleus (6-APA) or cephalosporin nucleus (7-ACA).

The high producing variants were prototrophic and exhibited decreased mycelial growth and reduced sporulation on plate culture. One, mutant CW-19, showed an antibiotic improvement of nearly three-fold and an improved ratio of cephalosporin C to penicillin N compared to the original Brotzu progenitor strain. The CW-19 mutant showed significantly more improve-

* Present address: Smith Kline and French Laboratories, Philadelphia, Pennsylvania 19101, USA.

ment over the parental Brotzu culture under more optimal production fermentation conditions for cephalosporin C. Parasexual recombination using complementary biochemical variants resulted in the selection of a number of putative recombinant cultures. The recombinant clones were slow growing, unstable in culture, and synthesized low levels of cephalosporins in shake-flask fermentation compared to those of the superior uv variants.

Introduction

The most important phase of any large-scale fermentation development programme is the selection of a stable high-producing production strain, An intensive antibiotic fermentation development programme was initiated in various laboratories at Eli Lilly and Company in 1960. This report summarizes the activities of an intensive strain development and genetics programme with the now famous cephalosporin fungus, *Cephalosporium acremonium*. This report covers the most productive years, 1961–1964, for the development of improved variant strains and optimum fermentation conditions for the synthesis of cephalosporin C.

The major objective was to obtain strains capable of producing high production levels of cephalosporin C. Other objectives were to select strains, either through mutation and selection or somatic hybridization, that would achieve: (a) the direct biosynthesis of the desired final product, eliminating cleavage of cephalosporin C to 7-aminocephalosporanic acid (7-ACA) and addition of the appropriate acyl chloride; (b) the direct biosynthesis of 7-ACA or a more readily cleaved derivative of 7-ACA; and (c) the biosynthesis of compound(s) related to but different from 7-ACA or penicillin nucleus (6-APA) and their respective derivatives.

This report summarizes the results of a highly successful strain improvement programme with cephalosporin C utilizing ultraviolet mutagenesis as the principal effective mutagen. To this extent, the major objective of the strain development programme was accomplished. The report also includes characteristics of the derived mutants and somatic recombinants and statistical interpretations of mutation induction with attempts to improve the efficiency of subsequent selection processes.

Materials and methods

STRAINS AND CULTURE CONDITIONS

The Brotzu strain of *Cephalosporium acremonium* (IMI-49, 137 and ATCC-11, 555) and an improved mutant (M-8650) were obtained from the National Research Development Corporation (NRDC), London, England. These and their derived mutants were maintained as lyophilized cultures in ampoules and were stored at 4°C. Suspensions of lyophilized spores were used to inoculate slants of a modified LePage and Campbell (1946) medium which was prepared at one-tenth of the original strength except for the addition of agar (2 per cent) and calcium chloride at a 1 per cent concentration (Elander and Wilgus, *unpublished results*). This medium supported abundant conidiation of the fungus and its derived variants. Pyrex glass tubes, 25 mm in diameter, containing 20 cm^3 of the medium were inoculated and incubated at 25°C for 10 days followed by storage at 4°C.

MUTAGENIC AND SELECTION TECHNIQUES

A variety of physical and chemical agents were employed as mutagenic agents. Ultraviolet radiation (253 nm) was an effective mutagen and elicited enhanced cephalosporin C formation in survivor colony populations. The details of the ultraviolet irradiation procedure were given by Elander (1967).

PARASEXUAL RECOMBINATION

The techniques used for parasexual recombination were the same as those described for *Penicillium chrysogenum* (Elander, 1967; Elander *et al.*, 1973).

ANTIBIOTIC FERMENTATION STUDIES

Culture conditions. Spores from a 25-mm slant, suspended in 10 cm^3 of nutrient broth, were used to inoculate flasks containing seed medium. The seed was propagated in narrow-mouth 500 cm^3 Erlenmeyer flasks containing 110 cm^3 of medium. The flasks were incubated at 28°C on a rotary shaker at 250 revolutions per minute for 72 hours.

Wide-mouth 500 cm^3 Erlenmeyer flasks containing 80 cm^3 of fermenter medium were inoculated with 8 per cent seed. The flasks were incubated at 25°C or 28°C for approximately 120 hours on a rotary shaker at 250 revolutions per minute. Samples were removed at periodic intervals for antibiotic assays and other chemical tests.

Seed medium formulations

BRITISH A: cerelose, 2.0 per cent; cornsteep liquor, 3.0 per cent; ammonium acetate, 0.5 per cent; pH adjusted to 6.8–7.0.

CVM: corn meal, 2.0 per cent; Nutrisoy flour (200 D), 1.5 per cent; $(NH_4)_2SO_4$, 0.1 per cent; methyl oleate, 2.0 per cent; $CaCO_3$, 0.3 per cent; pH adjusted to 6.0.

Fermenter medium formulation

BRITISH B: fish meal, 0.77 per cent; meat meal, 0.36 per cent; cornsteep liquor, 0.14 per cent; sucrose, 1.2 per cent; cerelose, 0.36 per cent; ammonium acetate, 0.2 per cent; *dl*-methionine, 0.5 per cent; pH adjusted to 6.8.

ANTIBIOTIC ASSAY

The total concentrations of β-lactam containing antibiotics (cephalosporin C, deacetylcephalosporin C, penicillin N) were determined according to the methods outlined by Dennen and Carver (1968).

PRECURSOR STUDIES

Potential acyltransferase activity in biochemical or morphological variants was tested, utilizing the British B formulation containing the following penicillin precursors at a concentration range from 0.5–3.0 per cent: salicylic acid, phenyl-mercaptoacetic acid, 4-phenyl-*n*-butyric acid, phenylacetic acid, phenoxyacetic acid, thiophene-2-acetic acid, allyl phenylacetic acid, and bromobenzoic acid. The broths were then chromatographed and assayed against *Bacillus subtilis* or *Salmonella gallinarum* as described by Caltrider and Niss (1966)

Results

ANTIBIOTICS PRODUCED BY *C. ACREMONIUM*

The Brotzu strain of *C. acremonium* is a versatile fungus capable of producing a total of eight different antibiotic substances which comprise three major classes. Table 1 lists some of the naturally occurring penicillin and cephalosporin antibiotics and a number of important marketed semi-synthetic cephalosporins. In addition to penicillin N and the two species of cephalosporin C, the fungus is capable of synthesizing five steroidal antibiotic substances known as cephalosporins P1–5. The latter compounds are inhibitory to Gram-positive bacteria, have possible chemotherapeutic value and are produced in abundant quantity along with the normal penicillin and cephalosporin metabolites.

SPONTANEOUS VARIATION

The original Brotzu strain (Sardinian isolate) of *C. acremonium* exhibits little spontaneous variability. Large colony populations of this strain and its derived mutants show extremely uniform population patterns. The predominant colony type is characterized by a glistening glabrous raised colony with extensive radial furrowing, extremely irregular peripheral margins with abundant synnemata formation. Spore aggregates appear in minute water droplets on the surface of the secondary mycelium. The spores are uninucleate,

TABLE 1
β-Lactam antibiotics produced by *Cephalosporium acremonium* and important semi-synthetic cephalosporins

---

(a) Penicillin

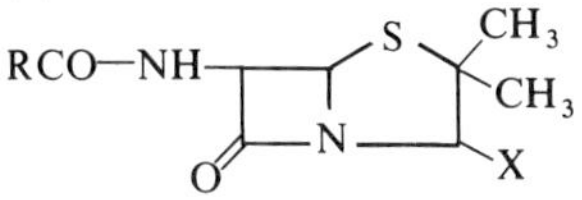

RCO—NH— [β-lactam structure with S, CH$_3$, CH$_3$, N, O, X]

	R	X
	H$_3$N$^+$—CH(CH$_2$)$_3$, O$_2^-$C	COOH

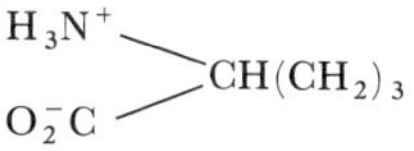

Penicillin N

(b) Cephalosporin

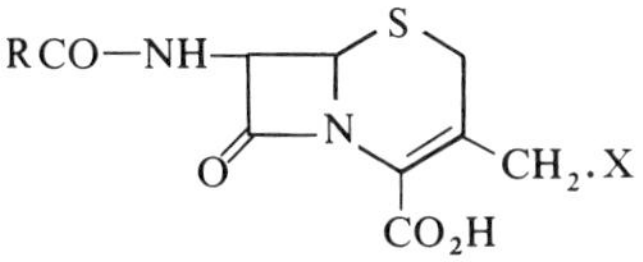

RCO—NH— [cephalosporin structure with S, N, O, CH$_2$·X, CO$_2$H]

H$_3$N$^+$—CH(CH$_2$)$_3$, O$_2^-$C   OCOCH$_3$

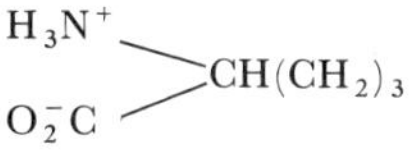

Cephalosporin C

H$_3$N$^+$—CH(CH$_2$)$_3$, O$_2^-$C   OH

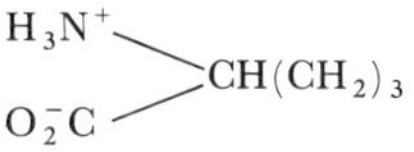

Deacetylcephalosporin C
(Acetylesterase Enzyme)

(c) Semi-synthetic cephalosporins

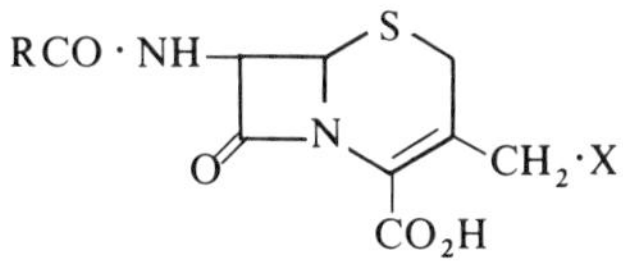

RCO·NH— [cephalosporin structure with S, N, O, CH$_2$·X, CO$_2$H]

[thiophene]—CH$_2$ OCOCH$_3$

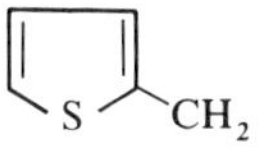

Cephalothin (Keflin®)

[thiophene]—CH$_2$—N$^+$[pyridine]

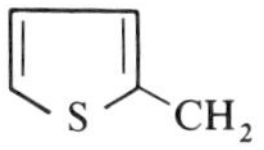

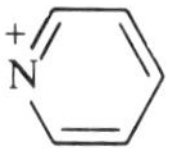

Cephaloridine (Loridine®)

R	X

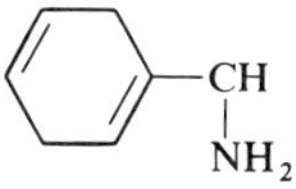

[cyclohexadiene]—CH(NH$_2$)   H

Cephradine (Anspor®)

[benzene]—CH(NH$_2$)   OCOCH$_3$

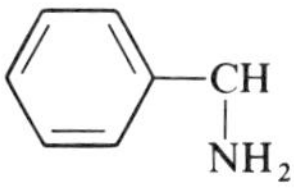

Cephaloglycin (Kafocin®)

[tetrazole]NCH$_2$ S—[thiadiazole]—CH$_3$

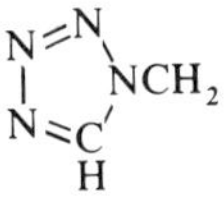

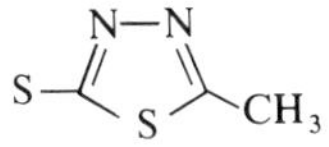

Cefazolin (Ancef® / Kefzol®)

[benzene]—CH(NH$_2$)   H

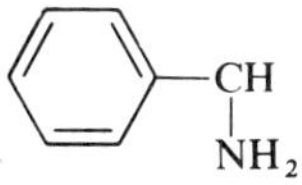

Cephalexin (Keflex®)

cigar-shaped, and devoid of discernible pigment. The colonies are cream coloured and synthesize diffusible yellow-green pigment visible on the reverse. Most large colony populations arising from untreated spores show less than 1 per cent variation from the above described type.

INDUCED VARIATION AND THE ROLE OF MUTAGENS

A variety of physical and chemical agents were used for mutation induction with strains of *C. acremonium* (Table 2). Of the mutagens tested, ultraviolet

TABLE 2

Mutagens employed for mutation induction in *Cephalosporium acremonium*

Radiation	Ultraviolet (253 nm)
	X-Ray
Mitotic inhibitors	Colchicine
Chemical agents	Nitrous acid (NA)
	Nitrogen mustard
	Methyl-bis-(β-chloroethyl)amine
	Epichlorohydrin
	N-methyl-N'-nitro-N-nitrosoguanidine (MNNG)
	Triethylenemelamine (TEM)
	Acriflavine
	β-Propriolactone
	Dimethyl sulphate (DMS)
	Ethyl Methane sulphonate (EMS)
	Low pH
Combination	Ultraviolet radiation (253 nm) and
	nitrosoguanidine (MNNG)
	Nitrous acid (NA) and nitrosoguanidine (MNNG)

radiation (235 nm) (uv) was the only effective mutagen with respect to enhanced cephalosporin formation. The ease of the mutation protocol and its effectiveness in eliciting strains with enhanced antibiotic synthesis were cogent reasons why uv became the mutagen of choice.

Throughout the mutation programme, a cyclical application of mutagens was employed, since regions within genetic loci may be more sensitive to one mutagen than another and since locus specificity of mutagens is now well established. Nitrous acid and N-methyl-N'-nitro-N-nitrosoguanidine were effective in that survivor colony populations showed a high degree of damaged variants. Ultraviolet combined with the above two chemical agents was effective in including biochemical variants.

MUTATION INDUCTION

The lethal and mutagenic effect of uv on strain M-8650 is presented in Fig. 1. The resulting sigmoid type of survival curve suggests a multiple-hit phenomenon, a response that has been noted in a variety of fungal organisms exposed to uv. The frequency of morphological variants expressed as a percentage of original spores (Fig. 1) indicates that mutation frequency increases with increasing uv doses to a point, and then decreases at higher doses. The mutation frequency peaked at a uv exposure period of 2.0–2.5 minutes which gave

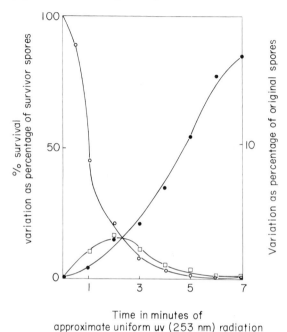

Time in minutes of
approximate uniform uv (253 nm) radiation

Fɪɢ. 1. Lethal and mutagenic effect of uv radiation. O, per cent survival; ●, morphological variants as per cent of survivor spores; □, morphological variants as per cent of original spores.

a survivor value of 15–25 per cent. The frequency of morphological variants expressed as a percentage of survivor spores increased approximately linearly with the dose rate.

UV MUTATION AND CEPHALOSPORIN C PRODUCTION

A decrease in the average cephalosporin C potency of survivor strains was observed with increasing uv exposure (Fig. 2). Twenty test strains were chosen randomly from dilution plates representing scheduled uv exposure times from 0 to 5 minutes (100 per cent to 0.68 per cent survival). The existing production strain (CB-344) in its known optimal fermentation conditions served as the control. All strains were run in duplicate except the control which was estimated as the mean of the results from 6 flasks. The regression line (Fig. 2) clearly demonstrates the effectiveness of uv as a mutagen, by the

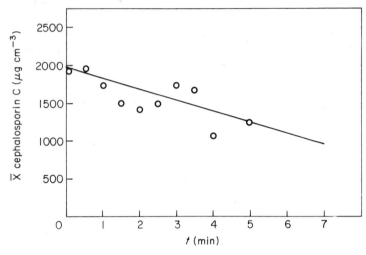

FIG. 2. Relationship of cephalosporin C potency and uv dose.

general decrease in average antibiotic potency for the various survivor populations.

The data shown in Fig. 3 indicate an increase in the coefficient of variation ($100\ \sigma/\overline{X}$). These data also show the mutagenicity of uv radiation in that a general increase in variability is associated with the 20 random isolates for each increasing exposure period. However, to make use of this information

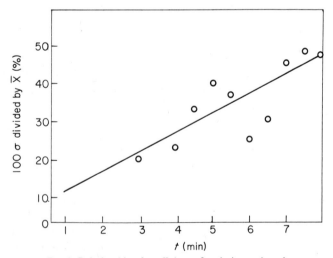

FIG. 3. Relationship of coefficient of variation and uv dose.

some estimate concerning the nature of distribution was needed. For all time periods, a normal distribution was found to be reasonable as an approximation (Brown and Elander, 1966).

CEPHALOSPORIN C PRODUCTION BY MORPHOLOGICAL AND BIOCHEMICAL
MUTANTS

Prior experience in our strain development programmes with other antibiotics (penicillin, tylosin, streptomycin, erythromycin, etc.) had shown that biochemical and morphological variants were generally inferior to strains exhibiting typical wild-type colony morphology. To assess the situation in *C. acremonium*, a large number of morphological and biochemical variants were selected and examined for their capacity to synthesize cephalosporin C. The results showed a general relative potency decrease with increased observed mutagenesis (Table 3).

TABLE 3

Cephalosporin C production by variant classes of *Cephalosporium acremonium*. (After Brown and Elander, 1966.)

Variant class	Mean relative potency (R)*
Normal (minor variants)	0.91
Abnormal (major variants)	0.70
a. Morphological	0.71
b. Morphological and known biochemical	0.66

* R, mean test strain potency divided by mean potency of replicated control.

PROBABILITIES ASSOCIATED WITH UV DOSE AND VARIANT CATEGORY

With a reasonable degree of knowledge acquired concerning the distributions for both the "normal" and "abnormal" groups, attention was focused upon inferences permitted by the ability to construct probability statements. Arbitrarily, it was decided that a test strain should truly exceed the present production control strain by at least 20% for real economic value and because of potential bioengineering problems associated with fermentation scale-up. The estimated probabilities associated with the stated criteria of superiority for cephalosporin C are shown in Fig. 4. These data indicate an approximate 11 to 1 (or one magnitude) advantage in the selection of a "normal" (minor) variant compared to the "abnormal" (major) variant. The optimal exposure time in this mutation cycle (CF Series) was in the vicinity of 2.5 minutes which corresponded to a 25–30 per cent survival value.

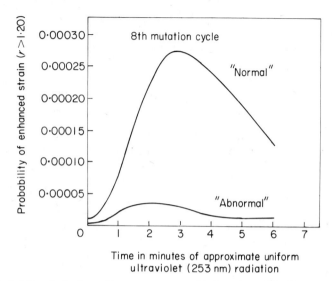

FIG. 4. Probability of selecting a 20 per cent excess antibiotic variant. (After Brown and Elander, 1966.)

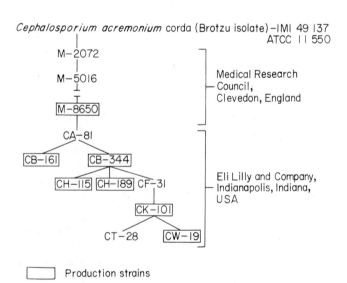

FIG. 5. Lineage of improved uv radiation variants.

THE SELECTION OF IMPROVED UV VARIANTS OF *C. ACREMONIUM*

The lineage of six Lilly production strains of *C. acremonium* is presented in Fig. 5. The strains were selected from uv survivor populations and were isolated from plates representing intermediate dose levels. All strains were characterized by wild-type colony morphology, homogeneous population patterns, and were prototrophic. The initial uv mutants (through M-8650) were selected by Miller *et al.* (1961) of the Clevedon (England) Research Station of the Medical Research Council.

Strains CB-161, CB-344 (M8650-1), CH-115, CH-189, CK-101, and CW-19 (M8650-2) were utilized for the commercial large-scale production of cephalosporin C during the years 1961–1966. The first superior laboratory variant, CA-81, was not utilized for commercial production because of scale-up problems associated with pilot plant fermentations. However, additional mutation treatments of this first Lilly progenitor culture culminated in the selection of two highly productive cultures, CB-161 and CB-344. CW-19 was the last strain entered in this lineage and was introduced for commercial fermentation in 1964.

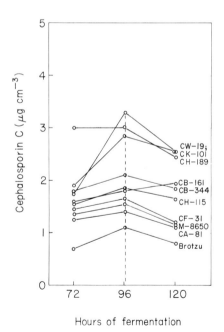

FIG. 6. Production of cephalosporin C by Brotzu strain and improved uv variants.

FERMENTATION CHARACTERISTICS OF THE IMPROVED VARIANTS

The synthesis of cephalosporin C in shake-flask fermentation by the various improved mutants and the original Brotzu strain in the early British fermentation conditions is summarized in Fig. 6.

The Brotzu strain, isolated from a sea water inlet off the coast of Sardinia, is a poor producer of cephalosporin C. Most of the strains show a tendency for less than peak antibiotic titres with more than 96 hours of fermentation. The reduction is associated with the formation of deacetylcephalosporin C or its lactone. The biological activity of the deacetylcephalosporin C moiety and its lactone is considerably less than cephalosporin C. Strain CW-19 produces nearly $350 \, \mu g \, cm^{-3}$ of cephalosporin C at 96 hours in the British fermentation conditions (Fig. 6). This represents a three-fold improvement over the original Brotzu strain.

An effective concomitant fermentation medium development programme is necessary to further optimize the fermentation potential of the improved mutants. In addition to the strain improvement programme, we also developed a number of improved fermentation media conditions for cephalosporin C. The conditions included improved complex nitrogen and carbon sources, increased levels of methionine and lowered fermentation temperatures during the idiophase stage of fermentation. The above conditions were also shown to be important for large-scale production fermentations. The CW-19 mutant showed significantly greater yield improvement for cephalosporin C compared to the original Brotzu progenitor or the early improved M-8650 British mutant in the improved fermentation conditions.

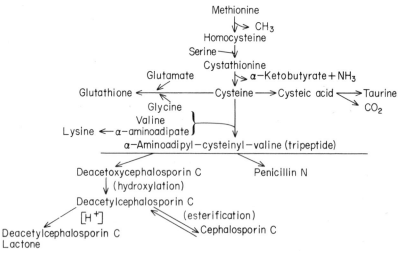

FIG. 7. Proposed scheme for the biosynthesis of cephalosporin C and penicillin N.

RATIO OF CEPHALOSPORIN C TO PENICILLIN N

Another major objective of the strain development programme was to discover strains that produced high levels of cephalosporin C at the expense of penicillin N. Both antibiotics are presumably derived from the α-aminoadipyl-cysteinyl-valine tripeptide and presumably compete for biosynthetic intermediates (Fig. 7). A comparison of strains M-8650 and the high-producing CW-19 with respect to both cephalosporin C and penicillin N is shown in Fig. 8. A

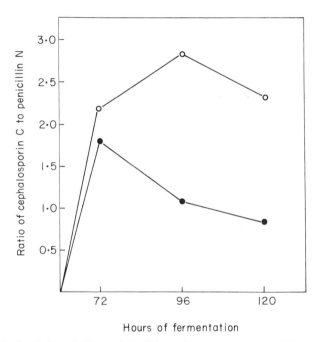

Hours of fermentation

FIG. 8. Ratio of cephalosporin C to penicillin N in two improved mutants. ○, CW–19; ●, M–8650.

ratio of cephalosporin C to penicillin N of nearly 3.0 was obtained with the CW-19 mutant compared to a ratio of 1.0 for the British M-8650 mutant at 96 hours. Penicillin N is a commercially unwanted antibiotic substance and thus represents biosynthetic waste and complicates cephalosporin C purification and subsequent crystallization.

CULTURAL CHARACTERISTICS OF IMPROVED UV VARIANTS

The comparative radial growth rate of strains CW-19 and M-8650 compared to the original wild-type culture are shown in Fig. 9. The radial growth of the wild-type culture was nearly double that of the high cephalosporin C variant

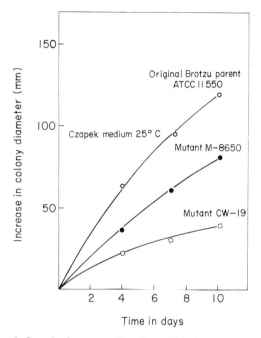

Fɪɢ. 9. Growth of parent strain and two high-yielding uv mutants.

CW-19. Decreased mycelial formation by the mutants, compared to M-8650 was also observed in flask and tank fermentations.

The improved mutants were also characterized by decreased sporulation. The data presented in Table 4 shows that wild-type parental culture produced approximately ten-fold more spores than CW-19. Lactose supplementation was shown to enhance the sporulation capacity of strain CW-19.

The strains also differed in important biochemical manifestations. Prior

TABLE 4

Conidium production by original parent strain and two high-yielding uv mutants of *Cephalosporium acremonium*

Strain	Conidia per slant* $\times 10^6$	Conidia per cm^2 mycelial surface $\times 10^6$
Brotzu strain	2.87	0.287
Mutant M–8650	1.92	0.192
Mutant CW–19	0.24	0.024

* Modified LePage and Campbell sporulation medium incubated for 10 days at 25°C.

publications concerning sulphatase levels and regulation and methionine stimulation will be considered later.

BIOCHEMICAL MUTANTS AND THE SEARCH FOR 6-APA, 7-ACA, PRECURSOR ACCEPTANCE, AND MODIFIED ANTIBIOTIC FORMATION

A number of biochemical and morphological variants were examined for free 7-ACA formation and modified penicillin or cephalosporin formation in a variety of fermentation conditions. A number of known penicillin precursors were also examined for possible acyltransferase activity by the mutant cultures. No transferase or amidase activity was detected in any of the mutants. Phenyl-acetylation of fermentation broths also yielded no evidence for penicillin or cephalosporin nucleus formation by any of the major variants. No evidence was obtained for modified penicillin or cephalosporin antibiotic formation by the many biochemical and morphological mutants examined.

PARASEXUAL RECOMBINATION STUDIES

These were made using the methods described previously (Elander, 1967). No clear evidence for diploidy was observed in contrast to the highly successful parasexual programme which was currently in progress with *Penicillium chrysogenum*. In contrast to the behaviour of *Penicillium*, putative diploid clones of *C. acremonium* did not show heterosis with respect to mycelial vigour or large conidium formation. Segregation analyses also gave little indication of somatic recombination and subsequent haploidization.

A number of presumptive heterokaryons or diploids were examined for their capacity to produce high levels of cephalosporin C. A variety of fermentation conditions were employed including supplementation with the requirements of the biochemically deficient parent clones. The clones were also tested for precursor acceptability, 6-APA, or 7-ACA formation, and the possible synthesis of modified penicillin or cephalosporin antibiotics. The recombinant cultures were generally poor producers of cephalosporins, and no evidence of free 6-APA or 7-ACA, precursor transferase activity, or modified penicillin or cephalosporin formation was found.

Discussion

The generation of stable high-producing variant strains and the rapid development of optimal fermentation conditions for mutants are the most important objectives of a fermentation development programme. In the present study, uv radiation was a particularly successful mutagen as it has been with other cephalosporin-producing fungi (Elander *et al.*, 1960; Schwartz and Stauffer, 1966; Stauffer *et al.*, 1966).

The natural variability in colony populations of *C. acremonium*, and its uv derivatives, based on colony morphology and cephalosporin production was found to be negligible. Low levels of spontaneous variability have been reported elsewhere for this organism (Stauffer *et al.*, 1966) and strains of *Emericellopsis*, the perfect stage of a number of *Cephalosporium* species (Elander *et al.*, 1960; Schwartz and Stauffer, 1966).

Despite the low level of spontaneous variability in *C. acremonium* and its derived strains, a number of mutant colony types, biochemical mutants, and strains with a high degree of variation with respect to cephalosporin productivity, were encountered in populations exposed to moderate dose levels of uv radiation. The highest frequency of variants expressed as a percentage of original spores, was encountered at the 15–20 per cent survival level (Fig. 1). Studies on *Emericellopsis glabra* (Schwartz and Stauffer, 1966) show a somewhat lower percentage survival (13 per cent) for the maximum frequency of morphological variants. Survivor populations of *P. chrysogenum* show a maximal mutation frequency at the 20–25% survival range (Backus and Stauffer, 1955).

The dose–mutation curve for *C. acremonium* M8650 (Fig. 1) is similar to those found for fungal spores in which mutation frequency increased with dosage for a time and then declines (Schwartz and Stauffer, 1966). Explanations for this unusual response include cumulative lethal and mutagenic effects, or other factors which affect radiation sensitivity. Others claim that the drop in mutation frequency at high uv dose is attributed to the presence of small proportions of darker pigmented spores which are more resistant to radiation (Markert, 1953). Although the conidia of *C. acremonium* appear devoid of pigment, there may be other factors, including photocatalytic effects on uv-repair enzymes, polymerases, etc., that affect the uv sensitivity of any given spore population.

The statistical considerations of the strain development programme with cephalosporin C are those fundamentally associated with criteria of judgement of strain superiority and the problem of attempting to maximize the efficiency of screening procedures. The trend for a decrease in the average potency of test strains as a function of dose (Fig. 2) and a concomitant increase in the coefficient of variation (Fig. 3) represent a reasonable extension of the overall mutation process. One would predict, in the biosynthesis of secondary metabolites (pencillins and cephalosporins), which are ultimately derived from the biosynthetic pathways of lysine, cysteine and valine, that minor mutations either affecting these pathways or other pathways competing for similar biosynthetic intermediates would adversely affect antibiotic yield. Moreover, many of the mutants exhibit cultural defects such as retarded growth rates or reduced sporulation capacity, features which are important for proper inoculum development and which are not taken into account in a fixed screening programme. The data presented for the maximization of the probability for enhanced antibiotic synthesis by mutants of normal colony morphology (Table 3 and Fig. 4) may be partially attributed to the fermentation characteristics of the normal cultures. The normal clones are phenotypically similar to the wild-type strain, and those conditions that are optimal for the control strain are also probably nearly optimal for minor variants. The probabilities associated with the selection of variants with a 20 per cent gain in productivity are of paramount importance to any screening programme. An improvement factor of 1.2 is reasonable for the strain programme described. It is undoubtedly too high for a screen that has been in progress for an extended period of time (Brown and Elander, 1966; Elander, 1967).

The trend towards decreased mycelial vigour (Fig. 9) and reduced sporulation (Table 4) by the superior uv-variants of *C. acremonium* (M-8650, CW-19) has also been reported for superior variants of *P. chrysogenum* by Backus and Stauffer (1955). The decreased mycelial vigour associated with high productivity indicates a highly efficient mycelium.

Nash and Huber (1971) reported that submerged cultures of *C. acremonium* exist in four distinct morphological states in fermentation culture: hyphae, conidia, germlings and arthrospores. The mycelial differentiation to arthrospores appears to be important in that it coincides with maximal cephalosporium C synthesis. Arthrospore formation appears to be proportional to cephalosporin formation and the capacity for strains to differentiate into arthrospores appear to be a determining factor in high-yielding mutants. Methionine supplementation also stimulates arthrospore formation (Caltrider and Niss, 1966). Thus, methionine appears to play a dual role in the metabolism of *C. acremonium*. It provides a source of cysteine for the tripeptide intermediate through reverse transulphuration and may "trigger" the onset of antibiotic formation through cellular differentiation.

Biochemical studies with the Brotzu strain and several of the *C. acremonium* mutants described in the report (M-8650, CB-161, CB-344 and CH-115) by Dennen and Carver (1968) showed a direct relationship between cephalosporin synthesis and sulphatase activity. This suggested that mutants with increased potential to produce higher levels of cephalosporin C from methionine, a sulphur-containing amino acid stimulating cephalosporin C production, have decreasing ability to use this amino acid for other sulphur requirements. Sulphatase is reported to be derepressed in these mutants (Dennen and Carver, 1968). A report by Nüesch *et al.* (1973) indicated that *C. acremonium* possesses a very efficient and specific amino acid oxidase for methionine, which deaminates methionine and cysteine to α-keto or α-hydroxy-γ-methylmercaptobutyric acid. Since increasing levels of methionine generally resulted in reduced mycelial growth and enhanced cephalosporin C and N production with strains of enhanced cephalosporin production potential (Caltrider and

Niss, 1966), the variants described in this study may also differ in their levels of amino acid oxidase for methionine and cysteine.

Many industrial strain development laboratories have utilized parasexual genetic techniques, in addition to highly successful procedures of mutation and selection for the selection of economically important fungi. Elander (1966) and Elander *et al.* (1973) summarized an intensive genetic programme with *P. chrysogenum* culminating in the selection of a stable heterozygous diploid culture which synthesized high levels of phenoxymethyl penicillin. The parasexual studies described in this report were disappointing with respect to the generation of high-yielding strains. An intensive parasexual programme with *C. acremonium* in England at the Microbiological Research Establishment at Porton Down was also disappointing with respect to the development of well-defined diploid or recombinant cultures (K. D. Macdonald, personal communication). However, Nüesch *et al.* (1973) reported the isolation of prototrophic recombinant strains of *C. acremonium* and claimed presumptive somatic diploids could not be clearly detected because of early haploidization. The use of mutants and parasexual genetics in the previous study was restricted to biosynthetic pathways for cephalosporin C, and the programme was not directed towards the generation of strains for improved cephalosporin C production.

The 3–4-fold improvement in antibiotic productivity described herein was substantial although far behind the 55–fold improvement in phenoxymethyl penicillin production by *P. chrysogenum* described by Elander (1969). Another important contribution of the present study was the improvement in cephalosporin C synthesis over that of penicillin N (Fig. 8), an unwanted metabolite competing for biosynthetic intermediates (Fig. 8) and a substance interfering with the efficient isolation of a crystalline salt of cephalosporin C.

In summary, the studies reported were essential to the development of a commercially feasible fermentation process for cephalosporin C. The highly successful strain programme coupled with the important discovery of cephalosporin C cleavage and its combination with appropriate acyl chlorides has already culminated in a number of potent semi-synthetic cephalosporins (Table 1) which appear to have significant important clinical advantages over many natural and semi-synthetic penicillins.

References

Backus, M. P. and Stauffer, J. F. (1955). *Mycologia*, **47**, 428.
Brown, W. F. and Elander, R. P. (1966). *Devs ind. Microbiol.* **7**, 114.
Caltrider, P. G. and Niss, H. F. (1966). *Appl. Microbiol.* **14**, 746.
Dennen, D. W. and Carver, D. D. (1968). *Can. J. Microbiol.* **15**, 175.
Elander, R. P., Stauffer, J. F. and Backus, M. P. (1960). *Antimicrob. Ag. A.* **1**, 91.
Elander, R. P. (1966). *Devs. ind. Microbiol.* **7**, 61

Elander, R. P. (1967). "Induced Mutations and Their Utilization", p. 403. Abhandlungen der Deutscher Akademie der Wissenschaften zu Berlin.
Elander, R. P. (1969). "Fermentation Advances" (Ed. D. Perlman), p. 89. Academic Press, New York and London.
Elander, R. P., Espenshade, M. A., Pathak, S. G. and Pan, C. H. (1973). "Genetics of Industrial Microorganisms" (Eds Z. Vaněk, Z. Hošťálek, J. Cudlín), vol. II— Actinomycetes and Fungi, p. 239. Elsevier Publishing Company, Amsterdam, London and New York.
LePage, G. A. and Campbell, E. (1946). *J. biol. Chem.* **162**, 163.
Markert, C. L. (1953). *Expl. Cell Res.* **5**, 427.
Miller, G. A., Kelley, B. K. and Codner, R. C. (1961). British Pat. Appl. 461/61.
Nash, C. H. and Huber, F. M. (1971). *Appl. Microbiol.* **22**, 6.
Nüesch, J., Treichler, H. J. and Liersch, M. (1973). "Genetics of Industrial Microorganisms" (Eds Z. Vaněk, Z. Hošťálek, and J. Cudlín), Vol. II—Actinomycetes and Fungi, p. 309. Elsevier Publishing Company, Amsterdam, London and New York.
Schwartz, L. J. and Stauffer, J. F. (1966). *Appl. Microbiol.* **14**, 105.
Stauffer, J. F., Schwartz, L. J. and Brady, C. W. (1966). *Devs. ind. Microbiol.* **7**, 104.

K

Penicillin: tactics in strain improvement

C. T. CALAM*, L. BARBARA DAGLISH and E. P. McCANN

Fermentation Products Department, ICI Ltd, Pharmaceuticals Division, Trafford Park Works, Westinghouse Road, Manchester 17, England

Summary

An exploratory programme, using high-yielding strains of *Penicillium chrysogenum*, was carried out to determine the utility of parasexual hybridizations for strain improvement. The objective was a high-yielding strain with improved sporulation. The programme involved (1) random crosses, (2) a series of mutations, (3) investigation of recombination with strains bearing spore colour and auxotrophic mutations, (4) homozygous diploids from sister matings.

Diploids were readily obtained. These showed the variations in yield previously reported elsewhere. In order to obtain high-yielding strains it was found necessary to submit the diploids to serial mutations and selections.

The best isolates, for production and sporulation, came from one of the random crosses, followed by three mutation steps, the final culture being still diploid as judged by spore size. A test showed no difference between the stability of haploid mutants and diploids. Crossing-over was observed among crosses with auxotrophs carrying spore colour mutations. The homozygous diploids gave high yields but grew less vigorously than hoped and also frequently failed to spore adequately.

The reason for the apparent success of individual crosses, at random, probably arises because we are not yet able to predict accurately the best mutants to cross. It is therefore better to carry out as many crosses as possible, than to spend time on the production of elaborately marked strains, whose performance cannot be reliably predicted.

* Present address: Department of Biology, Liverpool Polytechnic, Byrom Street, Liverpool L3 3AF, England.

Introduction

Ever since the discovery of the parasexual process, attempts have been made to use it for the improvement of the production of penicillin. Much has been written on the subject, for example, by Sermonti (1969), Macdonald et al. (1972), Ball (1973), Elander et al. (1973). In some cases promising results have been obtained, but it is still uncertain whether the new technique is more effective than mutation and selection alone. The present report describes an exploratory programme in which various approaches to strain improvement were investigated. This work was done as part of a joint programme organized by Dr K. D. Macdonald under the auspices of the NRDC in collaboration with Professor J. A. Roper, and we are glad to acknowledge the assistance received in the course of joint discussions throughout the work. It did not then seem possible to base the programme on a strictly genetical approach. A survey programme was therefore carried out in which hybridization and mutation techniques were compared. The object of the present report is to describe this work and to indicate the rates of progress that were obtained. It is hoped that this will help to provide a basis for discussing and evaluating possible new approaches to strain improvement.

At the time when the work was started, good progress was being made by direct mutation and selection, but many of the mutants showed only poor sporulation. The aim was as much to improve sporulation as it was to increase penicillin production. Hybridization work involved random crosses, as well as crosses which were thought possibly advantageous, for instance crosses between closely related strains. Alongside the hybridization work a number of ordinary mutations and selections were carried out, so that the efficacy of the two methods could be compared.

Material and methods

The procedures generally used in these laboratories for strain improvement, i.e. mutation, hybridization and selection, have already been described (Calam, 1970). Hybridization work with other fungi has already been reported (Calam et al., 1973). In the present case the methods used were based on those of Macdonald and collaborators (Macdonald et al., 1963a, 1963b, 1963c).

Isolates were initially tested in shaken flasks. Data quoted here are from a two-stage process.

Inoculum medium: corn-steep solids, 40; glucose monohydrate, 25; KH_2PO_4, 0.5; $NaNO_3$, 1.5; $ZnSO_45H_2O$, 0.04; $CaCO_3$, 10; $MgSO_47H_2O$, 0.25 g dm^{-3}; pH adjusted to 5.3–5.5 with NaOH; 50 cm^3 medium was used per 500 cm^3 conical flask.

Production medium: corn-steep solids, 37.2; lactose, 36.6; $CaCO_3$, 6.7; KH_2PO_4, 0.67; $MgSO_47H_2O$, 0.33; $NaNO_3$, 3.3; $Na_2S_2O_55H_2O$, 1:67; phenoxyacetic acid, 2.2 g dm^{-3}; 45 cm³ of medium were used per 500 cm³ conical flask, with addition of 1 cm³ per flask of arachis oil and 0.5 cm³ white oil.

Inoculum was started from 2 cm³ spore suspension, *c.* 2 × 10^7 spores, and grown for 44 hours, when thin growth was apparent; 5 cm³ of inoculum was added to each production flask. Production flasks were grown for 5–6 days. All shaken cultures were incubated at 25°C on rotary shakers, at 250 cycles (5 cm diameter) per minute.

Stirred cultures were carried out in 5-litre fermenters (15 cm diameter) using pitched-paddle agitators at 550 rpm. A lactose + corn-steep medium was used, supplemented by a nutrient feed from 72 hours. The method used was similar to one already described (McCann and Calam, 1972).

For tests of sporulation, Foster's medium was used, with the following composition: $NaNO_3$, 3; KH_2PO_4, 1; $MgSO_47H_2O$, 0.5; KCl, 0.5; $FeSO_47H_2O$, 0.01; sucrose, 30; $CaCl_2$, 40; Yeastrel, 1 g dm^{-3}. The medium was adjusted to 6.8 with NaOH. 50 cm³ of medium was used in 500 cm³ conical flasks, inoculated with spores and incubated on the shaker for 7 days, when a deep green suspension of spores was obtained.

For hybridization, the following media were used.

Minimal medium: glucose, 60; $NaNO_3$, 3; KH_2PO_4, 0.3; K_2HPO_4, 0.7; KCl, 0.5; $MgSO_47H_2O$, 0.5; $FeSO_47H_2O$, 0.01, g dm^{-3}; agar, 20 g dm^{-3}.

Complete medium; lactose, 30; corn-steep solids, 2.5 g dm^{-3}; solution C, 20 ml dm^{-3}; pH adjusted to 6.1–6.3 with NaOH. For slope cultures and general use, corn-steep solids were increased to 20 g dm^{-3}. Solution C contained $MgSO_47H_2O$, 2.5; $FeSO_47H_2O$, 0.6; $MnSO_44H_2O$, 0.2; $CuSO_45H_2O$, 0.2 g dm^{-3}.

Cultures. Mutants obtained from *P. chrysogenum* WIS 51/20, after a long series of mutations, were used. The relation between the various cultures employed are given in Table 1. Auxotrophic strains were isolated during these programmes and used for hybridization. Unless otherwise stated, the mutants were green spored, monoauxotrophic and nonleaky. Mutagens used during this work were, ethyleneimine followed by uv light, nitrogen mustard and X-rays.

In the later stages of the mutation programme the five to nine best isolates from each selection were mutated and colonies picked off. A total of 200 of these were screened, the best being passed forward to the next series. The original parent for all these series was the mutant JH272.

Penicillin was estimated iodimetrically after hydrolysis by penicillinase,

TABLE 1

Lineage of mutants used for hybridization

Strains	Penicillin production in shaken flasks u cm^{-3}
JJ 48	4 000
JV 64——————JV 192	5 000
| several steps	
JH 272	6 000
|	
4-series (4B28)	
|	
7-series	
|	
8-series	
|	
9-series	7 500
|	
10-series—11-series—13-series	
|	
14-series	7 700

using an automated procedure. Results are given in international units per cubic centimetre (u cm^{-3}).

Results

At the time when the programme started, the best strain available was JH272. While, as mentioned above, it was capable of high yields, it gave poor sporulation. In Foster's medium it gave only 0.6×10^7 viable spores cm^{-3}, against $5–15 \times 10^7$ spores cm^{-3} with strains of lower yield. This low level of sporulation was a disadvantage for production purposes. As a criterion for the programme, a ten-fold increase in sporulation was sought, with no loss in productivity, though increased productivity would be of value. The hybridization programme was carried out against the background of continuing mutation and selection work. As a result of the improvements obtained in this programme, the higher-yielding strain 9A36 later replaced JH272. Another mutant 11E30 was also used. The performance of these strains may be summarized.

Mutant	Penicillin production u cm^{-3}	Sporulation $\times 10^7$ cm^3
JH272	6 050	0.6
9A36	7 540	1.8
11E30	7 660	1.3

It will be noticed that sporulation does not necessarily fall as titres increase during mutation and selection. Both positive and negative effects are observed. The main lines of work carried out gave a broad survey of different lines of approach to strain improvement. It is dealt with under the following five main points:

1. Various auxotrophic mutants, yielding up to 7500 u cm^{-3} in shaken flasks, were crossed. This was a purely opportunist approach. Diploids were isolated and mutated, and the best isolates selected.

2. A series of direct mutations were carried out, starting from members of the 11-series (Table 1), giving around 7500 u cm^{-3}. This was intended to provide a comparison between mutation and hybridization. The main mutation and selection programme, summarized in Table 1, also provides a comparison.

3. Experience suggests that, with highly mutated strains, there may be difficulty in achieving an adequate degree of recombination. A number of auxotrophs bearing spore colour mutations were therefore crossed and the diploids tested for evidence of recombination.

4. Homozygous diploids were obtained by means of sister crosses, using auxotrophs from the 11-series of mutants. It has been suggested that the use of closely related parental strains might have the best possibilities for success.

5. Summary of performance of best strains in fermenters.

1. CROSSES OF AUXOTROPHS SELECTED AT RANDOM

a. *Diploidization*

The first experiment involved the crossing of two mutants of relatively low yield. From the heterokaryons a number of apparently diploid colonies were obtained, ten being investigated further. The results of the preliminary tests on these diploids are summarized in Table 2, which includes results from the parental strains and the common ancestor. The diploids gave titres better than the common ancestor but usually lower than those of the lower-yielding parent. While in a few cases the diameter of the spores was 1.3 times that of the parents, indicating a doubling of the volume, in others the diameter was less, suggesting that in these cases only partial diploidization had occurred. Irrespective of spore size, substantial increases in sporulation occurred in the diploids.

Further diploidizations were also carried out between different strains. A total of eight crosses were made, seven of which gave diploids. While some interesting crosses were obtained, none of the diploids nor the mutants obtained from them showed promise, and it is not proposed to discuss them in detail. They were numbered P11–18, and some are mentioned below.

b. *Mutation of diploids*

Most of the diploids were treated with nitrogen mustard in a search for high-yielding strains. In the case of the first series of diploids (Table 2), Nos 1–5 were mutated and 25 mutants from each were tested. The best mutants came from diploid P4, and a further series of mutants were prepared from this strain. The best of these mutants were remutated, and a third mutation was

TABLE 2
Diploids from the first series of crosses

Diploid	Spore size μm	Penicillin u cm^{-3}	Sporulation × 10^7 cm^{-3}
P 1	5.3	4 185	10.2
2	5.3	5 190	14.6
3	5.1	4 870	12.2
4	5.2	4 630	11.8
5	5.4	5 590	7.0
6	4.9	4 800	6.4
7	4.7	5 540	15.1
8	4.8	5 045	6.0
9	4.9	5 015	8.4
10	5.0	4 050	10.4
Parents			
Hm/9 (ex JH272)	4.42	6 050	0.6
D21/14 (ex JV64)	4.35	5 700	7.0
Common ancestor			
JJ48		4 400	2.2

then carried out. The results of the best mutants are given in Table 3, which indicates the succession of mutations and selections. The shake-flask titres obtained in the third mutation series were higher than usual. Repeat tests gave results 1 000–1 500 u cm^{-3} lower; however, these results were extremely promising, and were supported by trials in 5-litre fermenters, when compared with JH272. Several of the mutants, especially from diploid P4, achieved the original target of a strain equal in penicillin yield to JH272, with five to ten times the degrees of sporulation. In later tests in fermenters, higher yields were obtained with the strain DC2/14, which was adopted for use in the plant. Its spore size shows that the diploid character has been retained.

It is evident that the use of mutagens produced high-yielding strains and these are referred to as mutants; however this word is not intended to define the genetic process involved in their formation.

TABLE 3
Mutants from the diploid P4

Diploid	First mutants: Number	Spore size μm cm⁻³	Penicillin u cm⁻³	Sporulation × 10⁷ cm⁻³	Second mutants: Number and penicillin u cm⁻³	Third mutants: Penicillin Number	shake flask u cm⁻³	% of JH272	Sporulation × 10⁷ cm⁻³	Spore size μm
P4	P4/16	5.0	6 615	7.0	P4/16/61 7040	DC1/4	9 460	85	9.2	—
	P4/25	5.0	5 790	11.7	—	DC2/14	9 430	106	3.4	5.3
	P4/39	—	6 780	3.0	P4/39/34 6500	DC2/33	10 350	103	3.0	—

c. *Effect of mutation on diploids*

Experience has shown that mutation is valuable for obtaining high-yielding strains from diploids. In order to check the value of mutation, spontaneous recombinants were obtained from all the diploids in the first series of crosses. These consisted of (a) strains giving small colonies on isolation plates, plus a number of normal colonies, (b) white colonies from diploids P12–15. On testing it was found that these included a proportion of auxotrophic strains (20 per cent). About 90 recombinants were tested in shaken flasks, along with some of the original diploids. None gave high titres. For the series P1–5, the diploids, in this test, averaged 4250 u cm^{-3}, while the best of the eighteen recombinants reached 4700–5205 u cm^{-3}, clearly less, for instance, than the mutant P4/39 which gave 6780 u cm^{-3} under similar circumstances. It is therefore considered that the use of mutation is fully justified.

TABLE 4

Auxotrophic recombinants obtained from diploids

Diploids	Cross	Proportion of auxotrophs among small colonies tested	Auxotrophic requirements and (Parent)
P1–10	D21/14 × Hm9	16/104	Aneurin (D21/14)
P12–15	NH4/D4 × 11H/D21	35/120	Proline (NH4/D4)
P16–17	D35/1/3 × 11D/D3	6/46	Inositol (D35/1/3)
P18	D21/14 × 11D/D3	6/47	Aneurin (D21/14)

The type of auxotrophy occurring in the recombinants from the crosses was investigated. The results are given in Table 4. In all cases these carried the auxotrophic marker borne by the more robust parent. It has been found that when spores from heterokaryons are plated, usually one of the parental types considerably exceeds the other. It is probable that the proportion of genetical material exchanged is far from equally divided between the parents.

d. *Stability of diploids*

To compare the stability of diploid and haploid strains, typical cultures were investigated by plating and by serial subculture. These were diploid mutants P4/16 and P4/25, and a haploid mutant D18/1/18. The cultures were plated, colonies being picked off onto slopes and examined after incubation. From the diploids about 5% showed slightly paler green coloration and gave slightly lower titres than the rest. With the haploid mutant only 1% of white or pale green colonies were observed.

The three strains, along with JH 272 as control, were serially subcultured through six generations on slopes, each set being tested for productivity in shaken flasks. Subculturing was associated with the appearance of a greyish overgrowth. A decline in productivity occurred after 3–4 subcultures; individual strains behaved differently. There was no essential difference between diploids and haploids. Diploid cultures have subsequently been stored for several years on dry sand or soil, in freeze-dried ampoules or under liquid nitrogen, without loss of activity.

2. COMPARATIVE SERIES OF MUTATIONS AND SELECTIONS

Three high-yielding mutants, 9A36, 11E25 and 11E30, some of which had been used as parents for hybridizations, were treated with X-rays, and then given three further treatments with ethyleneimine followed by uv rays. At each stage nine mutants were selected for remutation. The best mutants obtained in this series gave $8\,300$–$8\,600\,\mathrm{u\,cm}^{-3}$ in shaken flasks, with sporulation at 1.6–$2.0 \times 10^{7}\,\mathrm{cm}^{-3}$. These mutants were thus about equal to some of the best strains obtained by hybridization, though none appeared attractive for plant work. Tests of some of these strains (XE and XF series) are given later in Table 7.

3. HYBRIDIZATION OF COLOURED STRAINS

Following the mutagenic treatments just described, a number of auxotrophs with spore colour mutations were obtained, giving high yields. Crosses were

TABLE 5

Hybridization of auxotrophs bearing spore colour mutations: crossing-over

Cross and description		Number	Colour	Segregants Requirement	Penicillin* u cm
A4/1 White Pyridoxin 6 420	× E2/1 White Leucine $6\,380\,\mathrm{u\,cm}^{-3}$	F12 F13 G29	Green Green Green	Leucine Pyridoxin Pyridoxin	— — 7 600
A4/1 White Pyridoxin 6 420	× A4/5 Green Ammonium $5\,320\,\mathrm{u\,cm}^{-3}$	H38	Green	Pyridoxin	7 590
E2/1 White Leucine 6 380	× J1 Lime green Inositol $5\,790\,\mathrm{u\,cm}^{-3}$	B7	White	Inositol	—

TABLE 6
Homozygous diploids from sister crosses

Parents	Phenotype of mutant*	Titre u cm⁻³	Diploids Number	Spore size μm	Titre u cm⁻³	Nos. of auxotrophs	Mutants (N-mustard) Best strains Strain	Titre
11E30/14	11E30/14D nic × 11E30/14D1 leu	(4 000) (6 250)	DD25 DD26	5.1 5.3	7 180 6 340	7 leu 3 nic	DD25/4 DD25/9 DD26/22 DD26/24	6 880 6 920 7 260 7 380
13F16	13F16D1 yellow, ane × CF4, paba	(4 600) (4 900)	DD28	5.3	4 380	5 ane	DD28/31	6 620
11E25	7½ME meth × 5MK amm	(5 700) (5 400)	DD29	5.0	5 540	2 meth 1 amm	DD29/12 13 14	6 700 6 820 6 880
11E2	11D/D3 nic × 11D/D2 inos	(4 500) (4 500)	DD30	5.2	6 480	1 inos	DD30/6 DD30/20	6 820 6 730

* Explanation of symbols. Nutritional requirements: amm, reduced inorganic nitrogen; ane, aneurin; inos, inositol; leu, leucine; meth, methionine; nic, nicotinamide; paba, para-amino-benzoic acid.

made and mutants selected. Although some fairly high titres were obtained, none of the mutants appeared likely to be of technical interest. In three cases crossing over was observed. These results are summarized in Table 5.

4. HOMOZYGOUS DIPLOIDS FROM SISTER CROSSES

Crosses were made using mutants from the 11- and 13-series. Auxotrophs were used giving 4000 to 6000 u cm^{-3}. These were crossed in pairs, from the same parent, giving homozygous diploids. This work, with the results of the first mutation (using nitrogen mustard), is summarized in Table 6. Five of the homozygous diploids were mutated and 34 isolates from each were screened; some were found to be auxotrophic, as is shown in the Table. Later two further mutations and selections were made, leading to the DF and DG series, some of which reached 7800 u cm^{-3} in shaken flasks. Results in fermenters were also very good (see Table 7).

Diploidization did not occur so readily as with the other crosses and the diploids showed less vigorous growth than usual. Inoculum development was sometimes weak and sporulation in Foster's medium fell to only 10^5 spores

TABLE 7
Test of high-yielding strains in 5-litre fermenters
(Results of individual tests)

Series	Number	Sporulation $\times 10^7$ cm^{-3}	Method of formation	Penicillin, u cm^{-3} at 120 h
Random crosses	DC2/14*	4.0	diploidization	10 600
		3.1	and mutation	11 300
				11 270
				11 080
				11 010
	DC11/11	3.0	diploidization	11 200
		1.5	and mutation	11 100
				11 000
				10 750
	DE10/9	0.5	diploidization	12 500
			and mutation	11 050
Mutants	XF5/12	1.3	mutation	10 500
	XF7/14	0.5	diploidization and mutation	10 200
Control mutant	9A36	1.8	mutation	10 900
Homozygous diploids	DG1/12†	2 × 10^5	diploidization	11 750
	DG3/5†	3 × 10^5	and mutation	11 500

Notes * DC2/14 achieved 12 200 and 13 000 u cm^{-3} in stronger medium.
    † Adequate supplies of spores for the test were obtained by growth on moistened pearl barley.

cm^{-3} on two occasions. For stirred culture tests spores were grown on moistened pearl barley. Altogether the hybrid vigour hoped for with these strains was not apparent.

5. SUMMARY OF PERFORMANCE OF BEST STRAINS IN FERMENTERS

The performance in 5-litre fermenters of some of the best strains from all programmes is summarized in Table 7. The mutant 9A36 was used as control. Although the DG strains from the homozygous diploids, i.e. mutants derived from the DD strains quoted in Table 6, gave the highest titres, DC2/14 was preferred as it gave high titres with good sporulation and general reliability.

Discussion

The experiments show that very substantial benefits can be obtained from hybridization followed by mutation. It is evident that a wide range of strains can be produced. It is also apparent that the procedure gives unpredictable results, for instance the highest yielder came from one of a number of random crosses. This agrees with previous experience (Calam et al., 1973). It is of interest that the high yield was, in this case, accompanied by improvements in sporulation, no doubt because the strain concerned was a diploid. Since the production of this strain was apparently a chance event, it might be thought that there is no pattern in the results of crosses. This is contradicted by the results of the crosses with sister strains, when the progeny gave high yields accompanied by greatly reduced sporulation. It was also found in crosses with spore colour mutants that there was definite evidence of crossing-over. It is therefore clear that in these crosses genetic exchanges are taking place, perhaps in a more restricted way than usual, but that we are as yet unable to predict the results that are likely to occur.

As was found in work with *Fusarium moniliforme* (Calam et al., 1973) it is obvious that certain crosses are more profitable than others, and that, in a campaign, success depends on finding successful crosses and concentrating selection upon them. A similar situation pertains in mutation work.

The difficulty of predicting results is not surprising when one considers the complexity of the processes taking place. We have previously expressed the view (Calam et al., 1973) that in the parasexual process, with high-yielding strains, full conjugation of nuclei may fail to occur, so that partial diploids are formed and recombination may be incomplete. In other words, it is probable that genetic exchanges are restricted. This is a subject about which little is known at present.

When the biochemical aspect of the problem is considered, it is seen that very complicated requirements must be met if high yields are to be obtained. This is well recognized by those concerned with the breeding of improved plants and animals. It is recognized that when a wild strain is mutated to give high yields, fundamental changes in metabolic routes may be essential. Thus Hoštálek (1973) has shown than an alternative biosynthetic route is used to provide acetyl units in chlortetracycline synthesis, in mutants of *Streptomyces aureofaciens.* In the case of penicillin production, it has been found that a high-yielding mutant differed from a wild strain, not only in rate of production, but also as regards growth-pattern in the fermenter and in the ratios of certain enzymes in the central metabolic system (Calam, 1973). Tardrew and Johnson (1958) also observed major changes in sulphur metabolism when comparing a wild strain with a mutant.

TABLE 8
Requirements of valine and cysteine for growth and production

Product	Wild strain g dm^{-3}	Mutant g dm^{-3}
Mycelium	20	20
Protein (25%)	5	5
Valine	0.25	0.25
Cysteine	0.05	0.05
Penicillin	0.12	12.0
Valine	0.038	3.8
Cysteine	0.041	4.1
TOTAL		
Valine	0.288	4.05
Cysteine	0.088	4.15

The main components of the penicillin molecule are valine and cysteine. While no precise data are available, it is possible to estimate roughly the quantities of these substances which would have to be synthesized during typical fermentations. It may be assumed that, during the production phase, some 20 g of cells must be produced along with the penicillin, containing 25 per cent of protein, of which 5 per cent may be valine and 1 per cent cysteine. Table 8 gives the amounts of valine and cysteine required for the biosynthesis of 200 and 20000 u cm^{-3} of benzyl penicillin. It is evident that enormously increased quantities of valine and cysteine are required. While in the wild strain the amounts of valine and cysteine required for penicillin are equal to or less than what is needed by the cells, with the high-yielding strain, penicillin production dominates the situation. While the data in Table 8 may exaggerate the position, it is clear that in the mutant the pattern of metabolic regulation must be completely rearranged, not only to provide amino acids, but also the increased requirement for sulphur will demand large amounts of energy. Goulden and Chattaway (1968, 1969) have investigated lysine and valine regulation in relation to penicillin biosynthesis; Demain and Masureka (1974) have continued work on the latter subject. Regulation of penicillin biosynthesis may also be affected by the presence of amino acids in the medium. A corollary of these observations is that when high-yielding mutants are being selected, adjustments to the medium may be necessary to meet increased demands for material for biosynthesis.

At present, when strains are crossed, we have no knowledge of the circumstances of the main metabolic pathways involved, and it is a matter of chance whether the recombinants are successful or not. Further research is necessary to clarify which areas are critical for production of penicillin. Most of our knowledge is qualitative; more knowledge is necessary on the rates of flow through the main metabolic routes. Hybridization is evidently useful, as it can both increase yields and improve the growth of the culture. When working in this field it still seems best to take an opportunist approach.

Having reached this conclusion it is worth while considering in more detail why the breeding methods discussed in this paper are preferred to an approach involving the production of a chromosome map which is used to guide the choice of strains for crossing and recombination. The problem is one of time. Judging by the references quoted in the introduction, mapping would be expected to be difficult and to require several years, while further time would be needed to obtain the most suitable mutants. Assuming technical success, there is no certainty as to what degree of productivity would result. From the information given in this report, the choice of mutants for crossing would be difficult, and from general experience the outcome of recombination would be unpredictable. It would not be unreasonable to expect three to four years to be required for this work. From the results reported here, it would be expected that during this time the level of production would have risen substantially, at least in other laboratories. Crosses with strains where linkage relationships were established would therefore take place with strains already obsolete as regards productivity. Alternatively, new high-yielding strains might be obtained, but genetic work would be needed to bring them into use. To choose an approach based on the construction of linkage groups would therefore involve the risk of losing several years of progress in strain improvement, and this would be commercially dangerous. It is difficult to see how further progress can be made until this problem of time can be overcome, and this sets aside other difficulties.

The breeding approach, on the other hand, can be in close touch with current mutation work, the latest strains being available for crossing at an early date. This is illustrated by the present report: see also Alikhanian (1958).

These points indicate why breeding as discussed here is favoured for industrial work. It is the purpose of the present report to describe typical industrial experiments, comparing mutation with hybridization as practical approaches to strain improvement. It is hoped that the availability of this data will stimulate discussion of the problem. The promising nature of the results reinforces the view of many workers that hybridization has something to offer to the industrial worker. If, at the same time, the difficulties of an approach based on the construction of chromosomal maps are brought out, it is our hope that this will bring attention to bear on the problem, and that in due course a solution will become apparent.

References

Alikhanian, S. I. (1958). *Bjull. Mosk. Obsa. Ispyt. Priorod. Ordel. Biol.* **63**, 79.
Ball, C. (1973). "Genetics of Industrial Microorganisms". (Eds Z. Vanék, Z. Hoštálek and J. Cudlín), p 227. Academia, Prague.
Calam, C. T. (1970). "Methods in Microbiology", vol. 3A, p. 435. Academic Press, London and New York.
Calam, C. T., Daglish, L. B. and Gaitskell, W. S. (1973). "Genetics of Industrial Microorganisms". (Eds Z. Vanék, Z. Hoštálek and J. Cudlín), p. 265. Academia, Prague.
Calam, C. T. (1973). Proceedings of the conference on the genetics of industrial microorganisms, Tsakazdor, Armenian, S. R., December, 1973. In press.
Demain, A. L. and Masureka, P. S. (1974). *J. gen. Microbiol.* **82**, 143.
Elander, R. P., Espenshade,M. A., Pathak, S. G. and Pan, C. H. (1973). "Genetics of Industrial Microorganisms" (Eds Z. Vanék, Z. Hoštálek and J. Cudlín), p. 239. Academia, Prague.
Goulden, S. A. and Chattaway, F. W. (1968). *Biochem. J.* **110**, 55P.
Goulden, S. A. and Chattaway, F. W. (1969). *J. gen. Microbiol.* **59**, 111.
Hoštálek, Z. (1973). Proceedings of the conference on the genetics of industrial microorganisms, Tsakazdor, Armenia S.R., December, 1973. In press.
McCann, E. P. and Calam, C. T. (1972). *J. appl. Chem. Biotechnol.* **22**, 1201.
Macdonald, K. D., Hutchinson, J. M. and Gillett, W. A. (1963a). *J. gen. Microbiol.* **33**, 365.
Macdonald, K. D., Hutchinson, J. M. and Gillett, W. A. (1963b). *J. gen. Microbiol.* **33**, 375.
Macdonald, K. D., Hutchinson, J. M. and Gillett, W. A. (1963c). *J. gen. Microbiol.* **33**, 385.
Macdonald, K. D., Holt, G. and Ditchburn, P. (1972). "Fermentation Technology Today" (Ed. G. Terui), p. 251. Society of fermentation technology, Osaka, Japan.
Sermonti, G. (1969). "Genetics of Antibiotic-Producing Micro-organisms". Wiley-Interscience, London.
Tardrew, P. L. and Johnson, M. J. (1958). *J. Bact.* **76**, 400.

GENETIC ASPECTS OF NONANTIBIOTIC
FERMENTATION PRODUCTS

Genetic approaches to the stimulation of bacterial protein synthesis

W. J. BRAMMAR

*Department of Molecular Biology, University of Edinburgh,
King's Buildings, Edinburgh EH9 3JR, Scotland*

Summary

The maximum rate at which a bacterial gene can be expressed is governed by the structure of the relevant promoter region. Genetic alteration of a promoter site can increase the rate of transcription of the gene and enhance the yield of the gene product.

A second genetic method of stimulating the yield of a bacterial protein is by increasing the number of copies of the structural gene. The formation of specialized transducing particles is a convenient method of achieving this aim, and the power of the approach can be enhanced by manipulation of the phage genes. The method has been made applicable to genes from any source by the discovery of methods for linking fragments of heterologous DNA into *E. coli* replicons.

Introduction

Recent advances in our understanding of the molecular genetics of bacteria and their viruses have encouraged hope and endeavour for rapid progress in the large-scale production of specific proteins for use in fundamental research, medicine and industry. The isolation and purification of a potentially useful protein from an organism in culture can be greatly facilitated by ensuring that the organism is synthesizing the required product at its maximum rate. This consideration is of particular importance during operations on the industrial scale: the higher the specific activity of the protein in the culture, the simpler and more efficient will be the purification process.

The rates at which many bacterial proteins are synthesized are affected by the composition of the growth medium and the physiological condition of the cells. The rates of synthesis of many catabolic and biosynthetic enzymes can be varied over at least a thousand-fold range by the well-known processes of induction and repression (Jacob and Monod, 1961). The *maximum* rate at which a given gene can be expressed is genetically determined, however, and can be altered by mutation (Scaife and Beckwith, 1966).

A second method of enhancing an organism's capacity to synthesize a particular protein is by bringing about an increase in the number of copies of the relevant structural gene per genome. A powerful method of achieving this aim involves incorporation of the bacterial gene into the genome of a specialized transducing phage. The transposed gene can then be replicated by the phage-specific DNA replication system and its number of copies per cell can be greatly increased.

In this paper examples of these approaches to increasing protein production will be discussed, and possibilities for extending their application to diverse systems and organisms will be emphasized.

Results and discussion

INCREASING THE EFFICIENCY OF GENE EXPRESSION

Central to the process of gene expression is the transcription of the DNA into single stranded messenger RNA molecules, catalysed by RNA polymerase. To initiate transcription of a gene or group of genes RNA polymerase binds to the DNA at the promoter site (Jacob et al., 1964; Scaife and Beckwith, 1966). It is the initiation of transcription that is the rate-limiting step in bacterial gene expression (Rose and Yanofsky, 1972) and it appears to be the promoter itself, or the nucleotide sequence in the vicinity of the promoter, that determines the maximum rate of expression of a bacterial gene (Scaife and Beckwith, 1966). Therefore by genetic alteration of the promoter region we can increase or decrease the maximal rate at which a given gene can be expressed.

The maximal rates at which different bacterial genes can be expressed vary over a very wide range. The constitutively expressed *lacI* gene of *E. coli*, coding for the repressor protein of the lactose operon, produces only about ten molecules of the gene product per cell (Gilbert and Müller-Hill, 1966). Structural genes for metabolic enzymes are usually capable of much higher rates of expression. For example, each of the enzymes involved in the biosynthesis of tryptophan in *E. coli* is represented by about 10 000 molecules per cell when the corresponding genes are fully derepressed (Morse and Yanofsky, 1969).

The capacity for expression of a gene, which shows such great variability, is determined by the base sequence of the relevant promoter region, and is therefore susceptible to genetic alteration. A mutation in the promoter, in addition to affecting the maximum rate of expression, should have the following properties (Scaife and Beckwith, 1966):

a. *cis-specificity*. The mutation should affect the expression of only those genes in the *cis* arrangement; the functioning of a nonmutant copy of the promoter in *trans* in the same cell should be unaffected.

b. *Pleiotropy*. The mutation should affect the expression of *all* the genes in the transcriptional unit or operon.

c. *Normal regulation*. The specific regulation system operating in the parental strain should function normally in the mutant strain.

TABLE 1

Mutations increasing the rate of gene expression

System*	Factor increase	Molecules of product per genome	Reference
lac I	10	100	Müller-Hill *et al.* (1968)
Nicotinamide deamidase	22	8 000	Pardee *et al.* (1971)
Glucose 6 phosphate dehydrogenase	18	35 000	Fraenkel and Parola (1972)
trp operon	3	22 000	Rabstein, M. A. and Brammar, W. J. (unpublished)
trp genes, lambda promoter	10	80 000	Davison *et al.* (1974)
lac operon	10	140 000	Bruenn *et al.* (1973)
Dihydrofolase reductase (*Diplococcus pneumoniae*)	100†	?	Sirotnak (1971)

* All examples are from *E. coli* systems unless stated otherwise.
† This mutant shows an increased yield of a structurally altered enzyme (Sirotnak, 1971).

Mutations with these properties, believed to involve either improved or impaired promoter function, have now been isolated in several systems. Since we are concerned here with the *stimulation* of macromolecular synthesis through genetic manipulation, I will refer only to the mutations resulting in improved promoter function. Examples of such mutations are shown in Table 1.

The efficacy of both weak and strong promoters can be enhanced by mutation: in each case the increase achieved as a result of a single mutational event is about ten-fold (Table 1). In both *lacI* (Miller, 1970) and the nicotinamide deamidase system (Pardee *et al.*, 1971) a second mutational event has been shown to improve promoter function further. The mutation affecting the expression of the *lac* operon is not a simple change of the *lac* promoter, since it maps in the *lacI* gene, and may well involve the accretion of DNA containing a powerful "foreign" promoter (Bruenn and Hollingsworth, 1973).

In the mutant with enhanced *trp* promoter activity, the five enzymes whose synthesis is governed by the mutant promoter represent 10 per cent of the total cellular protein. This proportion is further increased in a strain in which the *trp* promoter has been replaced by a highly efficient promoter from the bacteriophage λ. The way in which this substitution can occur during the formation of a specialized transducing phage, λ*trp*, is shown in Fig. 1. In this way *trp*-transducing phages can be isolated that express the *trp* genes entirely from

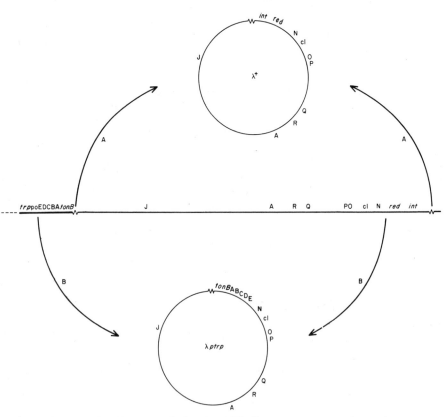

FIG. 1. The formation of a *trp*-transducing phage. The linear map represents the prophage map of a Φ80/λ hybrid phage integrated into the *E. coli* chromosome at the Φ80-attachment site near *tonB* and the *trp* genes. A, The formation of wild-type phage by the normal excision process following induction. B, The formation of a *trp*-transducing phage by a rare, aberrant excision event. The *trp* genes replace nonessential genes from the *N* operon of the parental phage, so that the transducing derivative retains the ability to make plaques.

p_L, the promoter for leftward transcription of the N operon of phage λ (Franklin, 1971; Davison *et al.*, 1974). By integrating such a phage into the bacterial chromosome and subsequently isolating derivatives that have lost the lambda control genes *cI* and *cro*, responsible for regulating the expression of the N gene (see Fig. 2), a prototrophic bacterial strain has been constructed that synthesises 20% of its soluble protein as *trp* operon enzymes (Davison *et al.*, 1974).

(a) *int xis red* cIII N p_L *rex* cI p_R *cro* cII O P Q S R

trp
(b) *tonB* A B C D E N p_L *rex* cI p_R *cro* cII O P Q S R

trp
(c) *tonB* A B C D E N p_L /////////////////////////////////

FIG. 2. Prophage map of the right arm of bacteriophage λ (a), λ*trp*BG2 (b), and a deletion derivative of λ*trp*BG2, Dx (c). The horizontal arrow represents the transcription of the N operon of the phage, which starts at P. λ*trp*BG2 contains all five structural genes of the *trp* operon, but has lost the *trp* promoter, the *trp* genes can be expressed by reading started at p_L (Davison *et al.*, 1974). In the deletion Dx (c), p_L and the N gene remain intact, but the control genes *cI* and *cro* have been eliminated. The *trp* genes are therefore expressed constitutively at a very high rate. – – – – – – represents bacterial DNA carried by the transducing phage, while ———— represents phage DNA. ////// represents deleted genes.

GENERAL APPROACHES TO ISOLATING MUTANTS WITH IMPROVED PROMOTER FUNCTION

The above examples of the potential of genetic improvement of promoter function have relied on a detailed knowledge of the genetics of *E. coli* and its temperate phages. Nevertheless, there are methods of obtaining such variants that are applicable to organisms with less well-studied genetic systems than that of *E. coli*.

One such method that has been successfully used is the selection for restoration of function at the restrictive temperature in a temperature-sensitive mutant. Such a mutant can revert by a genetic event that alters the structure of the temperature-sensitive protein, or by an event that increases the rate of production of the mutant protein and thereby phenotypically compensates for its defect. This approach was used by Müller-Hill *et al.* (1968) to isolate mutants of *E. coli* that make increased amounts of the *lac* operon repressor.

A variation on the same theme is the selection for fast-growing revertants of a very slow-growing ("leaky") mutant. Again the reversion event could alter either the structure of the protein or its rate of production. Where "leaky" mutants are not available they can often be obtained amongst the revertants of a nonleaky mutant.

Both the preceding methods have the disadvantage that the promoter mutation is necessarily obtained in conjunction with the original structural gene mutation that makes the desired gene product defective. For organisms with a good system of genetic transfer and recombination this is not a serious problem, since the mutant promoter can easily be recovered following recombination.

In many biosynthetic systems, improved promoter mutants should show increased resistance to a toxic analogue of the end product of the biosynthetic pathway. This is certainly true of the *trp* promoter mutants in *E. coli*, which shows an increased resistance to 5-methyl-DL-tryptophan (Rabstein and Brammar, unpublished). Of course many different molecular mechanisms can give rise to resistance to a toxic analogue, but it is often relatively easy to screen amongst resistant mutants, by assay of the gene product if necessary, for those that have the desired overproduction of the protein.

The key to obtaining mutants with improved gene expression is the imposition of the appropriate selection. In order to arrange this we must have a detailed knowledge of the relevant enzyme system. We need to know the range and activity of substrates, inhibitors, inducers and repressors, for example, as well as the effects of different sources of carbon and nitrogen on the behaviour of the system. Fortunately, these are properties that are readily obtainable from simple physiological studies. The use of the chemostat for imposing powerfully selective conditions should not be overlooked (see, for example, Horiuchi *et al.*, 1962).

In the absence of a suitable selection or enrichment procedure, it becomes necessary to resort to direct screening for mutants synthesizing a product at an increased rate. In this situation, methods allowing the screening of colonies on plates, such as indicator plates or plate-staining methods, can be invaluable. The very powerful chemical mutagens available, particularly the alkylating agents, make this approach to mutant isolation quite practicable, though their tendency to produce multiple linked mutations (Guerola *et al.*, 1971) can make subsequent genetic analysis hazardous.

INCREASING GENE DOSAGE VIA SPECIALIZED TRANSDUCING PHAGE

A different approach to improving the yield of a given gene product involves increasing the number of copies of the relevant structural gene. A convenient and powerful method of achieving this aim, at least for *E. coli* systems, is by incorporation of the structural gene into a specialized transducing derivative of a temperate phage.

Specialized transducing particles are derived by rare, aberrant variations of the normal excision process. Bacterial genes located close to the site of integration of the bacteriophage DNA into the host chromosome can become incorporated into the bacteriophage genome, usually at the expense of bacteriophage genes from the opposite end of the prophage genetic map (Campbell, 1962) (Fig. 1). Often, formation of a transducing derivative eliminates a gene essential for viral growth: the defective transducing particle can then only be grown in the presence of complementing helper phage.

Techniques have recently been developed to extend the use of specialized transducing phages to genes that are not normally located close to sites for bacteriophage integration. One such technique involves the forced integration of a thermosensitive episome carrying the gene of interest into a chromosomal gene, *ton B*, very close to the attachment site for transducing phage φ80 (Beckwith *et al.*, 1966). The existence of a positive selection for *ton B* mutants makes this a very convenient method. A second approach makes use of the fact that the two autonomous F factors cannot normally coexist in the same *E. coli* cell to force the fusion of an episome carrying the relevant structural gene to an episome carrying a phage-attachment site (Press *et al.*, 1971). A third method makes use of the observation that, in the absence of the normal site of integration, phage lambda will integrate with decreased frequency into many other chromosomal locations (Shimada *et al.*, 1972). By the application of these techniques a gene from any part of the *E. coli* chromosome can be brought into close proximity to a phage-attachment site and subsequently incorporated into a transducing particle.

THE USE OF MUTANT PHAGES TO ENHANCE OVERPRODUCTION

The power and convenience of a transducing phage as a means of stimulating enzyme production via increased gene dosage can often be enhanced by genetic manipulation of the phage itself. One obvious example of this is the use of a mutant having a temperature-sensitive repression system, so that it can be induced from the prophage into the vegetative state by increasing the temperature. In those cases where the incorporated structural gene can be transcribed from a phage promoter, the use of mutations derepressing phage functions can obviously be of advantage (Franklin, 1971; Davison *et al.*, 1974).

The number of copies of the bacteriophage genome per cell can be further increased by the use of mutations rendering the phage unable to lyse the host cell. Mutants of phage lambda defective in gene *S* develop normally and generate over a thousand phage per cell without producing lysis (Harris *et al.*, 1967; Müller-Hill *et al.*, 1968). The use of mutants defective in gene *Q*, the positive control gene for late functions of phage lambda, produces a similar effect with the possible advantage that the synthesis of phage head and tail structural proteins is minimized (Moir and Brammar, unpublished). The expression of the *trp* genes of *trp*-transducing phages can be used to monitor the usefulness of various phage mutations in enhancing the yield of specific

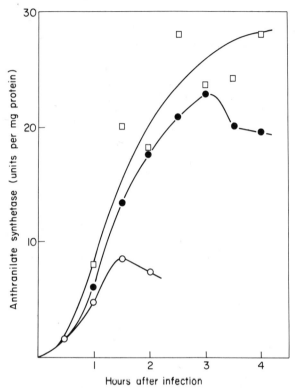

Fig. 3. The synthesis of anthranilate synthetase on infection of a *trp* (*EDCB*) deletion strain of *E. coli* by derivatives of λ*trp*AM1. The procedure for infection, sampling and assay has been described (Franklin, 1971) (λ*trp*AM1 carries all five *trp* structural genes, and expresses them exclusively from the *trp* promoter (A. Moir, personal communication)). The host strain was W3110, *trp*R, *trp*(EDCB) 9, and the multiplicity of infection was 2.00
○, λ*trp*AM1; ●, λ*trp*AM1 *Sam7*; ☐, λ*trp*AM1*Qam*.

proteins. Figure 3 shows the kinetics of expression of the *trpE* and *D* genes of *trp*-transducing phage λ*trp*AM1 during vegetative growth in a *trp*⁻ host. The parental phage, λ*trp*AM1, lyses the host after about two hours of infection. In contrast, cells infected with the *S*⁻ or *Q*⁻ derivatives of λ*trp*AM1 continue to synthesize anthranilate synthetase at a high rate for about four hours. After this time, the five enzymes coded by the *trp* operon constitute about 50 per cent of the protein of the cells infected with the *Q*-defective derivative of λ*trp*AM1.

BIOCHEMICAL APPROACHES TO INCREASING GENE DOSAGE

The use of specialized transducing phages as a means of increasing gene dosage has been limited by the requirement for the appropriate genetic technology.

Recently, however, this kind of approach has been made applicable to genes from any source by the exploitation of sequence-specific endonucleases, the type II restriction enzymes. Several such enzymes break double-stranded DNA into discrete fragments with short, mutually complementary, single-stranded projections, or "cohesive ends" (Hedgpeth et al., 1972; Bigger et al., 1973; Murray and Old, 1974). Fragments of DNA from any source prepared by the action of such an enzyme will anneal via their cohesive ends and become covalently joined after treatment with polynucleotide ligase (Mertz and Davis, 1972).

The circular DNA of the E. coli tetracycline-resistance plasmid, pSC101, has only one target for the RI restriction endonuclease (Cohen et al., 1973), R.EcoRI (Smith and Nathans 1973), an enzyme that produces cohesive ends (Hedgpeth et al., 1972). Heterologous DNA fragments produced by the action of the RI enzyme can be inserted into the R.EcoRI site of pSC101 DNA, and the recombinant molecules so formed become biologically functional replicons when introduced into E. coli by transformation (Cohen et al., 1973). In this way genes from a Staphylococcal plasmid (Chang and Cohen, 1974) and ribosomal RNA genes from Xenopus laevis (Morrow et al., 1974) have been amplified and expressed in E. coli.

The extensive knowledge of the genetics and biochemistry of phage lambda make the chromosome of the phage an obvious choice as a receptor for fragments of heterologous DNA. The DNA from wild-type lambda phage has five targets for the R.EcoRI endonuclease, at least three of which are in nonessential regions of the chromosome (Allet et al., 1973). Genetic manipulation of lambda has generated derivatives with single targets for the RI endonuclease, and R.EcoRI produced fragments of DNA have been incorporated at some of these sites to give, after transfection of an E. coli host, "recombinant" plaque-forming phages (Murray and Murray, 1974). One of the targets for R.EcoRI, sRI3, lies within the N operon of phage lambda (Allet et al., 1973), which can be expressed at very high rates under the appropriate conditions (Franklin, 1971; Davison et al., 1974). The use of sRI3 as the receptor site may well have the extra advantage of producing a high rate of gene expression by transcription started at the powerful phage promoter, p_L (Franklin, 1971). Experiments with model systems have shown that genes inserted in this way can be expressed from a phage promoter (N. E. Murray and W. J. Brammar, unpublished observations).

It is clear from these studies with R.EcoRI-produced DNA fragments that the means are now available for incorporating genes from any source into E. coli replicons and, after transformation or transfection, to propagate them in the bacterial cell. It remains to be demonstrated that eukaryotic genes are efficiently expressed by the prokaryotic transcription and translation apparatus.

References

Allet, B., Jeppeson, P. G. N., Katagiri, K. J. and Delius, H. (1973). *Nature,* **241**, 120.
Beckwith, J. R., Signer, E. T. and Epstein, W. (1966). *Cold Spring Harb. Symp. quant. Biol.* **31**, 393.
Bigger, C. H., Murray, K. and Murray, N. E. (1973). *Nature, New Biol.* **244**, 7.
Bruenn, J. and Hollingsworth, H. (1973). *Proc. natn. Acad. Sci. U.S.A.* **70**, 3693.
Campbell, A. (1962). *Adv. Gen.* **11**, 101.
Chang, A. C. Y. and Cohen, S. N. (1974). *Proc. natn. Acad. Sci. U.S.A.* **71**, 1030.
Cohen, S. N., Chang, A. C. Y., Boyer, H. W. and Helling, R. B. (1973). *Proc. natn. Acad. Sci. U.S.A.* **70**, 3240.
Davison, J. R., Brammar, W. J. and Brunel, F. (1974). *Molec. gen. Genetics,* **130**, 9.
Fraenkel, D. G. and Parola, A. (1972). *J. molec. Biol.* **71**, 107.
Franklin, N. C. (1971). *In* "The Bacteriophage Lambda" (Ed. A. D. Hershey), p. 621. Cold Spring Harbor Laboratories, New York.
Gilbert, W. and Müller-Hill, B. (1966). *Proc. natn. Acad. Sci. U.S.A.* **56**, 1891.
Guerola, N. Ingraham, J. L. and Cerda-Olmedo (1971). *Nature, New Biol.* **230**, 122.
Harris, A. W., Mount, D. W. A., Fuerst, C. R. and Simonovitch, L. (1967). *Virology,* **32**, 553.
Hedgpeth, J., Goodman, H. M. and Boyer, H. W. (1972). *Proc. natn. Acad. Sci. U.S.A.* **69**, 3448.
Horiuchi, T., Tomazawa, J-I. and Novick, A. (1962). *Biochim. biophys. Acta.* **55**, 152.
Jacob, F. and Monod, J. (1961). *J. molec. Biol.* **3**, 318.
Jacob, F., Ullman, A. and Monod, J. (1964). *C.r. hebd. Séanc. Acad. Sci., Paris,* **258**, 3125.
Mertz, J. E. and Davis, R. W. (1972). *Proc. natn. Acad. Sci. U.S.A.* **69**, 3370.
Miller, J. H. (1970). *In* "The Lactose Operon" (Eds J. R. Beckwith and D. Zipser), p. 173. Cold Spring Harbor Laboratory, New York.
Morrow, J. F., Cohen, S. N., Chang, A. C. Y., Boyer, H. W., Goodman, H. M. and Helling, R. B. (1974). *Proc. natn. Acad. Sci. U.S.A.* **71**, 1743.
Morse, D. E. and Yanofsky, C. (1969). *J. molec. Biol.* **41**, 317.
Müller-Hill, B., Crapo, L. and Gilbert, W. (1968). *Proc. natn. Acad. Sci. U.S.A.* **59**, 1259.
Murray, K. and Old, R. W. (1974). *Prog. Nucleic Acid Research Mol. Biol.* (Ed. W. E. Cohn), vol. 14, p. 117. Academic Press, New York and London.
Murray, N. E. and Murray, K. (1974). *Nature, London,* **251**, 476.
Pardee, A. B., Benz, E. J., St. Peter, D. A., Krieger, J. N., Neuth, M. and Trieshmann, Jr., H. W. (1971). *J. biol. Chem.* **246**, 6792.
Press, R., Glansdorff, N., Miner, P. de Vries, J., Kadner, R. and Maas, W. K. (1971). *Proc. natn. Acad. Sci. U.S.A.* **68**, 795.
Rose, J. K. and Yanofsky, C. (1972). *J. molec. Biol.* **69**, 103.
Scaife, J. and Beckwith, J. R. (1966). *Cold Spring Harb. Symp. quant. Biol.* **31**, 403.
Shimada, K., Weisberg, R. A. and Gottesman, M. E. (1972). *J. molec. Biol.* **63**, 483.
Sirotnak, F. M. (1971). *J. Bact.* **106**, 318.
Smith, H. O. and Nathans, D. (1973). *J. molec. Biol.* **81**, 419.

Genetic aspects of asparaginase- 2 production in *Escherichia coli*

J. C. JEFFRIES*

Department of Microbiology, University of Edinburgh, Edinburgh, Scotland

Summary

Production of asparaginase-2 (Asnase-2) by *E. coli* is greatest in a medium rich in a variety of amino acids, with a limited oxygen supply, over a pH range 7.0 to 7.8, at the end of exponential phase growth. There is a requirement for inorganic cations and possibly for methionine. Lactic acid has a beneficial effect on the yield, but readily fermentable carbohydrates such as glucose cause catabolic repression, which is not relieved by addition of cyclic AMP. Mutations which adversely affect growth markedly depress ASNase-2 production. The nature of the control mechanisms is not understood, nor is the *in vivo* function of the enzyme known.

Two selective media have been formulated which allow isolation of strains producing increased levels of ASNase-2, but the effective pressure exerted by these media may not be that for which they were designed.

The structural gene for ASNase-2 has been located by conjugation and transduction at about 25.5 minutes on the *E. coli* chromosome map. Duplication of this gene, by means of F' episomes containing this region of the chromosome, give rise to an increase in enzyme yield of 60–80 per cent. The instability of such episomes would not appear to be a major problem, despite the fact that they must be carried by a $recA^+$ strain, since $recA$ mutations (normally used to prevent recombination of the F') adversely affect the production of ASNase-2.

The high ASNase-2 producing wild-type *E. coli* strain F221 readily yields mutants of greater enzyme productivity. It seems likely that the genetic

* Present address: Department of Botany, University of Edinburgh, The King's Buildings, Mayfield Road, Edinburgh EH9 3JH, Scotland.

determinants of this strain could be transferred by Pl transduction to a K12 strain of *E. coli* for genetic manipulation studies.

Introduction

Ten years ago, Calam (1964) was able to summarize the industrial approach to the generation of high-yielding strains of microorganisms as follows: "Although a certain amount of theoretical information is available which can be used as a guide, the selection, improvement and preservation of cultures are still mainly matters of empirical experience."

The amount of theoretical information from academic research on the physiology and genetics of microorganisms has increased enormously since then, but is still often concentrated on systems of little interest to industry.

Recent techniques of environmental and genetic manipulation have been summarized by Pardee (1969) and Demain (1971) among others, and will doubtless be expounded elsewhere in these Proceedings.

Once a useful industrial product is discovered in an intensively studied organism such as *Escherichia coli*, it should be possible to remove some of the empiricism from strain improvement. Industrial interest in asparaginase-2 (ASNase-2) stemmed from its effectiveness in the treatment of certain leukaemias, and commercial strains of *E. coli* were developed to produce this enzyme. This was sufficient incentive to attempt strain improvement for ASNase-2 production in *E. coli* K12, since commercial strains would provide a useful basis for comparison of techniques, when production figures were eventually released. ASNase-2 is now thought unlikely to become commercially significant, but we have continued our research, using this enzyme as a model system to demonstrate some of the problems that need to be overcome before genetic manipulation can be successfully employed in a previously undefined genetic system. *E. coli* W3110, a derivative of strain K12 with a thoroughly investigated genetic system and amenable to genetic manipulation, and *E. coli* Crookes (NCIB 8545) with unknown genetics but a higher initial specific yield of ASNase-2, were studied initially. The reason for using the Crookes strain was to develop high yielding derivatives by mutagenesis and by environmental manipulation, with the aim of transferring the genetic determinants for ASNase-2 to the K12 derivative for gene amplification studies. Recently, a third strain of *E. coli*, F221 (Iijima) has been studied since it produces very high yields of ASNase-2 (Imada *et al.*, 1973).

To carry out genetic manipulations with strains of *E. coli* making ASNase-2, it is necessary to locate the position of the structural and regulatory genes on the chromosome. There have been no previous reports of such work in *E. coli*, although the structural gene for asparaginase in *Saccharomyces* has been mapped (Jones, 1973). Several difficulties have impeded progress in mapping.

Firstly, four enzymes able to hydrolyse L-asparagine were found in *E, coli*; besides the periplasmic enzyme ASNase-2, there is a cytoplasmic enzyme ASNase-1 (of no therapeutic value) and two glutaminases with asparaginase activity.

Secondly, the physiological function of ASNase-2 in *E. coli* is not known, but it does not appear to be simply related to the hydrolysis of external asparagine, for although mutants can be isolated which are unable to use asparagine as sole source of carbon (or nitrogen), they have normal levels of ASNases 1 and 2. The existence of two asparagine transport systems in *E. coli* has recently been demonstrated (Willis and Woolfolk, 1974).

Thirdly, as a corollary, there is no direct procedure for isolating mutants either lacking or overproducing the enzyme, since no selection pressure can be applied.

For these reasons, it was necessary to concentrate on understanding the physiological basis of ASNase-2 production before attempting genetic studies. Production of the enzyme by *E. coli* was known to depend upon a rich medium containing a wide variety of amino acids, a limited oxygen supply and the absence of readily fermentable carbohydrates, and was known not to be specifically induced by its substrate (L-asparagine) or products (L-aspartate and ammonia) (Schwartz, 1971).

Materials and methods

BACTERIAL STRAINS

Escherichia, irregular type 1 strain NCIB 8667 *cys* streptomycin-dependent and *E. coli* strain Crookes (NCIB 8545) were obtained from the National Collection of Industrial Bacteria, Aberdeen, Scotland. Strain F221 (Iijima) was obtained from T. Iijima, Institute for Fermentation, Osaka, Japan. Strain CSH 57B *leu purE trp his met(A or B) ilv argG thi ara lac xyl mtl gal tsx strA*; strain CSH 59 (X181a) *pyrC trp thi strA*; and strain CSH 68 (Hfr 6) *mtl met malB* were obtained from Cold Spring Harbor Laboratory, New York. Strain CGSC 5038 (H680 P. G. de Haan) *thi tyrA his trp purB lacY gal mtl xyl malA str tonA tsx supE*; strain CGSC 4253 (KLF26/KL181 K. B. Low) *thi pyrD his trp recA mtl xyl malA galK str*/F′ $\xrightarrow[\;gal\;]{\;\;\;\;\;\;\;\;\;\;\;\;\;\;\;\;\;rac\;\;}$ and strain CGSC 4320 (KLF25/ KL181 K. B. Low) as CGSC 4253, but F′ $\xrightarrow[\;pyrD\;]{\;\;\;\;\;\;\;\;\;\;\;\;\;\;\;(rac)\;}$, were obtained from the *E. coli* Genetic Stock Center, Yale University School of Medicine, New Haven, Connecticut. Strain AB 2463/F′*gal*⁺ was obtained from A. S. Breeze of this laboratory. Strain W3110 was obtained from G. Kaplan of this laboratory.

Strains unable to produce ASNase-2 were prepared from strain W3110 as follows:

L

1. ASA-5 series (G. Kaplan) (ASA = ASNase-2 not produced)

W3110 $\xrightarrow{\text{N-methyl-N'-nitro-N-nitrosoguanidine (MNNG) mutagenesis}}$ W3110 LAC⁻

$\xrightarrow{\text{(MNNG) mutagenesis}}$ W3110 LAC⁻ ASA-5

$\xrightarrow{\text{Streptomycin selection}}$ W3110 LAC⁻ ASA-5 SM^R

$\xrightarrow{\text{F'}lac^+ \text{ transfer}}$ W3110 LAC⁻ ASA-5 SM^R/F'lac^+

2. ASA-24 series (A. S. Breeze)

W3110 $\xrightarrow{\text{Spontaneous}}$ W3110 MAL⁻

$\xrightarrow{\text{MNNG mutagenesis}}$ W3110 MAL⁻ ASA-24 auxotroph

$\xrightarrow{\text{Spontaneous}}$ W3110 MAL⁻ ASA-24 prototroph

$\xrightarrow{\text{Streptomycin selection}}$ W3110 MAL⁻ ASA-24 SM^R

3. ASA-71 series (A. S. Breeze)

W3110 $\xrightarrow{\text{Ultraviolet radiation mutagenesis}}$ W3110 GAL⁻ ASA-71
or W3110 GAL⁻ CHL^R ASA-71

GROWTH MEDIA

For studies on the production of ASNase-2 in complex medium, cultures were grown in Nutrient Broth No. 2 (Oxoid) supplemented as required, in 100 cm³ batches in 250 cm³ conical flasks stoppered with polyurethane foam bungs, on a rotary incubator (200 rpm) at 37°C.

To distinguish between ASNase-2 producers and nonproducers by assay, single colonies were inoculated into 5 cm³ Nutrient Broth supplemented with sodium DL-lactate (10 cm³ dm⁻³ 70 per cent solution of mixed isomers) contained in 35 cm³ test tubes covered with aluminium caps and incubated for 6 to 8 hours at 37°C on a rotary incubator (200 rpm).

Basal Synthetic Medium was slightly modified from that described by Roberts et al. (1968) and contained per litre of distilled water: glutamic acid, 7 g; methionine, 1 g; K₂HPO₄, 17.5 g; lactic acid, 7 cm³ (88 per cent solution of mixed isomers); 200 × trace element solution, 5 cm³, adjusted to pH 7.0 with KOH, and supplemented with amino acids as necessary.

SELECTIVE MEDIA

a. Succinamic acid minimal media contained per litre of distilled water:

Na_2HPO_4, 7 g; KH_2PO_4, 3 g; NaCl, 0.5 g; $MgSO_47H_2O$, 0.37 g; succinamic acid, 0.5 g; sugar (galactose or glucose), 2.5 g; pH 7.2.

b. Methylamine minimal medium contained per litre of distilled water: Na_2HPO_4, 7 g; KH_2PO_4, 3 g; NaCl, 0.5 g; $MgSO_47H_2O$, 0.37 g; galactose, 2.5 g; methylamine solution to 100 mM, adjusted to pH 7.2 with HCl; agar, 16 g.

ROUTINE ENZYME ASSAYS

For assay of ASNase-2, bacteria were harvested by centrifugation and washed in 0.05 M sodium acetate buffer pH 5.5, or 0.1 M sodium borate–HCl buffer pH 8.5.

The washed cell suspension (0.1 cm^3), 0.7 cm^3 buffer and 0.2 cm^3 0.04 M L-asparagine were incubated together for up to 30 min at 37 °C. The ammonia released was estimated by the indophenol method of Muftic (1964). Suspension and substrate blanks were included in all assays. A standard curve was prepared using ammonium acetate. ASNase-1 activity was negligible in whole cell suspensions. Interference by L-aspartase was negligible at pH 5.5 and pH 8.5. Glutaminase assays were performed similarly, substituting L-glutamine for L-asparagine in the reaction mixture.

To distinguish between cultures producing or not producing ASNase-2 it was possible to perform assays at pH 5.5 only, at a time when glutaminase activity was negligible.

MUTAGENESIS WITH N-METHYL-N'-NITRO-N-NITROSOGUANIDINE (MNNG)

The cells from 5 cm^3 of log phase broth culture were washed with 0.067 M phosphate buffer pH 7.0, suspended in the same buffer containing 100 µg MNNG cm^{-3} and incubated at 37 °C for 30 min. The mutagenized culture was washed twice with phosphate buffer, then resuspended in broth and allowed to grow overnight at 37 °C, after which it was diluted and plated on nutrient agar, or subjected to penicillin enrichment in a minimal medium for selection of auxotrophs.

CONJUGATION EXPERIMENTS

Log phase cultures (5 cm^3) of male and female strains in broth were mixed in a 250 cm^3 conical flask and incubated for 3 hours at 37°C in a shaking water bath (40 rpm). Counterselection against the donor was achieved by incubation with phage T6 (m.o.i. of 100) for 1 hour at 37°C before plating, or by using streptomycin (200 µg cm^{-3}) in the selective plates. After restreaking, a number of single colonies from each recombinant class were screened for the presence of unselected markers and tested for ASNase-2 production after growth in Nutrient Broth supplemented with sodium lactate.

dadR mutants of strain CSH 59 were isolated by the method of Kuhn and Somerville (1971). These mutants are tryptophan auxotrophs capable of utilizing D-tryptophan.

P1 transduction experiments were carried out according to the methods described by Miller (1972).

Results

CONDITIONS GOVERNING ASNASE-2 PRODUCTION

Nutrient Broth No. 2 (Oxoid) was the best proprietary medium for ASNase-2 production by *E. coli*, although occasional batches gave poor results. Dialysis experiments showed that the high molecular weight components were not necessary for growth or ASNase-2 production. There was, however, an inorganic cation requirement for ASNase-2 production, which was satisfied by the presence of NaCl in Nutrient Broth. The optimum temperature was 37°C.

Supplementation of Nutrient Broth with sodium DL-lactate ($10 \ cm^3 \ dm^{-3}$ 70 per cent solution of mixed isomers) and L-glutamine ($7 \ g \ dm^{-3}$) increased enzyme yields. Addition of a wide range of other organic and amino acids was generally without substantial beneficial effect. Fermentable carbohydrates generally reduced the enzyme yield, glucose being the most effective, but addition of cyclic AMP at concentrations up to 20 mM had no effect on enzyme production in any strain, including *cyc* mutants (lacking adenyl cyclase).

ASNase-2 production was insignificant during exponential growth phase, but increased dramatically as the growth rate slowed down. This was partly due to oxygen limitation. Maximum production occurred when the pH of the culture lay in the range pH 7.0 to pH 7.8 at the end of log phase. As ammonia accumulated in the medium, the pH rose rapidly above 8.0 and ASNase-2 production ceased. Apart from this, ammonia had no effect on enzyme production.

MUTATIONS AFFECTING EXPRESSION OF ASNASE-2

Examination of a wide range of strains containing characterized mutations showed that a number of lesions causing unusual growth patterns resulted in abnormally low or negligible ASNase-2 production. Examples of such mutations are *bio, recA, dadR, purB* (of strain CGSC 5038) and streptomycin-dependence (studied because Coukell and Polglase (1969) reported that such mutants show nonspecific resistance to catabolite repression).

A number of uncharacterized mutations leading to a slow growth rate or inability to grow anaerobically also resulted in an inability to produce

ASNase-2. One class of ethionine/norleucine-resistant mutants with a normal growth rate, but apparently impaired in methionine uptake, also displayed a reduced enzyme level. (There is a methionine requirement for ASNase-2 production in Basal Synthetic Medium. The optimum concentration was 6 mm. It is possible that methionine deficiency may be partly responsible for the problems that occur with occasional batches of broth.)

PROPERTIES OF THE ASNASE-2 FROM *E. COLI* CROOKES

The purified enzyme from the Crookes strain differs in some respects from the typical *E. coli* ASNases as described by Laboureur *et al.* (1971). The major active species *in vitro* appears to be a dimer of molecular weight 65 000. With increasing enzyme concentration, the apparent molecular weight increases, glutaminase activity appears and the specific activity of ASNase falls. At a concentration of 50 μg cm^{-3} in 50 mm sodium acetate buffer pH 5.5, the enzyme showed activity towards various substrates (relative to L-asparagine as 100 per cent) as follows: L-glutamine, 60 per cent; β-cyanoalanine, 28 per cent; D-asparagine, 25 per cent; D-glutamine, 16 per cent; succinamic acid, 2 per cent; also towards L-β-aspartic hydroxamate, L-β-aspartic hydrazide, L-γ-glutamic hydrazide and L-5-diazo-4-oxonorvaline. There was no activity towards urea, L-aspartate, L-glutamate, L-pyroglutamate, L-dihydroorotate, acetamide, propionamide, butyramide, isobutyramide, succinamide, glycyl-L-asparagine, L-β-aspartic-β-naphthylamide or succinic mono *p*-nitroanilide, all at 5 mm. None of these compounds inhibited deamidation of L-asparagine, nor did α-ketoglutarate, fumarate and ammonia. Ammonia was also non-inhibitory at pH 8.5, in contrast to the results of Campbell and Mashburn (1969), with typical *E. coli* ASNases.

In the presence of 2 mm L-asparagine, the enzyme was 80 per cent inhibited by cysteine or oxaloacetate at 10 mm and by mercuric ion at 0.1 mm.

There appears to be substrate inhibition by L-asparagine, with a K'_s of 20 mm.

The enzyme did not release carbohydrate from fetuin under the conditions described by Bosmann and Kessel (1970).

MEDIA FOR SELECTION OF HIGH-YIELDING STRAINS

a. *Succinamic acid based media*

ASNase-2 shows slight activity towards succinamic acid. This fact was used as the basis of a selection procedure for high ASNase-2 producers. Succinamic acid was supplied as sole nitrogen source and galactose as carbon source (for succinamate cannot be simultaneously utilized as both carbon and nitrogen source). After a 2-day lag, growth occurred and some of the culture was re-grown for several cycles in succinamate + glucose medium. About 10 per cent of the single colony isolates from this medium, when assayed in broth, showed levels of ASNase-2 increased by up to 30 per cent. There was no increase in the percentage of high-yielding derivatives when the concentration of succinamic acid was reduced, either in batch or continuous culture. The major limitation of this procedure was the slow release of ammonia in the medium from the spontaneous breakdown of succinamic acid.

b. *Methylamine medium*

This medium was formulated following the report by Arst and Cove (1969) that mutants of *Aspergillus nidulans* resistant to methylammonium toxicity were derepressed for apparently all ammonium-repressible activities. Despite the fact that there is no evidence that ASNase-2 is ammonium repressible and that methylamine did not appear to be toxic to *E. Coli* strain W3110, strain Crookes and its high-yielding derivatives produced only a few isolated colonies on this medium, and 10 per cent of these colonies had increased levels of ASNase-2 activity, when assayed in broth. The highest specific activities obtained represented an increase of about 100% over the wild type level.

HIGH-YIELDING DERIVATIVES BY MUTAGENESIS

High-yielding derivates of strains W3110 and Crookes were not detected in this laboratory after assay of some 2000 survivors of MNNG mutagenesis of each strain. Strain F221, however, appeared to have a high spontaneous mutation frequency. Assay of the survivors of MNNG mutagenesis of this strain showed that about 10 per cent had elevated ASNase-2 levels. The majority of these quickly reverted to wild type. The highest yielding stable derivative produced 30 per cent more ASNase-2 than the wild type, to give a specific activity of 4.3 International Units per mg soluble protein.

MAPPING STUDIES WITH MUTANTS LACKING ASNASE-2

a. A series of ASNase-less mutants (ASA-71) was isolated from strain W3110 by Dr Breeze, while investigating the possibility of involvement of ASNase-2 with nitrate reductase activity, as suggested by Schwartz (1971). Mutants were selected in the *gal* to *chl* (nitrate reductase) region. A number of these mutants, which grew poorly and were thought to be deletions for this region, did not produce ASNase-2, but this was possibly due to the adverse effect of loss of the *bio* genes. A number of other ASNase-less mutants were found which grew reasonably well, and these were all found to be *gal* mutants. Preliminary experiments showed that transfer of F′ *gal*$^+$ (presumably containing other genes from this region) into these *gal* mutants restored ASNase-2 activity. Transfer of F′*gal*$^+$ into ASNase-2 producing strains, which were *gal* mutants, reduced the ASNase-2 activity to 60 per cent of the normal level. Dr Breeze was unable to show P1 co-transduction of the ASNase-2 character with *gal*. It is possible that this locus is concerned with periplasmic enzyme production in general, rather than ASNase-2 in particular.

b. Two other ASNase-2-less mutants (ASA-5 and ASA-24) have been isolated, which grow normally and are not associated with *gal*. Both fail to produce many recombinants when used as recipients in matings with a number of Hfr strains. They have therefore been converted to $lac/F'lac^+$ derivatives, for use as donors. Conversion to $F'lac^+$ also occurs at a low frequency. Matings with the female strains CSH 57B and CSH 59 (*tsx* derivative) place the ASA-5 locus at 25.5 to 26.0 minutes on the *E. coli* chromosome map. Introduction of the ASA-5 mutation into these female strains also reduces the frequency of recombination observed in subsequent matings with Hfr strains. After mating such an ASA-5 female with an Hfr, the recombinants which produce ASNase-2 do so at the level associated with the male strain. It was also found possible to distinguish between the male derived and female derived ASNase-2 levels after matings of two ASNase-2 producing strains of different activity, although great care was necessary with assays, which made the experiment tedious. From such a cross, it was possible to derive a map position of 25.5 to 25.8 minutes for the ASNase-2 locus. The ASA-24 locus has not yet been mapped.

The P1 co-transduction frequency of the ASA-5 locus with the *trp* locus (27 min) of strain CSH 59 was 1.4 per cent. This is in agreement with the map position derived from conjugation studies. Transduction of other nearby markers (*dadR* at 25.7 min, *purB* at 24.9 min) has not yet been achieved.

GENE DUPLICATION STUDIES AT THE ASA-5 LOCUS

Two long episomes, KLF25 and KLF26, containing the ASA-5 locus, have been introduced (separately) into the ASNase-2 producing strain CSH 59, which was thus made diploid for this locus. ASNase-2 production in these partial diploid strains was increased by up to 80 per cent in both cases. After storage for one week on nutrient agar plates at 4 °C, 70 per cent of the isolates still retained 60–80 per cent increase in ASNase-2 levels. After one month, 50 per cent still showed levels 60 per cent above wild type. After 3 months' storage, this enhancement of production was largely lost. No significant differences were detected between strains carrying the two different episomes, despite the fact that KLF26 extends beyond the *gal* region and should therefore duplicate a second presumptive ASNase locus associated with *gal*.

STUDIES WITH ASNASE-1

Because of the similarity of L-dihydrorotic acid to L-asparagine, a study was made of L-dihydroorotase activity. The *pyrC* gene specifies the enzyme dihydroorotase, which is normally able to function in either the synthetic or catabolic direction. This enzyme and ASNase-1 activity were found to be associated on partial purification. The pH-activity profiles of ASNase-1 and catabolic dihydroorotase activity were found to be similar, and addition of L-asparagine inhibited catabolic dihydroorotase activity. Studies with strain CSH 59, which contains a *pyrC* mutation, showed that this strain lacks synthetic dihydroorotase activity and has reduced levels of both ASNase-1 and catabolic dihydroorotase activity. It was concluded that ASNase-1 activity was associated with the *pyrC* gene product.

BACTERIOPHAGE SENSITIVITY OF *E. COLI* STRAINS, OTHER THAN K12

In preliminary studies, strains Crookes and F221 were not susceptible to any of a wide variety of phages held in this laboratory. Phage $\lambda C_I 857$ has since been found to plaque on strain Crookes, although a host restriction phenomenon was evident. Strain F221 spontaneously produces at least five different colony types, and one of these has been found to be susceptible to P1.

Discussion

I shall attempt to discuss the significance of some of the points raised in relation to the practical applications of genetic manipulation.

In the first place, a knowledge of the physiological control of enzyme production would be very useful. Calculations show that at the critical period when ASNase-2 is being produced by strain Crookes, this enzyme represents 20–25 per cent of protein synthesized (assuming *de novo* synthesis of ASNase-2). Our best derivative of strain Crookes yields about 1 per cent of its protein as ASNase-2. It is obvious therefore that if the critical conditions for enzyme production could be maintained, great advances could be made in yields.

Knowledge of the control mechanisms operating at the genetic level enables rational selection procedures to be devised for constitutive and hyperproducing strains, as has been the case with the *lac* system of *E. coli* (Novick and Horiuchi, 1961). Our understanding of the control of ASNase-2 synthesis is still rudimentary and although selection media have been formulated, which have been successful to a limited extent, the effective pressure exerted may not have been that expected. For example, the succinamate + glucose medium was designed to select for organisms better able than wild type to derive ammonia from succinamic acid (a poor substrate) under conditions where ASNase-2 production is normally severely restricted, i.e. in minimal medium under strong catabolite repression by glucose. The high-yielding derivatives obtained by this technique produced negligible amounts of enzyme in this medium and were still catabolite repressed by glucose in broth.

In theory, it would seem that little benefit would accrue from duplication of a structural gene, if the control mechanisms were still operative. Duplication of the ASA-5 locus by means of episomes does, however, appear to produce worthwhile results and furthermore, the instability of such episomes would not appear to present serious problems. Normally of course, F' episomes would be maintained in *recA* strains, to reduce the frequency of recombination, and this may well be a feasible proposition for other products, but in the case of ASNase-2 the *recA* mutation prevents expression of the enzyme.

The transfer of the male derived ASNase-2 level to the female on conjugation suggests that certain of the control mechanisms are closely associated with the ASA-5 locus. This would be an important feature if rescue of characteristics from strains such as F221 were to be undertaken, for example by P1 transduction. Such rescue would presumably not be possible from strains in which the increase in yield was the result of a number of independent unrelated mutations. It is, of course, necessary to demonstrate that a rescue method is available, before undertaking extensive studies on strains which are not amenable to genetic manipulation. Furthermore, it should not be assumed that the product from such strains necessarily displays the required properties, nor should it be assumed that enzymes from mutants possess the same properties as those from the wild type. It has been found in this study that the enzyme from strain Crookes is unusual in certain of its properties, but whether or not this vitiates its clinical effectiveness is not known. The enzymes from the high-yielding derivatives of strain Crookes show no obvious differences from the original, but to date the only possible means of rescue of the ASNase-2 genes from these strains would appear to be as defective λ phage.

It may be worthwhile during preliminary selection of strains to screen on the basis of mutability as well as on yield, since our studies with strains F221 and Crookes show that use of a readily mutable strain such as F221 enables results to be obtained more quickly. This would be especially important when methods of detection of high-yielding derivates are so time-consuming as to preclude the screening of large numbers of isolates after mutagenesis, as is the case with ASNase-2. It must be remembered though that highly mutable strains may present storage problems.

The spectacular increases achieved by means of genetic manipulation are the result of rare events and depend on powerful techniques of detection or enrichment. On the basis of my experience, I would not recommend that genetic manipulation be attempted in the absence of such techniques. The report of Takenaka *et al.* (1971) that ASNase-2 is able to hydrolyse L-β-aspartic-β-nitroanilide, albeit at a very slow rate, holds promise for the innovation of a direct plate visualization technique. Until such a technique is available, progress with the ASNase-2 system will be drastically hindered by the necessity of performing innumerable assays.

312   J. C. JEFFRIES

Acknowledgements

I thank Dr B. E. B. Moseley and Dr J. F. Collins for valuable advice and criticism. This work was supported by a grant from the Science Research Council.

References

Arst, H. N. Jr. and Cove, D. J. (1969). *J. Bact.* **98**, 1284.
Bosmann, H. B. and Kessel, D. (1970). *Nature, Lond.* **226**, 850.
Calam, C. T. (1964). "Progress in Industrial Microbiology" (Ed. D. J. D. Hockenhull), vol. 5, p. 1. Temple Press, London.
Campbell, H. A. and Mashburn, L. T. (1969). *Biochemistry*, **8**, 3768.
Coukell, M. B. and Polglase, W. J. (1969). *Biochem. J.* **111**, 279.
Demain, A. L. (1971). "Methods in Enzymology" (Ed. W. B. Jakoby), vol. 22, p. 86. Academic Press, New York.
Imada, A., Igarasi, S., Nakahama, K. and Isono, M. (1973). *J. gen. Microbiol.* **76**, 85.
Jones, G. E. (1973). *Mol. gen. Genetics* **121**, 9.
Kuhn, J. and Somerville, R. L. (1971). *Proc. natn. Acad. Sci. U.S.A.* **68**, 2484.
Laboureur, P., Langlois, C., Labrousse, M., Boudon, M., Emeraud, J., Samain, J. F., Ageron, M. and Dumesnil, Y. (1971). *Biochimie*, **53**, 1147.
Miller, J. H. (1972). "Experiments in Molecular Genetics", p. 201. Cold Spring Harbor Laboratory, New York.
Muftic, M. K. (1964) *Nature, Lond.* **201**, 622.
Novick, A. and Horiuchi, T. (1961). *Cold Spring Harb. Symp. quant. Biol.* **26**, 239.
Pardee, A. B. (1969). "Fermentation Advances" (Ed. D. Perlman), p. 3. Academic Press, New York.
Roberts, J., Burson, G. and Hill, J. M. (1968). *J. Bacteriol.* **95**, 2117.
Schwartz, J. H. (1971). "International Symposium on L-Asparaginase", vol. 197, p. 79. Centre Nat. Rech. Sci., Paris.
Takenaka, O., Tamaura, Y., Nishimura, Y. and Inada, Y. (1971). *J. Biochem.* **69**, 1139.
Willis, R. C. and Woolfolk, C. A. (1974). *J. Bacteriol.* **118**, 231.

Mutation, repair mechanisms and transformation in the methane-utilizing bacterium, *Methylococcus capsulatus.*

E. WILLIAMS* and B. W. BAINBRIDGE

Department of Microbiology, Queen Elizabeth College, London, England

Summary

The availability of methane as a cheap source of carbon has resulted in considerable interest in its utilization by bacteria, particularly for the production of single-cell protein and chemicals such as amino acids. Genetic manipulation of strains may be of value in such processes so a study has been made of the genetics of the methane-utilizing bacterium, *Methylococcus capsulatus.*

Spontaneous mutations conferring resistance to a range of amino acid analogues and antibiotics can be isolated at frequencies between 1 in 10^7 and 1 in 4×10^8, but attempts to increase these frequencies by exposures to mutagens have failed. Similarly, attempts to isolate auxotrophs have met with little success as only one mutant (with a requirement for *para*-amino benzoic acid, *pab-1*) was isolated from over 35 000 colonies after varied mutagenic and enrichment treatments. The difficulties experienced in inducing mutations appear to be of general occurrence in methane-utilizing bacteria as a survey of other strains has shown similar results. These difficulties may be due to the obligate methylotrophic nature of the organisms and/or the presence of accurate DNA repair mechanisms.

Evidence is presented indicating the absence of photoreactivation and filament formation and the presence of excision repair and recombination repair. It is possible that interference with these repair processes and careful

---

* Present address: Department of Microbiology, University of Edinburgh, Edinburgh, Scotland.

choice of media and mutagenic treatments may allow easier isolation of suitable mutant strains.

Transformation of the *pab-1* locus has been detected at a level of 0.0056 to 0.17 per cent.

Introduction

World shortage of protein and rapidly increasing costs of animal feedstuffs have stimulated interest in the production of single-cell protein. Micro-organisms have many attractions as protein supplements since they multiply rapidly, are easily handled and can be grown on inexpensive organic materials. Of these, hydrocarbons are in greatest supply and the cheapest fractions, gaseous and liquid alkanes, are being investigated as potential sources of microbial protein. The discovery of natural gas ($\sim$ 90 per cent methane), an extremely cheap source of carbon, has stimulated recent research into methane-utilizing organisms.

Up to 1970, only three species of methane-utilizing organisms were available in pure culture: *Pseudomonas methanica* (Dworkin and Foster, 1956), *Methanomonas methanooxidans* (Brown *et al.*, 1964), and *Methylococcus capsulatus* (Foster and Davis, 1966). However, in 1970 over 100 strains were obtained in pure culture, including many new species (Whittenbury *et al.*, 1970).

All methane-utilizing organisms are Gram-negative, strictly aerobic and have an obligate requirement for methane or methanol as carbon and energy source. Growth does not occur on complex organic media, e.g. nutrient agar; many individual sugars, carboxylic acids, amino acids, casein hydrolysate and yeast extract inhibit growth (Eroshin *et al.*, 1968; Whittenbury *et al.*, 1970; Eccleston and Kelly, 1972).

Most of the industrial interest in methane-utilizing bacteria is in their use as protein supplements. Ideally, the protein should be rich in lysine, tryptophan and methionine (Whittenbury, 1969). Examination of a large number of isolates may reveal an organism with an ideal amino acid profile, but variation of growth conditions and the selection of mutants may be used to produce the necessary changes. Besides proteins, many other products such as amino acids, vitamins, various metabolic intermediates and enzymes from genetically engineered mutants may prove practical industrial products. Mutants more suitable for long-term growth in fermentors might also be selected. Thus, for maximum exploitation, methane-utilizing bacteria should be readily mutable and possess genetic exchange mechanisms.

The present paper is intended to be a review of mutation, DNA repair mechanisms and the genetic exchange mechanism, transformation in the Foster and Davis strain of *Methylococcus capsulatus*.

Results and discussion

Spontaneous mutants of *M. capsulatus* resistant to antibiotics, amino acid analogues and a variety of other compounds have been found at frequencies between 1 in 10^7 and 1 in 4×10^8 (Harwood *et al.*, 1972). Since these frequencies are too low to allow the isolation of spontaneously occurring auxotrophs, attempts have been made to induce mutants by exposure of the cells to ultraviolet light (uv), γ-irradiation, *N*-methyl-*N'*-nitro-*N*-nitrosoguanidine (MNNG), methyl methanesulphonate (MMS), ethyl methanesulphonate (EMS), nitrous acid and *N*-nitroso-*N*-methylurethane (NMU). Attempts to isolate auxotrophs have met with little success as only one mutant (with a requirement for *para*-amino benzoic acid, *pab-1*) was isolated from over 35 000 colonies after varied mutagenic and enrichment treatments (Harwood *et al.*, 1972; Williams, 1973). Several unstable "auxotrophs" have been found after treatment with MNNG, but these rapidly reverted to the wild-type phenotype. This difficulty in inducing stable auxotrophs of *M. capsulatus* may be due to failure to detect the induced mutants or to failure to induce stable heritable DNA alterations. The composition of the supplemented medium has been extensively varied since it has been noted that the isolation of auxotrophs of blue-green algae is influenced by the composition of the supplemented medium (Herdman *et al.*, 1973). However none of these changes has resulted in the isolation of auxotrophs of *M. capsulatus*.

The second possibility, that the mutagenic agents are not producing stable heritable alterations to the DNA, has been examined by comparing a control population of cells with a mutagen-treated population for mutation to either streptomycin-resistance, L-canavanine-resistance or reversion to prototrophy of the *para*-amino benzoic acid requiring auxotroph. None of the mutagenic treatments used resulted in a significant increase in the number of mutants (Harwood *et al.*, 1972). Other methane-utilizing bacteria (*Methylobacter* sp., *Methylomonas* sp., *Methylocystis* sp. and *Methylosinus* sp.) appear to be stable to uv, γ-irradiation, MMS, EMS and nitrous acid (Shimmin, personal communication), although some induction does occur with MNNG (Williams, unpublished data).

To understand why this group of bacteria appears to be stable to most of the mutagenic treatments it is important to consider how mutations are induced in *Escherichia coli.*

When a cell is exposed to a mutagen a variety of chemical changes may occur in the DNA (for review see Smith, 1966). Mutations usually arise by modification of this premutational damage by DNA repair mechanisms. Lesions which escape accurate repair may be fixed as heritable DNA alterations by repair processes which produce a mistake rather than leave a lethal lesion (Bridges, 1969). The importance of repair processes in establishing

mutations is indicated by the observation that, at low doses, all of the mutations induced in *E. coli* by uv and at least 90 per cent of the mutations induced
by ionizing radiations depend on the presence of a repair mechanism designated Exr (Witkin, 1967; Bridges, 1969). Recent evidence also suggests that
many chemically induced mutations also depend on the repair mechanisms
for establishment. Mutations can arise by errors in recombination provoked
by: (a) excisable DNA damage, e.g. nitrous acid; (b) unexcisable DNA
damage, e.g. MMS; and (c) excision repair errors, e.g. mitomycin C. In
contrast, some of the damage produced by MNNG and EMS results in DNA
replication errors and the establishment of mutations is independent of the
repair mechanisms (Kondo *et al.,* 1970; Kondo, 1973).

Two of the repair mechanisms are named above, excision repair (UVR
or HCR) and recombination repair (*recA, recB, recC, exrA*). These are dark
repair processes. There is also a light-dependent repair process, photoreactivation, which is specific for the uv photoproducts, pyrimidine dimers. All
three repair processes influence survival after uv, but the important mutational pathway is dependent only on the presence of the *recA* and *exrA*
gene products (Witkin, 1967, 1969). A fourth factor which influences survival, but probably not mutation, is the process of filament formation (Fil).
This is undesirable because it sensitizes the cells to mutagens (Witkin, 1967).

Excision repair, recombination repair, filament formation and photoreactivation have been examined in a number of methane-utilizing bacteria
(Williams and Bainbridge, 1975; Shimmin and Williams, unpublished data).
Direct examination of some of these processes at the molecular level, particularly the important $exrA^+$-dependent mechanism, is not possible, and
indirect experiments based on the physiological modification of the processes
have been used.

We would like now to discuss a few of the results of such experiments by
comparing the reaction to uv of *M. capsulatus* and several *E. coli* strains with
different repair capacities These direct comparisons may not be valid for
some of the experiments and conclusions of individual experiments cannot be
assumed to be definitive. However, it is hoped that by using this approach
and basing conclusions of a large number of different experiments, a general
view of the repair mechanisms operating in *M. capsulatus* may be obtained.

A gross indication of the efficiency of the repair processes may be obtained
from an analysis of survival curves. The uv survival curve of *M. capsulatus* is
complex and consists of three component parts, a small shoulder, a period
of exponential loss of viability and a resistant tail at low levels of survival
(Fig. 1). Although it is generally accepted that a shouldered survival curve
indicates repair capacity, Witkin (1967) observed that shoulders were confined to strains of the genotype *fil⁻*, all unsuppressed *fil⁺* strains exhibiting
shoulderless one-hit curves. Fil⁺ strains, in which filament formation is

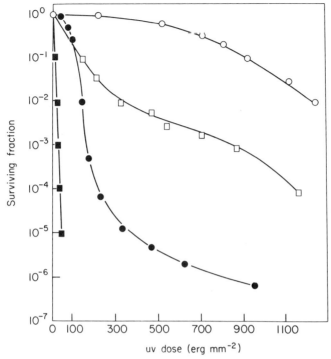

FIG. 1. Comparison of the ultraviolet survival curve of *M. capsulatus* with *E. coli* strains of different repair capacities. ○, *E. coli* B/r (*fil⁺ sul hcr⁺ exr⁺*); □, *E. coli* B (*fil⁺ hcr⁺ exr⁺*); ■, *E. coli* Bs₁ (*fil⁺ hcr⁻ exr⁻*); ●, *M. capsulatus*.

suppressed by *exrA⁻* or *recA⁻*, still die by the Fil⁺ mechanism and exhibit shoulderless survival curves, but when the Fil⁺ character is suppressed by *sul*, radiation resistance is restored and a shouldered survival curve is found if the cells have some repair capacity. Fil⁻ strains have shouldered survival curves if they can repair DNA by excision or recombination. The size of the shoulder is influenced by excision and recombination and, in *E. coli* Fil⁻ strains, is increased by mutation from *hcr⁻* (Bs₁/r) to *hcr⁺* (Bs₂/r) or from *exr⁻* (Bs₁/r) to *exr⁺* (B/r[HCR⁻]) (Witkin, 1967). The size of the shoulder is therefore an indication of the combined efficiency of the excision and recombination mechanisms.

The small shoulder on the *M. capsulatus* uv survival curve indicates that the organism is similar to the Fil⁻ (or Fil⁺ *sul*) strains of *E. coli*. This is supported by the observation that irradiated cultures fail to form filaments or giant cells. The small size of the shoulder indicates that the overall efficiency of repair is small and that either one or both of excision repair and recombination repair are inefficient.

The slope of a survival curve is also influenced by excision repair, recombination repair and filament formation and in *E. coli* is decreased (i.e. becomes more resistant) by mutation from hcr^- (B-HCR$^-$) to hcr^+ (B), from exr^- (Bs$_1$) to exr^+ (B-HCR$^-$), and from fil^+ (Bs$_1$) to fil^- (Bs$_1$/r) (Witkin, 1967).

A comparison of the slope of the *M. capsulatus* survival curve with the slope of the *E. coli* B/r (fil^+ sul hcr^+ exr^+) survival curve indicates that if *M. capsulatus* is Fil$^-$ (or Fil$^+$ sul), then again its repair mechanisms must be inefficient. Even compared with the sensitive Fil$^+$ strains of *E. coli*, the slope of the *M. capsulatus* curve is steeper (i.e. more sensitive) than *E. coli* B (fil^+ hcr^+ exr^+), but is similar to the repair deficient strain Bs$_1$ (fil^+ hcr^- exr^-). This again suggests inefficient excision and/or recombination mechanisms in *M. capsulatus*.

At high doses of uv the *M. capsulatus* survival curve flattens to produce a resistant tail. This increased resistance is phenotypic rather than genetic, since surviving colonies taken from the tail region and regrown exhibit identical survival curves to the original culture. This tail region is probably due to a neighbour restoration, whereby products released from dead cells aid the recovery of the less damaged cells (Alder *et al.*, 1966; Witkin, 1967; Mukherjee and Bhattacharjee, 1971a, b).

M. capsulatus does not appear to possess the light-dependent repair mechanism, photoreactivation. No increase in survival is found when uv-irradiated cells are exposed to intense visible or near uv light.

In *E. coli* B/r the size of the shoulder on the uv survival curve is greater for a stationary phase culture than for an exponential phase culture. This is thought to be due to an enhancement of excision repair in the stationary phase cells (Morton and Haynes, 1969; Billen and Bruns, 1970). This growth phase dependent variation in uv sensitivity is not found in the repair deficient strain *E. coli* Bs$_1$. A stationary phase culture of *M. capsulatus* has a larger shoulder than an exponential phase culture (intercepts 150 erg mm^{-2} and 100 erg mm^{-2} respectively). This may indicate the presence of an excision repair mechanism in *M. capsulatus*.

Evidence for the presence of dark repair mechanisms may also be obtained from the use of chemical inhibitors such as 5-bromodeoxyuridine (5-Budr) and caffeine.

The substitution of DNA thymine by 5-Budr has been reported to inhibit host-cell reactivation (HCR) of irradiated bacteriophage (Sauerbier, 1961; Yan, 1969), to reduce the efficiency of excision repair (Lett *et al.*, 1970), and to sensitize to uv only those cells which are able to excise pyrimidine dimers (Aoki *et al.*, 1966). Increased numbers of single-strand breaks are found in uv-irradiated 5-Budr substituted DNA (Hutchinson and Hales, 1970), and excessive DNA breakdown without concomitant resynthesis is found (Boyce, 1966). It has also been shown that brominated DNA drastically reduces the priming capacity of *E. coli* or mammalian DNA polymerase (Recondo *et al.*, 1971). This suggests that the repolymerization step of excision repair may be inhibited by 5-Budr. The presence of excision repair in *M. capsulatus* is suggested by the uv sensitization produced by the substitution of DNA thymine by 5-Budr (Williams and Bainbridge 1975).

Caffeine is also an inhibitor of dark repair in *E. coli* and a variety of other organisms (Malke, 1967; Freim and Deering, 1970; Loprieno and Schupbach, 1971; Walker and Reid, 1971), although unlike 5-Budr it probably inhibits recombination repair as well as excision repair (Witkin, 1967).

At concentrations greater than 1 mg cm^{-3} the incorporation of caffeine into the agar medium reduced the colony forming ability of *M. capsulatus* (Fig. 2). *E. coli* B is more sensitive to caffeine and has a shoulderless survival

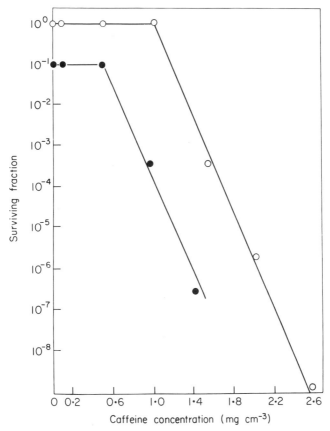

FIG. 2. Effect of caffeine on the colony forming ability of unirradiated and ultraviolet irradiated *M. capsulatus*. ○, unirradiated culture; ●, uv irradiated culture.

curve (Grigg, 1968). Mutants of *E. coli* deficient in the $exrA^+$ gene product (Bs_2) or deficient in excision repair (Bs_1, Bs_8, and Bs_{12}) are much more resistant to caffeine than *E. coli* B (hcr^+, exr^+) and have shouldered survival curves similar to the *M. capsulatus* survival curve (Grigg, 1968). If a comparison is valid, this suggests that *M. capsulatus* is excision defective or deficient in the exr^+ gene product. The presence of the excision repair mechanism is suggested by previous evidence and because concentrations of caffeine which have no effect on colony formation sensitize *M. capsulatus* to uv inactivation (Fig. 2). The sensitization to uv by low concentrations of caffeine is restricted to excision-effective (HCR^+) strains of *E. coli* and is due to inhibition of either the repolymerization or ligase stage of excision repair (Clarke, 1967; Grigg, 1968; Witkin and Farquharson, 1969). This leads to the conclusion that the caffeine resistance exhibited by *M. capsulatus* is due to the absence of the exr^+ gene product.

The experiments discussed so far indicate the presence of excision repair and probably a weak recombination repair mechanism (Exr^-?). Further evidence for the presence of recombination repair may be obtained by holding uv-irradiated cells in buffer, in the absence of an energy source, and assaying for increase in survival. This liquid holding recovery occurs in *E. coli* B because the expression of the Fil^+ character is inhibited, but, in *E. coli* K12 Fil^- strains, liquid-holding recovery is restricted to those which are excision-effective (hcr^+) and $recA^-$. Mutation in recombination genes other than $recA^-$ does not permit the expression of liquid holding recovery (Roberts and Aldous, 1949; Ganeson and Smith, 1968, 1969). Liquid-holding recovery could not be demonstrated in *M. capsulatus* (Williams and Bainbridge, 1975). This leads to the conclusion that the organism is not $recA^-$ hcr^+ but could be $recA^-$ hcr^- or $recA^+$ hcr^+ or $recA^+$ hcr^-. The latter possibility is unlikely on the basis of the previous evidence and also because *M. capsulatus* fails to show an increased survival when plated on minimal compared to supplemented medium (Williams and Bainbridge, 1974). This shift-down recovery is a characteristic of *E. coli* Fil^- $recA^+$ hcr^- strains (Ganeson and Smith, 1968). This leaves the genotypes $recA^-$ hcr^- or $recA^+$ hcr^+. All of the previous evidence suggests that the correct genotype is $recA^+$ hcr^+. This is also suggested by the high frequency of transformation found with *M. capsulatus* (0.0056 to 0.17 per cent), Williams and Bainbridge (1971) since $recA^-$ strains of *E. coli* have recombination frequencies (measured by conjugation and transduction) or 10^{-3} to 10^{-5} compared with a value of 1 for $recA^+$ cells (Willets and Mount, 1969).

In conclusion, the evidence suggests that in *M. capsulatus* filament formation and photoreactivation are absent and excision repair and recombination repair are present, although the recombination repair mechanism may be inefficient and of the accurate Exr^- type. Such a conclusion would explain the difficulties experienced in the induction of mutants of *M. capsulatus*. If the accurate $exrA^+$-dependent mechanism is present then the best mutagens to use are MNNG and EMS since these produce mutants independently of the repair mechanisms (Kondo *et al.*, 1970). However, *M. capsulatus* is sensitive to these mutagens and, although MNNG induces mutants, only low doses can be used. Some of this sensitivity may be due to the inhibition of early stages of methane oxidation (Hubley, personal communication), and it would be of interest to determine whether methanol grown cultures of methane utilizing organisms are more tolerant to MNNG and EMS than methane grown cultures.

Acknowledgement

The financial support of the Science Research Council is gratefully acknowledged.

References

Alder, H. I., Fisher, W. D., Hardigree, A. A. and Stapleton, G. E. (1966). *J. Bacteriol.* **91**, 737.
Aoki, S., Boyce, R. P. and Howard-Flanders, P. (1966). *Nature, Lond.* **209**, 686.
Billen, P. and Bruns, L. (1970). *J. Bact.* **103**, 400.
Boyce, R. P. (1966). *Nature, Lond.* **209**, 688.
Bridges, B. A. (1969). *Rev. nucl. Sci.* **19**, 139.
Brown, L. R., Stawinski, R. J. and McCleskey, C. S. (1964). *Can. J. Microbiol.* **10**, 791.
Clarke, C. H. (1967). *Molec. gen. Genet.* **99**, 97.
Dworkin, M. and Foster, J. W. (1956). *J. Bact.* **72**, 646.
Eccleston, M. and Kelly, D. P. (1972). *J. gen. Microbiol.* **75**, 211.
Eroshin, V. K., Harwood, J. H. and Pirt, S. J. (1968). *J. appl. Bact.* **31**, 560.
Foster, J. W. and Davis, R. H. (1966). *J. Bact.* **91**, 1924.
Freim, J. O., Jr. and Deering, R. A. (1970). *J. Bact.* **102**, 36.
Ganeson, A. K. and Smith, K. C. (1968). *J. Bact.* **96**, 365.
Ganeson, A. K. and Smith, K. C. (1969). *J. Bact.* **97**, 1129.
Grigg, G. W. (1968). *Molec. gen. Genet.* **102**, 316.
Harwood, J. H., Williams, E. and Bainbridge, B. W. (1972). *J. appl. Bact.* **35**, 99.
Herdman, M., Delaney, S. F. and Carr, N. G. (1973). *J. gen. Microbiol.* **79**, 233.
Hutchinson, F. and Hales, H. B. (1970). *J. molec. Biol.* **50**, 59.
Kondo, S. (1973). *Genetics Supplement*, **73**, 109.
Kondo, S., Ichikawa, H., Iwo, K. and Kato, T. (1970). *Genetics*, **66**, 187.
Lett, J. T., Caldwell, I. and Little, J. B. (1970) *J. molec. Biol.* **48**, 395.
Loprieno, N. and Schüpback, M. (1971). *Molec. gen. Genet.* **110**, 348.
Malke, H. (1967). *Zeitschrift. Naturforschung*, **22b**, 1139.
Morton, R. A. and Haynes, R. H. (1969). *J. Bact.* **97**, 1379.
Mukherjee, P. and Bhattacharjee, S. B. (1971a). *J. gen. Microbiol.* **65**, 275.
Mukherjee, P. and Bhattacharjee, S. B. (1971b). *Mutation Res.* **13**, 115.

Recondo, A. M., Londos-Gagliardi, D. and Aubel-Sadron, G. (1971). *FEBS Letters,* **14,** 149.
Roberts, R. B. and Aldous, E., (1949). *J. Bact.* **57,** 363.
Sauerbier, W. (1961). *Virology,* **15,** 465.
Smith, K. C. (1966). *Radiat. Res. Supplement.* **6,** 54.
Walker, I. G. and Reid, B. D. (1971). *Mutation Res.* **12,** 101.
Whittenbury, R. (1969). *Process Biochem.* **4,** 51.
Whittenbury, R., Davies, S. L. and Davey, J. F. (1970). *J. gen. Microbiol.* **61,** 219.
Willets, N. S. and Mount, D. W. (1969). *J. Bact.* **100,** 923.
Williams, E. (1973). Ph.D. Thesis, University of London.
Williams, E. and Bainbridge, B. W. (1971). *J. appl. Bact.* **34,** 683.
Williams, E. and Bainbridge, B. W. (1975). In preparation.
Witkin, E. M. (1967). *Brookhaven Symp. Biol.* **20,** 17.
Witkin, E. M. (1969). *A. Rev. Microbiol.* **23,** 487.
Witkin, E. M. and Farquharson, E. L. (1969). CIBA Foundation Symposium, Mutation as a Cellular Process, 36.
Yan, Y. (1969). *Jap. J. Genet.* **44,** 275.

Viruses of industrial fungi

P. A. LEMKE,* K. N. SAKSENA* AND C. H. NASH†

*Mellon Institute of Science, Carnegie-Mellon University, Pittsburgh, USA
† Antibiotic Development Department, Eli Lilly and Company, Indianapolis, USA

Summary

The discovery of viruses in fungi developed out of interest in industrial fungi. To date, the most extensively studied of fungal viruses are double-stranded RNA (dsRNA) viruses found not only in species of *Penicillium* but in several other moulds and in yeast. Although infection of fungi by viruses appears now to be ubiquitous, dramatic symptoms indicative of such infection have been reported in only a few fungi and mainly in cultivated species.

In *Penicillium chrysogenum* transmission of virus and the expression of lytic plaques have been examined through heterokaryon tests. Wild-type *P. chrysogenum* (NRRL-1951), although infected by virus, carries a nuclear gene (s^+) for resistance to plaque formation. Plaque formation, however, does occur in a mutant strain of *P. chrysogenum* (E-15), and the frequency of plaques therein is related to viral titre. Re-infection experiments have indeed confirmed that plaque formation in E-15 is a consequence of viral infection in the presence of a recessive nuclear determinant (s^-).

In the cultivated mushroom, *Agaricus bisporus*, three morphologically distinct viruses have been isolated. Although these viruses occur at low titre, they cause severe disease symptoms and are readily transmitted through heterokaryosis.

In yeast, *Saccharomyces cerevisiae*, virus particles containing either one of two molecular weight species of dsRNA have been found. These two dsRNAs have been correlated with killer phenotype in yeast strains that carry at least two nuclear genes for maintenance of infection by killer determinant. Re-infection experiments, however, have not been conducted in order to prove that viral dsRNA is the actual genetic determinant for killer phenotype in yeast.

To what extent viruses engage in genetic determination in fungi remains largely undetermined.

Introduction

Although fungal viruses appear generally to be latent, there are now specific examples of alteration in fungal phenotype brought about, at least in part, by the presence of viruses or double-stranded RNA (for review see Hollings and Stone, 1971; Lemke and Nash, 1974). Three examples involve industrially important fungal species. These examples include: (1) formation of lytic plaques in some strains of *Penicillium chrysogenum* (Lemke *et al.*, 1973); (2) production of degenerative symptoms in the cultivated mushroom, *Agaricus bisporus* (Gandy, 1960a, 1960b; Hollings, 1962; Dieleman-van Zaayen, 1972); and (3) determination of killer phenotype among strains of *Saccharomyces cerevisiae* (Berry and Bevan, 1972; Vodkin and Fink, 1973a; Bevan *et al.*, 1973).

It is our intention here to review recent studies concerning viruses in these three fungal systems and to discuss certain genetic implications of these studies.

Results and discussion

GENETIC DETERMINATION OF PLAQUE FORMATION IN *PENICILLIUM CHRYSOGENUM*

The wild-type strain of *Penicillium chrysogenum* (NRRL-1951) and its descendants, used in commercial production of penicillin, harbour a virus (Banks *et al.*, 1969; Lemke and Ness, 1970). This virus has been extensively characterized in three laboratories (Buck *et al.*, 1971; Wood and Bozarth, 1972; Nash *et al.*, 1973). Virus particles are isometric measuring 35 nm in diameter, and nucleic acid derived from these particles is double-stranded RNA of approximately 2×10^6 daltons (Fig. 1). This dsRNA is, however, heterogeneous in so far as it can be resolved by polyacrylamide gel electrophoresis into three components of slightly different molecular weights. Each component appears to be separately encapsulated (Wood and Bozarth, 1972). Thus, the combined molecular weight for the genome of this multicomponent virus is about 6×10^6 daltons.

Interest in the biology of this virus was prompted by two observations. First, strains of *P. chrysogenum* grown in liquid media, containing lactose as the principal source of carbohydrate, produced surprisingly large amounts of dsRNA and virus (respectively, 1 and 10 mg g^{-1} dry-weight of cells) without generalized lysis of mycelia (Lemke and Ness, 1970; Nash *et al.*, 1973). Secondly, a specific strain of *P. chrysogenum* (E-15), when grown on a

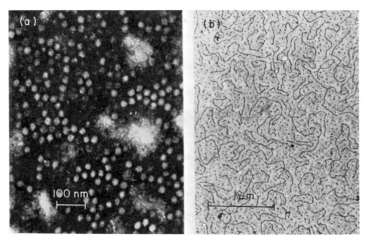

FIG. 1. Electron micrographs of purified virus particles from *P. chrysogenum* (a) and component *ds*RNA (b). Particles are 35 nm in diameter and nucleic acid strands have an average contour length of 0.86 μm.

solid medium containing 18 per cent lactose, exhibited localized formation of lytic plaques (Lemke *et al.*, 1973).

Although lytic plaque formation does not occur in all strains of *P. chrysogenum* known to be infected with virus, it should be mentioned that many strains of *P. chrysogenum*, including NRRL-1951, can develop asporogenic patches of mycelia. Such patches occur spontaneously and their frequency can be augmented by subculturing affected isolates onto lactose-containing medium. Only in culture E-15, however, do these asporogenic patches (proplaques) ultimately lyse, a lysis that is asynchronous (Fig. 2).

It is also possible that asporogeny in *P. chrysogenum* could result through mutation or through mitotic instability. However, from the genetic studies described below it would appear that asporogeny in *P. chrysogenum* when accompanied by lytic plaque formation is determined mainly by the presence of virus.

Variation in viral titre among strains of *P. chrysogenum* has been observed and can be measured readily by an immunodiffusion assay (Fig. 3). Based on this assay, some strains exhibit marked reduction in viral titre following treatment with heat (74°C) or growth in the presence of antimetabolites (Lemke *et al.*, 1973). Auxotrophic mutants frequently show reduction in viral titre as well. Among strains of *P. chrysogenum*, one strain gave no evidence for virus either by the immunodiffusion assay (Fig. 3) or in subsequent experiments. This strain (Δ-2) derived from strain E-15 was obtained following repeated heat treatment of spores. Strain Δ-2, moreover, forms neither asporogenic patches (proplaques) nor lytic plaques when grown on solid

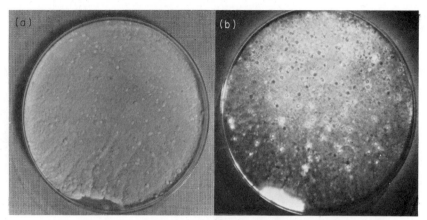

FIG. 2. Lytic plaque formation in culture E-15 of *P. chrysogenum*. Culture photographed after 4 weeks of growth on medium containing 18 per cent lactose. (a) Plaques observed by transmitted light in (b) develop asynchronously and vary in morphology from clear to turbid.

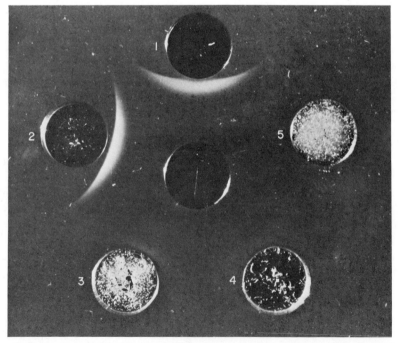

FIG. 3. Ouchterlony double-diffusion assay of *P. chrysogenum* virus: rabbit antiserum to purified virus (centre), purified virus (1), extract from strain E-15 (2), extract from strain treated with cycloheximide (3), extract from strain treated with pyrazomycin (4), and extract from heat-treated strain Δ-2 (5).

medium containing 18 per cent lactose. In addition, labelling experiments involving tritiated uracil have shown that strain Δ-2 lacks virus (Lemke et al., 1973).

The genetic basis for plaque formation in *P. chrysogenum* has been studied through the parasexual cycle. Parasexuality in *P. chrysogeum* was first described by Sermonti (1957) and details concerning the genetics of this system have been reviewed extensively by Sermonti (1969). In the present studies all mutants were obtained following treatment of spores with ultraviolet light (254 nm) at a dosage of 10 000 erg (Nash et al., 1974). A lactose-containing medium developed by Borré and co-workers (1971) was used both as a complete medium and as a medium to test for lytic plaque formation. A sporulation medium described previously (Lemke et al., 1973) served as a minimal medium for selecting the auxotrophic strains used in this study.

In order to examine the role of virus in the formation of lytic plaques, two genetic crosses were conducted involving four strains of *P. chrysogenum*. Each strain was doubly marked with a spore colour marker and an auxotrophic requirement. The first strain (NRRL-*lys*) was obtained from the wild-type strain of *P. chrysogenum* (NRRL-1951) and carried a white-spore marker. Two strains (E-15-*ade* and E-15-*cys*) carried yellow-spore markers and were obtained from the plaque-forming strain E-15. The fourth strain (E-15-*met*) carried a white-spore marker and was obtained from a nonplaque-forming, virus-free derivative (Δ-2) of strain E-15.

Heterokaryons involving these four parental strains were synthesized by co-propagation of paired auxotrophic strains on minimal medium. Spores from resultant prototrophic mycelia were isolated and the ratio of yellow-spored to white-spored progeny was determined in each case. Parental strains

TABLE 1

Heterokaryon test 1

Parent 1 (NRRL-*lys*)		×	Parent 2 (E-15-*ade*)	
White spored			Yellow spored	
Virus	+		Virus	+
Plaques	−		Plaques	+

		Progeny		
Spore colour	Ploidy	Virus	Plaques	Sample size
White	haploid	+	−	8
Yellow	haploid	+	+	12
Green	diploid	+	−	2

and progeny were tested for the presence of virus by the immunodiffusion assay, and plaque formation was determined for each isolate after four weeks of growth on 18 per cent lactose medium. Green-spored diploid strains were also recovered from heterokaryons and tested for virus content and plaque formation.

Heterokaryon I involving NRRL-*lys* and E-15 *ade* (Table 1) yielded white-spored and yellow-spored progeny at a ratio of 2 to 3. All progeny examined from heterokaryon I as well as both parental strains contained

TABLE 2
Heterokaryon test 2

Parent 2 (E-15 *cys*)	×	Parent 3 (E-15-*met*)
Yellow spored		White spored
Virus +		Virus −
Plaques +		Plaques −

		Progeny		
Spore colour	Ploidy	Virus	Plaques	Sample size
Yellow	haploid	+	+	15
White	haploid	+	+	20
Green	diploid	+	+	1

virus. Plaque formation, a condition present in just one parent (E-15-*ade*), was observed only among yellow-spored progeny from the heterokaryon. Such parental segregation for plaque formation indicates that the white-spored, nonplaque-forming parent (NRRL-*lys*) carries some nuclear determinant (s^+) for resistance to plaque formation. This condition appears to be dominant as evidenced by the absence of plaques in diploid strains obtained from heterokaryon I (Table 1).

Heterokaryon II involving E-15-*cys* and E-15-*met* (Table 2) yielded yellow-spored and white-spored progeny at a ratio of 3 to 4. Only one of the two parental strains (E-15-*cys*) contained virus. The second parent (E-15-*met*) represents a white-spored mutant obtained from a strain (Δ-2) cured of virus. All progeny examined from heterokaryon II, white-spored as well as yellow-spored progeny, contained virus (Fig. 4). Strain E-15-*met* was thus re-infected with virus through heterokaryosis. Once re-infected, E-15-*met* formed lytic plaques (Fig. 5). The occurrence of plaques in all progeny derived from heterokaryon II indicates that plaque formation is a cytoplasmically inherited phenomenon (Table 2). The coincidence of viral infection and plaque formation in all progeny derived from heterokaryon II suggests further that

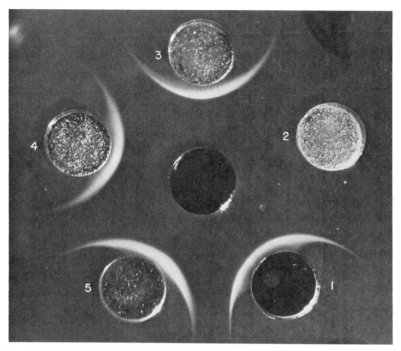

Fig. 4. Virus content in strains from heterokaryon II of *P. chrysogenum*: rabbit antiserum to purified virus (centre), purified virus (1), extract from parental strain E-15-*met* (2), extract from parental strain E-15-*cys* (3), extracts from representative progeny—yellow-spored (4), white-spored (5).

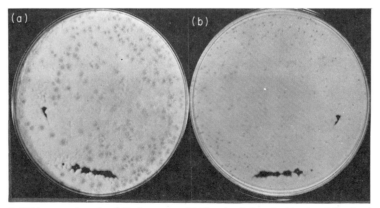

Fig. 5. White-spored strain of *P. chrysogenum* (E-15-*met*) reinfected with virus following hetero-karyon formation (a). Plaque formation in this case appears to be more uniform in morphology with the predominance of clear plaques evident when the culture is observed from below (b).

plaque formation is a consequence of viral infection among strains derived from E-15. Strain E-15 presumably carries a mutant allele (s^-) for sensitivity to virus.

These data clearly demonstrate that the dsRNA virus of $P.$ $chrysogenum$ is potentially virulent and that this virulence is dependent on at least one nuclear determinant (s^-). Such results, however, do not indicate that the dsRNA virus of $P.$ $chrysogenum$ engages in genetic determination beyond its replication. In the normal course of viral replication mycelial lysis might ensue, particularly if the host strain were mutant for native resistance to virus. We have no explanation for the fact that plaque formation in $P.$ $chryso$-$genum$ is localized or asynchronous except to mention that the mycelium itself constitutes an asynchronous network of cells.

The present studies have merely shown that the presence of virus in $P.$ $chrysogenum,$ particularly in a mutant strain such as E-15, can promote overt or phenotypic instability of a culture grown on a lactose-containing medium. Such instability among industrial strains of $P.$ $chrysogenum$ has long been recognized.

OCCURRENCE AND TRANSMISSION OF VIRAL DISEASE SYMPTOMS IN THE CULTIVATED MUSHROOM

Almost 25 years ago, Sinden and Hauser (1950) described a disease of $Agaricus$ $bisporus$ that eventually was shown to be caused by virus. Symptoms of this disease included slow growth of mycelium, production of abnormal mushrooms and overall reduction in yield of mushrooms (Fig. 6). Sinden (1957) and later Gandy (1960a) speculated on the viral nature of the disease, and Gandy (1960b) reported that transmission of this disease could occur through hyphal anastomoses in mixed mycelial cultures. Hollings (1962) isolated three types of viral particles from diseased mushrooms and thereby provided substantial evidence for the viral nature of the disease.

Schisler and co-workers (1967) studied the transmissibility of the disease further and demonstrated that spores from infected mushrooms were an active source for viral transmission. These workers determined that as few as 10 infected spores deposited on a 5 ft^2 area of a mushroom bed could transmit the disease. Spore transmission of virus is aggravated in industrial production of mushrooms by the fact that virus-infected mushrooms tend to open and release their spores prematurely.

Transmission studies involving genetically marked strains of $A.$ $bisporus$ have not been conducted nor have strains resistant to virus been developed. $A.$ $bisporus$ has, however, been shown to be amenable to genetic study (Raper et $al.,$ 1972), which should make such experiments feasible.

To date, at least five different sizes of virus-like particles have been reported from *A. bisporus* (for review see Hollings and Stone, 1971). Of these, three are common and geographically widespread (Fig. 7). These three particles frequently occur in combination, and as yet no definitive correlation of any specific symptom with any specific particle has been established. Indeed, it is unclear at this time whether the three particles constitute distinct viruses or whether they represent multiple forms of one virus.

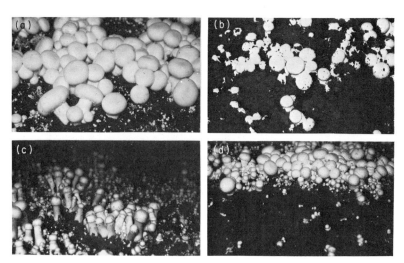

Fɪɢ. 6. Viral disease symptoms in *A. bisporus*: normal mushrooms in cultivation (a); virus-infected mushrooms with small caps and narrow, often twisted, stipes (c); scattered production of virus-infected mushrooms seen embedded or partially embedded below the surface of a mushroom bed (b); nonproductive region of a virus-infected mushroom bed (d, foreground) with a cluster of more normal mushrooms in the background.

It is now well established among higher plant viruses that the genetic information necessary for replication of a virus and for full expression of disease symptoms can be divided among two or more nucleoprotein components (for review see Bancroft, 1968, and Van Kammen, 1972). Included among the list of multicomponent plant viruses is alfalfa mosaic—a single-stranded RNA virus, which has a marked morphological similarity to mushroom viruses and has a functionally divided genome.

All mycoviruses characterized extensively thus far have been found to contain double-stranded RNA genomes and possess spherical morphology (for review see Wood, 1973, and Lemke and Nash, 1974). Although individual mushroom viruses have not yet been critically analysed as to their nucleic acid composition, the very fact that one of these viruses has a particle morphology distinct from the known *ds*RNA mycoviruses is intriguing. If nucleic acid components other than *ds*RNA exist among mushroom viruses,

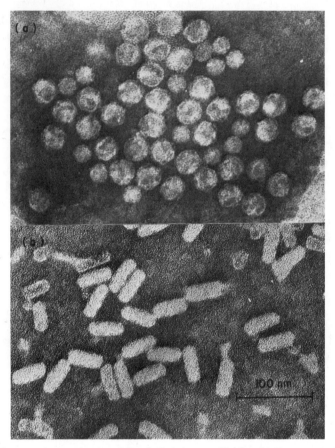

Fig. 7. Electron micrographs of partially purified virus particles from *A. bisporus:* spherical particles (a) with approximate diameters of 25 nm and 34 nm; bacilliform particles (b) about 19 × 50 nm in size. All particles are magnified 200000× and stained with 1 per cent phosphotungstic acid at pH 6.8.

then the mushroom and its viruses should prove to be an especially good experimental system for genetic analysis of a virus in a eukaryotic host. However, only after individual mushroom viruses are analysed and the extent of pathogenicity by individual particles determined will such genetic investigations be meaningful.

THE KILLER SYSTEM OF *SACCHAROMYCES CEREVISIAE*

The killer reaction of yeast, *Saccharomyces cerevisiae*, has been recognized as a genetic phenomenon for more than 10 years (Bevan and Makower, 1963), but only recently have viruses been implicated as genetic determinants in this system. Killer strains synthesize a toxic protein which has the ability to kill sensitive strains, yet killer strains are autoimmune and immune to other killer strains. In this discussion we will refer to the expression of the toxin (killer) phenotype as T^+ and the expression of the immune phenotype as I^+ according to the scheme proposed by Vodkin and his associates (1974). Genetic analysis of cells segregating for killer and immune characteristics has shown that this system is genetically controlled by at least two cytoplasmic determinants and at least two nuclear maintenance genes (Bevan and Somers, 1969; Somers and Bevan, 1969; Fink and Styles, 1972; Nesterova and Zekhnov, 1973; Mitchell et al., 1973; Somers, 1973; Naumov, 1974; Wickner, 1974b; Woods et al., 1974). Non-Mendelian segregation of the cytoplasmic determinants for the I^+ and T^+ functions is similar in behaviour to suppressive petite mutants in yeast (Somers, 1973).

Although the inheritance of killer determinant in yeast is cytoplasmic, at least two chromosomal genes ($M1$ and $M2$) are required for maintenance of the determinant. In cells with the alternate alleles ($m1$ and $m2$), the killer cytogene is not duplicated and is eventually diluted out from growing cultures (Somers and Bevan, 1969; Bevan et al., 1973; Wickner, 1974b). Naumov (1974) reported another chromosomal allele, R^{k2}, which controls neutrality of certain strains. Such strains neither kill nor are killed. A cytogene designated n is also involved in neutrality (Bevan and Somers, 1969). Yeasts of r^{k2} genotype are rendered sensitive nonkillers provided they do not contain the cytoplasmic determinant for toxin and immune functions (Naumov, 1974).

An unusual complex of dsRNA species was discovered in several killer strains of yeast as a result of a search for the biochemical basis of cytoplasmically inherited killer character (Berry and Bevan, 1972; Bevan et al., 1973; Vodkin and Fink, 1973a). The larger dsRNA species of this complex designated P_1 or L has a molecular weight of 2.5×10^6 daltons and a ratio of bases consistent with double-stranded structure, whereas the smaller dsRNA species (P_2 or M) has a molecular weight of 1.4×10^6 daltons and a base composition with an excess of adenine (Bevan et al., 1973; Vodkin and Fink, 1973b; Vodkin et al., 1974).

Investigators have studied the dsRNA species present in strains altered for killer and immune functions (Mitchell, et al., 1973; Vodkin et al., 1974; Table 3). Nonkiller ($I°T°$) cells either lack dsRNA completely or contain only the larger of the two dsRNA species known to be present in killer. Those nonkiller strains which arise spontaneously contain less L dsRNA than the killer and lack M dsRNA. In contrast, nonkiller strains derived from cycloheximide treatment contain about twice as much L dsRNA as the killer but also lack M dsRNA. The killer character can also be eliminated by growing killer strains in the presence of 5-fluorouracil or by exposure to elevated

TABLE 3

Representative phenotypes and *ds*RNA content among strains in the killer system of yeast*

| Phenotype | Cytoplasmic determinants | | | | Unidentified |
| | Viral *ds*RNA | | Nonviral *ds*RNA | | |
	L-*ds*RNA (2.5 × 10^6 mw)	M*ds*RNA (1.4 × 10^6 mw)	S*ds*RNA (5 × 10^5 mw)	I*ds*RNA (2.5 × 10^5 mw)	n (?)
Normal killer (I^+T^+)	+	+	–	–	–
Super killer (I^+T^{sup})	+	>+†	–	–	–
Temperature-sensitive killer (I^+T^{ts})	+	+	–	–	–
Spontaneous nonkiller ($I°T°$)	<+	–	–	–	–
Induced nonkiller ($I°T°$)	>+	–	–	–	–
Suppressive nonkiller ($I°T°$)	+	–	+	–	–
Immune-minus ($I°T^+$)	+	–	–	+	–
Toxin-minus ($I^+T°$)	+	<+(?)‡	–	–	+

* Table 3 is based principally upon the data of Vodkin et al. (1974) and Herring and Bevan (1974). The Table does not mention nuclear determinants and is not exhaustive (i.e. some nonkillers ($I°T°$) lack *ds*RNA completely).

† > and <+ mean, respectively, more or less than the amount present in normal killer.

‡ Strains of toxin-minus or neutral phenotype have not been extensively characterized; however, both L*ds*RNA and M*ds*RNA are present in some of these strains (Bevan et al., 1973). A trace of M*ds*RNA might confer neutrality ($I^+T°$) but the actual basis for immunity in toxin-minus strains is unknown at this time. The cytoplasmically inherited n could be either a separate determinant for immunity or a suppressor of M*ds*RNA synthesis.

temperature (Mitchell *et al.*, 1973; Wickner, 1974a), but the *ds*RNA content of all nonkiller strains thus derived has not been studied.

Mutant strains carrying nonmaintenance nuclear alleles (m_1 or m_2) often resemble the spontaneous nonkillers with respect to *ds*RNA, or such strains may lack *ds*RNA completely (Bevan *et al.*, 1973). Suppressive nonkillers, which suppress the killer determinant in diploids, contain a novel S *ds*RNA with a molecular weight of 5×10^5 daltons (Vodkin *et al.*, 1974). Diploids formed between a suppressor strain and a killer strain lack M *ds*RNA but contain levels of L *ds*RNA comparable to that of the killer parent. Other strains are altered for only one of the two functions. These include immune-minus ($I°T^+$), toxin-minus ($I^+T°$), temperature-sensitive killer (I^+T^{ts}) and super-killer (I^+T^{sup}) strains (Table 3). The super killers and temperature-sensitive killers contain both the L and M *ds*RNAs. The former, however, contains 2.5 times more M *ds*RNA than a normal killer. Immune-minus strains contain, in addition to the M and L *ds*RNAs, a very small I *ds*RNA (2.5×10^5 daltons). According to Wickner (1974b) mutation at a chromosomal locus (*rex*-1) can elicit an immune-minus phenotype. Toxin-minus or neutral strains ($I^+T°$) have been less extensively characterized with respect to *ds*RNA content. At least some neutral strains contain both L and M *ds*RNAs (Bevan *et al.*, 1973). The basis for neutrality seems to reside in more than one nuclear determinant (*kex*-1, *kex*-2, and R^{k2}) and in a cytoplasmic determinant (*n*) of yet undefined nature (Wickner, 1974; Naumov, 1974; Bevan and Somers, 1969).

Vodkin and co-workers (1974) have concluded that toxin production in yeast is controlled by the M *ds*RNA since all killer strains contain M *ds*RNA and nonkillers lack M *ds*RNA. Furthermore, super-killers contain an excess of M *ds*RNA. The origin and function of the S *ds*RNA species in suppressive nonkiller strains and the I *ds* RNA in immune-minus strains remain unknown.

Isometric virus particles were first isolated from certain strains of *S. cerevisiae* by Buck and co-workers (1971). These particles are similar in morphology to other *ds*RNA mycoviruses but they are known to be serologically distinct from the viruses of *Penicillium stoloniferum*, *Aspergillus foetidus* and *Aspergillus niger*. The yeast virus isolated by Buck and co-workers (1971) contains *ds*RNA with a molecular weight of 2.5×10^6 daltons which corresponds to the high molecular weight *ds*RNA described by Bevan and his associates (1973). Recently, Herring and Bevan (1974) demonstrated the presence of two isometric virus particles, both 39 nm in diameter, from killer strains. The two previously described *ds*RNA species, L and M, appear to be separately encapsulated into these two virus particles. Transmission of these virus particles and the cytoplasmic inheritance of killer determination by *ds*RNA would thus seem to be related. In addition, Herring and Bevan (1974) propose that the virus is closely integrated with the host cell since its

M

replication appears to be controlled by nuclear genes. The L dsRNA-containing virus can replicate in the absence of the M dsRNA virion.

The correlation between dsRNA associated with virus particles and killer and immune phenomena in yeast supports strongly the contention that viruses are the cytoplasmic determinants for killer and immune functions therein. These viruses, however, have not been isolated and used to infect virus-free sensitive strains, which would confirm unequivocally their genetic control of killer and immune functions.

The independent replication of the L dsRNA-containing virus indicates that the two yeast viruses do not represent a component system and that the M dsRNA virus probably represents a defective or satellite virus unable to replicate in the absence of L dsRNA virus. The presence of small and apparently extra-particulate species of dsRNA, such as S dsRNA and I dsRNA, could represent even further degenerate or vestigial remnants of viruses in yeast. It is interesting to note that an extra-particulate and small molecular weight dsRNA (1.4×10^5 daltons) has been observed among strains of Penicillium chrysogenum as well (Cox et al., 1970).

To date, there have been no reports of virus or of dsRNA in industrial strains of yeast. However, the possible influence of virus and dsRNA on the quality of yeast fermentations and the stability of yeast strains should now be investigated.

Acknowledgments

We are grateful to R. E. Bowen, Eli Lilly and Company, for preparation of antiserum to purified virus of Penicillium chrysogenum. Photographs of viral disease symptons in Agaricus bisporus were supplied by W. Gerner, Butler County Mushrooms Farms, Inc., Worthington, Pennsylvania.

References

Bancroft, J. B. (1968). "Molecular Biology of Viruses" (Eds J. Crawford and R. Stoker), p. 71. Cambridge University Press, London.
Banks, G. T., Buck, K. W., Chain, E. B., Darbyshire, J. J. E. and Himmelweit, F. (1969). Nature, Lond. 222, 89.
Berry, E. A. and Bevan, E. A. (1972). Nature, Lond. 239, 279
Bevan, E. A., Herring, A. J. and Mitchell, D. J. (1973). Nature, Lond. 245, 81.
Bevan, E. A. and Makower, M. (1963). Proc. 11th Int. Cong. Genet. 1, 202.
Bevan, E. A. and Somers, J. M. (1969). Genet. Res. Camb. 14, 71.
Borré, E., Morgantini, L. E., Ortalé, V. and Tonolo, A. (1971). Nature, Lond. 229, 568.
Buck, K. W., Chain, E. B. and Himmelweit, F. (1971). J. Gen. Virol. 12, 131.
Cox, R. A., Kanagalingam, K. and Sutherland, E. (1970). Biochem. J. 120, 549.

Dieleman-van Zaayen, A. (1972). "Mushroom Virus Disease in the Netherlands: Symptoms, Etiology, Electron Microscopy, Spread and Control". Centre for Agricultural Publishing and Documentation, Wageningen (Netherlands).

Fink, G. R. and Styles, C. A. (1972). *Proc. natn. Acad. Sci. U.S.A.* **69**, 2846.

Gandy, D. G. (1960a). *Nature, Lond.* **185**, 482.

Gandy, D. G. (1960b). *Ann. appl. Biol.* **48**, 427.

Herring, A. J. and Bevan, E. A. (1974). *J. gen. Virol.* **22**, 387.

Hollings, M. (1962). *Nature, Lond.* **196**, 962.

Hollings, M. and Stone, O. M. (1971). *A. Rev. Phytopathol.* **9**, 93.

Lemke, P. A. and Nash, C. H. (1974). *Bact. Rev.* **38**, 29.

Lemke, P. A. and Ness, T. M. (1970). *J. Virol.* **6**, 813.

Lemke, P. A., Nash, C. H. and Pieper, S. W. (1973). *J. gen. Microbiol.* **76**, 265.

Mitchell, D. J., Bevan, E. A. and Herring, A. J. (1973). *Heredity, Lond.* **31**, 133.

Nash, C. H., Douthart, R. J., Ellis, L. F., Van Frank, R. M., Burnett, J. P. and Lemke, P. A. (1973). *Can. J. Microbiol.* **19**, 97.

Nash, C. H., de la Higuera, N., Neuss, N. and Lemke, P. A. (1974). *Dev. Indust. Microbiol.* **15**, 114.

Naumov, G. I. (1974). *Genetika,* **10**, 130.

Nesterova, G. F. and Zekhnov, A. M. (1973). *Genetika,* **9**, 171.

Raper, C. A., Raper, J. R. and Miller, R. E. (1972). *Mycologia,* **63**, 1088.

Schisler, L. C., Sinden, J. W. and Sigel, E. M. (1967). *Phytopathology,* **57**, 519.

Sermonti, G. (1957). *Genetics,* **42**, 433.

Sermonti, G. (1969). "Genetics of Antibiotic-Producing Microorganisms". Wiley-Interscience, London.

Sinden, J. W. (1957). *Mushroom Grow. Assoc. Bull.* **216**, 608.

Sinden, J. W. and Hauser, E. (1950). *Mushr. Sci.* **1**, 96.

Somers, J. M. (1973). *Genetics,* **74**, 571.

Somers, J. M. and Bevan, E. A. (1969). *Genet. Res. Camb.* **13**, 71.

Van Kammen, A. (1972). *Ann. Rev. Phytopathol.* **10**, 125.

Vodkin, M. H. and Fink, G. R. (1973a). *Proc. natn. Acad. Sci. U.S.A.* **70**, 1069.

Vodkin, M. H. and Fink, G. R. (1973b). *Genetics,* **74**, s286.

Vodkin, M., Katterman, F. and Fink, G. R. (1974). *J. Bacteriol.* **117**, 681.

Wickner, R. B. (1974a). *J. Bacteriol.* **117**, 1356.

Wickner, R. B. (1974b). *Genetics,* **76**, 423.

Wood, H. A. (1973). *J. gen. Virol.* **20**, 61.

Wood, H. A. and Bozarth, R. F. (1972). *Virology,* **47**, 604.

Woods, D. R., Ross, I. W. and Hendry, D. A. (1974). *J. gen. Microbiol.* **81**, 285.

Genetic analysis of flocculation in *Saccharomyces cerevisiae* and tetrad analysis of commercial brewing and baking yeasts

J. R. JOHNSTON and C. W. LEWIS

Department of Applied Microbiology, University of Strathclyde, Glasgow G1 1XW, Scotland

Summary

Two strains of brewing origin have been found to be exceptional to the general rule that brewing yeasts are not amenable to tetrad analysis because of their low spore viability. One of these is a hybrid of two spore cultures of a brewery yeast and has been shown to be disomic for 11 linkage groups and, therefore, most likely diploid. This strain has been shown to be homozygous for a dominant gene, designated *Flo1*, which confers flocculation of dispersed cells during late fermentation. It is emphasized that this type of flocculation, so important to brewers, must be distinguished from that of cell aggregates due to the nonseparation of cells after division. Another dominant gene, *Flo2*, and a recessive gene, *flo3*, both of which confer flocculation late in fermentation, have been identified in strains of *Saccharomyces* breeding stock (i.e. Carbondale–Berkeley lines). The genes *Flo1* and *Flo2* are linked and separated by 8 centimorgans, gene *flo3* is unlinked to those and all three genes are noncentromere-linked. Attempts to map these genes have not yet proved successful.

The second strain is a brewery yeast which, it is suggested, is tetraploid and forms diploid spores most of which self-conjugate to perpetuate the tetraploid condition.

Three commercial baking yeasts were subjected to ascus dissection but, because of their relatively poor spore viabilities, genetic analysis was largely confined to populations of random spores. Since some spore cultures are capable of sporulating, other of mating with haploid strains, and the remainder are sterile, it is unlikely that these baking yeasts are diploid.

It is concluded that a sizeable gap at present exists between empirical breeding of industrial yeasts and genetic analysis of strains of *Saccharomyces* breeding stock.

Introduction

Laboratory-bred strains of *Saccharomyces* yeast have become firmly established as organisms for genetical studies which have been the subject of several reviews (for example: Mortimer and Hawthorne, 1969; Hartwell, 1970). Although the early pioneers understandably utilized industrial strains (for references, see Winge and Roberts, 1958; Lindegren, 1949), the field has been developed using strains separated from their industrial heritage by extensive breeding and strong selection for noncommercial characteristics. These latter laboratory strains have usually been strictly either diploid or haploid and selection of diploid strains has generally been for those which form an abundance of viable ascospores. On the other hand, breeding of new commercial hybrids in industrial laboratories has been much more empirical and the elucidation of a strain's ploidy and the location of particular genes involved in an economic characteristic have not been considered essential. Breeding has been most extensive within the baking yeast and distilling industries (Fowell, 1958) but, more recently, has also begun to be pursued within the brewing (Clayton *et al.*, 1972) and ethanol (Oberman, personal communication) industries. The industrial situation has been aptly described by Harrison (1971): ". . . hybridization is entirely empirical in the sense that no prediction can be made as to the outcome. Failures are vastly more common than successes, and a very large number of hybrids must be accurately assayed before the best can be selected; and this may not be strikingly better than the parents."

Few characteristics of commercial importance have therefore featured among the vast number of genetical investigations carried out on yeasts. An exception has been that of flocculence, the clumping together of individual cells. Unfortunately, although this phenotype is extremely important within the yeast industries, when examined in more detail, the term "flocculation" has been applied to several distinct phenomena. With respect to the traditional (noncontinuous) brewing process, the most important type of flocculation is that describing the aggregation of dispersed cells into flocs at a late stage of fermentation, i.e. the "Class II" and "Class III" types of Gilliland (1951). The commercial value of this characteristic is that fermentation is generally faster and more complete by dispersed cells and that separation of the yeast from the beer is facilitated by the late aggregation of these cells.

The most important distinction is between this characteristic and that of cells which form clumps as they grow because of the lack of separation of mother and daughter cells at cell "division", more accurately, cell duplication. This type of "flocculation" has been designated Type IV by Gilliland (1951). It is particularly important to make this distinction when classifying ascospore cultures during genetic analysis, if the characteristic under investigation is late fermentation aggregation, particularly since nonseparation of cells is a common characteristic of haploid strains. Thus there is frequent confusion in the brewing literature of Gilliland's (1951) single gene for "flocculation", when in fact his analysis was for (Class IV) clumpy growth. Neither is it clear whether Thorne (1951a, 1951b), in his extensive genetic analysis of flocculation, distinguished between these two types of clumping. This, and the possible uncertainty of the ploidy of strains used, reduces the value of his interpretation of the observed proportions of $4:0$, $3:1$ and $2:2$ tetrad ratios. Thorne's inference was that three polymeric dominant genes controlled flocculation in the strains investigated. In reports in literature not directly connected with the brewing industy, "flocculation" seems to have been generally used to mean clumpy growth. Thus the three genes described by Gilmore and Murphy (1972) may play no role in late fermentation aggregation.

In the light of these comments, it has been our aim to perform genetic analysis, where possible with strains of commercial origin, of late fermentation (Class II) flocculation, clearly differentiating this phenotype from that of nonseparation of cells during growth. An additional aim of the studies reported in this paper was to attempt to elucidate the ploidy of some strains of brewing and baking yeasts which are amenable to genetic (tetrad) analysis. A preliminary report of some of these studies has appeared in abstract form (Lewis and Johnson, 1974).

Materials and methods

STRAINS

The following flocculent brewing strains of *Saccharomyces cerevisiae* were obtained from The National Collection of Yeast Cultures, Nutfield: NCYC 1026, 1298 (strongly flocculent), 1245, 1307 (moderately flocculent). Another 8 flocculent strains were obtained from Allied Breweries Ltd, Burton-on-Trent, and a further 2 flocculent brewing yeasts were from the Departmental Collection. The flocculent strains K2NB (diploid) and W11 (haploid) were obtained from E. A. Bevan (London) and L. Silhankova (Prague). Three baking strains of *S. cerevisiae* were received from Distillers Company Ltd, Glenochil. Laboratory marker strains of *Saccharomyces* were either obtained from The Yeast Genetics Stock Center, Berkeley, or were already held within the Department, having been derived from Carbondale-Berkeley/Seattle stock. The marker strains, with their genotypes in brackets, were:

X3104-8C (*a leu2, his6, his6, ilv3, met14, pet8, tyr7, ade2, uvs9, can1*),
X3382-3A (*a ade1, gal1, trp1, his2, leu1, arg4, his6, asp5, pet17, tyr7, cdc14*),
X1437-6B (α *gal7, his6, trp1, ura1, met2, ade6, lys1, suc, mal*),
X764-S1 (α *arg4, his6, ura3, hom3*),
X764-S2 (*a arg4, leu1, ade6, hom3, lys1*),
S732C (*a ade1*),
S1780B (*a gal1, thr1, ura2, ade1, lys1, ura4*),
XS144-S1 (*a leu1, trp5, cyh2, met13, tyr3, lys5, ade5/7*),
XJ119-S77 (*a his8, ser1, gal1, lys2, arg4, CUP1, hom3, trp2, ura3, MAL1*).
Strains (X3104-8C) α and (X3382-3A) α were α mating-type segregants of crosses of strains X3104-8C and X3382-3A respectively.

The gene symbols *ade, arg, asp, his, hom, ilv, leu, lys, met, thr, trp, tyr, ura* denote requirement for, respectively, adenine, arginine, aspartate, histidine, homoserine, isoleucine + valine, leucine, lysine, methionine, threonine, tryptophan, tyrosine + phenylalanine, uracil; *gal, MAL, suc* denote nonfermentation of, respectively, galactose, maltose, sucrose; *pet* denotes respiratory deficiency (petite); *can* denotes canavanine-resistance; *uvs* denotes ultraviolet sensitivity; *cdc* denotes late nuclear division (temperature-sensitive lethal).

MEDIA

Most media for culture maintenance, growth, fermentation and sporulation were those described by Mortimer and Hawthorne, 1969. For fermentations in which flocculation was tested either brewers wort of specific gravity 1.040 or 10 per cent malt extract (Oxoid) was used.

METHODS

Routine methods for growth, hybridization and sporulation were those described by Mortimer and Hawthorne (1969). When testing strains for flocculation, fermentations were carried out in 10 cm^3 of media in test tubes $6 \times \frac{5}{8}$ in. and incubated stationary at 25°C for 3–4 days.

The following procedure was devised for differentiating between truly flocculating (in late fermentation) strains and those strains, principally haploid spore cultures, which grow in clumps due to nonseparation of parent and daughter cells. Cells were separated from spent medium by centrifugation, resuspended in 10 cm^3 distilled water and sonicated for 15 seconds by soniprobe (Dawe Instruments, England, Type 1130/1B). This treatment was shown to impair neither cell viability nor flocculating potential, and resulted in both redispersion of cells in flocs and disruption of most clumps of nonseparated cells. When necessary, any remaining clusters of cells were removed by passage through a sintered glass filter (grade 3 with 20–30 µm pore size). The dispersed cells were centrifuged and resuspended in acetate buffer at pH 4.5 containing 510 ppm $CaSO_4$, the latter supplying calcium ions for flocculation. The degree of flocculation, if any, in this medium was then recorded by examining the average size of flocs, if any, either microscopically or by naked eye. The scale used was 0 (nonflocculent) to 7 (extremely flocculent) after the method of Baker and Kirsop (1972).

Results

GENETICS OF FLOCCULATION

Brewing strains   Fourteen flocculent strains of brewing origin were sporulated and subjected to ascus dissection. All but one of these strains yielded a very low level of viable ascospores. Many strains produced no viable spores and the strain NCYC 1026, which has been used extensively in tower fermentations (Greenshields *et al.*, 1972), gave only 3 per cent viability. The exceptional strain from which almost 100 per cent of isolated ascospores were viable, was originally thought to be a yeast in commercial practice (Lewis and Johnston, 1973). Later clarification, however, confirmed that this strain was a hybrid produced from ascospore crosses of a commercial yeast (Clayton *et al.*, 1972). This hybrid brewing strain has been coded ABX and it is moderately flocculent in late fermentation.

Strain ABX produced tetrads showing a 2:2 segregation ratio for mating type (*a* and α). Four spore cultures derived from one tetrad of strain ABX

TABLE 1
Crosses between brewing yeast (ABX) spore cultures and marker strains

Brewing yeast spore strains		Marker strains
ABX-1A	×	(X3104-8C)α
	×	(X3382-3A)α
	×	X1437-6B
ABX-1B	×	X3104-8C
	×	X3382-3A
	×	(X1437-6B)*a*
ABX-1C	×	X3104-8C
	×	X3382-3A
	×	(X1437-6B)*a*
ABX-1D	×	(X3104-8C)α
	×	(X3382-3A)α
	×	X1437-6B

1A, 1B, 1C and 1D are from a single tetrad of ABX.

TABLE 2

Tetrad ratio of marker genes in crosses shown in Table 1

Marker gene	Chromosome number	Number of tetrads	Tetrad ratio
ade1	I	28	2:2
gal1	II	28	2:2
leu2, a/α	III	26	2:2
trp1	IV	23	2:2
his2	VI	26	2:2
leu1	VII	28	2:2
his6	IX	25	2:2
ura1	XI	21	2:2
pet8	XIV	28	2:2
ade2	XV	28	2:2
met2	XVII	23	2:2

were crossed with various haploid strains which carry a wide range of marker genes (Table 1). Subsequent tetrad analysis of these crosses gave, with very few exceptions, the results shown in Table 2. These show that, barring a low level of 3:1 or 1:3 segregation ratios presumably due to gene conversion, all 11 genetic markers segregated in a 2:2 ratio. Since these genes are located on 11 different chromosomes of *Saccharomyces* (Mortimer and Hawthorne, 1969; R. K. Mortimer, personal communication), the ABX segregant strains appear to be haploid and, by implication, strain ABX itself diploid. When 14 tetrads were tested for flocculation, all 56 spore cultures proved to be flocculent. When 4 of these cultures were crossed to nonflocculent haploid strains they produced flocculent hybrids and 30 tetrads out of a total of 32 gave a 2:2 ratio for flocculence versus nonflocculence (Table 3). Thus the hybrid strains

TABLE 3

Tetrad ratios of crosses of brewing yeast (ABX) spore cultures to nonflocculent haploid strains

Cross	Hybrid phenotype	Number of tetrads	Number of tetrads with 2:2 segregation (flocculent:nonflocculent)
ABX-2A × X764-S1	flocculent	12	10
ABX-2B × S732C	flocculent	6	6
ABX-2C × S732C	flocculent	7	7
ABX-2D × X764-S1	flocculent	7	7

2A, 2B, 2C and 2D are from a single tetrad of ABX.
Of the other two tetrads, one gave a 3:1 and the other a 1:3 segregation ratio.

were heterozygous for a single dominant gene conferring flocculence and strain ABX itself is homozygous for this gene, designated *Flo1*.

Nonbrewing strains   Tetrad analysis was performed upon diploid strain K2NB and all 13 tetrads contained 4 flocculent spores. In crosses of some of the latter to nonflocculent haploid strains, flocculent diploid hybrids were obtained and, in 41 out of 43 tetrads, a 2:2 segregation ratio for flocculation versus non-flocculation was observed. Thus strain K2NB is also homozygous for a dominant gene conferring flocculence. Tetrad analysis of crosses of segregants of strain ABX to segregants of strain K2NB shows that the latter strain carries a second flocculation gene, designated *Flo2*, and that the genes *Flo1* and *Flo2* are linked (Table 4). The ratio of 28 tetratype asci to 145 parental ditype asci gives a map distance between these two genes of 8 centimorgans.

TABLE 4

Tetrad analysis of allelism crosses for various flocculation genes

Cross	Number of tetrads with ratio (flocculent:nonflocculent)		
	4:0 (PD)	2:2 (NPD)	3:1 (T)
Flo1 × *Flo* (*Flo2*)	145	0	28
Flo1 × *flo* (*flo3*)	11	9	41
Flo2 × XJ119-S77	31 random segregants all flocculent		
Flo2 × XS144-S1	11	0	0
Flo2 × W11	8	0	0
Flo2 × S1780B	9	0	0

A stable flocculent variant of the nonflocculent strain X764-S1 was isolated during a continuous culture experiment with this strain. When this variant was crossed to a nonflocculent haploid strain, a nonflocculent diploid hybrid was produced which formed tetrads showing a 2:2 ratio for flocculation versus nonflocculation. Thus this isolate is a single gene mutant carrying a recessive gene for the ability to flocculate and, when crossed to a strain carrying the gene *Flo1*, analysis shows that these two genes are nonallelic and unlinked (Table 4). This recessive gene has been designated *flo3*. Other flocculent haploid strains were shown to carry the gene *Flo2* (Table 4) which therefore seems to be the more commonly occurring gene for flocculation in laboratory *Saccharomyces* strains, at least those derived from Carbondale–Berkeley stocks.

The numbers of 11 parental ditype, 9 nonparental ditype and 41 tetratype asci obtained from crossing strains carrying genes *Flo1* and *flo3* (Table 4) closely approximate a 1:1:4 ratio. This result indicates that either gene *flo3* or genes *Flo1* and *Flo2* or all three genes are not centromere-linked. The results of tetrad analysis of crosses involving genes *Flo2*, *flo3* and centromere-linked genes *leu2* and *ade1* (Table 5) show that neither gene *flo3* nor genes *Flo1* and *Flo2* are centromere-linked. An attempt was therefore made to detect linkage of the flocculation genes to one of a range of noncentromere-linked marker genes located upon six different chromosomes. Although the

TABLE 5

Tetrad analysis of crosses of *Flo2*, *flo3* to strains carrying centromere-linked markers

Flocculation gene	Centromere-linked gene	Number of tetrads		
		PD	NPD	T
Flo2	*leu2*	6	5	31
flo3	*ade1*	7	5	25

search for linkage is being continued, at present it appears that none of the flocculation genes *Flo1*, *Flo2* and *flo3* is linked to the marker genes *met8*, *hom2*, *trp4*, *hom3*, *trp2*, *ade3*, *ade5*, *ura1*, *met4* or *lys10* (Table 6).

GENETIC ANALYSIS IN BREWING YEAST NCYC 1085

Of over 40 strains of British brewing yeasts which have been subjected to ascus dissection (Johnston, 1965; Lewis, unpublished), only strain NCYC 1085 has yielded a high percentage of viable ascospores (Table 7). This strain might therefore be thought a rare diploid strain among British brewing yeasts. As reported earlier, however, most ascospores of strain 1085 produced cultures which again sporulated, thereby precluding simple tetrad analysis (Johnston, 1965). The simplest explanation would be that strain 1085 was homozygous for the diploidization gene, D (Winge and Roberts 1949). It would seem unlikely that strain 1085 is tetraploid, since sporulation generally produces both sporulating a/α and nonsporulating a/a and α/α diploid ascospores (Roman *et al.*, 1955; MacKinnon and Johnston, 1972). Since strain 1085 is such an exception among brewing strains, however, further analysis of its probable ploidy seemed worthwhile.

A high proportion (87 per cent) of strain 1085 ascospores form sporulating cultures (Table 7). This proportion and the highly skewed distribution of tetrad ratios (Table 7) makes it most unlikely that the strain is a tetraploid which undergoes random meiotic segregation for the mating-type alleles (Roman *et al.*, 1955). Nor does it appear to be a tetraploid strain yielding predominantly a/α diploid ascospores since haploid spores were not obtained from a total of 48 dissected asci produced by several ascospore cultures of strain 1085 (i.e. asci of strains 1085-S1, 1085-S2 etc.). In an attempt to show

TABLE 6

Tetrad analysis of crosses of *Flo2*, *flo3* to strains carrying noncentromere-linked markers

Flocculation gene	Number of tetrads $\dfrac{P:NP}{T}$ with marker gene (chromosome number)									
	met8 (II)	*hom2* (IV)	*trp4* (IV)	*hom3* (V)	*trp2* (V)	*ade3* (VII)	*ade5* (VII)	*ura1* (XI)	*met4* (XVII)	*lys10* (XVII)
Flo2	$\dfrac{5:3}{9}$	$\dfrac{3:5}{10}$	$\dfrac{0:3}{8}$	—	$\dfrac{2:5}{9}$	$\dfrac{3:5}{13}$	$\dfrac{5:3}{10}$	$\dfrac{4:4}{13}$	$\dfrac{1:1}{7}$	$\dfrac{0:2}{6}$
flo3	$\dfrac{5:3}{13}$	$\dfrac{1:3}{6}$	$\dfrac{1:3}{6}$	$\dfrac{1:2}{6}$	$\dfrac{4:3}{11}$	$\dfrac{3:2}{11}$	$\dfrac{2:2}{6}$	$\dfrac{2:4}{10}$	$\dfrac{2:3}{8}$	$\dfrac{0:3}{5}$

if strain 1085 produces haploid ascospores carrying the gene D (for diploidization), single cells of either strain X764-S1 or strain X764-S2 were paired with
newly isolated spores of strain 1085 using a micromanipulator. In some
pairings distinct zygotes were formed and two of these, from different pairings, were isolated and grown into colonies. One cross, X251, was of a 1085
spore and X764-S1 cell and the other, X252, was of a 1085 spore and X764-S2
cell. Both of these crosses sporulated well but produced low levels of viable
ascospores (4/64 or 6 per cent for X251, 6/64 or 9 per cent for X252). Two

TABLE 7

Tetrad analysis of brewing yeast NCYC 1085 for ability to sporulate

Spore viability of NCYC 1085 %	Number of tetrads with segregation ratios (sporulating : nonsporulating)				
	4:0	3:1	2:2	1:3	0:4
96	15	8	1	1	0

spore cultures of X251 and 5 spore cultures of X252 displayed nutritional
requirements thereby confirming that hybridization between strain 1085
spores and marker strains had taken place. These low spore viabilities and the
fact that most of the 10 viable spores grew slowly (none of the resulting
cultures could sporulate) makes it unlikely that the two parent 1085 spores
were haploid. It is more likely that the hybrids X251 and X252 are triploid
and therefore the two 1085 spores diploid.

A further investigation of this possibility was made by crossing 4 of the
spore cultures of either X251 or X252 to strains X764-S1 or X764-S2. Some
of the growing ascospores of strains X251 and X252 might be expected to
be aneuploid and their disomy might be detected in the segregation ratios of
their test crosses. These test crosses also yielded relatively low levels of viable
spores and therefore only segregation ratios for random spore populations
were obtained (Table 8). Most ratios are consistent with the monosomic
condition of spore cultures of X251 and X252. However, the appearance of
lysine-requiring spores of crosses X252-S1 × X764-S1 and X252-S3 × X764-
S1 and of adenine-requiring spores of the latter cross show that the spores
of X252 can be disomic and heterozygous for genes *lys1* and *ade6*. This
is further evidence that the crosses X251 and X252 are triploid. It therefore appears that strain 1085 is tetraploid and produces diploid spores, many
of which form cells which can self-conjugate to reproduce the tetraploid
state.

TABLE 8

Random spore segregation ratios for crosses of presumed aneuploid derivatives from NCYC 1085 and haploid marker strains, X764-S1 and X764-S2

Cross	Spore viability	Ratio (+ : mutant) for marker genes						
		ura3	hom3	leu1	ade6	arg4	his6	lys1
X251-SI (+) × X764-S1 (ura hom arg his)	$\frac{6}{32}$	3:3	4:2	6:0	6:0	1:5	3:3	6:0
X252-S1 (leu ade) × X764-S1 (ura hom arg his)	$\frac{15}{32}$	7:8	10:5	6:9	6:9	9:6	10:5	10:5
X252-S2 (lys) × X764-S2 (hom leu ade arg lys)	$\frac{9}{32}$	9:0	6:3	5:4	6:3	7:2	9:0	0:9
X252-S3 (+) × X764-S1 (ura hom arg his)	$\frac{13}{32}$	10:3	8:5	13:0	9:4	8:5	6:7	10:3

ura3-hom3 are on chromosome V, leu1-ade6 on chromosome VII, arg4 on VIII, and his 6-lys1 are on chromosome IX.

GENETIC ANALYSIS OF BAKING YEAST

Ascus dissection was carried out upon 3 commercial baking strains which have been coded as BAK 1, BAK 2 and BAK 3. These strains show only moderate spore viability (Table 9) but are amenable to tetrad analysis if a sufficient number of asci are dissected. It can be estimated that, to obtain a total of 20 tetrads for analysis, the approximate number of asci which would require to be dissected would be 100 for BAK 1, 320 for BAK 2 and 160 for BAK 3. The level of spore viability is surprising in that these baking strains have

TABLE 9

Ascus dissection of three commercial baking strains

Strain	Ascospore viability %	Number of tetrads tested	Number of random spores tested	Number of spores producing asci	Number of spores mating with a α	Number of spores neither sporulating nor mating
BAK 1	66	3	21	6	5 10	12
BAK 2	51	3	67	12	14 4	51
BAK 3	59	3	16	4	6 10	8

generally been considered to be diploid, although previous results (Johnston, 1965) suggested otherwise. That they are not simple a/α diploids is shown by the results of testing spore cultures for their ability to sporulate. For each strain, approximately 15 per cent of ascospores produce sporulating cultures, and are therefore not haploid unless there is some degree of diploidization occurring. The percentage of spores which could be haploid, as judged by their mating reactions with haploid tester strains, is 45 per cent for BAK 1, 22 per cent for BAK 2 and 57 per cent for BAK 3. Since ascus dissection of these latter crosses has not yet been performed, however, they cannot all be positively identified as haploid, since a/a or α/α diploid or disomic spores would also show the observed mating reaction. The remaining spores, which constitute 36 per cent for BAK 1, 64 per cent for BAK 2 and 28 per cent for BAK 3, produce cultures which neither sporulate nor mate with tester haploid strains. From the point of view of breeding, these spore cultures can therefore be classified as "infertile". The limited number of full tetrads obtained varied in their composition of ascospore phenotypes. For example, one tetrad of BAK1 contained 2 sporulating spores and 2 spores of a mating type. Another comprised one spore of mating type a and 3 infertile spores. A tetrad of BAK2 contained one sporulating spore, 2 spores of mating type α and one infertile spore.

Three sporulating cultures of BAK 1 and 3 of BAK 2 were subjected to ascus dissection. In all 6 strains, however, spore viability was very low. That this was not caused by sensitivity of these spores to Helicase treatment was shown by equally poor viability of isolated untreated asci. Crosses of baking strain spores to tester haploid strains are in the process of being subjected to tetrad analysis.

Discussion

As far as we can tell, identification of the genes *Flo1*, *Flo2* and *flo3* is the first which clearly pertains to genes controlling aggregation during a late stage of fermentation. However, it is wise to bear in mind that flocculent strains carrying these genes behave in a specific fashion only in a defined environment and particular fermentation system. Thus the expression of flocculation by a strain in a tower continuous fermentation may be different from that described above for small-scale batch fermentations. In addition, in common with other genes, genes for flocculation determine the exact nature of the phenotype relative to a particular environment. Thus the degree of flocculation, if any, is dependent on the state of various physical and chemical factors in the medium, for example pH and calcium ion concentration (reviewed by Rainbow, 1970). Moreover, in this report we have treated flocculation as an all-or-none qualitative characteristic, when in reality it is a quantitative characteristic and should be treated as such. By way of explanation, we have considered ours the simplest approach in the first instance. However, it means that our use of the term flocculation can be taken only as a guide to the quantitative expression of this characteristic. Therefore, although on average it can be approximated to moderate flocculation (point 4-5 on the scale proposed by Baker and Kirsop, 1972), measurements showed that this could vary from poorly flocculent to extremely flocculent for any particular ascospore strain. On the other hand, the approach was sufficiently quantitative to show that there was no additive effect from combining any of the genes *Flo1*, *Flo2* and *flo3*.

As well as the importance of flocculence in brewing strains, its lack in other strains, notably baking, can also be of commercial significance. Thus the alleles *flo1*, *flo2* and *Flo3* conferring nonflocculence should also be important genes industrially. There has been much interest in the degree of stability of both flocculent and nonflocculent strains. Generally, in the growth and fermentation systems used, population changes have been in the direction of flocculent to nonflocculent (Chester, 1963; Thorne and Nohr, 1963; Thorne, 1968, 1970), and these have sometimes been integrated as resulting from higher gene mutation rates from flocculent to nonflocculent alleles than vice versa. However, it is perhaps more likely that the observed results were due to selection pressure favouring the nonflocculent form. Certainly, in a system of continuous culture which may allow flocculent cells an advantage, accumulation of flocculent cells in cultures of nonflocculent strains has been observed (Thornton, 1969). The rates of appearance of nonflocculent homozygotes from *Flo1* and *Flo2* heterozygotes and of flocculent homozygotes from *flo3* heterozygotes would be interesting to determine. Since none of the three loci is centromere-linked, mitotic crossing over should produce these homozygotes at relatively high frequencies.

Our genetically defined strains should also provide useful material in the search for the biochemical explanation of flocculence. Although many ideas and pieces of supporting evidence have been forthcoming, there is still no firmly established and universally accepted explanation. Partly, the wide variety of theories (for references, see Rainbow, 1970; Stewart *et al.*, 1974) recently added to by Poon and Day, 1974, may be due to the widespread use of genetically undefined strains.

The beginning of a clear definition of ploidy in brewers breeding strains, as in the case of strain ABX, could place future breeding programmes on a more scientific basis. Certainly, the low spore viability of most brewing strains can be circumvented by ignoring ascus dissection and adopting mass spore isolation (methods given by Fowell, 1969). Mating ascospore cultures can then be recovered on a random basis and subsequent hybridization carried out (Clayton *et al.*, 1972). While this practice may be satisfactory for the empirical breeding of industrial strains, it has severe limitations as a method of genetic analysis. Great caution must be exercised when interpreting the results of random spore analysis of a low proportion of viable ascospores since it is often impossible to tell if a particular characteristic is distributed randomly among viable and inviable spores. Thus it would seem essential to develop good British ale strains with an orthodox diploid–haploid life-cycle.

A more encouraging report concerning the ploidy of some non-British brewing strains has recently appeared (Sakai and Takahashi, 1972). Of the two German and one American strains which could sporulate (out of a total of 19 brewing yeasts), one gave a high and another a moderate degree of spore viability, allowing tetrad analysis to be performed. The results indicated that both strains were diploid, one homothallic and the other heterothallic. Of 16 nonsporulating strains, 11 were concluded to be diploid by DNA estimation. These results and conclusions contrast with those obtained earlier by Emeis (1961) and Johnston (1963) who concluded that both Continental and British brewing yeasts were often polyploid and principally triploids.

In the circumstances, where selection appears to have favoured polyploid strains, it is perhaps surprising that no tetraploid brewing yeast forming viable diploid spores has been detected. The results obtained with strain NCYC1085 therefore seem doubly interesting. Although in the absence of more extensive genetic analysis the conclusion reached must be viewed as tentative, the results suggest that this brewing yeast is tetraploid and that it produces diploid spores which can self-conjugate subsequent to germination to again revert to the tetraploid state. This behaviour has not hitherto been observed in tetraploid strains subjected to tetrad analysis (Roman *et al.,* 1951; Pomper *et al.,* 1954; Roman *et al.,* 1955; MacKinnon and Johnston, 1972). It would seem unlikely that such a proposal can be explained solely by the action of the D gene for homothallism which has been shown to direct mutation of the *a* allele to α and vice versa (Hawthorne, 1963). Conceivably an *aa* diploid spore can "self-tetraploidize" by double mutation of progeny cells to αα genotype with subsequent conjugation and likewise for an αα diploid spore. But a majority of diploid spores would be expected to have the *a*α genotype and the action of the D gene should then be repressed. A possible explanation is that meiotic distribution of the mating-type chromosomes of strain 1085 is not random and most diploid ascospores are of genotype *aa* or αα. Confirmation of these proposals and also identification of the ploidy and genotypes of the fraction (13 per cent) of 1085 ascospores which do not produce sporulating cultures must await further genetic analysis. However, the basis of sexuality in brewing yeasts may be more complex than that established for laboratory-bred *Saccharomyces* strains since Clayton *et al.* (1972) have reported brewing yeast ascospore cultures which mate with both *a* and α haploid strains. The usefulness of strain 1085 in a commercial breeding programme would seem to be limited to producing tetraploid hybrids by pairing of its spores to diploid cells with which they might mate (assuming the desirability of producing hybrids with high spore viability).

The results obtained with commercial baking strains show that these also are not simple diploid yeasts which form haploid spores, although this has generally been assumed within the baking yeast industry. Earlier, the results of Johnston (1965) had indicated otherwise and these have more recently been supplemented by the results of Clayton *et al.* (1972). In examining random spore isolates of two commercial baking yeasts, the latter authors found those incapable of mating (sterile) to comprise 50 per cent in one strain and 29 per cent in the other. They also report that 14 per cent of isolates from one strain were capable of mating with both *a* and α haploids. Without further genetic analysis, the ploidy of these baking strains is uncertain. Even these preliminary results, however, show the kind of gap which can exist between industrial breeding and more academic yeast genetics. Thus, although empirical hybridization has provided some notable successes (see, for example. Burrows and Fowell, 1961; British Patent, 1965) the strains developed by this method do not provide an unambiguous diploid–haploid system and greatly increase the difficulty of genetic analysis and definition of individual genes involved in characteristics of economic importance.

Acknowledgements

It is our pleasure to thank Miss Patricia Hendry for her skilful technical assistance during part of these studies; Allied Breweries Limited, in particular Mr P. A. Martin, and Distillers Company Limited, in particular Dr P. Hatton, for their valuable cooperation; Drs R. K. Mortimer and J. Bassel from the University of California, Berkeley, for supplying essential strains; and the Science Research Council and Allied Breweries Limited for provision of a CAPS (CASE) Studentship to Christopher W. Lewis.

References

Baker, D. A. and Kirsop, B. H. (1972). *J. Inst. Brew.* **78,** 454.
British Patent, 989,247 (1965). (Konink. Ned. Gist-en-Spiritus Fabriek N.V.)
Burrows, S. and Fowell, R. R. (1961). British Patents, 868,133 and 868,821.
Chester, V. E. (1963). *Proc. R. Soc.* (B) **157,** 223.
Clayton, E., Howard, G. A. and Martin, P. A. (1972). *Proc. Am. Soc. Brew. Chem.* 78.
Emeis, C. C. (1961). *Proc. Euro. Brew. Conv., Vienna,* 205.
Fowell, R. R. (1958). "Recent Studies in Yeast". S.C.I. Monographs No. 3, Society of Chemical Industry, London.
Fowell, R. R. (1969). "The Yeasts" (Eds A. H. Rose and J. S. Harrison), vol. 1, p. 303. Academic Press, London and New York.
Gilliland, R. B. (1951). *Proc. Euro. Brew. Conv., Brighton,* 35.
Gilmore, R. A. and Murphy, J. (1972). *Genetics 71,* Supp. No. 3(2), S19.
Greenshields, R. N., Yates, J., Sharp, P. and Davies, T. M. C. (1972). *J. Inst. Brew.* **78,** 236.
Harrison, J. S. (1971). *J. appl. Bact.* **34,** 173.
Hartwell, L. H. (1970). *A. Rev. Genetics,* **4,** 373.
Hawthorne, D. C. (1963). *Genetics,* **48,** 1727.
Johnston, J. R. (1963). *Proc. Euro. Brew. Conv., Brussels,* 412.
Johnston, J. R. (1965). *J. Inst. Brew.* **71,** 130.
Lewis, C. W. and Johnston, J. R. (1973). *Microbial Genetics Bull.* **35,** 11.
Lewis, C. W. and Johnston, J. R. (1974). *Proc. Soc. gen. Microbiol.* **1,** 73.
Lindegren, C. C. (1949). "The Yeast Cell. Its Genetics and Cytology". Educational Publishers, St. Louis.
MacKinnon, J. M. and Johnston, J. R. (1972). *Heredity,* **28,** 347.
Mortimer, R. K. and Hawthorne, D. C. (1969). "The Yeasts" (Eds A. H. Rose and J. S. Harrison), vol. 1, p. 385. Academic Press, London and New York.
Pomper, S., Daniels, K. M. and McKee, D. W. (1954). *Genetics,* **39,** 343.
Poon, N. H. and Day, A. W. (1974). *Heredity.* In press.
Rainbow, C. (1970). "The Yeasts" (Eds. A. H. Rose and J. S. Harrison), vol. 3, p. 147. Academic Press, London and New York.
Roman, H., Hawthorne, D. C. and Douglas, H. C. (1951). *Proc. natn. Acad. Sci., U.S.A.* **37,** 79.
Roman, H., Phillips, M. M. and Sands, S. M. (1955). *Genetics,* **40,** 546.
Sakai, K. and Takahashi, T. (1972). *Bull. Brew. Sci., Tokyo,* **18,** 29.
Stewart, G. G., Russell, I. and Garrison, I. F. (1974). Labatt's Beverage Research Report.

Thorne, R. S. W. (1951a). *C.r. Lab. Carlsberg, Ser. Physiol.* **25**, 101.
Thorne, R. S. W. (1951b). *Proc. Euro. Brew. Conv., Brighton*, 21.
Thorne, R. S. W. (1968). *J Inst. Brow.* **74**, 516.
Thorne, R. S. W. (1970). *J. Inst. Brew.* **76**, 555.
Thorne, R. S. W. and Nohr, B. (1963). *Brew. Digest*, **38**, (2), 36.
Thornton, R. J. (1969). Ph.D. Thesis, University of Strathclyde, Glasgow.
Winge, O. and Roberts, C. (1949). *C.r. Lab. Carlsberg, Ser. Physiol.* **24**, 341.
Winge, O. and Roberts, C. (1958). "The Chemistry and Biology of Yeasts" (Ed.
A. H. Cook), p. 123. Academic Press, New York and London.

Mutants of *Saccharomyces cerevisiae* utilizing hydrocarbons

S. G. INGE-VECHTOMOV, E. G. RABINOWITZ, V. N. EGOROVA,
J. O. SOOM and T. R. SOIDLA

Department of Genetics and Selection, Leningrad State University, USSR

Summary

Hydrocarbon utilizing mutants, designated hyc^+, were obtained in two homo-thallic strains of *Saccharomyces cerevisae*, 768 and 41. Transition from an hyc^- to hyc^+ phenotype involved two sequential events. The first gave rise to the appearance of "conditional hydrocarbon utilizing" mutants (hyc^c). These were capable of hydrocarbon utilization and of 102 independent hyc^c isolates 99 were methionine and 3 were arginine auxotrophs. The conversion $hyc^- \rightarrow hyc^c$ was accompanied by a number of phenotypic changes including altered ability to utilize several organic and amino acids as carbon sources, resistance to some antimetabolites and inhibitors, sensitivity to elevated concentrations of glucose, loss of activity of exogenous acid phosphatase I and inability to produce pseudomycelium.

The second event, conversion of $hyc^c \rightarrow hyc^+$, was a simple reversion to prototrophy from methionine or arginine dependence. No sporulation ability, residual mating reaction or mitotic recombination have been found in hyc^c and hyc^+ mutants in contrast to the original hyc^- strains.

A number of revertants, $hyc^+ \rightarrow hyc^-$ and $hyc^c \rightarrow hyc^-$, were obtained with restored sporulating ability. These were shown to be heterozygous for all original markers.

It is possible to explain multiple phenotypic changes accompanying the $hyc^- \rightarrow hyc^c$ transition as a result of change in some membrane structure.

Introduction

Yeast cultures utilizing hydrocarbons are of well recognized practical importance. Although the problem of utilizing petroleum waste for producing food protein has been solved using various bacterial systems, for example *Pseudomonas*, yeast is traditionally considered as the most adequate source for protein supply.

Most industrial yeast strains are asporogenous and asexual. Accordingly, selection work applied to these strains is mainly restricted to different mutagenetic treatments combined with sometimes ingenious autoselection procedures.

An alternative approach is to use the recently discovered hydrocarbon-utilizing yeast strains capable of sporulation (Wickerman *et al.*, 1970). The work of Bassel *et al.* (1971), Bassel and Mortimer (1973) and Gaillardin *et al.* (1973) on *Saccharomycopsis lipolytica* was the first genetic approach to the problem. They selected mutants incapable of hydrocarbon utilization and made a biochemical and genetical study of these. A comparable system was recently developed in the USSR with another hydrocarbon utilizing yeast: *Pichia guilliermondii* (Schelokova and Zharova, 1973).

We developed another experimental system based on a quite different approach to the problem. Our system involved the induction of hydrocarbon utilizing mutants in homothallic strains of *Saccharomyces cerevisiae*. Some of our results are summarized in the present paper.

Results and discussion

Homothallic yeast strains 768 and 41 were used for the induction of hydrocarbon utilizing (hyc^+) mutants. The systematic position of these strains obtained from the "All-Union" collection of yeasts was investigated recently (Soom, 1973). Both strains proved to be typical *Saccharomyces cerevisiae*. They differed from race XII of *S. cerevisiae* only in the ability to utilize succinate and fumarate as the sole source of carbon.

Variants of type hyc^+ derived from both strains differed considerably from the original ones as well as from *S. cerevisiae* XII (Table 1). The hyc^+ strains would be classified as *Candida sp.* according to widely accepted criteria of yeast taxonomy.

Hybrids between each of the original strains 768 and 41 and haploids of the "Peterhof" breeding stocks derived from *Saccharomyces cervisiae* XII have been obtained. Exluding several instances of aneuploidy, the majority of these hybrids possessed high fertility and usually showed normal Mendelian segregation (2:2) for a number of markers studied including homothallism versus heterothallism. These facts confirmed the close taxonomic relationship between strains which were crossed and furthermore confirmed that the genetic organi-

TABLE 1
Comparison of taxonomically significant characters in some yeast strains

Substance	Saccharomyces cerevisiae XII race	768 and 41	Mutants hyc⁺ derived from 768 and 41
Glucose[f]	+	+	+
Galactose[f]	+	+	−
Sucrose[f]	+	+	−
Maltose[f]	+	+	−
Raffinose[f]	+	+	−
Sorbose[a]	−	−	+
Trehalose[a]	+	+	+
Melibiose[a]	+	+	−
Inulin[a] (2%)	+	+	+
Glycerol[a]	+	±	+
Mannitol[a]	−	−	+
Sorbitol[a]	−	−	+
Acetate[a]	−	−	+
DL-Lactic acid	−	±	+
Succinate[a]	−	+	+
Fumarate[a]	−	+	+

[a] Assimilation.
[f] Fermentation.

zation of *S. cerevisiae* was not incompatible with ability for hydrocarbon utilization.

The fine structure of the *ade2* locus in both homothallic and heterothallic strains was shown to share many features in common such as polarity and position of hot spots in leaky mutants, However, a clear-cut case of divergence in the complementation pattern of the locus was also shown (Simarov *et al.*, 1972).

Induction of *hyc*⁺ mutants was shown to be a two-step process in our case. Apparent phenotypic *hyc*⁺ clones were selected on minimal agar plates containing, in a gaseous phase, hexadecane as a sole carbon source. Re-examination on the hexadecane-containing medium revealed the inability of selected clones to utilize hydrocarbons. In the course of re-examination some clones, although not utilizing hexadecane on minimal medium, gave rise again to rare apparently *hyc*⁺ clones. These secondary *hyc*⁺ clones appeared to be quite stable in their hydrocarbon-utilizing ability.

The puzzling intermediate forms designated *hyc*ᶜ were found to be auxotrophs and therefore incapable of growth on the hexadecane supplemented minimal medium used. Of 102 independent *hyc*ᶜ clones isolated, 99 were

TABLE 2

Differences in utilization of various carbon sources by hyc^-, hyc^c and hyc^+ strains of *Saccharomyces cerevisiae*

Carbon source	Strains		
	hyc^-	hyc^c	hyc^+
Hexadecane, peptone, acetic aldehyde, acetate, pyruvate, citrate, malate, *cis*-aconitate, alanine, glutamate, glutamine, aspartate, asparagine, arginine, proline, or ornithine	−	+	+

methionine auxotrophs (hyc^{met}), and 3, arginine auxotrophs (hyc^{arg}). All these hyc^c clones readily utilized hexadecane on minimal medium supplemented respectively with either methionine or arginine.

The mutational step $hyc^c \rightarrow hyc^+$ was a simple reversion to prototrophy from methionine or arginine dependence. It occurred spontaneously with a frequency of $10^{-6} - 10^{-7}$ per cell per generation. The first step, $hyc^- \rightarrow hyc^c$ transition, was observed in only a few experiments. The corresponding mutation rate was approximately 10^{-9} per cell per generation. Attempts to stimulate the production of hyc^c clones with various mutagens such as ultraviolet light, ethylmethanesulphonate and 6-hydroxyamino-purine were ineffective. However, the same mutagens were highly efficient in inducing auxotrophic mutants and hyc^+ mutant types from hyc^c clones. Conversion of hyc^- to hyc^c was accompanied by pleiotropic changes giving a wide range of phenotypic traits (Tables 2 and 3). Obviously, rather drastic changes occurred in the ability to utilize various carbon sources, both hyc^c and hyc^+ strains being able to utilize all the Kreb's cycle intermediates tested; hyc^c and hyc^+

TABLE 3

Phenotypic differences in hyc^-, hyc^c and hyc^+ strains of *Saccharomyces cerevisiae*

Phenotypic trait	Strains		
	hyc^-	hyc^c	hyc^+
Growth without methionine (arginine)	+	−	+
Sporulation	+	−	−
Pseudomycelium development	−	+	+
Resistance to 50% glucose	+	−	−
50% ethionine	−	+	+
50% canavanine	−	+	+
50% cycloheximide	−	+	+
50% killer-factor	−	+	+
Acid phosphatase I activity	+	−	−

mutants appeared to be resistant to several inhibitory agents unlike the original hyc^- strains.

Identification of phenotypic differences among hyc^-, hyc^c and hyc^+ strains enabled us to use selective media to study both forward and backward spontaneous mutation rates for various characters comprising an hyc^+ phenotype (Fig. 1). All the rates measured with one obvious exception $(hyc^- \rightarrow hyc^c)$ were above 10^{-6}, therefore suggesting single-step mutational changes.

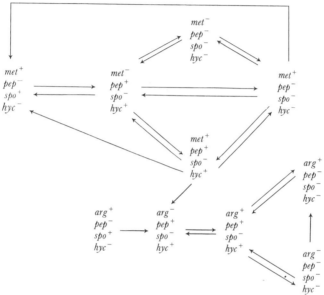

FIG. 1. Mutational transition between various hyc^- and hyc^+ phenotypes. met^-, auxotrophy for methionine; arg^-, auxotrophy for arginine; pep^-, ability to utilize peptone as a sole source of carbon; spo^-, ability to sporulate.

In addition to the phenotypic changes accompanying an $hyc^- \rightarrow hyc^c$ transition we observed alterations in the regulation of cytochrome biosynthesis in both hyc^c and hyc^+ strains. The alterations consisted of changes in the cytochrome spectra when grown on glucose and ethanol; the effects of erythromycin and chloramphenicol on cytochrome spectra were even more pronounced. In both heterothallic and parental homothallic hyc^- strains, erythromycin caused inhibition of both cytochromes b and aa_3 and slightly stimulated cytochrome c but there were no pronounced effects in hyc^c and hyc^+ mutants even with high concentrations of erythromycin (600–1400 mg dm^{-3}). Moreover, in hyc^+ strains erythromycin slightly stimulated the synthesis of all the cytochromes recorded (c_1, b and aa) (Fig. 2).

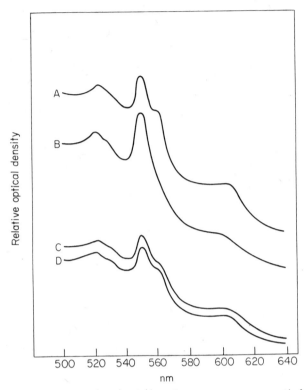

Fɪɢ. 2. Cytochromes spectra of *hyc⁻* and *hyc⁺* strains at room temperature. A, hyc^- (0.6 per cent glucose + 1.6 per cent ethanol); B, hyc^- (0.6 per cent glucose + 1.6 per cent ethanol + 600 mg dm⁻³ erythromycin); C, hyc^+ (0.6 per cent glucose + 1.6 per cent ethanol); D, hyc^+ (0.6 per cent glucose + 1.6 per cent ethanol + 900 mg dm⁻³ erythromycin).

Obviously, the synthesis of mitochondrial-coded components of cytochromes *b* and aa_3 (Wheeldon, 1973) was changed in hyc^c and hyc^+ mutants, but not that of the mitochondrial-coded repressor of the nuclear genes which control mitochondrial development (Barrath and Küntzel, 1971).

Another effect accompanying the transition $hyc^- \rightarrow hyc^c$ was found while studying residual copulation activity of diploid and polyploid *hyc⁻* and *hyc^c* strains. Strains of both phenotypes carrying various genetic markers were crossed with haploids of heterothallic "Peterhof" breeding stocks of *Saccharomyces cerevisiae*. Forty-seven combinations (including 7 homothallic *hyc⁻* strains) with heterothallic haploids gave rise to 39 hybrids whereas 563 combinations (including 65 various *hyc^c* strains) with heterothallic haploids produced no hybrids at all. The copulation activity, if present, was obviously greatly suppressed in *hyc^c* strains.

Both hyc^c and hyc^+ strains are also invariably deficient in sporulation ability (see Table 3). Loss of any sexual activity in hyc^c and hyc^+ strains was further confirmed by the inability of hyc^c and hyc^+ mutants to undergo both spontaneous and uv-induced mitotic recombination (Table 4).

TABLE 4

Mitotic recombination in hyc^-, hyc^c and hyc^+ strains

Strain	hyc	Number of tested colonies			Σ Recombinants for *ade, met, his, ura* (%)
		Control	uv-10″	uv-1′	
D131	hyc^-	5744	—	—	7 (0.12%)
		—	6021	—	44 (0.74%)
		—	—	1339	19 (1.40%)
D131-3	hyc^c	5700	—	—	0 (<0.02%)
		—	6052	—	0 (<0.01%)
		—	—	2569	0 (<0.03%)
D131-3-4	hyc^+	3035	—	—	0 (<0.03%)
		—	6005	—	0 (<0.03%)
		—	—	546	0 (<0.18%)

In view of the natural occurrence of sporulating yeast strains utilizing hydrocarbons (Wickerham *et al.*, 1970), the correlation between inability to sporulate and the hyc^+ phenotype may be a characteristic feature of our strains only.

We obtained several revertants, hyc^c or $hyc^+ \rightarrow hyc^-$, capable of sporulation. An analysis of these revertants, designated R, demonstrated persistence of all the markers for which the original hyc^- strains were heterozygous (Table 5).

TABLE 5

Recovery of genetic markers in strain D131 and revertants $hyc^- \rightarrow hyc^+$

Strain	Ascospore viability (%)	Allele ratio for genes segregating			
		$ade^+ : ade^-$	$his^+ : his^-$	$met^+ : met^-$	$hth : a : \alpha$
D131	30.7	12:3	1:14	12:3	6:2:7
D131-3-6R	38.4	12:8	3:17	7:13	9:9:2
D131-3-29R	45.0	13:10	7:16	13:10	12:5:6

ade, adenine; *his*, histidine; *met*, methionine; *hth*, homothallism; *a* and *α*, mating types.

The nature of the metabolic shift occurring in a $hyc^- \rightarrow hyc^c$ mutational conversion is rather obscure. At first, the low frequency of the $hyc^- \rightarrow hyc^c$ transition suggests a complex event involving several mutations. The explanation, therefore, of the origin of hyc^c strains as a result of one pleiotropic mutation may be misleading. However, since the number of gene changes cannot be large, some generalizations can be made. A change in lipid metabolism, for example, could produce many of the effects described here.

Lipid metabolism is regulated via metabolism of fatty acids by the acetyl-CoA system. The active group of acetyl-CoA is cysteine which is synthesized from methionine. It suggests an explanation for the methionine auxotrophy of hyc^{met} strains. An alternative target could be the succinyl-CoA system, closely connected with both methionine and arginine biosynthesis. It is also possible that methylation systems are altered in hyc^{met} mutants. Moreover, it is now well established that some mutations changing fatty acid–lipid metabolism do lead to methionine auxotrophy and, through modification of membrane structures, to various abnormalities in mitochondrial function (Resnick and Mortimer, 1966; Keith et al., 1969; Bard, 1972; Karst and Lacroute, 1973; Bard et al., 1974).

The latter is paralleled in the present investigation by an alteration in mitochondrial synthesis of a highly hydrophobic component of cytochromes b and aa_3, as well as a dramatic change in the availability of the yeast cell to utilize intermediates of the Kreb's cycle. More general changes in membrane structure are likely to produce the defects in the sexual cycle found in our mutants.

As the products of n-alkane oxidation are utilized via the fatty acid–Kreb's cycle pathway, modifications of the first steps in lipid synthesis are likely to be needed for the conversion of hyc^- to hyc^+ strains in Saccharomyces cerevisiae.

References

Bard, M. (1972). J. Bact. 111, 649.
Bard, M., Woods, R. A. and Haslam, J. M. (1974). Biochem. biophys. Res. Commun. 56, 324.
Bassel, J., Warfel, J. and Mortimer, R. (1971). J. Bact. 108, 609.
Bassel, J. and Mortimer, R. (1973). J. Bact. 114, 894.
Barath, Z. and Küntzel, H. (1972). Proc. natn. Acad. Sci. U.S.A. 69, 1371.
Gaillardin, C. M., Charoy, V. and Heslot, H. (1973). Arch. Mikrobiol. 92, 69.
Karst, F. and Lacroute, F. (1973). Biochim. biophys. Res. Commun. 52, 741.
Keith, A. D., Resnick, M. R. and Haley, A. B. (1969). J. Bact. 98, 415.
Resnick, M. R. and Mortimer, R. K. (1966). J. Bact. 92, 597.
Schelokova, I. F. and Zharova, V. T. (1973). "Konferencya po genetice promyschlennych mikroorganismov. Tezisy dokladov". 102. Tsahkadzor, USSR.

Simarov, B. V., Tichomirova, V. L. and Rabinowitz, E. G. (1972). "Vtoroy s'ezd vsesoyunogo obschestva geneticov i selectionerov", Vystavka T (tezisy rabot). 2, 98, Moskva.

Soom, I. O. (1973). *Genetika*, **9**, 12, 95.

Wheeldon, L. W. (1973). *Biochimie.* **55**, 805.

Wickerham, L. J., Kurtzman, C. P. and Herman, A. I. (1970). *Science*, **167**, 1141.

REGULATION OF METABOLISM

N

Genetic control of arginine metabolism in prokaryotes

S. BAUMBERG

Department of Genetics, University of Leeds, Leeds LS2 9JT, England

Summary

Arginine is synthesized by prokaryotes from glutamate in eight steps; it is also catabolized by some bacteria (thus serving as carbon or nitrogen source) by at least two pathways. Physiological and genetic studies on the regulation of flow through these biosynthetic and catabolic pathways have been carried out in *Escherichia coli* and in members of the genera *Proteus, Pseudomonas* and *Bacillus.*

Flow through a biosynthetic pathway may be controlled by (a) inhibition of activity of the first (and/or sometimes the second) enzyme by the end product, (b) repression of synthesis of some or all enzymes of the pathway by the end product or a derivative; and that through a peripheral catabolic pathway by (a) induction of synthesis of the enzymes by the substrate or a derivative, (b) if catabolism of the substrate can provide carbon skeletons, catabolite repression of synthesis of the enzymes. Also, some or all genes coding for enzymes of a pathway may be clustered into operons.

Arginine metabolism in the organisms mentioned exemplifies most of these points, with interesting exceptions. In *Pseudomonas*, (1) a step common to biosynthesis and catabolism is mediated by two enzymes, whose properties are such that one can catalyse the reaction in the biosynthetic but not the degradative direction, and the other vice versa, (2) whereas some biosynthetic enzymes are repressible, others are constitutive and one (which probably also doubles as a catabolic enzyme) is inducible and subject to catabolite repression. Constitutive enzyme synthesis in this sequence also occurs in *E.coli* B, though not in the K–12 and W strains. In the *Bacillus subtilis* catabolic pathway, catabolite repression is absent but induction is antagonized by glutamine (a nitrogen metabolism equivalent?).

Mutants with altered control of enzyme synthesis have been isolated in *E.coli, Proteus mirabilis* and *B. subtilis*, sometimes as resistant to arginine analogues. Some overproduce arginine and/or one or more of the biosynthetic enzymes. They demonstrate that (1) in *E.coli* a four-gene cluster is transcribed divergently from an internal control region, and (2) in *B.subtilis* the control systems for arginine biosynthesis and catabolism may have common components.

The knowledge of patterns of physiological control may aid in the search for optimal conditions for metabolite or enzyme production, while regulation mutations could be used in the construction of better strains for these purposes.

Introduction

Most prokaryotes have evolved systems for controlling the flow through individual metabolic pathways; these can be understood teleologically as enabling the organism to exploit its environment with maximum efficiency. Two major kinds of regulating device are found, operating respectively at the levels of (a) *activity* and (b) *synthesis* of the proteins involved—these latter are usually enzymes, but may be, e.g. transport proteins ("permeases"). In many prokaryotes and for many pathways, mutants have been isolated in which the wild-type regulation is altered, and our understanding of control mechanisms is largely based on their study. Many such mutants accumulate large amounts of some metabolite, or overproduce one or more enzymes, or metabolize substances than can be utilized by the wild type less readily or not at all. They are for these reasons of potential industrial interest. In the following discussion, the possible industrial relevance may pass out of sight while the details of the various control systems are being elaborated but I shall return to this topic in the concluding section.

PATHWAYS OF ARGININE METABOLISM IN PROKARYOTES

These are illustrated in Fig. 1. Note that this collates information for all the prokaryotes to be mentioned. Arginine biosynthesis commences with the acetylation of glutamate (step 1: either *N*-acetyl-glutamate synthetase or ornithine transacetylase*), which is converted to *N*-acetylornithine (step 2: *N*-acetyglutamokinase; 3, *N*-acetylglutamic γ-semialdehyde dehydrogenase; 4, *N*-acetylornithine δ-transaminase). This compound is converted to ornithine (5) either by an enzyme also catalysing reaction (1) (ornithine transacetylase), in which case the acetyl group is cycled between glutamate

---

* In the following, the enzyme's name is given after the number of the reaction catalysed according to Fig. 1.

and ornithine; or with the release of free acetate, in which (1) requires acetyl-CoA and is catalysed by N-acetylglutamate synthetase while (5) is catalysed by acetylornithinase. Ornithine condenses with carbamyl phosphate to yield citrulline (6, ornithine transcarbamylase), and arginine is synthesized from the latter in two steps (7, argininosuccinate synthetase; 8, arginino-succinase).

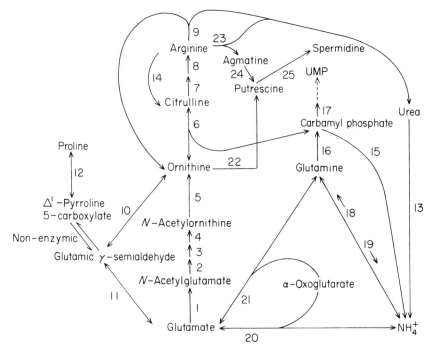

FIG. 1. Pathways of arginine metabolism in prokaryotes.

There are two common pathways for arginine catabolism. The first is to ornithine + urea (9, arginase), followed by conversion of the former to glutamic γ-semialdehyde (10, ornithine transaminase) and eventually glutamate (11, Δ^1-pyrroline 5-carboxylate dehydrogenase). Step 11, operating in the reverse direction, is also the first in proline biosynthesis, the second being step 12 (proline oxidase). Urea may also be degraded to $NH_4^+ + CO_2$ (13, urease). The second catabolic pathway is to citrulline + NH_4^+ (14, arginine deiminase); the former then forms ornithine + carbamyl phosphate through step (6) working in reverse, and the latter is hydrolysed to $NH_4^+ + CO_2 + P_i$ (15, spontaneously or mediated by carbamate kinase). The ornithine may be degraded to glutamate as in the first pathway.

Other points to note in Fig. 1 are:

i. Carbamyl phosphate (synthesized from glutamine; 16, carbamyl phosphate synthetase) lies at a metabolic branch point, since it is required for the synthesis of pyrimidines (the first step in which 17 is catalysed by aspartate transcarbamylase) as well as of arginine.

ii. The interconversion of glutamate, glutamine and NH_4^+. Glutamine is synthesized from glutamate, NH_4^+ and ATP (18, glutamine synthetase), and may be hydrolysed to glutamate $+ NH_4^+$ (19, glutaminase). NH_4^+ may be converted to glutamate either by direct reaction with α-oxoglutarate (20, glutamate dehydrogenase) or, following its incorporation into glutamine, but the condensation of the latter with α-oxoglutarate (21, glutamine: α-oxoglutarate amidotransferase, usually abbreviated to GOGAT).

The following topics will not be discussed here for reasons of space:

i. Arginine transport and its control (Celis et al., 1973; Rosen, 1973).
ii. "Channelling", particularly the different fates of endogenous and exogenous arginine (Sercarz and Gorini, 1964; Tabor and Tabor, 1969).
iii. The production of the polyamines putrescine and spermidine, often in large amounts, from the arginine pathway. Putrescine is produced either directly by decarboxylation of ornithine (22, ornithine decarboxylase), or through the decarboxylation of arginine to give agmatine (23, arginine decarboxylase) followed by cleavage of the latter by a reaction analogous to that mediated by arginase (24, agmatine ureohydrolase). Putrescine condenses with S-adenosyl-5'-S-methyl mercaptopropylamine (decarboxylated S-adenosylmethionine) to give spermidine. References will be found in Maas (1972) and Morris and Jorstad (1973).

Results and discussion

In this section, I shall describe how arginine metabolism is controlled in various prokaryotes under three headings: *Escherichia coli* (with occasional mention of other enterobacteria); *Pseudomonas aeruginosa, P. fluorescens* and *P. putida;* and *Bacillus subtilis* and *B. licheniformis.*

The description will cover the observed control properties of each system, followed by the physiological and genetic mechanisms by which these are achieved.

The control of a given system may appear dissimilar even for closely related organisms, though often the underlying mechanisms are related; while for more divergent groups there may be fundamental differences. It therefore seems regrettable that the analysis of control systems in *Streptomyces* species, where this might be thought of obvious practical relevance, has so far been fragmentary (Hopwood *et al.*, 1973). An extreme illustration of this diversity is afforded by the blue-green algae, where control of arginine biosynthesis appears to be entirely at the level of enzyme activity (Carr, 1973).

E. COLI

In *E. coli* neither pathway of arginine catabolism is found. We can therefore consider, in this system, just the biosynthetic pathway. This possesses a separate *N*-acetylglutamate synthetase and an acetylornithinase, rather than the ornithine transacetylase.

Control in the K12 strain on which most of the work in this system (and indeed most others) has been done is as in the model biosynthetic pathway sketched above. The first enzyme, *N*-acetylglutamate synthetase, is inhibited by arginine *in vivo* (Vyas and Maas, 1963) and *in vitro* (T. Leisinger, in press); while the synthesis of all eight enzymes is repressed by arginine (Vogel, 1961; Gorini *et al.*, 1961; Maas, 1961). In addition, carbamyl phosphate synthetase is inhibited by UMP and *cumulatively* repressed by arginine and uracil, i.e. the effect of the two together is approximately the sum of their individual effects (Piérard *et al.*, 1965).

End-product inhibition is, as expected, subject to modification or loss by mutation in the gene(s) coding for the enzyme. Mutants in which *N*-acetylglutamate synthetase is no longer inhibited by arginine have recently been isolated (T. Leisinger, personal communication). A uracil-sensitive mutant whose inhibition by uracil is reversed by arginine possesses a carbamyl phosphate synthetase hypersensitive to inhibition by UMP; the mutation maps in the structural gene for this enzyme (Piérard *et al.*, 1965).

Control of enzyme synthesis has a complex mechanism. It will first be necessary to describe the location of the enzymes' structural genes on the "circular" *E. coli* chromosome. This can be represented as follows (Taylor and Trotter, 1972):

pyrA (16) - *argF* (6) - *argA* (1) - *argG* (7) - *argD* (4) -

argE (5) ; *argC* (3) ; *argB* (2) ; *argH* (8) - *pyrB* (17) ; *argI* (6)

The hyphens indicate that many genes of unrelated function lie between, while the semicolons indicate that the genes are contiguous (the numbers refer to reactions in Fig. 1). There are two points of interest. First, unlike most amino acid biosynthetic systems in *E. coli* and *S. typhimurium* (but like the proline system), the genes for the arginine biosynthetic enzymes do not all form a contiguous *cluster*. However, the genes are not completely scattered; there is a cluster of four genes, *argECBH*. Second, in *E. coli* K12 there are two genes coding for ornithine transcarbamylase, *argF* and *argI* (Glansdorff *et al.*, 1967); in *E. coli* B and W, and in *S. typhimurium*, whose arginine genes otherwise map identically to K12, *argF* is missing (Jacoby, 1971; Syvanen and Roth, 1972). Interestingly, *argI* is adjacent to *pyrB*, which codes for aspartate transcarbamylase, also a carbamyl phosphate-utilizing enzyme. The polypeptide products of *argF* and *argI* give rise to a family of isoenzymes (four, since the protein is a trimer), the first instance of this in prokaryotes (Legrain *et al.*, 1972).

In *Proteus mirabilis*, *P. vulgaris*, *P. rettgeri* and *P. morgani* the cluster includes *argG*, thus: *argECBGH* (Prozesky, 1968; Prozesky *et al.*, 1973).

In a Providence strain the cluster is as in *E. coli*, suggesting a correlation between the presence of *argG* in the cluster and the possession of a urease. The structural gene for the latter, however, is not linked to the *arg* cluster (Prozesky *et al.*, 1973).

I shall now discuss the physiology of repression in *E. coli* in more detail. As might be expected, the degree of repression depends on the intracellular arginine concentration. The specific activities of these enzymes are considerably lower in minimal salts–glucose medium with arginine than without, while provision of the arginine precursors ornithine or citrulline results in activities slightly above the fully repressed ones. Even in minimal medium without arginine endogenous arginine production yields an appreciable pool, so that some repression is occurring. Repression can be eliminated by restricting endogenous arginine production, e.g. by growth of a bradytroph (a "leaky" arginine auxotroph) without arginine, or of a "tight" auxotroph in continuous culture with arginine limiting (note that this cannot be done in batch culture, as the kinetics of transport are such that growth takes place at the wild-type rate until the arginine is exhausted). Enzyme levels in these cultures are said to be *physiologically derepressed*, and are higher than in cultures grown in minimal medium without arginine.

Regulator gene mutations

The phenotypic character of repressibility of the arginine biosynthetic enzymes must be under genetic control, and one therefore would expect mutants with altered regulation to be capable of isolation. *Genetically derepressed* mutants may readily be obtained in which the enzymes are produced at rates characteristic of physiological derepression whether arginine is present or not. There are several methods of isolating such mutants (see e.g. Itikawa *et al.*, 1968; Piérard *et al.*, 1972); two of these will be described here.

1. In this as in other biosynthetic systems, analogues of an end product can be used to obtain control mutants. One analogue here is canavanine, which is a substrate for arginyl tRNA synthetase and can be introduced into nascent polypeptide chains (Hirshfield *et al.*, 1968); canavanine therefore acts as an

inhibitor by competing with arginine during protein synthesis. However, since it competes with arginine relatively ineffectively for the tRNA synthetase, it only inhibits cells with very low internal arginine pools; if these cells show any residual repression, the arginine pool can increase following mutation to genetic depression, and such mutants may therefore be selected as forming colonies on appropriate solid media containing canavanine (mutants with other phenotypes, including uptake-deficient mutants, may also be selected: Maas, 1961; Hirshfield *et al.*, 1968; Kadner and Maas, 1971; Maas, 1972). Although minimal medium + canavanine has been used successfully (Williams, 1973) it has been more common to employ media supplemented with all amino acids but arginine, and containing canavanine (e.g. Novick and Maas, 1961).

2. Acetylornithinase can de-acetylate several *N*-acetyl-amino acids other than its natural substrate *N*-acetylornithine. Among these is *N*-acetylhistidine; a histidine auxotroph depends therefore on acetylornithinase for growth with *N*-acetylhistidine instead of histidine. As acetylhistidine is a poor substrate for the enzyme, the repressed level of acetylornithinase is insufficient to permit growth under these conditions. Selection on acetylhistidine + ornithine conveniently selects for genetically depressed mutants (arginine cannot be used as it prevents acetylhistidine utilization in some additional way) (Baumberg, 1970). The mutants obtained, as well as producing the biosynthetic enzymes at high constitutive (i.e. in this context not repressible by arginine) levels, also excrete arginine to a limited extent. This would appear to indicate that end product inhibition alone is inadequate to control flow through the pathway.

Mutations conferring genetic depression usually (but not always: see below) map at a locus *argR*, the arginine *regulator gene,* which lies between *argG* and *argD*, close to but not contiguous with the former (Taylor and Trotter, 1972). That the functional *argR* product is a protein is shown by the fact that certain *argR* mutations can be suppressed by extragenic suppressors known to work during translation (Jacoby and Gorini, 1969). A reasonable hypothesis is that *argR* specifies a protein *apo-repressor* which is nonfunctional on its own but binds arginine or a related substance to give a functional *repressor.* The repressor acts to switch off expression of the enzymes' structural genes, by the mechanism described in Scaife's paper (p. 29). In some other amino acid biosynthetic systems, notably the *S. typhimurium* histidine system (Wyche *et al.*, 1974; Kasai, 1974) and the *E. coli* leucine–isoleucine–valine system (Levinthal *et al.*, 1973), though not the *E. coli* tryptophan system (Squires *et al.*, 1973; Rose *et al.*, 1973; McGeoch *et al.*, 1973), repression seems to require components other than apo-repressor and end product: the amino acyl tRNA, amino acyl tRNA synthetase and first enzyme in the pathways may take part. Certain genetically derepressed mutants (Williams, 1973; Williams and Williams, 1973) appear to possess altered arginyl tRNA synthetases, and this and other work (Williams *et al.*, 1973) suggest comparable phenomena here. There is evidence against this idea, though it is not conclusive (Hirshfield *et al.*, 1968; Leisinger and Vogel, 1969; Celis and Maas, 1971). The hypothesis that the *argR* product gives rise to a repressor in the classical sense, i.e. a *negatively acting* regulatory element (Jacob and Monod, 1961), is in accord with studies (Maas *et al.*, 1964; Maas and Clark, 1964) showing that the wild-type *argR*$^+$ allele is dominant to mutant *argR* alleles. The fact that *argR* nonsense mutants, which make only a shortened polypeptide chain, show the genetically derepressed phenotype (Jacoby and Gorini, 1969) strongly suggests that the *argR* product differs from the product of the *E. coli* L-arabinose system regulatory gene *araC* (Englesberg, 1971; Greenblatt and Schleif, 1971) in that it does not under appropriate circumstances act positively, to switch on gene expression, as well as negatively

In *E. coli* strain B, the *argR* allele *argR*$_B$ gives rise to a product which behaves differently from its K12 counterpart (Jacoby and Gorini, 1967). The activities of the arginine enzymes in cells of this strain grown in minimal medium without arginine are somewhat lower than in K12, but the addition of arginine either has no effect or induces slightly higher levels. Nevertheless, physiological derepression of ornithine transcarbamylase can occur to a slight extent; and at temperatures above 39°C arginine represses, rather than induces, this enzyme (Karlström and Gorini, 1969). Also, the *argR*$_B$ allele can mutate to an allele effectively the same as in wild-type K12, or to an allele whose phenotypic effect is the same as that of the *argR* mutant alleles in K12 (Jacoby and Gorini, 1969). It therefore seems likely that control of this pathway is basically the same in the K12 and B strains, notwithstanding the apparent phenotypic differences.

In *Proteus mirabilis*, the activities of the biosynthetic enzymes show only slight physiological variation, but such variation as exists is reminiscent of *E. coli* B. Levels in cells grown in media containing arginine at 10 µg cm^{-3} are higher than in cells grown without arginine; however, at higher concentrations the levels tend to fall again. Mutants isolated on arginine-free supplemented medium + canavanine excreted arginine and behaved like the two types of *argR* mutant described above as obtainable in *E. coli* B, although the effects of the mutations were slight in comparison (Prozesky, 1969).

Mechanism of action of the argR product

In earlier contributions to these Proceedings, Scaife (p. 29) and Brammar (p. 291) have described the role of promoter and operator in the control of gene expression. How does all this apply to the *E. coli* arginine system? The isolated genes must, in theory, be regulated individually through an adjacent promoter and operator. An interesting point is that the operators differ considerably in affinity for repressor; the repression ratios for the enzymes coded for by *A*, *D* and *F* + *I* are respectively 250, 20 and 750, while for the enzymes whose genes are clustered the repression ratios are 18 (*E*) and 40–50 (*B*, *C* and *H*) (Leisinger and Haas, in press; Cunin *et al.*, 1969). Mutations in the promoters or operators of isolated genes are very difficult to obtain, because they can affect the level of only one enzyme: hence the overall flow through the pathway will generally be only slightly perturbed, resulting in a phenotypic effect too slight on which to base a selection technique (contrast this with the much greater effect of such mutations in, say, the *E. coli* tryptophan system: Hiraga, 1969)

An ingenious solution has been found by Jacoby and Gorini (1969) who used the fact that strains carrying the *argR*$_B$ allele do not physiologically derepress even when the internal arginine pool is very low. They started with a strain which carried, as well as *argR*$_B$, a particular *argF* mutation— *argF40*, which is *streptomycin-suppressible*—i.e. in the presence of streptomycin (one of whose effects is to cause misreading of the genetic code) the triplet UAG, which appears in the mRNA as a result of the *argF40* mutation and which results in premature chain termination, is occasionally mistranslated as if it coded for an amino acid acceptable at that position in the polypeptide chain. However, this occurs so infrequently, or the resulting polypeptide(s) is so poorly functional, that the level of gene expression allowed by the *argR*$_B$ allele is not sufficient for streptomycin to counteract the arginine requirement. However, if another mutation arises either in *argR* (to permit pathway-wide physiological or genetic derepression) or in the *argF* operator, the net result in either case is that enough functioning polypeptide is made for the mutant to grow without arginine. In this way, an *o*^{c} *F40* mutant was obtained in which the expression of just the *argF* gene has been partially freed from repression control.

The same difficulty as for the isolated genes exists for the isolation of promoter or operator mutations in the *argECBH* cluster. The organization of this cluster has been unclear for a number of years. It was found (Cunin *et al.*, 1969) that *C*, *B* and *H* are transcribed on to a polycistronic mRNA molecule in the direction $\overrightarrow{CBH}$; this is consistent with the corresponding enzymes showing the same repression ratio (see above), an example of *coordinate control* (Ames and Garry, 1959). The obvious expectation, that the four genes constitute a single operon $\overrightarrow{ECBH}$ with control regions at the *E* end, was contradicted by several lines of evidence (Cunin *et al.*, 1969; Baumberg and Ashcroft, 1971; Elseviers *et al.*, 1972). The properties of a deletion ending in the *E–C* boundary region suggested that the latter might contain overlapping control regions for both *E* and *CBH* expression (Elseviers *et al.*, 1972), and the same was implied when Jacoby (1972) by a technique similar to that described above, isolated a mutant selected as o^c for C which turned out to be o^c for E as well. The inescapable conclusion is that the *E. coli* arginine cluster shows *divergent transcription* from an internal promoter–operator complex at the *E–C* boundary. Elseviers *et al.* (1972) proposed the genetic arrangement $\overleftarrow{E} - p_{\text{CBH}} - o_{\text{ECBH}} - p_{\text{E}} - \overrightarrow{\text{CBH}}$, whereby transcription from either promoter can be blocked by the binding of repressor to a common operator. However, this is probably an oversimplification. Recently, Bretscher (1974) has used *localized mutagenesis* (Hong and Ames, 1971) to isolate mutants that over-produce acetylornithinase by virtue of mutations in or near the cluster. He mutagenized with hydroxylamine a suspension of the generalized transducing phage P1 grown on a wild-type host, and used this to transduce a recipient which was (a) mutated in the gene *ppc* which is (probably) adjacent to *argE*, and (b) a histidine auxotroph. Transductants were selected on a medium selective for *ppc⁺* and containing ornithine with acetylhistidine as source of histidine. As noted above, the latter may select for *argR* mutants; but the simultaneous selection for *ppc⁺* attempts to ensure that the only mutations to appear in transductants that confer ability to grow on acetylhistidine + ornithine are linked to *ppc*. One mutation, 11, obtained in this way behaves as an o^c, fully constitutive for E and partially constitutive for *CBH*. Another, 8, behaves like a two-fold "up-promoter" mutation for E and a 1.5-fold "down-promoter" for *CBH*, a conjunction of properties that may be viewed as predictable from the genetic sequence proposed by Elseviers *et al.* (1972). However, deletion mapping suggests an order *E*-8-11-*CBH*. The precise nature and sequence of control regions at the *E-C* boundary therefore needs further elucidation.

Control at the level of transcription or translation?

I have so far assumed that control of gene expression is at the level of transcription. Although the isolation of the arginine repressor has been claimed (Udaka, 1970), it has not yet been demonstrated that the protein isolated binds to DNA corresponding to an arginine operator region, although this experiment should be feasible with the isolation of several specialized transducing phage genomes, derived from λ or ø80, that carry the *argECBH* cluster (Press *et al.*, 1971; Cunin and Glansdorff, personal communication). These phages have, however, been used in arginine mRNA assays. Here the fraction of pulse-labelled RNA, prepared from cultures growing under various conditions of repression or depression, that can hybridize with denatured (i.e. single strands of) phage DNA is determined. With the correct controls, this fraction can be taken as estimating the rates of transcription of the clustered genes. It is clear (Cunin and Glansdorff, 1971; Krzyzek and Rogers, 1972) that a large part at least of the control in this system is at the level of transcription. However, it seems possible that the arginine regulatory system also has a translational component, a view advocated by Vogel (Vogel *et al.*, 1971) on the basis of various lines of evidence (e.g. McLellan and Vogel, 1970; Faanes and Rogers, 1972). This effect, whereby the frequency of translation of arginine enzyme mRNA, and/or the total number of times such an individual messenger is translated, alter under different conditions of repression and derepression, is envisaged by Vogel *et al.* (1971) as involving "degradation of message or interference with translation or both". They suggest that the effect may operate through a "repressive complex" containing mRNA and some or all of the following: ribosomes, repressor, arginine, arginyl tRNA and arginyl tRNA synthetase. McLellan and Vogel (1972) report that the *in vivo* half-lives of *argECBH* messengers differ according to whether the culture is repressed or derepressed, being 1.3 min and 5.3 min respectively, suggesting differences in rate of specific mRNA degradation.

By use of poly(U,G) to separate the strands of specialized transducing phage DNA followed by assay of mRNA hybridizable with the separated strands, it is possible to estimate the amounts of *argECBH* transcription off each strand, and hence to show that *E* and *CBH* are transcribed off different strands (Pouwels *et al.*, 1974) and with divergent, rather than convergent, transcription (Panchal *et al.*, 1974). It is interesting that in the first cluster shown, by this means, to be divergently transcribed, the *E. coli* biotin cluster (Guha *et al.*, 1971), the control regions for transcription in the two directions are said not to overlap (Vrancic and Guha, 1973); however, in the third known divergently transcribed cluster, *malB* in *E. coli*, they do (Hofnung, 1974).

The final test of any model of control is whether it applies in a (relatively) purified *in vitro* system. In the *arg* system, a coupled *in vitro* transcription–translation system has been described (Urm *et al.*, 1973); this may eventually make possible the purification of functional repressor and thereby the solution of some unsolved questions, e.g. the nature of the co-repressor, the nature and location of control sites within the *argECBH* cluster, and the existence and extent of translational control.

PSEUDOMONAS AERUGINOSA, P. FLUORESCENS, P. PUTIDA

For convenience I shall in general not indicate for which organism results are reported, as there is at present no reason to believe that they differ substantially.

In the fluorescent pseudomonads, both *N*-acetylglutamate synthetase and ornithine transacetylase are present (Udaka, 1966; Chou and Gunsalus, 1971; Haas *et al.*, 1972). The rapid breakdown of arginine by the "arginine dihydrolase" system, which is characteristic of pseudomonads (Sherris *et al.* 1959), is mediated first by arginine deiminase to yield citrulline. The latter reacts with phosphate to give ornithine + carbamyl phosphate, this being the reverse of the reaction for citrulline biosynthesis; the catabolic and bio-synthetic reactions are catalysed by different ornithine transcarbamylases (Stalon *et al.*, 1967; Ramos *et al.*, 1967). Both the ornithine and carbamyl phosphate can be utilized further, the former as source of both carbon and nitrogen, the latter of nitrogen only. There are two possible paths for ornithine breakdown, both of which may operate. Ornithine transaminase activity has been reported by Voellmy and Leisinger (in press) to be present and to be a property of the enzyme which also possesses the biosynthetic N-acetylornithine δ-transaminase activity; the organism probably also contains a Δ^1-pyrroline 5-carboxylate dehydrogenase, so that ornithine can eventually yield glutamate. Alternatively, ornithine can be decarboxylated to putrescine, and this may be degraded via 4-aminobutyraldehyde and succinic semialdehyde to succinate (Stalon *et al.*, 1972). This pathway may also allow arginine to be utilized independently of the "dihydrolase" system, by decarboxylation to agmatine and cleavage of the latter to putrescine + urea. Carbamyl phosphate is broken down to CO_2 + NH_4^+ + ATP by carbamate kinase; this reaction, which provides ATP to be produced anaerobically from arginine or citrulline, enables these two compounds to restore motility to cells which have lost this through anaerobiosis (Shoesmith and Sherris, 1960).

Physiology of regulation of arginine metabolism

I shall first consider regulations of enzyme activity starting with the two ornithine transcarbamylases. The specialization of these enzymes is remark-able, in that the biosynthetic enzyme (at least *in vitro*) cannot catalyse the reaction in the catabolic direction, nor the catabolic enzyme (at least *in vivo*) in the biosynthetic direction (Ramos *et al.*, 1967). The explanation of the properties of the biosynthetic enzyme is as yet unknown. The inability of the catabolic enzyme to catalyse the biosynthetic step *in vivo* is probably explained by the extreme cooperativity of binding of carbamyl phosphate, its half saturation concentration being more than 100 times the K_m of the biosynthetic enzyme; the intracellular carbamyl phosphate pool is presumably too low to permit an adequate rate of citrulline formation (Stalon *et al.*, 1972). The catabolic enzyme also shows modulation of activity by various effectors. It is activated by phosphate, a substrate and also a low energy level signal; it is inhibited by ATP, a product of the catabolic pathway and a high-energy level signal, and by putrescine, also a product of a catabolic pathway (Stalon *et al.*, 1972). The enzyme is an oligomer made up of eight identical subunits: the equilibrium between the octamer and various states of lowered aggregation is affected by its substrates, products and effectors. These results can be explained in terms of the *allosteric* model of modulation of enzyme activity (Monod *et al.*, 1963, 1965; Stalon, 1972; Halleux *et al.*, 1972).

That the catabolic enzyme cannot function biosynthetically *in vivo* is shown by the fact that a mutant lacking the biosynthetic enzyme acts as an arginine auxotroph blocked between ornithine and citrulline (Ramos *et al.*, 1967). An arginine-independent revertant isolated from this mutant was found to possess an altered *catabolic* ornithine transcarbamylase with altered kinetics such that it possessed appreciable activity at much lower levels of carbamyl phosphate, thus confirming that the kinetics of the wild-type enzyme with respect to carbamyl phosphate are responsible for its inability to act biosynthetically (Stalon *et al.*, 1972).

Two other enzymes of arginine metabolism show control of activity in *Pseudomonas*. N-acetylglutamate synthetase shows feedback inhibition by arginine (Haas *et al.*, 1972); while also the enzyme catalysing the second biosynthetic step, N-acetyl γ-glutamokinase, is inhibited by arginine, as is found in all microorganisms possessing an ornithine transacetylase (Udaka, 1966; Chou and Gunsalus, 1970; Leisinger *et al.*, 1972; Isaac and Holloway, 1972).

As for control at the level of enzyme synthesis, this appears to be less extensive than in *E. coli*, as also reported for other amino acid biosynthetic pathways in these organisms (Crawford and Gunsalus, 1966; Isaac and Holloway, 1968; Marinus and Loutit, 1969). The levels of N-acetylglutamate synthetase, ornithine transacetylase, N-acetyl γ-glutamokinase, acetyl-ornithinase, and argininosuccinase in *P. aeruginosa* PAO-1 did not respond at all to changes in arginine supply; while under arginine limitation in batch or chemostat cultures, N-acetylglutamic γ-semialdehyde dehydrogenase showed two-fold, and the biosynthetic ornithinase transcarbamylase up to 50-fold, physiological derepression (Isaac and Holloway, 1972; Voellmy and Leisinger, 1972). Repression of the ornithine transcarbamylase by exogenous arginine was considerably increased if arginine was the sole carbon source N-acetyl-ornithine δ-transaminase was *induced* 15-fold by arginine, and also showed catabolite repression; this suggests that it is controlled for its catabolic (ornithine transaminase) rather than biosynthetic function.

Of the degradation enzymes, the catabolic ornithine transcarbamylase may show induction by arginine in *P. aeruginosa* strains PAO–1 (Isaac and Holloway, 1972) and ATCC 10145, and in *P. fluorescens* strain A.3.12, but does not in the strain of the latter species, IRC 204, with which most work has been done in this enzyme (Stalon *et al.*, 1967). However, in this strain the catabolic ornithine transcarbamylase, like arginine deiminase and carbamate kinase, is subject to catabolite repression (Ramos *et al.*, 1967).

Genetic information for these systems is not extensive. The structural genes for the biosynthetic enzymes are almost or perhaps totally unlinked (Feary *et al.*, 1969; Isaac and Holloway, 1972), a common situation for biosynthetic pathways in this group (Holloway *et al.*, 1971). The genes for the catabolic enzymes have not been mapped. No regulatory mutants for control of enzyme synthesis in either the biosynthetic or catabolic pathways have been described

BACILLUS SUBTILIS, B. LICHENIFORMIS

These organisms have the same biosynthetic pathway as *E. coli* (*B. subtilis:* Vogel and Vogel, 1963). As in *Pseudomonas,* there are two ornithine transcarbamylases (*B. licheniformis:* Laishley and Bernlohr, 1968a; *B. subtilis:* Stalon and Wiame, personal communication), but it will be seen below that the cases are not analogous. The catabolic pathway involves the degradation of arginine to ornithine mediated by arginase; the transamination of ornithine to glutamic γ-semialdehyde and Δ^1-pyrroline 5-carboxylate, mediated by ornithine transaminase; and the reduction of the last-named to glutamate, mediated by Δ^1-pyrroline 5-carboxylate dehydrogenase. Two separate enzymes catalyse the final step (*B. subtilis:* de Hauwer *et al.*, 1964); a correlation is suggested below with the fact that this is common also to the pathway of proline breakdown.

In addition to a carbamyl phosphate synthetase a carbamate kinase is present (*B. subtilis:* Issaly *et al.*, 1970). These two enzymes represent the only case so far reported for these organisms of modulation of enzyme activity by small molecules in this metabolic system. The synthetase is inhibited by UTP, arginine, uridine and CMP (in order of decreasing effect), arginine and UTP acting cumulatively. The kinase responds most to arginine, followed by UMP and UTP. The role of these enzymes is discussed further below. The pathways of arginine metabolism in *Bacillus* are similar to those in fungi such as *Saccharomyces cerevisiae, Neurospora crassa* and *Aspergillus nidulans*. A major point, therefore, of studying control of arginine metabolism in *Bacillus* is the comparison between prokaryotic and eukaryotic groups. It is therefore particularly interesting that the inhibition of ornithine transcarbamylase activity by arginase found in yeast (Wiame, 1971)—a hitherto unprecedented regulatory device—has now been found to occur also in *B. subtilis* (Stalon and Wiame, personal communication). The biosynthetic enzymes are repressed and the catabolic ones induced by arginine. However, ornithine and citrulline have different effects on the two pathways, in that these arginine precursors induced the catabolic enzymes but do not repress those of the biosynthetic path (*B. subtilis:* Harwood, 1974; Harwood and Baumberg, paper in preparation). This may reflect different affinities of arginine for the macromolecules that mediate these regulatory responses, or may indicate that the nature of the metabolite "signal" differs in the two cases.

Comparison of enzyme levels between glucose and citrate-grown *B. subtilis* cultures indicates that the catabolic enzyme show only slight (c. two-fold) catabolic repression. Under similar conditions, histidase, an enzyme of histidine breakdown shows at least a 20-fold effect (Chasin and Magasanik, 1968; Harwood, 1974). However, the arginine catabolic enzymes in *B. licheniformis* show considerable catabolic repression (Laishley and Bernlohr, 1968b). Cyclic AMP does not seem to be involved in any case. This is the usual picture in Gram-positive bacteria (Rickenberg, personal communication).

One might expect that, just as inducible enzymes which provide carbon and energy are subject to catabolite repression mediated by a "signal" of the availability of both of these, inducible enzymes which provide nitrogen might be subject to a similar form of control mediated by a "signal" of nitrogen availability. This kind of control occurs in yeast, where NH_4^+ antagonizes induction of the arginine catabolic enzymes (Wiame, 1971). Harwood (1974) has found that in *B. subtilis*, neither NH_4^+ nor glutamate antagonize induction of these enzymes, but glutamine does. To understand this, we should recall that *Bacillus* species in general seem to use a glutamine synthetase-GOGAT mediated path for NH_4^+ assimilation, glutamate dehydrogenase usually being low or undetectable (Meers and Tempest, 1970; Meers *et al.*, 1970; Meers and Pedersen, 1972). This pathway is not readily reversible, since these organisms have only very low levels of glutaminase (Wade *et al.*, 1971). It therefore seems likely that when these species grow on glutamate or on a nitrogen source yielding glutamate, NH_4^+ production necessary for synthesis of glutamine is limiting. Consistent with this is the observation that *B. subtilis* grows much more slowly with glutamate than glutamine as nitrogen source (Harwood, 1974). It is therefore understandable that glutamine should be (directly or indirectly) the "signal" of nitrogen availability in this case.

I will now discuss the roles of the dual enzymes in the three instances reported for *B. subtilis* and *B. licheniformis*. The Δ^1-pyrroline 5-carboxylate dehydrogenase case seems clear: one of the enzymes is induced by arginine, the other by proline (de Hauwer *et al.*, 1964). Of the two ornithine trans-carbamylases in *B. licheniformis*, one is repressed by arginine, ornithine or citrulline, while the other shows induction by arginine (though, unlike arginase, ornithine transaminase and Δ^1-pyrroline 5-carboxylate dehydrogenase, not by ornithine or citrulline) and strong catabolite repression by glucose (Laishley and Bernlohr, 1968a). This control pattern suggests that the second enzyme has a catabolic role, but it is not at all clear under what circumstances this could come into play, since *Bacillus* species lack an arginine deaminase. The same problem arises for the carbamyl phosphate synthetase and carbamate kinase of *B. subtilis*. The former is repressed by uracil (with a concerted effect of arginine at lower uracil concentration);

while the latter is induced by arginine, again suggesting a catabolic role which cannot seemingly be utilized.

B. subtilis genes and mutants

As often found for *B. subtilis* (Young and Wilson, 1971), the genes coding for the arginine biosynthetic enzymes show considerable clustering. Although functional analysis of the mutants is fragmentary, it seems likely that the genes for the first five enzymes are contiguous, with that for ornithine trans-carbamylase linked though probably not contiguous; the genes for the last two enzymes are contiguous, and unlinked to the others (Mahler *et al.*, 1963; Dubnau *et al.*, 1967; Young *et al.*, 1969). The genes for the catabolic enzymes have not been mapped.

Two control mutants were obtained by de Hauwer *et al.* (1964), one constitutive for the arginine catabolic enzymes (and also for arginine per-mease), the other noninducible for them.

Kisumi *et al.* (1971) showed that some *B. subtilis* mutants resistant to the arginine analogue arginine hydroxamate excrete arginine, suggesting a regulatory defect. Harwood (1974; Harwood and Baumberg, paper in preparation) isolated a large number of such resistant mutants, and found that they showed a bewildering variety of phenotypes. He divided them into the following seven classes:

Class 1 The catabolic enzymes are completely noninducible, the bio-synthetic enzymes show normal control. This class is the commonest.

Class 2 Arginase is noninducible, but ornithine transaminase is inducible by ornithine or citrulline though not by arginine; the biosynthetic enzymes show normal control.

Class 3 The catabolic enzymes show normal induction by arginine or citrulline, but ornithine only induces to a quarter of the wild-type levels. The biosynthetic enzymes show normal control.

Class 4 The catabolic enzymes are noninducible (as in class 1); ornithine transcarbamylase is at a very high level and is not repressible, but other biosynthetic enzymes show normal control.

Class 5 The catabolic enzymes show greatly diminished inducibility; biosynthetic enzymes are at a very high level and are not repressible.

Class 6 The catabolic enzymes show somewhat diminished inducibility; ornithine transcarbamylase is at a high level in the absence of arginine and shows diminished repressiblity.

Class 7 The catabolic enzymes show diminished inducibility, ornithine transcarbamylase perhaps shows slightly diminished repressibility.

There is good correlation between the inducibility or otherwise of the catabolic enzymes and the ability or inability of any mutant to utilize arginine, ornithine or citrulline as sole nitrogen source.

These patterns suggest a regulatory system physiologically and perhaps genetically more complex than those described in the enterobacteria. Two points stand out, however. Firstly, the ease with which pleiotropic non-inducibility mutations are isolated suggests a positive control. The isolation of similar mutants in the only other *B. subtilis* regulation system to be studied in detail, that for sucrose catabolism (Lepesant *et al.*, 1972, 1974), suggests that this may be general for this organism; and such control mutants are frequent in fungi (Metzenberg, 1972; Wiame, 1971, and these Proceedings; Cove, these Proceedings). Secondly, mutant classes 4–6 strongly suggest that the repression control of the biosynthetic enzymes and the induction control of the catabolic enzymes share at least some common components, again as in yeast (Wiame, 1971).

Conclusions

The potential industrial relevance of our knowledge of metabolic control systems in prokaryotes may by now seem to have submerged beneath a tide of detail. It may be worth concluding by pointing out the possible connecting links. A knowledge of patterns of physiological control should help in a rational search for optimal conditions of metabolite or enzyme production; and regulatory mutants may directly or indirectly give rise to increased metabolite or enzyme yields. The matter of metabolite, rather than enzyme, production has hardly been mentioned in this review, because it has often not been studied in detail in the investigations described; but clearly the control mutants described will have altered metabolite pool sizes, and in some cases might (especially in conjunction with other mutations) excrete particular compounds.

A semi-hypothetical example may be of interest. Kinoshita *et al.* (1957) described an auxotroph of *Corynebacterium glutamicus* responding to arginine or citrulline that accumulated large amounts of ornithine. However, excess arginine in the medium inhibited ornithine accumulation (and stimulated glutamate formation). This is presumably due to the end product inhibition of N-acetyl γ-glutamokinase by arginine (Udaka and Kinoshita, 1958; Udaka, 1966; see also Nakayama *et al.*, these Proceedings). Had a mutant been available with an end-product inhibition-resistant enzyme, the combination of such a mutation with the auxotropic mutation might have produced a strain whose ornithine accumulation could proceed without possible limitations of growth through arginine restriction.

"... 'tes wickedness. 'Tes flyin' in the face of Nature.' 'That's right ...
All the same, it might be worth tryin'."

Stella Gibbons, "Cold Comfort Farm"

Acknowledgements

C. R. Harwood and A. P. Bretscher planned and executed the as yet un-published work carried out in Leeds, the *B. subtilis* component of which was supported by M.R.C. grants G969/215/B and G970/367/B.

I am grateful to Drs J.-M. Wiame, N. Glansdorff, R. Cunin, V. Stalon, and T. Leisinger for stimulating discussions and permission to describe unpublished results.

References

Ames, B. N. and Garry, B. (1959). *Proc. natn. Acad. Sci. U.S.A.* **45,** 1453.
Baumberg, S. (1970). *Molec. gen. Genet.* **106,** 162.
Baumberg, S. and Ashcroft, E. (1971). *J. gen Microbiol.* **69,** 365
Bretscher, A. P. (1974). Ph.D. thesis, University of Leeds.
Carr, N. G. (1973). "The Biology of Blue-green Algae" (Eds N. G. Carr and B. A. Whitton), p. 39. Blackwell Scientific Publications, Oxford.
Celis, T. F. R. and Maas, W. K. (1971). *J. molec. Biol.* **62,** 179.
Celis, T. F. R., Rosenfeld, H. J. and Maas, W. K. (1973). *J. Bact.* **116,** 619.
Chasin, L. A. and Magasanik, B. (1968). *J. biol. Chem.* **243,** 5165.
Chou, I. N. and Gunsalus, I. C. (1970). *Bact. Proc.* 140.
Chou, I. N. and Gunsalus, I. C. (1971). *Bact. Proc.* 162.
Crawford, I. P. and Gunsalus, I. C. (1966). *Proc. natn. Acad. Sci. U.S.A.* **56,** 717
Cunin, R. and Glansdorff, N. (1971). *FEBS Letters,* **18,** 135.
Cunin, R., Elseviers, D., Sand, G., Freundlich, G. and Glansdorff, N. (1969). *Molec. gen. Genet.* **106,** 32.
de Hauwer, G., Lavallé, R. and Wiame, J. M. (1964). *Biochim. biophys. Acta,* **81,** 257.
Dubnau, D., Goldthwaite, C., Smith, I. and Marmur, J. (1967). *J. molec. Biol.* **27,** 163.
Elseviers, D., Cunin, R., Glansdorff, N., Baumberg, S. and Ashcroft, E. (1972). *Molec. gen. Genet.* **117,** 349.
Englesberg, E. (1971). "Metabolic Regulation" (Ed. H. J Vogel), p. 257. Academic Press, New York and London.
Faanes, R. and Rogers, P. (1972). *J. Bact.* **112,** 102.
Feary, T. W., Williams, B., Calhoun, D. H. and Walker, T. A. (1969). *Genetics,* **62,** 673.
Glansdorff, N., Sand, G. and Verhoef, C. (1967). *Mut. Res.* **4,** 743.
Gorini, L., Gundersen, W. and Burger, M. (1961). *Cold Spring Harb. Symp. quant. Biol.* **26,** 173.
Greenblatt, J. and Schleif, R. (1971). *Nature New Biol.* **233,** 166.
Guha, A., Saturen, Y. and Szybalski, W. (1971). *J. molec. Biol.* **56,** 53.
Haas, D., Kurer, V. and Leisinger, T. (1972). *Eur. J. Biochem.* **31,** 290.
Halleux, P., Legrain, C., Stalon, V., Piérard, A. and Wiame, J. M. (1972). *Eur. J. Biochem.* **31,** 386.

Harwood, C. R. (1974). Ph.D. thesis, University of Leeds.
Hiraga, S. (1969). *J. molec. Biol.* **39**, 159.
Hirshfield, I. N., de Deken, R., Horn, P. C., Hopwood, D. A. and Maas, W. K. (1968). *J. molec. Biol.* **35**, 83.
Hofnung, M. (1974). *Genetics*, **76**, 169.
Holloway, B. W., Krishnapillai, V. and Stanisich, V. A. (1971). *A. Rev. Genet.* **5**, 425.
Hong, J. and Ames, B. N. (1971). *Proc. natn. Acad. Sci. U.S.A.* **68**, 3158.
Hopwood, D. A., Chater, K. F., Dowding, J. E. and Vivian, A. (1973). *Bact. Rev.* **37**, 371.
Isaac, J. H. and Holloway, B. W. (1968). *J. Bact.* **96**, 1732.
Isaac, J. H. and Holloway, B. W. (1972). *J. gen. Micobiol.* **73**, 427.
Issaly, I. M., Issaly, A. S. and Reissig, J. L. (1970). *Biochim. biophys. Acta*, **198**, 482.
Itiawa, H., Baumberg, S. and Vogel, H. J. (1968). *Biochim. biophys. Acta*, **159**, 547.
Jacob, F. and Monod, J. (1961). *Cold Spring Harb. symp. quant. Biol.* **26**, 193.
Jacoby, G. A. (1971). *J. Bact.* **108**, 645.
Jacoby, G. A. (1972). *Molec. gen. Genet.* **117**, 337.
Jacoby, G. A. and Gorini, L. (1967). *J. molec. Biol.* **24**, 41.
Jacoby, G. A. and Gorini, L. (1969). *J. molec. Biol.* **39**, 73.
Kadner, R. J. and Maas, W. K. (1971). *Molec. gen. Genet.* **111**, 1.
Karlström, O. and Gorini, L. (1969). *J. molec. Biol.* **39**, 89.
Kasai, T. (1974). *Nature, Lond.* **249**, 523.
Kinoshita, S., Nakayama, K. and Udaka, S. (1957). *J. gen. appl. Microbiol., Tokyo,* **3**, 276.
Kisumi, M., Kato, J., Sugiura, M. and Chibata, I. (1971). *Appl. Microbiol.* **22**, 987.
Kryzek, R. and Rogers, P. (1972) *J. Bact.* **110**, 945.
Laishley, E. J. and Bernlohr, R. W. (1968a) *Biochim. biophys. Acta,* **167**, 547.
Laishley, E. J. and Bernlohr, R. W. (1968b). *J. Bact.* **96**, 322.
Legrain, C., Halleux, P., Stalon, V. and Glansdorff, N. (1972). *Eur. J. Biochem.* **27**, 93–102.
Leisinger, T. and Vogel, H. J. (1969). *Biochim. biophys. Acta,* **182**, 572.
Leisinger, T., Haas, D. and Hegarty, M. P. (1972). *Biochim. biophys. Acta,* **262**, 214.
Lepesant, J.-A., Kunst, F., Lepesant-Kejzlarová, J. and Dedonder, R. (1972). *Molec. gen. Genet.* **118**, 135.
Lepesant, J.-A., Lepesant-Kejzlarová, J., Pascal, M., Kunst, F., Billault, A. and Dedonder, R. (1974). *Molec. gen. Genet.* **128**, 213.
Levinthal, M., Williams, L. S., Levinthal, M. and Umbarger, H. E. (1973). *Nature New Biol.* **246**, 65.
Maas, W. K. (1961). *Cold Spring Harb. Symp. quant. Biol,* **26**, 183.
Maas, W. K. (1972). *Molec. gen. Genet.* **119**, 1.
Maas, W. K. and Clark, A. J. (1964). *J. molec. Biol.* **8**, 365.
Maas, W. K., Maas, R., Wiame, J. and Glansdorff, N. (1964). *J. molec. Biol.* **8**, 359.
McGeoch, D., McGeoch, J. and Morse, D. (1973). *Nature New Biol.* **245**, 137.
McLellan, W. L. and Vogel, H. J. (1970). *Proc. natn. Acad. Sci. U.S.A.* **67**, 1703.
McLellan, W. L. and Vogel, H. J. (1972). *Biochem. Biophys. Res. Commun.* **48**, 1027.
Mahler, I., Neumann, J. and Marmur, J. (1963). *Biochim. biophys. Acta,* **72**, 69.
Marinus, M. G. and Loutit, J. S. (1969). *Genetics,* **63**, 557.
Meers, J. L. and Pedersen, L. K. (1972). *J. gen. Microbiol.* **70**, 277.
Meers, J. L. and Tempest, D. W. (1970). *Biochem. J.* **119**, 603.
Meers, J. L., Tempest, D. W. and Brown, C. M. (1970). *J. gen. Microbiol.* **64**, 187.
Metzenberg, R. L. (1972). *A. Rev. Genet.* **6**, 111.

Monod, J., Changeux, J.-P. and Jacob, F. (1963). *J. molec. Biol.* **6,** 306.

Monod, J., Wyman, J. and Changeux, J.-P. (1965). *J. molec. Biol.* **12,** 88.

Morris, D. R. and Jorstad, C. M. (1973). *J. Bact.* **113,** 271.

Novick, R. P. and Maas, W. K. (1961). *J. Bact.* **81,** 236.

Panchal, C. P., Bagchee, S. N. and Guha, A. (1974). *J. Bact.* **117,** 675.

Piérard, A., Glansdorff, N. and Yashpe, J. (1972). *Molec. gen. Genet.* **118,** 235.

Piérard, A., Glansdorff, N., Mergeay, M. and Wiame, J.-M. (1965). *J. molec. Biol.* **14,** 23.

Pouwels, P. H., Cunin, R. and Glansdorff, N. (1974). *J. molec. Biol.* **83,** 421.

Press, R., Glansdorff, N., Miner, P., DeVries, J., Kadner, J. and Maas, W. K. (1971). *Proc. natn. Acad. Sci. U.S.A.* **68,** 795.

Prozesky, O. W. (1968). *J. gen. Microbiol.* **54,** 127.

Prozesky, O. W. (1969). *J. gen. Microbiol.* **55,** 89.

Prozesky, O. W., Grabow, W. O. K., van der Merwe, S. and Coetzee, J. N. (1973). *J. gen. Microbiol.* **77,** 237.

Ramos, F., Stalon, V., Piérard, A. and Wiame, J.-M. (1967). *Biochim. biophys. Acta,* **139,** 98.

Rose, J. K., Squires, C. I., Yanofsky, C., Yang, H.-L. and Zubay, G. (1973). *Nature New Biol.* **245,** 133.

Rosen, B. P. (1973). *J. Bact.* **116,** 627

Sercarz, E. E. and Gorini, L. (1964). *J. molec. Biol.* **8,** 254.

Sherris, J. G., Shoesmith, J. G., Parker, M. T. and Breckon, D. (1959). *J. gen. Microbiol.* **21,** 389.

Shoesmith, J. G. and Sherris, J. C. (1960). *J. gen. Microbiol,* **22,** 10.

Squires, C. L., Rose, J. K., Yanofsky, C., Yang, H.-L. and Zubay, G. (1973). *Nature New Biol.* **245,** 131.

Stalon, V. (1972). *Eur. J. Biochem.* **29,** 36.

Stalon, V., Ramos, F., Piérard, A. and Wiame, J.-M. (1967). *Biochim. biophys. Acta,* **139,** 91.

Stalon. V., Ramos, F., Piérard, A. and Wiame, J.-M. (1972). *Eur. J. Biochem.* **29,** 25.

Syvanen, J. M. and Roth, J. R. (1972). *J. Bact.* **110,** 66.

Tabor, H. and Tabor, C. W. (1969). *J. biol. Chem.* **244,** 6383.

Taylor, A. L. and Trotter, C. D. (1972). *Bacteriol. Rev.* **36,** 504.

Udaka, S. (1966). *J. Bact.* **91,** 617.

Udaka, S. (1970). *Nature, Lond.,* **228,** 336.

Udaka, S. and Kinoshita, S. (1958). *J. gen. appl. Microbiol., Tokyo,* **4,** 272.

Urm, E., Yang, H., Zubay, G., Kelker, N. and Maas, W. K. (1973). *Molec. gen. Genet.* **121,** 1.

Voellmy, R. and Leisinger, T. (1972). *J. gen. Microbiol.* **73,** xiii.

Vogel, H. J. (1961). *Cold Spring Harb. Symp. quant. Biol.* **26,** 163.

Vogel, R. H. and Vogel, H. J. (1963). *Biochim. biophys. Acta,* **69,** 174.

Vogel, R. H., McLellan, W. L., Hirvonen, A. P. and Vogel, H. J. (1971). "Metabolic Regulation" (Ed. H. J. Vogel), p. 463. Academic Press, New York and London.

Vrancic, A. and Guha, A. (1973). *Nature New Biol.* **245,** 106.

Vyas, S. and Maas, W. K. (1963). *Archs. Biochem. Biophys.* **100,** 542.

Wade, H. E., Robinson, H. K. and Phillips, B. W. (1971). *J. gen. Microbiol.* **69,** 299.

Wiame, J.-M. (1971). *Curr. Topics in Cell Reg.* **4,** 1.

Williams, A. L. and Williams, L. S. (1973). *J. Bact.* **113,** 1433.

Williams, A. L., Yem, D. W., McGinnis, E. and Williams, L. S. (1973). *J. Bact.* **115,** 228.

Williams, L. S. (1973). *J. Bact.* **113,** 1419.
Wyche, J. H., Ely, B., Cebula, T. A., Snead, M. C. and Hartman, P. E. (1974). *J. Bact.* **117,** 708.
Young, F. E. and Wilson, G. A. (1971). "Spores V" (Eds H. O. Halvorson, R. E. Hanson and L. L. Campbell), p. 77. American Society for Microbiology, Bethesda, Md., U.S.A.
Young, F. E., Smith, C. and Reilly, B. E. (1969). *J. Bact.* **98,** 1089.

The regulation of enzyme synthesis in arginine metabolism of *Saccharomyces cerevisiae*

J. M. WIAME and E. L. DUBOIS

Institut de Recherches, CERIA, and Laboratoire de Microbiologie, Université Libre de Bruxelles, 1070 Brussels, Belgium

Summary

Arginase synthesis is regulated in several distinct ways.

1. Arginine, ornithine, lysine, α,γ-diaminobutyrate are inducers of the first two enzymes of the arginine catabolism: arginase and OTAase. Induction operates through a Jacob and Monod mechanism. Mutations which provoke constitutivity of these enzymes allow the characterization of this system. However, *Saccharomyces* has a regulatory mechanism which provides an exclusion between arginine catabolism and anabolism. This mechanism accounts for $argR^-$ mutations, which provoke constitutivity of the anabolic enzymes and the loss of induction of the catabolic enzymes.

2. In addition to substrate induction, a process of nitrogen catabolite repression which is independent of induction may be defined. In $argR^-$ and $cargA^+O^-$ (operator arginase) mutants, arginase synthesis is repressed by the good nitrogen nutrients: NH_4^+, glutamine and asparagine. Repression is abolished by the $gdhA^-$ mutation affecting the structural gene for the NADP-specific (anabolic) glutamate dehydrogenase. The effect of the $gdhA^-$ mutation does not seem to be due to its metabolic defect. No variation of metabolite pools can explain the derepression of arginase synthesis by itself. As enzyme levels do not change from a state of repression to derepression, NADP-specific glutamate dehydrogenase must act by receiving metabolic signals which are tentatively identified as NH_4^+ and α-ketoglutarate.

3. The behaviour of $cargA^+O^-\ gdhA^-$ mutation indicates the existence of an additional mechanism, termed synergism. This regulation operates when an inducer is present and nitrogen catabolite repression is released. Synergism

implies the ARGR integrity. We possess a $cargA^+O^h$ mutation which is constitutive not only towards induction but also towards synergism.

4. Addition of some amino acids provokes an increase of arginase synthesis. This fourth regulation, "nonspecific induction," is independent of induction and nitrogen catabolite repression.

Introduction

S. cerevisiae can synthesize and degrade arginine. Synthesis (anabolism) and degradation (catabolism) operate through the enzymatic steps described in Fig. 1. NH_4^+ can be used as the only nitrogen nutrient. Indeed, NH_4^+, with glutamine and asparagine, is the best nitrogen nutrient. The generation time of the strain $\Sigma1278b$, currently used in this laboratory, is 120 minutes at 29°C with each of these nitrogen sources. Glutamate, arginine and most amino acids support a slower growth rate. Their utilization as nitrogen sources involve a degradation which leads to the formation of NH_4^+. NH_4^+ is at least necessary to synthesize glutamine through glutamine synthetase. Glutamine and glutamate are the two most general nitrogen donors for biosyntheses.

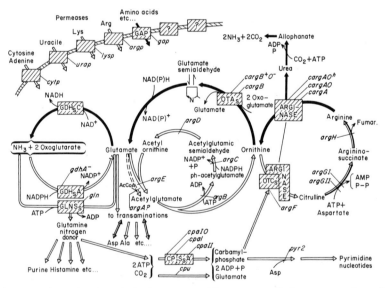

Fig. 1. Metabolism of arginine in *Saccharomyces cerevisiae*. ⟹ anabolic steps; ➡ catabolic steps; ⟹ mixed steps which operate when citrulline is used as the only source of nitrogen. A bent line such as ⌐ *argF* indicates a gene coding for the corresponding enzyme or a genetic element strongly linked with that gene, for instance *cargAO* for the operator of arginase, the first enzyme of the catabolic pathway. Table 1 lists mutations dealing with arginine metabolism.

In fungi, the conversion of glutamate into NH_4^+ involves two distinct glutamate dehydrogenases which have two distinct physiological functions (Fincham, 1957; Holzer and Schneider, 1957; Sanwal and Lata, 1961).

The NADP glutamate dehydrogenase is an anabolic enzyme (GDHase A). The *gdhA⁻* mutation which suppresses its activity reduces the growth rate on NH_4^+ while a normal growth is resumed if the mutation is compensated by addition of glutamate to NH_4^+ medium. The NAD glutamate dehydrogenase (GDHase C) is a catabolic enzyme; its synthesis is increased 40-fold when glutamate is used as the only nitrogen nutrient and has to be partially degraded into NH_4^+ to allow glutamine synthesis. It is likely that, in a *gdhA⁻* mutant growing slowly on NH_4^+, the GDHase C, present in small amounts, compensates partially for the lack of GDHase A (see Grenson and Hou, 1972, and Dubois *et al.*, 1973). The *gdhCR⁻* regulatory mutation which keeps GDHase C at a high level in spite of the presence of NH_4^+ allows the *gdhA⁻* mutants to grow at normal rate on NH_4^+ as sole nitrogen source (Grenson *et al.*, 1974).

Glutamine synthetase is essential for the biosynthesis of glutamine: *gln⁻* mutants which have no glutamine synthetase activity require glutamine for growth (Dubois and Grenson, 1974).

In this report we shall deal mainly with the regulation of the catabolism of arginine.

However, a brief account of the biosynthesis is necessary because *argR⁻* mutations which were selected as regulatory mutants of anabolic enzymes synthesis have been shown to affect the catabolic pathway. *argR⁻* mutations keep five of the seven known anabolic enzymes in a state of constitutivity and simultaneously keep the two first catabolic enzymes (Table 1) at a low and noninducible level. This is what one may logically expect for a regulatory element which provokes an exclusion between opposite concurrent pathways (Thuriaux *et al.*, 1968; Béchet *et al.*, 1970; Wiame, 1971). The way by which such a control might operate will be described in the sections on induction and synergy under Results and Discussion.

Results and discussion

Culture conditions, enzyme assays and selection of mutants have been described in previous publications as mentioned specifically later. The genealogy and characteristics of mutants are summarized in Fig. 2 and Table 1 (Wiame, 1973).

INDUCTION OF THE CATABOLIC PATHWAY

The arginine catabolic pathway in *S. cerevisiae* is under the control of a process of induction which operates on the two first enzymes: arginase and ornithine

TABLE 1

List of mutations and their main characteristics

We adopt a genetic nomenclature which is closer to the bacterial nomenclature than the official yeast genetic nomenclature.
Capitals of the first half of the alphabet distinguish classes of mutations which have been proved or are very likely to affect enzyme structural genes. However, the letter P is retained for permeases.
O⁻ indicates nonfunctional operator with indication of the structural gene affected by the mutation.
Capitals from the second half of the alphabet are used to differentiate classes of regulatory mutations.
If more than one class of mutations confer a very similar phenotype and are likely to affect the same biochemical function, the same capital is used followed by a roman number, for instance, mutations in both argGI and argGII genes affect the activity of argininosuccinate synthetase.

Mutation	Characteristics
$argA^-$?	The direct acetylation of glutamate has not yet been detected in yeast but it is likely to be necessary at least at a reduced rate to replenish the cyclic transacetylation of glutamate. Indeed some arginine auxotrophic mutants possess all other biosynthetic enzymes and are able to grow on ornithine or citrulline. Recently their auxotrophy was shown to be suppressed by acetylglutamate (Grenson, unpublished)
$argB^-$	(usual name *ar6*) Loss of acetylglutamate kinase activity; normal growth with ornithine, citrulline or arginine. The normal gene activity is repressed by 80% in the presence of arginine.
$argC^-$	(usual name *ar5*) Closely linked with *argB*. Loss of phosphoacetylglutamic semialdehyde dehydrogenase. 80% repression of normal gene activity by arginine.
$argD^-$	(*ar8*) Loss of acetylglutamic semialdehyde transaminase activity. Normal growth on ornithine, citrulline and arginine. 85% repression of normal gene activity by arginine.
$argE^-$	(*ar7*) Loss of acetylornithine glutamate transacetylase. Normal growth with ornithine, citrulline and arginine. The normal gene is not subject to regulation by arginine.
$argF^-$	(*ar3*) Loss of ornithine carbamoyltransferase activity. Normal growth with citrulline and arginine. 90% repression of normal gene activity by arginine.
$argGI^-$	(*ar1*) and $argGII^-$ (*ar10*) Two linked mutations. Both mutations provoke loss of argininosuccinate synthetase. Normal growth with arginine. The synthesis of this enzyme is 80% repressible by arginine in the wild type.
$argH^-$	(*ar4*) Loss of argininosuccinase. No repression of the normal gene by arginine.
$argRI^-$, $argRII^-$, $argRIII^-$	Three unlinked mutations, each one producing nonrepressibility of enzyme production coded by *argB*, *argC*, *argD*, *argF* and *argG*, and producing the incapacity to induce *cargA* and *cargB* gene products by arginine, ornithine and analogues. The products of the three normal genes can be interpreted as forming a heteropolypeptidic repressor (see text).
$cargA^-$	Loss of arginase activity. Normal gene subject to a number of regulatory mechanisms (see text).

TABLE 1—*contd.*

Mutation	Characteristics
$cargA^+O^-$	Operator constitutive mutation of $cargA^+$. Mutant insensitive to the presence of argine added to NH_4^+ medium (see text).
$cargA^+O^h$	As above but higher constitutivity.
$cargB^-$	Loss of ornithine transaminase activity. Normal gene subject to regulation (see text).
$cargB^+O^-$	Operator constitutive mutation of $cargB^+$. Mutant insensitive to the presence of inducer added to NH_4^+ medium.
$cargRI^-$, $cargRII^-$ and $cargRIII^-$	Three unlinked recessive mutations, each one producing a pleiotropic partial constitutivity for arginase and ornithine transaminase. The products of the three normal genes are interpreted as forming a heteropolypeptidic repressor for the catabolic pathway.
$cpaI^-$ and $cpaII^-$	Unlinked mutations coding for two polypeptides forming carbamoylphosphate synthetase belonging to the arginine pathway. $cpaII^-$ confers a complete loss of activity. $cpaI^-$ confers a loss of activity with glutamine as nitrogen donor without affecting the weak nonphysiological activity with NH_4^+ as nitrogen donor.
$cpaI^+O^-$	Operator partial constitutive mutation for $cpaI^+$.
$cpaR^-$	Recessive mutation producing a partial constitutivity of the arginine pathway carbamoylphosphate synthetase.
cpu^-	Loss of the activity of the carbamoylphosphate synthetase belonging to the pyrimidines pathway.
$gdhA^-$	Loss of NADP (anabolic) glutamate dehydrogenase (GDHase A) due to mutation in the structural gene for the enzyme.
$gdhCR^-$	Provokes a loss of NH_4^+ effect on the synthesis of the NAD (catabolic) glutamate dehydrogenase.
gln^-	Loss of activity of glutamine synthetase.

transaminase. Arginine, homoarginine, ornithine, lysine and α,γ-diaminobutyrate are inducers. Induction by arginine is independent of its transformation into ornithine. Arginaseless mutants retain induction by arginine of the second enzyme.

The control by induction is delineated by mutations which provoke constitutivity of these enzymes when cells are grown with NH_4^+ as nitrogen nutrient. Such mutations do not affect the growth rate.

These mutations are of three types. *Cis*-dominant mutations $cargA^+O^-$ and $cargB^+O^-$ indicate operator genetic elements for the two unlinked structural genes $cargA$ and $cargB$ coding respectively for arginase and ornithine transaminase. In both cases, addition of inducer does not increase the synthesis of the corresponding enzyme. Recessive pleiotropic mutations, $cargR$, provokes constitutivity for both enzymes. This constitutivity is not as high as in operator mutations and inducers retain the capacity to increase enzyme levels. Altogether these mutations suggest strongly that the Jacob and Monod type of regulatory process is present in microbial eukaryotic cells (Table 2).

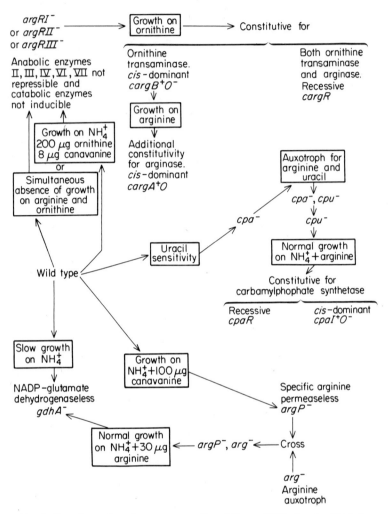

FIG. 2. Genealogy of regulatory mutants (from Wiame, 1973). See also Table 1.

At variance with what has been shown so far in prokaryotes, *Saccharomyces* has a regulatory mechanism which provides an exclusion balance between the catabolism of arginine and its biosynthesis (see, however, Baumberg, 1975). Evidence for such a mechanism came from the *argR⁻* mutations. These mutations were selected for constitutivity of anabolic enzymes such as ornithine carbamoyltransferase (Béchet *et al.*, 1970). The process of selection depends on canavanine resistance when cells are grown in a minimal medium supplemented with ornithine. The purpose of adding ornithine is to short-

TABLE 2
Induction of the catabolic pathway

Genotype	Name of strain	Nitrogen nutrient	Activities per mg of protein Arginase	Ornithine transaminase
1 wild type	Σ1278b	NH_4^+	6	0.4
2		NH_4^+ + arg	20	0.2
3		NH_4^+ + orn	20	0.2
4 *cargA$^+$O$^-$*	7204b	NH_4^+	138	0.04
5		NH_4^+ + arg	134	—
6 *cargB$^+$O$^-$*	7051a	NH_4^+	6	3.6
7		NH_4^+ + arg	—	4.1
8 *cargRI$^-$2*	0235b	NH_4^+	40	1.1
9		NH_4^+ + arg	92	1.7
10 *cargRII$^-$2*	14E7a	NH_4^+	46	0.5
11		NH_4^+ + arg	95	1.1
12 *cargRIII$^-$1*	20E9a	NH_4^+	34	0.7
13		NH_4^+ + arg	70	1.5
14 *argRII$^-$10*	BJ210	NH_4^+	3.6	0.03
15		NH_4^+ + arg	3.5	0.03
16 *cargRI$^-$* *cargRII$^-$* *cargRIII$^-$*	24E2b	NH_4^+	75	2.2

circuit the feedback inhibition of acetylglutamate kinase by arginine and, consequently, to allow a more effective competition between arginine and canavanine due to derepression of the last part of the biosynthetic enzymes, ornithine carbamoyltransferase and arginino-succinate synthetase.

argR$^-$ mutations not only provoke constitutivity of the anabolic enzymes but make the cell unable to degrade arginine and ornithine because arginase and ornithine transaminase are at a low noninducible level (Table 2). This property was used as a tool to select *cargR$^-$* mutations and also, sequentially, the *cargB$^+$O$^-$* and *cargA$^+$O$^-$* mutations mentioned above. These mutations overcome the effect of *argR$^-$* mutations. To avoid the trivial reversion of *argR$^-$* into *argR$^+$* the parent strain was made *argRI$^-$*, *argRII$^-$*.

Altogether, this led us to propose a reciprocal control of the anabolic and catabolic pathways as shown in Fig. 3 (Wiame, 1971). Although this control was not expected and was observed accidentally, it was a very logical one. It provides an automatic exclusion between the two concurrent pathways. In this model the molecule ARGR coded by *argR* genes is the common entrance of the signal for repression of anabolism and for induction of catabolism (Wiame, 1971). In that way, catabolism cannot be switched on without switching off anabolism. In the section on synergy we shall see that ARGR has an additional function.

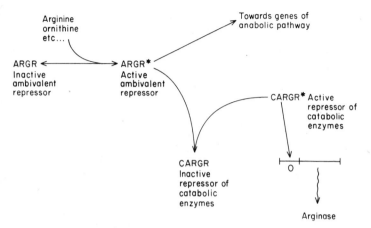

Fᴵɢ. 3. Cascade control of the arginine catabolic enzymes of *Saccharomyces cervisae*. Entrance of the metabolic signals into regulatory circuits is common for induction of catabolism and repression of anabolism. When activated, the common element (ARGR*) designated as ambivalent repressor, plays the role of inhibitor (or repressor) of the catabolic pathway specific repressor CARGR (from Dubois *et al.*, 1974, and Wiame, 1971).

argR⁻ mutations belong to three classes, *argRI⁻*, *argRII⁻* and *argRIII⁻*. The mutations of these classes have similar effects and, at present, it is difficult to assign to the corresponding genes other functions than to code for different polypeptides involved in the formation of a heteropolypeptidic repressor (Béchet *et al.*, 1970; Ramos *et al.*, 1970).

More mutations of the *cargR* type have been obtained recently. They also belong to different genetical classes: *cargRI⁻* (4 mutants), *cargRII⁻* (20) and *cargRIII⁻* (10). These mutants do not differ in their phenotypic properties and a combination such as *cargRI⁻*, *cargRII⁻*, *cargRIII⁻* has only a slight cumulative effect (Table 2). So far, we have not observed individual mutation or combination of mutations leading to arginase levels higher than 90 units per mg protein. Arginase operator mutations, with one exception to which we shall return later, uniformally confer an arginase level of 130 units. From these results and the ones mentioned above, one may think that eukaryotic repressors may frequently be heterpolypeptidic molecules (Deschamps, Dubois and Wiame, unpublished).

THE NITROGEN CATABOLITE REPRESSION OF ARGINASE

In addition to a control by substate induction, arginase is subject to other regulatory processes. One of them can be designated "nitrogen catabolite repression". The best way to distinguish this process from others is the effect of *gdhA⁻* mutations. These mutations affect the gene coding for the NADP (anabolic) glutamate dehydrogenase (GDHase A). This enzyme participates in the regulation of some nitrogen catabolite functions $gdhA^-$ mutations release the NH_4^+ inhibition (or repression) on the general amino acid permease (Grenson and Hou, 1972) and the repression of arginase observed when NH_4^+ or other good nitrogen sources such as glutamine or asparagine are present in the medium (Table 3, experiments 11, 14, 15 versus 1, 5, 6). The level of arginase is similar to the one obtained in a wild type or in a mutant strain growing with glutamate as sole nitrogen source (Table 3, experiment 12 versus experiment 8). The release of the NH_4^+ effect extends to other nitrogen catabolic enzymes such as allantoinase and urea amidolyase

TABLE 3

The nitrogen repression of arginase

	Genotype	Name of strain	Nitrogen nutrient	Activities per mg of protein Arginase	Ornithine transaminase
1	wild type	Σ1278b	NH_4^+	6	0.04
2			NH_4^+ + arginine	20	0.2
3			NH_4^+ + glutamate	8	0.04
4			arginine	250	8
5			glutamine	8	
6			asparagine	10	
7			chemostat NH_4^+ limited	35	0.12
8			glutamate	50	0.03
9			proline	20	
10			valine	63	
11	$gdhA^-$ 1	4324c	NH_4^+	40	
12			NH_4^+ + glutamate	35	0.035
13			NH_4^+ + proline	17	
14			NH_4^+ + glutamine	52	
15			NH_4^+ + asparagine	34	
16	$argRII^-$ 10	BJ210	NH_4^+	3.8	
17			NH_4^+ + glutamate	5	
18			glutamate	33	
19			chemostat NH_4^+ limited	15	
20	$cargA^+O^-$	7204b	NH_4^+	138	
21			NH_4^+ + glutamate	129	
22			glutamate	208	
23			chemostat NH_4^+ limited	222	
24	$argRII^-$ 10, $gdhA^-$	0315b	NH_4^+ + glutamate	17	
25	$cargA^+O^-$, $gdhA^-$ 1	0311a	NH_4^+ + glutamate	185	

o

(Dubois *et al.*, 1973). In contrast, the level of the second enzyme of the arginine catabolic pathway, ornithine transaminase, is not modified by the $gdhA^-$ mutation and this is in agreement with the fact that the level of transaminase does not increase when glutamate or proline replaces NH_4^+ as the nitrogen nutrient (Table 3, experiments 1, 8 and 12). It is worth recalling that total nitrogen starvation derepresses both arginase and transaminase (Middelhoven, 1967).

The NAD-(catabolic) glutamate dehydrogenase which is strongly repressed by NH_4^+ is not under the control of GDHase A.

A typical carbon catabolic enzyme, the α-glucosidase which is derepressed when galactose replaces glucose is unaffected by $gdhA^-$ mutations (Dubois *et al.*, 1973). In *Aspergillus nidulans*, a $gdhA^-$ mutation also causes the derepression of some nitrogen catabolic enzymes, such as xanthine dehydrogenase and nitrate reductase (Arst and MacDonald, 1973).

As mentioned above the $gdhA^-$ mutation allows us to define a regulatory process independent of substrate induction, because $gdhA^-$ mutations affect the level of arginase in mutants which have completely lost inducibility by arginine and ornithine (Table 2, experiments 14, 15). The combination of $argR^-$ and $gdhA^-$ provokes a three-fold increase of arginase synthesis, when compared to $argR$ mutants. In both cases, growth is performed on NH_4^+ + glutamate in order to permit comparison (Table 3, experiment 24 compared with 17). The high level of arginase in the arginase operator constitutive mutant is also increased in the presence of the $gdhA^-$ mutation (Table 3, experiment 25 compared with experiment 21). The combination of $gdhA^-$ with $cargR$ also gives rise to a large increase of arginase synthesis but this is not a useful tool because $cargR$ mutants retain some inducibility. Recently we have tried to understand the way in which GDHase A exerts its action. We have arrived at the following explanation: GDHase A itself, rather than the product of its catalytic function, is a regulatory molecule. Variations in the synthesis of GDHase A do not explain its action, because derepression may occur at constant GDHase A level. So metabolic signals are required. The enzyme is the receptor of metabolic signals which are its two substrates, NH_4^+ and 2 oxoglutarate. The physiological meaning of such a process is obvious. When GDHase A is working there is no reason to degrade elaborate nitrogen molecules. The experimental data which lead to this explanation can be briefly summarized as follows (Dubois *et al.*, 1974).

As already mentioned, the addition of glutamate to $gdhA^-$ mutants growing on NH_4^+ restores a normal rate of growth and a normal amino acids pool but not the repression of the afore-mentioned enzymes.

In addition, it has been shown that glutamine and asparagine which are even better nitrogen nutrients than NH_4^+ do not cancel the effect of a $gdhA$ mutation. As the pools of NADP or NADPH remain similar in condition of repression, of derepression and in a $gdhA^-$ mutant, a secondary effect due to a modification of the pool of these co-factors is unlikely The pool of NH_4^+ can be increased in a wild type strain by replacing glucose by lactate, or in an aconitaseless mutant by growing it on glucose $+ NH_4^+$; in both cases derepression of arginase occurs, showing that an intact GDHase A $+ NH_4^+$ is not a sufficient signal for repression and that another factor must have been changed. In both cases, the pool of 2 oxoglutarate is 3 to 4 times lower than in condition of repression (NH_4^+ + glucose). Conversely, a high pool of 2 oxoglutarate can be produced by growth on glutamate but, in this case, NH_4^+ is low. In an aconitaseless mutant, repression may be recovered by an appropriate nutrition which re-establishes a normal pool of 2 oxoglutarate, by growth on either NH_4^+ + glutamate or, better, on glutamine. Asparagine, which does not restore repression, keeps 2 oxoglutarate low.

So far repression only occurs when both NH_4^+ and 2 oxoglutarate pools are as high as in the wild type strain growing on NH_4^+ + glucose.

As glutamine synthetase is another important early step in NH_4^+ assimilation it was important to determine whether this enzyme does participate in the nitrogen catabolite repression. As mentioned above, glutamine is not the metabolic signal of nitrogen catabolite repression. However the enzyme itself could have been involved also in this regulation. The absence of effect on repression of a gln^- mutation which eliminates glutamine synthetase shows that this enzyme is not involved in the regulation of yeast nitrogen catabolism (Dubois and Grenson, in press). This is at variance with the catabolite repression of histidase in *Klebsiella aerogenes* (Tyler *et al.*, 1974).

SYNERGY BETWEEN THE PRESENCE OF INDUCER AND NITROGEN CATABOLITE
DEREPRESSION

Induction and "nitrogen (or ammonia) catabolite repression" of arginase can be distinguished by appropriate mutations. If these mechanisms are the only ones which control arginase synthesis, a $cargA^+O^-$ (operator constitutive) and $gdhA^-$ double mutant should give the maximum level of arginase synthesis when cells are growing on NH_4^+ + glutamate. As reported in Table 4, this is not the case; there is more arginase either in $gdhA^-$ growing on arginine and NH_4^+ (Table 4, experiment 3) or in $cargA^+O^-$ growing on arginine alone (Table 4, experiment 6) than in the double mutant growing on NH_4^+ + glutamate (Table 4, experiment 9). Obviously arginine which does not induce the operator constitutive mutant in the presence of NH_4^+ (section on induction of the catabolic pathway, p. 397, Table 2) can promote the synthesis when the NH_4^+ effect is released either by excluding NH_4^+ or by using a $gdhA^-$ mutant. This observation led us to propose that the inducer not only operates through a negative type of control involving operator–

TABLE 4

Synergy between the presence of inducer and nitrogen catabolite derepression in arginase synthesis

Genotype	Name of strain	Nitrogen nutrient†	Arginase activities per mg of protein
1 Wild type	Σ1278b	NH_4^+ + glutamate	8
2 $gdhA^-$ 1	4324c	NH_4^+ + glutamate	35
3		NH_4^+ + arginine	350
4		arginine	350
5 $cargA^+O^-$ 2	7204b	NH_4^+ + glutamate	130
6		arginine	355
7		ornithine	275
8		valine	288
9 $gdhA^-$ 1, $cargA^+O^-$ 2	0311a	NH_4^+ + glutamate	185
10 $cargA^+O^-$ 2, $cargB^+O^-$*	DH438	arginine	185–200
11 $argRI^-$ 2, $argRII^-$ 10		ornithine	170
12		valine	290
13 $cargA^+O^h$	7094a	NH_4^+	240
14		arginine	347
15		valine	433
16		proline	357
17		glutamate	332
18 $cargA^+O^h$, $cargB^+O^-$*	DH437	NH_4^+	240
19 $argRI^-$ 2, $argRII^-$ 10		arginine	340
20 $cargA^+O^h$, $gdhA^-$ 1	0325c	NH_4^+ + glutamate	353
diploids			
21 $\dfrac{cargA^+O^h, \alpha}{cargA^+O^+, \alpha}$		NH_4^+	110
22 $\dfrac{cargA^+O^h, a}{cargA^+O^+, \alpha}$		NH_4^+	30

* Introduction of operator constitutive mutation for ornithine transaminase ($cargB^+O^-$) in cells bearing $argR^-$ mutation allows the cell to use arginine and ornithine as sole nitrogen sources. Otherwise it has no action on arginase synthesis.

† 3 per cent glucose is the carbon source. Amino acids are given at 1 mg ml^{-1}. NH_4^+ is 0.05 M.

repressor interactions but also acts in a different way when the nitrogen catabolite repression is released. This mechanism was presented under the name "Synergism" (Wiame, 1973). Although evidence for the occurrence of synergy is based on experiments with mutants in which its action is rather limited, it is likely to be of a great physiological significance in the wild type strain. It is a very logical process. It keeps arginase production very limited when a substrate is present simultaneously with a good nitrogen nutrient. Conversely it limits arginase production when a need for nitrogen exists but no substrate to be degraded is available. When arginine is added to NH_4^+, induction leads to the synthesis of only 8 per cent of the amount of arginase that is produced in the presence of arginine alone (Table 2). Conditions of catabolite derepression by growth on proline or in a chemostat or in a $gdhA^-$ mutant growing on NH_4^+ + glutamate, causes only 8 to 15 per cent induction (Table 3). This behaviour is likely to be due to synergism. The real quantitative participation of synergism in normal cells is difficult to evaluate because NH_4^+ and GDHase A also control the penetration of the inducer into the cell (Grenson and Hou, 1972; Dubois *et al.*, 1974).

In the section on induction of the catabolic pathway, p. 397, it is shown that the process of induction by the negative type of control begins by the reception of the inducer on the ambivalent repressor ARGR and is followed by the transfer of this signal to the operators of catabolic genes through the catabolic repressor CARGR. It can be shown that synergism also implies the integrity of ARGR. $argR^-$ mutants loose both induction and synergism. A mutant $cargB^+O^-$, $cargA^+O2^-$ argRI, argRII (DH438), when grown on arginine alone, has 185 units of arginase, which is similar to the arginase level of a $cargA^+O^-$, $gdhA^-$ mutant growing on NH_4^+ + glutamate (Table 4, experiments 10 and 9). In the absence of $argR^-$ mutations, as in strain $cargA^+O^-$ growth on arginine, leads to a synthesis of 350 arginase units (Table 4, experiments 6 versus 10). So far there is no indication of a participation of CARGR in synergism (not reported here). Thus, ARGR is the first and common receptor for specific (substrate) induction as well as for synergism. The distinction between these two processes is based on the effect of arginase operator constitutive mutants which cancel induction but not synergism. There is another way to individualize these regulatory circuits. A number of operator constitutive mutants $cargA^+ O^-$ have been selected; all have around 130 units of arginase. One exceptional mutant has 240 units (Table 4, experiment 13). Genetic analysis shows that this mutation is strongly linked with the *cargA* gene and affects arginase only as an operator mutation does. Yet, this mutation has an unexpected property. In diploids, one expects 120 units of arginase, as indeed occurs in diploid $\alpha\alpha$ or aa, homozygotes for the mating type. However, the level of arginase is usually 30 in αa diploids. This low but significant constitutivity can be shown to result from a *cis* effect. Whatever the mechanism of this effect is, what is important for the present analysis, is the adjacence of this mutation with the *cargA* gene. The mutation is designated as $cargA^+O^h$, *h* meaning high constitutivity. Like other $cargA^+O^-$ mutants, this mutant is not more sensitive to the addition of arginine to NH_4^+ medium and is derepressed by $gdhA^-$ mutation. What is new in the effect of this mutation is that it is constitutive not only towards induction but also towards synergism. A combination of this mutation with the $gdhA^-$ mutation results in the same level of arginase during growth on NH_4^+ + glutamate as a $cargA^+O^-$ growing on arginine. In this mutant the presence of inducer is not required to reach the highest level (340 units). In agreement with that,

$argR^-$ mutations have no effect. The nitrogen catabolite repression is maintained.

The genetical combination $cargA^+O^h$, $gdhA^-$ cancels the mechanisms described in the sections on the induction of the catabolic pathway and on the nitrogen catabolite repression of arginase, and in this section. However, it can be seen in Table 4, experiment 15, that arginase level is highest in a $cargA^+O^h$ mutant growing on valine as sole nitrogen source. Valine is not a very good nitrogen nutrient and one expects a nitrogen catabolite derepression. However, this should not produce more than 350 units arginase as in the $cargA^+O^h$, $gdhA^-$ combination. Indeed, a long time ago, we observed that nitrogen catabolite derepression caused by valine is always higher than that obtained in a chemostat limited by NH_4^+ or by growth on proline or glutamate and yet the growth rate on valine is not lower than on proline. This point will be considered in the section on nonspecific induction.

The δ-ornithine transaminase is under a control by induction (section on the nitrogen catabolite repression of arginase) but contrary to arginase, this enzyme is not subject to nitrogen catabolite repression. The level of ornithine transaminase is similar in cells growing on NH_4^+ or on glutamate and is not affected by $gdhA^-$ mutations. However, it can be shown that ornithine transaminase is not under the sole control of induction by the process of repressor–operator interactions. As for arginase, the available operator constitutive mutants for ornithine transaminase no longer respond to the addition of inducer to NH_4^+ medium. However, when arginine is the only nitrogen nutrient, there is a two-fold increase in the level of ornithine transaminase which does not occur in the presence of the $argR$ mutation. Here again one can distinguish a control by substrate which is distinct from induction and is only expressed when no better substrate than arginine is available for the cell. This mechanism is similar to synergism in arginase synthesis, except that the catabolite derepression is not expressed by itself. We have seen that the increase in arginase level obtained by nitrogen catabolite derepression is only 8 to 15 per cent of the maximal arginase synthesis. For ornithine transaminase it is nil. Detailed results on this matter will be presented elsewhere.

NONSPECIFIC INDUCTION

Growth on valine as sole nitrogen source always leads to a higher arginase level than expected on the basis of a nitrogen catabolite derepression resulting from the fact that valine is not a good nitrogen nutrient. Valine produces 63 units of arginase instead of 35 in a $gdhA^-$ mutant growing on NH_4^+ + glutamate or in a wild type strain growing in a chemostat under sharp NH_4^+ limitation. This effect is due to a mechanism which can be designated as "nonspecific induction". It occurs when valine is added to a medium con-training NH_4^+. It has been shown in that case that valine does not reduce the NH_4^+ pool. This effect occurs in any genetical combination so far described, the most striking one being the presence of $argR^-$ mutations which abolish substrate specific induction. This unexpected effect has no immediate biological meaning but is important methodologically because it can operate in addition to other mechanisms. Occasionally, it is responsible for the production of more arginase in presence of valine than in presence of arginine, as shown in Table 4, experiment 12 versus experiment 10. In that case, the mutant $cargA^+O^-$, $gdhA^-$ is constitutive for induction, catabolically derepressed and constitutive for synergism but valine still leads to an additional production of arginase. This disturbing complication gains clear experimental support by an incidental finding disclosed by the following experiment: α,γ-diaminobutyrate, as an analogue of ornithine, is an inducer and this induction is lost in $argR^-$ mutants. In order to appreciate the contribution of the two amino groups of this compound, α-aminobutyrate and γ-aminobutyrate were tested for induction. γ-Aminobutyrate has no effect but α-aminobutyrate behaves as an inducer. However this induction in contrast to the one produced by α,γ-diaminobutyrate is not lost in $argR^-$ mutants. A systematic study using various amino acids has shown that many amino acids have some effect. Leucine and methionine are the best nonspecific inducers; they respectively cause the production of 26 and 32 arginase units in $argR^-$ mutants instead of 3 to 5 units when grown on NH_4^+ or in the presence of the specific inducer. Proline, glutamate and aspartate are very poor inducers. Part of the results have been presented elsewhere (Wiame, 1973); a more detailed account will be given later. Such effects have not been found for other enzymes like allantoinase, urea amidolyase, NAD and NADP glutamate dehydrogenase. Ornithine transaminase is poorly or not sensitive to this induction. Mutations which affect the nonspecific induction have not been found.

References

Arst, H. N. and MacDonald, D. W. (1973). *Molec. gen. Genet.* **122,** 261.

Baumberg, S. (1975). These Proceedings.

Béchet, J., Grenson, M. and Wiame, J. M. (1970). *Eur. J. Biochem.* **12,** 31.

Dubois, E., Grenson, M. and Wiame, J. M. (1973). *Biochem. biophys. Res. Commun.* **50,** 967.

Dubois, E. L. and Grenson, M. (1974). *Biochem. biophys. Res. Commun.* In press.

Dubois, E. L., Grenson, M. and Wiame, J. M. (1974). *Eur. J. Biochem.* In press.

Fincham, J. R. S. (1957). *Biochem. J.* **65,** 721.

Grenson, M. and Hou, C. (1972). *Biochem. biophys. Res. Commun.* **48,** 749.

Grenson, M., Dubois, E. L., Piotrowska, M., Drillien, R. and Aigle, M. (1974). *Molec. gen. Genet.* **128,** 73.

Holzer, H. and Schneider, S. (1957). *Biochem. Zeit.* **329,** 361.

Middelhoven, W. J. (1968). *Biochim. biophys. Acta,* **156,** 440.
Ramos, F., Thuriaux, P., Wiame, J. M. and Béchet, J. (1970). *Eur. J. Biochem.* **12,** 40.
Sanwal, B. D. and Lata, M. (1961). *Can. J. Microbiol.* **7,** 319.
Thuriaux, P., Ramos, F., Wiame, J. M., Grenson, M. and Béchet, J. (1968). *Archs Int. Physiol. Biochem.* **76,** 955.
Tyler, B., Delco, A. B. and Magasanik, B. (1974). *Proc. natn. Acad. Sci. U.S.A.* **71,** 225.
Wiame, J. M. (1971). "Current Topics in Cellular Regulation" (Eds B. L. Horecker and E. R. Stadtman), vol. 4, p. 1. Academic Press, New York and London.
Wiame, J. M. (1973). "Proceedings of the Third International Specialized Symposium on Yeasts"—Otaniemi-Helsinki, part II, p. 307.

The control of catabolism in *Aspergillus nidulans*

D. J. COVE

Department of Genetics, University of Cambridge, Cambridge, England

Summary

In *Aspergillus nidulans*, the enzymes which catabolize a particular metabolite are generally produced only when that metabolite is in excess. In addition, those metabolites which can serve as a carbon source are not usually catabolized if an alternative better carbon source is available. Analogously, those metabolites which can serve as a nitrogen source are not usually catabolized in the presence of ammonium, nor in some cases are they catabolized in the presence of nitrate. Where a metabolite can serve as a source of both carbon and nitrogen, then, provided it is present in excess, its catabolism is usually only prevented when both an inorganic nitrogen source and an alternative better carbon source are present.

To help understand how this complex pattern of regulation is achieved, mutants with abnormal regulatory characteristics have been selected. Most progress has been made with the system mediating ammonium repression. We conclude that the *areA* gene product is required for the syntheses of ammonium-repressible enzymes. Repression is achieved because ammonium inactivates the *areA* gene product. Another gene, *creA*, is involved in carbon catabolite repression. The mode of action of the *creA* gene is less clear, and further genes may also be involved.

The repression of certain catabolic activities by nitrate appears to involve the complex control system which regulates nitrate assimilation, such that catabolism does not normally occur when the enzymes of nitrate assimilation are induced. Preliminary studies indicate that uptake may be the target of this regulation.

Both ammonium and nitrate repression can under some circumstances be bypassed by the alleviation of carbon catabolite repression.

Introduction

The breakdown of metabolites to produce carbon- and/or nitrogen-containing intermediates is a well regulated process in a wide range of organisms. The mechanisms which mediate this control have been studied in both pro- and eukaryotes, but most progress has been made with *Escherichia coli* where some of the mechanisms involved have been characterized at the molecular level. Recently, however, progress has begun to be made towards understanding the way in which catabolism is controlled in fungi, and I shall attempt to review here work being carried out on *Aspergillus nidulans* to elucidate the cellular mechanisms involved.

In general, for the enzymes necessary for the catabolism of a particular metabolite to be produced at high levels, a number of conditions need to be fulfilled. Firstly the metabolite must be present. In some cases where the metabolite is a normal cellular constituent, it may be further deduced that a higher than normal pool size of the metabolite must be present in order to effect full induction of the catabolic enzymes. In addition to this pathway specific regulation, there are further general constraints. Where a compound can serve as a carbon source, the catabolic enzymes are usually subject to carbon catabolite repression, and where it serves as a nitrogen source, to repression by ammonium. Metabolites serving as both carbon and nitrogen sources are

TABLE 1

Summary of the control characteristics of five enzyme systems of *Aspergillus nidulans*

Enzymes of:	Specific control Induction by	Sensitivity to repression by Ammonium	Glucose	Reference
Purine catabolism	uric acid	yes	no	Darlington and Scazzocchio (1967); Scazzocchio and Darlington (1967, 1968); Scazzocchio (1973)
Nitrate assimilation	nitrate	yes	no	Cove (1966, 1967, 1969, 1970); Pateman and Cove (1967); Cove and Pateman (1969)
Ethanol oxidation	ethanol	no	yes	Page (1971); Page and Cove (1972)
Proline catabolism	proline	yes	yes	Arst and Cove (1973); H. N. Arst and D. W. MacDonald, unpublished data
Acetamide catabolism	acetamide	yes	yes	Hynes and Pateman (1970a, 1970b, 1970c); Hynes (1972); Dunsmuir and Hynes (1973)

often subject to both carbon catabolite and ammonium repression. I shall present evidence later in this paper that there may be a third general control system affecting catabolism in *Aspergillus nidulans*, involving repression by nitrate. Table 1 summarizes these effects for a number of systems, and gives references to the origin of the data; nitrate assimilation is not thought of as a

TABLE 2

Proline oxidase levels in wild-type strains of *Aspergillus nidulans*

Initial nitrogen source	Initial concentration of D-glucose %	Added after 16 h growth 5 mM L-proline	Added after 16 h growth 10 mM NH$_4^+$	Proline oxidase specific activity
100 mg dm^{-3}	1	no	no	3
uric acid	1	no	yes	2
	1	yes	no	167
	1	yes	yes	71
	0.3	no	no	7
	0.3	no	yes	2
	0.3	yes	no	297
	0.3	yes	yes	71

Mycelium was cultured according to the method of Cove (1966) for 21 hours with additions as indicated in the Table. Fresh mycelium was extracted by hand grinding in a mortar with powdered glass and ten times its weight of 0.1 M tris HCl buffer (pH 8.5) containing 0.5 M sucrose. The supernatant obtained after centrifugation at 12000 × g for 10 min was used as the cell-free extract. Proline oxidase was assayed by measurement of the rate of reduction of 2-(4-iodophenyl)-3-(4-nitrophenyl)-5-phenyltetrazolium chloride spectrophotometrically (D. W. MacDonald, unpublished data). Protein was determined by the Biuret method (Layne, 1957) and specific activities are given in nanomoles of substrate reduced per min per mg of protein.

catabolic activity but is included for later reference. Table 2 gives preliminary data for proline oxidase (D. W. MacDonald, unpublished results) which indicate that the various control constraints operate to some extent independently of one another, such that the highest activities are found in the presence of proline and limiting glucose, and absence of ammonium.

The specific control of individual catabolic pathways will not be reviewed here. Some are better characterized than others, and have been shown to involve relatively complex mechanisms. The references given in Table 1 describe what is known about the specific regulation of each system. Instead I shall concentrate on what I and my colleagues, in particular Dr H. N. Arst, have been finding out about the mechanisms of ammonium, carbon catabolite and nitrate repression.

Results and discussion

AMMONIUM REPRESSION

Most of the work summarized in this section has been described in greater detail by Arst and Cove (1973) and, except where indicated to the contrary, this reference should be consulted. As a result of evidence, much of which follows, we believe that a gene, designated *areA*, plays a central role in the mediation of ammonium repression. It is proposed that the *areA* gene specifies a product which allows (and in some cases is essential for) the expression of a large number of genes whose enzyme products are involved in the catabolism of nitrogen-containing metabolites. Ammonium represses the expression of these genes by inactivating the *areA* gene product. The evidence for this hypothesis is mainly genetical.

A number of mutant alleles of the *areA* gene have been isolated and characterized. Their effects are varied, and in many cases extremely pleiotropic. Thus *areA* 1 strains are unable to utilize a wide range of nitrogen sources including acetamide, adenine, L-alanine, allantoin, L-arginine, L-α-aminobutyrate, L-asparagine, L-aspartate, formamide, L-glutamate, glycine, 6-hydroxynicotinate, hypoxanthine, nicotinate, nitrate, nitrite, L-ornithine, L-phenylalanine, L-proline, L-serine, skimmed milk, L-threonine, and urate. They show a reduced ability to grow on ethylammonium, L-glutamine and urea, but grow almost as well as the wild type on ammonium. We conclude that the *areA* 1 mutation greatly impairs the function of the *are* product. We do not at present know what the effect of deleting the *areA* gene is, but it is possible that such deletion mutants might have a greatly reduced viability. Such a situation would occur for example if the uptake of ammonium was itself subject to ammonium repression, mediated by the *are* product. A deletion of the *areA* gene would then impair growth even on ammonium, and it might be difficult or perhaps impossible to devise a medium upon which such a strain could grow. Other mutant *areA* alleles with phenotypes similar to *areA* 1 have been obtained and for convenience we have called these *areA*[r] mutants. In addition we have isolated further alleles which are unable to use a narrower range of nitrogen sources. Such alleles would specify *areA* products which were less drastically affected than *areA* 1.

As well as alleles of the *areA*[r] type there are further *areA* alleles which have little effect on nitrogen source utilization, but which lead to insensitivity to ammonium repression of some catabolic activities. We have designated this class of alleles *areA*[d]. Examples of such alleles are *areA*[d]101 which leads to ammonium-insensitive production of extracellular protease, and *areA*[d]102 (formerly designated *amdT* 102) which leads to ammonium-insensitive synthesis of acetamidase. It is thought that such alleles specify an *areA* product which differs only slightly from the wild type, and which can function satisfactorily to promote enzyme synthesis, but which is impaired in its interaction with ammonium. A necessary corollary of the proposed mode of action of the *areA* gene product, is that it must therefore interact with each gene system which it controls in a slightly different manner, otherwise the heterogeneous effects of the various alleles could not be explained.

The isolation of alleles, some of which lead to a loss of gene expression, and others of which lead to derepressed gene expression, whilst providing strong evidence that the gene involved has a regulatory role, does not establish whether this role is positive or negative. That the *areA* gene product acts as a positive regulator, that is to say is required for, rather than prevents, gene expression is supported by two lines of evidence. Firstly dominance studies show that alleles of the $areA^r$ class which result in loss of gene function are recessive in both diploids and heterokaryons. With alleles of the $areA^d$ class, which lead to derepressed gene expression, dominance relationships are less straightforward. Dominance varies depending on which other *areA* allele is present. Diploids between $areA^d101$ and 102 on the one hand, and $areA^+$ on the other, have a phenotype intermediate between the corresponding homoallelic diploids. If $areA^r1$ replaces the $areA^+$ allele in the diploid, then diploids with $areA^d101$ more closely resemble $areA^r1$ homoallelic diploids, while diploids with $areA^d102$ more closely resemble $areA^d102$ homoallelic diploids. Whilst such a pattern of dominance is consistent with the *areA* gene playing a positive regulatory role, it indicates that further complications must exist. Two possibilities are either that the *areA* gene product forms a polymer, and subunit–subunit interactions occur to give in some cases negative intra-cistronic complementation, or that the *areA* product not only plays a positive regulatory role in the absence of ammonium, but also plays a negative role in preventing gene expression when ammonium is present. Diploids heterozygous for an *areA* gene deletion would help to resolve which of the alternatives is the more likely. Further support for the *areA* gene product playing a positive role is provided by the relative frequencies with which alleles leading to loss of function or to derepressed expression can be obtained. If the *areA* gene role were wholly negative, reversion of an $areA^r$ allele should yield a relatively high number of derepressed mutants. It does not however; $areA^d101$ is the only allele resulting in derepression, out of 268 revertants selected from $areA^r1$.

In summary we therefore conclude that ammonium repression of a large number of catabolic activities is mediated by the *areA* gene product, which is required for the expression of many genes which specify catabolic enzymes. In the presence of ammonium the *areA* gene product is either inactive or actively prevents expression of these same genes.

Genetic studies have also shed considerable light on how the *areA* gene product interact with pathway specific regulation systems. Double mutants containing an *areA* allele, which prevents growth on nitrate, and an *nir* allele which results in constitutive synthesis of nitrate and nitrite reductase, are still unable to grow on nitrate. (The *nir* gene specifies a positive regulatory element controlling nitrate assimilation—see below and references given in Table 1.) Double mutants containing an *areA* allele which results in ammonium-insensitive nitrate reductase synthesis, and an *nir* allele which results in non-inducible synthesis, are also unable to grow on nitrate. Thus it is likely that both the pathway specific regulator specified by the *nir* gene, and the *areA* gene product must be active for the enzymes of nitrate assimilation to be synthesized. Similar studies reveal that the situation is broadly similar for the xanthine dehydrogenase I/urate oxidase system and for the nicotinate catabolic pathway. For the acetamidase system, however, it can be shown that there can be no absolute requirement for *areA* product. Not only are double mutants containing a mutant *areA* allele which normally prevents growth on acetamide, and a mutation leading to constitutive synthesis of acetamidase able to grow to a certain extent on acetamide, but also mutant *areA* strains such as *areA*1, which cannot utilize acetamide as a nitrogen source in the presence of 1 per cent D-glucose, can use it as a combined nitrogen and carbon source in the absence of glucose. A similar situation holds for a number of other metabolites which can serve as both carbon and nitrogen source. The significance of these observations will be discussed further, when the mechanism of carbon catabolite repression is considered below.

Finally in this section, I wish to consider another aspect of the interaction between the *areA* gene product, and individual catabolic systems. Reversion of *areA* alleles can occur not only as a result of mutation within the *areA* gene, but also as a result of the accumulation of a mutation in a second gene. Such suppressed *are* strains are not able to utilize all nitrogen sources, and some are only able to use the nitrogen source upon which the revertant was selected. The best characterized example of such a strain is one which has only regained the ability to utilize proline. Genetic analysis reveals that this strain carries in addition to the original *areA*ʳ mutation, a proline-specific suppressor which maps between the *prnA* and *B* genes, the structural genes specifying the enzymes of proline catabolism and uptake (H. N. Arst, unpublished data). This suppressor only affects structural genes *cis* to it in the genetic material, and so it is likely that some mutation of the operator constitutive type is involved which at least partially bypasses the requirement for the *areA* gene product.

CARBON CATABOLITE REPRESSION

Carbon catabolite repression whereby glucose and other readily utilizable sugars, such as sucrose and D-xylose, reduce the catabolism of various metabolites can be studied in various ways in *Aspergillus nidulans*. It will be seen from

the levels of proline oxidase given in Table 2 that raising the concentration of
D-glucose from 0.3 to 1 per cent results in an approximate halving of the
proline oxidase specific activity. The effect on enzymes involved in the
catabolism of metabolites which can serve only as a carbon source may be
more drastic. For example, the specific activity of alcohol dehydrogenase is
reduced by more than 98 per cent when 1 per cent D-glucose replaces 0.1 per
cent D-fructose (C. R. Cailey and H. N. Arst, unpublished data).

Mutations which result in an altered pattern of carbon catabolite repression
have been selected using two different methods (Arst and Cove, 1973; C. R.
Bailey and H. N. Arst, unpublished data). When *areA* strains unable to utilize
proline are reverted, as well as *are*$^+$ revertants, and revertant strains containing
the pathway specific suppressor mutation, a third class of revertants are
obtained which have regained the ability to utilize not only proline, but also
acetamide. Genetic analysis of this third class of revertants reveals that they
too contain a suppressor mutation retaining the original *areA* mutation. These
suppressor mutations designated *creA*^{d} have occurred in a gene which is
linked to neither the *prn* genes nor to *amdS*, the structural gene for acetamidase
(Dunsmuir and Hynes, 1973). On its own the suppressor mutation reduces the
sensitivity to carbon catabolite repression of some but not all normally carbon

TABLE 3

Carbon catabolite repression in wild-type and *creA*^{d}1 strains

Strain	Status with respect to carbon catabolite repression	Specific activities			
		Alcohol dehydro- genase	β-galactosidase	Quinate dehydro- genase	Proline oxidase
wild type	derepressed	118	6.3	117	89
wild type	repressed	2	0.3	22	59
creA^{d}1	derepressed	126	6.2	135	73
creA^{d}1	repressed	84	0.2	15	85

Unpublished data of C. R. Bailey and H. N. Arst. Mycelium was cultured for from 21 to 27 hours,
harvested and extracted according to the general method of Cove (1966). Specific growth conditions were: initial nitrogen source—100 mg dm^{-3} uric acid for proline oxidase, 10 mM NaNO$_3$
for other enzymes; initial carbon source for (a) carbon catabolite derepression 0.1 per cent
D-glucose for proline oxidase, 0.1 per cent D-fructose for other enzymes; (b) carbon catabolite
repression—1 per cent D-glucose. Alcohol dehydrogenase, β-galactosidase and quinate dehydrogenase were induced by the inclusion of 1 per cent (volume for volume) ethanol, 1 per cent
lactose and 0.3 per cent D-quinate, respectively, in the initial growth medium and proline oxidase
was induced with 5 mM L-proline added to the growth medium 5 hours before harvesting. Enzymes
were extracted and assayed by the following methods: alcohol dehydrogenase (Page, 1971);
β-galactosidase (Wallenfels, 1962); quinate dehydrogenase (Mitsuhashi and Davis, 1954);
proline oxidase (D. W. MacDonald, unpublished)—see legend to Table 2. Protein was measured
by the Biuret method (Layne, 1957), and specific activities are given in nanomoles of substrate
removed or product formed per min per mg of protein.

catabolite repressible enzymes (C. R. Bailey and H. N. Arst, unpublished results). Table 3 gives representative data for a number of enzymes of the sensitivity of wild type and *creA*^d mutant strains to carbon catabolite repression. Presumably the basis of suppression of *areA*^r mutations by *creA*^d mutations is that the latter have rendered the cell at least partially insensitive to carbon catabolite repression, thus bypassing the need for the *areA* product by the proline and acetamide catabolic systems. It will be recalled that *areA* mutants, unable to utilize metabolites such as proline as nitrogen sources in the presence of 1 per cent D-glucose, can utilize such metabolites as both carbon and nitrogen sources in the absence of glucose (Arst and Cove, 1973). This finding provides further evidence that the alleviation of carbon catabolite repression can bypass the requirement for the *areA* gene product.

creA^d mutations do not, however, suppress the effects of *areA*^r mutations on the utilization of other metabolites which can serve as both carbon and nitrogen sources such as L-alanine, L-arginine and L-glutamate, even though *areA*^r mutant strains can grow on such compounds in the absence of glucose. This correlates with the finding that whereas *areA*^r strains are able to use proline and acetamide as nitrogen sources in the presence of carbon sources such as L-arabinose, glycerol, melibiose, lactose and ethanol, they cannot use other compounds such as L-alanine, L-arginine or L-glutamate as nitrogen sources under similar circumstances. A possible explanation of both this, and the ability of *areA*^r *creA*^d double mutants to utilize only proline and acetamide, is that catabolism of these compounds is less sensitive to carbon catabolite repression than are other catabolic systems.

Further *in vivo* confirmation that mutations in the *creA* gene can relieve the sensitivity of ethanol catabolism to carbon catabolite repression is provided by an analysis of the phenotype of *pdhA*1 *creA*^d double mutants. *pdhA*1 strains lack the enzyme pyruvate dehydrogenase (Romano and Kornberg, 1968 and 1969), and consequently need a source of acetate. Ethanol can substitute for acetate but only in the absence of carbon catabolite repression. Thus a *pdhA*1 strain can grow on ethanol as carbon source, but not on ethanol + D-glucose. *pdhA*1 *creA*^d strains can utilize ethanol even in the presence of D-glucose, providing further evidence that the *creA*^d mutation has rendered the cell insensitive to carbon catabolite repression.

This finding has provided the basis of an alternative method of selecting mutants insensitive to carbon catabolite repression (C. R. Bailey and H. N. Arst, unpublished data). If *pdhA*1 strains are reverted on ethanol + D-glucose, at least some of the strains obtained retain the original *pdhA*1 mutation, and have additionally suppressor mutation, which can be shown to be allelic to the *creA* mutants. When crossed to *areA*^r strains, these new *creA*^d mutations can be shown to suppress not only *pdhA*1 but also *areA*^r, but only for proline and acetamide utilization.

Bailey and Arst have shown that not all carbon catabolite repressible activities are derepressed in $creA^d$ strains. Thus quinate dehydrogenase and β-galactosidase are still sensitive to carbon catabolite repression in the $creA^d$ strains so far examined (see Table 3 for data). It is not possible at the present time to say whether this indicates that there are other genes, as well as $creA$, involved in mediating carbon catabolite repression, or, if instead, the $creA$ alleles selected so far have for some reason a restricted specificity. It has not yet been possible to obtain $creA$ mutations which render the cell unable to catabolize carbon sources (C. R. Bailey, unpublished data), although if the $creA$ gene product had some vital role, the selection of such mutants might be impossible. Finally, it has not yet been possible to implicate cyclic AMP in carbon catabolite repression in *Aspergillus nidulans*, as has been done in *Escherichia coli* (Contesse et al., 1970). It is probable that *Aspergillus nidulans* is unable to take up 3′, 5′ cyclic AMP, as this compound cannot be used to repair adenine auxotrophs, nor can it serve as a nitrogen source, whereas 5′ AMP can do both. Attempts to select mutants able to use 3′, 5′ cyclic AMP as an adenine source have so far been unsuccessful (D. J. Cove and H. N. Arst, unpublished results).

NITRATE REPRESSION

The final general control system I wish to discuss is both less well characterized at present, and likely to be more complex than the ammonium and carbon catabolite repression systems. There is evidence that nitrate, like ammonium and glucose, causes a shut-down in catabolism. Direct evidence is difficult to obtain, but strains carrying mutations which eliminate nitrite reductase (*niiA*), and which are therefore unable to use nitrate as a nitrogen source (Pateman et al., 1967), show a greatly reduced ability to utilize certain other nitrogen sources in the presence of nitrate (D. J. Cove, unpublished results). The most drastic effects so far detected occur with L-ornithine and L-glutamate. It is unlikely that toxicity, due to the accumulation of nitrite, is the cause of this effect, as the morphology of *niiA* strains growing in the presence of nitrate on ornithine or glutamate is typical of nitrogen starvation, rather than inhibition as a result of the accumulation of a toxic intermediate. Furthermore, nitrate has no effect on the utilization by *niiA* strains of some other metabolites such as uric acid. Nitrate reductase levels in mycelium of wild type or *niiA* strains are similar whether the mycelium has been cultured on glutamate + nitrate or uric acid + nitrate (D. J. Cove, unpublished results). Chlorate, which is a reasonably close structural analogue of nitrate, also has an effect on catabolism qualitatively similar to, but more drastic than that of nitrate in *niiA* strains, but space does not permit a detailed account of its action here.

Since nitrate has little effect on the utilization as nitrogen sources by *niiA* strains of compounds metabolized by the same pathway, such as L-arginine and L-proline, the inhibition of L-ornithine and L-glutamate utilization is most likely to be at the uptake level. Amino acid uptake studies are now in hand and preliminary results (D. W. MacDonald, and D. J. Cove, unpublished results) indicate that nitrate reduces ornithine uptake by between 60 per cent and 90 per cent.

As a result of studies on mutant strains affected in the synthesis and control of nitrate reductase, it seems likely that the effect of nitrate on ornithine and glutamate utilization is mediated by way of the control system which controls nitrate assimilation. When the enzymes of nitrate assimilation are induced, the utilization of ornithine and glutamate is reduced. The system controlling nitrate assimilation in *Aspergillus nidulans* is complex involving not only the *nir* regulatory gene, but also the nitrate reductase molecule itself (Cove, 1970). The *nir* product acts in a positive manner, being required for the expression of the structural genes specifying nitrate and nitrite reductase. The nitrate reductase molecule is thought to act as the component of the regulation system which provides the nitrate recognition site, such that in the absence of nitrate, nitrate reductase prevents the *nir* product from functioning. Mutations in the nitrate reductase structural gene (*nia*) which abolish nitrate reductase activity are of two types. A minority (designated *nia*^{i}) retain the wild type pattern of nitrate inducibility of nitrite reductase, indicating that the mutant nitrate reductase produced by such strains retains its control capabilities, whereas a majority (designated *nia*^{c}) now synthesize nitrite reductase (and where detectable, mutant nitrate reductase) constitutively. Examination of utilization of ornithine and glutamate by *nia* strains reveals a correlation with their control status. "Constitutive" *nia* strains show reduced growth on these amino acids, whereas "inducible" *nia* strains are similar to wild type. This effect is not confined to these two amino acids and is observable to some extent on a wide range of nitrogen-containing metabolites. If *nia* strains are grown on ornithine or glutamate in the presence of nitrate, no inhibitory effect is observed with *nia*^{c} strains, whereas *nia*^{i} strains show reduced growth in the same way as *niiA* strains. Furthermore *nia*^{c} mutations protect *niiA* strains against this effect of nitrate, while *nia*^{i} mutations do not. It therefore seems likely that just as it plays a role in controlling nitrate assimilation, the nitrate reductase molecule also plays a role in controlling at least some parts of amino acid catabolism. The reduced utilization of nitrogen compounds by *nia*^{c} mutants, which include *nia* deletions, is consistent with nitrate reductase being required for the full catabolism of these compounds, nitrate having its effect on catabolism by preventing nitrate reductase playing its positive role.

Preliminary studies of ornithine uptake (D. W. MacDonald and D. J. Cove, unpublished data) provide support for the regulatory involvement of nitrate reductase. Reduced levels of ornithine uptake are present in nia^c strains, but this uptake is insensitive to nitrate repression. It is likely that the nitrate reductase molecule does not play a direct, positive role in regulating catabolism. Strains carrying mutations in the *nir* regulator gene which lead to noninducibility of the enzymes of nitrate assimilation (nir^- mutants) and which hence lack nitrate reductase, are unimpaired in their utilization of nitrogen sources. Such strains are also insensitive to the inhibitory effects of nitrate on ornithine and glutamate utilization. nir^- nia^i and nir^- *niiA* double mutant strains are as insensitive to the effects of nitrate as nir^- single mutants. These results are consistent with the nitrate reductase molecule playing the same positive role in catabolic regulation as it does in the regulation of nitrate assimilation, that is to say the inactivation of the *nir* gene product. It follows then that the *nir* gene product must play a negative role and prevent full catabolism of ornithine and glutamate, although this negative role need not necessarily be direct.

There is evidence that carbon catabolite repression interacts with nitrate repression in a way similar to that with which it interacts with ammonium repression. nia^c strains are indistinguishable from wild-type and nia^i strains when D-glucose is omitted from the medium, and L-ornithine and L-glutamate serve as carbon as well as nitrogen sources. Furthermore the utilization of ornithine and glutamate by nia^i and *niiA* strains is unaffected by nitrate when D-glucose is absent from the medium. Thus it seems that not only ammonium repression but also nitrate repression can be alleviated when carbon catabolite repression is relieved.

The independent action of nitrate and ammonium in the shut-down of catabolism perhaps arose as a result of nitrate assimilation itself being sensitive to ammonium repression. When growing on nitrate, ammonium pool sizes sufficient to repress catabolic activities also repress nitrate assimilation, and so either the relative thresholds at which ammonium repression became operative would have had to become modified, or an alternative system of catabolic control would need to evolve.

Conclusions

Although some of the results presented in this paper are preliminary, the general pattern of how catabolic activities are controlled in *Aspergillus nidulans* is emerging. Individual control systems generally working in a positive mode, allow the enzymes of a particular pathway to be synthesized only when excess metabolite is present. General control systems ensure that the rate of catabolism is modulated according to whether alternative better sources of nitrogen and carbon are present. These general control systems regulate not only the amount of catabolic enzymes produced, but also the amount of transport into the cell. At least in the case of ornithine we know that although transport is reduced considerably in the presence of both ammonium and nitrate, it is not eliminated completely, as neither ammonium (Arst and Cove, 1973) nor nitrate (D. J. Cove, unpublished results) prevent the repair of ornithine auxotrophies by exogenous ornithine. Thus it seems that transport of a metabolite into the cell is kept at such a level that only the cell's biosynthetic needs are satisfied, unless alternative sources of carbon or nitrogen are limiting, in which case transport is increased and catabolism proceeds.

Acknowledgements

I wish to thank the Science Research Council, who financed much of the work reported in this paper, and my colleagues, in particular Dr H. N. Arst and Dr D. W. MacDonald, for allowing me to use their unpublished data.

References

Arst, H. N., Jr. and Cove D. J. (1973). *Molec. gen. Genet.* **126**, 111.
Contesse, G., Crepin, M., Gros, F., Ullmann, A. and Monod, J. (1970). "The Lactose Operon" (Eds J. R. Beckwith and D. Zipser), p. 401. Cold Spring Harbour Laboratory, New York.
Cove, D. J. (1966). *Biochim. biophys. Acta (Amst.)* **113**, 51
Cove, D. J. (1967). *Biochem. J.* **104**, 1033.
Cove, D. J. (1969). *Nature Lond.* **224**, 272.
Cove, D. J. (1970). *Proc. R. Soc. Lond. B.* **176**, 267.
Cove, D. J. and Pateman, J. A. J. (1969). *J. Bacteriol.* **97**, 1374.
Darlington, A. J. and Scazzocchio, C. (1967). *J. Bacteriol.* **93**, 937.
Dunsmuir, P. and Hynes, M. J. (1973). *Molec. gen. Genet.* **123**, 333.
Hynes, M. J. (1972). *J. Bacteriol.* **111**, 717.
Hynes, M. J. and Pateman, J. A. J. (1970a). *Molec. gen. Genet.* **108**, 97.
Hynes, M. J. and Pateman, J. A. J. (1970b). *Molec. gen. Genet.* **108**, 107.
Hynes, M. J. and Pateman, J. A. J. (1970c). *J. gen. Microbiol.* **63**, 317.
Layne, E. (1957). "Methods in Enzymology, vol. III" (Eds S. P. Colowick and N. O. Kaplan), p. 447. Academic Press, New York and London.
Mitsuhashi, S. and Davis, B. D. (1954). *Biochem. biophys. Acta,* **15**, 268.
Page, M. M. (1971). Ph.D. Thesis, University of Cambridge, England.
Page, M. M. and Cove, D. J. (1972). *Biochem. J.* **127**, 17P.
Pateman, J. A. J. and Cove, D. J. (1967). *Nature, Lond.* **215**, 1234.
Pateman, J. A. J., Rever, B. M. and Cove, D. J. (1967). *Biochem. J.* **104**, 103.
Romano, A. H. and Kornberg, H. L. (1968). *Biochim. biophys. Acta,* **158**, 491.
Romano, A. H. and Kornberg, H. L. (1969). *Proc. R. Soc. Lond. B.* **173**, 475.
Scazzocchio, C. (1973). *Molec. gen. Genet.* **125**, 147.
Scazzocchio, C. and Darlington, A. J. (1967). *Bull. Soc. Chim. biol. (Paris)* **49**, 1503.
Scazzocchio, C. and Darlington, A. J. (1968). *Biochim. biophys. Acta,* **166**, 557.
Wallenfels, K. (1962). "Methods in Enzymology, vol. V" (Eds S. P. Colowick and N. O. Kaplan), p. 212. Academic Press, New York and London.

Regulation of bacterial sporulation

K. F. BOTT
Department of Bacteriology and Immunology, University of North Carolina, Chapel Hill, 27514, USA

Summary

Endospore formation like other forms of cellular differentiation is a complex process in which several new classes of messenger RNA are synthesized at precisely the right time to assure successful completion of a series of pleiotropic events. Spore-specific changes appear continuously throughout the process, though apparently not just in association with the synthesis of new classes of messenger RNA. During the process many enzymatic functions characteristic of vegetative metabolism continue to be expressed and help to stabilize the normal metabolic activities of the sporangium. There is still disagreement over the reports that a stable class of messenger RNA is involved.

Although several aspects of transcriptional control for the process have been elucidated, including structural modifications to the DNA dependent RNA polymerase and changes of sigma factors associated with it, an apparent paradox has also developed. Sporulation appears to be one of the few representatives of differentiating processes in which the transcriptional controls are not regulated by cyclic AMP or its close relatives. The actual molecular events which do regulate it are not known. Some evidence suggests this might be the role played by the liberation of cyclic peptide antibiotics always associated with early spore-specific metabolism. Sporulation is also known to be regulated at the level of *translation* since structural alterations of ribosomes, induction of new translation factors, and changes in soluble enzyme components accompany the spore-specific changes and progressively reduce the effectiveness of the protein synthesizing apparatus on vegetative mRNA. It remains to be shown that these same changes enhance the efficiency of a sporulation-specific mRNA. *Post-translational* modification of proteins is a third important aspect of the regulation of sporulation. Current evidence suggests that for several distinctly different enzymes, the vegetative form and spore form (unlike in size, shape and three-dimensional structure) may be derived from the same polypeptide. These studies are especially relevant to our understanding of the manner in which genetic information is expressed since the current evidence favours an interpretation that more than one structural form of certain enzymes is coded by a single gene.

Introduction

Since the time of Louis Pasteur and Ferdinand Cohn, the bacterial endospore has been the subject of experimental interest because of its structural and functional uniqueness (Sussman and Halvorson, 1966; Gould and Hurst, 1969). Although a few species pose a threat to man because of their patho-genicity, the sporulating organisms have been of scientific interest mainly for other purposes (Gould and Hurst, 1969). Since the bacterial spore is recognized as an extremely resistant biological structure and capable of maintaining the state of cryptobiosis for hundreds of years, efficient means of controlling the process of sporulation have always been of interest to industrial food processors. It is now known that intermediate stages in the sporulation process can be exploited for industrial purposes. These include the production of antibiotics, proteolytic enzymes, ecologically safe insecticides and many other compounds (Sussman and Halvorson, 1966; Gould and Hurst, 1969; Rogoff and Yousten, 1969; Vanek et al., 1973). Some sporulating organisms have been exploited because of their ability to synthesize a cellular product that is characteristic of the vegetative stage of growth (Vaněk et al., 1973). In those instances appropriate cultivation conditions must be devised to prevent sporulation from occurring. The academician has been prompted to study the process of sporulation because it represents a unicellular system capable of phenotypic differentiation (Halvorson, 1965; Sussman and Halvorson, 1966; Murrell, 1967; Freeze, 1972; Szulmajster, 1973). In any case, both the industrially and academically prompted motivations for studying sporulation have now arrived at the realization that a thorough understanding of the genetic regulation of endospore formation might better enable man to exploit these bacteria for his own purpose. Whether the ultimate goal is preventing sporulation to enhance production of vegetative functions, exploiting one of the intermediates of the sporulation process, destroying the fully mature spores in commercially useful products, or enabling the artificial control of all processes of cellular differentiation for man's benefit, the in-depth understanding of sporulation required for successful genetic manipulation of these species has become a necessity (see also Halvorson et al., 1972).

It is the purpose of this paper to review some of the more important bio-chemical mechanisms which are currently thought to regulate expression of spore-specific functions.

Results and discussion

TRANSCRIPTION

Bacterial sporulation leads to the biosynthesis of many new macromolecules, including enzymes, antigens and structural proteins, each of which can be synthesized only when the unique mRNA molecule encoding its structure has been produced (Halvorson, 1965; Halvorson et al., 1966; Murrell, 1967; Szulmajster, 1973). Many of these components are not detectable during vegetative growth, in asporogenic mutants, or during stationary phase metabolism under nonsporulating conditions. Usually these spore-specific alterations can be produced or "triggered" only after cessation of exponential growth. Their synthesis is categorically described as being under catabolite repression since they require the simultaneous presence of a carbon and nitrogen source to remain repressed during vegetative growth (Schaffer et al., 1965). The early events of sporulation can be initiated only in cells where this repression is lifted *and* where the existing round of DNA synthesis can be completed under these "starvation" conditions. Once the repression is lifted, a rapid turnover of RNA occurs. The actual molecular event (or events) which initiated this change is not known (Mandelstam, 1969; Halvorson et al., 1972; Szulmajster, 1973).

At least 100 structural and regulatory genes are known to be involved in sporulation (Halvorson, 1965; Young and Wilson, 1972). However, there is no evidence that any single genetic segment is reserved solely for the genes coding for sporulating functions. Therefore a single operon model of coordinated induction or repression cannot be used to explain the regulation of bacterial sporulation (Mandelstam, 1969).

Sterlini and Mandelstam (1969) pulsed *B. subtilis* cultures with actinomycin D at intervals after inducing sporulation. Their results have been interpreted as demonstrating that several distinct classes of spore specific message are produced because the pulse permitted expression of certain functions in the temporal sequence but not of others. Aronson (1965), Yamakawa and Doi (1971) and Gould and Hurst (1969) have also provided evidence that unique spore-specific messenger RNA is required.

Populations of cells rapidly become defective in their ability to synthesize phage SP01-specific RNA during the transition period from exponential growth to sporulation (Losick and Sonenshein, 1969; Sonenshein, 1970; Losick, 1972). This defect has been associated with observations that *in vitro* the DNA-dependent RNA polymerase loses its ability to transcribe phage DNA while retaining its ability to direct RNA synthesis from the synthetic copolymer poly dA-dT (Losick, 1972; Brevet and Sonenshein, 1972).

In summary, a number of totally different lines of evidence including synthesis of new proteins, new classes of mRNA and functional alterations of individual enzymes such as the RNA polymerase establish that the process of sporulation, like the more complex forms of differentiation characteristic of eukaryotes, is continuously modulated by changes in the mRNA.

Specific hybridization analysis with DNA that has been denatured and separated into two complementary fractions (H and L strands) by MAK column chromatography suggests that this new class of sporulation-specific RNA hybridizes predominantly to the L strand while RNA isolated from vegetative cells hybridizes predominantly with the heavy strand. More recent experiments also indicate that even late into sporulation (stage IV), 70 per cent of the vegetative phase messenger RNA is still being transcribed (Doi, 1973; Pero, 1973).

Since several new classes or new species of mRNA have been implicated in spore specific metabolism, it is likely that the DNA-dependent RNA polymerase is involved in these changes. The polymerase has been isolated and characterized from several *Bacillus* species (Losick, 1972; Brevet and Sonenshein, 1972; Klier and Lecadet, 1973; Aubert *et al.*, 1973). Mutants of RNA polymerase have also been isolated from strains of *B. subtilis* resistant to the drug rifampin (Brevet and Sonenshein, 1972). These mutants have been shown to be defective in sporulation *and* in the change of template specificity associated with the loss of ability to transcribe mRNA from phage DNA templates.

The DNA-dependent RNA polymerase isolated from wild-type vegetative *Bacillus* species consists of a core enzyme with four subunits ($\alpha\alpha\beta\beta$) plus an associated protein (sigma factor) which confers specificity of transcription to the enzyme when tested *in vitro* (Losick, 1972). Polymerase isolated from sporulating cells (regardless of the species tested) has no specificity *in vitro* and has lost its vegetative sigma factor (Losick, 1972). Since specificity can be restored to the "core" enzyme by addition of purified vegetative sigma factor until T_3 or T_4, sigma is believed to control vegetative specificity (Losick and Sonenshein, 1969; Sonenshein, 1970; Losick, 1972; Aubert *et al.*, 1973). A paradox exists because a diligent search for one or more sporulation-specific sigma factors has been fruitless (Aubert *et al.*, 1973; Greenleaf *et al.*, 1973). Furthermore, the fate of the vegetative sigma is not known even though various hypotheses suggesting its inactivation or degradation have been tested. The RNA polymerase isolated from sporulating cells does not have sufficient specificity *in vitro* to transcribe a major fraction of its RNA from the L strand (Losick, 1972; Aubert *et al.*, 1973).

Reports that one β subunit of the RNA polymerase from sporulating cells is modified by a unique proteolytic cleavage has now been shown to reflect an *in vitro* alteration caused by extracellular proteolytic enzymes which contaminated the preparation (Millet *et al.*, 1972; Aubert *et al.*, 1973). When those experiments were repeated under more rigorous conditions and in the presence of several protease inhibitors, it was shown that the enzyme from both sporulating cells and spores contain β subunits of identical molecular weight to those of the vegetative enzyme. It has been recently reported by Klier *et al.* (1973) that in *B. thuringiensis* during the later stages of sporulation the relative ratio of α subunits to core RNA polymerase decreases while 2 new subunits of lower molecular weight appear. (The new subunits may be present in the spore enzyme, which is supposedly deprived of α subunits, but the functional significance of this finding is not presently clear and the observation has not yet been made in any other species.)

Although it is generally accepted that transcriptional controls are necessary to provide the right message at the right time during sporulation, the existing data concerning the modification of RNA polymerase and its transcriptional specificity are not totally satisfactory to explain the regulation of sporulation (Aubert *et al.*, 1973). Well-documented observations that several spore-specific biochemical steps (e.g. induction of protease production, antibiotic production and alkaline phosphatase activity) as well as the loss of ability to produce phage-specific mRNA upon infection *precede* any of the detectable alterations in RNA polymerase still lack an adequate explanation to account for their regulation.

To complicate the story slightly, the elegant work of Sarkar and Paulus (1972) suggests that in *B. brevis* the antibiotic elaborated during early sporulation will inhibit vegetative cells of the same species. *In vitro* this antibiotic efficiently and selectively inhibits the RNA polymerase. Antibiotic production is thought to be at its maximum in sporulating cells before any alterations in the RNA polymerase can be detected. Since the antibiotics of sporulating bacilli are usually cyclic peptides—normally thought to interfere with the membranes of sensitive cells (Sadoff, 1972), it is tempting to postulate that one or more membrane alterations may be involved in the initial regulatory trigger that induces subsequent developmental changes.

From the structural and functional changes of RNA polymerase that do occur and from our knowledge of the manner in which the specificity of *E. coli* RNA polymerase is altered upon phage infection (synthesis of new phage specific σ etc.), it is reasonable to assume that one or more sporulating specific factors must exist to direct some of the sequential changes in enzyme specificity. Greenleaf *et al.* (1973) have approached this problem directly by preparing antiserum to the purified core enzyme of vegetative *B. subtilis* RNA polymerase and using it to precipitate the core enzyme from extracts of sporulating cells. They have looked for proteins in the precipitates which might have been associated with the enzyme and therefore precipitated together by virtue of their binding affinity for the enzyme. Several spore-specific proteins have been isolated in this manner, but their functional significance is still not understood. These proteins do not appear to in any way alter the specificity of the core enzyme in *in vitro* tests. Another protein having similar characteristics has also been isolated by Nishimoto and Takahashi (1973) using phosphocellulose chromatography. It, too, has no ascribed function to date. Needless to say, there is now a feverish pace of research among "sporologists" to identify the "essential" function of such molecules.

At this point it is clear that transcriptional controls probably operate during sporulation to provide a coarse type of adjustment providing RNA for each new stage of spore synthesis. In addition, it is evident that controls of this magnitude must be among the first to influence the onset of sporulation. However, the events which trigger them are still unclear. Attempts to attribute these changes to alterations in the cellular level of cyclic nucleotides as suggested by the extensive studies of catabolite repression in Gram-negative organisms have not been convincing (Clark and Bernlohr, 1972). Hypotheses such as that advocated by Freese or Hanson and their colleagues (Klofat *et al.*, 1969; Hutchison and Hanson, 1973) that changes in energy charge (or in ATP levels) may be a metabolic signal that can turn on spore-specific enzyme synthesis are attractive, but will require more direct testing.

The search for molecular events which "trigger" the onset of bacterial sporulation is still in progress.

One novel approach towards this objective appears to offer considerable promise (Brehm *et al.*, 1974). These experiments have exploited columns containing denatured *B. subtilis* DNA to isolate DNA binding proteins from extracts of broken cells. Several proteins have been isolated; now it remains to find a function for them.

In the meantime, a search for post-transcriptional regulatory events has begun.

TRANSLATION

Controls of eukaryotic development at the level of translation have been extensively documented (Charles and Knight, 1970; Cox and Hadjiolov, 1972; Bosch, 1972). Messenger RNA modification, the presence of stable species of mRNA, different classes of ribosomes, initiation factors and soluble enzymes have been shown to be essential prerequisites for maintaining several distinctly different types of cellular differentiation (Pasternak, 1970). However, control at the level of translation has not yet been conclusively demonstrated to be an important factor regulating bacterial sporulation. In fact, translational control has not been adequately documented for any prokaryotic system.

It is now clear that more than 200 individual macromolecules are required for the interplay in the formation of peptide bonds. Since the limitation of most of these molecules can interfere with efficient translation of mRNA *in vitro* (Cox and Hadjiolov, 1972; Bosch, 1972), it is reasonable to assume that many of the intermediates in the process of translation have the potential to be used as regulatory molecules

Numerous changes in the translational apparatus have been associated with bacterial sporulation, but few if any of these changes have yet been shown to be an essential prerequisite for the process. Part of the difficulty in obtaining this rigorous proof comes from observations that spore synthesis is associated with metabolic activities of a unique type of stationary phase metabolism. Before a cause-and-effect relationship can be demonstrated to prove the importance of the changes to spore formation, it must be demonstrated that the alterations are not merely part of the normal cellular modifications accompanying stationary phase metabolism.

Even though mRNA modification has not been reported and specific inducer or repressor molecules remain to be defined and characterized as extensively as they have for the *lambda* repressor or the *lac* operon of *E. coli*, a large number of changes in translational apparatus have been reported to occur among the *Bacillus* species. Many of these are shown in Table 1. Since they serve this discussion primarily to illustrate the extent to which the translational apparatus is modified and are all documented with selected reference citations, most of the entries in the Table are sufficiently self-explanatory and will not be discussed further.

In evaluating these reports the reader should keep in mind that frequently the work necessitated the isolation and comparison of subcellular components from vegetatively growing and stationary or sporulating cells. Many of the observed differences could also reflect nonspecific modifications by nucleases or proteases during the extraction procedure since the intracellular turn-over of macromolecules is dramatically increased during the stationary phase and sporulation (Halvorson, 1965; Halvorson *et al.*, 1966; Mandelstam, 1969; Schaeffer, 1969; Gould and Hurst, 1969).

Despite the fact that stable mRNA provides the most conclusive evidence for the existence of translational control in eukaryotic species, there is not yet adequate data to establish that it plays a significant role in sporulation.

Aronson and Del Valle (1964) have suggested that sporulation in *B. cereus* becomes insensitive to Actinomycin D at an early stage. Szulmajster *et al.* (1963) could not verify the same effect in *B. subtilis*. Aronson (1965) continued the work using DNA–RNA hybridization and again defined a persistently stable fraction which appeared to be spore specific messenger. Some workers report stable mRNA during sporulation but not in spores. Others claim that a substantial fraction of RNA in spores is inactive message. Controversy still exists regarding the presence of stable mRNA during the sporulation process or in dormant spores (Halvorson, 1965; Gould and Hurst, 1969; Aubert *et al.*, 1973; Doi, 1973). Likewise, the significance of protein modifications such as adenylation, phosphorylation, specific cleavage, etc. is still to be

TABLE 1
Changes of the translational apparatus in *Bacillus*

---

mRNA species
   Change in the relative abundance of mRNA (Aronson, 1965; Sterlini
      and Mandelstam, 1969; Gould and Hurst, 1969; Doi, 1973)
   Selective translation of existing mRNA (Doi, 1973; Pero, 1973)
   ?Stable message (Szulmajster *et al.*, 1973; Aronson and Del Valle, 1964;
      Aronson, 1965; Gould and Hurst, 1969; Halvorson, 1972; Glatron and
      Rapoport, 1972; Doi, 1973)

Ribosome alterations
   Subunits modified in structure or function (Kobayshi and Halvorson,
      1968; Kobayshi, 1972; Chambliss, 1972; Graham, 1974)
   Availability of 1 or both subunits (Shaw and Armstrong, 1972; Bonamy
      et al., 1973)
   Binding sites altered (Idriss and Halvorson, 1969)
   Discrimination of mRNA populations (Vogel and Vogel, 1965; Kornberg
      et al., 1968; Lodish, 1970)

Ribosome associated factors
   New IF's produced (Chambliss, 1972; Chambliss and Legault-Demare,
      1973)
   Elongation factors altered (Fortnagel, 1973; Fortnagel and Bergman,
      1973)
   High salt wash of ribosomes altered (Chambliss, 1972; Chambliss and
      Legault-Demare, 1973)

Availability of tRNA
   Selective synthesis of new species (Kaneko and Doi, 1966; Vold and
      Minatogawa, 1972; Aronson, 1973; Vold, 1973)
   Change in relative abundance (Kaneko and Doi, 1966; Lazzarini, 1966;
      Arceneaux and Sueoka, 1969; Vold, 1970, 1973a, 1973c; Vold and
      Minatogawa, 1972)

Enzyme or protein modification
   Alteration of tRNA synthetases (Vold, 1973b; Steinberg, 1974)
   Alteration of amino-acylating enzymes (Vold, 1973b, 1973c)
   ? Phosphorylation, Adenylation etc. (Stragier *et al.*, 1973)
Conformational changes in cell membranes (Cundliffe, 1970; Highton, 1972)

---

defined as a major source of translation regulation (Stragier *et al.*, 1973).
This type of alteration plays a well-established and widespread role by pro-
viding regulators of translation in eukaryotic development (Bosch, 1972;
Cox and Hadjiolov, 1972; Fortnagel, 1973).

Pre-spore synthesis includes extensive membrane alterations. Cytological
studies suggest that, within minutes after the induction of sporulation, mesosomes and membranes begin to change in density (Highton, 1970, 1972). The
DNA changes its cytological response and becomes redistributed to a more
discrete longitudinal position throughout the cell. Concomitant with the

redistribution of DNA, *de novo* membrane synthesis occurs at the site of eventual forespore engulfment. These membrane changes were first detected by cytological studies using the electron microscope but are now associated with changes in macromolecular composition and changes in function. A whole series of membrane-associated alterations is among the very earliest detectable spore-specific functions (Schaeffer, 1969; Mandelstam, 1969; Highton, 1972). Genetically blocked asporogenic mutants which cannot initiate the synthesis of spores often have defects in one or more of these membrane functions (Guespin-Michel, 1971). There is an increasing awareness that membranes hold a central position in a multitude of biological phenomena of great interest including respiration, macromolecular synthesis, normal and abnormal cell–cell interactions related to differentiation, coordination of viral synthesis, and others (Singer, 1971). A major role for membranes in maintaining and coordinating the differentiated state is accepted.

Messenger RNA complexes and polysomes do exist bound to membranes (Cundliffe, 1970). Many proteins are synthesized at unique membrane-associated sites in the cell. Therefore, it is logical to include the membrane as part of the translational apparatus for proteins. (In fact, it is probably logical to include it as part of the transcriptional apparatus as well.) It is tempting to postulate that membrane components (which are among the most sensitive to environmental changes—the earliest to come in contact with "starvation" conditions of the environment) might play a dominant regulatory role in influencing the transcriptional and translational products of a cell during sporulation (Kornberg *et al.*, 1968). More direct investigations of the roles of membrane components in translational control are definitely warranted.

Chambliss (1972) described the use of an *in vitro* protein synthesizing system to illustrate clearly that, in *B. subtilis,* the soluble enzyme components, the protein factors which wash off ribosomes with high salt, as well as the ribosomes themselves, become defective in their ability to translate vegetative mRNA after the sporulation metabolism has been initiated. The exact nature of these defects was not clearly elucidated, although it was shown that few if any of the defects result from the production of specific inhibitors.

Our own research for the past few years has been directed towards an elucidation of the changes which occur in ribosomal structure concomitantly with sporulation. These experiments have been performed with the collaboration of Glenn Chambliss, Scott Graham, Janne Cannon, Marianna Matthews and Roselyn Little.

Experiments have been performed using two separate approaches: (1) direct biochemical analysis of washed ribosome preparations; and (2) genetic investigation (mutant characterization).

The direct analyses have proved to be the most difficult and least rewarding

428   K. F. BOTT

to date, but both approaches independently demonstrate that multiple proteins of the 30S and the 50S subunit of the ribosome are altered concomitant with sporulation. These results are consistent with the functional tests of Chambliss showing that both the 30S and 50S ribosomal subunits become defective *in vitro* during spore specific metabolism.

Other investigators have also reported that sporulating ribosomes differ from vegetative ribosomes. Kobayashi and Halvorson (1968) have shown that *B. cereus* spore ribosomes lack the ability to bind aminoacyl tRNA. Kobayashi (1972) has tried to correlate this defect directly with the presence of subunits in the spore which are inactive because they lack certain ribosomal proteins. Unusual ribosomal proteins have also been reported by others (Woese, 1961; Idriss and Halvorson, 1969). Osawa and co-workers (Tanaka *et al.*, 1973; Osawa *et al.*, 1973) have presented good evidence that several different classes of ribosomes can exist in *B. subtilis*.

The rationale for our genetic experiments have been as follows: if ribosomal proteins are different at various stages of growth in *Bacillus subtilis*, it should be possible to obtain antibiotic-resistant mutant strains whose ribosomes are altered such that vegetative growth but not sporulation will occur in the presence of specific antibiotics. Such a class of mutants has been found among spontaneous mutants selected for resistance to more than six different antibiotics. In each case the mutants represent a small but distinct subclass of the resistant population. All antibiotics we have tested have been clearly shown by others to interfere with normal protein synthesis by virtue of their ability to interact with the prokaryotic ribosome.

Approximately 2–3 per cent of spontaneous mutants isolated for resistance to erythromycin ($1 \mu g\, cm^{-3}$), kanamycin ($1 \mu g\, cm^{-3}$), spectinomycin ($100 \mu g\, cm^{-3}$), or streptomycin ($500 \mu g\, cm^{-3}$) exhibited an antibiotic-resistant vegetative phase and an antibiotic-sensitive sporulative phase. These mutants showed normal vegetative growth when characterized spectrophotometrically and developed heat-resistant spores in a normal manner if cultured in the absence of antibiotic. When cultivated in the presence of antibiotic, they failed to develop heat resistance or form microscopically recognizable spore structures.

In addition to this class of "conditionally resistant" mutants, we have been able to isolate and characterize for comparative purposes two other mutant classes for each of the antibiotics indicated above. Class 1 mutants are the classic, totally resistant mutants which grow and sporulate normally in the presence of antibiotic. Class 2 mutants grow normally in the presence of antibiotic but are permanently and irreparably asporogenic.

We have found that a few of the mutants are resistant to much lower concentrations of antibiotic in liquid cultures than on solid medium. The reason for this reduction in resistance is unknown but may reflect differences in the cell membrane under the different growth conditions. Staal and Hoch (1972) have described a medium dependent antibiotic sensitivity in their streptomycin resistant mutant StrB3 and attributed it to membrane changes. The conditional spectinomycin and erythromycin strains are more typical and exhibit resistance to antibiotic concentrations 10 to 100 times greater than the level to which they were originally selected. This characteristic has frequently been associated with ribosomal directed antibiotic resistance in other species.

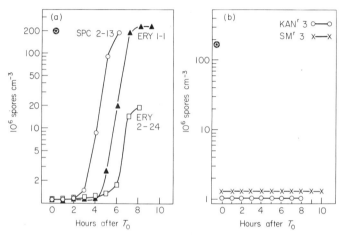

FIG. 1. Antibiotic at the appropriate concentration for each mutant was added to the resuspension medium of Sterlini and Mandelstam (1969) at T_0 and at hourly intervals afterwards. Sporulation was determined in all cultures by measuring the number of colony forming units in the population which survived 10 minutes at 80°C 24 hours later. The star to the left of T_0 represents the potential level of sporulation in a population to which no antibiotic was added.

In an attempt to characterize the conditional mutants, we have tried to determine whether each of the antibiotics had its primary effect at a specific portion of the sporulative cycle. In these experiments the replacement culture technique of Sterlini and Mandelstam (1968) was modified by adding antibiotic at various intervals after T_0 and then testing for heat-resistant spore production after 24 hours. The mutants were shown to exhibit several types of response. After T_4 (Fig. 1(a)) both erythromycin strains became increasingly refractory to the effects of erythromycin. By T_6 addition of drug had no effect on eventual ability to complete the synthesis of heat-resistant spores. The spectinomycin mutants showed a similar type of response but begin to be refractory to the drug as early as T_2. In contrast, the kanamycin and streptomycin mutants were not released from their inhibition prior to germination (Fig. 1(b)). The classic type resistant mutants were always refractory to the appropriate drug under these experimental conditions.

We have characterized the mutants further by determining the extent to which antibiotic addition altered the expression of spore-specific metabolism. Alkaline phosphatase has been associated with Stage III of sporulation, $T_{1.5} - T_3$ (Mandelstam, 1969). It is clear (Fig. 2(a)) that addition of antibiotic at T_0 prevents or represses alkaline phosphatase synthesis in the conditional erythromycin and spectinomycin mutants but has virtually

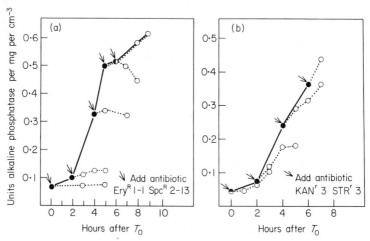

Fig. 2. Antibiotic at the appropriate concentration was added to the resuspension medium of Sterlini and Mandelstam (1969) at points indicated by the arrows. Alkaline phosphatase was determined by using the colorimetric assay kit provided by Worthington Biochemicals. Enzyme levels in the absence of antibiotic are indicated by solid lines, and in the presence of antibiotic by the dotted lines.

no effect on the kanamycin or streptomycin mutants (Fig. 2(b)). When antibiotic was added at various times after T_0, we found that addition of erythromycin prevented subsequent enzyme synthesis until T_4 (Fig. 2(a)). After T_4 the cells became increasingly refractory to the effects of drug. In the spectinomycin mutants, however, the inhibition of alkaline phosphatase was never released (Fig. 2(b)).

Since these results could reflect a generalized reduction in total protein synthesis as well as the specific discrimination of spore-specific mRNA, we measured histidase formation and the effect on total protein synthesis during vegetative growth and during sporulation. Histidase can be induced to the same extent in either vegetative cells or sporulating cells (Sterlini and Mandelstam, 1969). Its presence or absence has no effect on sporulation. If alkaline phosphatase was selectively inhibited by the presence of antibiotic in the conditional strains, then we might have expected the histidase levels to be identical in vegetative and sporulating cells. Furthermore, any reduction in histidase should correlate with a reduction in total protein synthesis. The class 1 strains, which are totally resistant, and the wild-type parent all act as controls.

The addition of antibiotic to the conditional spectinomycin mutants during sporulation caused a complete cessation of alkaline phosphatase production, but only a 12–30 per cent decrease in histidase. Total protein synthesis paralleled the histidase reductions. In each case sporulation was reduced more than 90 per cent below control samples. Addition of antibiotic during vegetative growth had no effect on histidase production, growth rate, or total cell count.

As a control, experiments were performed with a mutant from the resistant class 1 strain, in which no effect of antibiotic could be detected during either vegetative growth or sporulation. Similar experiments with 168 *ind*- showed that this antibiotic-sensitive strain was inhibited in all measured parameters during vegetative growth and sporulation.

It is apparent that protein synthesis in the conditional mutants for spectinomycin continues after T_0 in the presence of antibiotic although neither alkaline phosphatase nor spores are produced. It is known that more than 70 per cent of the vegetative messenger RNA continues to be produced during sporulation (Doi, 1973). Continued protein synthesis could reflect the translation of those vegetative functions.

It is possible to explain many of the results by hypothesizing that some change occurs during the transition between vegetative growth and sporulation which renders the sporulating cell permeable to antibiotic, i.e. a membrane effect. However, we have several kinds of evidence against such an interpretation in most of our conditional mutants. First, no cross resistance between mutants has been detected, i.e. mutants isolated for resistance to one antibiotic do not show resistance to others. Second, if we add antibiotic during vegetative growth, wash the cells, and resuspend them in a sporulation medium, sporulation is still inhibited. This implies the existence of an irreversible binding of antibiotic to cells— supposedly at the interior. Third, genetic transduction studies using phage PBSI link the spectinoymcin mutant loci and possibly others to the *cysA* locus of the genome—a known site for other ribosomal markers. Similar map positions have been observed by Osawa and co-workers (Tanaka *et al.*, 1973; Osawa *et al.*, 1973; Kimura *et al.* 1973) in antibiotic-resistant strains having altered ribosomal proteins.

These results are consistent with an interpretation that in the conditional strains some ribosomal change normally occurs between vegetative growth and sporulation and that this alteration prevents the cells from continually expressing the phenotype of antibiotic resistance.

The fact that conditional-type mutations have been found for several

P

totally different antibiotics whose site of action is directed towards the ribosome supports previous evidence that structural modifications occur at both the 30S and 50S subunits concomitant with spore specific metabolism. Conditional-type mutations should prove to be extremely valuable for determining the importance of the ribosomal change to sporulation—the time that each alteration occurs in the sequence of spore synthesis and the exact type of structural modification which can result in a conditional phenotype. Based on the background of knowledge relative to the mode of action of these antibiotics, we would predict that each of the three types of mutation described above could result from structural changes in just one specific ribosomal protein. The protein should be highly specific for each antibiotic. Do the results mean that by randomly modifying a ribosomal protein three or more different phenotypes are produced? We are currently testing this hypothesis.

The conditional-type mutants may not all be the result of ribosomal modification since the phenotypic expression of antibiotic resistance in some of our kanamycin and streptomycin-resistant strains suggest that a membrane modification has also occurred. These mutants do not map genetically near known ribosomal loci, they grow in unusually long chains, never develop motility and have abnormal levels of resistance to antibiotic when grown in some media. These mutants may enable us to define more clearly the relevant membrane alterations which accompany sporulation.

Research activities will certainly be continued using both direct biochemical analyses and genetic analyses to characterize the changes in translational apparatus between vegetative growth and sporulation. However, positive demonstration of translational control will undoubtedly required the isolation of, or demonstration of, function for a spore-specific mRNA to show that the sporulating cell-machinery can translate it more efficiently than vegetative message.

It has not been shown possible to separate and purify a uniquely spore-specific message which is functional *in vitro*. Several of the most promising current approaches involve the following:

1. Chemically fractionating purified mature spores and raising highly specific antiserum to these fractions in rabbits. Ultimately the products of *in vitro* translation using messenger RNA isolated from sporulating cells will be tested for antigenic substances which interact immunologically with the antiserum (P. Shaeffer, personal communication).

2. Some species, including *B. thuringiensis*, synthesize concomitantly with sporulation a crystalline protein toxin which has insecticide activity. During the synthesis of this protein (which never occurs during vegetative growth), a very large proportion of the mRNA found in the cells is message for the protein (Rogoff and Yousten, 1969). Attempts are being made to

isolate and purify that abundant population of mRNA molecules for further *in vitro* testing of the translational apparatus (Dedonder, personal communication).

POST-TRANSLATION

Post-translational modifications of proteins in all probability also provides important regulatory functions for bacterial sporulation although they have been less well characterized than the previously discussed transcriptional or translational controls.

For years proteolytic activity has been considered an essential prerequisite for spore-specific metabolism (Schaffer, 1969; Doi, 1972). Elevated levels of extracellular and intracellular protease are characteristic of the earliest stages of sporulation. Some purified enzymes from spores appear to be the proteolytically cleaved products of higher molecular weight vegetative enzymes (Doi, 1972). However, the isolation of mutant *Bacillus* strains which lack these enzymes and still sporulate casts doubt on their significance to spore synthesis. Recently, Aronson (1973) has attempted to put these observations into perspective. Briefly reiterated, it will be essential to repeat these studies under conditions that prevent proteolytic alteration during the extraction and purification procedures before the true significance of the results can be evaluated.

From the previous discussion it will be recalled that various cellular proteins are known to be modified concomitantly with spore synthesis. These include the RNA polymerase, ribosome subunits, membrane components and others. Each of these modifications could originate at the post translational level. The production of peptide antibiotics, phosphorylation, adenylation or other chemical interactions between molecules also have a potential ability to regulate cellular functions by modifying proteins that already exist in the cell.

In conclusion, I suggest that the process of sporulation like differentiation of all higher forms requires an integrated functioning of controls at all three levels: transcription, translation and post-translation. A detailed knowledge of the regulation of spore formation will be of fundamental importance to our understanding of the processes by which normal cellular differentiation is regulated. Perhaps someday these results will even make it a little easier for man to exploit microorganisms as tools for genetic engineering since the sporulating bacteria contain many of the regulatory functions necessary for higher forms of cellular development but within a relatively simplistic prokaryotic background.

References

Arceneaux, J. L. and Sueoka, N. (1969). *J. biol. Chem.* **244**, 5959.

Aronson, A. (1965). *J. molec. Biol.* **11**, 576.
Aronson, A. (1973). "Regulation de la Sporulation Microbienne" (Eds J.-P. Aubert, P. Schaeffer and J. Szulmajster). Colloq. Intern., vol. 227, p. 33. CNRS, France.
Aronson, A. and Del Valle, M. R. (1964). *Biochim biophys. Acta,* **87**, 267.
Aubert, J.-P., Schaeffer, P. and Szulmajster, J. (eds) (1973). "Régulation de la Sporulation Microbienne". Colloq. Intern., vol. 227, p. 147. CNRS, France.
Bernlohr, R. W. (1973). "Régulation de la Sporulation Microbienne" (Eds J.-P. Aubert, P. Schaeffer and J. Szulmagster), Colloq. Intern., vol. 227, p. 59. CNRS, France.
Bonamy, C., Hirschbein, L. and Szulmajster, J. (1973). *J. bact.* **113**, 1296.
Bosch, L. (ed). (1972). "Frontiers of Biology", vol. 27. Elsevier, Amsterdam.
Brehm, S. P., Le Hegarat, F. and Hoch, J. (1974). *Abstr. of ann. Mtg.* G113, American Society for Microbiology.
Brevet, J. and Sonenshein, A. L. (1972). *J. Bact.* **112**, 1270.
Chambliss, G. H. (1972). Ph.D. dissertation, University of Chicago.
Chambliss, G. H. and Legault-Demare, L. (1973). "Régulation de la sporulation Microbienne" (Eds J.-P. Aubert, P. Schaeffer and J. Szulmajster), Colloq. Intern., vol. 227, p. 103. CNRS, France.
Charles, H. P. and Knight, B. C. (eds) (1970). *Symp. Soc. gen. Microbiol.* **20**, 457.
Chuang, R. Y. and Doi, R. (1972). *J. biol. Chem.* **247**, 3476.
Clark, V. L. and Bernlohr, R. W. (1972). "Spores V" (Eds H. Halvorson, R. Hanson and L. Campbell), p. 167. American Society for Microbiology.
Cox, R. A. and Hadjiolov, A. (eds) (1972). "Functional Units in Protein Biosynthesis", vol. 23, 7th FEBS Mgs. Academic Press, London and New York.
Cundliffe, E. (1970). *J. mol. Biol.* **52**, 467.
Doi, R. H. (1972). "Current Topics in Cellular Regulation" (Eds B. L. Horecker and E. R. Stadtman), vol. 6, p. 1. Academic Press, New York and London.
Doi, R. (1973). "Régulation de la Sporulation Microbienne" (Eds J.-P. Aubert, P. Schaeffer and J. Szulmajster), Colloq. Intern., vol. 227, p. 43. CNRS, France.
Fortnagel, P. (1973). "Régulation de la Sporulation Microbienne" (Eds J.-P. Aubert, P. Schaeffer and J. Szulmajster), Colloq. Intern., vol. 227, p. 113. CNRS, France.
Fortnagel, P. and Bergman, R. (1973). *Biochim biophys. Acta,* **299**, 136.
Freeze, E. (1972). "Current Topics in Developmental Biology" (Eds A. A. Moscona and A. Montroy), vol. 7. Academic Press, New York and London.
Glatron, M. F. and Rapoport, G. (1972). *Biochimie,* **54**, 1291.
Gould, G. W. and Hurst, A. (eds) (1969). "The Bacterial Spore". Academic Press, London and New York.
Graham, S. (1974). Ph.D. dissertation, University of North Carolina, Chapel Hill.
Greenleaf, A., Linn, T. and Losick, R. (1973). *Proc. natn. Acad. Sci. U.S.A.* **70**, 490.
Guespin-Michel, J. (1971). *J. Bact.* **108**, 241.
Halvorson, H. O. (1965). *Symp. Soc. gen. Microbiol.* **15**, 343.
Halvorson, H. O., Vary, J. C. and Steinberg, W. (1966). *A. Rev. Microbiol.* **20**, 169.
Halvorson, H. O., Hanson, R. and Campbell, L. L. (eds) (1972). "Spores V", p. 471. American Society for Microbiology.
Hendler, R. W. (1968). "Protein biosynthesis and membrane biochemistry". John Wiley, New York.
Highton, P. F. (1970). *J. Ultrastruct. Res.* **31**, 247.
Highton, P. F. (1972). "Spores V" (Eds H. O. Halvorson, R. Hanson and L. Campbell), p. 13. American Society for Microbiology.
Hutchison, K. W. and Hanson, R. S. (1973). "Régulation de la Sporulation Micro-

bienne" (Eds J.-P. Aubert, P. Schaeffer and J. Szulmajster), Colloq. Intern. vol. 227, p. 63. CNRS, France.

Idliss, J. and Halvorson, H. O. (1969). *Archs. Biochem. Biophys.* **133**, 422.

Kaneko, I. and Doi, R. (1966). *Proc. natn. Acad. Sci. U.S.A.* **55**, 564.

Kimura, A., Kobata, K., Takata, R. and Osawa, S. (1973). *Mol. gen. Genetics*, **124**, 107.

Kleir, A. F. and Lecadet, M. M. (1973). "Régulation de la Sporulation Microbienne" (Eds J.-P. Aubert, P. Schaeffer and J. Szulmajster), Colloq. Intern., vol. 227, p. 29. CNRS, France.

Kleir, A., Lecadet, M. M. and Dedoner, R. (1973). *Eur. J. Biochem.* **36**, 317.

Klofat, W., Picciolo, G., Chapelle, E. and Freeze, E. (1969). *J. biol. Chem.* **244**, 3270.

Kobayashi, Y. (1972). "Spores V" (Eds H. Halvorson, R. Hanson and L. Campbell), p. 269. American Society for Microbiology.

Kobayashi, Y. and Halvorson, H. O. (1968). *Archs. Biochem. Biophys.* **123**, 622.

Kornberg, A., Spudick, J., Nelson, D. and Deutscher, M. (1968). *A. Rev. Biochem.* **37**, 51.

Lazzarini, R. A. (1966). *Proc. natn. Acad. Sci. U.S.A.* **56**, 185.

Lodish, H. (1970). *Nature, Lond.* **226**, 705.

Losick, R. (1972). *A. Rev. Biochem.* **41**, 409.

Losick, R. and Sonenshein, A. L. (1969). *Nature, Lond.* **224**, 25.

Markert, C. L. and Ursprung, H. (1971). "Developmental Genetics". Prentice-Hall, New York.

Mandelstam, J. (1969). *Symp. Soc. gen. Microbiol.* **19**, 377.

Millet, J., Kerjan, P., Aubert, J.-P. and Szulmajster, J. (1972). *FEBS Letters*, **23**, 47.

Murrell, W. G. (1967). *Ann Rev. microbiol. Physiol.* **1**, 1.

Nishimoto, H. and Takahashi, I. (1973). "Régulation de la Sporulation Microbienne" (Eds J.-P. Aubert, P. Schaeffer and J. Szulmajster), Colloq. Intern., vol. 227, p. 9. CNRS, France.

Osawa, S., Takata, R., Tanaka, K. and Tamaki, M. (1973). *Mol. gen, Genetics.* **127**, 163.

Pasternak, C. A. (1970). "Biochemistry of differentiation". Wiley-Interscience, New York.

Pero, J. (1973). "Régulation de la Sporulation Microbienne" (Eds J.-P. Aubert, P. Schaeffer and J. Szulmajster), Colloq. Intern., vol. 227, p. 7. CNRS, France.

Rogoff, M. H. and Yousten, A. (1969). *A. Rev. Microbiol.* **23**, 357.

Sadoff, H. (1972). "Spores V" (Eds H. O. Halvorson, R. Hanson and L. Campbell), p. 157. American Society for Microbiology.

Sarker, H. and Paulus, H. (1972). *Nature, New Biol.* **239**, 228.

Schaeffer, P. (1969). *Bact. Rev.* **33**, 48.

Schaeffer, P., Millet, J. and Aubert, J.-P. (1965). *Proc. natn. Acad. Sci. U.S.A.* **54**, 704.

Shaw, M. V. and Armstrong, R. L. (1972). *J. Bact.* **109**, 282.

Singer, S. J. (1971). "Structure and Function of Biological Membranes" (Ed. J. I. Rothfield), p. 145. Academic Press, New York and London.

Sonenshein, A. L. (1970). Ph.D. dissertation, Massachesetts Institute of Technology.

Staal, S. P. and Hoch, J. (1972). *J. Bact.* **110**, 202.

Steinberg, W. (1974). *J. Bact.* **118**, 70.

Sterlini, J. and Mandelstam, J. (1969). *Biochem. J.* **113**, 29.

Stragier, P., Brevet, J. and Hischbein, L. (1973). "Régulation de la Sporulation Microbienne" (Eds J.-P. Aubert, P. Schaeffer and J. Szulmajster), Colloq. Intern, vol. 227, p. 23. CNRS, France.

Sussman, A. S. and Halvorson, H. O. (1966). "Spores: their Dormancy and Germination". Harper and Row, New York.

Szulmajster, J. (1973). *Symp. Soc. gen. Microbol.* **23**, 45.

Szulmajster, J., Canfield, R. and Blicharska, J. (1963). *C.R.A.S. (Paris)*, **256**, 2057.

Tanaka, K., Tamaki, M., Osawa, S., Kimura, A. and Takata, R. (1973), *Mol. gen. Genetics*, **127**, 157.

Vaněk, Z., Hošťálek, Z. Cudlín, J. (eds) (1973). "Genetics of Industrial Microorganisms" vol. 1. Elsevier, Amsterdam.

Vogel, R. and Vogel, H. (1965). *Biochem. biophys. Res. Commun.* **18**, 768.

Vold, B. S. (1970). *J. Bact.* **102**, 711.

Vold, B. S. (1973a). *J. Bact.* **114**, 178.

Vold, B. S. (1973b). *Arch. Biochem. Biophys.* **154**, 691.

Vold, B. S. (1973c). *J. Bact.* **113**, 825.

Vold, B. S. and Minatogawa, S. (1972). "Spores V" (Eds H. O. Halvorson, R. Hanson and L. Campbell), p. 254. American Society for Microbiology.

Woese, C. (1961). *J. Bact.* **82**, 695.

Yamakawa, R. and Doi, R. (1971). *J. Bact.* **106**, 305.

Young, F. E. and Wilson, G. (1972). "Spores V" (Eds H. O. Halvorson, R. Hanson and L. Campbell), p. 77. American Society for Microbiology.

Amino acid fermentations using regulatory mutants of *Corynebacterium glutamicum*

K. NAKAYAMA, K. ARAKI, H. HAGINO, H. KASE AND H. YOSHIDA

Tokyo Research Laboratory, Kyowa Hakko Kogyo Co., Ltd, Tokyo, Japan

Summary

Mutation and selection based on rational speculation led to success in obtaining mutants of *Corynebacterium glutamicum* which produce aromatic amino acids (L-tryptophan, L-tyrosine or L-phenylalanine), L-threonine, L-histidine or L-arginine in large amounts. A phenylalanine auxotroph multiply resistant to analogues of phenylalanine and tyrosine produced 17 g L-tyrosine per litre in cane molasses medium containing 10 per cent sugar (as glucose). A tyrosine auxotroph multiply resistant to phenylalanine and tyrosine analogues produced 9.5 g dm^{-3} of L-phenylalanine. A phenylalanine and tyrosine double auxotroph multiply resistant to tryptophan analogues produced L-tryptophan at a yield over 10 per cent (w/w) of initial sugar in a cane molasses medium. The regulatory mechanism of the biosynthesis of aromatic amino acids in *C. glutamicum* was elucidated in outline. A methionine auxotroph resistant to both α-amino-β-hydroxyvaleric acid and S-(β-aminoethyl)-cysteine produced L-threonine to a level of 14 g dm^{-3} in a medium containing 10 per cent glucose. A histidine producer, selected for resistance to 1,2,4-triazolealanine, was further stepwise improved in histidine productivity by mutations endowing resistance to certain purine, pyrimidine and tryptophan analogues. The mutant finally selected produced 25 g dm^{-3} of L-histidine in a cane molasses medium containing 15 per cent sugar (as glucose).

Deviation from the normal biosynthetic regulation explained the production of amino acids in the above mutants.

437

Introduction

Industrial production of amino acids by fermentation methods started with the discovery of a glutamic acid producing bacterium, *Corynebacterium glutamicum* (Kinoshita *et al.*, 1957), and was enlarged by the utilization of auxotrophic mutants for the production of other amino acids such as L-lysine, L-ornithine, L-citrulline, L-proline, L-valine, etc. (Nakayama, 1973). However, amino acids such as histidine and arginine could not be produced using auxotrophic mutants because the pathways for the synthesis of these amino acids, which are end products, have no branches giving rise to other essential metabolites. Production of these amino acids was first accomplished using regulatory mutants (Nakayama, 1972), which can be isolated by selecting for resistance to an analogue of the regulatory metabolite, usually the end product of the pathway. The combination of auxotrophy and regulatory defect is generally more efficient in production, especially in contributing to stability of productivity in long or continuous fermentations.

In this paper, the production of aromatic amino acids, L-threonine, L-histidine and L-arginine using auxotrophic regulatory mutants of *C. glutamicum* is described.

Results and discussion

L-TYROSINE PRODUCTION

L-Tyrosine production by a phenylalanine auxotroph of *C. glutamicum* (Nakayama *et al.*, 1961b) was affected by the concentration of L-phenylalanine in the growth medium. Maximal L-tyrosine production was attained at a low concentration of L-phenylalanine. The phenylalanine auxotroph was improved in its L-tyrosine productivity by imposing other auxotrophic requirements (Hagino *et al.*, 1973). Especially, double auxotrophs requiring purine, histidine or cysteine in addition to phenylalanine produced significantly higher amounts of L-tyrosine compared to the parent. A phenylalanine and purine double auxotrophic strain LM-96, which was derived from a phenyl-alanine-leaky auxotroph KY 10233, produced 15.1 g dm^{-3} of L-tyrosine in a medium containing 15 per cent sucrose and fed to 20 per cent total. Production decreased at high concentrations of phenylalanine.

p-Fluorophenylalanine (PFP) and *m*-fluorophenylalanine were the most effective growth inhibitors for *C. glutamicum* ATCC 13032 (a wild-type strain) among the analogues of L-phenylalanine and L-tyrosine tested. Their inhibitory effects were released by L-phenylalanine and slightly by L-tyrosine and L-tryptophan. 3-Aminotyrosine (3AT), *p*-aminophenylalanine (PAP), *o*-fluorophenylalanine and β-2-thienylalanine were weak inhibitors. Resistant mutants of *C. glutamicum* isolated on a medium containing both PFP and 3AT, or PFP and L-tyrosine, were found to produce both L-tyrosine and L-phenyl-alanine while resistant mutants isolated on a medium containing only PFP produced only L-phenylalanine (Hagino and Nakayma, 1973a). The production of L-tyrosine by these analogue-resistant prototrophs was less than 5 g dm^{-3}.

A combination of auxotrophy and multiple resistance to analogues of aromatic amino acids was necessary to yield a large amount of L-tyrosine. A

		L-Tyrosine produced (g dm^{-3})*
KY 10108 ↓	wild	0
KY 10233 ↓	Phe^L	3.0
3AT-337 ↓	Phe^L, 3AT^r	5.7
PAP-45 ↓	Phe^L, 3AT^r, PAP^r	7.4
PFP-175 ↓	Phe^L, 3AT^r, PAP^r, PFP^r	10.6
PFP-175-33 ↓	Phe^L, 3AT^r, PAP^r, PFP^r	12.2
Tx-200-98 ↓	Phe^L, 3AT^r, PAP^r, PFP^r, TyrHx^r	(8.4)
98-Tx-71 ↓	Phe^L, 3AT^r, PAP^r, PFP^r, TryHx^r	13.5
Pr-20	Phe^L, 3AT^r, PAP^r, PFP^r, TyrHx^r, Tyr^s	17.6

Fɪɢ. 1. Genealogy of L-tyrosine-producing mutants and their L-tyrosine productivity. *With a cane molasses medium containing 10 per cent sugar (as glucose). Abbreviations: 3AT, 3-aminotyrosine; PAP, p-aminophenylalanine; PFP, p-fluorophenylalanine; TyrHx, tyrosine hydroxamate; L, leaky; r, resistance; s, sensitive.

phenylalanine auxotroph, 98-Tx-71, multiply resistant to analogues of phenylalanine and tyrosine [PFP, PAP, 3AT and tyrosine hydroxamate (TyrHx)], produced 13.5 g dm^{-3} of L-tyrosine in a cane molasses medium containing 10 per cent sugar (as glucose) (Fig. 1).

Strain 98-Tx-71 of *C. glutamicum* possesses the same leaky L-phenylalanine-synthesizing system as its parent, KY 10233. In fact, excretion of a trace amount of L-phenylalanine (below 500 mg dm^{-3}) was often observed. The L-phenylalanine pool of this mutant may reach such a level as to inhibit the biosynthesis of L-tyrosine owing to deviation of the regulation of L-phenyl-alanine synthesis in this mutant. Thus mutants which are more strictly defective in L-phenylalanine biosynthesis were expected to produce higher amounts of L-tyrosine. Such mutants may be selected as L-tyrosine-sensitive strains which grow slowly in minimal medium supplemented with excess

L-tyrosine, because the L-tyrosine antagonizes L-phenylalanine uptake into the cells of *C. glutamicum* and inhibits the growth of a phenylalanine auxotroph in proportion to the degree of the requirement for L-phenylalanine (Nakayama *et al.*, 1960). Colonies which grew slowly in the presence of L-tyrosine (100–400 mg dm^{-3}) were selected as mutants sensitive to L-tyrosine and screened for L-tyrosine production. Some were found to produce higher amount of L-tyrosine than strain 98-Tx-71. In particular, strains Pr-20 and Pr-102 produced L-tyrosine at a concentration of 17.6 and 17.3 g dm^{-3} respectively (Hagino and Nakayama, 1973b).

L-PHENYLALANINE PRODUCTION

The amount of L-phenylalanine produced by a tyrosine auxotroph of *C. glutamicum* was small (Nakayama *et al.*, 1961a). A prototrophic mutant No. 66, resistant to PFP (4 g dm^{-3}), produced 5.5 g of phenylalanine per litre and a trace amount of L-tyrosine in a cane molasses medium containing 10 per cent of sugar (as glucose). A tyrosine auxotrophic mutant, strain 31-PAP-20-22, resistant to PFP (100 mg dm^{-3}) and PAP (1 g dm^{-3}), produced 9.5 g dm^{-3} of L-phenylalanine in the molasses medium (Hagino and Nakayama, 1974a). L-Phenylalanine production in these mutants was inhibited by L-tyrosine and stimulated by L-tryptophan.

L-TRYPTOPHAN PRODUCTION

Mutants producing a large amount of L-tryptophan were derived from a phenylalanine and tyrosine requiring double auxotroph of *C. glutamicum*, KY 9456, which produced only a trace amount of L-tryptophan (150 mg dm^{-3}) and anthranilate. A mutant, 4 MT-11, which had stepwise acquired resistance to 5-methyltryptophan, tryptophan hydroxamate, 6-fluorotryptophan and 4-methyltryptophan, produced L-tryptophan at a concentration of 4.9 g dm^{-3} in a molasses medium containing 10 per cent sugar (as glucose). L-Tryptophan production in strain 4MT-11 was inhibited by L-phenylalanine and L-tyrosine. Accordingly, mutants resistant to phenylalanine and tyrosine analogues such as PFP, PAP, TyrHx and phenylalanine hydroxamate were derived from strain 4MT-11 (Fig. 2). One of the mutants thus obtained, strain Px-115-97, produced 12 g dm^{-3} of L-tryptophan in the molasses medium. L-Tryptophan production with the mutant was still sensitive to L-phenylalanine and L-tyrosine (Hagino and Nakayama, 1947b).

REGULATION OF AROMATIC AMINO ACID BIOSYNTHESIS IN *C. GLUTAMICUM*

Regulatory properties of the enzymes involved in aromatic amino acid biosynthesis in *C. glutamicum* wild strain, ATCC 13032, were investigated (Hagino and Nakayama, 1974c, 1974d, 1974e, 1974f). 3-Deoxy-D-arabinoheptulosonate-7-phosphate (DAHP) synthetase, which catalyses the first reaction in

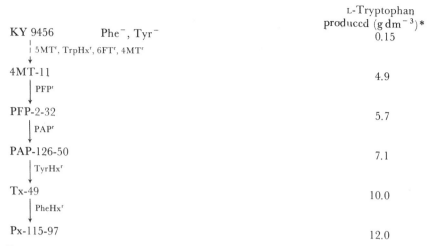

KY 9456   Phe⁻, Tyr⁻

<table>
<tr><td>KY 9456</td><td>Phe⁻, Tyr⁻</td><td>L-Tryptophan produced $(g\,dm^{-3})$*</td></tr>
</table>

<table>
<tr><td colspan="2"></td><td>L-Tryptophan
produced $(g\,dm^{-3})$*</td></tr>
<tr><td>KY 9456</td><td>Phe⁻, Tyr⁻</td><td>0.15</td></tr>
<tr><td colspan="3">| 5MTʳ, TrpHxʳ, 6FTʳ, 4MTʳ</td></tr>
<tr><td>4MT-11</td><td></td><td>4.9</td></tr>
<tr><td colspan="3">| PFPʳ</td></tr>
<tr><td>PFP-2-32</td><td></td><td>5.7</td></tr>
<tr><td colspan="3">| PAPʳ</td></tr>
<tr><td>PAP-126-50</td><td></td><td>7.1</td></tr>
<tr><td colspan="3">| TyrHxʳ</td></tr>
<tr><td>Tx-49</td><td></td><td>10.0</td></tr>
<tr><td colspan="3">| PheHxʳ</td></tr>
<tr><td>Px-115-97</td><td></td><td>12.0</td></tr>
</table>

Fig. 2. Genealogy of L-tryptophan-producing mutants and their L-tryptophan productivity. *With a cane molasses medium containing 10 per cent sugar (as glucose). Abbreviations: 5MT, 5-methyltryptophan; TrpHx, tryptophan hydroxamate; 6FT, 6-fluorotryptophan; 4MT, 4-methyltryptophan; PFP, *p*-fluorophenylalanine; PAP, *p*-aminophenylalanine; TyrHx, tyrosine hydroxamate; PheHx phenylalanine hydroxamate.

the biosynthesis of aromatic amino acids, was inhibited synergistically by L-phenylalanine and L-tyrosine; L-tryptophan enhanced the inhibition exerted by these pair of amino acids. Maximum inhibition was close to 90 per cent in the simultaneous presence of the three amino acids. Prephenate dehydrogenase, which is the first enzyme in the L-tyrosine terminal pathway, was weakly inhibited by L-tyrosine, and prephenate dehydratase, the first enzyme in the L-phenylalanine terminal pathway, was completely inhibited by L-phenylalanine (100 per cent inhibition at 0.05 mM) and cross-inhibited by L-tryptophan (100 per cent inhibition at 0.1 mM). Moreover, L-tyrosine stimulated the prephenate dehydratase activity and reversed the inhibition by L-phenylalanine or L-tryptophan competitively with the inhibitors. Anthranilate synthetase, which is the first enzyme in the L-tryptophan terminal pathway was strongly inhibited by L-tryptophan, competitively with chorismate and noncompetitively with glutamine. Formation of the anthranilate synthetase was repressed by L-tryptophan. Chorismate mutase, which catalyses the reaction located at the branch point of the L-phenylalanine and L-tyrosine biosynthetic pathways, was partially inhibited by L-phenylalanine (90 per cent inhibition at 0.1 mM) and L-tyrosine (50 per cent inhibition at 0.1 mM) and completely inhibited by L-phenylalanine and L-tyrosine together (each at 0.1 mM). Chorismate mutase was also stimulated by L-tryptophan (260 per cent of the control at 0.1 mM), which restored the activity inhibited by

L-phenylalanine and L-tyrosine, and the formation of chorismate mutase was repressed by L-phenylalanine. The overall control pattern (Fig. 3) is a new addition to the list of control patterns in aromatic amino acid biosynthesis in microorganisms.

L-Phenylalanine biosynthesis is controlled by L-phenylalanine itself through the feedback inhibition of prephenate dehydrogenase activity. Therefore,

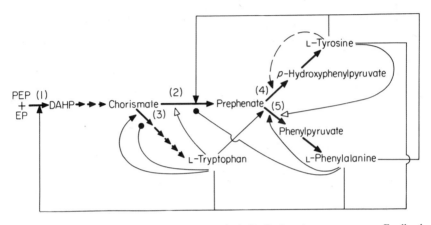

FIG. 3. Control of aromatic amino acid biosynthesis in *C. glutamicum*. ←———— Feedback inhibition; ←-------- partial inhibition; ◁———— activation; •———— repression. (1) DAHP synthetase; (2) chorimate mutase; (3) anthranilate synthetase; (4) prephenate dehydrogenase; (5) prephenate dehydratase. Abbreviations: PEP, phosphoenolpyruvate; EP, erythrose 4-phosphate; DAHP, 3-deoxy-D-arabinoheptulosonic acid 7-phosphate.

L-tyrosine is produced more easily than L-phenylalanine, and the L-tyrosine thus produced reverses the inhibition of prephenate dehydratase activity competitively with L-phenylalanine. Then L-phenylalanine biosynthesis will continue until the L-phenylalanine concentration reaches a level which inhibits prephenate dehydratase activity in competition with L-tyrosine at which point L-tyrosine biosynthesis is resumed. Thus L-tyrosine seems to play a role in partitioning prephenate between prephenate dehydrogenase and prephenate dehydratase and the mechanisms described seem to give a balanced biosynthesis of L-tyrosine and L-phenylalanine in *C. glutamicum*. Balanced production of L-phenylalanine and L-tyrosine was observed *in vivo* in mutants of *C. gluta-micum* having desensitized DAHP synthetase; these yielded almost equal amounts of L-tyrosine and L-phenylalanine.

The competitive inhibition of anthranilate synthetase activity by L-trypto-phan means that the reaction would proceed when sufficient chorismate is supplied. This rationally explains the excretion of L-tryptophan and an-thranilate by a phenylalanine and tyrosine double auxotroph of *C. glutamicum*, strain KY 9456, in a medium supplemented with limiting amounts of L-phenylalanine and L-tyrosine.

Chorismate mutase seems to have two physiological roles: one is the control of the metabolic flow to L-phenylalanine and L-tyrosine biosynthesis and the other is the balanced partition of chorismate between L-phenylalanine/L-tyrosine biosynthesis and L-tryptophan biosynthesis. L-Tryptophan biosynthesis seems to proceed in preference to L-tyrosine and L-phenylalanine biosynthesis because the K_m value of anthranilate synthetase for chorismate $(6.25 \times 10^{-5} \text{ M})$ was lower than that of chorismate mutase $(2.9 \times 10^{-3} \text{ M})$. Feedback regulation of chorismate mutase in *C. glutamicum* is achieved mainly by L-phenylalanine through inhibition and repression as described above, and the second role of chorismate mutase is ensured by the stimulation of the enzyme activity by L-tryptophan. L-Tryptophan not only stimulates the enzyme activity but also reverses the inhibition exerted by L-phenylalanine and L-tyrosine. This mechanism appears to be favourable for the balanced partition of chorismate between L-phenylalanine/L-tyrosine biosynthesis and L-tryptophan biosynthesis. L-Tryptophan completely reversed the inhibition exerted by L-phenylalanine at one tenth molar concentration of the inhibitor and reversed half of the inhibition exerted by L-tyrosine and L-phenylalanine together. The ratio of these amino acids may reflect the optimal one of aromatic amino acids necessary for protein biosynthesis.

As described above, L-tryptophan increased L-tyrosine and L-phenylalanine production by the mutants. This seems to be a demonstration of the role of L-tryptophan in balancing the ratio between L-tryptophan and L-phenylalanine + L-tyrosine *in vivo* through the stimulation of chorismate mutase activity. The stimulation and the inhibition of prephenate dehydratase activity by L-tyrosine and L-phenylalanine respectively were considered to give a balanced synthesis of L-tyrosine and L-phenylalanine as described above.

Thus it is concluded that these two negative and positive control mechanisms, demonstrated on the two enzymes of metabolic branch-points in the aromatic amino acid biosynthetic pathway, maintain balanced synthesis of L-tyrosine, L-phenylalanine and L-tryptophan in *C. glutamicum*. Furthermore, the aromatic amino acids thus produced cooperatively inhibit the activity of the first enzyme in aromatic amino acid biosynthesis, DAHP synthetase.

DERANGEMENT OF METABOLIC CONTROLS IN AROMATIC AMINO ACID PRODUCERS

The enzymes involved in aromatic amino acid biosynthesis in the mutants described above were also studied for their regulatory properties.

A phenylalanine auxotrophic L-tyrosine producer, strain Pr-20, had DAHP synthetase released from feedback inhibition by L-phenylalanine, L-tyrosine and L-tryptophan, and had two-fold derepressed chorismate mutase. L-Phenylalanine and L-tyrosine together still inhibited chorismate mutase activity though the enzyme was partially released from this inhibition by L-phenylalanine alone. Inhibition of the production of L-tyrosine by the mutant in a medium containing a high concentration of L-phenylalaine was found to be caused by the inhibition of chorismate mutase activity by L-phenylalanine. Furthermore, L-tyrosine production by whole cells of the mutant was stimulated by L-tryptophan competitively with L-phenylalanine. This phenomenon also appeared to be caused by the action on chorismate mutase. Thus the role of chorismate mutase to partition chorismate between the L-tryptophan pathway and the L-phenylalanine/L-tyrosine pathway in balanced amounts was demonstrated *in vivo*.

A tyrosine auxotrophic L-phenylalanine producer, strain PFP-19-31, had DAHP synthetase sensitive to the inhibition, and prephenate dehydratase and chorismate mutase both partially released from the inhibition by L-phenylalanine. The mutant produced a large amount of prephenate in addition to L-phenylalanine (Sugimoto *et al.*, 1974). This phenomenon is explicable as follows. By limiting the supply of L-tyrosine the feedback inhibition of DAHP synthetase is released, while chorismate mutase activity is feedback inhibited by the L-phenylalanine synthesized by the mutant. Accordingly, a considerable amount of chorismate synthesized in the cell under these conditions is converted either to prephenate, competitively with the inhibition by L-phenylalanine, or partially to L-tryptophan, which reverses the feedback inhibition of chorismate mutase by L-phenylalanine. Then a part of the prephenate synthesized is converted to L-phenylalanine competitively with the inhibition by L-phenylalanine. If the phenylalanine synthesized were quickly excreted from the cells, the accumulation of L-phenylalanine by the mutant PFP-19-31 would be easily explained because 58 per cent of the activity of prephenate dehydratase remains in the presence of 0.1 mM L-phenylalanine.

The prototrophic mutant, strain No. 66, resistant to PFP, produced a large amount of L-phenylalanine. Because the mutant has a wild-type DAHP synthetase, though it has desensitized prephenate dehydratase, production of a large amount of L-phenylalanine requires that L-tyrosine in the growth medium is low enough not to inhibit the activity of DAHP synthetase synergistically with L-phenylalanine. The K_m value of prephenate dehydratase for prephenate from the mutant ($K_m = 8.3 \times 10^{-5}$ M) was slightly decreased compared with that from the parent strain, ATCC 13032 ($K_m = 1.0 \times 10^{-4}$ M). Accordingly, L-phenylalanine biosynthesis in the mutant appears to proceed in preference to L-tyrosine biosynthesis because prephenate has a higher affinity for the prephenate dehydratase than for the prephenate dehydrogenase (K_m for prephenate $= 8.3 \times 10^{-4}$ M) and because the prephenate dehydratase was competitively released from the feedback inhibition by L-phenylalanine and L-tryptophan. Thus a large amount of L-phenylalanine production in the mutant is rationally explained.

The double (phenylalanine and tyrosine) auxotrophic L-trytophan producer strain, Px-115-97, has anthranilate synthetase partially released from
the inhibition by L-tryptophan and had wild-type DAHP synthetase. Though
other enzymes concerning L-tryptophan biosynthesis were not examined,
L-tryptophan production by the mutant appeared to be caused by the
release from feedback inhibition of anthranilate synthetase by L-tryptophan.

L-THREONINE PRODUCTION

A mutant of *E. coli* W, polyauxotrophic for diaminopimelic acid, methionine
and isoleucine produced 14 g dm^{-3} of L-threonine in a medium containing
7.5 per cent fructose (Kase *et al.*, 1971). Similar auxotrophic mutants of
C. glutamicum were unable to produce a large amount of L-threonine owing
to feedback inhibition by L-threonine on homoserine dehydrogenase. A
mutant resistant to a threonine analogue, α-amino-β-hydroxyvaleric acid
(AHV), produced L-threonine. A combination of polyauxotrophy and analogue-resistance increased the ability to produce L-threonine (Kase and
Nakayama, 1972). Thus strain KY 10440 which was obtained by stepwise
mutagenic improvement (Fig. 4) and is a methionine auxotroph resistant to
AHV and *S*-(β-aminoethyl)-L-cysteine (AEC, a lysine analogue) produced
14 g dm^{-3} of L-threonine in a medium containing 10 per cent glucose. Another
AHV and EAC resistant mutant, strain KY 10251 which was derived from
strain KY 10230, produced both 9 g dm^{-3} of L-threonine and 5.5 g dm^{-3} of
L-lysine.

The deviation of feedback control in these mutants from that in the wild-
type strain of *C. glutamicum* was examined. The regulation of threonine
biosynthesis in wild-type *C. glutamicum* is shown in Fig. 5. The activities of

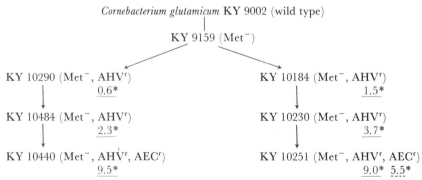

FIG. 4. Genealogy of mutants of *Corynebacterium glutamicum* producing L-threonine or L-threonine
and L-lysine. *The amount (g dm^{-3}) of L-threonine (solid underline) or L-lysine (broken underline)
produced in a medium containing 10 per cent glucose. Abbreviations: AHV, α-amino-β-hydroxyvaleric acid; AEC, *S*-(β-aminoethyl)-L-cysteine.

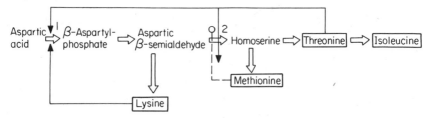

FIG. 5. Regulation of threonine biosynthesis in *C. glutamicum.* ⟶ Feedback inhibition; ---------○ repression. 1, aspartokinase; 2, homoserine dehydrogenase.

homoserine dehydrogenase in the mutants which produced L-threonine, or L-threonine and L-lysine, were slightly less susceptible to inhibition by L-threonine than the activity in the original strain, KY 9159. Thus genetical alteration of the enzyme may be a cause of L-threonine production in these mutants. The aspartokinase in threonine producing mutants, strains KY 10484 and KY 10230, which were resistant to AHV and more sensitive to AEC than the parent, was sensitive to concerted feedback inhibition by L-lysine and L-threonine to the same degree as strain KY 9159. The aspartokinase of strain KY 10440 was less susceptible to the concerted feedback inhibition than strains KY 10484 or KY 9159, although the activity was still under the feedback control. In strain KY 10251, which produces both L-threonine and L-lysine, L-threonine and L-lysine added simultaneously hardly inhibited the activity of aspartokinase. The difference in L-lysine production between strains KY 10440 and KY 10251 seems mainly to be due to a difference in the susceptibility of the aspartokinase to the concerted feedback inhibition by L-lysine and L-threonine. Furthermore, higher levels of L-threonine production in AHV and AEC-resistant mutants as compared with the parent AHV-resistant mutants could be brought about by the genetical desensitization of aspartokinase to end product inhibition.

L-HISTIDINE PRODUCTION

A 1,2,4-triazole-3-alanine (TRA)-resistant mutant, strain KY 10260, derived from the wild-type strain of *C. glutamicum,* ATCC 13761, produced several grams per litre of L-histidine in a cane molasses medium (Araki and Nakayama, 1971). The histidine productivity of strain KY 10260 could be improved stepwise by successively introducing such characters as purine analogue-resistance, pyrimidine analogue-resistance, increased resistance to histidine analogue and tryptophan analogue-resistance as shown in Fig. 6 (Araki *et al.,* 1974a, 1974b). The improvement of L-histidine productivity in each step was rather minor, but the mutant strain finally selected, AT-83, produced approximately twice as much L-histidine as the original strain

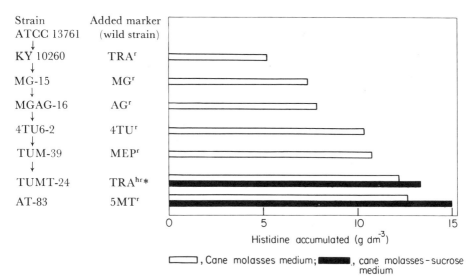

FIG. 6. Increase in histidine productivity by the successive additions of purine, pyrimidine, histidine and tryptophan analogue-resistance to *C. glutamicum* KY 10260. *High resistance to TRA. Abbreviations: TRA, 1,2,4-triazole-3-alanine; MG, 6-mercaptoguanine; AG, 8-aza-guanine; 4TU, 4-thiouracil; MEP, 6-mercaptopurine; 5-MT, 5-methyltryptophan.

KY 10260. Amongst the steps, the introduction of 4-thiouracil-resistance resulted in the most significant increase in L-histidine productivity.

The principle of the improvement was to increase the supply of 5-phospho-ribosylpyrophosphate and adenine nucleotide for L-histidine biosynthesis by releasing feedback regulation on their biosynthesis, based on the speculation that the regulatory mechanism of L-histidine biosynthesis and related reactions known in some other microorganisms (Brenner and Ames, 1971; Gots, 1971; Stadman, 1966) would be applicable to *C. glutamicum*. The improvement on increasing resistance to TRA could be explained in terms of a further release of end product regulation in the histidine pathway in consequence of a mutation additional to the original one in strain KY 10260.

2-Fluoroadenine-resistant mutants derived from histidine-producing mutants and from the wild-type strain of *C. glutamicum*, ATCC 13761, produced a large amount of adenine in the culture medium. This is explained in terms of the lack of feedback regulation in the biosynthesis of adenine nucleotide, overproduction and decomposition of the nucleotides and excretion in the form of adenine base.

L-ARGININE PRODUCTION

A wild-type strain of *C. glutamicum* was found to be highly resistant to the arginine analogues, canavanine and arginine hydroxamate. A D-serine-sensitive mutant DSS-8 derived from an isoleucine auxotroph was found to be sensitive to canavanine and arginine hydroxamate and to produce a small amount of L-arginine. The productivity of L-arginine in this mutant was improved stepwise by mutation and selection (Fig. 7). Strain KY 10576, a mutant derived from the D-serine-sensitive mutant, and resistant to both D-arginine and arginine hydroxamate, produced 25 g dm^{-3} of L-arginine in a cane molasses medium containing 15 per cent sugar calculated as glucose (Nakayama and Yoshida, 1972).

Corynebacterium glutamicum		L-Arginine produced (g dm^{-3})
KY 10025		
↓		
KY 10150	(Ile$^-$)	
↓		
DSS-8	(Ile$^-$, D-Ser^s)	1.5*
↓		
KY 10479	(Ile$^-$, D-Ser^s, D-Arg^r)	6.8*
↓		
KY 10480	(Ile$^-$, D-Ser^s, D-Arg^r, ArgHx^r)	16.6†
↓		
KY 10508	(Ile$^+$, D-Ser^s, D-Arg^r, ArgHx^r)	19.6†
↓		
KY 10576	(Ile$^+$, D-Ser^s, D-Arg^r, ArgHx^r)	25.0†

FIG. 7. Genealogy of L-arginine-producing mutants and their L-arginine productivity. *With a medium containing 7.5 per cent glucose.† With a cane molasses medium containing 15 per cent sugar (as glucose). Abbreviations: ArgHx, arginine hydroxamate.

Strain DSS-8, its parent isoleucine auxotroph KY 10150, and the original wild strain KY 10025 all showed the same level of arginase activity in determinations both with L-arginine and with arginine analogues (L-canavanine, L-homoarginine, D-arginine and arginine hydroxamate) as the substrate. The accumulation of both D- and L-arginine by cells of strain DSS-8 was approximately 1.5 times larger than that by strain KY 10150. Increased permeability of DSS-8 cells to D- and L-arginine is the explanation of the senstitivity to L-arginine analogues and of the production of the D-serine-sensitive mutant, DSS-8.

Conclusion

Selection of the proper regulatory mutants of *Corynebacterium glutamicum* utilizing the analogue technique, and a combination of auxotrophy and regulatory defects, led to success in developing new industrial processes for the production of L-tyrosine, L-phenylalanine, L-tryptophan, L-threonine, L-histidine and L-arginine.

References

Araki, K. and Nakayama, K. (1971). *Agr. Biol. Chem.* **35**, 2081.
Araki, K. and Kato, F., Ari, Y. and Nakayama, K. (1974a). *Agr. Biol. Chem.* **38**, 189.
Araki, K., Shimojo, S. and Nakayama, K. (1974b). *Agr. Biol. Chem.* **38**, 837.
Brenner, M. and Ames, B. N. (1971). "Metabolic Pathway" (Ed. H. H. Vogel), vol. 5, p. 349. Academic Press, New York and London.
Gots, J. S. (1971). "Metabolic Pathway" (Ed. H. H. Vogel), p. 225. Academic Press, New York and London.
Hagino, H., Yoshida, H., Kato, F., Arai, Y., Katsumata, R. and Nakayama, K. (1973). *Agr. Biol. Chem.* **37**, 2001.
Hagino, H. and Nakayama, K. (1973a). *Agr. Biol. Chem.* **37**, 2007.
Hagino, H. and Nakayama, K. (1973b). *Agr. Biol. Chem.* **37**, 2013.
Hagino, H. and Nakayama, K. (1974a). *Agr. Biol. Chem.* **38**, 157.
Hagino, H. and Nakayama, K. (1974b). *Agr. Biol. Chem.* In press.
Hagino, H. and Nakayama, K. (1974c). *Agr. Biol. Chem.* In press.
Hagino, H. and Nakayama, K. (1974d). *Agr. Biol. Chem.* In press.
Hagino, H. and Nakayama, K. (1974e). *Agr. Biol. Chem.* In press.
Hagino, H. and Nakayama, K. (1974f). *Agr. Biol. Chem.* In press.
Kase, H., Tanaka, H. and Nakayama, K. (1971). *Agr. Biol. Chem.* **35**, 2089.
Kase, H. and Nakayama, K. (1972). *Agr. Biol. Chem.* **36**, 1611.
Kinoshita, S., Tanaka, K., Udaka, S. and Akita, S. (1957). *Proc. Int. Symp. Enzyme. Chem.* **2**, 464.
Nakayama, K. (1972). "Fermentation Technology Today" (Proc. IV International Fermentation Symposium) (Ed. G. Terui), p. 433. Society of Fermentation Technology, Japan, Osaka.
Nakayama, K. (1973). "Genetics of Industrial Microorganisma" (Eds Z. Vanék, Z. Hošťálek and J. Cudlin), vol. 1, Bacteria, p. 219. Elsevier, London.
Nakayama, K., Sato, Z. and Kinoshita, S. (1960). *Nippon Nogeikagaku Kaishi*, **34**, 938.
Nakayama, K., Sato, Z. and Kinoshita, S. (1961a). *Nippon Nogeikagaku Kaishi*, **35**, 142.
Nakayama, K., Sato, Z. and Kinoshita, S. (1961b). *Nippon Nogeikagaku Kaishi*, **35**, 146.
Nakayama, K. and Yoshida, H. (1972). *Agr. Biol. Chem.* **36**, 1675.
Stadman, E. R. (1966). *Adv. Enzymol.* **28**, 41.
Sugimoto, M., Tsuruta, T. and Imada, K. (1974). Abstract of Papers, Annual Meet. Agr. Chem. Soc. Japan, April, 1974. p. 180.

A biochemical and genetical approach to the biosynthesis of cephalosporin C

J. NÜESCH, A. HINNEN, M. LIERSCH and H. J. TREICHLER

*Research Department, Pharmaceutical Division, Ciba-Geigy Ltd,
Basel, Switzerland*

Summary

Methods of investigating the biosynthesis of cephalosporin C in *Cephalosporium acremonium* by biochemical and genetical means are demonstrated with the aid of two biochemical models. The relationship between methionine uptake and cephalosporin C synthesis and the pathway leading to cephalosporin C through oxidation and acetylation of the free methyl group of the valinyl moiety are examined. The implication of this terminal reaction sequence of cephalosporin C synthesis for the regulation of the excretion of intermediate products is shown. Finally an important aspect concerning the enzymatic deacetylation of cephalosporin C under certain physiological conditions is discussed.

Introduction

In considering regulatory and enzymatic aspects of the biosynthesis of secondary metabolites two distinct features must be kept in mind. In the first sequence of events, primary metabolism is involved in generating such metabolites as will subsequently serve as precursors for secondary metabolism. The latter combines the primary metabolites directly or after certain specific modifications to form new products, e.g. secondary metabolites. It is therefore obvious that investigations of the genetical and biochemical mechanisms leading to secondary metabolites are much more complicated than those leading to a primary metabolite, e.g. an amino acid.

This contribution is an attempt to characterize, on the one hand, a particular

451

aspect of primary metabolism involved in the biosynthesis of cephalosporin C and, on the other hand, enzymatic reactions as well as intermediary products of the biochemical machinery of secondary metabolism.

In the excellent monograph on cephalosporins and penicillins edited by Flynn, Lemke and Brannon (1972) give an extensive survey of our knowledge of the biosynthesis of the β-lactam antibiotics. It now seems clear that three pathways leading to the primary amino acids, L-lysine, L-cysteine and L-valine, are connected with the biosynthesis of all β-lactam antibiotics. In the case of the lysine pathway an intermediary product, L-α-aminoadipic acid, is the direct precursor whereas in the other two cases L-cysteine and L-valine are the end products of the corresponding primary pathways and are direct precursors of the secondary metabolites, the β-lactam antibiotics. This situation has now become even more cómplicated by the discovery of the cephamycins, β-lactam antibiotics from *Streptomycetes,* a group of prokaryotic microorganisms (Stapley *et al.,* 1972). In these producers the α-aminoadipic acid seems to be a catabolic product of lysine (Kirkpatrick *et al.,* 1973).

With regard to regulatory aspects, the few investigations existing show a clear relation between a deregulated formation of the primary amino acids lysine and valine and the production of β-lactam antibiotics. In both cases the regulation occurs at an early enzyme in the pathway and the mechanism belongs to the feedback inhibition type (lysine: Goulden and Chattaway, 1968; Masurekar and Demain, 1972; Lemke and Nash, 1972; Nüesch *et al.,* 1972; valine: Goulden and Chattaway, 1969).

Another important aspect of primary metabolism in relation to the synthesis of β-lactam antibiotics is the formation of the cysteinyl moiety and its relation to sulphur metabolism. The β-lactam antibiotics produced by the *Penicillium*-type, as well as by the prokaryotic *Streptomycetes,* form cysteine preferentially through a condensation of reduced sulphur and serine by the enzyme, cysteine synthase. Eukaryotic producers of the *Cephalosporium*-type utilize methionine most efficiently as the sulphur donor for the cysteinyl moiety in β-lactam antibiotics (Lemke and Brannon, 1972). Methionine uptake in *Cephalosporium acremonium* offers an interesting model for an investigation of regulatory aspects of the biosynthesis of secondary metabolites and will be discussed in detail.

Considering the biosynthesis of β-lactam antibiotics in its proper sense, e.g. the reaction sequences which condense the amino acid precursors to the chemically complicated heterocyclic peptide-like compounds, *C. acremonium* represents a system which is particularily suited for biochemical and genetical investigations. In analogy to Arnstein's tripeptide from *Penicillium chrysogenum* (Arnstein and Clubb, 1958), peptides from *C. acremonium* have been isolated which are presumed to be precursors of β-lactam antibiotics (Abraham *et al.,* 1964; Loder and Abraham, 1971a, 1971b). Further, three β-lactam antibiotics, penicillin N, cephalosporin C and deacetylcephalosporin C can be found in culture broths of *C. acremonium*. Assuming that the biosynthesis of penicillin N and cephalosporin C follow a common pathway at first, it is of particular interest to investigate those steps of reactions where the two compounds show differences. It is generally agreed that the essential difference in the biosynthesis of penicillin N with respect to cephalosporin C involves the oxidation of one methyl group of the valinyl moiety. It is a matter of speculation whether this oxidation occurs early, at the level of the tripeptide, or later at the level of cyclic intermediates. Demain (1963) proposed that 3-cephem as well as penem antibiotics would be derived from the same α,β-dehydrovaline derivative of the tripeptide. He predicted isodeacetoxycephalosporin C as the first cephalosporin compound which would be further oxidized and acetylated to yield isocephalosporin C and through inversion of the free α-amino group, by a racemase, cephalosporin C would be formed (Lemke and Brannon, 1972). Our investigations (Liersch *et al.*, 1975) as well as results from other laboratories (Huber *et al.*, 1968; Fujisawa *et al.*, 1973; Konecny *et al.*, 1973; Neuss *et al.*, 1973; Nagarajan *et al.*, 1975) made it possible to elucidate the pathway for the formation of the acetoxy group in cephalosporin C and to draw conclusions concerning the regulation of its biosynthesis.

Material and methods

CULTURAL CONDITIONS FOR PRODUCTION OF β-LACTAM ANTIBIOTICS WITH
C. ACREMONIUM

The conditions were as described by Nüesch *et al.* (1973). The complete medium was as follows:

Peanut meal, $30 \, g \, dm^{-3}$; molasses, $20 \, g \, dm^{-3}$; corn meal, $20 \, g \, dm^{-3}$; methyloleate, $6.7 \, g \, dm^{-3}$; DL-methionine, $10 \, g \, dm^{-3}$; borax, $0.5 \, g \, dm^{-3}$; CaCo$_3$, $5 \, g \, dm^{-3}$; tap water, pH adjusted to 7.0 with 1 N KOH before sterilization at $120 \, C$ for 20 minutes.

This medium was also solidified for the prescreening of blocked mutants with 2 per cent agar.

MUTAGENESIS
See Nüesch *et al.* (1973).

MICROBIOLOGICAL ASSAYS OF β-LACTAM ANTIBIOTICS
See Nüesch *et al.* (1973).

HIGH-PRESSURE LIQUID CHROMATOGRAPHY OF CEPHEM ANTIBIOTICS
See Konecny *et al.* (1973).

PAPER CHROMATOGRAPHY AND BIOAUTOGRAPHY

See Nüesch *et al.* (1973).

DETERMINATION OF METHIONINE

See Nüesch *et al.* (1973).

DETERMINATION OF 2-KETO- AND 2-HYDROXY-4-METHIOLBUTYRIC ACID

See Benz *et al.* (1971).

PERMEASE ASSAY

See Marzluf (1970). The reaction was carried out in 0.1 M phosphate buffer pH 7 in 20 cm^3 shake flasks with 5 cm^3 reaction mixture. Cell suspensions of 10 mg cm^{-3} expressed as dry weight were used. Usually 0.1 μC cm^{-3} of radioactivity was employed. The measurements were carried out in the linear phase of uptake after 3 to 6 min.

ASSAYS OF ESTERASES

Acetyl-hydrolase activity was measured according to Pocker and Stone (1967) with *p*-nitrophenylacetate as substrate.

Cephalosporin C acetyl-hydrolase activity was followed by a modified acidimetric method (Rubin and Smith, 1973). The reaction mixture contained cephalosporin C 100 mM, tris 0.005 M pH 7.5 and phenol red 0.0006 per cent (w/v).

Both tests were carried out at 25°C.

DEAE-SEPHADEX A-50 CHROMATOGRAPHY

All operations were carried out between 0 and 4°C. The culture broth was centrifuged for 20 min at 13 000 × g to remove the cells. The supernatant was concentrated ten-fold by precipitating with ammonium sulphate to 90 per cent saturation. The precipitate was dissolved in 0.1 M tris pH 8.1 and desalted by Sephadex G-25. The salt-free extract was placed on a DEAE-Sephadex A-50 column in the presence of the same buffer and eluted by a linear NaCl gradient from 0 → 0.5 M.

ULTRACENTRIFUGATION

Ultracentrifugation in sucrose-gradient was carried out according to Martin and Ames (1961) in a Heraeus Christ Omega II centrifuge for 20 hours at about 100000 × g with myoglobin as standard.

GEL ELECTROPHORESIS

The tris–glycine system as described by Maurer (1971) was used. Acetyl-hydrolase activity was detected by activity-staining (Gabriel, 1971).

CHEMICALS

All labelled compounds were purchased at the Radiochemical Centre, Amersham, England.

Sephadex G-25 and DEAE-Sephadex A-50 were obtained from Pharmacia (Uppsala, Sweden), diisopropyl fluorophosphate from Fluka (Buchs, Switzerland), myoglobin from Schwarz/Mann (New York) and *p*-nitrophenyl-acetate from Schuchardt (München, Germany). All other chemicals (analytical grade) were purchased from Merck (Darmstadt, Germany).

β-Lactam antibiotics: see Liersch *et al.* (1975).

Results and discussion

METHIONINE UPTAKE AND ITS INFLUENCE ON CEPHALOSPORIN C FORMATION

For a long time methionine has been known to be the optimal sulphur donor in the biosynthesis of cephalosporin C by *C. acremonium* (Caltrider and Niss, 1966; Nüesch *et al.*, 1973).

C. acremonium possesses, like other fungi, a complex sulphur metabolism, characterized by reverse *trans*-sulphuration (Kerr and Flavin, 1970). Both isomers of methionine permit growth and antibiotic synthesis. D-Methionine is converted into L-methionine by a two-enzyme system, a D-amino acid and an L-amino acid transaminase. These two enzyme systems are also responsible for the extracellular accumulation of 2-keto-4-methiolbutyric acid which is subsequently reduced to 2-hydroxy-4-methiolbutyric acid by means of a dehydrogenase (Benz *et al.*, 1971; Liersch *et al.*, 1973).

We have shown (Nüesch *et al.*, 1973) that a mutant of *C. acremonium* impaired in sulphur assimilation gave a four-fold increase in cephalosporin C synthesis over the wild strain. Auxanographic studies showed that the mutant is able to grow in the presence of sulphite and sulphide but not sulphate. In view of results with other fungi (Benko *et al.*, 1967) we assumed that the transport of methionine into the cells may be regulated by an intermediate, in particular sulphide, of the sulphate reduction and assimilation pathway. A series of experiments has been carried out to investigate the influence of sulphur compounds, such as sulphide, on the methionine uptake system and to characterize the latter. On the other hand it was important to know if any relationship exists between the uptake rate of methionine and the formation of cephalosporin C.

The results in Table 1 show that Na_2S strongly inhibits the formation of cephalosporin C in a chemically defined medium. Although the sulphate nonassimilating mutant 8650slp grows very well with sulphide as sole sulphur source, the formation of cephalosporin C is practically nil. If the medium is supplemented with methionine and sulphide, cephalosporin

TABLE 1

Influence of Na_2S on growth and cephalosporin C production of *C. acremonium* strain 8650slp*

Incubation time h	Basal medium	Additions		Growth: pmv†	Cephalosporin C μg cm^{-3}
		DL-Methionine g dm^{-3}	Na_2S g dm^{-3}		
		4	—	35	670
		–	6.24	25	60
120	III	–	3.12	31	—
		–	1.56	20	—
		4	6.24	31	156
		4	3.12	35	234
		4	1.56	20	90

* Shake flask trial with chemically defined medium III (Nüesch *et al.*, 1973).

† 10 cm^3 of broth centrifuged 10 min at 1300 × g and the packed mycelial volume (pmv) expressed as percentage of total volume.

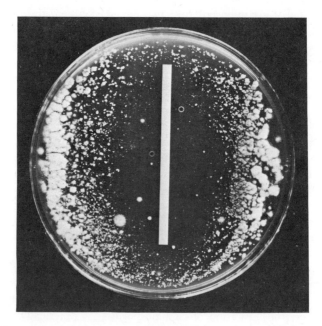

FIG. 1. Selection of DL-seleno-methionine resistant mutants of *C. acremonium*.

formation is only partially restored. Thin-layer chromatography reveals a remarkable reduction in methionine uptake in the presence of sulphide.

In order to investigate further methionine transport into the cells, and its relation to cephalosporin C synthesis, mutants with impaired transport systems for methionine have been selected with the aid of DL-seleno-methionine (Fig. 1). It was possible to isolate strains with various degrees of sensitivity to seleno-methionine (Fig. 2). A highly resistant mutant, HR. F204, with a ten-fold increase in seleno-methionine resistance (MIC 45 μg cm^{-3}), has been tested in chemically defined, as well as in several complex nutrient media, for the ability to synthesize cephalosporin C.

The drastic reduction of methionine uptake in strain HR. F204 is paralleled by a strong reduction in both cephalosporin C formation and excretion of 2-hydroxy-4-methiolbutyric acid, a deamination product of methionine

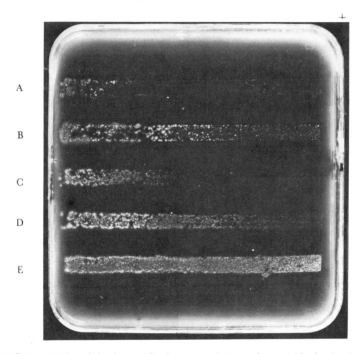

FIG. 2. Determination of the degree of resistance against DL-seleno-methionine by the gradient method.

		MIC μg cm^{-3}
A,	wild-type K17/42	4
B,	mutant LR F204	18
C,	wild-type F204	12
D,	mutant LR F204	18
E,	mutant HR F204	45

TABLE 2

Methionine uptake, growth and cephalosporin C synthesis in a DL-seleno-methionine resistant mutant of *C. acremonium* strain 8650slp F 204*

Incubation time h	Strain	Growth pmv†	DL-Methionine uptake as a % of methionine	Cephalosporin C μg cm^{-3}	2-Hydroxy-4-methiolbutyric acid excreted μg cm^{-3}	Total sugar uptake as a % of amount added
120	8650slp F 204 (control)	24	78.25	1064	1750	99.75
120	F 204/4hr seleno-methionine resistant	44	7.0	60	750	98.2

* Shake flask culture with chemically defined medium IIIa (Nüesch *et al.*, 1973).
† See footnote to Table 1.

(Table 2). Nevertheless the amount of methionine consumed is high enough to permit optimal growth. The experiment illustrates that in comparison with the control, biomass production in the seleno-methionine resistant mutant seems to increase at the expense of cephalosporin C synthesis showing a certain "uncoupling" of primary and secondary metabolism.

In the light of these results a series of experiments were carried out to characterize methionine transport in *C. acremonium*. The following questions seemed to be of particular interest. Firstly, what physiological conditions influence the methionine uptake system? Secondly, are there specific inhibitors of methionine permeases? Thirdly, how complex is the transport system? In contrast to the extensive studies of amino acid permease systems in fungi, e.g. by Benko *et al.* (1967), Hunter and Segel (1973) and Pall (1971), it was our aim to characterize methionine. uptake of *C. acremonium* in the active phase of cephalosporin C synthesis. Therefore the mycelial cell mass was harvested from the chemically defined basal medium III supplemented with DL-methionine (Nüesch *et al.*, 1973) at the time of maximal rate of cephalosporin C formation. The transport of methionine and other amino acids was determined according to a slightly modified procedure of Marzluf (1970) using ^{14}C-labelled substances dissolved in 0.1 M phosphate buffer pH 7.

The uptake of L-methionine proceeds linearly for about 6 minutes (Fig. 3); $2 \mu mol \, cm^{-3}$ of sodium azide completely inhibits methionine transport

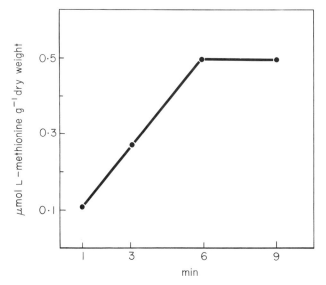

FIG. 3. Time-course of L-methionine uptake.

which suggests that the intracellular accumulation depends on metabolic energy, a characteristic of an active transport. On the other hand, 1 μmol cm^{-3} of 2,4-dinitrophenol has no effect on methionine uptake or on growth of the organism. The transport system can be destroyed by keeping the mycelium in boiling water for five minutes.

An analysis of the effect of external concentration of L-methionine on the velocity of methionine uptake revealed that the system follows saturation

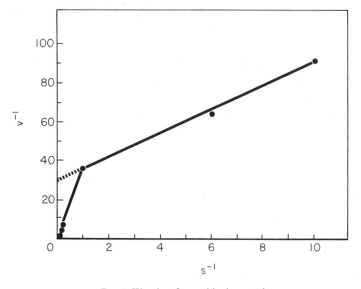

FIG. 4. Kinetics of L-methionine uptake.

kinetics. However saturation is achieved only at very high levels of substrate concentration. The Lineweaver–Burk plot of the uptake rate versus external substrate concentration reveals that at least two processes with different affinities for L-methionine are involved (Fig. 4). As mentioned before it was not our intention to separate different transport systems, e.g. by keeping the mycelium under specific nutrient-deficient conditions. However, in contrast to results with *Penicillium chrysogenum* (Hunter and Segel, 1973) under nutrient-sufficient conditions, where the uptake was of a near first-order nature (this being characterized by free diffusion), *C. acremonium* mycelium from a production medium still displays second-order kinetics of L-methionine transport. This statement is supported by the sensitivity to Na-azide and competition between alternate substrates.

The activity of the methionine transport system varies according to the sulphur compound used in the cultivation medium (Table 3). If in the basal

TABLE 3

Effect of sulphur compounds on the induction of the L-methionine transport system*

Culture medium		L-Methionine uptake†
Basal medium	Addition 4 g dm^{-3}	(in % of control)
	DL-methionine (control)	100
III	L-cysteine	27
	Na$_2$S$_2$O$_3$	6
	D-methionine	19

* Shake flask culture with chemically defined medium III (Nüesch et al., 1973).
† Using standard permease assay.

medium III supplemented with 4 g dm^{-3} DL-methionine this amino acid is replaced by other sulphur compounds in equimolar amounts, then the transport activity for methionine is influenced. A particularly strong reduction of L-methionine uptake is exerted by Na thiosulphate. Thiosulphate is split into sulphite and sulphide by a dismutase and represents therefore a source of sulphide. L-Cysteine as well as D-methionine have intermediate effects. The action of the above compounds on the methionine permease system is concentration dependent. At half the chosen concentrations the effect is only marginal.

TABLE 4

Inhibition of L-methionine uptake in the presence of various compounds

Unlabelled compound (10 μmol cm^{-3})	L-Methionine uptake (0.1 μmol cm^{-3}) % of control with no unlabelled compound
Control	100
Na$_2$SO$_4$	100
NaHSO$_3$	100
Na$_2$S$_2$O$_3$	100
Na$_2$S	100
L-Cysteine	7
DL-Homocysteine	24
D-Methionine	27
2-Keto-4-methiolbutyric acid	100
D-2-Hydroxy-4-methiolbutyric acid	100
S-Methyl-L-cysteine	4
DL-Phenylalanine	7

TABLE 5

Trans-inhibition of L-cysteine, L-methionine and DL-phenylalanine uptake in *C. acremonium* mutant 8650lp*

Labelled amino acid (0.1 μmol cm⁻³)	Unlabelled amino acid (10 μmol cm⁻³)	Uptake as a percentage of control without unalbelled amino acid		
		L-Cysteine	L-Methionine	DL-Phenylalanine
L-Methionine	—		100	
L-Methionine	L-cysteinine		5	
L-Methionine	DL-phenylalanine		7	
L-Methionine	D-methionine		20	
L-Cysteine	—	100		
L-Cysteine	L-methionine	6		
L-Cysteine	D-methionine	25		
DL-Phenylalanine	—			100
DL-Phenylalanine	L-methionine			5
DL-Phenylalanine	D-methionine			37

* According to Pall (1971).

To establish whether the interaction concerns permease activity, rather than induction or derepression of the system, investigations of L-methionine uptake in the presence of various sulphur compounds and nonrelated amino acids have been carried out. The results in Table 4 show that the inorganic sulphur compounds including Na sulphide are not inhibitors of the L-methionine transport system. With regard to amino acids the spectrum of activity is very broad. Beside the amino acids shown in Table 4, L-norleucine (a nonsulphur analogue of methionine), L-arginine, L-lysine, L-tryptophan or L-valine, are inhibitory whereas L-α-aminoadipic acid and L-proline do not

TABLE 6

The relation between methionine uptake and cephalosporin C production in *C. acremonium*

Strain*	Cephalosporin C production as a percentage of control	L-Methionine uptake as a percentage of control under standard conditions
8650slp (control)	100	100
8650slp-1	120	110
8650slp-2	150	190
8650slp-3	120	240

* Productivity examined in shake flask cultures using a complex production medium.

interfere with methionine transport. *Trans*-inhibition studies (Table 5) with L-methionine, L-cysteine and DL-phenylalanine revealed that these three amino acids appear to compete for the same permease system. The control with D-methionine shows once again that L-methionine transport is effected by more than one permease. On the basis of the above experiments one may conclude that *C. acremonium* possesses, during the phase of active synthesis of cephalosporin C in methionine-containing media, a complex but very efficient system of methionine uptake. The system shows a very low degree of specificity, reflected in the results of inhibition and *trans*-inhibition studies. An inorganic sulphur compound, probably sulphide, exerts a regulatory effect on L-methionine uptake which cannot be explained by *trans*-inhibition. This regulation seems to be at the level of permease synthesis. In view of this result the increase in cephalosporin C synthesis in mutant 8650slp, blocked in the assimilation of inorganic sulphur, can be explained on the basis of methionine transport. That methionine uptake is a rate limiting step in cephalosporin C synthesis is illustrated by a range of high producing mutants derived from mutant 8650slp (Table 6). There is a positive correlation between cephalosporin C productivity and methionine uptake for three mutants. On the other hand one mutant with an exceptionally efficient methionine transport system shows no further increase in cephalosporin C synthesis.

FORMATION OF THE C-3-ACETOXY GROUP IN CEPHALOSPORIN C

In the introduction we mentioned that the C-3-acetoxy group of cephalosporin C offers an excellent model to study the final steps in the biosynthesis of this antibiotic. Such studies are not only of theoretical but also of great practical interest. Deacetoxycephalosporin C, for example, is a possible intermediate in the biosynthesis of cephalosporin C and at the same time an interesting product for chemical modification. Recently, information of considerable interest concerning the biosynthesis of the acetoxy group in cephalosporin C appeared in the literature. Fujisawa et al. (1973) were able to isolate mutants of C. acremonium M.8650 producing deacetylcephalosporin C exclusively. These authors also demonstrated the existence of a cephalosporin C O-acetyltransferase which is able to acetylate deacetylcephalosporin C to cephalosporin C using acetyl-CoA as the acetate donor. Mutants producing exclusively deacetylcephalosporin C showed no acetyltransferase activity. Independently Liersch et al. (1975) confirmed these results. On the other hand, the Eli Lilly group was able to detect deacetoxycephalosporin C in various fungi and Streptomycetes but they did not mention the cephalosporin C producer C. acremonium M.8650, or derivatives of this strain, as producers of deacetoxycephalosporin C (Dutch patent application, 1973; Higgens et al., 1974; Nagarajan et al., 1974). At the beginning of 1972 in our laboratories we detected small amounts of deacetoxycephalosporin C for the first time in a sample of cephalosporin C from a high producing mutant derived from C. acremonium M.8650 (Liersch, M., unpublished results). This interesting result opened a new field of research. In was of particular interest to know if deacetoxycephalosporin C would be an intermediate in the pathway leading to cephalosporin C or an occasional by-product. A genetic investigation of the cephalosporin C producing fungus C. acremonium was started, aiming to induce and select monogenic mutants blocked in certain biogenetic steps.

The investigator of secondary metabolism is faced with certain specific difficulties. In the case of primary metabolites of microorganisms their biosynthesis can be elucidated using blocked mutants. This well-known technique cannot be applied in the same way to secondary metabolites as it is based on the fact that the pathway leads to a compound essential for growth. Secondary products do not fulfil this condition.

Mutants of C. acremonium unable to synthesize cephalosporin C but retaining the potential to synthesize penicillin N have been isolated by Lemke and Nash (1972). The same technique was successfully applied by Fujisawa et al. (1973) to isolate deacetylcephalosporin C producing mutants. If one assumes that a sequence of steps leads from penicillin N or from a common yet unknown penem or cephem precursor to cephalosporin C, one would expect that cephalosporin C-minus mutants which still retain the capacity to produce penicillin N belong to a group impaired in the final step, e.g. introduction of the acetoxy moiety, of cephalosporin C formation. If Demain's hypothesis is correct (Demain, 1963) such mutants could possibly accumulate compounds like D- or L-deacetoxy- or deacetylcephalosporin C or as yet unknown metabolic products.

We were aware that the hypothetical intermediates, deacetoxy- and deacetylcephalosporin C, show some activity against the commonly used test organism for cephalosporin, *Alcaligenes faecalis* ATCC 8750. In comparison with cephalosporin C the two compounds show about 10 per cent and 20 per cent respectively of the activity of cephalosporin C. Therefore in the selection programme it was necessary to consider not only nonproducers but also low producing mutants. The presence of penicillin N was detected with the aid of *Sarcina lutea* ATCC 9341, a bacterium showing a high resistance to cephalosporin C and the steroid antibiotics of the cephalosporin P group. In view of the large number of strains which had to be examined for the selection of one blocked mutant a special production procedure was developed.

Briefly, mutagenically treated conidia were spread onto a complete medium, solidified with agar, allowing optimal cephalosporin C and penicillin N production. After antibiotic synthesis had reached a maximum in the colonies growing from surviving conidia, pieces of equal size were cut out of every colony using very small cylinders, and tested for their activity against *A. faecalis* in an agar diffusion test. About 40 per cent of the tested colonies were stable nonproducers in this test. In a second step these nonproducing colonies were examined in shake flask cultures using a complex medium for optimal cephalosporin C production. Table 7 summarizes the results. Seven different groups of mutants have been distinguished. The first three groups are generally low producers of β-lactam antibiotics. Nearly 70 per cent of the total colonies examined form a group of low producers, in which the reduction in antibiotic synthesis is due to an impairment in methionine uptake. Of particular interest are the strains belonging to the yield groups C and D. These two groups comprise the strains producing deacetyl- or deacetoxycephalosporin C instead of cephalosporin C. In comparison with the total number of isolates tested 4.8 per cent are deacetyl- and 3.4 per cent are deacetoxycephalosporin C producers.

On the basis of this genetic investigation and given the biochemical characterization of the presumed enzymatic steps (Fujisawa *et al.*, 1973; Liersch *et al.*, 1974) the pathway of the C-3-acetoxy group formation in cephalosporin C synthesis in *C. acremonium* is now fully elucidated. The reaction sequence leads from deacetoxycephalosporin C to deacetylcephalo-

TABLE 7

Classification of various mutant strains

Group characterization	Yield group	Number of strains tested	Percentage of total	Antibiotic potency as a percentage of reference strain	
				A. faecalis	S. lutea
Original parent strain (reference strain)	Cephalosporin C-high producer	—	—	100	100
Mutants impaired in methionine uptake	LP 1	168	68.8	10–50	10–50
Crippled strains and auxotrophic mutants	LP 2	25	10.2	10	10
Mutants with unknown properties	LP 3	19	7.8	10–30	10–30
Ceph C⁻ pen N⁻	A	9	3.8	0	0
Ceph C⁻ pen N⁺	B	3	1.2	0	50–100
Deacetylcephalosporin C-producer	C	12	4.8	4–7	100
Deacetoxycephalosporin C-producer	D	8	3.4	3–5	100
Total number of isolates		244	100		

sporin C and subsequently to cephalosporin C. Two enzyme systems are involved in these two steps: a hydroxylase (class 1 oxido-reductase) and an O-acetyl-transferase (Liersch *et al.*, 1975; Fujisawa *et al.*, 1973). Both intermediate compounds possess an *N*-acyl-α-amino-adipoyl moiety with the D-configuration of the free amino group. In contrast to Demain's hypothesis,

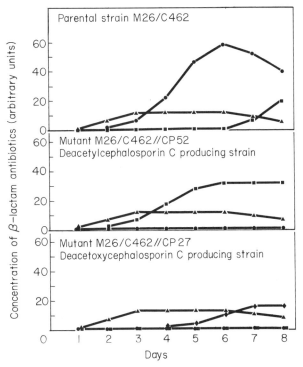

F IG. 5. Fermentation curves of cephalosporin C, deacetylcephalosporin C and deacetoxycephalosporin C producing mutants. ●, Cephalosporin C; ■, deacetylcephalosporin C; ◆, deacetoxycephalosporin C; ▲, penicillin N.

conversion of the α-aminoadipic acid from the L to the D form must occur before the cephem nucleus is built up.

From the point of view of regulation, a comparison of the fermentation pattern of a high producing cephalosporin C strain with a particular deacetoxycephalosporin C or deacetylcephalosporin C producing mutant derived from it is very instructive. Figure 5 shows that the cephalosporin C producing parental strain starts to synthesize cephalosporin C (in a shake flask culture with a complex nutrient medium) on the second day of incubation. Only small amounts of deacetylcephalosporin C are detectable during the phase of rapid cephalosporin C production between the 3rd and 5th day. From the 5th day on, however, there was a remarkable increase in the accumulation of deacetylcephalosporin C followed by a decrease in cephalosporin C. This aspect is dealt with in the final section. The deacetylcephalosporin C producing mutant showed a very similar picture with regard to the time-course of accumulation of deacetylcephalosporin C in comparison to cephalosporin C formation in the parental strain. However, a striking contrast was seen in the amount of deacetylcephalosporin C accumulated. In comparison with cephalosporin C it reached only about one half of the latter. The third mutant, which produced exclusively deacetoxycephalosporin C, was characterized by a rather late formation of this compound, starting at the fifth day of incubation and reaching its maximum at about seven days.

As in the case of the deacetylcephalosporin C mutant no decrease in activity was observed, but the maximal titre of deacetoxycephalosporin C reached only one seventh of the cephalosporin C titre in the parental strain. In conclusion one may assume that blocked mutants accumulate the intermediate product. However, they exert a strong product-inhibitory effect on their own synthesis. This effect is strictly restricted to the formation of the cephem antibiotics. As shown in Fig. 5, penicillin N formation does not differ between the parental strain and the two mutants.

The final transformation of the free methyl group of the cephem nucleus seems therefore to facilitate the excretion of the product thus avoiding regulatory effects on its own synthesis.

CATABOLIC REACTION ON THE C-3-ACETOXY GROUP OF CEPHALOSPORIN C

Huber et al. (1968) investigated the origin of deacetylcephalosporin C in cephalosporin C fermentation broths. They concluded that the formation of deacetylcephalosporin C is due to nonenzymatic hydrolysis of cephalosporin C. Konecny et al. (1973), however, concluded, on the basis of their investigation on the kinetics of the hydrolysis of cephalosporin C, that at pH 7 of a typical broth, the deacetylcephalosporin C concentration of the magnitude reported by Huber et al. (1968) and found in their own culture broths must originate other than by the hydrolysis of the product. From the culture filtrate of a cephalosporin C producing mutant of C. acremonium, Fujisawa et al. (1973) were able to isolate and purify an enzyme which catalysed the formation of deacetylcephalosporin C from cephalosporin C. They also studied the fermentation pattern of this mutant and found that in the late phase of fermentation practically all cephalosporin C produced was converted to deacetylcephalosporin C. In our laboratories analogous results have been obtained. From a culture filtrate of C. acremonium mutant C462 a spectrum of at least six acetyl-hydrolases has been isolated (Fig. 6). These enzymes showed very different substrate specificities (Table 8). Only the first fraction

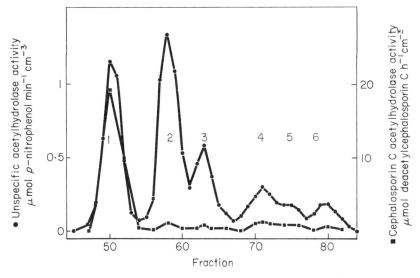

FIG. 6. Elution pattern of DEAE-Sephadex A-50 chromatography.

seems to be responsible for the deacetylation of cephalosporin C. The pH optimum of the cephalosporin C acetyl-hydrolase is 7.5. The activity of the enzyme is completely inhibited by 10^{-4} M di-isopropylfluorophosphate (DFP), a typical esterase inhibitor. With the aid of ultracentrifugation in a sucrose gradient a sedimentation constant of about 2.6 S was obtained. This value corresponds to a molecular weight of about 25 000.

To obtain further information on the formation of the cephalosporin C acetyl-hydrolase, mycelium harvested at different times during growth in shaken flask cultures was disrupted with the aid of an X-Press. The cell-free extract was tested for intracellular acetyl-hydrolase activity using cephalo-

TABLE 8

Activities of the peaks (see Fig. 6) with different substrates

Fraction number	p-Nitro-phenylacetate	p-Nitro-phenylbutyrate	Cephalosporin C
50	65	0	1.6
58	90	100	0.1
63	41	37	0.07
71	21	0	0.1
74	14	2	0.08
75	12	2	0.08
80	22	4	0.05

sporin C as substrate. The reaction mixtures were analysed for the formation of deacetylcephalosporin C by high-pressure liquid chromatography and acidimetrically. No intracellular cephalosporin C acetyl-hydrolase activity could be detected during the growth phase of the fungus, though various intracellular acetyl-hydrolases could be found with the aid of polyacrylamide electrophoresis and staining techniques. The same method confirmed the total absence of cephalosporin C acetyl-hydrolase in the cells.

It was interesting to compare this specific hydrolytic enzyme with the acetyl-transferase activity (Liersch et al., 1974). Under the conditions chosen no such activity was found. Therefore it is unlikely that the two reactions are performed by the same enzyme. This conclusion is sustained by the fact that the acetyl-transferase is an intracellular protein and seems to have a much higher molecular weight. A partially purified transacetylase activity can be concentrated with an Amicon XM50-Ultrafilter which suggests a molecular weight over 50000. Therefore the synthesis and the degradation of the

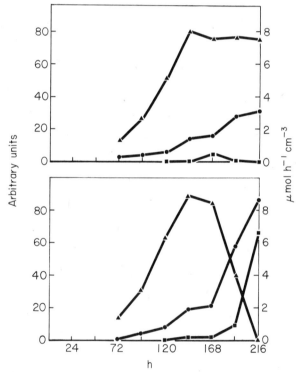

FIG. 7. Regulatory effect of added carbohydrates on the appearance of cephalosporin C acetyl-hydrolase activity. (above) Glucose not limiting. (below) Glucose limiting (see text). ▲, Cephalosporin C; ●, deacetylcephalosporin C; ■, cephalosporin C acetyl-hydrolase activity.

acetoxy ester group of cephalosporin C seems to depend on two different enzymes.

A first attempt to investigate the regulation of the catabolic cephalosporin C acetyl-hydrolase is presented in Fig. 7. Experiments in shake flasks with a complete nutrient medium show that excretion of the enzyme can be suppressed by maintaining a sufficient carbohydrate level in the flask through the addition of a suitable carbohydrate source such as glucose. On the other hand depletion of the medium leading to carbohydrate-deficient conditions induces an extracellular accumulation of the enzyme. Consequently an enzymatic degradation of cephalosporin C reflected in its conversion to de-acetylcephalosporin C occurs. This catabolic reaction on a secondary metabolite offers not only an excellent model for studies of the regulation of extracellular enzymes but also opens up a new field for investigating the biological significance of secondary metabolites.

Acknowledgements

The excellent technical assistance of Lucia Winkler, Silvia Rosteeter and Daniel Harth is acknowledged with many thanks.

References

Abraham, E. P., Newton, G. G. F. and Wanner, S. C. (1964). IAM Symp. *Appl. Microbiol. (Tokyo)*, **6**, 79.
Arnstein, H. R. V. and Clubb, M. E. (1958). *Biochem. J.* **68**, 528.
Benko, P. V., Wood, C. and Segel, I. H. (1967). *Archs Biochem. Biophys.* **122**, 783.
Benz, F., Liersch, M., Nüesch, J. and Treichler, H. J. (1971). *Eur. J. Biochem.* **20**, 81.
Caltrider, P. G. and Niss, H. F. (1966). *Appl. Microbiol.* **14**, 746.
Demain, A. L. (1963). *Trans. N.Y. Acad. Sci.* **25**, 731.
Dutch patent application (1973). Nederland Octrovianvrage Nr. 7305881.
Fujisawa, Y., Shirafuji, H., Kida, M., Nara, K., Yoneda, M. and Kanzaki, T. (1973). *Nature New Biol.* **246**, 154.
Gabriel, O. (1971). "Methods in Enzymology" (Eds S. P. Colowick, N. O. Kaplan), vol. XXII, p. 590. Academic Press, New York and London.
Goulden, S. A. and Chattaway, F. W. (1968). *Biochem. J.* **110**, 55.
Goulden, S. A. and Chattaway, F. W. (1969). *J. gen. Microbiol.* **59**, 111.
Higgens, C. E., Hamill, R. L., Sands, T. H. Hoehn, M. M., Davis, N. E., Nagarajan, R. and Boeck, L. D. (1974). *J. Antibiotics*, **27**, 298.
Huber, F. M., Baltz, R. H. and Caltrider, P. G. (1968). *Appl. Microbiol.* **16**, 1011.
Hunter, D. R. and Segel, I. H. (1973). *Archs Biochem. Biophys.* **154**, 387.
Kerr, D. S. and Flavin, M. (1970). *J. biol. Chem.* **245**, 1842.
Kirkpatrick, J. R., Doolin, L. E. and Godfrey, O. W. (1973). *Anti-microb. Ag. Chemother.* **4**, 542.
Konecny, J., Felber, E. and Gruner, J. (1973. *J. Antib.* **26**, 135.
Lemke, P. A. and Brannon, D. R. (1972). "Cephalosporins and Penicillins" (Ed. E. H. Flynn), p. 370. Academic Press, New York and London.

Lemke, P. A. and Nash, C. H. (1972). *Can. J. Microbiol.* **18**, 255.

Liersch, M., Nüesch, J. and Treichler, H. J. (1973). *Path. Microbiol.* **39**, 39.

Liersch, M., Nüesch, J. and Treichler, H. J. (1975). These Proceedings.

Loder, P. B. and Abraham, E. P. (1971a). *Biochem. J.* **123**, 471.

Loder, P. B. and Abraham, E. P. (1971b). *Biochem. J.* **123**, 477.

Martin, R. G. and Ames, B. N. (1961). *J. biol. Chem.* **236**, 1372.

Marzluf, G. A. (1970). *Archs. Biochem. Biophys.* **138**, 254.

Masurekar, P. S. and Demain, A. L. (1972). *Can. J. Microbiol.* **18**, 1045.

Maurer, H. R. (1971) "Disc Electrophoresis and Related Techniques of Polyacrylamide Gel Electrophoresis". Walter de Gruyter, Berlin and New York.

Nagarajan, R., Boeck, L. D., Hamill, R. L., Higgens, C. E. and Yong, K. S. (1974). *J.C.S. Chem. Commun.* 321.

Neuss, N., Nash, C. H., Baldwin, J. E., Lemke, P. A. and Grutzner, J. B. (1973). *J. Am. chem. Soc.* **95**, 3797.

Nüesch, J., Liersch, M. and Treichler, H. J. (1972). "Fourth International Fermentation Symposium, Kyoto, Japan" Abstracts, G 6–13, 228.

Nüesch, J., Treichler, H. J. and Liersch, M. (1973). "Genetics of Industrial Microorganisms. Actinomycetes and Fungi" (Eds Z. Vaněk L. Hošťálek and J. Cudlín), p. 309. Academia, Prague.

Pall, M. L. (1971). *Biochim. biophys. Acta,* **233**, 201.

Pocker, Y. and Stone, J. T. (1967). *Biochemistry,* **6**, 668.

Rubin, F. A. and Smitz, D. H. (1973). *Antimicrob. Ag. Chemother.* **3**, 68.

Stapley, E. O., Jackson, M., Hernandez, S., Zimmerman, S. B., Currie, S. A., Mochales, S., Mata, J. M., Woodruff, H. B. and Hendler, D. (1972). *Antimicrob. Ag. Chemother.* **2**, 122.

Biogenesis of linear tri- and tetracyclic oligoketides and their glycosides

Z. VANĚK, J. TAX, J. CUDLÍN, M. BLUMAUEROVÁ,
N. STEINEROVÁ, J. MATĚJŮ, I. KOMERSOVÁ, AND K. STAJNER
*Institute of Microbiology, Czechoslovak Academy of Sciences, Prague,
Czechoslovakia*

Summary

From mutant strains of *Streptomyces aureofaciens,* aureovocine, a glucoside of
pretetramide type, was isolated. The ability of *S. aureofaciens* strain B-96 to
glucosidate various dihydroxyanthraquinones (alizarin, anthraflavine, etc.)
was examined. The corresponding mono-β-glucosides were isolated in all
cases. Good yields of glucosidation products were achieved with aklavinone
and ε-pyrromycinone, the aglycones of galirubines.

Preliminary experiments with enzyme preparations showed glucosyl
uridyl pyrophosphate to be the glucose donor.

Using the methods tested on *S. aureofaciens,* we started a genetic study of
S. galilaeus JA3043. This strain produces the glycosidic antibiotics galirubines
A and B, whose aglycones are aklavinone and ε-pyrromycinone. Mutant
strains provide new compounds, both free anthracyclinones and glycosides.
Special attention was paid to the selection of mutants producing neither
glycosides nor aglycones but still possessing transglycosidation ability. Cell
permeability itself does not prevent transglycosidation, as was shown by
incorporation of labelled pyrromycinone into galirubins.

Introduction

Phenolic glycosides are synthesized in all living organisms. It is often claimed
in a simplified way that the formation of glucosides in plants and of glucuron-
ides in animals represents first of all a detoxication mechanism (Harborne

and Simmonds, 1964). Glycosylation increases the solubility of many compounds in the cell water and thus facilitates their transport to various organs. After glycosylation, the chemical reactivity of phenols is decreased, which may affect their enzymic aerobic oxidation. The view has also been advanced that glycosides are less aggressive as surfactants towards cell membranes.

There is no doubt that many of the considerations pertaining to the role or significance of transglycosylation mechanisms in plants and animals are applicable to the biosynthesis of phenolic glycosides in microorganisms. Generally, glycosylation can be divided into two types: a low-energy one, when the transfer of glycosyl is effected by the energy contained in the glycoside bond of disaccharides or of glycosides; and a high-energy one, where glycosylnucleotides are required. The substrate donors for most of the plant enzymes synthesizing phenolic glycosides are sugar nucleotides. On the other hand, most of the known microbial transglycosidases can utilize the corresponding disaccharide as donor of the sugar moiety.

The validity of this division is certainly limited and reflects only the present state of knowledge in the field. Decoding of the chemical structure of antibiotics, particularly from *Streptomycetes*, such as macrolides, aminoglycosides, and phenolic glycosides, showed these compounds to contain some unusual sugars, frequently 2-, 3-, 4- or 6-deoxy hexoses, with substituents of methoxy, acetyl or amino type. Past studies of the biosynthesis of these sugar components support the theoretical assumption that transformation of glucose here involves energy-rich nucleotides.

Results and discussion

BIOGENESIS OF TETRACENE COMPOUNDS AND TRANSGLUCOSYLATION IN *STREPTOMYCES AUREOFACIENS*

We showed in a consideration of the genetic control of compounds produced by *S. aureofaciens* that a combination of 11 blocks in the enzyme reactions that may be assumed to proceed during transformation of the hypothetical tricyclic intermediate to the chlortetracycline molecule may lead to a total of 72 different compounds (Vaněk et al., 1971). So far, 27 such compounds have been isolated, and for the remaining 45 chemical structures have been suggested.

A mutagenic block or inhibition of one of the steps leading to chlortetracycline may result either in a potentiation of production of intermediates before this block or in quantitative changes in the production of compounds in branching metabolic pathways that may lead away from the block. A mutation in this region cannot result in an increase of chlortetracycline production. This suggests the existence of an operon, a *ctc*-cluster of structural genes under the control of a single operator gene.

When working on tetracene metabolite formation in mutant strains of *Streptomyces aureofaciens* we isolated strain B-96 which produced substantial amounts of a glucoside which was called aureovocin (Vokoun *et al.*, 1973). Its aglycone, aureovocidin (**1**), a pretetramide derivative, can be derived from the intermediate where oxidation of the hydroxyl group in position 4 is blocked.

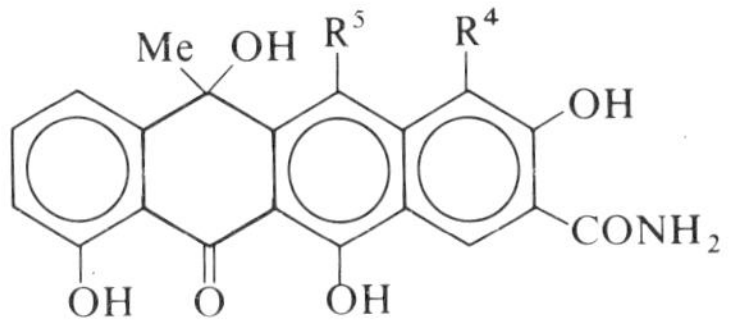

R^4=OH or H
R^5=H or OH
Aureovocidin
(**1**)

It was of interest to examine whether this mutant might be used for the glycosylation of other compounds (Cudlín *et al.*, 1973; Vaněk, 1973). As model substances we used derivatives of dihydroxyanthraquinones, alizarin, anthraflavin, anthrarufin, quinizarin and chrysazin as well as 1-hydroxy-anthraquinone and 2-hydroxyanthraquinone (**2**) (Hovorková *et al.*, 1974b). Initially, the compounds studied were added directly to the cultivation medium; later tap-water washed mycelium from the beginning of the

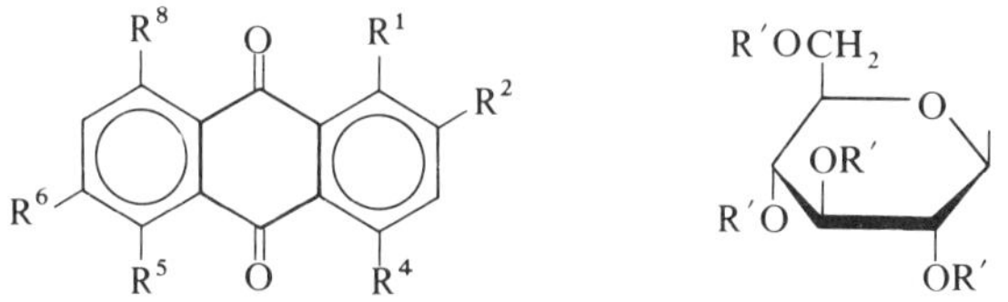

	R^1	R^2	R^4	R^5	R^6	R^8		R
1-Hydroxyanthraquinone	OX	H	H	H	H	H	A	Ac
2-Hydroxyanthraquinone	H	OX	H	H	H	H	B	H
Alizarin	OH	OX	H	H	H	H		
Quinizarin	OH	H	OX	H	H	H		
Anthrarufin	OH	H	H	OX	H	H		
Chrysazin	OH	H	H	H	H	OX		
Anthraflavin	H	OH	H	H	OX	H		

	X
Aglycones	H
2′,3′,4′,6′-Tetra-O-acetyl--β-D-glucopyranosides	A
β-D-Glucosides	B

(**2**)

stationary phase of growth (about 20 h old) was employed (Matějů et al., 1974a). After the incubations, the mycelium was centrifuged and the fermentation liquor was extraced with ethyl acetate. The transglycosylation products were investigated by thin-layer chromatography in chloroform-methanol. The spots were detected in ammonia vapour or in uv light. The isolated products from alizarin, anthraflavin and monohydroxyanthraquinones were identified by comparison of the physicochemical properties with those of chemically synthesized standards (Hovorková et al., 1974a, 1974b).

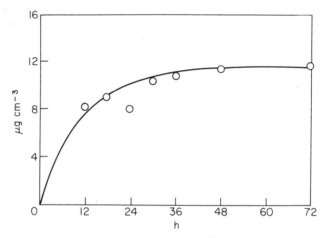

FIG. 1. Production of alizarin-2-β-D-glucoside (μg cm^{-1}) during time of fermentation (h).

It was found that, in the case of alizarin, the product was 1-hydroxy-2-(β-D-glucopyranosyloxy)anthraquinone; in the case of anthraflavin it was 2-hydroxy-6-(β-D-glucopyranosyloxy)anthraquinone. The transglycosylation proceeded best with anthraflavin where the conversion amounted to 48 per cent, with alizarin it was 24 per cent.

Figure 1 shows that a half of the total glucoside produced from alizarin was synthesized within 12 h of fermentation. Later, the rate of transglycosylation decreased; at about 48 h, glucoside synthesis ceased completely.

The best source of glucose was sucrose, and good production of glucosides was demonstrated during cultivation with glucose or fructose. Lactose, maltose and cellobiose were poor glucose donors.

The composition of the buffers (McIlvaine, Sörensen; tris-maleate, tris-HCl) had no effect on the course of glycosylation, with the exception of acetate buffer which inhibited it. Good transglycosylation yields were obtained at initial pH values of 4.5–6.0.

A partially purified enzyme from homogenates of the mycelium of Strepto-

myces aureofaciens B-96 was prepared by differential centrifugation, salting out with ammonium sulphate to 50 per cent saturation and chromatography on DEAE-cellulose. The enzyme catalyses the transfer of glucose from gluco-syluridylpyrophosphate to 1,2-dihydroxyanthraquinone with formation of 1-hydroxy-2-(β-D-glycopyranosyloxy)anthraquinone (Matějů, *et al.*, 1974b).

Using an analogous procedure, glucosides were prepared from pyrro-mycinone and aklavinone obtained by hydrolysis of galirubins, antibioti-cally active glycosides produced by *Streptomyces galilaeus*.

To obtain a more general picture of the transglycosylation capacity of *S. aureofaciens* mention should be made of compounds of the quinocycline complex (Matern *et al.*, 1972) which contain at the aglycone a branched sugar, viz. 2,6-dideoxy-4-*C*-(1'-hydroxyethyl)-L-xylohexopyranose or 2,6-dideoxy-4-*C*-(1'-oxoethyl)-L-xylohexopyranose (**3**). It was shown that the branching

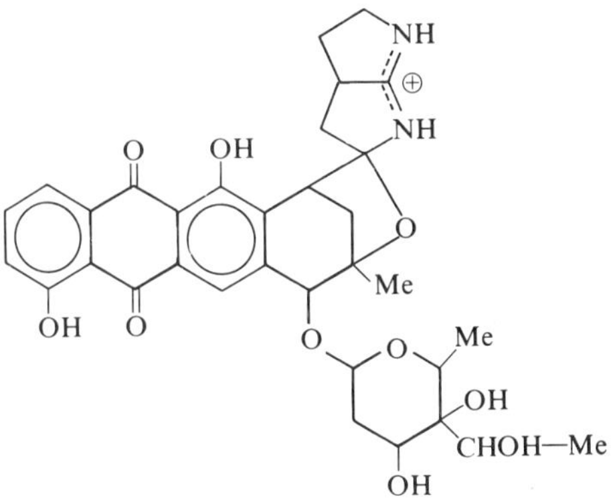

Isoquinocyclin A

(**3**)

is derived from C-2 and C-3 of pyruvic acid. Further glycosidic metabolites described in *S. aureofaciens* are venturicidin A and B, antifungal antibiotics probably of polyene nature (Brufani *et al.*, 1968). The sugar moiety of venturi-cidin A is 3-*O*-carbamyl-D-olivose, in venturicidin B it is D-olivose. This sugar forms a building block for other antibiotic compounds, chromomycin and olivomycin; in avilamycin and curamycin, D-olivose is esterified with dichloroisoeverninic acid.

ANTHRACYCLINES

The group of antibiotics designated according to Brockmann (1963) as anthracyclines, comprises glycosides of derivatives of 7,8,9,10-tetrahydro-5,12-naphthacenequinones. For aglycones of anthracyclines and their deoxy and anhydro derivatives, Brockmann introduced the general name anthracyclinones. Anthracyclines, as well as free anthracyclinones were isolated from the cultivation medium of some *Streptomyces* strains, e.g. *Streptomyces purpurascens* (Brockmann, 1963; Brockmann *et al.*, 1969), *S. antibioticus* (Ettlinger *et al.*, 1959), *S. galilaeus* (Ettlinger *et al.*, 1959; Eckardt, 1967), *S. niveoruber* (Ettlinger *et al.*, 1959), *S. ryensis* (Sato *et al.*, 1964) *S. rubrireticuli* (Mitscher *et al.*, 1964), *S. peuceticus* (Arcamone *et al.*, 1968, 1969), *S. violaceus* (Trakhtenberg *et al.*, 1961), *S. nogalater* (Wiley *et al.*, 1968) and some others.

Biogenesis of anthracyclinones

Ollis *et al.* (1960) showed that the terminal group of the hypothetical decaketide precursor of anthracyclinones is formed by propionic acid or propionyl-CoA, and the remaining nine units are formed by condensation and decarboxylation of malonyl-CoA (**4**). One can envisage that by the closure of the hypothetical decaketide chain, either aklavinone is formed, if the terminal carboxylic group is suitably protected by methylation, or else the ring is closed with simultaneous decarboxylation and formation of 10-demethoxy-carbonylaklavinone.

10-Demethoxycarbonylaklavinone   Aklavinone

(**4**)

According to the acetate rule, the oxygen functions at positions 4, 5, 6, 7, and 9 are preserved and are utilized during formation of the conjugated system in positions 10a, 11a and 12a. The carbonyl group in position 12 is apparently formed by a subsequent introduction of oxygen. Oxidation (action of oxidases) of aklavinone in position 1 leads to ε-pyrromycinone, oxidation in position 11 to ε-rhodomycinone. Further oxidation of these compounds in the free positions 11 or 1 gives rise to ε-isorhodomycinone (**5**).

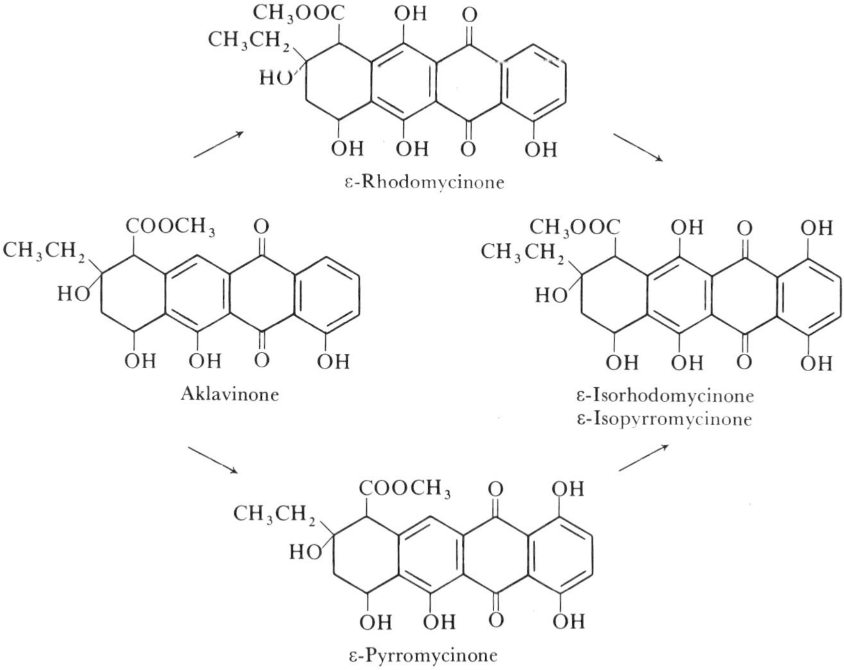

ε-Rhodomycinone

Aklavinone

ε-Isorhodomycinone
ε-Isopyrromycinone

ε-Pyrromycinone

(5)

The same two tetrads of oxidation products can be derived for 7-deoxy-aklavinone and bisanhydroaklavinone (6). All 12 compounds forming these tetrads have been isolated and described.

Another group of 12 compounds can be derived from the hitherto unknown 6-deoxyaklavinone. The existence of this series is based on the isolation of ruticulomycinone, δ-rhodomycinone and of its bisanhydro derivative (7). From the biogenetic point of view one may assume that the hydroxyl group was lost either at the level of the ketide chain or by reduction of the keto form of the enolic hydroxyl at C-6 and subsequent dehydration.

The total number of possible anthracyclinones discussed so far (with a 10-methoxycarbonyl group) amounts to 24, 15 of which have been isolated.

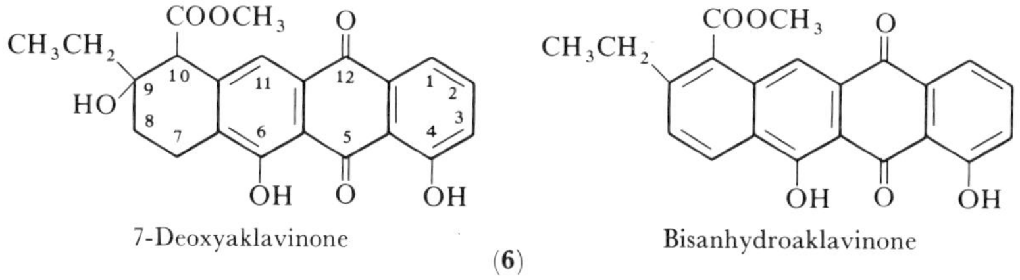

7-Deoxyaklavinone

Bisanhydroaklavinone

(6)

In *Streptomyces galilaeus*, ε_1-pyrromycinone (Tax *et al.*, 1973) was found, and in an unidentified *Streptomycetes*, η_1-pyrromycinone (Hegyi and Gerber, 1968), both of which are substituted with a methyl group rather than an ethyl group in position 9. Therefore, during the formation of the hypothetical oligoketide chain, the terminal group is not formed by propionyl-CoA but rather by acetyl-CoA. Cultivation media of *Streptomycetes* will probably yield other compounds of this series so that the number of possible anthracyclinones with a methoxycarbonyl group in position 10 will reach 48.

Analogous series can be derived for compounds which are not substituted in position 10 and further for compounds carrying a hydroxyl group in position 10. Thus the number of anthracyclinones would increase by another 96 and the total would amount to 144.

From the biogenetic point of view, many compounds that are not substituted in position 10 after decarboxylation are original, the hydroxyl being introduced into position 10 subsequently. Nevertheless, only one has been isolated in the unsubstituted series, viz. 10-deoxy-γ-rhodomycinone (Brockmann *et al.*, 1965), whereas in the hydroxylated series as many as 14 substances are known (8). Apparently *Streptomycetes* producing anthracyclinone derivatives possess an efficient oxidase system.

Of the lower homologues containing methyl in the place of ethyl in position

9, two compounds were isolated in this group, α_1- and β_1-rhodomycinones (Brockmann et al., 1965, 1968). Of the compounds not possessing a hydroxyl group in position 6, α_2-rhodomycinone, α-citromycinone and its 7-deoxy derivative, γ-citromycinone, have been isolated (Brockmann and Niemeyer, 1968).

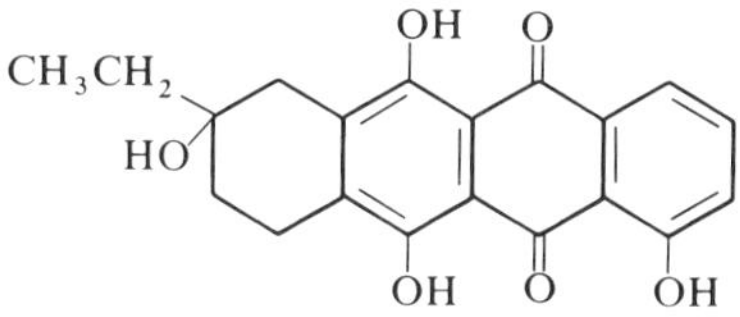

10-Deoxy-γ-rhodomycinone

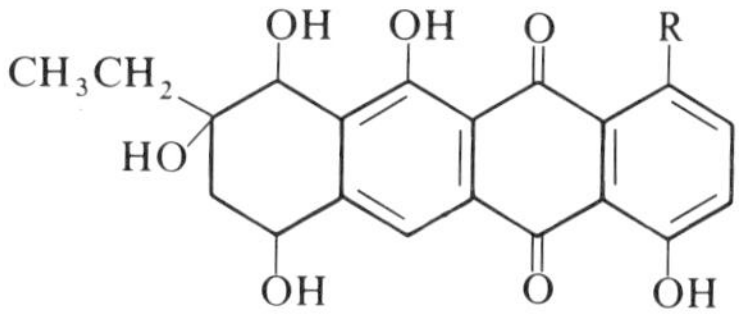

R = H   α-Citromycinone
R = OH   α₂-Rhodomycinone

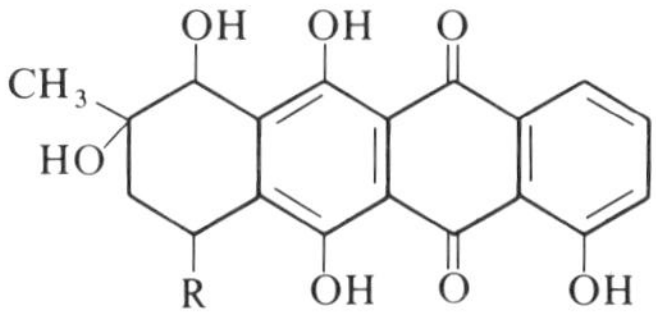

R = H   β₁-Rhodomycinone
R = OH   α₁-Rhodomycinone

(8)

Work dealing with the constitution and configuration of compounds of anthracyclinone type (Bowie and Johnson, 1966; Brockmann et al., 1968; Brockmann and Niemeyer, 1967; Eckardt et al., 1974) has shown that stereo-isomers may occur in this group. So far, compounds with different configurations in positions 7 and 10 have been isolated. There is another centre of asymmetry in the anthracyclinone molecules at C-9 but all known compounds have the same configuration in that position (R). Apparently, one of the stereoisomers is preferred by the enzyme system and the probability of formation of another steric configuration is very low or nil. The same consideration may be applied to the hydroxyl group in position 7 where a reduction of the original carbonyl group may take place with low stereoselectivity but, since this is an enzyme reaction, one of the stereoisomers will significantly pre-dominate.

The occurrence of stereoisomers in the group of anthracyclinones increases the possibilities of isolating novel compounds. It would be interesting to know how these stereoisomers, either aglycones or glycosides, differ in their biological activity.

Glycosides

It follows from the work dealing with the production of antibiotics of anthra-cycline type that cultivation media of production *Streptomycetes* always contain mixtures of these glycosidic substances. The individual glycosides differ both in the constitution and in the conformation of their aglycones, as well as in the number, position and structure of the sugar residues (Brockmann, 1963; Brockmann *et al.*, 1969). The aglycones of the glycosides isolated so far were β-rhodomycinone, α$_2$-rhodomycinone, β-isorhodomycinone, α-isorhodomycinone, γ-rhodomycinone, aclavinone, ruticulomycinone and ε-pyrromycinone. The sugar residues are glycosidically linked in position 7 or, in the case of the demethoxycarbonyl series, in position 10. In the substances so far described the sugar residue bound to the aglycone was always L-rhodosamine. Whereas one sugar residue is always bound in position 10, the rhodosamine in position 7 may bind a further di- or trisaccharide. The sugar residues are then formed by L-rhodinose, L-deoxyfucose or L-cinerulose A as in the case of cinerubin A (**9**) (Keller-Schierlein and Richle, 1970). The glycosidic α-bond with the aglycone always involves carbon 1 of L-rhodosamine.

Cinerubin A
(**9**)

An exception is ε-pyrromycinone-7-2,3,6-trideoxyhexopyranoside isolated from the cultivation medium of *Streptomyces galilaeus*.

Anthracyclines also include daunomycin (*S. peuceticus*), an antitumour antibiotic, active during acute leukemia and neuroblastoma of infants, and nogalamycin (*S. nogalater*) which is highly active against Gram-positive bacteria and mycrobacteria *in vitro*. Daunomycin (Arcamone *et al.*, 1968) carries in position 4 a methoxy group; in position 7 there is a nonmethylated amino sugar daunosamine, and in position 9 an acetyl group which indicates that the terminal group might be formed by a unit of pyruvic acid. In adria-mycin (Arcamone *et al.*, 1969) the methyl of this group is oxidized to the alcoholic group (**10**).

Nogalamycin carries two sugar residues in the molecule (Wiley *et al.*, 1968). Nogalose, 6-deoxy-2,3,4-tri-*O*-methyl-3-*C*-methylhexose, is bound in position 7; the link with the amino sugar (its structure is unknown) at the D ring of nogalarol, the aglycone of nogalamycin, has not been determined.

The above-mentioned group of quinocyclines may also be grouped with the anthracyclines.

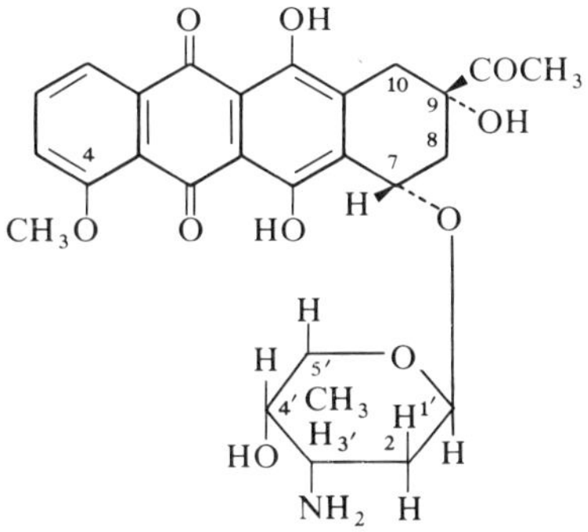

Daunomycin

(**10**)

Glycosylation of ε-pyrromycinone by Streptomyces galilaeus

A glycosylation experiment similar to those described above using *S. aureo-faciens* was carried out with *S. galilaeus* JA 3043. This strain produces antiviral antibiotics of the anthracycline type, galirubins A and B, which are glyco-sides of ε-pyrromycinone and aclavinone (Eckardt, 1967). We prepared labelled ε-pyrromycinone which was added to a submerged culture of *S. galilaeus* (Vaněk *et al.*, 1973) and we isolated a mixture of radioactive glyco-sides. Since it is difficult to separate a mixture of galirubins, we separated chromatographically the aglycones formed after hydrolysation. ε-Pyrro-mycinone was found to be labelled while aclavinone showed no activity, suggesting that the organism attached its sugars only to the added ε-pyrro-mycinone. This result indicates that the permeability of the cell envelope does not interfere with glycoslyation and that glycosylation can be con-sidered as one of the final steps in the biosynthesis of galirubins.

GLYCOSIDES FROM THE GROUP OF AUREOLIC ACID

Another class of glycosidic compounds containing an oligoketide aglycone are the structurally related antitumour antibiotics, aureolic acid, mithra-

TABLE 1

Metabolites of the aureolic acid group*

Name	Synonym	Producing organism	References
Mithramycin	Aureolic acid LA-7017	*Streptomyces* sp.; *Streptomyces* sp. LA-7017; *Streptomyces atroolivaceus* 11294/62	Grundy *et al.* (1953) Sensi *et al.* (1958) Rao *et al.* (1962) Gauze *et al.* (1967)
Chromomycin†	Aburamycin SK-229 M 5-18903	*Streptomyces* sp. No. 7; *Streptomyces griseus*; *Streptomyces griseus* var. 229; *Streptomyces aburaviensis* S-66; *Streptomyces* sp.	Nishimura *et al.* (1957) Gale *et al.* (1958) Shibata *et al.* (1960) Yoshida *et al.* (1965)
Olivomycin‡	NSC A-649	*Streptomyces olivoreticuli*; *Streptomyces* sp.	Schmitz *et al.* (1960) Gauze *et al.* (1962)
Variamycin	—	*Streptomyces* sp. 6604-9	Zhdanovich *et al.* (1971)
Chromocyclomycin	—	*Streptomyces* sp. LA-7017	Berlin *et al.* (1968b)

* The generic name of the group was proposed by Berlin *et al.* (1968a).

† Chromomycin complex consists of components A_2, A_3 and A_4, which are identical with aburamycins A, B, and D, respectively. Aburamycin C corresponds in its properties to deacetylchromomycin A_2 (7-methylolivomycin C). Both antibiotic SK-229 and antibiotic M 5-18903 are identical with a mixture of chromomycins A_2 and A_3.

‡ Olivomycin complex consists of components A, B, C, and D. (Berlin *et al.*, 1969e.)

mycin, chromomycins, olivomycins and variamycin, isolated from different species of *Streptomycetes* (Table 1). These are hydroxytetrahydroanthracene glycosides, the aglycone of which is olivin (for olivomycins) or its homologue chromomycinone (for mithramycin, chromomycins and variamycin) and which contain two carbohydrate chains in positions 2 and 6 (Fig. 2). Mithramycin, chromomycins and variamycin differ with respect to the carbohydrate moiety of their molecules while olivomycins contain sugars identical

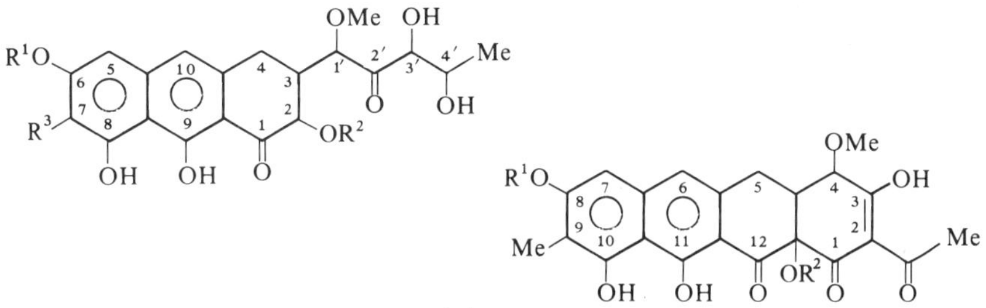

R^1, R^2, R^3 = H: olivin
R^1, R^2 = H, R^3 = Me: Chromomycinone

Aglycones

R^1, R^2 = H: chromocycline

Glycosides (*see* Table 2)
R^1 = S1—S2→
R^2 = ←S3—S4—S5

FIG. 2. Common structure of the substances of the aureolic acid family.

with those of chromomycins (Tables 2 and 3). Termination of the carbohydrate chain in position 2 appears to be an important factor determining antibiotic activity; compounds containing this chain terminated by a branched sugar (mycarose, 4-isobutyrylolivomycose or 4-acetylolivomycose) are much more potent biologically than derivatives without the third sugar in the chain.

According to structural relationships the group may include also the biologically inactive* glycoside chromocyclomycin, the aglycone of which (chromocycline) resembles both chromomycinone and tetracycline antibiotics (Fig. 2). The chromocyclomycin molecule contains the same sugars as mithramycin but in a different quantitative ratio (Table 2).

Metabolites of Streptomyces atroolivaceus

From microorganisms producing antibiotics of the aureolic acid group, we selected as a model the producer of mithramycin, *Streptomyces atroolivaceus*.

* Ineffective *in vivo* (probably due to limited penetration into the cell); *in vitro* it interacts with DNA (Kusch *et al.*, 1972).

TABLE 2
Structure of the glycosides of the aureolic acid group

Substance	Aglycone	Sugar component*					References
		S1	S2 →	← S3	S4	S5	
Mithramycin	chromomycinone	OLV	OLV	OLV	OLS	MCR	Bakhaeva et al. (1968)
Chromomycin A$_2$		OVM	Ac-OLS	OLV	OLV	iBu-OMC	Miyamoto et al. (1964a, 1964c, 1967)
Chromomycin A$_3$						Ac-OMC	
Chromomycin A$_4$		OVM	OLS			iBu-OMC	Zhdanovich et al. (1971)
Deacetylchromomycin A$_2$		OLV	OLV	OLV	OLS		Lokshin et al. (1973)
Variamycin						VRS	
Olivomycin A	olivin	OVM	Ac-OLS	OLV	OLV	iBu-OMC	Berlin et al. (1967, 1969a, 1969b, 1969e)
Olivomycin B						Ac-OMC	
Olivomycin C			OLS			iBu-OMC	
Olivomycin D			Ac-OLS				
Chromocyclomycin	chromocycline	MCR	MCR	OLV	OLS	MCR	Berlin et al. (1968b, 1973a, 1973b)

* See Table 3.

TABLE 3

Sugars of the aureolic acid group glycosides*

Symbol	Trivial name	Synonym	Chemical name
OVM	olivomose	chromose A	2,6-dideoxy-4-O-methyl-D-lyxohexose
Ac-OMC	acetylolivomycose	chromose B	4-O-acetyl-2,6-dideoxy-3-C-methyl-L-arabinohexose
iBu-OMC	isobutyrylolivomycose	chromose B'	4-O-isobutyryl-2,6-dideoxy-3-C-methyl-L-arabinohexose
OLV	olivose	chromose C	2,6-dideoxy-D-arabinohexose
OLS	oliose	—	2,6-dideoxy-D-lyxohexose
Ac-OLS	acetyloliose	chromose D	3-O-acetyl-2,6-dideoxy-D-lyxohexose
MCR	mycarose	—	2,6-dideoxy-3-C-methyl-D-ribohexose
VRS	variose	—	2,6-dideoxy-4-O-methyl-D-ribohexose

* For mycarose and variose see Berlin et al. (1972) and Lokshin et al. (1973), respectively. The other sugars were identified by Berlin et al. (1967, 1969c, 1969d) and by Miyamoto et al. (1964a, 1966).

The standard strain 11294/62, resembling the wild type (Gauze *et al.*, 1967) forms beside mithramycin (some 50 μg cm^{-3}) at least ten biologically inactive minor metabolites (compounds A-J: Fig. 3, group I) with different chromatographic behaviour (Stajner *et al.*, 1974). Most (with the exeption of C which is found only in the mycelium) are more readily detected in

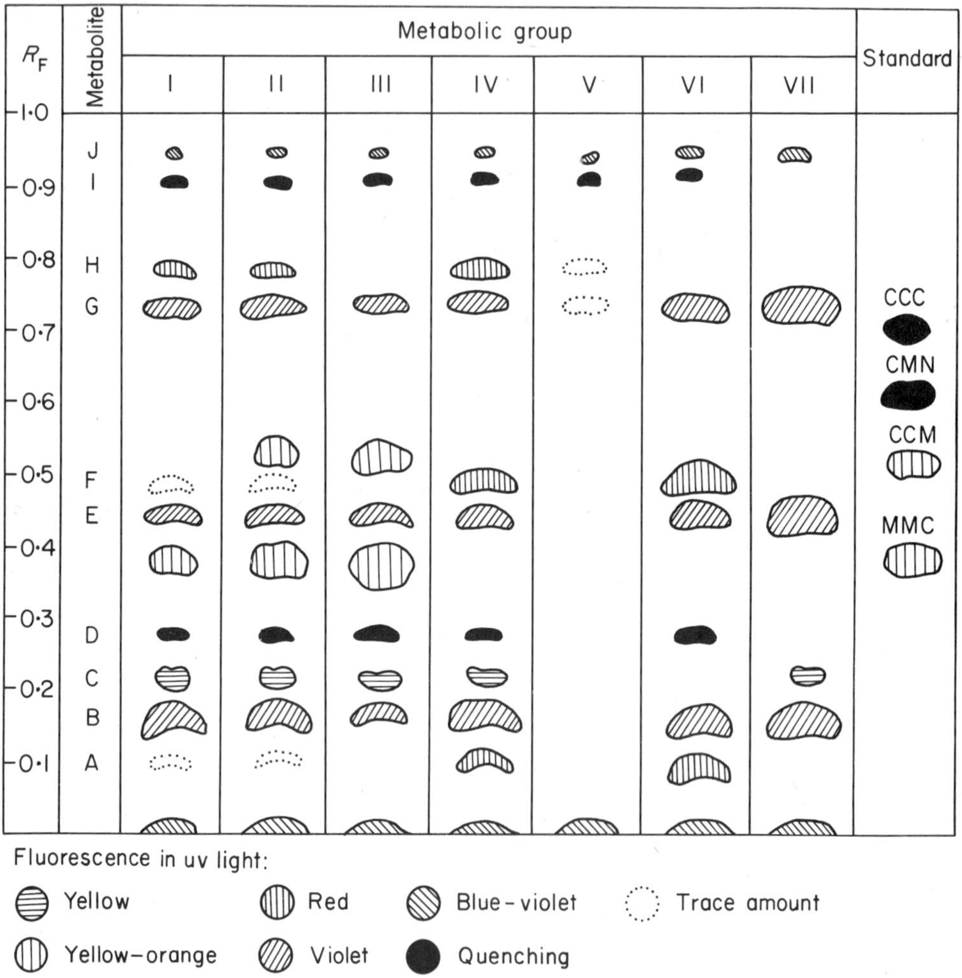

Fluorescence in uv light:

⊖ Yellow   ⦷ Red   ⊘ Blue-violet   ⦂ Trace amount

⦶ Yellow–orange   ⦸ Violet   ● Quenching

Fig. 3. Metabolites of *Streptomyces atroolivaceus* detected by thin-layer chromatography on "Silufol" (Kavalier, Czechoslovakia) in chloroform-methanol (6:1). Mithramycin production in different strains (μg cm^{-1}): 50 (group I), 80–500 (group II), 600–800 (group III) or none (groups IV–VII). Abbreviations: MMC, mithramycin; CCM, chromocyclomycin; CMN, chromomycinone; CCC, chromocycline; A–J, unidentified substances. For strain origin and cultivation *see* Blumauerová *et al.* (1974). Chromatographic methods and more detailed characteristics of the substances have been described by Stajner *et al.* (1974).

extracts of the fermentation liquor. Compounds C, D, I and J occur in cultures of strain 11294/62 irrespective of the level of production of mithramycin; they are chromatographically detectable after 36–48 h of cultivation and their level increases up to 96 h. On the other hand, compounds E and F have been obtained in highest yield after 48–60 h of cultivation and decreased as the biosynthesis of mithramycin rose. The time course of biosynthesis of compounds B, G and H is identical with that of mithramycin (i.e. it reaches its maximum at about 96 h), their yields also increasing under conditions that are unfavourable for the production of the antibiotic.

For transglycosylation experiments with *Streptomyces atroolivaceus* it was first necessary to obtain from the low-production strain 11294/62 variants that would have an increased biosynthesis of mithramycin and simultaneously to isolate blocked mutants unable to form the aglycone of the antibiotic molecule (chromomycinone) but retaining their ability to synthesize the corresponding sugar nucleotides.

In the course of strain improvement it was possible by a stepwise selection procedure (repeated uv irradiation and a single application of nitrous acid, with natural selection following every mutagenic treatment) to increase the production of mithramycin from the original 50 µg cm^{-3} to 700–800 µg cm^{-3}, i.e. 15–19 times (Blumauerová *et al.*, 1974). Chromatographic analysis (Stajner *et al.*, 1974) showed this increase in antibiotic titre to be due to the increased production of mithramycin and not a novel biologically active compound. At the same time, all the high-production variants displayed changes in the spectrum of antibiotically inactive compounds (Fig. 3, groups II and III). A new metabolite found was chromocyclomycin. This biologically inactive glycoside, isolated by Berlin *et al.* (1968b) from *Streptomyces* sp. LA-7017, had not been described from *Streptomyces atroolivaceus* before. Under the present conditions, the production of chromocyclomycin was directly related to the production of mithramycin. Up to 48 h it was present only in trace amounts but then its level rose steeply and, after 60 h cultivation, it reached about the same concentration as mithramycin. With high-production variants the production of chromocyclomycin was accompanied by the formation of a new, biologically inactive minor component (substance K) which appears to be related to chromocyclomycin. Changes in the dynamics of biosynthesis of B and G were also observed, the substances occurring in cultures of medium- and high-production varieties in highest amounts at the beginning of cultivation (i.e. before the beginning of intense biosynthesis of mithramycin and chromocyclomycin) while later their levels decreased sharply. In contrast with the standard strain and its medium-producing varieties, high-producing strains contained no A, F and H.

Inactive mutants were obtained from the standard strain 11284/62 and from some of the high-producing derivatives both by natural selection and by exposure to uv radiation, γ-radiation and nitrous acid (Blumauerová *et al.*, 1974, and unpublished results). They were divided into four principal types by chromatographic analysis (Fig. 3, groups IV, V, VI and VII). Loss of ability to form mithramycin was never accompanied by the formation of new substances different from the parent strain metabolites. Individual mutants differed only by changes in the proportion of the standard products. Most (with the exception of group V) were characterized by an increased production of B, E and G; in the case of group VI also by an increased production of A and F, up to 96 h of cultivation. In mutants of group IV, the highest yields of A and F were obtained after 60 h; at that time the level decreased sharply with a concomitant increase of biosynthesis of H. None of the mutants was found to contain chromocyclomycin, chromomycinone or chromocycline.

The results of chromatographic analysis of various strains of *Streptomyces atroolivaceus*, differing in their production activity, permit some preliminary conclusions on the biogenetic relationships between the biosynthesis of mithramycin, chromocyclomycin and other metabolites. The time course of the biosynthesis of mithramycin and chromocyclomycin showed that chromocyclomycin is not a precursor of mithramycin. A direct quantitative correlation between the yields, as well as the fact that all the nonproducing mutants so far tested have simultaneously a blocked production of mithramycin and chromocyclomycin, indicate on the contrary that the biosynthesis of the two structurally related aglycones (chromomycinone and chromocycline) proceeds first by a common sequence and splits only during the terminal stages into two parallel branches. As in the biosynthesis of tetracyclines (Vaněk *et al.*, 1971) one can assume here that an important factor bearing on the proportion of the two final products in different strains is the rate of synthesis of acetyl-CoA which is preferentially used for the mithramycin pathway. Only when the supply of the precursor is increased, and cannot be all transformed to mithramycin, are the accumulating intermediates drained through the chromocyclomycin pathway. Sequential mutation treatments affected none of the steps of mithramycin biosynthesis but rather induced a number of changes in primary metabolism, thus influencing the availability of acetyl-CoA for increased biosynthesis.

The inverse quantitative correlation between the production of minor metabolites and the formation of mithramycin and chromocyclomycin indicate that compounds A, B, E, F, G and H probably do not represent intermediates of the principal metabolic pathway leading to mithramycin but rather that they are formed by competitive pathways utilizing the same key precursor as the mithramycin and chromocyclomycin ones.

Since none of the tested nonproduction mutants accumulated chromomycinone or chromocycline one might have assumed that the mutants are blocked during early stages of the biosynthesis of the two aglycones and that their glycosylation ability would be unimpaired. However, in preliminary experiments attempting a biological transformation of chromomycinone added to washed cultures of some mutants, no mithramycin was produced but instead some new, biologically inactive compounds, different from the standard metabolites. The block in biosynthesis of mithramycin is apparently the result of more complex changes in the biosynthetic apparatus; this can be elucidated only after identification of the transformation products, which is in progress.

MECHANISM OF ACTION

Anthracyclines belong to a group of substances (acridine, derivatives of ate-brine, ethidium bromide, actinomycins, chromoycins, olivomycin, luteo-skyrin) which inhibit DNA-dependent RNA synthesis. Experimental data indicate that the mechanism of action of these compounds may be explained (with chromomycin, mithramycin and olivomycin only partially) by an inter-calation of chromophores between the nucleotide pairs of DNA (Kersten *et al.*, 1969; Waring, 1970; Neogy *et al.*, 1973). This can be achieved only with chromophores which are planar. Some of these compounds react only with certain nucleotides or with a certain pair of nucleotides.

It has been shown for anthracyclines that the loss of sugar residues resulted in a loss of antibiotic properties (Berg and Eckardt, 1970), and the aglycones of these compounds are biologically almost inactive. The view was advanced that a prerequisite for intercalation is the presence of a basic sugar which forms an electrostatic bond at the DNA helix, resulting in a sufficient "lag" for the intercalation of the chromophore. Besides a change in the electrostatic charge, the complex with DNA undergoes a change of hydrophobic properties, hydro-gen bonds, viscosity, sedimentation, density, melting point and optical properties.

With chromomycin, mithramycin and olivomycin, which do not contain a basic amino sugar, the binding with DNA presumably depends on an equiva-lent or higher concentration of Mg^{2+} which reacts directly with the chromo-phore. The binding also depends on residues of deoxyguanosine, particularly on its 2-amino group.

The present results of studying the mechanism of action of anthracyclines and related compounds on various microorganisms or tumour cells do not allow one more than to speculate about the role that may be played by the various functional groups of the chromophore, or sugar residues during their biological action.

Conclusion

Attempts at utilizing the transglycosylation ability of *Streptomycetes* for the preparation of new biologically active compounds may be applicable in other groups of antibiotics. Some success has been achieved in the study of bio-synthesis of macrolides. Washed cells of *Streptomyces narbonensis* can transform in good yield added narbonolide to narbomycin and added picronolide to picromycin, which means that the last step of the biosynthesis of the antibiotic is the transfer of the sugar moiety (desosamine) or its precursor to the added aglycone (Maezawa *et al.*, 1973).

Many years of studying the biosynthesis of erythromycin led to the pre-paration of biogenetic precursors and to the isolation of point-blocked mutant strains of *Streptomyces erythreus* which do not synthesize the aglycone erythrono-lide but retain the ability to transform the biogentic intermediates to erythromycin. One of the mutants transformed 25 mg erythronolide B in 100 cm³ fermentation medium to erythromycin A within 120 h. This means that both desosamine and mycarose were transferred onto the aglycone, the mycarose being further transformed to cladinose. After adding 8-*epi*-erythrono-lide B to the mutant strain of *Streptomyces erythreus*, a practically quantitative yield of 2-*O*(α-L-mycarosyl)-8-*epi*-erythronolide B was obtained (Martin *et al.*, 1973). In this case it was mycarose (a biogenetic precursor of cladinose) which was transferred. One of the possible explanations may be that the desosamine-transferring enzyme has a much greater substrate specificity. Enzyme systems forming and transferring these unusual sugars are relatively little understood. Greatest progress was achieved with cell-free extracts of *Streptomyces rimosus* which produced the macrolide antibiotic tylosin, containing in its molecule a disaccharide composed of mycaminose and mycarose (the terminal sugar). It was shown that the extracts catalyse the formation of TDP-mycarose from TDP-D-glucose and S-adenosyl-L-methionine. The reaction proceeds via TDP-4-keto-6-deoxy-D-glucose (Pape and Brillinger, 1973).

Acknowledgement

This work was supported by the International Atomic Energy Agency, Research Contract No. 845/RB.

References

Arcamone, F., Cassinelli, G., Franceschi, G. and Orrezzi, P. (1968). *Tetrahedron Letters*, 3353.
Arcamone, F., Franceschi, G. and Penco, S. (1969). *Tetrahedron Letters*, 1007.
Bakhaeva, G. P., Berlin, Yu. A., Boldyreva, E. F., Chuprunova, O. A., Kolosov, M. N., Soifer, V. S., Vasilyeva, T. E. and Yartseva, I. V. (1968). *Tetrahedron Letters*, 3595.
Berg, H. and Eckardt, K. (1970). *Z. Naturf.* **25b**, 362.
Berlin, Yu. A., Esipov, S. E., Kiseleva, O. A. and Kolosov, M. N. (1967). *Khim. Prirod. Soedin.* 331.

Berlin, Yu. A., Kiseleva, O. A., Kolosov, M. N., Shemyakin, M. M., Soifer, V. S., Vasina, I. V., Yartseva, I. V. and Kuznetsov, V. D. (1968a). *Nature, Lond.* **218**, 193.

Berlin, Yu. A., Kolosov, M. N., Vasina, I. V. and Yartseva, I. V. (1968b). *Chem. Commun.* 762.

Berlin, Yu. A., Esipov, S. E. and Kolosov, M. N. (1969a). *Khim. Prirod. Soedin.* 567.

Berlin, Yu. A., Esipov, S. E., Kolosov, M. N. and Chuprunova, O. A. (1969b). *Khim. Prirod. Soedin.* 561.

Berlin, Yu. A., Esipov, S. E., Kolosov, M. N. and Peck, G. Yu. (1969c). *Khim. Prirod. Soedin.* 103.

Berlin, Yu. A., Borisova, G. B., Esipov, S. E., Kolosov, M. N. and Krivoruchko, V. A. (1969d). *Khim. Prirod. Soedin.* 109.

Berlin, Yu. A., Vasina, I. V., Kiseleva, O. A., Kolosov, M. N., Lupach, E. J., Smirnova, G. M., Soifer, V. S., Yartseva, I. V. and Kuznetsov, D. V. (1969e). *Khim. Prirod. Soedin.* 554.

Berlin, Yu. A., Kolosov, M. N., Soifer, V. S. and Yartseva, I. V. (1972). *Khim. Prirod. Soedin.* 535.

Berlin, Yu. A., Kolosov, M. N. and Severtsova, I. V. (1973a). *Khim. Prirod. Soedin.* 524.

Berlin, Yu. A., Kolosov, M. N. and Yartseva, I. V. (1973b). *Khim. Prirod. Soedin.* 539.

Blumauerová, M., Callieri, D. A. S., Stajner, K. and Vaněk, Z. (1974). *Folia microbiol., Praha*, **19**, 133.

Bowie, J. H. and Johnson, A. W. (1966). *J. chem. Soc.* 3927.

Brockmann, H. (1963). *Fortschr. Chem. org. Naturstoffe*, **21**, 122.

Brockmann, H. and Niemeyer, J. (1967). *Chem. Ber.* **100**, 3578.

Brockmann, H. and Niemeyer, J. (1968). *Chem. Ber.* **101**, 1341.

Brockmann, H. and Patt, P. (1955). *Chem. Ber.* **88**, 455.

Brockmann, H., Niemeyer, J., Brockmann, H., Jr. and Budzikiewicz, H. (1965). *Chem. Ber.* **98**, 3785.

Brockmann, H., Brockmann, H., Jr. and Niemeyer, J. (1968). *Tetrahedron Letters*, 4719.

Brockmann, H., Waehneldt, T. and Niemeyer, J. (1969). *Tetrahedron Letters*, 415.

Brufani, M., Keller-Schierlein, W., Löffler, W., Mansperger, I. and Zähner, H. (1968). *Helv. chim. Acta*, **51**, 1293.

Cudlín, J., Vaněk, Z., Steinerová, N. and Blumauerová, M. (1973). *Czechoslov. Pat. Appl.* PV 8739–73.

Eckardt, K. (1967). *Chem. Ber.* **100**, 2561.

Eckardt, K., Tresselt, D., Tax, J. and Jancke, H. (1974). *Z. Chem.* **14**, 57.

Ettlinger, L., Gäumann, E., Hütter, R., Keller-Schierlien, W., Kradolfer, F., Neipp, L., Prelog, V., Reusser, P. and Zähner, H. (1959). *Chem. Ber.* **92**, 1867.

Gale, R. M., Hoehn, M. N. and McCormick, M. H. (1958). "Antibiotics Annual 1958–1959", p. 489. Medical Encyclopedia, New York.

Gauze, G. F., Ukholina, R. S. and Sveshnikova, M. A. (1962). *Antibiotiki*, **7**, 34.

Gauze, G. F., Maksinova, T. S., Ukholina, R. S., Brazhnikova, M. G. and Kruglyak, E. B. (1967). *Antibiotiki*, **12**, 1059.

Grundy, W. E., Goldstein, A. W., Rickher, C. J., Hanes, M. E., Warren, H. B. and Sylvester, J. C. (1953). *Antibiotics Chemother.* **3**, 1215.

Harborne, J. B. and Simmonds, N. W. (1964). "Biochemistry of Phenolic Compounds" (Ed. J. B. Harborne), p. 77. Academic Press, London and New York.

Hegyi, J. R. and Gerber, N. N. (1968). *Tetrahedron Letters*, 1587.

Hovorková, N., Cudlín, J., Matějů, J., Blumauerová, M. and Vaněk, Z. (1974a). *Colln. Czech. chem. Commun.* 39, 662.

Hovorková, N., Cudlín, J., Matějů, J., Blumauerová, M. and Vaněk, Z. (1974b). *Colln. Czech. chem. Commun.* 39.

Keller-Schierlein, W. and Richle, W. (1970). *Chimia*, 24, 35.

Kersten, W., Kersten, H., Wanke, H. and Ogilvie, A. (1969). *Zentbl. Bakt. Parasitede. Abt.* 212, 259.

Kusch, A. A., Fedoseeva, G. E., Kiseleva, O. A. and Zelenin, A. V. (1972). *Antibiotiki*, 17, 504.

Lokshin, G. B., Zhdanovich, Yu. V., Kuzovkov, A. D. and Scheychenko, V. I. (1973). *Khim. Prirod. Soedin.* 418.

Maezawa, I., Hori, T., Kinumaki, A. and Suzuki, M. (1973). *J. Antib.* 26, 771.

Martin, J. R., Egan, R. S., Perun, T. J. and Goldstein, A. W. (1973). *Tetrahedron.* 29, 935.

Matějů, J., Cudlín, J., Hovorková, N., Blumauerová, M. and Vaněk, Z. (1974a). *Fol. microbiol.* 19, 307.

Matějů, J., Mikulík, K., Blumauerová, M. and Vaněk, Z. (1974b). *Folia microbiol., Praha,* 19.

Matern, U., Grisebach, H., Karl, W. and Achenbach, H. (1972). *Eur. J. Biochem.* 29, 1.

Mitscher, L. A., McCrae, W., Andress, W. W., Lowery, J. A. and Bohonos, N. (1974). *J. Pharm. Sci.* 53, 1139.

Miyamoto, M., Kawamatsu, Y., Shinohara, M., Nakanishi, K., Nakadaira, Y. and Bhacca, N. S. (1964a). *Tetrahedron Letters*, 2355.

Miyamoto, M., Morita, K., Kawamatsu, Y., Noguchi, S., Marumoto, R., Tanaka, K., Tatsuoka, S., Nakanishi, K., Nakadaira, Y. and Bhacca, N. S. (1964b). *Tetrahedron Letters*, 2355.

Miyamoto, M., Morita, K., Kawamatsu, Y., Sasai, M., Nohara, A., Tanaka, K. and Tatsuoka, S. (1964c). *Tetrahedron Letters*, 2367.

Miyamoto, M., Kawamatsu, Y., Shinohara, M., Nakadaira, Y. and Nakanishi, K. (1966). *Tetrahedron*, 22, 2785.

Miyamoto, M., Kawamatsu, Y., Kawashima, K., Shinohara, M., Tanaka, K., Tatsuoka, S. and Nakanishi, K. (1967). *Tetrahedron*, 23, 421.

Neogy, R. K., Chowdhury, K. and Thakurta, G. G. (1973). *Biochim. biophys. Acta*, 299, 241.

Nishimura, H., Kimura, T., Tawara, K., Sasaki, K., Nakajima, K., Shimaoka, N., Okamoto, S., Shimohira, M. and Isono, J. (1957). *J. Antibiotics (Ser. A)*, 10, 205.

Ollis, W. D., Sutherland, J. O., Codner, R. C., Gordon, J. J. and Miller, G. A. (1960). *Proc. chem. Soc. (London)*, 347.

Pape, H. and Brillinger, G. U. (197ɔj. *Arch. Mikrobiol.* 88, 25.

Rao, K. V., Cullen, W. P. and Sobin, B. A. (1962). *Antibiotics Chemother.* 12, 182.

Sato, K., et al. (Shionogi Seiyaku Co.) (1964). Japan Pat. 14, 496.

Schmitz, H., Heinemann, B., Lein, J. and Hooper, I. R. (1960). *Antibiotics Chemother.* 10, 740.

Sensi, P., Greco, A. M. and Pagani, H. (1958). *Antibiotics Chemother.* 8, 241.

Shibata, M., Tanabe, K., Hamada, Y., Nakazawa, K., Miyake, A., Hitomi, H., Miyamoto, M. and Mizuno, K. (1960). *J. Antibiotics (Ser. B)*, 13, 1.

Stajner, K., Blumauerová, M., Callieri, D. A. S. and Vaněk, Z. (1974). *Folia microbiol., Praha,* 19, 498.

Tax, J., Sedmera, P., Vokoun, J., Eckardt, K., Komersová, I. and Vaněk, Z. (1973). *Colln Czech. chem. Commun.* **38**, 2661.

Trakhtenberg, D. M., Birkova, L. V. and Baikova, V. M. (1961). *Antibiotiki,* **6**, 603.

Vaněk, Z. (1973). "Advances in Antimicrobial and Antineoplastic Chemotherapy I/2", Proc. VIIth Internat. Congress of Chemotherapy (Eds M. Hejzler, M. Semonský, and S. Masák), p. 783.

Vaněk, Z., Cudlin), J., Blumauerová, M. and Hošťálek, Z. (1971). *Folia microbiol.,* *Praha,* **16**, 225.

Vaněk, Z., Tax, J., Komersová, I. and Eckardt, K. (1973). *Folia microbiol., Praha,* **18**, 526.

Vokoun, J., Vaněk, Z., Podojil, M., Blumauerová, M., Vondráček, M. and Benda, A. (1963). Czechoslov. Pat. 153722.

Waring, M. (1970). *J. molec. Biol.* **64**, 247.

Wiley, P. F., MacKellar, F. A., Caron, E. L. and Kelly, R. B. (1968). *Tetrahedron Letters,* 663.

Yoshida, T., Matsuura, S., Sunagawa, N., Suetomi, S., Kimura, Y. and Katagiri, K. (1965). *Ann. Rep. Shionogi Res. Lab.* **15**, 212.

Zhdanovich, Yu. V., Lokshin, G. B., Kuzovkov, A. D. and Rudaya, S. M. (1971). *Khim. Prirod. Soedin.* 646.

R

Cascade expression of the mating-type locus in Mucorales

J. D. BU'LOCK

Microbial Chemistry Laboratory, Department of Chemistry,
The University, Manchester, England

Summary

In heterothallic Mucorales the complex biochemical and morphogenic sequence leading to sexual spores (zygospores) is controlled by a single mating-type gene MT and by a requirement for the diffusion of extracellular metabolites between mycelia having two different alleles of MT, *plus* and *minus*. The genome thus regulated differs from, but probably overlaps with, that for asexual sporulation with which it also shares regulation by nutritional levels (catabolite repression). Because heterothallic systems involve extracellular mediators, considerable insight into mechanisms whereby the action of one gene can control the expression of very many others is attainable.

The product of MT is a repressor for, *inter alia*, two (probably more) structural genes for enzymes in an interpretable metabolic sequence from β-carotene to trisporic acids. Partly repressed versions of this pathway corresponding to *plus* and *minus* alleles, and their products, now characterized, cause its full derepression in mixed cultures. Trisporic acids are then formed; they derepress a wide spectrum of genes including those for the two part-pathways, and elicit similar morphogenic sequences in both mating types. The resultant zygophores are related to, but distinct from sporangiophores provided that trisporate-mediated derepression is maintained.

Expression of the MT alleles in the zygophores also gives them mating-type-specific surface properties. Mutal contact between such surfaces, if also species-similar, switches further sequences, including localized wall-formation and dissolution, for completion of the sexual process.

This cascade mechanism also allows us to interpret chemical and morphogenic features of homothallic species, in which the nutritional signal triggers localized development of *plus* and *minus* biochemistry in a common mycelium.

Introduction

Probably the simplest form of sexuality in the true fungi occurs in hetero-thallic Mucorales. It requires that the two organisms involved should differ genetically in a single character, the so-called "mating type", and though the data are not conclusive there are none to contradict the accepted view that this is determined by a single gene which has two functioning alleles: these we shall denote MT^+ *(plus)* and MT^- *(minus)*. However the inter-action between these two minimally different genotypes leads to complex molecular and morphological events. Consequently the following review is intended, at least in a tentative manner, to map out the kind of regulatory processes which seem to link these multiple expressions to the single deter-mining locus.

There are additional determinants for the mating process. Some are environmental and some are genetic. Often they can be shown to act at defined stages in the process, and it is particularly striking that the require-ment that the participating mycelia shall be of the same species only enters at quite a late stage. It is also possible to extend our analysis to homothallic species, in which phenotypically determined *plus* and *minus* characters are expressed in different parts of a genetically homogeneous mycelium.

The vegetative mycelia of the Mucorales are haploid, aseptate and co-enocytic; asexual reproduction is by haploid sporangiospores and the diploid state occurs only transiently within the sexually produced zygospore.

All but the most recent data on this problem—which has a long history involving some of the most distinguished of descriptive mycologists—are assembled in reviews by Gooday (1973) and van den Ende and Stegwee (1971). Observations not otherwise documented in the present account are fully dealt with there.

Results and discussion

THE MATING PROCESS

The morphological sequence in the mating process is described in most text-books of mycology, but a summary of the key features and events is useful here for later reference:

1. If vegetative mycelia of opposite mating type grow adjacent and if nutritional conditions are correct, low-molecular-weight "prohormones" specific to each mating type (Fig. 1) can diffuse between them, either aerially or through the substrate or aqueous medium.

2. In the zone where the colonies are close, sexual initials or zygophores branch from the mycelia and sporangium formation is inhibited.

3. Ensuing sexual reactions involve zygophores rather than vegetative hyphae or sporangiophores but if the stimulus is withdrawn zygophores can revert to vegetative hyphae or to sporangiophores, or they may collapse.

4. From cultures with both mating types, in correct nutritional conditions, trisporic acids (Fig. 1) can be isolated and these are hormones which will induce mycelia of either mating type to form zygophores.

5. The developing zygophore, though continuous with the basal hypha, is a region of localized cell-wall synthesis, carotenoid accumulation, intensified nuclear replication and (see below) specialized surface properties.

6. Zygophores of opposite mating-type are distinguishable by their interaction with other zygophores but not otherwise (isogamy).

7. Zygophores of opposite mating type grow towards each other (or towards a source of the appropriate prohormone) (zygotropism).

8. Zygotropism leads to mutual contact of zygophores of opposite mating type, normally near their apices.

9. If the contacting zygophores are of the same or rather similar species they adhere rather firmly and simple zygophore extension gives way to events (10)–(14), but otherwise more or less abortive versions of events (2)–(8) may continue (thigmotropic reaction).

10. The zygophores distend as cytoplasmic events (above, 5) continue; an imperforate septum forms sub-apically across each, delimiting the (multinucleate) gametangia.

11. The wall between the two gametangia is lysed and symmetrical plasmogamy follows.

12. The resulting heterokaryotic compartment develops the distinctive chemistry and morphology of the zygospore.

13. Specialized chemical and morphological changes may also occur in the suspensors adjacent to the zygospore.

14. The karyotic events in the zygospore compartment are rather obscure and fall outside the scope of this review. A good summary of the problem is given by Emerson (1966).

THE HORMONES AND PROHORMONES

Crucial to present views of the hormone mechanism was the discovery in 1971–72, contrary to earlier opinions and some current prejudices, that all the natural trisporic acids (TA, see Fig. 1) act similarly and on *both* mating types of test species such as *Mucor mucedo*. The TA-induced changes in single strains are subject to nutritional regulators and comprise the induction and elongation of fully normal zygophores (and inhibition of sporangial development). TA-induced zygophores have the mating-type properties of the

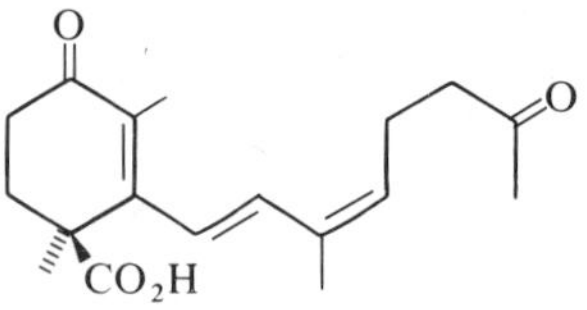

Trisporic acid B
(also 9-*trans*)

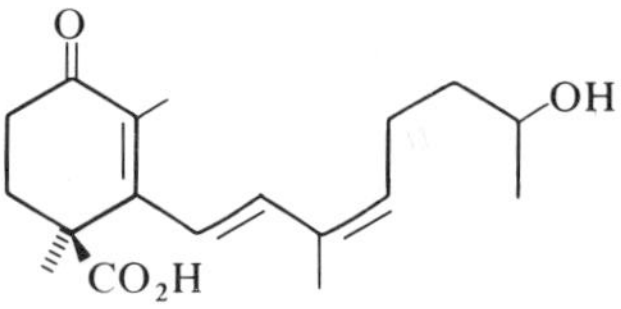

Trisporic acid C
(also 9-*trans*)

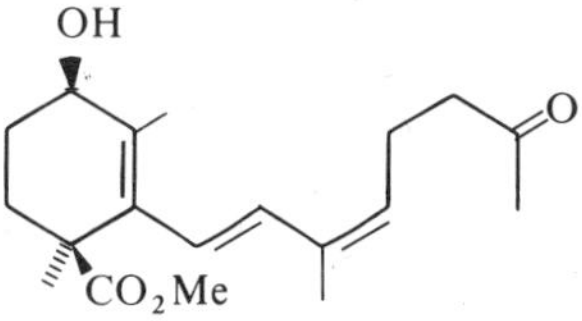

Methyl dihydrotrisporate B
(P^+)

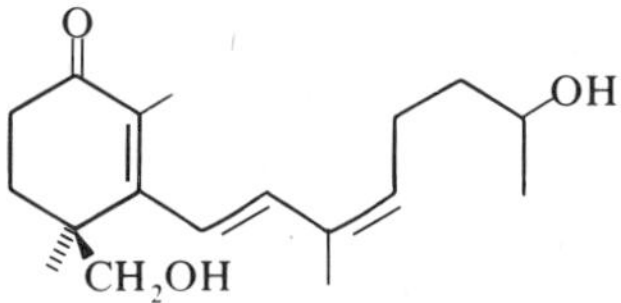

Trisporol C
(P^-)

Note P^- also includes trisporol B (13-keto) and analogues with *gem*-dimethyl at C(1).

Fig. 1. Structures of trisporic acids (TA) and the *plus* and *minus* prohormones.

genotype, carotenoids accumulate and nuclei multiply there, but there is no zygotropism towards the TA source (though in most tests the TA reach the zygophores via the vegetative mycelium so zygotropism could not be observed). Stages of the mating process involving contact with a zygophore of opposite mating type do not, of course, occur in such a system, but if zygophores are induced separately in a *plus* and a *minus* culture and then brought together mechanically their mutual reactions are normal.

The cooperative synthesis of TA which occurs when cultures of *plus* and *minus Blakeslea trispora* are mixed is only fully established following *de novo* enzyme synthesis in both mycelia. However, both mating types of *B. trispora* seem to contain all the genes required for TA synthesis, since single cultures spontaneously produce them in very small amounts—about 0.1 per cent or less of the mixed-culture level (Sutter *et al.*, 1973). We conclude that some or all of these genes are repressed in both the single strains and that in the "mated" cultures all are derepressed, either in both strains or partly in one and the remainder in the other.

Probably some 12–20 enzymes are required to make TA from their precursor β-carotene (see below) and the genes coding for them are not intrinsically different in the two mating types; it appears that the MT locus controls the pattern of repression of these genes and the most economical hypothesis is that the MT gene product is itself a repressor, with different detailed activities towards the various structural genes corresponding to the MT^+ and MT^- alleles.

The most direct experimentally tested expression of the MT alleles is that the meta-bolic products of the repressed versions of TA formation which exist in single strains are different in the two mating types. These single-strain metabolites are the mating-type-specific prohormones, which are neutral compounds formed at about 1/50 to 1/100 of the potential TA level in *B. trispora;* they are the substances designated P^+, P^- by Werkman and van den Ende (1973) (a useful designation we shall use here) and P, π, M, μ by Sutter *et al.* (1973). To understand their origin and function, and the significance of their chemical structures, it is useful first to consider the formation of TA in mixed cultures (Bu'Lock *et al.*, 1974a).

To produce TA from β-carotene requires the following "unit steps", each probably involving some 1–4 distinct enzymes: (a) 15,15'-oxygenase cleavage (carotenoid numbering) of the C_{40} precursor to C_{20} units, e.g. retinal; (b) β-oxidation, C_{20} to C_{18}; (c) H addition at C(11), C(12); (d) oxidation at C(4), CH_2 to CHOH; (e) oxidation of this CHOH to $C=O$; (f) oxidation of C(1)-methyl to CH_2OH; (g) oxidation of this CH_2OH (through CHO?) to CO_2H.

In addition, there are enzymes which by carrying out additional reactions remove material from the sequence and give rise to inactive by-products. *A priori* we expect most of these enzymes to have high specificity for the region of the substrate which they modify but rather lower specificity for the molecule as a whole, and consequently the sequence in which they act is not absolutely fixed.

In 1973 we showed (Bu'Lock *et al.*, 1973), that the very complex mixtures of neutral metabolites produced at low levels by single strains of *B. trispora* had mating-type-specific features, such as would result from the omission of step (g) in the *minus* strain and from the omission of step (e) in the *plus* (coupled with methylation of the carboxyl group). The repressed-level versions of the TA pathway appear to be enzyme-limited, not substrate-limited, overall, and the inactivating processes still occur. More recently (Bu'Lock *et al.*, 1974b) it has proved that the functionally active mating-type-specific prohormone substances P^+ and P^- (Fig. 1) have structures in accord with the situation thus defined; the active products from the *plus* are the methyl dihydro-trisporates and those from the *minus* are the trisporols.

In regulatory terms we can alternatively conclude from these data that: synthesis of the enzyme system for step (e) is strongly repressed in MT^+; synthesis of that for step (g) is strongly repressed in MT^-; synthesis of that for step (a) is moderately repressed in both MT^+ and in MT^-. Since step (a) appears to be rate limiting overall, the state of the remaining steps in the single strains, relative to the derepressed system, is less certain. However, the patterns of repression corresponding to the two MT alleles are at least partly defined.

Now the *minus* prohormones (trisporols, P⁻) accumulate because of the strong MT⁻ repression of a step (g), which the MT⁺ allele does not repress so strongly and which *plus* mycelium can carry out. Similarly the *minus* mycelium can constitutively carry out the step (e), which MT⁺ strongly represses, the absence of which in *plus* mycelium leads to the formation of methyl dihydrotrisporates, P⁺. Hence *minus* produces, constitutively, traces of products which *plus* can transform into TA, and vice versa, and so when the prohormones can diffuse between the mycelia low levels of TA are formed by the "gratuitous" enzymes already present.

The production of TA in one strain from the prohormones of the other will have similar effects to those which can be studied in both *plus* and *minus* strains by the exogenous TA; these are known to be far-reaching. The TA were originally detected because of their effect on carotenogenesis, but this is only one aspect of a general derepression of early rate-limiting steps in isoprenoid synthesis (Thomas *et al.*, 1967). This can lead, in *B. trispora,* to a ten-fold or greater increase in the total output of carotenoids, sterols, prenols, etc. (Bu'Lock and Osagie, 1973); later enzymes in the biosynthesis of these products may now become rate-limiting so that the pattern of individual products may change markedly. For example in some conditions in *B. trispora* the proportion of the more saturated carotenoids like phytoene is markedly increased. Moreover the considerable increase in consumption of isoprenoid precursors—AcCoA, NADPH, and ATP—must have consequences in intermediary metabolism which may themselves actuate more far-reaching regulatory adjustments. The total change, in which the expression of very many genes must be implicated, is of course seen morphologically in the induction of zygophores and the suppression of the structurally similar asexual sporangiophores.

An important addition to the range of TA effects was the discovery by Werkman and van den Ende (1973) that TA derepresses, through *de novo* enzyme synthesis, the formation of the mating-type-specific prohormones in the single strains. Thus if P⁻ is taken up by *plus* mycelium it is converted, as above, into TA and this increases the production of P⁺ by the *plus* mycelium. The cooperative production of TA in the mixed cultures is explained by this variant of the well-known mechanism of "product derepression". In terms of our earlier designation, TA derepresses at least the previously rate-limiting step (a), and possibly the intermediate steps (b)–(d) and (f), but even in the TA-treated single strains the steps which are blocked with mating-type specificity ((e) in MT⁺, (g) in MT⁻) seem unaffected. The prohormones are responsible for zygotropism (Mesland *et al.*, 1973) and the derepression effects are particularly located in the elongating zygophores, where TA levels must progressively increase.

There is some uncertainty as to whether the strongly MT-repressed reactions are ever derepressed, or whether virtually all TA synthesis is by way of cross-diffusion of the prohormones. Recently Jockusch (private communication, 1974) has obtained mutants of *minus M. mucedo* with either complete or temperature-sensitive blocks in the mating process. Some of these will not cross-react at all with wild type *plus* or with TA, but others will cross-react with *plus* even though they show no response to TA. However, we have found that this latter type will respond quite normally to added *plus*-prohormones, and also to some analogues which normal *minus* can constitutively convert into TA. We believe these may be a class of mutants with an altered permeability to exogenous TA, and their rather normal cross-reaction with wild type *plus* suggests that in the natural system it is only the prohormones which are exchanged. Similar conclusions follow, together with further valuable details, from work soon to be published on the mating of carotenoid mutants of *Phycomyces* (R. P. Sutter, private communication, 1974). So perhaps *B. trispora* is anomalous in excreting such large amounts of what is normally an endogenously formed effector. Significantly Gooday (1968) isolated TA from the *mycelium* of *M. mucedo* cultures, not from the medium. On the other hand, nearly forty years ago Köhler (1935) described selection of a spontaneous mutant of *plus M. mucedo*, which he designated *Laniger* and which we would now guess as having constitutively derepressed TA synthesis, since it produced much carotenoid and large numbers of spontaneous zygophores. In crosses with wild type *minus* the *Laniger* character segregated with MT^+; this we would expect if the repressor for step (e), which in our view is what is defective in *Laniger*, is in fact the gene product from MT^+.

Heterokaryons of the two mating types have been produced in *Phycomyces* and other species, and though their properties have not been so fully characterized as one would wish, they are consistent with the mechanisms of negative control we have preferred in our interpretation.

We can summarize the position thus far as follows:

i. The two-allele system at MT is primarily expressed through its effects on several enzymes in the "constitutive" prohormone system.

ii. The prohormone system is made self-intensifying through interdiffusion and the derepressor effects of TA.

iii. TA derepress a wide range of genes rather directly, and indirectly a still wider range, some effects being positive and some (e.g. on certain vegetative functions and conidiation) negative.

iv. Interaction of these effects with nutritional regulation explains the mating-type requirement, zygophore formation, and zygotropism, i.e. events (1)–(7) of our summary sequence.

THIGMOTROPISM

Successful zygotropism leads of course to contact between zygophores of opposite mating type. Up to this stage the process has included no mechanism to limit it to matings within a species, which is desirable in a functioning sexual system. From the properties of differentiated zygophores it appears that this mechanism is primarily provided by the "thigmotropic" system which governs their contact behaviour, which is absolutely mating-type-specific and also relatively species-specific. This system, and the subsequent stages in zygospore formation, are fully reviewed by Gooday (1973). It is observed that a *plus* zygophore will make firmly adhering contact only with a *minus* zygophore, and not with vegetative hyphae of either mating type. Moreover, if the contacting zygophores are of the same or similar species, events (10)–(14) of our sequence follow, but if they are not, then various "imperfect" reactions are seen, ranging from indefinite continuations of earlier stages to successively closer approximations to the "normal" process.

We suggest that the thigmotropic system is governed by the presence on the zygophore surface of mating-type- and species-specific macromolecules we may designate θ^+ and θ^-. These could well be similar to the specifically agglutinative surface glycoproteins of the two mating types in *Hansenula* (Crandall and Brock, 1968). Their formation in, or at least their transfer to the surface of, the zygophores seems to be another of the processes which is derepressed directly or indirectly by TA. The identity of these mating-type-specific substances is also controlled, of course, by the MT allele. According to Jockusch (private communication) wild type *M. mucedo* does not show normal thigmotropic effects at 29°C or above, suggesting that the formation or function of θ^+/θ^- is temperature sensitive. Some of his mutants, however, show normal adhesion but later steps are blocked. It is less easy to suggest how the θ^+/θ^- interaction leads to changes in the TA-induced programme, but the *Hansenula* system, though different in detail, involves similar sequels.

Functional contact leads, in particular, to the formation of septa delimiting the gametangia at the zygophore apices. In all but the more advanced members of the Mucorales septa are formed only in nonvegetative contexts and are specifically functional, either in old or damaged hyphae or in specialized reproductive structures, both sexual and asexual. The rather late stage at which septum formation occurs in the sexual process in heterothallic species is an important distinction from the system seen in homothallics and discussed later. The septa have plasmodesmata but not central pores and effectively seal off cytoplasmic compartments. Development of the characteristic wall-structure of the zygospore normally begins at this stage, while the gametangia are still separate; it continues while the intervening wall is lysed and in the single zygospore compartment thus formed. Rarely, zygospore-like structures are completed in both gametangia before plasmogamy can occur, and a pair of "azygospores" is formed, presumably because the processes of wall-modification outstrip that of dissolution of the wall between the gametangia.

We suggest that these events are all part of the TA-induced programme as selectively modified or extended by the action of the hypothetical θ^+/θ^- system. It has frequently been pointed out that even the normal process of vegetative growth of hyphae involves a delicate balance between wall synthesis and wall lysis; the series of events, vegetative branching, zygophore outgrowth, septum formation, and gametangial fusion, represent increasingly precise and localized adjustments to that balance. Some interesting observations (Bu'Lock and Jones, unpublished) with an inhibitor, SKF-3301A, seem to show how the whole TA-induced programme can be subjected to interference by this single agent, known to be a relatively specific inhibitor of isoprenoid biosynthesis. In plate cultures of *M. mucedo*, concentrations of SKF-3301A in the agar above $300\ \mu\mathrm{g\,cm^{-3}}$ inhibit vegetative mycelium markedly, but lower levels interfere rather selectively with various aspects of the mating process between adjacent *plus* and *minus* colonies. Even with 50 or $100\ \mu\mathrm{g\,cm^{-3}}$ many zygophores fail to show clear zygotropic reactions, and degenerate after failing to pair. In successful pairings many progametangia degenerate, or sometimes only one develops and a single "azygospore" forms from it. Double azygospores are relatively frequent. Other paired zygophores continue extension growth after making mutual contact, just as in some interspecific matings. Thus both the developmental and the mutual recognition aspects of the mating process seem to be affected. At higher inhibitor levels even the vegetative mycelia show "avoidance" growth, which is common between colonies of different fungi but which is characteristically absent between colonies of different mating type in *M. mucedo* and similar species.

HOMOTHALLISM

The widespread occurrence of homothallic species in the Mucorales and their obvious relationship to the heterothallic system, has provided critical tests for understanding the sexual process ever since the earliest observations (e.g. Satina and Blakeslee, 1930). The homothallic species are homozygous haploids in which sexuality is phenotypic and local, and there is no "mating type". In simple homothallics such as *Zygorhynchus*, a vegetative hypha puts out a sexual branch which soon swells into an obvious zygophore. This extends tropically towards another part of the same hypha, or less commonly to an adjacent hypha, which puts out a small gametangial bud in response; the two meet, delimit, and fuse to give rise to a typical zygospore. There is no doubt that a hormonal mechanism similar to that in heterothallic species is involved. Many years ago Satina and Blakeslee (1930) showed that there were some homothallics which cross-reacted as *plus* with test heterothallic species, and others which behaved as *minus*. This "constitutive" sexual tendency was displayed by the main hyphae in each case, and by the smaller (second) gametangia that grow out from the hypha, whereas the opposite sexual tendency was shown more locally by the larger outgrowing (initial) zygophore. More recently Werkman and van den Ende (1974) have shown that the corresponding patterns of prohormone metabolism exist in these two types; in mass culture, species with the "constitutive" *plus* tendency produce P^+ and convert P^- into TA, while those constitutively *minus* in tendency produce P^- and convert P^+ into TA Coupling this with the earlier data we have little doubt that the opposite patterns are localized in the larger zygophore outgrowths in each case. Strikingly, the Dutch workers also observed that added TA induced homothallic structures in a strain of *Syzigites megalocarpus* which otherwise did not produce zygospores at all.

We suggest that the required different expressions of the common genome in a homothallic mycelium are elicited by a nutritional regulator alone, without the intervention of a mating-type locus. Attention has already been drawn to the overriding role, even in the heterothallic system, of a "nutritional regulator" which, although not well investigated in these fungi, appears to be of the same kind as the broad "catabolite repression" mechanism which in fungi generally has been linked with the whole spectrum of nonvegetative processes including so-called secondary metabolism (Demain, 1972; Bu'Lock, *passim*). Moreover there are already examples, for instance in *Gibberella fujikuroi,* of the selective response of different multi-gene systems to different levels of a growth-linked regulatory mechanism (Bu'Lock *et al.,* 1974c).

In the homothallic system the outgrowing larger zygophore almost invariably curves towards a part of the parent hypha nearer to the growing tip; in other words, the "constitutive" sexuality is shown by that part of the hypha which has access to higher nutrient levels and where vegetative growth processes are more active. Moreover we have confirmed in several species what is apparent generally from the older descriptions, namely that the *first* step in homothallic sexual reproduction is the *formation of a septum* between the point at which a branch is emerging and the tip of the main hypha. Such a branch *then* becomes gametangial, and the characteristic accumulations of lipid and carotenoid frequently extend right up to the septum, leaving "normal" cytoplasm in front. Other septa, delimiting the gametangia proper, usually form at a later stage just as in the heterothallic process, but the *ab initio* role of the first septum has no such parallel; on the other hand it can readily be envisaged as a means of preventing some hyphal tip product, that could be an effector for vegetative growth and "catabolite repression", from diffusing further into the mycelium. Presumably the formation of the septum is itself a response to reduced vegetative growth, which in turn, by compartmentalizing the older cytoplasm, accentuates this effect in the interior portion.

On this hypothesis the functioning genome of the homothallic species is similar to that of the heterothallics, but the MT locus is absent or inactive, and its function in setting up two reaction patterns is carried out by selective "catabolite repression" mechanisms. From the evolutionary viewpoint, this makes the homothallic species intelligible, since the self-sexuality of these fungi offers virtually no evolutionary advantage, and is better seen as a vestigial modification of the outbreeding mechanism evolved in the heterothallic species. A communication by S. Branner–Jörgensen and R. Illum Nielsen at this Symposium presents data to show that within the species *Mucor pusillus* there are both heterothallic and homothallic strains.

An extrapolation of this hypothesis, in line with some current ideas on differentiation processes and the mechanisms of catabolite repression, would be that the hyphal tips produce phosphodiesterase, and that when the level of this is reduced that of cyclic AMP rises; this in turn could activate the expression of genes for nonvegetative functions. As a crude test, we have applied 0.1–0.6 mmol of *N,N*-dibutyryl cyclic AMP to wells a few mm in front of growing colonies of *M. mucedo* and *M. hiemalis* on agar. This has dramatic effects. Extension growth of the hyphae is stopped almost immediately, and up to 20 mm from the well. The colony front develops an arborescent appearance with thickened hyphae and swollen clubshaped hyphal tips. Septa are formed and are sometimes very numerous, dividing hyphae into strings of swollen "cells" or partitioning the base of clustered clubshaped tip outgrowths. Throughout, the hyphae become filled with large and small lipid droplets and carotenoids are conspicuous.

To some extent the forms induced by Bu_2cAMP resemble the yeast growth forms which can be induced in many Mucorales by adjustments of the CO_2/O_2 ratio etc. (Bartnicki-Garcia and Nickerson, 1962), and indeed Larsen and Sypherd (1974) have recently described such forms, induced by Bu_2AMP, as "yeastlike" in *M. racemosus*. However, they also note the larger size, lipid content and "granular" cytoplasm as being different from the true yeast forms. To us, the induced forms appear at least equally related to gametangia, and we regard the induction of septum formation as a particularly critical feature; on the other hand it must be admitted that the experiments so far conducted lack refinement. Possibly cAMP mediates both yeast–hyphal dimorphism and aspects of the sexual system, and our present techniques are too crude to single out just one aspect of a wide spectrum of activities that are more selectively effected in less perturbed systems.

FUTURE TASKS

The Mucorales are not well suited for genetic experiments of a classical kind and progress in applying such methods to the sexual system has been slow.

508   J. D. BU'LOCK

Some relevant data have been noted above, and more may be expected now that a range of mutants blocked at various stages in the heterothallic process is becoming available. At the same time, renewed chemical and physiological studies of sex heterokaryons and sex diploids would seem to offer a further promising approach.

Because an essential step in the process requires two thalli, the heterothallic system has allowed considerable experimental manipulation. This in turn has allowed us to see something of the complexities that are involved in the seemingly simple idea of the "expression" of a gene, and—I believe—to begin to see a way through these complexities in terms of what I have termed "cascade" mechanisms. The resemblance of these mechanisms, or at least their cybernetic equivalence, to the general views of Britten and Davidson (1969) on regulation in eukaryotes is not merely coincidental, even though the actual data for the regulatory patterns are of quite a different kind. I hope also that this review has thrown some light on the problem of phenotypic sexuality in homozygous organisms, and perhaps indirectly on the very complex realities which we may suspect are concealed in heterokaryotic ones, where different nuclei can interact directly through a common cytoplasm. Equally I hope this review will show how much remains to be done in this field despite the remarkable progress that has been made in the last few years.

References

Bartnicki-Garcia, S. and Nickerson, W. J. (1962). *J. Bact.* **84**, 829.
Britten, R. J. and Davidson, E. H. (1969). *Science,* **165**, 349.
Bu'Lock, J. D., Jones, B. E., Quarrie, S. A. and Winskill, N. (1973). *Naturwissenschaften,* **60**, 550.
Bu'Lock, J. D. and Osagie, A. U. (1973). *J. gen. Microbiol.* **76**, 77.
Bu'Lock, J. D., Jones, B. E., Taylor, D., Winskill, N. and Quarrie, S. A. (1974a). *J. gen. Microbiol.* **80**, 301.
Bu'Lock, J. D., Jones, B. E. and Winskill, N. (1974b). *Chem. Commun.* In press.
Bu-Lock, J. D., Detroy, R., Hošťálek, Z. and Munim-al-Shakarchi, A. (1974c). *Trans. Br. mycol. Soc.* **62**, 377.
Crandall, M. A. and Brock, T. D. (1968). *Science,* **161**, 473.
Demain, A. L. (1972). *J. appl. Chem. Biotechnol.* **22**, 345.
Emerson, S. (1966). "The Fungi" (Ed. G. C. Ainsworth and A. S. Sussman), vol. 2, p. 554. Academic Press, New York and London.
Gooday, G. W. (1968). *New Phytol.* **67**, 815.
Gooday, G. W. (1973). *Symp. Soc. gen. Microbiol.* **23**, 269.
Kohler, F. (1935). *Z. indukt. Abstamm.-u. VererbLehre,* **70**, 1.
Larsen, A. D. and Sypherd, P. S. (1964). *J. Bact.* **117**, 432.
Mesland, D. A. M., Huisman, J. G. and van den Ende, H. (1973). *J. gen. Microbiol.* 79.
Satina, S. and Blakeslee, A. F. (1930). *Bot. Gaz.* **90**, 299.
Sutter, R. P., Capage, D., Harrison, T. L. and Keen, W. A. (1973). *J. Bact.* **114**, 1074.

Thomas, D. M., Harris, R. C., Kirk, J. T. O. and Goodwin, T. W. (1967). *Phytochem.* **6**, 361.
van den Ende, H. and Stegwee, D. (1971). *Bot. Rev.* **37**, 22.
Werkman, B. A. and van den Ende, H. (1973). *Arch. Mikrobiol.* **90**, 365.
Werkman, B. A. and van den Ende, H. (1974). *J. gen. Microbiol.* **82**, 279.

GENETICS OF ACTINOMYCETES

Recent advances in *Streptomyces rimosus* genetics

M. ALAČEVIĆ

Institute of Biotechnology, Faculty of Technology,
University of Zagreb, Yugoslavia

Summary

The elaboration of already collected and new genetic data by a computer allowed confirmation and extension of the map of *Streptomyces rimosus*. Segregation data from crosses and heteroclones with eight or more markers can be analysed in about one minute. The computer output includes the choice of gene permutations minimizing the number of crossovers, the ordering of allele frequencies in gradients, the calculation of recombination frequencies between pairs of alleles (possibly including chi square tests), and the testing of additivity between adjacent "distances". The co-mutation technique (reported in detail by A. Carere and R. Randazzo in these Proceedings) proved a good tool for isolating and localizing new genes with respect to reference markers, and for checking the positions of already located genes.

An up to date map of *S. rimosus* is reported including some temperature-sensitive and some oxytetracycline nonproducing mutants. The map is compared to that of *S. coelicolor* (Hopwood, *et al.*, 1973), and to that of *S. rimosus* according to Friend and Hopwood (1971). An integrated picture is presented.

Introduction

Mapping in *Streptomyces rimosus* has been achieved through the analysis of a very large number of crosses (Friend and Hopwood, 1971) or heteroclones (Alačević *et al.*, 1973), involving from four to six and sometimes more markers. The information collected was so large (Table 1) that only part of the available data could be elaborated, and the maps had to be constructed by successive additions of new markers to known ones taking the position of the latter for granted.

Alačević *et al.* (1973) developed analytical tables suitable for the choice of the best circular permutation of four or five markers, but even by that method many parameters had to be neglected, and crosses with six or more markers could not be analysed.

TABLE 1

Increasing information by addition of markers

Markers	Genotypes	Permutations
3	8	1
4	16	3
5	32	12
6	64	60
7	128	360
8	256	2520
9	512	20160
10	1024	181440
n	2^n	$(n-1)!/2$

To re-elaborate the collected data, to test the position of markers by further crosses and to add new loci to the map, computer processing of data was introduced. Once the programme is chosen, crosses involving eight or even more markers can be analysed in detail, providing, in a few minutes, analytical and statistical information otherwise obtainable only after days of hard calculation. Due to the automatic nature of the process the genetic information can be made available even to people not familiar with the analytical procedures of *Streptomyces* genetics. The programme may thus work also as a guide to genetic analysis. To the expert geneticist it can open new fields of analytical research otherwise inhibited by the quantity of information involved.

The markers mapped so far have been obtained by random mutation. In order to concentrate mutations in regions of the map of special interest a new technique is being developed, already introduced in *S. coelicolor* by Randazzo *et al.* (1973) (see also A. Carere and R. Randazzo, these Proceedings), the co-mutation method. By means of this device mutations can be focused in regions of the map still lacking markers, or in regions expected to harbour genes of special interest for biochemical or industrial purposes, e.g. genes involved in oxytetracycline synthesis.

Results and discussion

COMPUTERIZATION OF GENETIC DATA: THE FLOWCHART

The computer processing of segregation data is based on a programme which will be presented in detail in a future paper (Topolovec, Alačević and Sermonti, in preparation). The computer we have used is a UNIVAC 1110, of the Zagreb University Computer Centre. The programme language was Fortran V. Once the programme is chosen the data are arranged in a simple manner in a suitable form. They may refer to segregants from one or more heteroclones of the same cross (Hopwood and Sermonti, 1962), or recombinants from one or more samples on selective media of the same cross (Hopwood, 1967). We will refer hereafter to heteroclones (HET), which have been the main source of our information (Alačević *et al.*, 1973), but the same considerations hold for selective analysis. Heteroclones are more suitable for estimating absolute distances and selective analysis for the choice of the best permutations (i.e. for location of new markers).

The upper part of the record form includes such general information as species name, cross code, key parameters (number of markers from each parent and heteroclone number), code and gene symbols of parent strains, as well as further optional elaboration. The lower part of the form is filled with the genotypes obtained in arbitrary order, but with the markers arranged in the order used above, and their frequencies in each heteroclone. All the data are punched on cards and fed into the computer to be processed according to the flowchart shown in Fig. 1.

Input 1, followed by *parameter calculation*, corresponds to the upper part of the record form, *input 2* to the lower part. Genotypes are translated into binary

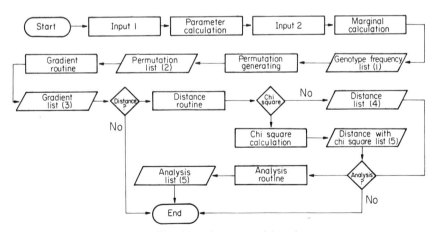

Fig. 1. Flowchart of computer elaboration.

code, ordered from 0000.... to 1111...., and totals calculated (*marginal calculations*) and arranged in the first output, the *genotype frequency list*. Then all possible circular permutations are generated (*permutation generating*), and arranged for each heteroclone and the summary one, in order, starting from the permutation minimizing the number of multiple crossovers and proceeding to a number of permutations equal to the total number of parental markers. *Gradient routine* is the calculation of allele frequencies and their ordering in gradients referring to each heteroclone and to the summary one. They are presented in the *gradient list*.

After these calculations have been performed, the computer can proceed, if requested, to the optional ones. Recombination frequencies for each pair of loci (*distance*) can be calculated (*distance routine*) and presented in a *distance list*, possibly including their 2:2 *chi square* test, according to Hopwood and Sermonti (1962) (*distance with chi square list*). The last optional analysis is a test of additivity of adjacent distances, calculated for trios of loci by comparing the recombination frequency (distance) between the external markers with the sum of the distances (A and B) between these and the central marker (A + B − 2AB) (*analysis routine*). The data are presented in a final *analysis list*, referring to different possible gene orders, according to the *permutation list*.

CO-MUTATION

The co-mutation method appears as a promising short-cut for the isolation and preliminary location of new loci. It also permits the collection of mutants in a desired region, provided that a selectable locus is available (or a revertable mutation) nearby. This is discussed in detail by A. Carere in another paper of these Proceedings. I will only refer to some of his results, and to some un-published results by J. Pigac especially pertinent to the clarification of the *S. rimosus* map.

By reverting the *hisA2* mutant, at 1 o'clock on the map, a co-mutation pattern comparable to that obtained by reverting mutants *hisA1* and *hisA132* of *S. coelicolor* was found. The revertant locus turned out to belong to a cluster of other *his* loci. Around this locus the following loci were found: *met, amm, trp, tyr, arg* and *ala*. Loci *met, tyr,* and *trp* had already been located in the vicinity of *hisA* and their location was confirmed; the locus *amm* was known to be near *hisA* in *S. coelicolor* but not yet detected in *S. rimosus*; the locus *ala*, comprising the most frequent co-mutant class, was unknown both in *S. rimosus* and in *S. coelicolor* and it is very likely absent in the corresponding region of the latter species, being undetectable by the co-mutation test.

The co-mutants appearing among revertants of the *pdx-1* locus (Pigac, personal communication), *phe* and *ilv*, were of special interest, being hitherto unknown in *S. rimosus*, mapping in a region poorly known, and corresponding to loci in *S. coelicolor* located on different sides of the 9 o'clock point, separated

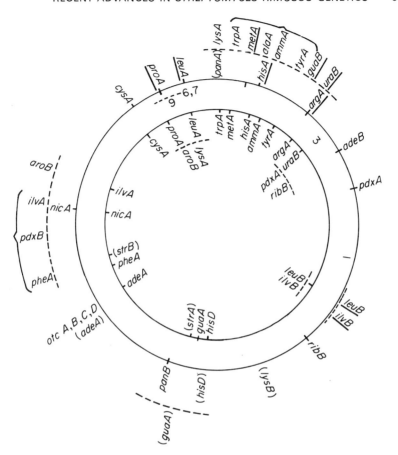

FIG. 2. The map of *Streptomyces rimosus* (outer circle) compared to that of *S. coelicolor* with empty regions omitted (inner circle) (Hopwood *et al.*, 1973). The locus letters in *S. rimosus* have been adopted to conform to those of corresponding genes in *S. coelicolor* (Alačević *et al.*, 1973). Underlined symbols refer to *S. rimosus* genes located in the same order also by Friend and Hopwood (1971). Genes located by Friend and Hopwood (1971) opposite mutations in genes concerned with the same biosynthetic pathway mapped by us, and also genes not mapped by us, are indicated in parentheses. Loci outside broken arcs have not been ordered relative to each other. Bracketed loci were shown to be linked by co-mutation. Numbers inside the outer circle are allele numbers of temperature-sensitive mutants.

by one of the empty regions, that region containing the sex-factor in NF strains (Hopwood *et al.*, 1973).

The loci recognized by the co-mutation test as linked are shown as bracketed in the map in Fig. 2.

THE CURRENT MAP OF *STREPTOMYCES RIMOSUS*

The map of *S. rimosus* ATCC 10970 R7 and R6 (Alačević *et al.*, 1973) has been reassessed on the basis of computer processing of some old data, enriched by new accessions and checked in two regions by the co-mutation test. It has also been compared with the map of *S. coelicolor* A3(2) (Hopwood *et al.*, 1973) and with the map of *S. rimosus* presented by Friend and Hopwood (1971).

The genome sizes of *S. coelicolor* and *S. rimosus* were calculated (R. Benigni, unpublished results) by application of the technique of renaturation of single-stranded DNA (Wetmur and Davidson, 1968). The amount of nonrepetitive DNA is not significantly different in the two species (c. $5.21 \pm 0.56 \times 10^9$ daltons as compared with 2.28 ± 0.19 in *Escherichia coli*). No repetitive DNA was demonstrated in *S. rimosus* although a small amount might be present in *S. coelicolor*.

The new accessions involve some *tps* (temperature sensitive) mutants. The temperature tolerance of *S. rimosus* is different from that of *S. coelicolor* because *S. rimosus* grows very well at 37°C and the limiting temperature is 43–45°C. By mutation we obtained 5 stable *tps* strains unable to grow at 43°C. On the map in Fig. 2 their location is indicated by numbers inside the outer circle.

A few temperature-resistant strains grow normally at 45°C and some of them also retain antibiotic activity, while others, as well as the wild type, lose their activity with increasing temperature above 28°C.

A large number of *otc* (oxytetracycline nonproducing) mutants belonging to at least four complementation groups have also been located (Pigac, personal communication) and all are in the region between *panB* and *pdxB*, a region unfortunately poorly mapped. This region overlaps that between two *str* loci in *S. coelicolor* (Fig. 2) (Hopwood *et al.*, 1973). This location agrees with that indicated by Boronin and Mindlin (1971), who have placed two groups of mutations in a region between two nonallelic *str* mutations, on the assumption that they correspond to the *strA* and *strB* loci in *S. coelicolor*.

Nine loci located by us (Alačević *et al.*, 1973) correspond in their order to similar loci on the map of *S. rimosus* published by Friend and Hopwood (1971) (underlined in Fig. 2), and four (*lys, his, ade, pan*) correspond to loci diametrically opposed (in parentheses in Fig. 2).

Comparison with the *S. coelicolor* A 3(2) map does not indicate important discrepancies, but only minor differences which may perhaps be reconciled or confirmed in the future. One concerns the occurrence of "empty regions". In the comparison in Fig. 2 they have been deleted from the map of *S. coelicolor*. The arcs around these regions are, however, the less consistent regions in the two maps. The loci designated as *aroB* and *ribB* do not fit properly, but their location is still doubtful in both maps. The loci *ilvA* and *pheA*, which belong to two different arcs in *S. coelicolor* were considered as linked to each other and to *pdxB* in *S. rimosus* on the basis of the co-mutation test alone, a conclusion which needs to be substantiated by further analysis. The *ala* gene, located in *S. rimosus* near *hisA* by the co-mutation method, seems to be elsewhere in *S. coelicolor*, not being detected by the same method (Carere and Randazzo, these Proceedings).

The *otc* loci have obviously no counterpart in *S. coelicolor*. It seems remarkable that they all belong to the lower arc of the map, as do the genes for zorbonomycin synthesis (Coats and Roeser, 1971), after reassessment of the *S. bikiniensis* map by Friend and Hopwood (1971). Also most of the morphological mutants of *S. coelicolor* (Hopwood *et al.*, 1973) are located in the same lower arc, which appears to be the preferred site for genes involved in differentiation and secondary metabolism.

Acknowledgements

I thank Professor Giuseppe Sermonti for his continuous guidance and great help in preparation of the manuscript and Professor Topolovec for his skilful work on the elaboration of the computer programme. I am grateful to Mrs M. Strašek-Vešligaj, Mrs J. Pigac and Mrs Z. Matijašević for their collaboration and to Dr R. Randazzo and Dr R. Benigni for details of unpublished data.

I wish to thank the Directors of "Pliva", Chemical and Pharmaceutical Works, Zagreb, for permission to publish these results.

References

Alačević, M., Strašek-Vešligaj, M. and Sermonti, G. (1973). *J. gen. Microbiol.* **77**, 173.
Boronin, A. M. and Mindlin, S. Z. (1971). *Genetika*, **7**, 125.
Coats, J. H. and Roeser, J. (1971). *J. Bact.* **105**, 880.
Friend, E. J. and Hopwood, D. A. (1971). *J. gen. Microbiol.* **68**, 187.
Hopwood, D. A. (1967). *Bact. Rev.* **31**, 373.
Hopwood, D. A., Chater, K. F., Dowding, J. E. and Vivian, A. (1973). *Bact. Rev.* **37**, 371.
Hopwood, D. A. and Sermonti, G. (1962). *Adv. Genet.* **11**, 273.
Randazzo, R., Sermonti, G., Carere, A. and Bignomi, M. (1973). *J. Bact.* **113**, 500.
Wetmur, G. and Davidson, N. (1968). *J. molec. Biol.* **31**, 349.

Genetic recombination in
Streptomyces achromogenes var. *rubradiris*

J. H. COATS

The Upjohn Research Laboratories, Kalamazoo, Michigan, USA

Summary

A genetic recombination system in *Streptomyces achromogenes* var. *rubradiris* is described. This culture produces several antibiotics including rubradirin, a new antibiotic of undetermined structure. The genetic system of *S. achromogenes* differs from that of *S. coelicolor* in that in many *S. achromogenes* crosses, essentially all colonies growing on selective media give rise to a mixture of two or more recombinant classes or a mixture of recombinants and parentals. The presence of closely linked markers in repulsion is not a prerequisite for the appearance of these heterogenous clones. In contrast to the behaviour of the *S. coelicolor* partial diploids, the *S. achromogenes* heteroclones grow quite vigorously on selective media. Analysis of allele frequency gradients in segregants from these heteroclones suggests that multiple copies of the donor fragment are produced in growing clones and that crossover positions for the integration of the fragments are not fixed at either end. A large number of *S. achromogenes* crosses have been examined both by selective and heteroclone analysis, and the presumptive gene order determined for several auxotrophic markers. The linkage map constructed for *S. achromogenes* agrees in most respects with that of *S. coelicolor*.

Introduction

Modification of the antibiotic producing capability of Streptomycetes through genetic manipulation has been a goal of several investigations over the past few years. While the most thoroughly explored genetic system in this group of organisms remains that of *Streptomyces coelicolor* (Hopwood *et al.*, 1973), genetic data on Streptomycetes of industrial interest are accumulating (Coats and Roeser, 1971; Friend and Hopwood, 1971; Alačević *et al.*, 1973). Work has been carried out in our laboratories over the last three years on the genetics of *Streptomyces achromogenes* var. *rubradiris*. This organism produces the antibiotic rubradirin (Bhuyan *et al.*, 1965; Meyer, 1965) in a mixture of several antimicrobial activities. It was hoped that genetic recombination techniques might be utilized both to increase the capacity of this organism to make rubradirin and to eliminate the formation of the additional antibiotics.

This report describes the genetic system in *S. achromogenes*. A genetic map has been constructed showing the presumptive map order of fifteen marker loci.

Materials and methods

ORGANISM

Streptomyces achromogenes var. *rubradiris* UC 2630 (NRRL 3061) is a soil isolate characterized by A. Dietz of The Upjohn Company (Bhuyan *et al.*, 1965). The culture grows well at temperatures ranging from 18 to 37°C, is melanin-positive and has grey aerial growth containing chains of smooth, oval-to-oblong spores. The sporophores of *S. achromogenes* form open loops and are classified RA in the sense of Pridham *et al.* (1958).

ISOLATION OF MUTANTS

The majority of *S. achromogenes* mutants were obtained by *N*-methyl- *N'*-nitro-*N*-nitrosoguanidine (MNNG) treatment following the procedure employed with *S. bikiniensis* (Coats and Roeser, 1971). Optimum mutagenesis was achieved with 3 mg MNNG cm^{-3} at pH 9.0. A few mutants were also obtained by ultra-violet irradiation. Mutants were characterized using the procedures given for *S. bikiniensis* (Coats and Roeser, 1971). All stock cultures were stored above liquid nitrogen on agar.

MEDIA

The auxotrophic strains of *S. achromogenes* vary considerably in their ability to produce aerial mycelium and spores. Most strains grow and sporulate well on Hickey–Tresner agar (HT) (Hickey and Tresner, 1952) or on HT supplemented with 3 cm^3 dm^{-3} yeast nucleic acid hydrolysate (HTN) prepared as described by Pontecorvo (1953). A number of strains produce little aerial growth on HT but sporulate heavily on either MM-1 agar (Coats and Roeser, 1971) supplemented with growth factors required by the given strain, Bennett's agar (Jones, 1949), or on NCV agar (Coats and Roeser, 1971).

CROSS PROCEDURE

The crossing techniques used in these studies and the method for carrying out selective analysis are essentially the same as those described for *S. bikiniensis* (Coats and Roeser, 1971). Crosses were made on either HT, HTN, NCV or Bennett's agar. Cross plates were generally incubated seven days at 28°C before spores were harvested. Heteroclones were analysed by the procedure of Sermonti (1969).

Results and discussion

MUTANT LOCI

The marker loci used in mapping experiments are listed in Table 1. All of the mutations with the exception of *ilv-2* which resulted from ultraviolet irradiation were obtained by MNNG treatment.

TABLE 1
Mutant loci used in mapping experiments

Mutant allele	Characteristic
arg-2	Requirement for arginine
his-3	Requirement for histidine
ilv-2	Requirement for isoleucine plus valine
lys-2	Requirement for lysine
met-1	Requirement for methionine
nic-1	Requirement for nicotinamide
nic-2	Requirement for nicotinamide
pur-1	Requirement for purines
pyr-1	Requirement for pyrimidines
str-1	Resistance to streptomycin
thi-1	Requirement for thiamine
thi-2	Requirement for thiamine
thi-4	Requirement for thiamine
thr-1	Requirement for threonine
ura-4	Requirement for uracil

CROSS ANALYSIS

The initial crosses attempted with *S. achromogenes* strains were plate crosses (Sermonti and Casciano, 1963) between seventeen primary mutants in all possible combinations. In these preliminary experiments only crosses involving strain 191–17 (*thi-2 pur-1*) yielded stable prototrophic recombinants. Crosses of 191–13 (*thr-1 met-1*) × 191–17 (*thi-2 pur-1*) when subsequently carried out as described in Materials and Methods, yielded good numbers of presumptive recombinants on MM-1 agar. All the colonies were large and well sporulated.

However, when spores from these colonies were replated on MM-1, they gave rise in many cases to scattered heavily sporulating colonies in an easily discernible background growth. Further analysis of the colonies on the original selective medium plates revealed the presence of one or both parental genotypes mixed with stable prototrophic recombinants. These colonies resemble the heteroclones described by Hopwood and Sermonti (1962) as "aberrant heteroclones". Since many of the mutant strains examined in crosses subsequent to these initial studies were derived from 191–13 and 191–17, most crosses were analysed by techniques for both selective analysis and heteroclone analysis.

ORDERING OF LOCI

To map mutant loci, data from both of the above types of analyses were collected. Map order was deduced by choosing the marker arrangement in which all major recombinant classes could be accounted for by single crossovers in each of two regions of an assumed circular genome. The *S. achromogenes* map showing the location of several marker loci is given in Fig. 1.

The results of a typical selective analysis of a cross are shown in Table 2. Very few recombinant classes were obtained from each selective medium. The 191–13 derivative (191–46) appears to act as a recipient in a strongly polarized cross. The occurrence of few classes of recombinants in generally polarized crosses rendered the haploid analysis technique, as used for *S.*

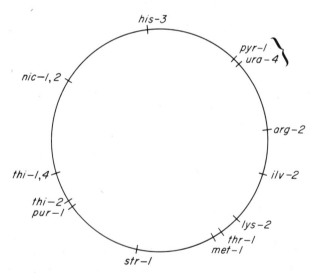

Fig. 1. Linkage map of *S. achromogenes* var. *rubradiris*. Marker loci are explained in Table 1. The order of the *pyr-1*, *ura-4* markers (bracket) is not known. The placement of markers relative to each other does not reflect actual map distance.

TABLE 2

Results of cross 191–46 (*thr-1 met-1 ura-4 str-1*) × 191–50 (*thi-2 pur-1 ilv-2*)

Recombinant genotypes	Selected markers			
	pur^+ ura^+	pur^+ thr^+	ilv^+ thr^+	ilv^+ ura^+
thr met + str + + −	120	—	—	118
+ + ura + + + ilv	—	1	—	—
+ + ura str + + +	—	11	11	—
+ + ura str + + ilv	—	20	—	—
+ + ura + thi pur +	—	—	1	—
thr met + str thi +	—	—	—	1
+ + + + + + +	0	0	0	1
TOTALS	120	32	12	120

bikiniensis and *S. coelicolor* mapping (Hopwood, 1967; Coats and Roeser, 1971) of little value for mapping this organism.

HETEROCLONE ANALYSIS

The segregants from a series of heteroclones from the cross 191–30 (*thr-1 met-1 str-1*) × 191–54 (*lys-2 ura-4*) are listed in Table 3. Since strain 191–30 (*thr met str*) appears to act as recipient in this cross, the *lys ura* donor parent class is most probably a "pseudo-parental" recombinant class. Such recombinants would be expected if donor fragments contained both the *thr⁺ met⁺ str⁺* prototrophic alleles and the *lys ura* mutant alleles. These "pseudo-parentals" would not only appear along with obvious haploid recombinants but the ratio between the two might be expected to vary from heteroclone to heteroclone. This is the precise situation that obtains in the so-called "aberrant heteroclones".

Plating units giving rise to heteroclones in *S. coelicolor* are thought to contain a terminally redundant genome resulting from an odd number of crossovers between a donor fragment and a complete recipient genome (Hopwood, 1967). Heteroclones are generally seen in this organism only when two closely linked genes in repulsion are selected or when special techniques are employed for their isolation (Sermonti, 1969). The majority of progeny recovered from *S. coelicolor* crosses are haploid recombinants arising through even numbers of crossover events. By contrast, in many *S. achromogenes* crosses virtually all plating units give rise to heterogenous clones regardless of the selection imposed. It seems unreasonable therefore to expect that only odd numbers of crossovers occur in such crosses to give plating units containing exclusively terminally redundant genomes. Nevertheless, in the initial analysis of heteroclones from this organism an effort was made to fit segregation data to the *S.*

TABLE 3

Heteroclones from cross 191–30 (*thr-1 met-1 str-1*) × 191–54 (*lys-2 ura-4*)

Segregants	Heteroclone number						
	1	2	3	4	5	6	7
+ + + *lys* +	100	100	0	115	97	70	0
+ + *str lys* +	0	42	64	0	0	10	43
thr met str + +	30	0	0	0	29	130	2
+ + + *lys ura*	0	0	8	17	41	3	15
TOTALS	130	142	72	132	167	213	60

Allele ratios:

Heteroclone 2 =

$\dfrac{100}{str}=\dfrac{+}{42}$	$\dfrac{142}{met}=\dfrac{+}{0}$	$\dfrac{142}{thr}=\dfrac{\oplus*}{0}$	$\dfrac{142}{+}=\dfrac{lys}{0}$	$\dfrac{0}{\oplus*}=\dfrac{ura}{142}$

Heteroclone 5 =

$\dfrac{138}{str}=\dfrac{+}{29}$	$\dfrac{138}{met}=\dfrac{+}{29}$	$\dfrac{138}{thr}=\dfrac{\oplus}{29}$	$\dfrac{138}{+}=\dfrac{lys}{29}$	$\dfrac{41}{\oplus}=\dfrac{ura}{122}$

Heteroclone 6 =

$\dfrac{73}{str}=\dfrac{+}{140}$	$\dfrac{83}{met}=\dfrac{+}{130}$	$\dfrac{83}{thr}=\dfrac{\oplus}{130}$	$\dfrac{83}{+}=\dfrac{lys}{130}$	$\dfrac{3}{\oplus}=\dfrac{ura}{210}$

Heteroclone 7 =

$\dfrac{15}{str}=\dfrac{+}{45}$	$\dfrac{58}{met}=\dfrac{+}{2}$	$\dfrac{58}{thr}=\dfrac{\oplus}{2}$	$\dfrac{58}{+}=\dfrac{lys}{2}$	$\dfrac{15}{\oplus}=\dfrac{ura}{45}$

* Alleles selected on original plating medium.

coelicolor heteroclone model. The origin of the major recombinant classes recovered from many *S. achromogenes* heteroclones, however, could not be explained by a model requiring one crossover common to all segregants from a heterozygous plating unit. Upon tabulation of allele ratios in heteroclones from several crosses, it became apparent that changes in allele gradients occur frequently within heterozygous regions of fairly closely linked markers. In *S. coelicolor*, this type of heteroclone segregation pattern is seen only rarely. It is postulated to result from a double crossover occurring in a terminally redundant genome which causes a change in coupling within the heterozygous region

(Hopwood, 1967). Double gradients around a maximum central value have also been reported for some *S. rimosus* heteroclones thought to originate from genomes with two disomic regions (Alačević *et al.*, 1973). In *S. achromogenes*, however, the location of the change in allele gradient is associated with the selected marker in a polarized cross. This is illustrated by the allele ratios given in Tables 3 and 4. All of the recombinant classes bear the selected donor allele. The mutant alleles that do occur at the selected loci occur in the recipient parental class only.

TABLE 4

Allele ratios among segregants from heteroclones in the cross 191–24 (*thi-2 pur-1 nic-1*) × 191–66 (*thr-1 met-1 str-1 ura-4 arg-2*)

	0	78	78	146	146	146	78	0
	nic	*thi*	*pur*	+	+	⊕*	+	+
Heteroclone 1								
	+	+	⊕*	*str*	*met*	*thr*	*arg*	*ura*
	146	68	68	0	0	0	68	146
	0	17	17	17	117	117	17	0
	nic	*thi*	*pur*	+	+	⊕	+	+
Heteroclone 2								
	+	+	⊕	*str*	*met*	*thr*	*arg*	*ura*
	117	100	100	100	0	0	100	117
	0	10	10	10	10	10	63	0
	nic	*thi*	*pur*	+	+	+	⊕	+
Heteroclone 3								
	+	+	⊕	*str*	*met*	*thr*	*arg*	*ura*
	63	53	53	53	53	53	0	63

* Alleles selected on original plating medium.

The allele frequency gradients observed in both segregants from heteroclones and recombinants from selective analysis procedures are similar in *S. achromogenes*. The gradients fall in one or both directions depending upon the location of the selected allele (Tables 4 and 5). When the selected marker occurs at the end of a group of marker loci (Table 4, heteroclone 3) the allele gradient obtained (a falling gradient in one direction only) resembles that seen in most *S. coelicolor* heteroclones. The ratio of parental classes to recombinant classes in *S. achromogenes* heteroclones also varies with the pattern of selection. When selection is made for two closely linked markers in repulsion and all marker loci in the parents map within a fairly short region of the genome, only "parental" classes of segregants are observed.

The above results suggest that multiple copies of the donor fragment are produced in a growing *S. achromogenes* heteroclone and that crossover positions for the integration of the fragment are not fixed at either end. A similar model has been proposed recently by Lotan *et al.* (1972) to explain the origin of segregant classes from *Escherichia coli* heterogenous clones. The *E. coli* donor genome fragment is postulated to replicate for two or three generations only thus limiting the number of donor pieces available for recombination. Donor fragment replication may also be limited in *S. achromogenes*. In general, only a few of the possible recombinant classes are recovered from a single heteroclone.

TABLE 5

Allele ratios among selected recombinants in the cross 191–17 (*thi-2 pur-1*) × 191–66 (*thr-1 met-1 str-1 ura-4 arg-2*)

Selection for *pur⁺ ura⁺*						
0	0	2	2	2	113	116
thi	pur	+	+	+	+	⊕*
+	⊕	str	met	thr	arg	ura
116	116	114	114	114	3	0
Selection for *pur⁺ arg⁺*						
0	0	1	12	12	128	117
thi	pur	+	+	+	⊕*	+
+	⊕*	str	met	thr	arg	ura
128	128	127	116	116	0	11

* Alleles selected on original plating medium.

From an examination of allele frequency gradients, estimates of the length of the donor fragments in different *S. achromogenes* heteroclones can be made. In heteroclone 2, Table 4, the donor fragment ends (zero points) are between *nic-2* and *thi-2* and between *arg-2* and *ura-4*. A comparison of heteroclones 5 and 6, Table 3, suggests that the donor fragment extends farther to the left of *str* in clone 5 than in clone 6. These estimates of fragment length are based on the previous observation (Sermonti, 1969) that donor alleles are contributed to recombinant progeny at higher frequencies as their distance from the fragment ends increases.

FERTILITY

A fertility system comparable to that in *S. coelicolor* has not been demonstrated as yet in *S. achromogenes*. The role of 191–17 (*thi-2 pur-1*) derivatives as donors in crosses with 191–13 (*thr-1 met-1*) derivatives, however, seems clear. Although recombinants from *S. achromogenes* crosses vary markedly in their ability to participate in fertile crosses, segregation of a fertility factor is not apparent in the crosses carried out to date.

COMPARISON OF MAPS

As shown in Fig. 2, the linkage map for *S. achromogenes* agrees in most respects with that of *S. coelicolor* (Hopwood *et al.*, 1973). The *thi-2 pur-1* markers of *S. achromogenes* may actually correspond to the *athA* locus in the *S. coelicolor* map.

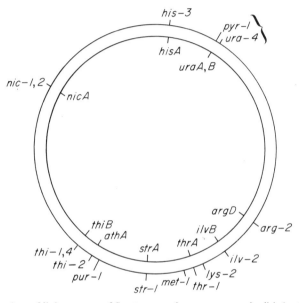

FIG. 2. Comparison of linkage maps of S*treptomyces achromogenes* var. *rubradiris* (outer circle) and *S. coelicolor* A3(2) (inner circle). Marker intervals are drawn to conform with those of the *S. coelicolor* map from Hopwood *et al.* (1973). No counterparts for the *met-1* and *lys-2* loci are apparent. *Lys-2* maps at the position given for *lysB* in the *S. rimosus* map of Friend and Hopwood (1971) which was compatible with the *S. coelicolor* map. Only *S. coelicolor* loci which appear to be counterparts of the *S. achromogenes* markers are given.

Although the *S. coelicolor* map does not exhibit an equivalent locus for the *lys-2* marker, its location between *thr-1* and *ilv-2* coincides with the *lysB* locus in the *S. rimosus* map (Friend and Hopwood, 1971). The data thus far obtained from *S. achromogens* crosses do not indicate the two large empty regions present in the *S. coelicolor* map. This was also the finding in *S. rimosus* (Friend and Hopwood, 1971; Alačević *et al.*, 1973). The discovery of *S. achromogenes* heteroclones heterozygous for the *ura-4—arg-2*, the *ura-4—nic-1*, the *nic-1— pur-1* and the *arg-2—pur-1* segments of the map suggests that the genome in this organism is circular or circularly permuted.

Acknowledgement

I would like to thank W. A. Murphy for his capable technical assistance during the course of this investigation.

References

Alačević, M., Strašek-Vešligaj, M. and Sermonti, G. (1973). *J. gen. Microbiol.* **77**, 173.
Bhuyan, B. K., Owen, S. P. and Dietz, A. (1965). *Antimicrob. Agents Chemother.* 1964, 91.
Coats, J. H. and Roeser, J. (1971). *J. Bact.* **105**, 880.
Friend, E. J. and Hopwood, D. A. (1971). *J. gen. Microbiol.* **68**, 187.
Hickey, R. J. and Tresner, H. D. (1952). *J. Bacteriol.* **64**, 891.
Hopwood, D. A. (1967). *Bact. Rev.* **31**, 373.
Hopwood, D. A. and Sermonti, G. (1962). *Adv. Genet.* **11**, 273.
Hopwood, D. A., Chater, K. F., Dowding, J. E. and Vivian, A. (1973). *Bact. Rev.* **37**, 371.
Jones, K. L. (1949). *J. Bact.* **57**, 142.
Lotan, D., Yagil, E. and Bracha, M. (1972). *Genetics,* **72**, 381.
Meyer, C. E. (1965). *Antimicrob. Agents Chemother.* 1964, 97.
Pontecorvo, G. (1953). *Adv. Genet.* **5**, 141
Pridham, T. G., Hesseltine, C. W. and Benedict, R. G. (1958). *Appl. Microbiol.* **6**, 52.
Sermonti, G. (1969). "Genetics of Antibiotic-Producing Microorganisms", p. 263. Wiley-Interscience, London.
Sermonti, G. and Casciano, S. (1963). *J. gen. Microbiol.* **33**, 293.

Genetic analysis in *Nocardia mediterranei*

T. SCHUPP

Ciba-Geigy AG, Basel, Switzerland

Genetic recombination has been shown to occur in *Nocardia mediterranei*, the producer of the rifamycin antibiotics (Sensi *et al.*, 1967). The rifamycins form an important group of macrocyclic antibiotics which are active against *Mycobacterium tuberculosis* and a wide range of other bacteria. The antibiotic activity of the rifamycins is due to a specific inhibition of the DNA-dependent RNA polymerase of prokaryotic cells. Clinically the rifamycins proved to be a very valuable class of antibiotics, especially for the treatment of tuberculosis. The apparent industrial importance of *N. mediterranei* was the main reason for the work on the genetics of this organism which is summarized here. The aim of the work was to obtain information on genetic recombination in *N. mediterranei* ATCC 13685 and to apply techniques of genetic analysis worked out for *Streptomyces coelicolor* A3(2) to construct a genetic map of *N. mediterranei* ATCC 13685. This was done in the hope that knowledge of genetic recombination, and of the linkage map, could be used later to improve rifamycin production by industrial strains of the organism and to study rifamycin biosynthesis.

Originally, *N. mediterranei* was classified as *Streptomyces mediterranei*, but chemical analysis of the cell wall by Thiemann *et al.* (1969) later clearly showed that the strain belongs to the genus *Nocardia*, and Thiemann *et al.* (1969) proposed its classification in the genus *Nocardia* as *N. mediterranei*.

Ultraviolet-induced auxotrophic mutants and a spontaneous mutation to streptomycin resistance were used as markers for the construction of a genetic map.

It was found that genetic recombination occurs when two marked strains of *N. mediterranei* are grown together in mixed culture on slants of complete medium. The crosses are quite self-fertile, yielding 1–10 recombinants per 10 000 cells of parental genotype.

The majority of the recombinants behaved as stable haploid genotypes. In addition a minority of recombinant colonies were found which showed a mixture of phenotypes. These mixed colonies very probably arise from multi-nucleate plating units, which are not unexpected since we are dealing with fragments of mycelium and not spores as plating units.

For the construction of the linkage map of *N. mediterranei* only haploid recombinants were analysed. The mapping procedures applied were similar to those used for *S. coelicolor* A3(2) (Hopwood, 1967, 1969) and can be divided into two parts. To detect the linkage relationships of a first set of loci, 4-factor crosses were performed and analysed according to the method devised by Hopwood (1969); this tests for the pattern of segregation of nonselected loci on 4 selective media. This analysis gave clear evidence on the linkage relationships of 4 loci on a circular linkage map. After this first indication of linkage, further markers were added to the linkage map by performing 5- and 6-factor crosses. These crosses were analysed by the method applied to *S. coelicolor* A3(2) (Hopwood, 1967) which allows the positioning of a new marker by fitting its allele frequency into the gradient of the allele frequencies of the other markers.

All the mapping data were combined to give a unique sequence of 15 loci on a circular linkage map. The results of the crosses showed that the genetic recombination system of *N. mediterranei* ATCC 13685 is very similar to that of *S. coelicolor* A3(2) and other Streptomycetes. Incompletely diploid zygotes are formed and each parent can behave as donor or recipient of a fragment of the chromosome. The fertility of the crosses was fairly constant and it seems that no fertility types have segregated amongst the mutant and recombinant strains so far.

A set of crosses between high producing strains of *N. mediterranei* and strain ATCC 13685 has shown that these combinations are also fertile. The overall features of these inter-strain crosses are similar to the crosses involving only ATCC 13685 mutants described above. This result is very encouraging, as it indicates that the genetic recombination system developed for *N. mediterranei* ATCC 13685 can also be applied to the high producing strains. The way is now open for the use of genetic recombination as an additional weapon besides the classical methods of mutation and selection to improve rifamycin production by *N. mediterranei*.

A detailed account of the recombination and mapping experiments with the ATCC 13685 mutants is in the paper by Schupp *et al.* (1974).

References

Hopwood, D. A. (1967). *Bact. Rev.* **31**, 373.
Hopwood, D. A. (1969). Genome toplogy and mapping in *Streptomyces coelicolor*, p. 5. *In* "Symposium on Genetics and Breeding of Streptomyces". Dubrovnik, Yugoslav Academy of Sciences and Arts, Zagreb.

Schupp, T., Hütter, R. and Hopwood, D. A. (1974). *J. Bact.* **121**, 128.
Sensi, P. and Thiemann, J. E. (1967). "Progress in Industrial Microbiology" (Ed. D. J. D. Hockenhull), vol. 6, p. 21. Heywood, London.
Thiemann, J. E., Zucco, G. and Pelizza, G. (1969). *Arch. Mikrobiol.* **67**, 147.

Genetics of *Streptomyces glaucescens* and regulation of melanin production

R. BAUMANN* and H. P. KOCHER

Microbiology Department, Swiss Federal Institute of Technology, Zürich, Switzerland

Summary

Genetic analysis of *Streptomyces glaucescens* strain ETH 22794 revealed a circular linkage map, which is similar to that of *S. coelicolor* A3(2). Tyrosinase is synthesized *de novo* after addition of various 2-aminocarboxylic acids to a growing culture.

From several melanin-negative mutants, an excretion-deficient tyrosinase producing mutant (*mel⁻ tye⁺*) and an excretion-competent tyrosinaseless mutant (*mel⁺ tye⁻*) were chosen for mapping studies. The results revealed a location of the tyrosinase marker (*tye*) on the chromosome, and suggest an extrachromosomal situation for the excretion character (*mel*).

Introduction

Streptomyces glaucescens, strain ETH 22794, was shown to yield the highest specific tyrosinase activity amongst a number of selected melanin-positive *Streptomyces* species. Precursors of melanin (Bu'Lock, 1960) are produced in *S. glaucescens* by the enzyme tyrosinase (EC 1.10.3.1), which can use mono- and *o*-diphenol substrates, and is therefore referred to as a "mixed function oxidase" (Hayaishi, 1968). The tyrosinase of *S. glaucescens* was purified and characterized by Lerch and Ettlinger (1972).

Gregory and Shyo (1961) and Gregory and Huang (1964) studied melanin production in *Streptomyces scabies*, and provided strong circumstantial evidence that melanin production is controlled by an extrachromosomal factor.

* Present address: Société d'Assistance Technique pour Produits, Nestlé SA, 1350 Orbe, Switzerland

Genetical studies with *S. scabies* by Townsend (1973) have so far yielded no reproducible system of recombination analysis. The establishment of a good experimental genetic system in *Streptomyces coelicolor* A 3(2), summarized by Hopwood *et al.* (1973), initiated an extension of mapping studies to other Streptomycetes (Friend and Hopwood, 1971; Alačević, 1973; Alačević *et al.*, 1973; Matselyukh *et al.*, 1973; Baumann *et al.*, 1974).

The mapping studies described in this investigation were done to establish a genetic system and to locate the structural marker of the single *S. glaucescens* tyrosinase. The biochemical study of tyrosinase production provided a basis for investigations of the regulation of enzyme synthesis.

Material and methods

MEDIA

The composition of the solid minimal medium (MM) used during this investigation has been described previously (Baumann *et al.*, 1974). The liquid minimal medium had the following composition, per litre: glucose, 15 g; mono-Na-glutaminate, 15 g; $K_2HPO_43H_2O$, 0.5 g; $MgSO_47H_2O$, 0.2 g; $CaCl_22H_2O$, 0.01 g; $FeSO_47H_2O$, 0.01 g; $ZnSO_47H_2O$, 0.01 g; $CuSO_45H_2O$, 0.005 g; $MnSO_44H_2O$, 0.04 g. Glucose and $K_2HPO_43H_2O$ were autoclaved separately in 125 cm^3 distilled water. The pH of the medium was 7.2, adjusted with NaOH. Supplements were added at the following final concentration to the liquid minimal medium: amino acids, 10^{-3} M; purines and pyrimidines, 5×10^{-4} M: vitamins, 5×10^{-5} M.

STRAINS

All strains were derived from a single clone of *Streptomyces glaucescens* strain ETH 22794.

MUTAGENIC TREATMENTS AND CHARACTERIZATION OF GROWTH-FACTOR REQUIREMENTS

Mutations were induced by uv, X-rays and *N*-methyl-*N'*-nitro-*N*-nitroso-guanidine (MNNG), or obtained spontaneously (streptomycin resistance), following the methods described elsewhere (Baumann *et al.*, 1974). The wild type and some mutants were treated in liquid culture and on solid media with several plasmid curing agents at the following concentrations: ethidium bromide (Sigma), 10^{-6} M; acridine orange (CIBA), 10^{-3} M; methylene blue (Merck), 10^{-5} M; acriflavine (FLUKA), 10^{-5} M. The strains growing in liquid minimal medium and treated with curing agents were submitted to mycelial fragmentation by ultra-sonication (Branson–Sonifier S-75) for 15 s before incubation on plates. Mutants were characterized by the method of Pontecorvo (1953).

GENETIC MARKERS

The auxotrophic and antibiotic-resistant markers isolated and used in this study are designated by standard symbols.

CROSSING PROCEDURE

The crossing procedure and the analysis of recombinants were those described by Baumann *et al.* (1974).

INDUCTION AND MEASUREMENT OF TYROSINASE ACTIVITY

Inducing substances were added at a final concentration of 10^{-2}–10^{-3} M to a batch culture incubated on a rotary shaker at 30°C. At the time of induction the total wet weight of the batch was 3–4 g dm^{-3}. The mycelium was harvested 2–8 h after induction by filtration through a Buchner funnel with filter paper No. 589^2 (Schleicher and Schuell), washed with distilled water, and suspended in 0.05 M phosphate buffer, pH 7.5. This mycelial suspension, cooled by an ice–salt mixture, was then ruptured by ultra-sonication (Branson–Sonifier 5-75) for one minute at maximum energy. The enzyme activity in the supernatant of the centrifuged crude extract (34800 g for 10 min) was measured by the methods described by Lerch and Ettlinger (1972).

DETERMINATION OF PROTEIN

Soluble protein was determined by the method of Lowry *et al.* (1951) using crystalline bovine serum albumin as a standard, or estimated by determining E_{260} and E_{280} of the sample. The protein concentration was then obtained from a nomograph compiled by Adams (California Corporation for Biochemical Research) from the data of Warburg and Christian (1942).

ENZYME PURIFICATION

The tyrosinase was purified by the method of Lerch and Ettlinger (1972).

ELECTROPHORESIS

Polyacrylamide gel electrophoresis and staining procedures were carried out as described by Lerch and Ettlinger (1972).

ASSAY OF RADIOACTIVITY

(U-^{14}C) Glycine (New England Nuclear Corporation, NEN) was added to a batch culture (wet weight of 3 g dm^{-3}) at a final concentration of 6–10^{-5} M (total activity was 200 μCi). Fifteen minutes after addition of ^{14}C-glycine, half of this batch was induced by L-methionine, whereas the other half served as noninduced control. Both cultures were incubated for 2 further hours. Then

TABLE 1

Analysis of a multi-factor cross: $hom\text{-}1^+$ $lys\text{-}3$ $ura\text{-}3$ $met\text{-}2$ $pro\text{-}1$ $str\text{-}4$ $\times$ $hom\text{-}1$ $lys\text{-}3^+$ $ura\text{-}3^+$ $met\text{-}2^+$ $pro\text{-}1^+$ $str\text{-}4^+$

Selection I: $pro\text{-}1^+/str\text{-}4$

Genotypes	Number	Crossovers in intervals
+ lys + +	211	3,6
+ lys ura +	144	2,6
+ lys ura met	22	1,2
+ lys + met	8	1,3
hom lys + met	5	1,4
hom + + met	5	5,6
hom lys + +	3	4,6
hom + + met	3	1,5
+ + + met	0	1,3,4,5
hom lys ura +	0	2,3,4,6
+ + + +	0	3,4,5,6
hom lys ura met	0	1,2,3,4
hom + ura met	0	1,2,3,5
+ + ura +	0	2,4,5,6
+ + ura met	0	1,2,4,5
hom + ura +	0	2,3,5,6
Total	381	

Selection II: $lys\text{-}3^+/str\text{-}4$

Genotypes	Number	Crossovers in intervals
ura met pro hom	273	3,5
+ + + hom	18	5,6
+ met pro hom	16	2,5
ura met pro +	8	4,5
+ met + hom	6	1,5
ura + + +	1	2,4,5,6,
ura + pro +	1	1,4,5,6,
ura met + +	0	1,2,4,5
+ + pro hom	0	1,2,5,6
+ met + +	0	1,3,4,5
ura + pro hom	0	1,3,5,6
+ + + +	0	3,4,5,6
+ + pro +	0	1,2,3,4,5,6
ura met + hom	0	1,2,3,5
+ met pro +	0	2,3,4,5
ura + + hom	0	2,3,5,6
Total	323	

Selection III: $ura\text{-}3^+/str\text{-}4$

Genotypes	Number	Crossovers in intervals
lys + + +	180	3,6
lys met pro +	23	2,3
lys met pro hom	17	2,4
lys met + +	12	1,3
lys met + hom	10	1,4
+ met + hom	5	1,5
lys + + hom	5	4,6
+ + + hom	4	5,6
+ met pro hom	3	2,5
lys + pro +	1	1,2,3,6
+ met + +	0	3,4,5,6
+ met + +	0	1,3,4,5
lys + pro hom	0	1,2,4,6
+ + pro +	0	1,2,3,4,5,6
+ met pro +	0	2,3,4,5
+ + pro hom	0	1,2,5,6
Total	260	

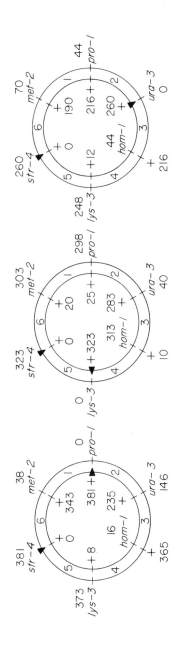

the mycelium was harvested and treated for enzyme extraction and purification as already described. The partially purified enzyme preparation was subjected to polyacrylamide gel electrophoresis. The gel was then sliced into segments of 1 mm thickness, which were solubilized in Protosol (NEN) and their radioactivity measured in a Beckman counter LS-250 with Aquasol (NEN) as scintillant.

Results

EVIDENCE OF LINKAGE AND MAP CIRCULARITY

The four-factor crossing procedure of Hopwood (1959) was applied to *Streptomyces glaucescens,* and the results indicated a reproducible linkage of certain markers. The analysis of the marker sequences by 2×2 tables as described by Hopwood (1969) showed all the loci to be located on a circular linkage map (Baumann *et al.,* 1974).

The analysis of a multi-factor cross allowing the location of more than one unknown marker, which is an extension of the rationale described by Hopwood (1967), is demonstrated in Table 1. The results of this cross represent three of eight possible selections between these six loci, whose locations on the circular map are unknown. The genotypes of the recombinants of each selection (upper section of Table 1) produce particular allele ratios at each non-selected locus. These ratios must form an uninterrupted gradient between the selected loci. With n markers there are $2^{(n-3)}$ possible sequences to consider. In the present example the most probable, from eight possible marker arrangements, is that with the lowest number of multiple crossover progeny in a selection and that showing the same marker sequence in all three selections (lower section of Table 1). This kind of analysis, which reveals the sequence, but not the relative distance of loci, was used for preliminary and rapid location of several new markers.

THE LINKAGE MAP OF STREPTOMYCES GLAUCESCENS

The marker sequence on the circular map (shown in Fig. 1) of *S. glaucescens* strain ETH 22794 was obtained by a series of four- and multi-factor crosses. The linkage distances of the markers on the chromosome are based on five reference distances evaluated from the results of several sets of three four-factor crosses (Baumann *et al.,* 1974).

PHYSIOLOGY OF MELANIN PRODUCTION

The specific activity of intracellular tyrosinase can be raised by adding substances which have a 2-aminocarboxylic acid configuration to the culture medium of growing cells (Fig. 2). In *Neurospora crassa* tyrosinase synthesis is induced by growth inhibitors (Fox *et al.*, 1963), whereas in *S. glaucescens* inhibition of growth does not necessarily produce a rise in specific tyrosinase activity (N. Ankwanda, personal communication, 1972).

The results of an incorporation experiment with (U-^{14}C) glycine is shown in Figs 3 and 4. Glycine was chosen for the following reasons: it is a bad inducer of tyrosinase; it is taken up extremely well by growing cells (H. P.

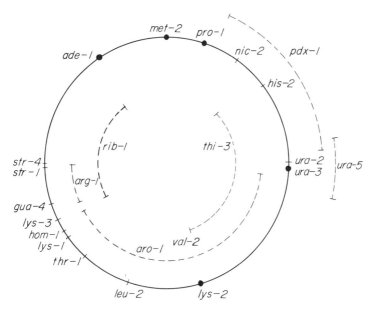

FIG. 1. Linkage map of *Streptomyces glaucescens* strain ETH 22794. The five reference loci are indicated by the symbol ●.

Kocher and J. Vetterli, personal communication, 1974), and it represents 15 per cent of the amino acids of the pure enzyme (Lerch and Ettlinger, 1972). In the noninduced culture (Fig. 3) (U-^{14}C) glycine or metabolites thereof are only incorporated into an unknown protein fraction and, as revealed by activity staining of the polyacrylamide gel, not into tyrosinase. The disc-gel electrophoresis of the partially purified tyrosinase from the induced culture (Fig. 4) yielded two labelled protein fractions, one of which was tyrosinase. These results indicate a *de novo* synthesis of tyrosinase upon addition of inducing substances, and exclude an activation of an inactive precursor of the enzyme.

So far, the physiological data obtained on melanin production in *S. glaucescens* point to a regulation of tyrosinase synthesis by induction. The repressor theory, as proposed by Horowitz *et al.* (1970), cannot be definitely excluded because the substrate, tyrosine, which has a low uptake rate of 1.3 nmol min^{-1} mg^{-1} (H. P. Kocher and J. Vetterli, personal communication, 1974), has been found to be a poor inducer.

GENETICS OF MELANIN PRODUCTION

S. glaucescens produces, in contrast to eukaryotic organisms (Fling *et al.*, 1963; Jolley *et al.*, 1969), a single tyrosinase (Lerch and Ettlinger, 1972),

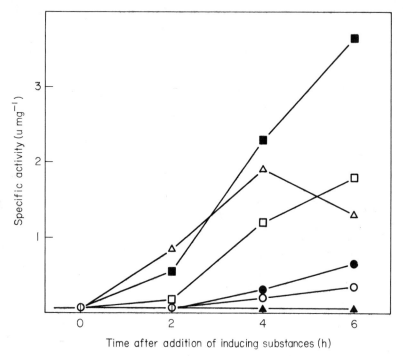

FIG. 2. Influence on the specific tyrosinase activity with inducing substances, such as 2-aminopropionic acid (O), 2-aminobutyric acid (●), 2-aminovaleric acid (□), 2-aminocaproic acid (■), 2-aminoenanthic acid (△), 2-aminocaprylic acid (▲).

which is not an endoenzyme as found in higher fungi (Lyr and Luthardt, 1965), but is excreted into the culture medium. Melanin-negative mutants did not discolour the minimal medium supplemented with a 3×10^{-3} M concentration of tyrosine and were shown to lack extracellular tyrosinase activity. They could therefore be distinguished from the melanin-positive, tyrosinase excreting colonies, which were surrounded by a brownish-black pigment. The phenotypically melanin-negative mutants could be classified theoretically into three genotypes: first, a class which showed no intra- or extra-cellular tyrosinase activity (*tye⁻ mel⁺*); second, a class which maintained intracellular tyrosinase activity but did not excrete the enzyme (*tye⁺ mel⁻*); third, the double mutant (*tye⁻ mel⁻*). The gene *tye* would code for the

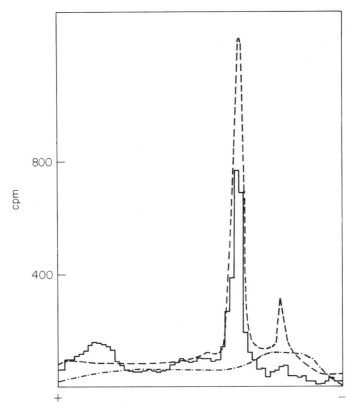

Fɪɢ. 3. Amount of partially purified tyrosinase of the uninduced or repressed control culture present in analytical disc-gel electrophoresis. Conditions are indicated under methods. Radioactivity (————), protein staining with Coomassie brilliant blue (— — —), activity staining of tyrosinase with 3,4-dihydroxy-ʟ-phenylalanine (— · — — · —).

enzyme tyrosinase; the gene designated *mel* would influence the extracellular activity of the enzyme. The excretion-deficient mutant classes *tye⁺ mel⁻* and *tye⁻ mel⁻* cannot be distinguished from one another or from the excretion competent *tye⁻ mel⁺* type by simple plate tests for melanin production but are clearly different from the wild type *tye⁺ mel⁺*. Several different melanin-negative mutants were crossed with *mel⁺ tye⁺* strains.

The results of the cross shown in Table 2 gave a perfect segregation of the marker for tyrosinase, which is located on the map between the loci *met-2*

T

and *gua-4*. In this cross a representative random sample of phenotypically melanin-negative recombinants was tested for intracellular tyrosinase activity, and all were found to be tyrosinase negative, which indicates that

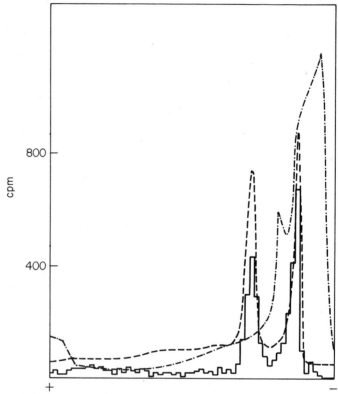

Fɪɢ. 4. Amount of partially purified tyrosinase of the induced or derepressed culture present in analytical disc-gel electrophoresis. Conditions are indicated under methods. Radioactivity (————), protein straining with Coomassie brilliant blue (— — —), activity staining of tyrosinase with 3,4-dihydroxy-ʟ-phenylalanine (— · — · —).

both parents were *mel*⁺ (no deficiency in excretion), and that therefore the genotype is directly deducible from the phenotype on the tyrosine medium. Thus it is most likely that the chromosomal locus revealed by this cross is the tyrosinase structural gene. Crosses involving other melanin-negative mutants, in contrast, yielded an unclear segregation of the marker for tyrosinase, due to the presence of phenotypically ambiguous recombinants with regard to melanin production. Further analysis proved these unclear recombinants to be genotypically *tye*⁺ *mel*⁻ (results not shown), which could only arise if the *tye*⁻ parent was also *mel*⁻.

The kind of cross shown in Table 3 involves an excretion-deficient mutant ($tye^{+}mel^{-}$). Although the standard markers used in this cross behaved normally, the segregation of the mel^{-} character is inconsistent with any chromosomal location. The ratio for mel^{+}/mel^{-} in each selection provides two possible locations on the gradient. However, when the segregation of the *mel* marker is considered in relation to the known chromosomal markers by 2×2 tables, the character of enzyme excretion (*mel*) shows, with one exception (*str-1/mel-1* in section I), always an independent segregation, and even in this one case the segregation is incompatible with a chromosomal location. It thus seems that although the locus for tyrosinase is on the chromosome (Table 2) at least one factor determining tyrosinase-excretion is extrachromosomal (Table 3).

There are different classes of tye^{+} mel^{-} mutants, because crosses with two such parents yielded tye^{+} mel^{+} recombinants at a rate too high to be explained by intragenic recombination.

Discussion

This study has shown that the circular linkage map in *streptomyces glaucescens* is similar to that of *Streptomyces coelicolor* A3(2) (Hopwood, 1965), *Streptomyces rimosus* (Friend and Hopwood, 1971), *Streptomyces bikiniensis* (Coats and Roeser, 1971) and *Streptomyces olivaceus* (Matselyukh *et al.*, 1973). Heteroclones were present, as demonstrated by qualitative analysis, but were not quantitatively evaluated. The average fertility level of the crosses in *S. glaucescens* was similar to that of IF × IF crosses in *S. coelicolor* A3(2) (Vivian and Hopwood, 1970; Hopwood *et al.*, 1973). The significance of rarely occurring high fertility levels has not yet been studied.

The incorporation experiment showed that the rise in tyrosinase activity on addition of 2-aminocarboxylic acids to the culture medium is due to a *de novo* synthesis and not to an activation of a precursor of the enzyme. By what mechanism this induction is achieved is unclear. For *Neurospora crassa*, Horowitz *et al.* (1970) postulate the presence of an unstable precursor, which is drastically reduced by long-continued inhibition of protein synthesis, e.g. by addition of amino acid analogues. The situation in *S. glaucescens* seems different, because an inhibition of growth by amino acids or their analogues does not, as in *Neuropora crassa,* necessarily produce an induction of tyrosinase.

The tyrosinase in *Aspergillus nidulans* is, as demonstrated by Bull and Carter (1972), inhibited by an endogenous protein, which was separated from a tyrosinase-inhibitor complex. Such a protein was not detected during purification procedures of the *S. glaucescens* tyrosinase (Lerch and Ettlinger, 1972) and there is as yet no indication of an endogenous inhibitor (H.P. Kocher, personal communication, 1974).

TABLE 2

Analysis of cross: met-2 ura-+ 2 lys-1 gua-± 4 tye-1 mel+ × met-+ 2 ura-2 lys-+ 1 gua-4 tye-+1 mel+

One hundred colonies were isolated from each selective medium and classified into the possible genotypes to give the numbers in columns a. Columns b give the crossovers in the intervals numbered on the zygote models in the lower section of the Table.

Genotypes of selectable progeny					Selective media supplemented with							
					Lysine and guanine		Methionine and guanine		Lysine and uracil		Methione and uracil	
					a	b	a	b	a	b	a	b
+	+	+	+	+	1	1,2,3,4	3	1,2,3,4	1	1,2,3,4	1	1,2,3,4
+	+	+	+	tye	0	1,2,3,5	0	1,2,3,5	0	1,2,3,5	1	1,2,3,5
+	+	+	gua	+	10	1,2	20	1,2				
+	+	+	gua	tye	0	1,2,4,5	1	1,2,4,5				
+	+	lys	+	+	49	1,4			21	1,4		
+	+	lys	+	tye	36	1,5			22	1,5		
+	+	lys	gua	+	4	1,3						
+	+	lys	gua	tye	0	1,3,4,5						
+	met	+	gua	+			20	2,5				
+	met	+	gua	tye			32	2,4				
+	met	+	+	+			0	2,3,4,5			1	2,3,4,5
+	met	+	+	tye			20	2,3			43	2,3
ura	+	+	+	+					7	3,4	29	3,4
ura	+	+	+	tye					4	3,5	14	3,5
ura	+	lys	+	+					18	2,4		
ura	+	lys	+	tye					27	2,5		
ura	met	+	+	+							0	1,3,4,5
ura	met	+	+	tye							10	1,3
Sample size					100		96		100		99	

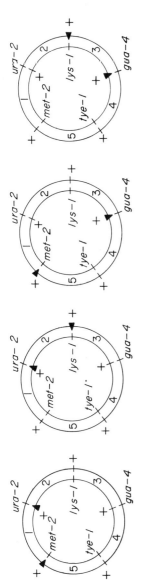

TABLE 3

Analysis of a multi-factor cross: $ade\text{-}1\ ura^+\ 2\ leu^+\ 2\ lys\text{-}1\ mel\text{-}1\ str\text{-}1 \times ade^+\ 1\ ura\text{-}2\ leu\text{-}2\ lys^+\ 1\ mel^+\ 1\ str^+\ 1$

Selection I: $ura^+\ 2/ade^+\ 1$

Genotypes	Number	Crossovers in intervals*
lys + + + +	26	3,5
lys + + + mel	10	3,5
+ + + + +	10	2,5
lys + str + +	23	4,5
+ leu + + +	12	1,5
+ leu + mel +	5	1,5
+ + str + +	2	2,3,4,5
Total	88	

Selection II: $ura^-\ 2/lys^+\ 1$

Genotypes	Number	Crossovers in intervals*
+ + + .	38	2,5
ade + + mel	12	2,4
ade + str +	10	2,3
ade + str mel	7	2,3
+ leu + +	8	1,5
+ leu + mel	9	1,5
ade leu str +	6	1,3
+ leu str mel	1	1,3,4,5
+ + str +	3	2,3,4,5
Total	94	

Selection III: $lys^+\ 1/leu^+\ 2$

Genotypes	Number	Crossovers in intervals*
+ + + +	12	2,5
ura + + +	16	1,2
ura + + mel	8	1,2
+ ade + +	9	2,4
+ ade str +	10	2,3
+ ade str mel	18	2,3
ura ade str mel	1	1,2,3,5
ura + str +	2	1,2,3,4
ura + str mel	1	1,2,3,4
+ + str mel	2	2,3,4,5
Total	79	

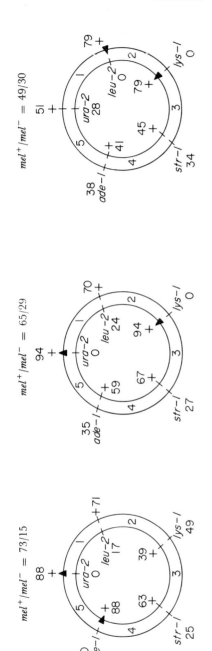

$mel^+/mel^- = 73/15$

$mel^+/mel^- = 65/29$

$mel^+/mel^- = 49/30$

Segregation of mel^+/mel^- in relation to known chromosomal markers

	leu^+	leu^-
mel^+	61	12
mel^-	10	5

	str^+	str^-
mel^+	48	25
mel^-	15	0

	str^+	str^-
mel^+	46	19
mel^-	21	8

	leu^+	leu^-
mel^+	51	14
mel^-	19	10

	str^+	str^-
mel^+	37	12
mel^-	8	22

	ura^+	ura^-
mel^+	31	18
mel^-	20	10

* The mel^- marker is not considered.

The frequency of tyrosinaseless (tye^-) mutants is, in contrast to *S. scabies* (Gregory and Huang, 1964), not increased in *S. glaucescens* when treated with plasmid curing agents, such as acridine orange or acriflavine. The structural locus for tyrosinase is located on the circular linkage map of the chromosome.

However, the incidence of phenotypically melanin-negative mutants in general is increased by acriflavine treatment. These mutants were shown to be of different classes, all of them lacking extracellular tyrosinase activity. Most are assumed to be defective in tyrosinase excretion. The genetic localization of these latter mutants is as yet uncertain, but at least one appears to be extrachromosomal.

Acknowledgements

We wish to thank Professors L. Ettlinger and R. Hütter for their interest and encouragement and for their generous financial support during this work.

References

Alačević, M., Strašek-Vešligaj and Sermonti, G. (1973). *J. gen. Microbiol.* **77**, 173.
Alačević, M. (1973). Actinomycetes and Fungi. *In* "Genetics of Industrial Micro-organisms" (Eds Vaněk, Z. et al.), p. 59. Academia, Prague.
Baumann, R., Hütter, R. and Hopwood, D. A. (1974). *J. gen. Microbiol.* **81**, 463.
Bull, A. T. and Carter, B. L. A. (1972). *J. gen. Microbiol.* **75**, 61.
Bu'Lock, J. D. (1960). *Archs. Biochem. Biophys.* **91**, 189.
Coats, J. H. and Roeser, J. (1971). *J. Bact.* **105**, 880.
Fling, M., Horowitz, N. H. and Heinemann, S. F. (1963). *J. biol. Chem.* **238**, 2045.
Fox, A. S., Burnett, J. B. and Fuchs, M. S. (1963). *Ann. N.Y. Acad. Sci.* **100**, 840.
Friend, E. J. and Hopwood, D. A. (1971). *J. gen. Microbiol.* **68**, 187.
Gregory, K. F. and Shyu, W. J. (1961). *Nature, Lond.* **191**, 465.
Gregory, K. F. and Huang, J. C. C. (1964). *J. Bact.* **87**, 1287.
Hayaishi, O. (1968). *In* "Biol. Oxidations" (Ed. T. P. Singer), p. 581. Interscience, New York.
Hopwood, D. A. (1959). *Ann. N.Y. Acad. Sci.* **81**, 887.
Hopwood, D. A. (1965). *J. molec. Biol.* **12**, 514.
Hopwood, D. A. (1967). *Bact. Rev.* **31**, 373.
Hopwood, D. A. (1969). Symposium on Genetics and Breeding of Streptomyces, Dubrovnik, p. 5. Yugoslav Acad. Sci. and Arts, Zagreb.
Hopwood, D. A., Chater, K. F., Dowding, J. E. and Vivian, A. (1973). *Bact. Rev.* **37**, 371.
Horowitz, N. H., Fling, M., Feldman, H. M., Pall, M. L. and Froehner, S. C. (1970). *Dev. Biol.* **21**, 147.
Jolley, R. L., Nelson, R. M. and Robb, D. A. (1969). *J. biol. Chem.* **244**, 3251.
Lerch, K. and Ettlinger, L. (1972). *Eur. J. Biochem.* **31**, 427.
Lowry, O. H., Rosebrough, N. J., Farr, A. L. and Randall, R. J. (1951). *J. biol. Chem.* **193**, 265.

Lyr, H. and Luthardt, W. (1965) *Nature, Lond.* **207**, 753.

Matselyukh, B. P., Podgorskaya, M. E., Stenko, A. S., Mukvich, N. S. and Laurinchuk, U. Y. (1973) *Mikrobiologichni Zhurnal, Kiev,* **35,** 26.

Pontecorvo, G. (1953). *Adv. Genet.* **5,**

Townsend, M. E. (1973). M. Phil. Thesis, University of East Anglia, Norwich, England.

Vivian, A. and Hopwood, D. A. (1970). *J. gen. Microbiol.* **64**, 101.

Warburg, O. and Christian, W. (1942). *Biochem. Z.* **310**, 384.

Structure and function of the
Actinomyces olivaceus genome

B. P. MATSELYUKH

*D. K. Zabolotny Institute of Microbiology and Virology,
Academy of Sciences of the Ukrainian SSR, Kiev, USSR*

Summary

The linkage map of *Actinomyces olivaceus* V KX was constructed by means of heteroclone analysis and selecting haploids. The intervals between 40 markers located on the map add up to about 240 units of recombination. By means of successive mutagenesis on synchronized spores it was shown that the chromosome is replicated at the same rate in two opposite directions.

Interrupted crosses have demonstrated the progressive transfer of chromosome from the donor to the recipient strain beginning from the "O" point localized in the 9 o'clock region and proceeding in both directions. The hypothesis has been proposed of a connection between the origin of chromosome replication and bi-directional transfer of genes. It is supposed that pili on the surface of *A. olivaceus* spores are determined by a sex factor, inactivation of which results in loss of these structures and in conversion of a donor strain into a recipient.

Introduction

Genetic research on different *Streptomyces* species is needed to work out effective breeding methods for industrial strains as well as to establish phylogenetic relationships and the path of evolution within the genus on the one hand and to carry out a comparative analysis of genome structure and the mechanism of genetic recombination of this genus as compared with bacteria with a simpler prokaryote organization on the other hand.

Fundamental investigations in *Streptomyces* genetics carried out to date in a

553

number of laboratories all over the world have resulted in the construction of linkage maps for five different *Streptomyces* species (Hopwood *et al.*, 1973).

The present paper deals with the main results of genetic mapping and the study of the direction and time of replication and chromosome transfer in *Actinomyces olivaceus* V KX.

Results and discussion

STRAINS

The initial prototrophic strain of *A. olivaceus* V KX was isolated from the rhizosphere of maize in the laboratory headed by Yekaterina I. Andreyuk. By treatment of wild-type spores with mutagens a series of independent auxotrophic mutants was obtained (Danilenko and Matselyukh, 1970; Matselyukh and Danilenko, 1970). The list of mutant alleles used in crosses is shown in Table 1. The frequency of spontaneous reversion for each marker was less than 10^{-8}.

DETERMINATION OF LINKAGE BY MEANS OF HETEROCLONE ANALYSIS

Heteroclones have been described in *A. olivaceus* (Podgorskaya *et al.*, 1972) similar to those of *Streptomyces coelicolor* (Hopwood and Sermonti, 1962) and *Streptomyces rimosus* (Alačević *et al.*, 1973). They were used for chromosome mapping (Matselyukh *et al.*, 1972, 1973b). As an example the results of analysis of four heteroclones are shown in Table 2 and in Fig. 1. The sequence of markers can be established by three criteria: (1) minimum frequency of quadruple crossovers; (2) gradient of allele frequencies; (3) percentages of recombination between neighbouring loci. The criterion of minimizing the frequency of multiple crossovers is more convenient and convincing for the choice of the correct marker sequence.

So far direct evidence for the existence of terminally redundant (TR) genomes in *Streptomyces* is absent; the possibility of merozygote formation in a circular form with tandem duplicated regions after the Campbell model must be considered equally probable from the data of heteroclone segregation. This model was proposed to explain the mechanism of genetic recombination in *Escherichia coli* K-12 (Bresler *et al.*, 1970). The gradient of allele frequencies, as can be seen from Table 2 in one case (heteroclone N24), is formed completely by donor (or recipient) markers and in another case (heteroclone N 13) by alleles of both parents. This depends on the location of crossovers between homologous regions of recipient chromosome and donor fragment in circular or linear form.

Complete analysis of about 200 heteroclones from three-, four- and six-factor crosses revealed one linkage group consisting of 20 markers and repre-

TABLE 1

Genetic markers of *A. olivaceus* V KX

Locus	Requirement (enzyme deficiency)	Mutagen
ade-1	Purines (phosphoribosylaminoimidazole carboxylase)	uv
ade-2	Purines (phosphoribosylaminoimidazolesuccinocarboxamide synthetase)	MNNG
ade-3	Purines (block before aminoimidazole ribotide synthesis)	MNNG
arg-1	Arginine (citrulline or ornithine)	uv
arg-3	Arginine (citrulline or ornithine)	MNNG
cca-1	Cyanocobalamine (or methionine)	uv
cca-2	Cyanocobalamine (or methionine)	NMU
cca-3	Cyanocobalamine (or methionine)	uv
cca-4	Cyanocobalamine (δ-aminolaevulinate synthetase)	MNNG
cca-5	Cyanocobalamine (or methionine)	MNNG
cys-2	Cysteine (or methionine)	uv
cys-3	Cysteine (or methionine)	uv
cys-4	Cysteine (or methionine)	uv
glu-1	Glutamine	MNNG
gly-1	Glycine	MNNG
his-1	Histidine	uv
his-2	Histidine	MNNG
his-3	Histidine	MNNG
his-4	Histidine	MNNG
inl-1	Inositol	MNNG
inl-2	Inositol	MNNG
leu-1	Leucine	uv
leu-2	Leucine	MNNG
lys-1	Lysine	MNNG
lys-2	Lysine	MNNG
met-1	Methionine	MNNG
met-2	Methionine	MNNG
nic-1	Nicotinic acid	MNNG
pab-1	*p*-Aminobenzoic acid	MNNG
pdx-1	Pyridoxine	uv
phe-1	Phenylalanine	MNNG
rib-1	Riboflavin	MNNG
rib-2	Riboflavin	MNNG
rib-3	Riboflavin	uv
str-1	Streptomycin resistance	uv
thi-1	Thiamine	uv
thi-2	Thiamine	MNNG
tyr-1	Tyrosine	MNNG
ura-1	Uracil	MNNG

Abbreviations: uv, ultraviolet light; MNNG, N-methyl-N'-nitro-N-nitrosoguanidine: NMU, N-nitroso-N-methylurea.

TABLE 2

Analysis of six-factor heteroclones in cross, 24–14 *leu-1 rib-1 met-1* × 204 *his-2 cca-5 inl-2*

Genotypes of segregants						Number of segregants in heteroclones				Crossovers in intervals
						N13	N22	N24	N26	
+	+	+	*l*	*r*	*m*	6	18	18	9	—
+	+	*i*	*l*	*r*	*m*⎫	7	8	2	—	⎫ a, b
h	*c*	+	+	+	+⎭	—	—	2	—	⎭
+	*c*	*i*	*l*	*r*	*m*⎫	26	4	1	2	⎫ a, c
h	+	+	+	+	+⎭	—	—	2	1	⎭
h	*c*	*i*	*l*	*r*	*m*	25	10	8	10	a, d
+	+	+	+	+	*m*	3	—	—	5	a, e
+	+	+	+	*r*	*m*	1	—	1	1	a, f
+	*c*	+	*l*	*r*	*m*	11	7	—	16	b, c
h	*c*	+	*l*	*r*	+	4	8	—	—	b, e
h	*c*	+	*l*	+	+⎫	2	—	7	—	⎫ b, f
+	+	*i*	+	*r*	*m*⎭	8	—	—	—	⎭
h	+	+	*l*	*r*	*m*	—	2	1	1	c, d
h	+	+	*l*	+	+⎫	—	23	30	38	⎫ c, f
+	*c*	*i*	+	*r*	*m*⎭	3	—	—	—	⎭
+	+	+	*l*	*r*	+	—	9	—	—	d, e
+	+	+	*l*	+	+	—	5	16	14	d, f
+	+	+	*l*	+	*m*	3	13	7	—	e, f
h	+	*i*	*l*	*r*	*m*	4	—	—	2	a, b, c, d
h	+	*i*	*l*	*r*	+	—	—	2	4	a, b, c, e
+	*c*	+	+	*r*	*m*⎫	3	—	—	—	⎫ a, b, c, f
h	+	*i*	*l*	+	+⎭	—	4	—	—	⎭
+	+	*i*	*l*	*r*	+	—	—	—	2	a, b, d, e
+	+	*i*	*l*	+	+	—	—	—	2	a, b, d, f
+	+	*i*	*l*	+	*m*	2	—	2	4	a, b, e, f
+	*c*	*i*	*l*	+	*m*⎫	1	1	—	1	⎫ a, c, e, f
h	+	+	+	*r*	+⎭	—	—	—	1	⎭
h	*c*	*i*	*l*	+	*m*	—	1	1	2	a, d, e, f
h	+	*i*	+	+	*m*	—	—	2	1	b, c, d, e
h	+	+	*l*	+	*m*	—	—	2	—	c, d, e, f
TOTALS						109	113	104	116	

35	75	76	91	98	103		97	86	85	47	45	33
h	*c*	*i*	*l*	*r*	*m*		*l*	+	+	+	*m*	*r*

Heteroclone N 13

+	+	+	+	+	+		+	*i*	*c*	*h*	+	+
74	34	33	18	11	6		7	18	19	57	59	71

Heteroclone N 24

senting about 240 recombination units (Fig. 2). The frequencies of recombination between some loci are shown in Table 3.

MAPPING BY MEANS OF HAPLOID SELECTION

Selective analysis of haploid recombinants confirmed the order of markers established by means of heteroclone analysis as well as giving an opportunity to map a number of new loci (Matselyukh *et al.*, 1973b). Two main criteria

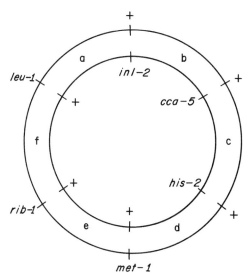

FIG. 1. Location of markers of the two parents in the cross in Table 2. Letters a–f indicate map intervals.

were taken into consideration for determining marker sequence by means of haploid selection: (1) minimum frequency of quadruple crossovers; (2) bidirectional gradients of allele frequencies (Table 4 and Fig. 3). The order of most of the loci and the map scale in *A. olivaceus* resemble those in *S. coelicolor*. However, the two large empty regions at 3 and 9 o'clock positions are absent on the map of *A. olivaceus* (Fig. 2).

BIDIRECTIONAL REPLICATION AND CHROMOSOME TRANSFER

Using the method of spore synchronization by sucrose density-gradient centrifugation (Matselyukh and Mukvich, 1972; Mukvich and Matselyukh, 1973) and the tests of forward and back mutation induced successively by N-methyl-N'-nitro-N-nitrosoguanidine it was shown that the *A. olivaceus* chromosome replicates at the same rate in two opposite directions (Matselyukh

TABLE 3

Distances between some pairs of loci

Cross and number of hetero-clone	Pair of loci	.	Frequency of: parental classes			recombinant classes			Recombinants (%)	χ^2, P*
24–	2	*ade-1*	*a u*	47	+ + 30	*a* + 9	+ *u* 21		28	
14	5	*ura-1*		43	18	20		19	39	
×	6			63	16	22		9	28	
196	10			56	30	23		2	22	$\chi^2_6 = 7.9$
	11			35	18	20		25	45	
	28			15	41	9		23	36	$P = 0.3$–0.2
	31			4	54	20		0	25	
Pooled									32	
24–	1	*met-1*	*m* +	14	+ *a* 68	*m a* 19	+ + 6		23	
14	2	*ade-1*		21	53	3		30	31	$\chi^2_5 = 6.8$
×	5			2	93	7		4	10	
196	10			18	60	19		14	29	
	11			39	30	25		4	29	$P = 0.3$–0.2
	21			29	42	11		3	16	
Pooled									22	
24 ⎧	4	*his-2*	*h c*	41	+ + 47	+ *c* 7	*h* + 23		25	
× ⎨	8	*cca-5*		15	52	13		10	24	$\chi^2_5 = 2.8$
204 ⎪	9			26	48	7		23	28	
⎩	10			7	74	26		3	24	$P = 0.8$–0.7
24– ⎰	22			19	63	12		29	36	
14 × ⎱	24			18	46	1		39	39	
204										
Pooled									30	
24 ⎧	4	*cca-5*	*c i*	42	+ + 40	+ *i* 30	*c* + 6		30	
× ⎨	7	*inl-2*		54	37	16		2	17	
204 ⎪	11			76	38	19		4	17	$\chi^2_5 = 2.6$
⎩	12			44	43	9		13	20	
76 ⎰	2			21	70	8		10	17	$P = 0.8$–0.7
× ⎱	5			78	19	1		12	12	
204										
Pooled									18	

* See Hopwood and Sermonti (1962).

and Mukvich, 1973). The origin and the end of replication are in the 9 and 3 o'clock regions respectively and one cycle of replication takes about 60 min (Fig. 2).

The polarity of 196 *ade-1 ura-1 his-1* × 24–14 *leu-1 met-1 rib-1* crosses and the location of markers in different map regions have been used to study chromosome transfer by means of interrupted crosses (Sermonti *et al.*, 1971).

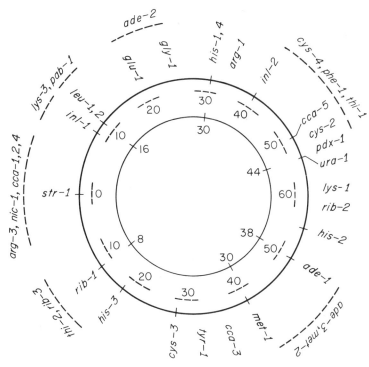

FIG. 2. Genetic map of *A. olivaceus* V KX. Outer circle: linkage map of genetic markers mapped by means of heteroclone analysis (radial lines) and selection of haploids (markers without lines or outside broken lines). Figures 0–60 between circles indicate the time of chromosome replication (min). Inner circle: the time of transfer of markers from donor to recipient (h).

It was shown that in this cross the progressive transfer of chromosome from the donor (N 196) to the recipient (N 24–14) strain occurs, beginning after 8 hours of mixed growth, in both directions from the 9 o'clock region and finishing at marker *ura-1* in the 3 o'clock region after 38–44 hours of growth (Fig. 4). The hypothesis has been proposed that the "O" point of chromosome replication is associated with the origin of chromosome transfer in the 196 × 24–14 cross (Matselyukh *et al.*, 1973a). In this cross a considerable

TABLE 4

Selective analysis of haploid recombinants in a six-factor cross of strains, 24–14
leu-1 rib-1 met-1 and 196 *ade-1 ura-1 his-1*

Genotypes of recombinants						leu^+ ade^+	leu^+ ura^+	rib^+ ade^+	rib^+ ura^+	met^+ ade^+	Crossovers in intervals
h	u	+	m	r	+	22	—	—	—	—	b, e
h	+	+	m	r	+	31	23	—	—	—	a, e
h	u	+	m	+	+	11	—	—	—	—	b, d
h	+	+	m	+	+	14	14	11	—	—	a, d
+	+	+	m	r	+	9	—	—	—	—	e, f
h	u	+	+	+	+	4	—	—	—	12	b, c
+	+	+	m	+	+	1	3	66	—	—	d, f
h	+	+	+	+	+	1	27	2	12	8	a, c
h	+	a	+	+	+	—	22	—	10	—	a, b
+	+	+	+	+	+	—	—	11	35	43	c, f
+	+	+	m	+	l	—	—	4	—	—	d, e
+	+	+	+	+	l	—	—	1	27	6	c, e
+	+	a	+	+	+	—	—	—	5	—	b, f
+	+	+	+	r	l	—	—	—	—	17	c, d
+	u	+	+	+	+	4	—	—	—	6	a, b, c, f
+	u	+	m	r	+⎫	2	—	—	—	—	⎫ a, b, e, f
h	+	a	+	+	l⎭	—	—	—	7	—	⎭
h	u	+	+	r	+	2	—	—	—	3	b, c, d, e
h	+	+	+	r	+	2	—	—	—	3	a, c, d, e
h	+	a	m	+	+	—	6	—	1	—	a, b, c, d
h	+	a	m	r	+	—	4	—	—	—	a, b, c, e
h	+	a	+	r	+⎫	—	5	—	—	—	⎫ a, b, d, e
+	u	+	m	+	l⎭	—	—	2	—	—	⎭
h	u	+	m	+	l	—	—	1	—	—	b, d, e, f
h	+	+	+	+	l	—	—	2	3	—	a, c, e, f
h	u	+	+	r	l	—	—	—	—	2	b, c, d, f
h	+	+	+	r	l	—	—	—	—	3	a, c, d, f
TOTALS						103	104	100	100	104	

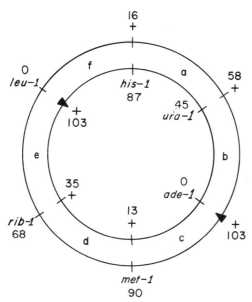

Fig. 3. Allele frequencies among selected recombinants in the cross in Table 4. Triangles indicate the selected alleles. Letters a–f indicate map intervals.

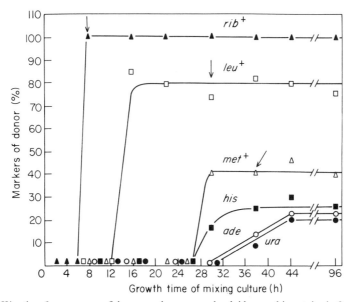

Fig. 4. Kinetics of appearance of donor markers among haploid recombinants in six-factor cross of strain 196, *ade-1 ura-1 his-1* (donor) and 24–14, *leu-1 rib-1 met-1* (recipient). Arrows indicate the time of first appearance of recombinants containing one of the selected alleles of the donor (delay of phenotypic expression of the same alleles transferred earlier in nonselective conditions).

delay in phenotypic expression of transferred genes was also observed, indicated by the impossibility of obtaining haploid recombinants containing the wild selected alleles *leu-1*⁺ or *met-1*⁺ for 8–14 h after their appearance in zygotes. Electron microscopy showed that donor strain N 196 formed "pili" on the spores like a wild strain (Matselyukh and Andreyuk, 1968) while recipient strain N 24–14 had almost lost the ability to form "pili" on the spore surface

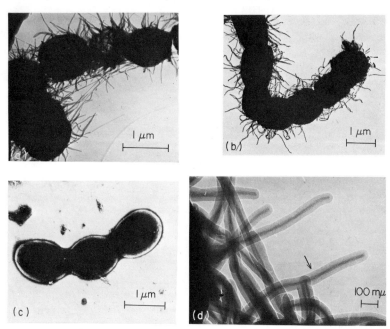

Fig. 5. Electron micrographs of *A. olivaceus* V KX spores; (a) wild type; (b) donor strain 196; (c) recipient strain 24–14; (d) fine structure of "pili" on spore surface (arrow indicates the quadruple spiral inside a "pilus").

(Fig. 5, a, b, c). By analogy with *E. coli* K-12 it is supposed that a sex factor is a possible cause of cross polarity by means of "pilus" formation on the spore surface and that inactivation of this factor results in loss of these structures and in conversion of donor strains into recipients. The "pili" of *A. olivaceus* spores do not have a hollow core and contain a quadruple spiral; like F-pili they have remarkable adhesive ability (Fig. 5, a, d).

References

Alačević, M., Strašek-Vešligaj, M. and Sermonti, G. (1973). *J. gen. Microbiol* **77**, 173.
Bresler, S. E., Lanzov, V. A. and Manukyan, L. R. (1970). *Genetika*, **7**, 116.

Danilenko, I. I. and Matselyukh, B. P. (1970). *Tsytologia i Genetika* (Kiev), **4**, 195.

Hopwood, D. A. and Sermonti, G. (1962). *Adv. Genet.* **11**, 273.

Hopwood, D. A., Chater, K. F., Dowding, J. E. and Vivian, A. (1973). *Bact. Rev.* **37**, 371.

Matselyukh, B. P. and Andreyuk, Y. I. (1968). *Dokl. Akad. Nauk SSSR*, **181**, 1263.

Matselyukh, B. P. and Danilenko, I. I. (1970). *Genetika.* **6**, 171.

Matselyukh, B. P. and Mukvich, N. S. (1972). *Microbiol. Zh.* (Kiev), **34** 448.

Matselyukh, B. P. and Mukvich, N. S. (1973). *Microbiol. Zh.* (Kiev), **35**, 411.

Matselyukh, B. P., Podgorskaya, M. E., Stenko, A. S. and Lavrinchuk, V. Y. (1972). *Genetika*, **8**, 123.

Matselyukh, B. P., Podgorskaya, M. E., Stenko, A. S. and Mukvich, N. S. (1973a). Conference on genetics of industrial microorganisms. Tsakhkadzor (USSR) Abstract Book, p. 124.

Matselyukh, B. P., Podgorskaya, M. E., Stenko, A. S., Mukvich, N. S. and Lavrinchuk, V. Y. (1973b). *Microbiol. Zh.* (*Kiev*), **35**, 26.

Mukvich, N. S. and Matselyukh, B. P. (1973). *Microbiol. Zh.* (Kiev), **35**, 293.

Podgorskaya, M. E., Matselyukh, B. P., Stenko, A. S. and Lavrinchuk, V. Y. (1972). *Genetika*, **8**, 78.

Sermonti, G., Puglia, A. M. and Ficarra, G. (1971). *Genet. Res.* **18**, 133.

Progressive fertilization in *Streptomyces coelicolor*

G. SERMONTI* and A. M. PUGLIA

Istituto di Genetica, University of Palermo, Palermo, Italy

Summary

On starving the basal mycelium of mixed cultures of *Streptomyces coelicolor* A3(2), heteroclones emerge as small tufts, even if heterokaryosis is prevented, but no pure recombinant is detectable. This shows that heteroclone formation does not require heterokaryosis, while recombinants need a previous heteroclone stage. The latter conclusion was confirmed by plating, at different time intervals, finely ground hyphae from mixed cultures; recombinants appear only in late samples. The donor contribution to heteroclones (and recombinants therefrom) increases in mixed basal mycelium with pre-incubation time. In NF × UF crosses it always includes the sex-factor (SCP1) region, possibly flanked on either or both sides by chromosomal segments, the average length of which increases with time. The rate of chromosome "transfer" was evaluated as about four times slower than in *Escherichia coli* K 12 conjugation. The sex-factor is the first element to be transferred to recipient cells, initially as a free particle. With the passage of time, recipient cells appear harbouring a short donor chromosome segment borne in the free sex-factor (SCP1'). When the donor segment has exceeded a critical size, it is integrated in the resident genome to form heteroclones, with the sex-factor attached to the chromosome, eventually leading to NF recombinants.

Introduction

The genetics of *Streptomyces* has dealt so far mainly with structural analysis of the genome and, more recently, with the occurrence of the sex plasmid

* Present address: Istituto de Istologia, via Elce di Sotto, The University, Perugia, Italy.

(SCP1) and its relation with the genome (Hopwood *et al.*, 1973). Recombination as a dynamic process has been largely neglected, probably owing to inherent difficulties in studying the progress of a process taking place within the network of hyphae of a filamentous organism. The first evidence of an intermediate phase in recombination came from the detection of unstable heterozygous clones, the "heteroclones" (Sermonti *et al.*, 1960), which were then adopted essentially as an analytical tool (Hopwood *et al.*, 1963; Hopwood, 1967; Alačević *et al.*, 1973). The structural analysis of heteroclones indicated that they were formed from merozygotes by a crossover joining one of the donor chromosome ends (or a point nearby) with the recipient chromosome, producing an open structure with terminal redundancy (Hopwood, 1967). Further crossovers in the disomic region produce simple circular structures, the haploid recombinants.

The first information on the time course of recombinant production in *S. coelicolor* A3(2) was obtained after the introduction of some techniques intended to interrupt the process at various stages (Sermonti *et al.*, 1966, 1971). The development of such investigations is the subject of the present paper.

Results and discussion

PROGRESSIVE COMPLETION OF HETEROCLONES

The first heteroclones isolated (Sermonti *et al.*, 1960; Hopwood *et al.*, 1963) derived from sporulated cultures, very likely from single spores bearing redundant genomes. They were a late product of the self-reproduction of preceding structures.

Sermonti *et al.* (1966) obtained heteroclones directly from the basal mycelium of mixed cultures, by seeding two complementary strains on a cellophane disc lying on complete medium and transferring the disc, with the developed basal mycelium, to a minimal (sometimes partially supplemented) medium after about one day. By this procedure, not only was parental growth arrested, and heteroclone growth allowed in the form of distinct tufts, but the process of heteroclone formation and completion was also affected. The latter possibly require protein synthesis by each parent.

The detection of heteroclones from starved mixed basal mycelium provided several pieces of information. First, heteroclones are formed within basal hyphae; second, they do not require a previous heterokaryotic phase. This second conclusion was based on the following considerations: heterokaryons start appearing from the starved mycelium after a longer pre-incubation time than heteroclones; in NF × UF (very fertile) mixed cultures virtually no heterokaryons are found among heteroclones, while in UF × UF (almost infertile) mixed cultures, only heterokaryons were detected; heteroclones emerge on selective media on which heterokaryotic growth is prevented (Sermonti *et al.*, 1966).

A third important finding is the virtual absence of pure recombinant clones among heteroclones emerging from starved mixed cultures. This supports the assumption that recombinants are generally formed as an indirect result of mating. A fourth finding is that the longer the pre-incubation on complete medium, the greater was the contribution from the donor strain. This indicates that merozygotes are formed progressively and their completion is hindered by starvation (Sermonti *et al.*, 1966).

The recombination process was also "interrupted" by finely grinding the hyphae of developing mixed cultures and plating them on selective media (Sermonti *et al.*, 1971). Whatever the cause of the recombination block, mechanical breakage or starvation, the gradual completion of heteroclones was confirmed, late heteroclones being more complete than early ones.

The requirement of the heteroclone stage for recombinant formation was also confirmed by the following experiment. A cross was carried out with alleles arranged as follows:

$$\text{NF} \quad \text{SCP1} \quad ura^- \quad phe^+$$

$$\text{UF} \qquad\qquad ura^+ \quad phe^-$$

(other markers omitted). From samples of hyphae harvested up to 38 hours after the initiation of the mixed culture, virtually only ura^+ phe^+ phenotypes were detected, and all those tested were ura^- phe^+/ura^+ phe^- heterozygotes, i.e. heteroclones. At sporulation, however, the great majority of phe^+ phenotypes were ura^-, as expected in pure recombinant clones because of the linkage relations of the markers, thus showing the occurrence of heteroclone segregation at a late stage of the mixed culture.

INCREASING DONOR CONTRIBUTION IN NF × UF CROSSES

The progressive contribution of donor markers to the recombinant output (irrespective of their physical connection with selected recipient markers) was studied by plating hyphal fragments from NF × UF mixed cultures, after different pre-incubation times, on selective media (Sermonti *et al.*, 1971). From such experiments it was concluded that the closer a marker is to the SCP1 (9 o'clock) position, the earlier is it contributed to the recombinant progeny, irrespective of its clockwise or counterclockwise location. Donor markers on both sides could be contributed to individual recombinants, so that it can be stated, more generally, that the shorter the donor region, the earlier is it contributed, provided it spans the 9 o'clock point. The first statement is a corollary of the latter.

The time elapsing between the first appearance among recombinants of a donor marker and that of another distal to the first (in respect of the 9 o'clock point) was evaluated in some NF × UF crosses, and assumed to correspond to the time required for the "transfer" of the chromosome segment between the markers. (When two donor markers on either side of the compulsory 9 o'clock region were considered, the time elapsing from the appearance of one to that of both was considered as that required for the "transfer" of a segment joining the second marker to the 9 o'clock point.) Although they were estimated crudely (sampling intervals were not less than two hours), the time intervals appeared to be proportional to the length of the corresponding map intervals (Table 1). The transfer of a length equal to the entire chromosome would take

TABLE 1

Preliminary estimates of time intervals between pairs of donor markers in "interrupted" NF × UF mixed cultures (data from Sermonti *et al.*, 1971)

Markers		Fraction of genome spanned*	Sampling intervals h	Time intervals† h	Fraction of genome transferred h^{-1}
pheA1	*hisD3*	0.16	3.0	6.0	0.03
pheA1	*metA2*	0.37	2.0	6.0	0.06
SCP1	*metA2*	0.25	2.0	4.0	0.06
SCP1	*pheA1*	0.12	2.0	2.0	0.06
hisA1	*uraA1*	0.36	c.4.0	8.5	0.04

* Calculated from the map presented by Hopwood (1967).

† From the appearance of the first marker to that of the second (see text). The cross in the last row is NF × IF.

of the order of 20 hours, roughly one order of magnitude longer than that in *E. coli* K12 Hfr × F⁻ crosses at 37°C (Wollman *et al.*, 1956). The amount of nonrepetitive DNA in *S. coelicolor* A3(2), calculated according to the method of Studier (1965), is $7.23 \pm 0.51 \times 10^9$ daltons (R. Benigni, personal communication), against $2.28 \pm 0.19 \times 10^9$ daltons in *E. coli* K12, i.e. about three times as much. This would make the rate of chromosome "transfer" in *S. coelicolor* about three times (10:3.1) slower than in *E. coli* K 12.

TRANSFER OF THE SEX-FACTOR IN NF × UF CROSSES

The first event in NF × UF mixed cultures is the transfer of the sex-factor (SCP1) to recipient cells, after about 12 hours. Eight hours later the majority of the ex-recipient cells harbour the plasmid, as shown by the loss of their recipient ability (Sermonti *et al.*, 1971).

Two features of plasmid transfer are striking. First, its transfer is invasive, soon involving the majority of recipient cells and outnumbering by far the chromosomal recombinants. Second, the plasmid is free in the first infected cells, which show the initial type of fertility (IF). They produce less than 10^{-4} recombinants with UF testers (Table 2), and infect them with the plasmid efficiently (up to 75 per cent). Only later do a minority of NF clones with the recipient phenotype appear, to become eventually (but not in all crosses) the

TABLE 2

SCP1-infected recipients from cross: 39 NF *hisA1* × 312 UF *argA1 uraA1 strA1*. Recombination frequencies with a UF tester. Test cross: *arg ura str* × 316 UF *pheA1 strA1 hisD3*

Tested clones (*arg ura str*)			Number of selected alleles		Number of recipients	Recombination frequency
Code number	Sampling time (h)	Fertility type	phe^+	his^+		(phe^+/recipients)
1	12	IF	25	22	2.0×10^6	1.3×10^{-5}
2	12	IF	29	31	2.5×10^6	1.2×10^{-5}
3	14	IF	39	41	2.1×10^6	1.9×10^{-5}
4	20	IF	78	196	1.4×10^5	5.5×10^{-4}
5	20	IF	90	150	7.5×10^4	1.2×10^{-3}
6	20	NF	200	100	2.0×10^3	1.0×10^{-1}
7	90	NF	450	45	5.0×10^2	9.0×10^{-1}

Seven SCP1-infected *arg ura str* clones, isolated from cross 39 NF × 312 UF after different mixed culture times, were tested in crosses with 316 UF for their ability to transfer the *phe*⁺ and *his*⁺ markers.

majority at spore formation. With only a few exceptions, all the chromosomal recombinants bear the plasmid. The integration of donor markers in the recipient genome appears thus to depend on the transfer of the plasmid.

The recombinants from NF × UF crosses detected after the shortest pre-incubation times are expected to bear a very short donor chromosome fragment, extending from the plasmid site (9 o'clock) to the marker closest to it (*phe*⁺ or *ura*⁺ in different crosses). Most of them, however, show the IF poor donor ability (for markers other than those received from the donor parent). After further incubation, recombinants with the same phenotype, but probably bearing a longer donor fragment, change to the NF donor type (Table 3).

The SCP1 plasmid precedes and conditions the transfer of chromosomal markers. Its physical connection to the chromosome, however, appeared obscure (Sermonti *et al.*, 1971). Recent observations on the early IF recombinants, to be referred to in the next paragraph, throw some light on this point.

TABLE 3

Relative frequencies of NF and IF fertility types among SCP1-infected recipients (convertants) and among recombinants*

Cross: 39 NF *hisA1* × 312 UF *argA1 uraA1 strA1*

Time of sampling h	Convertants (phenotype *ura arg str*)			Recombinants (phenotype *ura⁺ arg str*)		
	IF	NF		IF	NF	
	(number)	(number)	(%)	(number)	(number)	(%)
12	8	0	0	3	0	0
14	8	0	0	27	2	7
16	16	0	0	19	1	3
18	18	0	0	38	20	35
20	59	4	6	31	65	68
90	34	5	13	0	54	100

* Tested versus 39 NF *his* donor and 219 UF *metA2 pheA1 strA1* recipient.

PECULIAR BEHAVIOUR OF PRECOCIOUS RECOMBINANTS

Some ura^+ IF recombinants, obtained from the cross 39 NF $hisA1 \times$ 312 UF $uraA1$ $argA1$ $strA1$ were carefully investigated. Their phenotype was ura^+ arg str, but they spontaneously segregated a small (less than 5 per cent) proportion of ura arg str phenotypes, of the UF fertility type. When crossed to a tester UF strain, 316 $met A2$ $pheA1$ $strA1$, they transferred met^+ and phe^+ at the low rate characteristic of IF strains. When, however, their donor ability was tested against a ura^- UF tester, about one half of recipient cells (from 40 to 55 per cent) turned out to have received the ura^+ marker from the donor strain (ura^+ arg str). Thus, the marker originally received from the NF (39) parent retained its high donor ability, but this did not extend to other regions of the recombinant genome. This situation may be interpreted by assuming that the early ura^+ IF recombinants bear the plasmid in a free state, and that the ura^+ marker is incorporated in the free plasmid. These strains are therefore analogous to the SCP1′ (sexductant) strains described by Hopwood and Wright (1973); they harbour an SCP1-ura^+ plasmid and are ura^+/ura^- heterogenotes. Markers not borne on the SCP1-ura^+ plasmid are transferred at low frequency.

Recombinants bearing ura^+ arising later (phenotype ura^+ arg str), classified as NF (Table 3), are stable, and the high donor ability extends to regions of the genome other than ura. Since they arose later, they had presumably received a longer donor contribution than the early ura^+ recombinants. The ratio between ura^+ IF and ura^+ NF recombinants probably reflects the ratio between sexductants and heteroclones. The same should also hold for the ratio ura^- IF to ura^- NF convertant ex-recipients, the disomic region being unmarked.

Conclusion

The sex-factor (SCP1) has been considered as essential to zygote formation (Hopwood *et al.*, 1969; Sermonti *et al.*, 1971), but not as a transfer origin in NF × UF crosses, the donor contribution being able to extend to both sides of the plasmid location. We thus assumed that any point on the donor chromosome could act as transfer origin after NF–UF cell contact, but only zygotes containing the plasmid region were able to undergo effective merozygote and heteroclone formation.

It seems unlikely, however, that the plasmid has no function in transfer initiation, particularly considering its invasive spread in the young NF × UF basal mycelium. It is simpler to imagine the SCP1 plasmid as the first mobilized region after NF–UF cell contact. Plasmid mobilization could then trigger a unidirectional or bidirectional process in the connected donor chromosome (perhaps, its reproduction) which proceeds with time, making an increasing region of it available for transfer.

When the plasmid alone is transferred, IF convertants are formed; when a very short region of the donor chromosome is borne by the plasmid, SCP1' strains are established; when a longer region is connected to the plasmid, the immigrant segments present a sufficient homology to interact with the resident chromosomes and form heteroclones.

The process of chromosome transfer in NF × UF crosses of *S. coelicolor*, which emerges from these considerations, appears more comparable to an extended sexduction (Jacob and Adelberg, 1959) than to the Hfr × F⁻ conjugation process in *Escherichia coli* K12.

Acknowledgements

We thank Professor M. Alačević, Dr F. Misuraca and Dr R. Benigni for details of some of their unpublished experiments, and Mrs Z. Matijašević for skilled assistance. One of us (G.S.) is grateful to the Faculty of Technology of Zagreb University for a period of hospitality during this work. The present research was supported by a grant from the Italian National Research Council (CNR).

References

Alačević, M., Strašek-Vešligaj, M. and Sermonti, G. (1973). *J. gen. Microbiol.* **77**, 173.

Hopwood, D. A. (1967). *Bact. Rev.* **31**, 373.

Hopwood, D. A., Chater, K. F., Dowding, J. E. and Vivian, A. (1973). *Bact. Rev.* **37**, 371.

Hopwood, D. A., Harold, R. J., Vivian, A. and Ferguson, H. M. (1969). *Genetics*, **62**, 461.

Hopwood, D. A., Sermonti, G. and Spada-Sermonti, I. (1963). *J. gen. Microbiol.* **30**, 249

Hopwood, D. A. and Wright, H. M. (1973). *J. gen. Microbiol.* **77**, 187.

Jacob, F. and Adelberg, E. A. (1959). *C.r. hebd. séanc. Acad. Sci., Paris,* **249**, 189.

Sermonti, G., Bandiera, M. and Spada-Sermonti, I. (1966). *J. Bact.* **91**, 384.

Sermonti, G., Mancinelli, A. and Spada-Sermonti, I. (1960). *Genetics,* **45**, 669.

Sermonti, G., Puglia, A. M. and Ficarra, G. (1971). *Genet. Res.* **18**, 133.

Studier, F. W. (1965). *J. molec. Biol.* **11**, 373.

Wollman, E., Jacob, F. and Hayes, W. (1956). *Cold Spring Harb. Symp. quant. Biol.* **21**, 141.

Co-mutation in *Streptomyces*

A. CARERE* and R. RANDAZZO†

*Istituto Superiore di Sanità, Roma, Italy
†Istituto di Genetica, Università, Palermo, Italy

Summary

Selection of revertants in a gene (*hisA*) of the *his* operon, after nitrosoguanidine treatment, produces populations containing more than 6 per cent mutants (co-mutants) within the operon, and about 4 per cent co-mutants in a locus adjacent to the *his* operon (Randazzo *et al.*, 1973). By relaxing the selection, i.e. by supplying the selective medium with substances required by mutants in some genes linked or unlinked to *hisA*, numerous co-mutants were found requiring one of the supplements relevant to the linked genes. The co-mutation effect apparently extends to about fifteen units on both sides of the selected reversion.

A method was developed to select revertants without imposing any restriction on the possible co-mutations accompanying them. This was achieved by supporting the growth of the co-mutants in heterokaryosis with the original *his* strain. Approximately half the revertants turned out to be co-mutants. The spectrum of mutations accompanying the selected reversion comprises a high frequency of mutants closely linked to the revertant site and very few mutants, if any, in distant regions. A method is thus available permitting the detection of an extremely high rate of new mutations located in a restricted and defined region of the chromosome.

Introduction

The techniques available so far to produce genome variability in *Streptomyces* are genetic recombination (Sermonti and Spada-Sermonti, 1955; Hopwood *et al.*, 1973) and random mutagenesis, the latter made particularly efficient after the adoption of new mutagens, e.g. N-methyl-N'-nitro-N-nitrosoguani-dine (MNNG) (Delić *et al.*, 1970; Randazzo *et al.*, 1973). Procedures to induce mutations in specific regions of the map have been described recently. One, making use of MNNG applied to synchronized cultures, was reported in *S. olivaceus* (Matselyukh and Mukvich, 1973). Another possible use of MNNG is related to its ability to give mutations in clusters corresponding to replicating loci (Cerdà-Olmédo *et al.*, 1968). If one mutation (selectable) is induced in a given locus, a large excess of other mutations (so-called "co-mutations") at closely linked genes are observed in bacteria (Hirota *et al.*, 1968; Calendar *et al.*, 1970; Guerola *et al.*, 1971). The same effect was observed in *S. coelicolor* A3(2) (Randazzo *et al.*, 1973) around the *hisA* locus. By profiting from the co-mutation effect, mutations can be "focused" around a given point of the map, wherever a selectable mutation is available. This method appears promising for both short-range and fine-structure mapping, for detection of unknown loci in desired regions of the map, for map comparison between species, and for practical breeding purposes when mutations in a given region turn out to be favourable in yield improvement programmes with industrial *Streptomyces* or eubacteria.

Results and discussion

DETECTION OF NEW LOCI LINKED TO A GIVEN GENE

The first application of the co-mutation method is the "scanning" of the map around a given gene in search of new loci. When a supplemented selective medium is used for detection of new auxotrophs among revertants from a given mutant (the requirement of which is obviously unsatisfied), the types of new mutant are limited by the chosen supplements. The addition of too many supplements often creates difficulties in selecting against the original mutant. The following technique has therefore been developed. The hyphae treated by MNNG are plated on a cellophane disc lying on a complete medium. After about one day's incubation the disc is transferred on to a minimal medium. Let us designate the original mutant as his^- aux^+ to indicate a requirement for histidine (his^-) and the wild condition of any other nutritional gene (aux^+). Only his^+ revertants will be able to overgrow the background mycelium developed in one day. They belong to two classes: his^+ aux^+ (simple revertants) and his^+ aux^- (co-mutant revertants). The his^+ aux^+ revertants grow without any help; his^+ aux^- co-mutants are also able to form colonies, being supported in balanced heterokaryosis by the original his^- aux^+ hyphae. In *S. coelicolor* the two types of colonies are easily distinguishable, the simple revertants growing larger and more regularly than the co-mutants. In *S. rimosus* the two types are visually indistinguishable, which is not surprising because of the better growth of heterokaryons in *S. rimosus* (Friend and Hopwood, 1971; Alačević *et al.*,

TABLE 1

Random co-mutations among revertants in the *hisA1* site* in *S. coelicolor*

Centimorgans from *hisA*: Loci:	(5) *gluA*	2 *metA*	1.5–0 *hisB, I*	— *hisA*	0–1.5 *hisG, C*	2 *trpA, B*	3 *ammA, B*	4 *hisF*	5 *tyrA, B*	8 *argA, B, C*	Others (*cys, phe*)	Total
Total detected	1	7	0	—	15	5	7	0	2	3	2	42
Percentage among classified sample	2	16	0	—	36	12	16	0	5	7	5	100
Percentage among revertants	0.8	5.5	0	—	11.8	3.9	5.5	0	1.6	2.4	—	33.1

* The co-mutants (aux^-) were detected as components of heterokaryons ($hisA^- aux^+ + hisA^+ aux^-$) arising on cellophan discs after transfer from complete medium on to minimal medium of 20 h grown MNNG-treated hyphae. They were classified according to their requirement and tentatively assigned to loci controlling the corresponding synthesis situated in the vicinity of *hisA*. Some mutations have been mapped by complementation tests and turned out to belong to the expected locus (2 *metA*, 2 *argA*, 15 *hisG*, C, 12 *ammA*, 1 *cysA*).

1973). Heterokaryons can easily be distinguished from the revertant population by their inability to replicate on unsupplemented minimal medium. Visual detection permits an efficiency of heterokaryon scoring in *S. coelicolor* close to 100 per cent. When the heterokaryons are analysed, by isolation and classification of sub-clones or by direct auxanography of their mixed spore population, the usual output is a mixed population, part to the spores belonging to the $hisA^-$ aux^+ original type, part to a $hisA^+$ aux^- co-mutant. Some of the presumptive heterokaryons do not give rise to the second component; this can be due to a large deficiency of the missing component, or to the occurrence of lethal recessive co-mutations. They may account for up to 25 per cent of the colonies scored as heterokaryons. An example of a population of co-mutants obtained as heterokaryotic components after selection of $hisA^+$ revertants on cellophane is given in Table 1. The approximate distance (centimorgans) of genes corresponding to the detected mutations is given in the first line. Eighty per cent of the classified mutants are included in an interval of 5 centimorgans around *hisA* and 95 per cent in an interval of 12 centimorgans. As a first approximation, one could therefore expect that, by selecting a co-mutant by the heterokaryotic method, the probability is 80 per cent to be dealing with a locus no further than 2–3 centimorgans from the reference arc, and 95 per cent to have picked a gene no further than 8–10 centimorgans from it. This is what we call "focusing" mutations.

CO-MUTATION AND LINKAGE DETECTION

Co-mutations are confined to genes closely linked to the one in which a mutation is induced by MNNG. The closeness of the linkage and the corresponding degree of probability are only empirically determined. According to the data of Guerola *et al.* (1971) in *Escherichia coli* K12, 40 per cent of the co-mutations are within 2 minutes of the selected mutation (*azi*), i.e. in 1/60 of the map (50 000 nucleotide pairs), and no mutant phenotype represented at a frequency higher than 5–10 per cent among the co-mutants corresponds to genes more than two minutes from the selected mutation. Guerola *et al.* (1971) suggest as an index of closeness the ratio of the frequency of double mutants in the population selected for one of them to the frequency of the other in an unselected population. This index is about 15 for genes *azi* and *leu* (0.5 minute apart) and 0.4 for unlinked *azi* and *his*. Guerola *et al.* (1971) assume that two minutes (1/60 of the genome, 50 000 nucleotide pairs) correspond to the length of the replication region.

In *S. coelicolor* A3(2) a similar fraction of the genome would correspond to 4–5 centimorgans (260 centimorgans/60). If, however, we consider that the genome of *S. coelicolor* A3(2) has a size of about 10.8×10^6 nucleotide pairs, i.e. about three times that of *E. coli* (R. Benigni, personal communication) a similar amount of DNA involved in a duplicating region (50 000 nucleotide pairs) would cover about 0.6 per cent of the genome, i.e. about 1.5 centimorgans. Mutant phenotypes represented at frequencies higher than 5–10 per cent total co-mutants span a region (from *metA* to *ammA*) approximately that size (Table 1) but the co-mutation effect appears to spread to genes located within an interval roughly twice as wide (from *gluA* to *argA*, *B*, *C*).

Without indulging in subtle calculations at the present preliminary stage of the work, we can safely reach some conclusions from the data in Table 1. They show the occurrence of a cluster of genes controlling histidine biosynthesis adjacent to *hisA*; the close linkage to *hisA* of genes involved in the biosynthesis of methionine, tryptophan and reduced nitrate, and the possible linkage of glutamic acid, tyrosine and arginine genes. Of course they do not indicate on which side of the *hisA* landmark the loci mentioned are located. The conclusions arrived at are fully consistent with the data on linkage already available in *S. coelicolor* A3(2) (Hopwood *et al.*, 1973). It is, however, evident that new data are obtainable in a much shorter time and by much simpler procedures than that involving the collection of a large crop of random mutants and the sophisticated recombination analysis of a large number of multi-point crosses. The assignment of the emerging co-mutants to one or other side of the landmark gene may be accomplished by the detection of co-mutations around another reference gene linked to the first (see later). This gene can be chosen among those detected as rare co-mutants of the former.

Another important aspect of the co-mutation method of linkage detection is its possible application to unmapped species, even in the absence of any recombination process.

SPECIFICITY OF MUTATION PATTERN AFTER DIFFERENT REVERTANT SELECTIONS

An obvious implication of the phenomenon of mutation clustering is the occurrence of different patterns of mutation among revertant populations from different genes. The data so far available are shown in Table 2. They concern small populations of neo-auxotrophic revertants from some genes in the upper arc of the map of *S. coelicolor* A3(2). The patterns of co-mutations among revertants from two sites of the same gene, *hisA*, are well nigh super-imposable. When a gene (*metA*) 2 centimorgans to the left of *hisA* is used as reversion site, two new types of mutant appear (*leu* and *pro*) absent in the unselected co-mutant population of *hisA* revertants (Table 1). Both correspond to genes known to be further to the left of *metA* in respect to *hisA*. Several pro-line requiring (*pro*) mutants were recovered in a small population of revertants from *cysA*, which is located close to and to the left of *proA*, the furthest left gene detected among *metA*⁺ revertants; *cysA* was obtained as an exceptional co-mutant among *hisA* revertants (see Table 1). Finally, in a population of 416 revertants from *argA1*, which is located close and to the right of *tyrA*, *B* (see Table 1), 12 co-mutants were recovered. From this co-mutation pattern it is

TABLE 2

Co-mutants after different revertant selections*

	Streptomyces coelicolor					S. rimosus
Revertant site:	hisA1	hisA132	metA1	cysA	argA1	hisA2
Plating units:	hyphae	hyphae	spores	spores	spores	hyphae
Co-mutants:	phenotypes / total	phenotypes / total	phenotypes / total	phenotypes / total	phenotypes / total	phenotypes / total
	his 67	his 65	his 3	his 3	his 5	his 60
	amm 32	amm 36	amm 2	pro 3	ura 3	amm 8
	met 2	met 3	leu 1	met 1	tyr 2	met 6
	trp 1	arg 2	pro 1		cys 1	arg 3
	arg 1	trp 1			rib 1	trp 2
Medium:	AMM, ARG, HOL, MET, TRP	AMM, ARG, HOL, MET, TRP	AMM, ARG, HIS, LEU, LYS, PRO, SER	ADE, HIS, MET, NIC, PRO	HIS, URA, TYR, CYS, MET, PHE, RIB	AMM, ARG, HOL, MET, TRP
Revertants ($\times 10^{-6}$):	40	20	500	18	90.6	4.5
Co-mutants (%):	10.3	10.7	2.1	1.3	2.8	7.9

* For technical details see Randazzo et al. (1973).

apparent that, with the exception of one (*cys*), all the mutants correspond to genes known to be close to and to the left (*hisB, I, A, G, C, F; tyr A, B*) or to the right (*uraB* and *ribB*) of *argA* (Hopwood *et al.*, 1973). It is noteworthy also that, among *metA* revertants, two new types appear (*ura* and *rib*) which were absent in the unselected co-mutant population of *hisA* revertants (see Table 1).

The patterns of co-mutants in revertant populations so far collected provide encouraging indications about the possibility of using the co-mutation method for mapping genes in respect to a few markers, along an arc of the map a few tens of centimorgans long. Virtually a whole map could be built up stepwise.

CO-MUTATION IN FINE-STRUCTURE MAPPING

The occurrence of a cluster of *his* genes (Carere *et al.*, 1973), one of which, *hisA*, specifying the enzyme histidinol dehydrogenase, provided a method for detecting *his* co-mutants among MNNG-induced revertants from *hisA*, selected in the presence of histidinol (Randazzo *et al.*, 1973). Among the revertant hyphae, up to 5 per cent were co-mutants in the gene *hisG* (three cistrons) immediately to the right of *hisA*, and 1 per cent in the gene *hisC* (two cistrons) immediately to the right of *hisG*. Only 0.1 per cent mutations were found in the *hisF* gene, 2–3 centimorgans from the cluster *hisB, I, A, G* and *C*, and none in the other *his* genes, further from the *his* cluster. (A strange and still unexplained fact was the lack of co-mutants in genes *hisB* and *hisI*, supposed to be immediately to the left of *hisA*.) The concentration of co-mutations to the right of the *hisA* gene appears more pronounced than that observed by Guerola *et al.* (1971) in *Salmonella*, who reported 1.8 per cent *his* co-mutants in an operon comprising nine genes. The rate of co-mutation per gene within the *his* operon is not, however, significantly higher than the rate in the nearby genes (*metA, ammA, B*), in agreement with the assumption of Guerola *et al.* (1971).

The co-mutation method appears very effective in collecting mutants closely linked to a given gene, suitable for fine-structure genetic analysis and biochemical studies on enzyme regulation.

INTERSPECIFIC COMPARISON BY CO-MUTATION

The second best mapped species of *Streptomyces* after *S. coelicolor* is *S. rimosus* (Friend and Hopwood, 1971; Alačević *et al.*, 1973). The two maps appear exactly superimposable (Friend and Hopwood, 1971) with the possible difference of the absence of "empty" regions in *S. rimosus* (Alačević *et al.*, 1973). Mutations corresponding to the same gene (histidinol dehydrogenase) are available in the two species (*hisA*). By reverting the two mutations with MNNG on a selective medium designed for *S. coelicolor* (Table 2) a very similar pattern of mutation was observed, showing the occurrence of a histidine cluster around *hisA*, as well as the co-mutation with *hisA* of *amm, met, arg* and *trp* genes. When the heterokaryon method is used (Table 3) the picture is more interesting. The paucity of *amm* and *met* mutations is apparent, suggesting that *amm* and *met* genes lie at a greater distance from *hisA* in *S. rimosus*. More striking is the occurrence of several *ala* (alanine) mutants in *S. rimosus*, undetected in *S. coelicolor*. Such a gene was never recorded before in either species, and it is probably in the region around *hisA* in *S. rimosus*. Of the other six phenotypes detected in *S. rimosus*, four (*trp*, *met* and *tyr*, with *arg* detected on the selective

TABLE 3
Co-mutants obtained from heterokaryons

Species:	S. coelicolor		S. rimosus	
Revertant site:	hisA1*		hisA2	
Co-mutants:	Phenotypes	Total	Phenotypes	Total
	his**	15	his**	21
	amm	7	ala	4
	met	7	amm	2
	trp	5	trp	2
	arg	3	met	1
	tyr	2	tyr	1
	glu	1	leu	1
	cys	1		
	phe	1		
Total:		42		32
Revertants ($\times 10^{-6}$):	168		8	
Co-mutants (%):	33.1		18.0	

* See Table 1.
** Growing on L-histidinol.

medium: Table 2) correspond to genes mapped in the region around *hisA* of *S. rimosus* (Alačević *et al.*, 1973) and the other two (*amm* and *arg*) recall genes of *S. coelicolor* linked to *hisA*, possibly missed in the present sample of *S. rimosus* mutants. The co-mutant methods promise to be very effective in the detection of both homologies and heterologies between similar species.

Acknowledgements

We wish to thank Professor G. Sermonti for his guidance and help in the preparation of the manuscript and Mr G. Di Giuseppe, Mr G. Conti, Mr O. Cervelli and Mr A. Anselmi for technical assistance.

This work was partially supported by a grant from the Italian National Research Council (CNR).

References

Alačević, M., Strašek-Vešligaj, M. and Sermonti, G. (1973). *J. gen. Microbiol.* **77**, 173.
Calendar, R., Lindqvist, B., Sironi, G. and Clark, A. J. (1970). *Virology*, **40**, 72.
Carere, A., Russi, S., Bignami, M. and Sermonti, G. (1973). *Mol. gen. Genet.* **123**, 219.
Cerdà-Olmedo, E., Hanawalt, P. C. and Guerola, N. (1968). *J. molec. Biol.* **33**, 705.
Delić, V., Hopwood, D. A. and Friend, E. J. (1970). *Mutat. Res.* **9**, 167.
Friend, E. J. and Hopwood, D. A. (1971). *J. gen. Microbiol.* **68**, 187.
Guerola, N., Ingraham, J. L. and Cerdà-Olmedo, E. (1971). *Nature New Biol.* **230**, 122.
Hirota, Y., Jacob, F., Ryter, A., Buttin, G. and Nakai, H. (1968). *J. molec. Biol.* **35**, 175.
Hopwood, D. A., Chater, K. F., Dowding, J. E. and Vivian, A. (1973). *Bact. Rev.* **37**, 371.
Matselyukh, B. P. and Mukvich, N. S. (1973). *Microbiol. Zh.* Kiev, **35**, 411.
Randazzo, R., Sermonti, G., Carere, A. and Bignami, M. (1973). *J. Bact.* **113**, 501.
Sermonti, G. and Spada-Sermonti, I. (1955). *Nature, Lond.* **176**, 121.

Approaches to the study of differentiation in *Streptomyces coelicolor* A3(2)

K. F. CHATER and M. J. MERRICK

Department of Genetics, John Innes Institute, Colney Lane, Norwich NR4 7UH, England

Summary

Two classes of morphological mutants of *Streptomyces coelicolor* A3(2) have been studied: *bld* mutants (devoid of aerial mycelium), and *whi* mutants (defective in spore formation). Most *bld* mutations have map locations in one of two regions, both of which also contain *whi* mutations. *bld* mutations mapping close together share the same phenotype with respect to colony morphology, responses to changes in the growth medium, and production of an antibiotic.

Mutations in four (*A, B, G, H*) of the eight *whi* loci so far unambiguously identified prevent sporulation septation, and those in a fifth locus (*I*) cause aberrant spacing of these septa. The phenotypes of constructed double mutants give a consistent pattern of epistasis of *whiG* to *H, A, B, I*; *H* to *A, B, I*; and *A* and *B* to *I*. A *whiAB* double mutant was indistinguishable from either singly mutant parent strain. These results suggest that complex interactions between the products of the *whiA, B, G, H* and *I* genes do not occur. Three oligosporogenous *whi* mutants have been identified, all apparently with mutations in the same region of the map. One of these defines the *whiC* locus. The two remaining *whi* loci, *D* and *E*, affect late stages of spore development.

Introduction

The vegetative or substrate mycelium of *S. coelicolor* A3(2) growing on agar medium consists of long, branching cells with occasional cross walls. On this develops the aerial mycelium, the function of which is reproductive. Aerial hyphal cells prior to spore formation differ little in fine structure from substrate hyphae, except in possessing a fibrous sheath surrounding the cell wall (Wilder-muth *et al.*, 1971). Some aerial hyphal cells become subdivided into regular spore-sized compartments by morphologically distinctive sporulation septa. Spore wall thickening follows, and the old cell wall material between adjacent spores breaks down to give chains of ellipsoidal spores (Wildermuth and Hopwood, 1970; McVittie, 1974). A tentative minimum list of functions and processes which must occur during this whole developmental sequence is as follows:

1. signal to start reproductive phase;
2. changes in patterns of transcription and/or translation;
3. initiation of branching;
4. control of specifically aerial growth direction;
5. formation of sheath precursors and extracellular assembly of fibrous sheath;
6. provision of metabolites, and their transport to aerial hyphal growth zones;
7. signal for aerial hyphal cells to form sporulation septa;
8. regulation of spacing of sporulation septa;
9. regulation of partitioning of chromosomal material to spore compart-ments;
10. regulation of structure of sporulation septa;
11. breakdown of old cell wall material between spores;
12. synthesis of spore wall;
13. development of grey coloration.

In this paper, studies with morphological mutants are described and the results related to the above list. Current research on the role of RNA polymerase in differentiation (Chater, 1974) has not yet yielded any positive results, and will not be discussed.

Results and discussion

THE INITIATION OF AERIAL MYCELIUM FORMATION

We have started a systematic study of the so-called "bald" colony (*bld*) mutants that lack macroscopically visible aerial mycelium. Among the moder-ate number so far examined, several morphological classes are recognizable, a major operational distinction being between soft and hard colony *bld* mutants. The mycelium of soft mutants breaks into fragments to an unusual extent and is therefore easily transferred by velvet in replica plating. The colonies of hard mutants do not break up easily and therefore replicate poorly. All the hard colony *bld* mutations so far mapped are located in the *leuB–cysD* interval (Fig. 1). This short region of the map is known also to contain at least three genes (*whiG, H, I*) involved in sporulation of aerial hyphae (Chater, 1972; see below). The exact mapping relationships of these *bld* and *whi* mutations are not yet clear.

Mapping has revealed at least three groups of soft colony *bld* mutants. The best represented group includes "S48", which was mapped by Hopwood (1967) between *cysA* and *nicA*. More recent mapping (Table 1, crosses i and ii) has located "S48" (now termed *bldA1*) more precisely between *ilvA* and *agaA*. Another gene, *whiB*, affecting sporulation is also located anticlockwise of

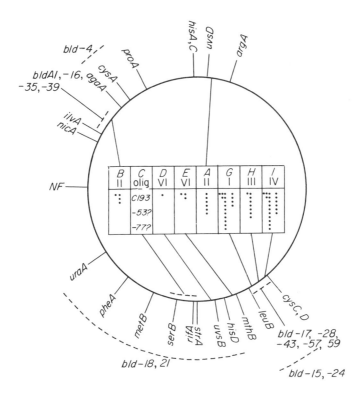

FIG. 1. The genetic and phenotypic properties of *whi* and *bld* mutants. In the boxes, the italicized capitals are *whi* locus designations; the dots indicate the number of mutations identified at each locus, two or more dots side by side indicating mutations that may have arisen from the same clone; and Roman numerals indicate the predominant phenotype of the aerial mycelium of mutants at each locus, according to the following scheme (Chater, 1972): I, no fragmentation or coiling; II, no fragmentation, tight coiling; III, no fragmentation, loose coiling; IV, fragmentation into curled pieces longer than spores; VI, "normal" spores by optical microscopy; olig, oligosporogenous. It is not yet known how closely *whi-53* and *-77* are linked to *whiC193*. Map locations of *bld* mutations are based on the unpublished data of M. J. Merrick, *bld* mutants *A1,-1,-16,-18,-21,-24,-35* and *-39* have soft, and the remainder hard, colonies. (Diagram after Hopwood *et al.*, 1973.)

TABLE 1

Mapping of *bldA1* and *whiB* mutations

Cross number	Strains	Diagram of cross	Crossover in interval	Genotype	Number of recombinants
i.	J397	*pheA1* 0 *ilvA1* 4 + 19 + 100 (Δ) 100 + (Δ1) 96 + (2) 81 *bldA1* (3) 0 *cysA15*	1	*ilv*	3
	966		2	+	11
			3	*bld*	60
				TOTAL	74
ii	J397	*uraA1* 0 *nicA1* 9 + 14 + 20 *agaA1* *proA1* 47 + 99 100 + (Δ1) 91 + (2) 86 *bldA1* (3) 80 + (4) 53 + (5) 0 *hisA1*	1	*nica aga pro*	7
	1514		2	*age pro*	6
			3	*bld aga pro*	6
			4	*bld pro*	27
			5	*bld*	51
			1, 4, 5	*nic aga*	1
			1, 2, 4	*nic bld pro*	1
				TOTAL	99

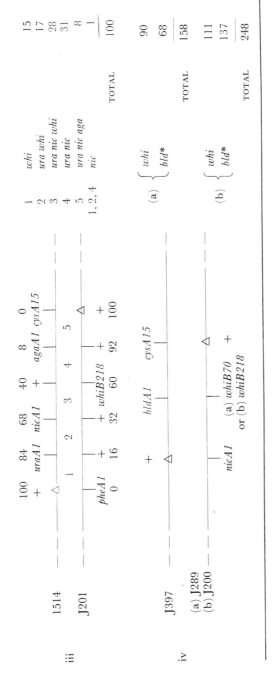

		uraA1	nicA1	whiB218	agaA1	cysA15			
	100	84	68	40	8	0			
1514	+	△	+	+	+	—	—		
J201	pheA1	+	+	+	+	+	—	—	
	0	16	32	60	92	100			
		1	2	3	4	5			

iii

			TOTAL
1	*whi*		15
2	*ura whi*		17
3	*ura nic whi*		28
4	*ura nic*		31
5	*ura nic aga*		8
1, 2, 4	*nic*		1
		TOTAL	100

		bldA1	cysA15	
J397	+	+	—	
	+	△	—	

(a) { *whi* — 90 ; *bld** — 68 } TOTAL 158

iv

	nicA1	(a) whiB70 or (b) whiB218	+	
(a) J289	—		△	
(b) J200	—			

(b) { *whi* — 111 ; *bld** — 137 } TOTAL 248

* May include *bld whi* recombinants.
In the diagrams, triangles indicate selected markers, and numbers, the allele frequencies (percentage). Irrelevant markers are omitted.

agaA (Fig. 1; Table 1, cross iii). In crosses of *whiB70* or *whiB218* with *bldA1* (so far made in only one coupling arrangement) the absence of sporulating recombinant colonies (Table 1, cross iv) showed that *whiB* was either very close to *bldA,* or between *bldA* and *cysA.* In view of this close linkage, it is relevant to point out the great differences in the *bldA* and *whiB* phenotypes; *whiB* mutants have nonfragmenting aerial hyphae and probably lack a function required for sporulation septation (see below), whereas ultrastructural studies (B. Wells and M. J. Merrick, unpublished) indicate that fragmentation of the mycelium of *bldA1* is related to the presence of numerous crosswalls at intervals reminiscent of the spacing of sporulation septa rather than of vegetative crosswalls. Similar structures were observed by Cherny *et al.* (1972) in morphological variants of *S. roseoflavus* var. *roseofungini* obtained on media containing fructose as sole carbon source.

In relation to the list of functions set out in the Introduction, the hard colony *bld* mutants may lack an essential function required for any reproductive growth to occur (e.g. items 1, 2, 3 or 6), while *bldA* mutants can apparently perform all the functions except perhaps items 4 and 5, i.e. their defects are possibly in the control of the direction of aerial mycelium growth or in fibrous sheath synthesis. Alternatively, *bldA* mutants may be in some way "derepressed" for sporulation septation. The fine structure of the remaining soft colony *bld* mutants has not been examined, and it is too early to speculate on the nature of their defects.

Recent studies have revealed interesting interactions between some *bld* mutations and antibiotic production. The wild-type *S. coelicolor* A3(2) strain harbours a plasmid (SCP1) that specifies production of an antibiotic (see Hopwood and Wright, 1974) active against strains lacking the plasmid (Vivian, 1971) and various unrelated bacteria (L. F. Wright, personal communication). Surprisingly, *bldA1* SCP1$^+$ strains do not produce the antibiotic, though they are resistant to it. (A *bldA1* SCP1$^-$ strain is sensitive to the antibiotic.) Thus the chromosomally located *bldA1* mutation prevents production (or extracellular accumulation) of the SCP1 antibiotic, indicating a possible regulatory link between sporulation and antibiotic production. This link can apparently be dislocated in certain circumstances: *bldA1* (and all other mutants of the same group) can be induced to sporulate on media containing mannitol, in the absence of glucose, and a preliminary experiment suggested that this sporulation was not accompanied by antibiotic production in a *bldA1* SCP1$^+$ strain. The possibility that the antibiotic is itself required for sporulation, as may be the case for antibiotics in sporulating Bacilli (Sadoff, 1972), is ruled out, since morphologically wild-type strains can lose the plasmid without any effect on sporulation.

Sporulation is possibly, at least in part, a response by some system monitoring intracellular energy levels, to changes in the growth medium. F. H. Flury (personal communication) has isolated mutants unable to grow on several carbon sources utilized by the wild type, in the hope that they may be defective in some system, analogous to the cAMP system of *Escherichia coli* (Pastan and Perlman, 1970), involved in the general control of carbohydrate metabolism. One of these mutants was bald, and mapping and reversion tests showed that a single mutation caused the nutritional and morphological effects. Clearly, deeper knowledge of the regulation of carbohydrate utilization could aid understanding of the biochemical and physiological basis of differentiation in *Streptomyces*.

WHITE COLONY MUTANTS AND THE LATER STAGES OF SPORULATION

White colony (*whi*) mutants of *S. coelicolor* fall into at least eight genetic and six phenotypic classes (Fig. 1), all forming aerial hyphae but none producing mature grey spores (Hopwood *et al.*, 1970; Chater, 1972; McVittie, 1974). The status of a ninth locus, *whiF*, originally proposed by Chater (1972) on the basis of a single mutation, *whi-99*, is in doubt (Chater and Hopwood, 1973), since the phenotype of the original mutant (type V: rod-shaped spores) has not been found amongst recombinants from crosses of this mutation with wild-type; these, where examined, were of type I phenotype. Another mutant (*whi-79*) with type V phenotype was described by McVittie (1974). However, its type V phenotype was replaced by type I during her studies. The map location of *whi-79* was then thought to be close to *strA*, but on the basis of more recent data it maps, like *whi-99*, between *leuB* and *cysC, D*. Perhaps *whi-79* and *-99* are *whiG* mutations whose phenotype is modified in the original background.

Three other *whi* mutations giving rise to somewhat indistinct phenotypes are located near *strA*. *whiC193*, which gives a slightly aberrant type I phenotype (long, straight aerial hyphae with occasional spores), was previously mapped between *metB* and *strA* (Chater, 1972). The other two mutations, both from the collection isolated by Hopwood *et al.* (1970), are *whi-77*, which phenotypically resembles *whiC193*, and *whi-53*, which gives a clearly oligosporogenous phenotype (McVittie, 1974). Preliminary crosses located *whi-53* and *-77* between *uraA* and *mthB*, but not close to either marker. The crosses in Table 2 show that *whi-53* is situated between *strA* and *uraA* (cross i); *whi-53* is either very close to *whiC193* or between it and *strA* (cross iia); and *whi-77* is located close to *whi-53*, or between it and *uraA* (cross iib). The defect in these three mutants appears to occur at a very early stage of aerial mycelium development since much of the aerial mycelium is of phenotype I. Since these mutants are all to some extent oligosporogenous, whereas *whiA, B, G* and *H* mutants usually are not, it is perhaps unlikely that they are defective in structural sporulation-specific proteins, and it is tempting to suspect some alteration

TABLE 2

Mapping of *whi-53, -77* and *-193*

Cross i — Diagram of cross:

```
        100   32    27     0
  △------+-----+-----+-----hisD3
  uraA1  whi-53 strA1  +
  0       68    73    100
      1      2     3
```

Cross ii — Diagram of cross:

```
  (a) whi-193
  +   (b) whi-77        +
  △---------------------△------ str
  ura       whi-53      str
```

Cross number	Crossover in intervals	Genotype	Number of recombinants
i	1	*whi str*	103
	2	*str*	9
	3	+	40
	1, 2, 3	*whi*	1
		TOTAL	153
ii	(a) {	*whi**	199
		+	0
	(b) {	*whi**	100
		+	0

* May include double *whi* recombinants.

Triangles indicate selected markers, and numbers on diagrams are allele frequencies (percentage). See text for further explanation.

at a regulatory level. None of the three mutations has yet been mapped with respect to the *rifA* locus, which specifies a component of RNA polymerase and is located a short distance clockwise of *strA* (Chater, 1974, and unpublished).

From the mapping results with *whi* mutants it seems that most of the early sporulation genes have been identified, since the *A, B, G, H* and *I* loci have 6, 3, 14, 7 and 16 independently obtained mutations respectively (Fig. 1). However, confirmation that each locus is a single functional unit awaits the development of a suitable complementation test. One possible approach, discussed by Chater and Hopwood (1973), depended on the differential retention of spores and nonsporulating hyphae by filters: in practice, however, no consistent data have been obtained by this method. Hopwood and Wright (1973, 1974) have recently isolated strains bearing SCP1 plasmids into which chromosomal regions had become inserted. Perhaps such plasmids may be obtainable for regions containing genes concerned with differentiation, thereby providing the basis for a reliable complementation test.

On the assumption that *whiA, B, G, H* and *I* are indeed single loci, representative double mutants have been synthesized in all possible pairwise combinations in order to define epistatic relationships (Chater, 1975). It seemed possible *a priori* that epistatic interactions among morphological mutations might be more complex than among mutations in genes controlling metabolic pathways. Hence it was important to find out (1) if the double mutants had the expected phenotype in clearly predictable combinations and (2) if the results were completely consistent in all combinations. Of the singly mutant parent strains, only the *whiI* mutant formed sporulation septa, so the other mutations should all have been epistatic to *whiI* if simple sequential gene action were involved. This was observed. Secondly, the results were indeed internally consistent, *whiG* being epistatic to *whiA, B, H* and *I, whiH* to *whiA, B* and *I*, and *whiA* and *B* to *whiI*; a *whiAB* double mutant was indistinguishable morphologically from the singly mutant parent strains (which had identical phenotypes). Since all the double mutants were identical in morphology to one of the singly mutant parent strains, the likelihood of complex interactions between gene products is not very great, and a simple interpretation of the results with *whiA, B, G* and *H* is possible. On this hypothesis, *whiG* specifies a product which, directly or indirectly, results in the production of helical hyphae, and the action of the *whiH* gene product can then, again directly or indirectly, further shorten the wavelength of the helices. The *whiA* and *B* gene products can only act when the *whiG* and *H* processes are completed, and their combined action results in the development of sporulation septa. An earlier study showed that at least one *whiI* mutant, *whiI6* (Hopwood *et al.*, 1970), had unusually widely spaced sporulation septa, and phase-contrast microscopy of several other *whiI* mutants suggests that this is true of all of them

(Chater, 1972), so that one result of *whiI* gene product activity is the correct spacing of sporulation septa.

Speculating further, the degree of coiling of aerial hyphae seems unlikely to be a primary part of the sporulation process, but rather a secondary result of some change(s) in cell wall structure required for the initiation of sporulation septa and specified by the *whiG* and *H* gene products. (Another possibility, that essential sheath changes are involved, has not been eliminated, though sheath-like material can be seen in electron micrographs of thin sections of *whiA*, *B* and *G* mutants taken by A. McVittie (personal communication).) The cell wall change(s) might well also determine the locations of sporulation septa, whose structure and development would be primarily controlled by the *whiA* and *B* gene products. On this model, the function of the *whiI* gene product in controlling septum spacing is apparently **redundant**; however, since incomplete partitioning of chromosomal material would effectively prevent the completion and perhaps the initiation of some septa, a role for the *whiI* gene product may be found in the completion of chromosomal partitioning.

Among later stages, mutants defective in the breakdown of old cell wall material between adjacent spores (item 11 in the list in the Introduction), probably would not have white colonies and so would not have been isolated even if genetic control is involved. Only one mutant defective in spore wall thickening (*whiD16*) has been identified (Chater, 1972; McVittie, 1974). Thus it is possible that only a single major spore-specific protein, specified by *whiD*, is involved in wall thickening.

It is fortunate in these genetic studies that the change of colony colour from white to grey, which occurs as spores develop, takes place only after spore wall material has been laid down. Two independent *whi* mutants have been described that produce morphologically wild-type spores whose only abnormality seems to be failure to produce this grey colour (Chater, 1972; McVittie, 1974). On the basis of map location these were both classified as mutants of a single locus, *whiE* (Chater, 1972). The very close linkage of *whiE107* and *whiE124* has now been confirmed in crosses in both coupling arrangements between *cysD18* and *hisD3* derivatives, selection being for prototrophic recombinants. Only 0·02 per cent recombination was observed between the two *whi* mutations.

Concluding remarks

At present the studies of *bld* mutants show the greatest immediate promise of useful information; phenotypic suppression of the *bld* phenotype, for example by changes in carbon source as described here, should permit experimental approaches to the links between basic metabolism and differentiation. At the same time, light may also be shed upon the regulation of other secondary processes, such as antibiotic production. Moreover, the defects in *hld* mutants may be detectable in vegetative cells and thus be more amenable to biochemical analysis than are the defects in most *whi* mutants.

Acknowledgements

We are grateful to Fred Flury and Fred Wright, whose unpublished results we have quoted; to David Hopwood for reading the manuscript; and to Judy Elsey-Warren for expert technical assistance.

References

Chater, K. F. (1972). *J. gen. Microbiol.* **72**, 9.
Chater, K. F. (1974). *J. gen. Microbiol.* **80**, 277.
Chater, K. F. (1975). *J. gen. Microbiol.* **87**, 312.
Chater, K. F. and Hopwood, D. A. (1973). *Symp. Soc. gen. Microbiol.* **23**, 143.
Cherny, N. E., Tikhonenko, A. S., Nikitina, E. T. and Kalakoutskii, L. V. (1972). *Cytobios*, **5**, 7.
Hopwood, D. A. (1967). *Bact. Rev.* **31**, 373.
Hopwood, D. A. and Wright, H. M. (1973). *J. gen. Microbiol.* **79**, 331.
Hopwood, D. A. and Wright, H. M. (1974). These Proceedings.
Hopwood, D. A., Wildermuth, H. and Palmer, H. M. (1970). *J. gen. Microbiol.* **61**, 397.
Hopwood, D. A., Chater, K. F., Dowding, J. E. and Vivian, A. (1973). *Bact. Rev.* **37**, 371.
McVittie, A. (1974). *J. gen. Microbiol.* **81**, 291.
Pastan, I. and Perlman, R. (1970). *Science*, **169**, 339.
Sadoff, H. L. (1972). "Spores V" (Ed. H. O. Halvorson, R. Hanson and L. L. Campbell), p. 157. American Society for Microbiology, Washington D.C.
Vivian, A. (1971). *J. gen. Microbiol.* **69**, 353.
Wildermuth, H. and Hopwood, D. A. (1970). *J. gen. Microbiol.* **60**, 51.
Wildermuth, H., Wehrli, E. and Horne, R. W. (1971). *J. Ultrastruct. Res.* **35**, 168.

Suppressor-sensitive mutations of *Streptomyces coelicolor* A3(2) and actinophage φC31

S. I. ALIKHANIAN, N. D. LOMOVSKAYA and V. N. DANILENKO

Institute of Genetics and Selection of Industrial Microorganisms, Moscow, USSR

Summary

Revertants of polyauxotrophic derivatives of *Streptomyces coelicolor* A3(2) which had lost requirements for arginine and homoserine or for arginine, homoserine and proline were isolated and shown to carry allele-specific suppressor (*su*) genes. The mutations suppressed by the *su* genes appeared also to be suppressed by 5-fluorouracil. The two *su* genes were mapped at different loci on the A3(2) chromosome. Suppressor-sensitive mutants of φC31 actinophage were obtained. By means of these mutants a further *su* gene was revealed and located on the A3(2) chromosome. All three *su* genes differed from each other in their suppressing ability.

The suggestion of the existence of *su* genes in wild-type strains *S. coelicolor* A3(2) and *S. lividans* 66 was confirmed by crossing these strains and by an analysis of recombinants which were shown to contain one or both parental *su* genes. Certain characteristics of these recombinants were studied. Some seemed to differ from the parental strains in respect of antibiotic production characteristics. They inhibited some actinomycete strains which were affected by neither of the parents. The results of the cross between *S. coelicolor* A3(2) and *S. lividans* 66 suggested that a study of its peculiarities would provide new approaches to a study of the recombination process in *Streptomyces*.

Introduction

In the last few years remarkable progress has been achieved in studies of actinomycetes which combine a simple cellular organization with a complex life cycle. Over 100 genes, controlling pathways of synthesis of amino acids, bases and vitamins, resistance to drugs and antibiotics, ultraviolet-sensitivity and various stages of differentiation, were located on the *Streptomyces coelicolor* A3(2) genetic map (Hopwood *et al.*, 1973). Temperature-sensitive mutants were found, as expected, to map at many different loci (Hopwood, 1966).

It is well known that the isolation of allele-specific suppressor genes and suppressor-sensitive mutations in bacteria, bacteriophages and fungi (Hawthorne and Mortimer, 1963; Gorini and Beckwith, 1966; Seale, 1968; Georgopoulos, 1969) allowed advances in studies on various problems of genetics and molecular biology. With this in mind one can predict that the isolation and use of mutants of this type in actinomycetes and actinophages will lead to more extensive genetic study of this system.

The present work describes the isolation of allele-specific suppressor (*su*) genes in *S. coelicolor* A3(2), and suppressor-sensitive (*sus*) mutants in A3(2) and actinophage ϕC31. To identify supressor genes, hybrids obtained between *S. coelicolor* A3(2) and *Streptomyces lividans* 66 were employed which proved to be useful tools to approach some problems of the genetics and breeding of *Streptomyces*.

Materials and methods

Strains Genetically marked strains used in this work are listed in Table 1. Genetic symbols are as given by Hopwood *et al.* (1973). Strains 853 and 928 were taken from a group of polyauxotrophic derivatives of A3(2) kindly supplied by D. A. Hopwood. Nonlysogenic polyauxotrophic derivatives of A3(2) (S12, S49, S221, S179, S277, S278, S111, S31) and derivatives of *S. lividans* 66 were obtained in our laboratory. Strains *S. griseus* 20, *S. cyanocolor* 14 and *S. caesius* 39 were employed as test cultures to measure antibiotic production.

Media, phage assays and crossing procedures were as described previously (Lomovskaya *et al.*, 1971, 1972). Heterokaryon and heteroclone analyses were done as described by Sermonti (1969a). In crosses between strains A3(2) and 66 conducted to test qualitatively the ability of these strains to recombine, auxotrophs of strains 66 with various nutrient requirements (except for proline, uracil, adenine, arginine) and strain S12 were used as parents. Auxotrophs of strain 66 grown on master plates containing complete medium were replicated to plates seeded with S12 spore suspensions. After incubation for 3 days, colonies were replicated on to plates containing a medium selecting recombinants. In each case *cysD18* and an auxotrophic marker of strain 66 served as counter-selective markers. Those auxotrophs of strain 66 that proved to yield the largest number of recombinants were selected for further work.

To test the ability of A3(2) and 66 and their recombinants to inhibit the growth of other strains a master plate streaked in patches with spores of tested cultures was overlayed after 1 day's incubation with spores of the indicator strain in soft agar. The appearance of zones in which the growth of the indicator strain was absent around tested patches after a further day of incubation was considered to reflect growth inhibition.

TABLE 1

Strains of *Streptomyces coelicolor* A3(2) and *Streptomyces lividans* 66

Strain	Genetic markers
S. coelicolor A3(2)	
853	*hisA1 uraA1 adeA3 cysD18 tps33 ly*[+] †
928	*uraA1 hisC9 cysA15 nicA3 tps 33 ly*[+]
S111	*uraA1 adeA3 cysD18 mthB2* strA1 ly*[−]†
S137	*argA1 cysD18 mthB2 pheA1 proA1 ly*[−]
S221	*proA1 uraA1 argA1 ly*[−]
S179	*hisA1 uraA1 pheA1 ly*[−]
S277	*proA1 uraA1 cysD18 ly*[−]
S278	*hisA1 proA1 uraA1 ly*[−]
S12	*uraA1 adeA3 cysD18 argA1 proA1 ly*[−]
S26	*hisA1 strA1 ly*[−]
S49	*argA1 mthB2 proA1 ly*[−]
S31	*uraA1 adeA3 cysD18 argA1 proA1 strA1 ly*[−]
S. lividans 66	
A7	*phe1 ly*[−]
A13	*cys1 ly*[−]

* *mthB2*—requirement for methionine plus threonine, or homoserine.

† *ly*[+], lysogenic for actinophage φC31; *ly*[−], nonlysogenic.

To isolate suppressor-sensitive phage mutants a clear-plaque mutant of φC31 actinophage was treated with a dose of ultraviolet light (uv) giving 0.1 per cent survival. To allow segregation of mutant heterozygotes during a one-cycle growth period, the phage was propagated on uv-treated strain S49 Rv1 (survival 50 per cent). *Sus* phage mutants were sought only in those mutagenized phage stocks where the frequency of temperature-sensitive mutations was high enough to indicate effective mutagenesis.

Phenotypic suppression of auxotrophic mutations by 5-fluorouracil (5FU) was carried out on minimal agar plates supplemented with 5FU (20 µg cm^{-3}), amino acids required for growth of the polyauxotrophic strain (except for that being studied), casein hydrolysate with vitamins in amounts insufficient for auxotrophic growth, cytosine and guanine (10 µg cm^{-3}) and thymidine to abolish the bacteriocidal action of 5FU. Uracil at 100 µg was placed on a small paper disc in the centre of the plate to counteract the bacteriostatic action of 5FU. A ring of suppressed mutant colonies appeared at some distance from the disc.

Results

To identify suppressor gene mutations in the *S. coelicolor* A3(2) genome the reversion frequencies of different pairs of loci were measured in polyauxotrophic derivatives of the strain. The markers tested were *proA1*, *uraA1*, *argA1*, *mthB2*, *pheA1*, *hisA1*, *cysD18*, *adeA3*, *hisC9*, *cysA15*, *nicA3*. Revertants which lost requirements for both arginine and homoserine appeared to arise in S49 with a high frequency: *argA1* and *mthB2* alleles separately gave revertants with a frequency of 3×10^{-8} and 2×10^{-7} respectively, while the reversion frequency for both loci simultaneously was 3×10^{-8}. Were the

TABLE 2

Analysis of *proA1*⁺ *adeA3*⁺ recombinants selected from the cross S49Rv1 × 853*

Genotype†	Crossover in intervals‡	Number of recombinants
mth his	a,e	6
mth arg his	a,f	26
mth arg su	a,h	11
ura mth arg his	b,f	2
ura mth arg	b,g	55

* The cross is illustrated in Fig. 1(a).
† Wild-type alleles omitted.
‡ See intervals in Fig. 1(a).

latter value a result of two independent events the frequency would have been 6×10^{-15}. As this was not the case, we assumed the occurrence of double revertants to be the result of a single mutation that suppressed the expression of both mutant phenotypes. The genotype of the strain obtained, designated S49Rv1, would therefore be *pro arg mth su* although phenotypically it was only *pro*. To provide evidence of the existence of a suppressor gene in S49Rv1, crosses were made between this strain and strain 853. As seen in Fig. 1(a) and Table 2, the recombinant classes *mth his*, *mth arg his*, *ura mth arg his* and *ura mth arg* detected amongst the sample of progeny analysed could have arisen only if S49Rv1 had the genotype *pro arg mth su*.

Analysis of recombinant genotypes allowed a preliminary location of the *su1* gene on the A3(2) chromosome. Amongst the recombinants from this cross a large *ura mth arg* class carried the fragment *c d e f* of the S49Rv1 chromosome. If the *su1* gene were situated in this fragment it would have been difficult to explain the existence of these recombinants. Thus the location of the *su1* gene between *adeA3* and *hisA1* in the right-hand arc seems very unlikely. If *su1* lay in interval *a* of the left-hand arc then *his* recombinants could have carried either the mutant or wild-type allele of the *su1* gene. As seen from Table 2, all *his* recombinants contained the wild-type allele of the gene. Further, if *su1* were located in interval *b* of the left-hand arc then all the *su*⁺ recombinants would have been *ura*. However, the *su*⁺ recombinants were both *ura* and *ura*⁺. As all recombinants arising by crossover in intervals *e* or *f* of the right-hand arc were *su*⁺, and *his* recombinants were *su* or *su*⁺, the location of the *su1* gene between *proA1* and *hisA1* was considered most likely.

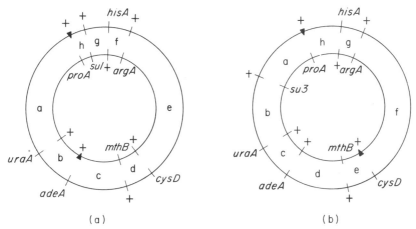

(a)   (b)

FIG. 1. Location of *su1* (a) and *su3* (b) genes on the A3(2) chromosome. Markers of the two parents are indicated on the two circles. Solid triangles indicate selected markers. Letters between circles show map intervals between markers.

The *su1* gene identified in S49Rv1 suppressed only *argA1* and *mthB2*. Later, reversions of the three loci, *pro*, *arg* and *mth*, arising simultaneously with a frequency of 5×10^{-9}, were recognized in strain S49. The occurrence of two recombinant classes, *arg mth pro* and *pro*, in the cross between the strain designated S49Rv2 and strain S26 (selected markers *hisA1*⁺ *strA*) indicated the presence in S49Rv2 of an *su* gene and suggested its location in the left-hand arc between *proA1* and *mthB2*. Hence, the *su1* and *su2* genes appeared to be located in different positions.

In the genome of a revertant which lost the requirement only for homoserine, a suppressor gene was detected using *sus* mutants of actinophage φC31 which grew on S49Rv3 but failed to do so on S49 at 37°C. A detailed characterization of *sus* mutants is presented later.

It turned out that in the cross S49Rv3 × 853 (Table 3 and Fig. 1(b)) recombinant classes *ura ade mth arg his*, *ura ade mth his*, *ura ade mth arg* and *mth arg* could have arisen only if S49Rv3 had the genotype, *pro arg mth su*. If crossovers occurred in the region between *pro* and *ura*, then the *mthB2* mutation was suppressed in some of the recombinants arising by crossovers in intervals *a*,*g*

TABLE 3

Analysis of $cysD18^{+}proA1^{+}$ recombinants selected from the cross S49Rv3 × 853*

Genotype†	Crossover in intervals‡	Number of recombinants
ura ade mth arg his	d,g	6
ura ade mth his	d,f	69
ura ade mth arg	d,h	12
mth arg	b,h	4
mth arg su3	a,h	9
mth arg his su3	a,g	4

* The cross is illustrated in Fig. 1(b).
† Wild-type alleles omitted.
‡ See intervals in Fig. 1(b)

and a,h but not in those arising by crossovers in intervals b,h. The possible position of $su3$ between $uraA1$ and $proA1$ was inferred from this analysis.

All of the mutations used in this work were tested for their ability to be suppressed by 5FU. Phenotypic suppression was demonstrated only for $proA1$, $mthB2$ and $argA1$.

Since A3(2) strains carrying su genes had been isolated we sought sus mutants of actinophage ϕC31 able to grow on strain S49Rv1 but unable to produce progeny when plated on strain S49. No mutants of this type were observed at 28°C but were detected at a higher temperature. These mutants, numbers 2, 3, 5, 6, 8, 9, grew on S49 and S49Rv1 at 28°C and, when incubated at 37°C, grew on S49Rv1 but failed to do so on S49. Similar mutants, numbers 41 and 49, were isolated also amongst ts mutants in a lawn of $S.$ $lividans$ strain 66 (Table 4).

The data presented above suggest that strain S49, as well as all derivatives of A3(2), originally contained a suppressor gene, which may cause insertion of an

TABLE 4

Host range of ϕ C31 actinophage sus mutants

	Strain					
	66		S49		S49Rv1	
Phage	28°C	37°C	28°C	37°C	28°C	37°C
sus 41, sus 49	+	−	+	−	+	+
sus 2, sus 3 } sus 5, sus 6 } sus 8, sus 9 }	+	+	+	−	+	+
sus 11	+	−	+	+	+	+

amino acid into a protein molecule of mutant phage allowing its function at low but not at high temperature. This amino acid is not acceptable at either temperature for actinomycete strains with *argA1* and *mthB2* mutations. Since *sus* mutants 2, 3, 5, 6, 8 and 9 grow well on strain 66 at 37°C we assume that it also contains an *su* gene, differing from those of S49 and S49Rv1 in its action, as seen from Table 4.

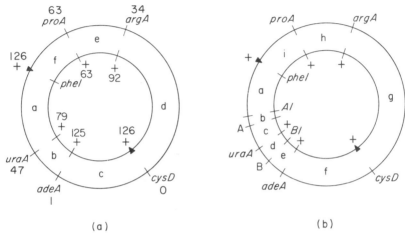

(a)   (b)

F𝚒𝚐. 2(a) Allele frequencies of nonselected markers in selected recombinants inheriting the alleles *phe1⁺* and *cysD18⁺* in cross *S. coelicolor* A3(2) × *S. lividans* 66 and (b) preliminary location of two groups of genes A, A1 and B, B1 controlling antibiotic production.

To confirm the presence of suppressor genes in *S. coelicolor* A3(2) and *S. lividans* 66, crosses were carried out between these two strains. The possibility of recombination between strains A3(2) and 66 (their strain 1326), which acts as a recipient of UF fertility type, was shown by Hopwood and Wright (1973).

The donor strain S12 of NF fertility type and auxotrophic derivatives of strain 66 were employed as parents in crosses. Table 5 presents the results of analysis of *phe1⁺ cysD18⁺* haploid recombinants from the cross S12 × A7. The frequency of recombinants was 3 × 10⁻⁵. As seen from Table 5 and Fig. 2(a) recombinant classes bearing different contributions from the parental chromosomes were obtained. The existence of Rc *pro arg* recombinants (Rc = interspecific recombinant) suggests that the gene of A3(2) corresponding to *phe1* in strain 66 is located in interval *a f e* between *uraA1* and *argA1*. If we suppose that in the cross A3(2) *NF* × 66 UF the 9 o'clock segment from the NF strain is usually inherited, then a large proportion of recombinants with wild-type alleles of nonselected markers must reflect the location of *phe1⁺* between *uraA1* and *proA1*.

TABLE 5

Analysis of *phe1*$^+$ *cysD18*$^+$ recombinants selected from the cross S12 × A7*

Genotype†	Crossover in intervals‡	Number of recombinants
Rc *ura pro arg*	b,d	24
Rc *ura pro*	b,e	22
Rc *pro arg*	a,d	9
Rc	a,f	63
Rc *pro*	a,e	7
Rc *ura pro arg ade*	c,d	1

* The cross is illustrated in Fig. 2(a).
† Wild-type alleles omitted; Rc, inter-specific recombinant.
‡ See intervals in Fig. 2(a).

To identify *su* genes in representatives of the various recombinant classes, actinophage *sus* mutants were employed. Since *sus5* and *sus11* grow only in the presence of *su* genes from strain 66 (named *su6*) and from strain A3(2) (named *su5*) respectively, the behaviour of these mutants in recombinant strains must clearly show whether one or both of the parental *su* genes are present in these strains. The data of Table 6 indicate that *su5* is situated on the chromosome in the vicinity of *phe1*, because recombinants with wild-type alleles of nonselected markers Rc *su5 su6* still suppressed *sus11* phenotype. Recombinant Rc *ade su6*, which did not include the *a f e* fragment where the *su5* gene is thought to lie, failed to suppress the expression of the *sus11* mutation. All the recombinants derived from the S12 × A7 cross and carrying the *a f e* fragment of the A3(2) chromosome bore the *su6* gene as well, which suppressed the *sus5* mutant phenotype. As to the location of this gene, it may be noted only that it is situated in the fragment of the A3(2) chromosome corresponding to that

TABLE 6

The ability of recombinants from the cross *S. coelicolor* A3(2) × *S. lividans* 66 to suppress *sus* mutants of phage φ C31 at 37°C

Genotypes of recombinants	Phage	
	sus 5	*sus 11*
Rc *su5 su6*	+	+
Rc *ura pro su5 su6*	+	+
Rc *pro arg su5 su6*	+	+
Rc *ura pro arg su5 su6*	+	+
Rc *ura ade pro arg su5*	−	+
Rc *ura pro arg cys str su5*	−	+
Rc *ade su6*	+	−

between *uraA1* and *argA1* in the right-hand arc. Rc *ura ade pro arg su5* and Rc *ade su6* were obtained in the progeny of the S12 × A13 cross where *cysD18*$^+$ and *cys1*$^+$ were selected markers. In contrast to the cross S12 × A7, in this cross only heterokaryons and heteroclones were formed on selective media after 3 to 4 days of incubation, their ratio changing gradually during the incubation period: 60 per cent heterokaryons after 4 days and 20 per cent after 8 days. Recombinants were observed after 8 to 10 days of growth, their colonies sporulating abundantly in contrast to heteroclones. By scoring progeny of this cross the map position of the gene corresponding to *cys1* in strain 66 was inferred to be between *adeA3* and *cysD18*. It is evident that the formation of *ade ura pro arg* recombinants is compatible only with this location. In the cross S12 × A13, where *adeA3*$^+$ *strA1* were the selected alleles, after 3 to 4 days of incubation only heteroclones were formed, with no heterokaryotic colonies. Consideration of the suppressor characteristics of Rc *ade su6* recombinants indicated that *su6* was not situated between *adeA3* and *cys1*$^+$ in this fragment of the 66 chromosome. In strain 66 also the gene was absent in fragments contributed to recombinants Rc *ura ade pro arg su5* and Rc *ura pro arg cys str su5* despite the fact that these fragments too are located between *uraA1* and *argA1* in the right-hand arc.

TABLE 7

Results of tests on the ability of representatives of *cysD18*$^+$ *phe1*$^+$ selected recombinant classes to produce antibiotic*

Genotype	Crossover in intervals	Number of tested recombinants	Indicator strain		
			S. cyanocolor 14	*S. caesius* 39	*S. griseus* 20
Rc A1 B1	a,i	26	−	−	+
Rc B1	b,i	2	−	−	−
Rc A B1	c,i	3	+	+	+
Rc *ura pro* A B1	d,h	9	+	+	+
Rc *ura pro* A B	e,h	2	−	−	+
Rc *pro arg* A B1	c,g	5	+	+	+
Rc *pro arg* A1 B1	a,g	1	−	−	+
Rc *ura pro arg* A B1	d,g	7	+	+	+
Rc *ura pro arg* A B	e,g	2	−	−	+
Rc *pro* A B1	c,h	2	+	+	+
Rc *pro* A B	a,h	2	−	−	+
Rc *ura pro arg cys str* A B1†		5	+	+	+
Rc *ura pro arg cys str* A B†		5	−	−	+

* The cross is illustrated in Fig. 2(b).

† Recombinants from cross S31 × A13, selected markers *adeA3*$^+$ *strA1*.

Another striking characteristic of recombinants from the cross A3(2) × 66 is worth pointing out. *S. coelicolor* A3(2) (*Streptomyces violaceoruber*, according to Kutzner and Waksman, 1959) and *S. lividans* are known to produce the antibiotic coelicomycin, with similar but not identical structure (Krasilnikov *et al.*, 1965; Blinov *et al.*, 1971), which affected a number of actinomycete cultures. A proportion of recombinants inhibited those actinomycete strains which were affected by neither of the parents. To account for this, it is proposed that at least two groups of genes participate in the control of antibiotic synthesis, *A B* in A3(2) and *A1 B1* in 66, their cooperation altering thereby the properties of the antibiotics. On the basis of the data obtained, we attempted to explain the interaction of the genes and to locate them tentatively on the chromosomes of both strains. It seems plausible that *A* and *A1* are situated between *uraA1* and *phe1*, and *B* and *B1* between *uraA1* and *adeA3*. If genes *A* and *B1* were combined it might have led to a change in the antibiotic properties of recombinants reflected by their ability to inhibit growth of strains 14 and 39 (Table 7 and Fig. 2(b)). In addition the *A* group seems to lie more closely to *ura* than the *A1* group. Such nonhomologous locations of the *A* and *A1* genes on the chromosomes of strains A3(2) and 66 is supported by the existence of *RcB1* recombinants which were shown to have lost the ability of parental strains to inhibit growth of *S. griseus* strain 20.

Discussion

Analysis of the genotypes of recombinants S49Rv1, S49Rv2 and S49Rv3 suggests that they carry genes suppressing mutant phenotypes in A3(2) and actinophage ϕC31. The study of these *su* genes and *sus* mutations is not sufficiently advanced to understand their nature. One can only say that *su* genes are allele-specific and that the mutant codon of the mRNA contains uracil. Crosses between strains with *su1*, *su2* and *su3* and polyauxotrophic derivatives of A3(2) located these genes between *proA1* and *hisA1*, and *proA1* and *mthB2* in the left-hand arc and *proA1* and *uraA1*, respectively. All 3 *su* genes differ from each other in their suppressing ability. The gene *su1* suppresses mutations *mthB2* and *argA1*, *su2* suppresses mutations *argA1*, *mthB2* and *proA1*, and *su3* suppresses only *mthB2*. This could be related to the fact that as a result of the action of *su* genes different amino acids are incorporated into mutant proteins.

We isolated actinophage suppressor-sensitive mutants while selecting them at a high temperature only. This might be explained by the presence of *su* genes in the initial strains A3(2) and 66. As a result of their action a mutant protein can function at a low temperature. This suggestion was confirmed by the analysis of recombinants arising in the progeny of the *S. coelicolor* A3(2) × *S. lividans* 66 cross which were shown to contain one or both *su* genes. The isolation of a strain lacking *su* genes, which is now under study, would be of particular interest for further study of the relationship between *su* genes and *sus* mutants. Use of this strain will naturally permit the isolation of a wider set of mutants, especially if our *su* genes turn out to suppress nonsense mutations.

The possibility of crosses between *S. coelicolor* A3(2) and *S. lividans* 66, first shown by Hopwood and Wright (1973), provides new approaches to the study of the recombination processes in *Streptomyces*. The data obtained in our crosses, involving A3(2) NF and 66 UF parents, seem to be rather interesting. In the cross S12 × A7 we detected a large proportion of heteroclones arising together with recombinants bearing the fragment which is usually donated by A3(2). We think that incomplete homology between the A3(2) and 66 chromosomes causes crossovers to be rarer than in crosses between A3(2) strains. As a result recombination frequencies are decreased and heteroclones are observed easily on selective plates.

When *strA1* or *cys1$^+$*, situated on the A3(2) fragment which is considered to be rarely donated to UF, served as selected markers, colonies of heteroclones and/or heterokaryons arose on selective plates after 3–4 days of incubation. At this time recombinants were observed comprising both the entire A3(2) chromosome with a small fragment of 66 chromosome and the whole 66 chromosome with a fragment of A3(2). On the basis of these data we suggested that recombinants do not arise exclusively as a result of the transfer of chromosomal material from donor to recipient by a process resembling conjugation. The fusion of substrate mycelium hyphae and heterokaryon formation might be an alternative route leading finally to the production of recombinants. Recombination between whole parental chromosomes might readily occur in heterokaryons and in this way any fragment from both chromosomes might be included in recombinants. The possibility of recombinant formation via a heterokaryotic stage was discussed by Sermonti (1969b). However, only now, after the identification of fertility types in A3(2) (Hopwood *et al.*, 1973), have we the experimental basis to distinguish the modes of recombinant formation.

We suggest that, in NF × UF, NF × IF and NF × NF crosses between A3(2) strains, recombinants may be produced both by conjugational transfer and as a result of chromosomal interaction in heterokaryons. In NF × UF and NF × IF crosses, recombinants derived in the former way must predominate. In NF × NF crosses both processes may lead to recombinant formation, while in UF × UF and IF × IF crosses it is more plausible that recombination occurs only in heterokaryons as a result of the interaction of whole parental chromosomes. A failure to detect heterokaryons and heteroclones in this case is likely to be attributed to the high frequency of recombination. Evidence for these suggestions may be obtained in further experiments using A3(2) × A3(2) and A3(2) × 66 crosses where parents lacking the plasmid SCP1 would be employed, and under conditions preventing heterokaryon formation.

Acknowledgement

We thank N. M. Mkrtumian for advice and many helpful discussions.

References

Blinov, N. O., Lomtatidze, Z. S. and Khokhlov, A. S. (1971). *Antibiotiki* (in Russian), **12**, 1105.
Georgopoulos, C. P. (1969). *J. Bact.* **97**, 1397.
Gorini, L. and Beckwith, J. R. (1966). *A. Rev. Microbiol.* **20**, 401.
Hawthorne, D. C. and Mortimer, R. K. (1963). *Genetics*, **48**, 617.
Hopwood, D. A. (1966). *Genetics*, **54**, 1169.
Hopwood, D. A., Chater, K. F., Dowding, J. E. and Vivian, A. (1973). *Bact. Rev.* **37**, 371.
Hopwood, D. A. and Wright, H. M. (1973). *J. gen. Microbiol.* **77**, 187.
Krasilnikov, N. A., Sorokina, E. I., Alferova, V. A. and Bezubenkova, A. P. (1965). "The Biology of Certain Groups of Actinomycetes" (Ed. N. A. Krasilnikov), p. 74. Science Press, Moscow.
Kutzner, H. J. and Waksman, S. A. (1959). *J. Bact.* **78**, 528.
Lomovskaya, N. D., Emeljanova, L. K. and Alikhanian, S. I. (1971). *Genetics*, **68**, 341.
Lomovskaya, N. D., Mkrtumian, N. M., Gostimskaya, N. L. and Danilenko, V. N. (1972). *J. Virol.* **9**, 258.
Seale, T. N. (1968). *Genetics*, **58**, 85.
Sermonti,   G. (1969a). "Genetics of Antibiotic-Producing Microorganisms". Wiley-Interscience, London.
Sermonti, G. (1969b). *In* "Genetics and Breeding of *Streptomyces*". p. 21. Proc. Internat. Symp., Dubrovnik. Yugoslav Acad. Sci. and Arts, Zagreb.

Interactions of the plasmid SCP1 with the chromosome of *Streptomyces coelicolor* A3(2)

D. A. HOPWOOD and H. M. WRIGHT

*Department of Genetics, John Innes Institute,
Colney Lane, Norwich NR4 7UH, England*

Summary

SCP1$^+$ (IF) strains of *Streptomyces coelicolor* A3(2), bearing the autonomous plasmid SCP1, give rise to strains that donate chromosomal markers to SCP1$^-$ (UF) strains with high frequencies. In various of these donors, SCP1 has interacted with the chromosome in at least three different ways.

1. In SCP1$'$ strains, analogous to F$'$ strains of *Escherichia coli* K-12, chromosomal regions have been inserted into SCP1; markers on these regions are donated to SCP1$^-$ strains with the same high efficiency as is SCP1 by SCP1$^+$ strains, and these markers become heterozygous in suitably marked recipients. Heterozygosity is prolonged in the case of SCP1$'$-*cysB*, but transient for SCP1$'$-*argA*, *uraB*, the plasmid-linked (exogenote) alleles of *argA* and *uraB* apparently replacing the chromosomal (endogenote) alleles by crossing-over. Most non-plasmid-linked loci are rarely donated by SCP1$'$ strains, although markers near to the chromosomal region corresponding to that borne by the plasmid, on one side only, may be donated slightly more often.

2. Unidirectional donors donate chromosomal markers with frequencies depending on their linkage, in one direction, to a point on the chromosome that varies with different donors. New evidence supports the hypothesis that at least the unstable subclass of unidirectional donors are SCP1$'$ strains in which SCP1 has incorporated unmarked chromosomal regions, and that these, perhaps because they contain specific nucleotide sequences, readily undergo "donor crossing-over" with corresponding regions of the main chromosome, leading to efficient marker mobilization. A stable subclass of unidirectional donors may have the plasmid permanently associated with the chromosome.

607

3. Bidirectional donors, of which NF is the type specimen, donate markers according to the closeness of their linkage, in either direction, from a chromosomal site. In stable donors of this type the plasmid is probably permanently associated with the chromosome.

Introduction

Streptomyces coelicolor A3(2), and many of its mutational and recombinant derivatives, bear the autonomous plasmid SCP1. The fertility type of such strains has been called IF (initial fertility) but the more descriptive term of SCP1$^+$ will be applied to them in this paper. The plasmid is occasionally lost by SCP1$^+$ strains to yield UF (ultrafertility) strains, henceforth referred to as SCP1$^-$. (For a detailed historical account of the fertility system of *S. coelicolor* A3(2), including its terminology, see Hopwood *et al.*, 1973.)

SCP1$^-$ strains donate chromosomal markers to each other at a low but detectable frequency (Vivian and Hopwood, 1970). When SCP1 is introduced into such a strain, converting it to SCP1$^+$, the frequency of chromosomal marker donation to SCP1$^-$ strains usually increases, although not by a large factor, while SCP1 donation in the same cross is extremely efficient (Hopwood *et al.*, 1973). This latter finding provided part of the evidence for the existence of SCP1 as an autonomous entity (Vivian, 1971). *A priori* it was expected that at least part of the chromosomal marker donation by SCP1$^+$ cultures might be due to clones within them in which SCP1 had interacted with the chromosome. In these clones the plasmid would retain its capacity for efficient invasion of an SCP1$^-$ culture, but would tend to take with it chromosomal markers of the donor strain. The markers transferred by any particular donor clone would depend on the geometry of the interaction between chromosome and plasmid that occurred in the origin of that donor.

Although the nature of marker transfer in an SCP1$^+$ × SCP1$^-$ cross is far from being completely understood (as is also still true of the corresponding F$^+$ × F$^-$ cross in *Escherichia coli* K-12: Curtiss, 1969; Evenchik *et al.*, 1969), the working hypothesis that at least part of the transfer is due to donor clones has proved, operationally, very fruitful. A variety of donor strains has indeed been isolated from a single SCP1$^+$ culture. The procedure, first used by Vivian and Hopwood (1973), is an indirect screening of colonies, derived from an irradiated SCP1$^+$ spore population, for their ability to donate particular wild-type alleles to SCP1$^-$ cultures bearing various auxotrophic markers.

In this paper we shall briefly describe some new data on the better characterized of these donor types and discuss experiments which bear on their genome structure. As will emerge, a number of questions still remain unanswered about the nature of the interactions between chromosome and plasmid in most of the donor types.

Material and methods

Strains derived from two different wild types were involved. *Streptomyces coelicolor* A3(2) is the well-known strain on which nearly all genetic studies of this species have been performed (Hopwood *et al.*, 1973). *Streptomyces lividans* 66, kindly supplied by Dr N. D. Lomovskaya, was referred to as "*Actinomyces coelicolor* strain 66" by Lomovskaya *et al.* (1971, 1972, 1973) and as "*S. lividans* 1326" by Hopwood and Wright (1973a, 1973b). It will henceforth be referred to as *S. lividans* 66, the name now adopted by the Russian group (Alikhanian *et al.*, 1975). Although the taxonomic criteria described by Krasilnikov (1965), which led to the proposal of a new specific designation for this strain, like any taxonomic criteria, might be disputed, the finding of poor chromosomal homology between strains A3(2) and 66 (Hopwood and Wright, 1973b, and this paper) makes it appropriate to assign the strains to different species.

For media and standard cultural procedures, see Hopwood (1967); for phage techniques and methods of mutagenesis and crossing, see Hopwood *et al.* (1973). The isolation and characterization of donor strains were essentially as described by Vivian and Hopwood (1973) and Hopwood and Wright (1973b).

Transfer of SCP1 and its derivatives between *S. coelicolor* A3(2) and *S. lividans* 66 was studied in various ways. Transfer, in either direction, of SCP1′ plasmids was detected by selection of prototrophic plasmid-linked markers, with auxotrophic chromosomal markers for counter-selection. Transfer of the wild-type SCP1 and other plasmids derived from it from *S. coelicolor* to *S. lividans* was followed by the visual selection procedure of Hopwood and Wright (1973a) which depends on the recognition of "pocks" on a lawn of wild-type *S. lividans* growing on minimal medium; each "pock" represents a microcolony of plasmid-bearing *S. lividans* producing the SCP1 antibiotic (see below) and so causing a minute zone of inhibition in the sensitive *S. lividans* background population. One or more chromosomal auxotrophic markers were used to select against the *S. coelicolor* donor parent. Plasmid transfer from *S. lividans* to *S. coelicolor* occurs at a much lower frequency (Hopwood and Wright, 1973a, 1973b), necessitating the use of a more powerful selection based on the resistance conferred by SCP1 to its own antibiotic. A streptomycin-sensitive plasmid-carrying *S. lividans* strain was crossed with a streptomycin-resistant SCP1⁻ strain of *S. coelicolor* and the output of the cross was densely spread on complete medium plates containing streptomycin, on which patches of a differently marked streptomycin-resistant SCP1⁺ strain were then inoculated. Antibiotic produced by these patches arrested development of the majority *S. coelicolor* SCP1⁻ population, while those few clones that had received the plasmid from *S. lividans* developed to maturity (Fig. 1).

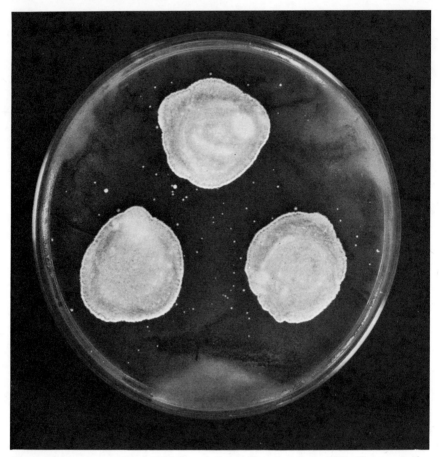

FIG. 1. Selection for transfer of SCP1 from *S. lividans* 66 to *S. coelicolor* A3(2). The output of a cross of SCP1$^+$ *S. lividans* (streptomycin sensitive) with SCP1$^-$ *S. coelicolor* (streptomycin resistant) was densely plated on complete medium plus streptomycin and three patches of a differently marked SCP1$^+$ strain of *S. coelicolor* were then added. Antibiotic produced by these patches arrested the development of the majority SCP1$^-$ *S. coelicolor* population, but resistant SCP1$^+$ progeny have developed to maturity and are recognizable where competition by the background population is relieved.

Results and discussion

THE SCP1 ANTIBIOTIC

Unpublished experiments by L. F. Wright in this laboratory have shown the "inhibitor" produced by SCP1-bearing strains (Vivian, 1971) to be a comparatively small molecule whose action is not specific against aerial mycelium production by SCP1$^-$ strains, as was first thought; young vegetative growth is also inhibited, as are various eubacteria. Moreover, genetic studies by R. Kirby in this laboratory indicate a relatively complex genetic determination of inhibitor production. These considerations suggest that the inhibitor can appropriately be called an antibiotic. It continues to be an extremely useful marker for SCP1.

DONOR TYPES ISOLATED FROM SCP 1⁺ (IF) CULTURES

The best characterized donor types are as follows: (1) SCP1′ strains (named by analogy with F′ strains of *E. coli* K-12); (2a) stable unidirectional donors; (2b) unstable unidirectional donors; (3a) stable bidirectional donors (NF is the type specimen); (3b) unstable bidirectional donors. Other donor types undoubtedly exist; for example, we have isolated a strain that transfers markers to SCP1⁻ with a high and uniform frequency, irrespective of map position. However, none of these other donor types has been adequately studied.

1. *SCP1′ strains* Two more SCP1′ strains have been added to the first example of this type, SCP1′-*cysB* (strain 1873) (Hopwood and Wright, 1973b). These clones (strains 1928 and 1937) were isolated from 11 300 survivors of uv irradiation of SCP1⁺ strain 12 in one experiment. The two strains resemble each other, except that strain 1937 produces no antibiotic, although retaining antibiotic resistance.

Strains 1928 and 1937 differ from strain 1873 (SCP1′-*cysB*) in several ways (Table 1). The most obvious is the specificity of marker donation (Fig. 2).

TABLE 1
Some properties of SCP1′ strains

Property	SCP1′-*cysB* (strain 1873)	SCP1′-*argA, uraB* (strains 1928 and 1937)
Known plasmid-linked loci	*cysB*	*argA, uraB*
Nearest loci known not to be plasmid-linked		
—clockwise	*adeA*	*att-VP5*
—anticlockwise	*metB*	*hisA*
Instability (proportion of SCP1⁻ derivatives)	6%	high
Heterozygosity of plasmid-linked markers after		
transfer to* —SCP1⁻ *S. coelicolor*	prolonged	transient
—*S. lividans*	prolonged	prolonged
Antibiotic resistance	+	+
Antibiotic production	+	+ (1928); − (1937)

* See Table 2.

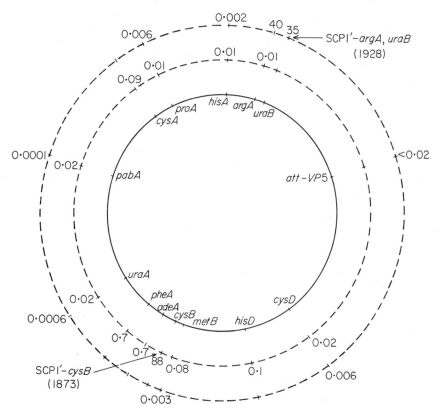

FIG. 2. Approximate percentage frequencies of inheritance of donor markers from SCP1´-cysB (1873) or SCP1´-argA, uraB (1928) in crosses with SCP1⁻ recipients. The frequency for att-VP5, studied only as a nonselected marker, is so far known imprecisely.

Strains 1928 and 1937 transfer *argA* and *uraB* at least 1000-fold more frequently than most other loci tested; the former are therefore candidates for plasmid-linkage, just as *cysB* is plasmid-linked in SCP1´-*cysB*. This conclusion was confirmed by the study of heterozygotes produced by mating with *argA* and *uraB* SCP1⁻ strains of *S. coelicolor* and *S. lividans* (see below). Strains 1928 and 1937 are therefore designated SCP1´-*argA, uraB*. More precise determination of the limits of the chromosomal insertions into SCP1 in these strains must await study of the transfer of members of a group of incompletely mapped loci in the *argA-uraB* region (Hopwood *et al.*, 1973). For the present we can simply say that they do not include *att-VP5* on one side and *hisA* on the other.

The spontaneous "instability" of SCP1´-*cysB*, that is the proportion of SCP1⁻ clones in a culture, is rather constant at about 6 per cent (Hopwood and Wright, 1973b). In contrast, the SCP1´-*argA, uraB* strains resemble the least stable of the unidirectional donors (Vivian and Hopwood, 1973); large clonal fluctuations make an average estimate of instability meaningless.

Perhaps the most significant difference between the SCP1'-*cysB* and SCP1'-*argA, uraB* strains concerns the behaviour of plasmid-linked donor markers after transfer to *S. coelicolor* or *S. lividans* recipients. The SCP1' strains (each bearing the counter-selectable chromosomal marker *pheA1*) were crossed with SCP1⁻ *S. coelicolor* strains carrying *cysB6, argA1* or *uraB2*, as appropriate, and with *S. lividans cys-3* or *arg-9* mutants. Phenotypically prototrophic progeny were selected on minimal medium. Several colonies were

TABLE 2

Fate of heterozygous prototrophs produced by transfer of SCP1' plasmids to SCP1⁻ strains on prolonged subculture

S. coelicolor donor	SCP1⁻ recipient	Prototrophs/ recipient	Number of prototrophic clones losing heterozygosity during subculture
SCP1'-*cysB* (1873)	*S. coelicolor cysB6*	8.8×10^{-1}	0/9 after 4 subcultures
SCP1'-*cysB* (1873)	*S. lividans cys-3*	8.0×10^{-2}	0/3 after 3 subcultures
SCP1'-*argA, uraB* (1928)	*S. coelicolor argA1*	4.0×10^{-1}	4/10 after 2 subcultures
SCP1'-*argA, uraB* (1937)	*S. coelicolor argA1*	1.5×10^{-1}	10/10 after 2 subcultures
SCP1'-*argA, uraB* (1928)	*S. coelicolor uraB2*	3.5×10^{-1}	10/10 after 3 subcultures
SCP1'-*argA, uraB* (1937)	*S. coelicolor uraB2*	3.0×10^{-1}	2/5 after 1 subculture
SCP1'-*argA, uraB* (1928)	*S. lividans arg-9*	7.7×10^{-3}	0/5 after 5 subcultures

streaked on minimal medium to eliminate possible contamination by auxotrophic recipient spores and a colony from each clone was re-streaked on medium containing cysteine, arginine or uracil, as appropriate, to allow the possible segregation of the recessive allele. This was detected by subsequent replication of the colonies to minimal medium. For those streakings that showed segregation the procedure was repeated for a further round or rounds (Table 2).

Although the numbers so far analysed are not large, the following conclusions can be drawn. In the case of SCP1'-*cysB* (strain 1873) the phenotypically Cys⁺ progeny remained heterozygous indefinitely, with *cys*⁺ on the plasmid (exogenote) and *cys*⁻ on the chromosome (endogenote), whether the recipient was *S. coelicolor* or *S. lividans*. In contrast, phenotypically Arg⁺ or

Ura$^+$ progeny produced by transferring the SCP1'-*argA, uraB* plasmids of strains 1928 or 1937 into *S. coelicolor* recipients remained heterozygous for only a few sub-cultures before pure Arg$^+$ or Ura$^+$ clones emerged. However, in *S. lividans*, there was prolonged heterozygosity for *arg* (no suitable *S. lividans ura* mutant is so far available). The pure Arg$^+$ or Ura$^+$ clones produced from prototrophic heterozygotes in *S. coelicolor* probably arose by integration of the plasmid-linked *arg$^+$* or *ura$^+$* allele into the chromosome by crossing-over to replace the recessive chromosomal allele, followed by loss of the plasmid, since the great majority of the pure Arg$^+$ or Ura$^+$ clones showed no evidence of the presence of plasmid functions (antibiotic production for strain 1928 and antibiotic resistance for both strains). Other classes of derivative strains also arose from the *S. coelicolor* Arg$^+$ heterozygotes, some interpretable as having lost the chromosomal region inserted into the plasmid, thereby reverting to SCP1$^+$.

We postulate that the chromosomal insertion into the plasmid in the SCP1'-*argA, uraB* strains is long enough to allow fairly frequent crossing-over between it and the corresponding region of the main chromosome, provided that they are completely homologous. Lack of such crossing-over with the *S. lividans* chromosome is consistent with the conclusion of poor chromosomal homology between *S. coelicolor* and *S. lividans* (Hopwood and Wright, 1973b). Presumably the chromosomal insertion in the SCP1'-*cysB* strain is shorter so that, even in *S. coelicolor,* crossing-over between exogenote and endogenote is not easily detected.

The frequency of transfer of SCP1'-*argA, uraB* from strain 1928 into *S. lividans* was nearly 1 per cent (Table 2), within the range determined for SCP1'-*cysB* (Hopwood and Wright, 1973b). Transfer back to *S. coelicolor,* determined by selecting either the *argA$^+$* or *uraB$^+$* allele, occurred at a frequency of 10^{-3} to 10^{-5}; this appears to be higher than for SCP1'-*cysB* (10^{-5} to 10^{-6}: Hopwood and Wright, 1973b), but neverthelss lower than in the forward direction.

2. *Unidirectional donors* A strain (2106) designated a *cysD* donor by analogy with the *pabA* and *uraA* donors described previously (Vivian and Hopwood, 1973) has been isolated (Fig. 3), bringing to three the patterns of marker transfer amongst known unidirectional donors. Strain 2106 belongs to the "stable" category, no nondonors having been found among 2000 colonies examined after uv irradiation.

As discussed previously (Hopwood *et al.,* 1973), three pieces of evidence indicate that chromosomal markers transferred efficiently by unidirectional donors, unlike those transferred by SCP1' strains, are not plasmid-linked: (1) no chromosomal marker is donated with the same high efficiency as the plasmid antibiotic marker; (2) marker transfer falls systematically with map distance from the maximally transferred locus (Fig. 3); (3) no persistent

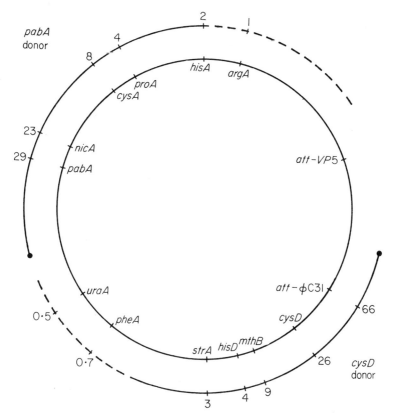

FIG. 3. Approximate percentage frequencies of inheritance of donor markers from unidirectional donors 2106 (stable *cysD* donor) and A607 and A608 (unstable and stable *pabA* donors respectively) in crosses with SCP1⁻ recipients. Where no figure is given for a particular locus or donor, the frequency is less than 0.5 per cent.

heterozygosity is found after transfer. An experiment bearing on the last point was performed with the new *cysD* donor. The average frequency of transfer of the *cysD⁺* allele by strain 2106 into a *cysD18* SCP1⁻ strain is 26 per cent (Fig. 3). In a reverse coupling cross between a recombinant derivative of strain 2106 carrying the mutant *cysD18* allele and a *cysD⁺* SCP1⁻ recipient, 25 out of 100 progeny inherited the donor *cysD18* allele. This result confirms the previous conclusion that progeny produced by crossing unidirectional donors with SCP1⁻ strains inherit donor markers by substitution rather than by addition.

In principle, unstable unidirectional donors might have arisen: (1) by a change in the plasmid alone (for example an insertion into it of a chromosomal region, the hypothesis favoured by Vivian and Hopwood, 1973); (2) by complementary changes in plasmid and chromosome; or (3) by a purely chromosomal change (for example by insertion into it of a plasmid region). Vivian and Hopwood (1973) favoured hypothesis (1) because of the finding that secondary donors produced by crossing the plasmid into new SCP1⁻ strains behaved like the original donors. However, owing to the very efficient transfer of chromosomal loci in such crosses, there was no guarantee that a region of the donor chromosome corresponding to the point of interaction with the plasmid had not been transferred to the new strain along with the plasmid. For the unstable *pabA* donor, A607 (Vivian and Hopwood, 1973), this objection has been overcome by transferring the plasmid to *S. lividans* 66 by means of the "pock" method (see Material and Methods) and back to a new SCP1⁻ strain of *S. coelicolor* by the antibiotic resistance method. A resistant clone was isolated that showed the unstable white colony phenotype shown by the original A607 and its characteristic gradient of marker donation. The frequency of plasmid transfer in both directions was similar to that of SCP1 and SCP1'. In view of the poor chromosomal homology between *S. coelicolor* and *S. lividans* it is very unlikely that a fragment of *S. coelicolor* chromosome could have replicated in *S. lividans* independently of the plasmid, enabling it to be later transferred back to *S. coelicolor*. This provides strong evidence in favour of hypothesis (1), that the special properties of at least one unstable unidirectional donor are due to a change in the plasmid alone.

Another experiment, which argues against hypothesis (3), consisted of reinfecting nondonor derivatives of A607, and also of the unstable *uraA* donor A610, with wild-type SCP1 from an SCP1⁺ strain. On hypothesis (3) the strains so produced should have behaved as unidirectional donors, whereas they were found to be SCP1⁺, the result expected on hypothesis (1).

3. *Bidirectional donors* The original example of this class, NF, belongs to the stable category of donors, with a nondonor segregation frequency of less than 10^{-4} (Vivian and Hopwood, 1970). From an SCP1⁺ culture we recently isolated a donor strain that appears to be the first example of an unstable bidirectional donor. This strain gives rise to about 5 per cent nondonors, apparently by plasmid loss. Chromosomal markers are transferred to SCP1⁻ in a bidirectional gradient resembling that in an NF × SCP1⁻ cross, but at a considerably lower frequency.

MARKER TRANSFER BY DONOR STRAINS

The physical basis of conjugation leading to SCP1 transfer in *S. coelicolor* A3(2) remains unknown. Apart from this major gap in our understanding there appear to be no particular problems associated with the transfer of plasmid-linked chromosomal markers by SCP1' strains, which seem to be very comparable with F' strains of *E. coli* K-12. The same cannot be said of marker transfer by any of the other donor types. The hypothesis of "donor crossing-over" to account for marker transfer by unstable unidirectional donors still appears the most plausible, and has been strengthened by the unchanged behaviour of the plasmid of such a strain after transfer into *S. lividans* and back to *S. coelicolor* (see above). On this hypothesis, SCP1′ strains should differ from the unidirectional donors only in bearing marked chromosomal insertions, instead of unmarked regions, and should therefore also donate preferentially chromosomal markers on one side of the region corresponding to the plasmid insertion. The SCP1′-*cysB* strain shows perhaps a very slight tendency to donate *adeA* and *pheA*, immediately clockwise of *cysB*, at higher frequencies than other markers (Fig. 2). Since it appears that the chromosomal region in the plasmid of this strain is not long enough for crossing-over often to integrate the exogenote (see above), "donor crossing-over" might also be rare, so that efficient chromosome mobilization by this process would not be expected. In the SCP1′-*argA, uraB* strains the chromosomal insertion is longer, by the criterion of exogenote marker insertion, so that "donor crossing-over" should also occur more frequently. The *hisA* gene, anticlockwise of *argA*, is certainly not donated at high frequency; unfortunately a suitable marker close to and clockwise of *uraB* is yet to be found but we can say that transfer of *att-VP5*, admittedly not very close to *uraB*, occurs at a frequency of less than 0.02 per cent (Fig. 2).

It appears, then, that none of the known SCP1′ strains transfers genes not linked to the plasmid with frequencies approaching those shown by the unidirectional donors. We may speculate that efficient interaction between plasmid and chromosome in the latter strains is due to the special nature of the chromosomal insertions carried by their plasmids. It is suggestive that, with the exception of the single *uraA* donor A610, all such strains have the presumptive origin of their chromosomal insertion in one or other of the two "silent regions" of the linkage map. These regions were postulated by Dowding and Hopwood (1973) to be preferentially involved in the integration of plasmids and prophages, with the possibility that recombination might be unusually frequent in these sites. This could conceivably cause efficient "donor crossing-over" also. Suggestively the presumptive chromosomal insertion into the plasmid in strain A610, of a region somewhere between *pheA* and *uraA*, may include an alternative attachment site for the prophage ϕC31 (Lomovskaya *et al.*, 1973). The recently isolated unstable bidirectional donor also has its site of interaction with the chromosome in one of the "silent regions".

The view has previously been discussed that the stable donors, both unidirectional and bidirectional, have the plasmid permanently associated with the chromosome, i.e. integrated (Hopwood *et al.*, 1973). This interpretation rests primarily on the observation of stability itself: the rate of loss of the plasmid-linked antibiotic marker, together with the donor properties characteristic of each strain, is considerably lower than the rate of loss of the wild-type SCP1 plasmid from SCP1⁻ strains. Discrimination between autonomous and integrated plasmids would be greatly aided by the isolation of plasmid DNA. Covalently closed circular (extrachromosomal) DNA of about 20×10^6 daltons molecular weight has recently been found in *S. coelicolor* A3(2) (Schrempf *et al.*, 1975), but it probably does not correspond to SCP1; we are continuing the search for the DNA of SCP1.

An alternative approach would be the use of recombination-deficient *(rec⁻)* mutants, which are unfortunately still lacking in *S. coelicolor*. *S. lividans* 66 appears to have poor overall DNA homology with *S. coelicolor* A3(2) and therefore, in crosses with *S. coelicolor*, can partially fulfil the role of a *rec⁻* mutant, as in the study of the SCP1′ strains described above. We are currently studying the transfer of plasmids from the various donor types into *S. lividans* to try to discriminate between autonomy and integration. Selection is for antibiotic production, using the "pock" method. "Pocks" are produced in crosses of donors of all types, including NF, at first sight suggesting that all donors have autonomously replicating plasmids. However, a number of factors may make such a conclusion premature. For example, evidence is accumulating that at least some classes of donors can readily give rise to derivatives with different properties, for example, SCP1⁺ and bidirectional donors from unstable unidirectional donors (Vivian and Hopwood, 1973) and SCP1⁺ and even SCP1′ in crosses of NF with SCP1⁻ strains (Sermonti and Puglia, 1975). Thus, to prove autonomy of the plasmid in an *S. coelicolor* donor, it would be necessary to transfer it into *S. lividans* and back into SCP1⁻ *S. coelicolor*, where it must confer the same donor properties as in the original *S. coelicolor* donor. This criterion has so far been satisfied only for unstable unidirectional *pabA* donor A607 (see above).

Acknowledgement

We thank Keith F. Chater for helpful comments on the manuscript.

References

Alikhanian, S. I., Lomovskaya, N. D. and Danilenko, V. N. (1975). Suppressor-sensitive mutations of *Streptomyces coelicolor* A3(2) and actinophage ϕC31. Proceedings of GIM 74. Academic Press, London and New York.
Curtiss, R. (1969). *A. Rev. Microbiol.* **23**, 69.
Dowding, J. E. and Hopwood, D. A. (1973). *J. gen. Microbiol.* **78**, 349.
Evenchik, Z., Stacey, K. A. and Hayes, W. (1969). *J. gen. Microbiol.* **56**, 1.
Hopwood, D. A. (1967). *Bact. Rev.* **31**, 373.
Hopwood, D. A., Chater, K. F., Dowding, J. E. and Vivian, A. (1973). *Bact. Rev.* **37**, 371.
Hopwood, D. A. and Wright, H. M. (1973a). *J. gen. Microbiol.* **77**, 187.

Hopwood, D. A. and Wright, H. M. (1973b). *J. gen. Microbiol.* **79**, 331.

Krasilnikov, N. A. (ed.) (1965). "Biology of Separate Groups of Actinomycetes". (In Russian). Nauka, Moscow.

Lomovskaya, N. D., Emeljanova, L. K. and Alikhanian, S. I. (1971). *Genetics,* **68**, 341.

Lomovskaya, N. D., Mkrtumian, N. M., Gostimskaya, N. L. and Danilenko, V. N. (1972). *J. Virol.* **9**, 258.

Lomovskaya, N. D., Emeljanova, L. K., Mkrtumian, N. M. and Alikhanian, S. I. (1973). *J. gen. Microbiol.* **77**, 455.

Schrempf, H., Bujard, H., Hopwood, D. A. and Goebel, W. (1975). *J. Bact.* **121**, 416.

Sermonti, G. and Puglia, A. M. (1975). Progressive fertilization in *Streptomyces coelicolor.* Proceedings of GIM 74. Academic Press, London and New York.

Vivian, A. (1971). *J. gen. Microbiol.* **69**, 353.

Vivian, A. and Hopwood, D. A. (1970). *J. gen. Microbiol.* **64**, 101.

Vivian, A. and Hopwood, D. A. (1973). *J. gen. Microbiol.* **76**, 147.

Subject Index

A

Acetate,
  in rifamycin biosynthesis, 141, 144, 145, 150
  in tetracycline biosynthesis, 156
Acridine, 536, 550
Acriflavine, 10, 258, 536, 550
Actinomyces coelicolor, see Streptomyces lividans
Actinomyces olivaceus, see also Streptomyces olivaceus
  bidirectional replication and chromosome transfer in, 557–562
  genetics of, 553ff
  haploid selection in, 557
  heteroclone analysis in, 554–557
  map of, 559
  mutants of, 554, 555
  pili of, 562
Actinophage φC31,
  host range of suppressor-sensitive mutants, 600
  mutation of, 597
  suppressor-sensitive mutants of, 595ff
Acyltransferase, 256, 267
Adenosine 3′:5′-cyclic phosphate (cAMP), role of in gene regulation, 30, 32, 35, 383, 415, 507, 589
Agaricus bisporus, virus diseases of, 324, 330–332
Alcaligenes faecalis, 465, 466
Alizarin, 475, 476
Amidase, 21, 22
α-Aminitin, resistance to in cultured cells, 80
Amino acid production, 437ff
  arginine, 447, 448
  derangement of metabolic control in producing organism, 443–445
  histidine, 446, 447
  phenylalanine, 440
  regulation of, 440–443, 446
  threonine, 445, 446
  tryptophan, 440
  tyrosine, 438–440
α-Aminoadipic acid, 130–132, 134, 179, 210, 452, 467
Aminocarboxybutylpenicillin (Penicillin N), 130–137, 192, 193, 256
  assay organism for, 465
  biosynthesis of, 264, 453, 464, 465
  co-production with cephalosporin C, 265, 270, 464, 465
  structure of, 257
7-Aminocephalosporanic acid (7-ACA), 254, 267
6-Aminopenicillanic acid (6-APA), 130, 254, 267
Aminopterin,
  resistance to in cultured cells, 79
  use of in cell fusion, 75
2-Aminopurine, 7
cAMP, *see* Adenosine 3′:5′-cyclic phosphate
Analogues of metabolites, *see* Metabolite analogues
Aneuploidy, 247, 249
Ansamycins, *see also* Rifamycins
  biosynthesis of, 139, 140ff
  relationship with macrolides, 153
  scheme of biogenesis, 149–152
Anthracyclines, 477–483
  biogenesis of, 478–481
  mechanism of action, 491
  producing organisms, 478
Antibiotics, *see* specific names
Arginase,
  of bacteria, 371, 372, 382–384
  of yeast, 391ff
Arginine, metabolism of, 369ff, 391ff
  in *Bacillus* spp, 372, 382–385

Arginine—*continued*
  in *E. coli*, 372–379
  in *Proteus* spp, 374
  in *Pseudomonas* spp, 372, 379–382
  in *Saccharomyces*, 391ff
  pathway of metabolism, 370–372
  production of, 447, 448
  regulation of,
      effect of mutation, 374–378, 393–398
      physiology of, 380–382, 398–405
Arthrospores, 269
Asparaginase, 45, 301ff
  assay of, 305
  location of genes controlling synthesis,
      302, 308, 309
  properties of, 307, 309, 310
  selective media for, 304, 305
  strains with high yields of, 307ff
  therapeutic use, 302
Aspergillus amstelodami
  linkage of brown spore colour (*brw*)
      and high growth rate genes in, 103
  quantitative analysis of growth rate in,
      97–105
Aspergillus foetidus, 335
Aspergillus nidulans
  aneuploidy in, 247
  arginine metabolism in, 382
  balanced lethals of, 249
  carbon catabolite repression in,
      412–415
  involvement of cAMP, 415
  comparison of sexual and parasexual
      crosses in, 106, 107, 230
  detection of epistasis in, 103–105
  heritability of quantitative characters
      in, 100
  mutants of, 201–208, 215–223, 249,
      250, 410ff
  nitrogen catabolism in, 400, 407
  penicillin production by, 200–210,
      213ff, 229ff
  rate of mitotic crossing-over in, 245
  relevance of work on, 243
  resistance to methylammonium in, 308
  selection for growth rate, 108, 109
  selection for penicillin titre, 108, 236–
      241
  tyrosinase of, 545
Aspergillus niger, 209, 243, 245, 335

Aureolic acid group of glycosides, 483ff
  antibiotic activity of, 491
Aureovocin, 157, 159, 163, 175, 475
Aureovocidin, 475
Auxotrophy,
  associated with resistance, 210
  effect on penicillin titre, 221, 224
  effect on virus titre, 325
8-Azaguanine, resistance to by cultured
      cells, 77–79
Azygospores, 504

B

Bacillus brevis
  and synthesis of gramicidin S, 115ff
  mutants affected in gramicidin S pro-
      duction, 127
  sporulation in, 423
Bacillus cereus, 425
Bacillus licheniformis, 372, 382–384
Bacillus subtilis
  acetyl hydrolase of, 181, 184
  altered DNA-polymerase mutants, 45
  arginine metabolism in, 372, 382–385
      effect of mutation, 384, 385
  assay of cephalosporin using, 256
  assay of penicillin using, 232
  replication of, 43
  sporulation of, 46, 421ff
Bacillus thuringiensis,
  parasporal protein of, 45
  sporulation in, 423, 432.
Bacteriophage λ, *see* Lambda phage
Bacteriophage Mu 1, 51, 52
Bacteriophage φ80, 49–51, 297, 378
Bacteriophage φX174, 12
Bacteriophage SV40, 54
Balanced lethals, 249
Barbiturates, role in rifamycin biosyn-
      thesis, 140, 149
Blakeslea trispora, 500–503
Blue-green algae, 373
Bradytrophic mutants, 17, 374
Breeding of microbial strains, *see* Hybrid-
      ization, Mutation
5-Bromodeoxyuridine (5-BUdR)
  and dark-repair mechanisms, 318, 319
  resistance to in cultured cells, 79

7-Bromomethyl benzanthracene, 12
5-Bromouracil, 7, 8

C

Caffeine, 10, 318–320
Canavanine, 374–376, 396, 447
Captan, 12
"Cascade" gene expression, 508
Catabolite repression,
    in bacteria, 23, 24, 26, 42, 46, 306, 381,
        383, 401, 421, 424
    in fungi, 407ff, 506, 507
    in yeast, 398–401, 404
Cell-free synthesis of gramicidin S, 118
Cephalosporin C, 130, 134–137, 184–189,
    193
    assay organisms for, 256, 465
    biosynthesis of, 129ff, 179ff, 264, 451ff
        regulation, 467, 468
    coproduction with penicillin N, 265, 452
    effect of mutation on synthesis of, 131,
        132, 253ff
    media for production of, 255, 256, 264,
        453
    methionine in synthesis of, 137, 269,
        270, 455–464
    structure of, 257
Cephalosporins, semi-synthetic, 270
    structures of, 257
Cephalosporium acremonium, 135, 179, 180,
        184, 187, 190, 194, 201, 452ff
    antibiotics of, 130, 134, 183, 256
    effect of aeration on antibiotic produc-
        tion by, 137
    isolation of tripeptide from, 131
    lineage of mutants used for cephalo-
        sporin production, 262, 263
    methionine uptake in, 457, 464
        kinetics of, 460
    morphological mutants of, 259, 261,
        265
    mutants blocked in antibiotic forma-
        tion, 131, 132, 201
    mutants deficient in cephalosporin syn-
        thetases, 181, 192, 261
    mutants enhanced in cephalosporin
        production, 253ff
    parasexual recombination in, 255, 267,
        270

    protoplasts of, 132
    sulphur metabolism of, 455ff
    variation in, 256, 258
Cephamycins, see also 7-Methoxycephalo-
        sporins, 452
Cephem antibiotics, see, Cephalosporin,
        β-Lactam antibiotics
Chlamydomonas reinhardi, and chloroplast
        genetics, 60, 63, 68
Chloramphenicol,
    multistep resistance to, 108
    resistance to in cultured cells, 79, 80
    resistance to in mitochondria, 62, 64,
        66, 69
Chlortetracycline (CTC), 156ff
    and primary metabolism of Strepto-
        myces, 171
    effect of mutations on synthesis, 157–
        161, 174–176
Chromocyclomycin, 485, 489, 490
Chromomycins, 485, 486, 490, 491
Chromosome assay, 107, 108
Chromosome duplication, see Aneuploidy
Chrysogenin, 208
Cinerubin A, 482
Citric acid, 209
Citrobacter freundii, 52
Cleistothecial analysis, 217–221, 231
Cochliobolus carbonum, 100
Coefficient of variation, 260, 268
Coelicomycin, 604
Coenzyme A, involvement in biosynthesis
    of
    amino acids, 364
    arginine, 371
    cephalosporin C, 189
    mithramycin, 490
    rifamycins, 145
    tetracyclines, 171–174, 478, 480
Co-fermentation,
    of penicillinless strains, 200
    of rifamycins, 149
Colchicine,
    as a mutagen in Aspergillus, 209
    as a mutagen in Cephalosporium, 258
    resistance to in cultured cells, 80
Collybia velutipes, 100, 102, 104
Complementation analysis,
    of gramicidin S synthetases, 127
    of oxytetracycline nonproducers, 518

Complementation analysis—*continued*
  of penicillinless mutants, 200, 201, 204, 208, 209, 210
  of petite mutants, 61
  of somatic cell auxotrophs, 81
  of white mutants in *Streptomyces*, 591
Computerization of genetic data, 515, 516
Co-mutation, 573ff
  detection of linkage by, 576, 577
  fine structure mapping by, 579
  in *E. coli*, 576
  in *Salmonella*, 579
  in *Streptomyces coelicolor*, 514, 573ff
  in *S. rimosus*, 514, 516, 517
  interspecific comparison by, 579, 580
Continuous culture, use in enrichment of mutants, 16–18, 296
Continuous variation, *see* Quantitative variation
Coordinate control, of gene expression, 377
Co-repressor, 379
Corynebacterium glutamicum, 385
  mutants of, 437ff
Co-synthesis, *see* co-fermentation
CRP factor, *see* cyclic AMP receptor protein
Cyclic AMP, *see* Adenosine 3′:5′-cyclic phosphate
Cyclic AMP receptor protein (CRP factor), 23, 32, 34, 35
Cysteine, involvement in antibiotic biosynthesis, 130, 210, 264, 268, 269, 285, 452
Cytochromes, in mutants of
  Saccharomyces, 361, 362
  Streptomyces, 174
Cytoplasmic inheritance, *see also* Mitochondria, Plasmids
  of killer factor, 333
  of melanin production, 535, 545, 550

D

Daunomycin, 482, 483

Deacetoxycephalosporin C, 130, 134, 179–189, 192, 193, 264, 464–468
  assay of, 465
Deacetylcephalosporin C, 130, 134, 179, 180, 184–189, 192, 256, 264, 453, 464–471
  assay of, 465
  structure of, 257
Diaminopimelic acid, in cell walls of *Nocardia*, 140
Dichlorvos, 12
Differentiation, in *Streptomyces*, 583ff
  mutations affecting, 584–592
Dimethyl sulphate (DMS), 258
Diplococcus pneumoniae, 293
Diploidization, *see also* Parasexual cycle, 245–247, 250, 277, 283, 284
DNA,
  action of restriction enzymes on 33, 52–55, 299
  binding of with anthracyclines, 491
  gaps in, 12
  hybrid molecules of, 52–55, 299
  hybridization, 69, 378
  in genomes of *Streptomyces* and *E. coli*, 518, 568, 576
  interspecific transfer of, 52–54
  of chloroplasts, 63
  of mitochondria, (mitDNA), 62, 66, 68–70, 85, 86
  of λ phage, 32, 33, 49
  of plasmids, 53, 54, 618
  of SV40 phage, 54
  polymerases of, 9, 45, 319
  repair of, 8, 10–12, 316ff
  replication of, 10, 11, 43, 44
  role in gene expression, 29ff, 292, 299
  thymine in synthesis of, 43, 44
  transformation of cultured cells by, 88
Dominance, in quantitative genetics, 96, 97, 105, 108
Dominance, tests of, in
  ammonium repressed mutants, 411
  mutants with decreased penicillin yield, 204, 209
  mutants with increased penicillin yield, 221, 222, 226
Double-stranded RNA viruses, 323ff
Drosophila melanogaster,
  genetic determination of abdominal

chaetae number in, 95, 96
genetic variation in, 95
Duplication strain(s), 248, 249

E

Effector molecules, 31, 37
Emericellopsis glabra, see also Cephalosporium acremonium, 268
End-product inhibition, 373, 446, 468
Enzymes, *see also* specific names
    allelic variation in populations, 96
    and the *in vitro* synthesis of gramicidin S, 115ff
    improvement in yield of, 17ff, 301ff
    involved in cephalosporin biosynthesis, 180ff, 468–471
    mutants altered in production of, 17ff, 302ff
    of amino acid biosynthesis, 440–445
    of arginine metabolism, 369ff, 393ff
    of cultured cells, 75, 82–87
    of *Streptomyces*, 171–174, 476, 477
    of trisporic acid synthesis, 500, 501
Epichlorohydrin, 258
Epistasis, 591
    in quantitative genetics, 96, 97, 103–105, 110, 236, 239
    of mutations increasing penicillin yield, 222, 223
Error-prone repair, 11, 12
Erythromycin,
    biosynthesis of, 492
    inhibition of cytochromes by, 361
    resistance in mitochondria, 62, 64, 66, 69
Escherichia coli
    arginine metabolism in, 372–379
    asparaginase production by, 301ff
    bacteriophage sensitivity of, 310
    co-mutation in, 576
    conjugation in, 305
    F factors in, 45, 48, 50, 297, 608, 616
    genetic manipulations of, 53, 54, 291ff
    genome size of, 518, 568, 576
    heterogenous clones of, 528, 554
    mapping of asparaginaseless mutations in, 308, 309

mating time of, 568
mechanisms of mutation in, 8, 315, 316
overproduction of β-galactosidase by, 17, 18, 46, 47
polymerase enzymes I, II and III of, 9
replication of, 43
resistance to chloramphenicol in, 108
resistance to 5'-methyltryptophan in, 19
survival of after mutagenesis, 316–320
threonine production by, 445
Ethidium bromide, 61, 62, 68, 536
Ethyl methanesulphonate (EMS), as a mutagen, 13, 202, 203, 208, 258, 315, 316, 321, 360
Ethyleneimine, as a mutagen, 246
    in conjunction with ultraviolet light, 275, 281
Euflavine, 61
Excision repair, in *E. coli*, 9, 10, 316
    in *Methylococcus*, 317–321

F

F factors, *see under Escherichia coli*
Filament formation, in methane-utilizing bacteria, 316–318
Fine structure mapping, by co-mutation, 579
Flocculation, in yeast,
    estimation of, 342, 343
    genetic analysis of, 339–346, 351, 352
    importance of, 340, 341
meta-Fluorophenylalanine, 438
para-Fluorophenylalanine (PFP), 204, 216, 223, 245, 438ff
5-Fluorouracil, 246, 333, 597
Frameshift mutations, 8
Fusarium moniliforme, 284

G

β-Galactosidase, 30
    from cultured plant cells, 88
    induction of, 21, 23, 24
    overproduction of, 17, 18, 46, 47
Galirubins, 483
Gamma irradiation, *see* Ionizing radiation

Gene action, *see also* Epistasis, 103, 109, 235, 236, 241

Gene amplification, .
  biochemical methods of enhancement, 298, 299
  by chromosomal gene duplications, 46, 47
  in bacteria, 18, 41ff, 309
  in yeast, 69, 70
  physiological control of, 42–46
  using mutator phage, 51, 52
  using plasmids, 47–49
  using transducing phage, 49–51, 292, 296–298

Gene conversion, 245

Gene dosage, *see* Gene amplification

Gene duplication, *see also* Gene amplification, 46, 47, 309–311

Gene expression,
  and yield of gene products, 36, 37
  autogenous control of, 35
  control of, 30ff, 291ff, 378, 379
    negative, 31–33
    positive, 34
    purpose, 34–36
  enhancement of, 41ff, 292ff
  involvement of cAMP in, 30, 32, 35, 383, 415, 507, 589
  of genes controlling arginine metabolism, 376–379
  of mating type in *Mucor*, 498–504, 508

Genetic engineering,
  of methane-utilizing bacteria, 314
  role of sporulating bacteria in, 433
  use of gene dosage in, 42
  use of plasmids in, 37, 38

Genetic instability, in fungi, 243ff, 330
  as a source of variation, 244
  due to aneuploidy, 247, 248
  reduction of,
    environmentally, 248, 249
    genetically, 249, 250
  use of in yield improvement, 247–250

Genetic mapping, *see* Mapping

Gibberella fujikuroi, 506

Glycolic acid, in rifamycin biosynthesis, 148

Glycosides,
  biogenesis of, 473ff
  of the aureolic acid group, 483ff

  structures of, 486
  sugars of, 487

Gramicidin S,
  biosynthesis of, 118–120
  cell-free synthesis of, 118
  effect of medium composition on, 120, 121, 123
  effect of mutation on producer organism, 127

H

Haemophilus influenzae, restriction endonuclease of, 33

Haemophilus sp., nonmutability of, 13

Haploid selection, in mapping of *Streptomyces*, 557

Haploidization, *see also* Parasexual cycle
  of *Aspergillus*, 204, 214, 216, 217, 223, 247
  of *Cephalosporium*, 267, 270
  of *Penicillium*, 231, 244

Hansenula, 504

HeLa cells, 75, 82

Heritability,
  estimation of, 99–101
  use in selection programmes, 110

Heteroclones, 513, 515, 523, 571, 603, 605
  aberrant, 524
  analysis of, 525–528, 554–557, 596
  isolation of, 566
  origin of, 566
  progressive completion of, 566, 567

Heterokaryon(s), *see also* Parasexual cycle,
  of *Cephalosporium*, 267
  of cultured cells, 75, 71–82
  of *Mucor*, 499, 508
  of *Penicillium*, 277
    transmission of viruses by, 327, 328
  of *Phycomyces*, 503
  of *Streptomyces*, 566, 574, 576, 596, 603, 605
  relationship with heteroclones, 566, 567
  tests, of mutants impaired in penicillin biosynthesis, 203, 204

Heterokaryon incompatibility,
  and quantitative variation, 108
  and sexual outcrossing, 233

and variation in penicillin titres, 233–235, 240, 241
Heterothallism, in the Mucorales, 498
Heterosis, 267
Histidase, 25, 26, 383
Histidine, production of, 446, 447
Homothallism, in the Mucorales, 505–507
    evolutionary significance of, 507
Human genetics,
    application of parasexuality to, 1, 2
    using cultured cells, 73ff
Hybrid(s), see also Recombinants
    cleistothecia, 217–221, 231
    DNA molecules, 52–55
    of bacteria, 49
    of somatic cells, 74ff
    of Streptomyces coelicolor and S. lividans, 596, 601–605
    of yeast, 340, 348, 358, 362
    plasmids, 53–54
Hybridization, see also Recombination, Somatic cell hybridization,
    applications of, 108
    combined with mutagenesis, 241, 273ff
    DNA/DNA and DNA/RNA, 69, 378, 379, 422, 425
    in strain improvement, 229, 236–241, 254, 274, 276–284, 286, 287
    of yeast, 348, 353
Hydrocarbon-utilization,
    by bacteria, 13, 313ff
    by yeast, 357ff
6-Hydroxyamino-purine, 360
Hydroxylamine, as a mutagen, 378

I

Idiophase, 210, 264
Immunodiffusion assay of virus titre, 325, 326, 328, 329
Interrupted crosses, of Streptomyces, 559, 567, 568
Ionizing radiation, 11, 12, 61, 258, 275, 281, 315, 316, 490, 536
    induction of penicillinless mutants by, 200, 202, 203, 209
Isochinocyklin A, 477
Isopencillin N, 130

K

Karyotype analysis, 82, 84
Killer phenotype of yeast, 324, 332–336
    genetics of, 333
    involvement of double-stranded RNA, 333–336
Klebsiella aerogenes,
    catabolite repression in, 26, 401
    genes controlling nitrogen fixation in, 49
    mutants of, 18, 22

L

β-Lactam antibiotics, see also Cephalosporin C, Penicillin
    biosynthesis of, 129ff, 179ff, 451ff
    component amino acids, 130, 131
    improvement in yield of, 273ff
    inhibition of cephalosporin synthetase by, 192, 193
    mutants impaired in biosynthesis of, 131, 132, 200ff, 464–471
    structures of, 130, 257
Lambda (λ) phage, 31–33, 34, 49, 50, 294, 295, 297–299, 311, 378
    DNA of, 32, 33, 49
    recombinant phage involving, 299
Lineweaver–Burk plot, 460
Localized mutagenesis, 378
Lysine,
    in single cell protein, 314
    involvement in antibiotic synthesis, 131, 132, 264, 268, 285, 452

M

Macrolide antibiotics,
    biogenesis of, 141, 474, 492
    relationship to ansamycins, 153
Malignancy, of somatic cells, 84, 85
Mapping,
    by computer in Streptomyces, 514–516
    by co-mutation, 573–577
    by antibiotic titre ratios, 217–221, 223–225
    of genes
        coding for asparaginase, 302

Mapping, of genes—*continued*
  in *Aspergillus,* 204–208, 213ff, 249, 250
  in cells grown in tissue culture, 82, 83
  in *E. coli,* 302, 303, 308, 309
  in *Saccharomyces,* 64, 67, 68, 69, 345, 346
  in *Streptomyces achromogenes,* 521ff
  in *S. coelicolor,* 576, 577, 579, 580 585–588, 592, 598–599, 602, 604
  in *S. glaucescens,* 538–541
  in *S. rimosus,* 513ff, 579, 580
  increasing penicillin yield, 214, 216–221, 223–226
  reducing penicillin yield, 204–208
  value of in strain improvement, 286, 287
Mating types
  of mitochondria, 67
  of *Mucor,* 498ff
  of *Saccharomyces,* 60, 67, 343, 346, 350, 353, 403
Melanin,
  nonproducing mutants of, 542–550
  production
    genetics of, 542–550
    physiology of, 540–542
Metabolite analogues, use of in mutant isolation, 16, 17, 19–21, 296, 374, 438–440, 445–448
Methane-oxidizing bacteria,
  availability, 314
  nonmutability of, 13, 315
  significance of, 314
Methanomonas methanooxidans, 314
Methionine,
  auxotrophs of hydrocarbon-utilizing yeast, 364
  in cephalosporin and penicillin production, 137, 269, 270, 455–464
  in single cell protein, 314
7-Methoxycephalosporins, *see also* Cephamycins, 130, 131
8-Methoxypsoralen, 10, 202, 203, 208
Methyl methanesulphonate (MMS), 11, 12, 315, 316
N-Methyl-*N'*-nitro-*N*-nitrosoguanidine (MNNG),
  as a mutagen in
    algae, 63

    bacteria, 13, 18, 304, 305, 308, 315, 321
    fungi, 202, 203, 258
    streptomycetes, 157, 161, 162, 522, 523, 536, 555, 557, 574
    yeast, 61
  co-mutation using, 574ff
  in conjunction with
    nitrous acid, 258
    ultraviolet light, 258
  toxicity of, 14
Methylene blue, 536
Methylobacter sp. 13, 315
Methylococcus capsulatus,
  nonmutability of, 13, 315ff
  survival after mutagenesis, 316–321
  transformation frequency of, 320
Methylocystis sp., 13, 315
Methylomonas sp., 13, 315
Methylosinus sp., 13, 315
Micrococcus luteus, exonuclease of, 9
Micrococcus radiodurans, nonmutability of, 13
Mithramycin, 485–491
  biosynthesis of, 490
  mechanism of action, 491
Mitochondria,
  biogenesis of in somatic cells, 85–86
  DNA of, 62, 66, 68–70, 85, 86
  drug resistance in, 62–65
  genetics of, 59
  isolation of mutants of, 60–64
  mating type, 67
  methods used in genetic analysis of, 65
  recombination and segregation in, 66–68, 86
Mitomycin C, 12, 316
Mitotic crossing-over, 108, 206, 207, 245, 246, 363
MNNG, *see N*-Methyl-*N'*-nitro-*N*-nitrosoguanidine
Morphology, and its relation to antibiotic production by
  Aspergillus, 203, 209, 220, 222, 225, 226
  Cephalosporium, 259, 261
  Penicillium, 226
  Streptomyces, 163–171
Mucor hiemalis, 507
Mucor mucedo, 499, 503–505, 507

Mucor pusillus, 507
Mucor racemosus, 507
Mucorales,
   expression of mating-type locus in, 497ff
   heterothallism in, 498
   homothallism in, 505–507
   hormones and prohormones of, 499–503
   mating process in, 498, 499
   thigmotropism in, 503–505
Multiple factor hypothesis, 95
Multiple-hit phenomenon, 259
Mushroom, *see Agaricus bisporus*
Mutagens, *see also* specific names
   carcinogenicity of, 14
   choice of, 12–14, 296
   specificity of, 200
Mutation, *see also* Co-mutation
   affecting amino acid production, 437ff
   affecting antibiotic production
      by *Aspergillus*, 200, 203–210, 214, 215
      by *Bacillus*, 127
      by *Cephalosporium*, 131, 181, 192, 201, 253ff, 455, 457, 463, 464–471
      by *Nocardia*, 141, 146, 147
      by *Penicillium*, 200–202, 208–210, 226, 280–287
      by *Streptomyces*, 156ff, 474–477, 489–490
   affecting enzyme production, 15ff, 301ff
   affecting gene expression, 295–298, 374–376
   affecting mating of *Mucor*, 503
   affecting melanin production, 542–550
   affecting metabolism of arginine, 370
   affecting sporulation, 428–432
   affecting ultrastructure of *Streptomyces*, 163–171
   and cytochromes of *Streptomyces*, 174
   and morphology of
      Aspergillus, 203, 209, 220, 222, 225, 226
      Cephalosporium, 259, 261, 265
      Penicillium, 226
      Streptomyces, 583ff
   as a source of variation, 244

   combined with hybridization, 241, 274ff
   in somatic cells, 76–81
   mechanisms of, 7ff, 315, 316
   mitochondrial, 59ff
   of bacteriophage, 297–298
   of hydrocarbon-utilizing yeast, 357ff
   of methane-utilizing bacteria, 313ff
   specificity of after revertant selection, 577, 579
Mutator phage, 51, 52
Mycobacterium tuberculosis, 531

N

Narrow heritability, 234
Neurospora crassa, 100, 103, 105, 108, 382
   tyrosinase of, 540, 545
Nicotiana tabacum, cell culture of, 87, 88
nif genes, *see* Nitrogen fixation genes
Nitrofurans, 12
Nitrogen fixation genes (*nif*), interspecific transfer of, 49
Nitrogen mustard, 12, 247, 248, 275, 278
Nitroquinoline-1-oxide, 12
N-Nitroso-N-methylurea (NMU), 555
N-Nitroso-N- methylurethane (NMU), 315
Nitrous acid, as a mutagen, 202, 203, 246, 258, 315, 316, 489, 490
   in conjunction with N-Methyl-N'-nitro-N-nitrosoguanidine, 258
Nocardia mediterranei,
   antibiotics of, 140, 141, 146
   distinction from *Streptomyces*, 140, 531
   genetic analysis of, 531, 532
   mutants of with altered antibiotic production, 141, 147
Nocardia NT19, 141
Nogalamycin, 482, 483
Nonbalanced lethals, 249
Nondisjunction, 244
Nonproducing mutants,
   of asparaginase, 303, 304, 308, 309
   of cephalosporin, 131, 132, 192, 201, 464–471
   of erythromycin, 492
   of gramicidin S, 127
   of melanin, 542–550

Nonproducing mutants—*continued*
  of mithramycin, 490, 491
  of oxytetracycline, 518, 519
  of penicillin, 200ff
    involvement of lysine, 210
  of rifamycins, 149
  of tripeptide and cephalosporin, 131,
    132
  of tyrosinase, 550
Nonsense mutations, 8, 376
Nonspecific induction, of arginase, 404,
  405

O

Ochre suppressors, 12
Oligomycin-resistance, in yeast mitochondria, 62, 64, 67–69
Oligomycin-sensitive ATPase, 59, 60
Omega (ω) factor, in yeast, 66–68
Operator-constitutive mutations, 32, 33,
  37, 377, 378, 401, 403, 404
Operator genes, 31–33, 34, 35, 37, 42,
  376, 377
  mutation in, 398
Operon,
  ara in *E. coli*, 21, 23
  arg in *E. coli*, 36, 377
  ctc in *Streptomyces*, 474
  gal in *E. coli*, 21
  his in *Salmonella*, 19, 35
  lac in *E. coli*, 21, 23, 24, 31, 292–294
  trp in *E. coli*, 293–295, 298
Ouabain, resistance to in cultured cells,
  80

P

Panmictic pool of *mit*DNA, 68
Paramecium aurelia, mitochondrial drug-
  resistance in, 65
Parasexual cycle,
  advantages of, in breeding, 244
  and genetic instability, 244–250
  and yield improvement, 247–250, 274,
    276–284
  comparison with sexual cycle, 106, 107,
    230
  disadvantages of, 230

discovery of, 200, 230
in *Cephalosporium*, 255, 267, 270
transmission of viruses by, 327–330
use in mapping, 204–206, 214
Parental genome segregation, 231
Paromycin, 64
Pasteurella, 49
Penem antibiotics, *see* β-Lactam antibiotics, Penicillin
Penicillaminic acid, 132–134
Penicillin,
  biosynthesis of, 129ff, 210
  media for production of, 275
  mutants impaired in synthesis of, 199ff
  mutants with increased production of,
    213ff, 273ff
  selection for increased titre of, 229ff
  strain improvement in production of,
    2, 273ff
  structure of, 257
Penicillin N, *see* Aminocarboxybutylpenicillin
Penicillin V, *see* Phenoxymethylpenicillin
Penicillinase, 46, 53, 54, 133, 275
Penicillium chrysogenum, 135, 202, 214, 269,
  460
  antibiotics of, 130
  balanced lethals of, 249
  discovery of parasexual cycle in, 200,
    230
  genetics of, 203, 208–210, 230, 231,
    244–246, 255, 267
  improvement of penicillin yield in, 226,
    244, 270, 273ff
  instability in commercial strains of,
    243ff
  isolation of tripeptide from, 131, 452
  mutation frequency in, 268
  penicillinless mutants of, 200, 201, 208,
    209
  rate of mitotic crossing-over in, 245, 246
  resistance to selenate, 209
  viruses of, 323–330
Penicillium notatum, 200, 210
Penicillium stoliniferum, 335
Peptide antibiotics, *see also* Gramicidin S
  cell-free synthesis of, 118
  importance of, 117–118
Perithecial analysis, *see* Cleistothecial
  analysis

Petite mutants in yeast,
  and antibiotic resistance, 63, 64
  cytoplasmic petites, 61
  isolation and characteristics of, 60–62
  nature of, 69, 70
  nuclear petites, 61
  suppressiveness, 61, 62
  use in deletion mapping, 68, 69
PFP, see para-Fluorophenylalanine
Phenoxymethylpenicillin (Penicillin V),
  135, 270
Phenylalanine, production of, 440
Photoreactivation, 316–318
Phycomyces, 503
Pichia guilliermondi, 358
Pili, of Actinomyces, 562
Plasmids,
  and gene amplification, 47–49, 299
  and genetic engineering, 37, 299
  coL factors, 48
  hybrid, 53, 54, 299
  interspecific transfer of, 48, 49
  pSC101, 53, 54, 299
  R factors, 48, 53
  R100, 48
  SCP1 of Streptomyces, 565–571, 588, 591,
    605, 607ff
    DNA of, 618
Plasmogamy, 504
"Pocks", due to antibiotic production by
  Streptomyces, 609, 616, 618
Polyene antibiotics, 477
Post-replication repair, 10, 11, 316–321
Post-translation, 433
Precocious recombinants of Streptomyces,
  570
Product derepression, 502
Prohormones, 498–503, 506
Promoters,
  mutants of, 33, 295, 296, 377
  role in gene expression, 31–34, 36, 42,
    55, 292–296, 299, 376, 377
β-Propiolactone, 258
Propionate, in rifamycin biosynthesis,
  141, 144, 145, 150
Proteus mirabilis,
  and the R100 plasmid, 48
  arginine metabolism in, 374, 376
Proteus morgani, 374
Proteus rettgeri, 374

Proteus sp.
  nonmutability of, 13
  plasmids of, 48, 49
Proteus vulgaris, 374
Protoplasts, of Cephalosporium, 132
Pseudomonas aeruginosa,
  arginine metabolism in, 372, 379–382
  catabolite repression in, 24
  mutants with altered catabolic en-
    zymes, 21, 22
  mutants of the histidine degradative
    pathway, 24–27
  resistance to analogues by, 19, 20
Pseudomonas fluorescens, 372, 379–382
Pseudomonas methanica, 314
Pseudomonas putida
  arginine metabolism in, 372, 379–382
  constitutive mutants of, 17
  histidine-degrading genes of, 27
  resistance to analogues by, 19
Pseudomonas reptilivora as an assay organ-
    ism for rifamycin SV, 147
Pyocyanine, 20
Pyrromycinones, 478–481

Q

Quantitative variation,
  applications of, 108–110
  environmental contribution to, 99–101
  genetic determination of, 95, 96
  in penicillin production, 230, 232–235
  methods of analysis, 96, 97

R

Recombinant(s), see also Hybrids
  carrying different genes determining
    increased penicillin yield, 222, 223
    226
  from crosses of Nocardia, 531, 532
  from crosses of Streptomyces, 515, 523–
    528, 538, 544, 545, 556–560, 565–
    570, 586–590, 598–605
  from diploids of Penicillium, 280
  from E. coli matings, 309
  precocious, of Streptomyces, 570

Recombination, *see also* Hybridization, Mitotic crossing-over
  and selection, 110
  and yield improvement, 229ff, 248, 276–284, 286, 287
  as a source of variation, 244, 573
  barriers to, 247
  between phage and bacterial DNA, 49–52
  deficient mutants of *Streptomyces*, 618
  frequencies, 163, 207, 208, 231, 516, 525–528, 538, 546, 548, 556, 558, 560, 569, 586, 587, 601
  in *Actinomyces*, 554, 556, 558, 560
  in *Aspergillus*, 204, 206–208, 230, 236–241
  in *Cephalosporium*, 255, 267, 270
  in mitochondria, 66–68, 86
  in *Nocardia*, 531, 532
  in *Streptomyces achromogenes*, 521ff
  in *S. aureofaciens*, 163
  in *S. coelicolor*, 566–571, 592, 596, 598
  in *S. glaucescens*, 540
  in *S. lividans*, 596
  involvement in mutation, 10–12, 316–321
  of natural variation, 241
  of whole chromosomes, 204, 216, 244, 245
Recombination repair, *see* Post-replication repair
Regulator gene, 375
Repressors, 31, 295, 362
  mode of action of *lac* repressor, 32, 33
  mode of action of λ repressor, 33
  of arginine synthetase enzymes, 373–377, 379, 381, 398–401
  of trisporic acid genes in Mucor, 500, 501
  of tyrosinase synthesis, 541, 542
  structure of *lac* repressor, 32
Restriction enzymes, 33, 52–55, 299
Rhizobium trifolii, 49
Rhodomycinones, 478–481
Rifampicin, inactivation of RNA polymerase by, 36
Rifamycins,
  antibiotic activity of, 531
  biosynthesis of, 139ff
  biosynthetic interrelationships, 146–152
  effect of phosphate on synthesis of, 149
  genetics of producing organisms, 531, 532
  structures of, 142, 143
RNA,
  double-stranded RNA viruses, 323ff
  hybridization with DNA, 69, 378, 379, 422, 425
  messenger (m)RNA, 42, 69, 377, 379, 421ff
  polymerase, 31, 33, 34, 36, 37, 46, 80, 292, 421–423, 584, 591
    structure of, 35, 422
  role in gene expression, 29ff, 292
  transfer (t)RNA, 30, 35, 47, 69, 375, 379, 426
Rubradirin, 522
Rutamycin, 64

S

Saccharomyces cerevisiae,
  arginine metabolism in, 391ff
    genes affecting, 394, 395
    induction of catabolism, 393–398
  nitrogen catabolite repression of, 398–401
  pathway of, 392
    role of inducer, 401–404
  auxotrophy of associated with resistance, 210
  breeding of, 340, 353
  flocculation of, 340–347
  gene amplification in, 46, 69, 70
  genetical analysis of, 339ff
  hydrocarbon-utilizing mutants of, 357ff
  killer phenotype in, 324, 332–336
  life cycle of, 60
  mapping of asparaginase gene in, 302
  mitochrondrial genetics of, 59ff
  mutant of with altered acid phosphatase, 18
  nonmutability by ethylmethanesulphonate, 13
  tryptophan synthetase genes in, 46
Saccharomyces lipolytica, 358

Salmonella, 49
  co-mutation in, 579
Salmonella gallinarum, 256
Salmonella phage P22, 34
Salmonella typhimurium
  ability to use *E. coli* genes, 37, 38
  arginine metabolism in, 373, 374
  catabolite repression in, 24
  his operon in, 19, 35
  replication of, 43
  repression in by histidine analogues, 19
Sarcina lutea, 465, 466
Schizophyllum commune,
  detection of linkage in, 103
  distribution of growth rate of, 98
  factors contributing to variation in, 102, 104, 105
  heritability of growth rate, 100
  selection in, 108
SCP1 sex factor of *Streptomyces,* 565–567, 571, 591, 605
  and production of an antibiotic, 588, 609–611
  DNA of, 618
  donor types of SCP1$^+$, 611–616
    bidirectional donors, 616
    SCP1$'$ strains, 611–614
    unidirectional donors, 614–616
  genetics of, 608
  interactions with the chromosome of *S. coelicolor,* 607ff
  marker transfer by donor strains of, 616–618
  properties of, 611
  transfer of in crosses, 568–570
Secondary metabolites,
  application of quantitative genetics to production of, 240
  effect of mutation on, 156, 268
  enzymatic synthesis of, 116, 117
  relationship with primary metabolism, 20, 174–176, 451–452, 464
Selenate, resistance to
  in *Aspergillus,* 206, 207
  in *Penicillium,* 209
Seleno-methionine, resistance to in *Cephalosporium,* 456–459
Sendai virus, use in cell fusion, 74, 75, 81
Serratia, 49
Sex factor of *Streptomyces, see* SCP1

Shigella, 48
Shikimate, in rifamycin synthesis, 145, 146
Sigma (σ) factor of *Bacillus,* 422
"Silent regions", of the *Streptomyces* linkage map, 557, 617
Single-cell protein, 314
Somatic cells,
  assignment of genes to chromosomes in, 76, 82, 83
  improvement of cell lines, 86, 87
  isolation of mutants, 76–81
  malignancy of, 84, 85
  organelle biogenesis in, 85, 86
Somatic cell hybridization, 74ff
  applications of, 81–87
  methods of cell fusion for, 74, 75
  of plant cell cultures, 87, 88
Spiramycin, 64
Sporulation,
  and antibiotic production, 423, 433, 588
  in relation to penicillin production, 274ff
  mutations affecting, 428–432, 585–588, 589–593
  of *Bacillus* spp., 45, 46, 421 ff
  of *Streptomyces,* 583, 584, 589–592
  of yeast, 340ff, 358
  regulation of, 419ff
  significance of, 420
Staphylococcus aureus,
  nonadditivity of penicillinase genes in, 46
  use of penicillinase plasmid from, 53, 54, 299
Streptomyces, see also individual species,
  control systems in, 372
  distinction from *Nocardia,* 140, 531
  interspecific recombination in, 596, 601–605
  production of
    cephamycins by, 130, 131, 452
    glycosides by, 473ff
Streptomyces aburaviensis, 484
Streptomyces achromogenes var. *rubradiris,*
  fertility of, 528, 529
  heteroclone analysis in, 525–528
  map of, 524, 529
  mutation in, 522

Streptomyces achromogenes—*continued*
recombination in, 521ff
Streptomyces antibioticus, 478
Streptomyces atroolivaceus, metabolities of,
484–491
Streptomyces aureofaciens,
biochemical activity of, 171–176
biogenesis of tetracenes and trans-
glucosylation in, 474–477
biosynthetic activity, 157, 159, 160,
285, 473ff
genetics of, 161–163
mutants altered in tetracycline production, 156ff, 474–477
sensitivity to chlortetracycline, 159
ultrastructure of, 163–171
viability of, 159–160
Streptomyces bikiniensis, 519, 522, 523, 525,
545
Streptomyces causius, 596
Streptomyces coelicolor, 521, 531, 532, 536,
545
comparison of map with
A. olivaceus, 557
S. achromogenes, 529
S. rimosus, 517–519, 579
co-mutation in, 514, 573–580
differentiation in, 583ff
genome size of, 518, 568, 576
heteroclone analysis in, 525–527, 554,
565ff
heterokaryons of, 574, 576, 579–580
hybridization with *S. lividans,* 596,
601–605
initiation of formation of aerial mycelium in, 584–589
mapping in, 516–519, 576, 577, 585–
588, 592, 598, 599, 602–604
morphology of, 583, 584
progressive fertilization in, 565ff
recombination deficient mutants of,
618
SCP1 plasmid of, 565–571, 588, 591,
605, 607ff
suppressor-sensitive mutations of,
595ff
Streptomyces cyanocolor, 596
Streptomyces erythreus, 492
Streptomyces galilaeus, 477, 478, 480, 482,
483

Streptomyces glaucescens,
genetics of, 535ff
mapping of, 538–541
medium for, 536
mutagenesis of, 536
Streptomyces griseus, 484, 596, 604
var. 229, 484
Streptomyces lividans, 600
and the SCP1 plasmid, 609, 612–614,
616–618
hybrids with *S. coelicolor,* 596, 601–605
mutant strains of, 597
*Streptomyces mediterranei, see Nocardia
mediterranei*
Streptomyces narbonensis, 492
Streptomyces niveoruber, 478
Streptomyces nogalater, 478
*Streptomyces olivaceas, see also Actinomyces
olivaceus,* 545, 574
Streptomyces olivoreticuli, 484
Streptomyces peuceticus, 478, 482
Streptomyces purpurascens, 478
Streptomyces rimosus, 492, 545, 554
co-mutation in, 516, 517, 579, 580
current map of, 517–519, 529
genetics of, 513ff, 527, 579, 580
genome size of, 518
heterokaryons of, 574, 579, 580
Streptomyces roseoflavus var. *roseofungini,* 588
Streptomyces rubrireticuli, 478
Streptomyces ryensis, 478
Streptomyces scabies, 535, 536, 550
Streptomyces spp., 484
6604–9, 484
4107 A2, 140
LA–7017, 484
X–63, 117
*Streptomyces violaceoruber, see also S.
coelicolor,* 604
Streptomyces violaceus, 478
Streptomycin,
and the *argF*40 mutation, 377
resistance as a genetic marker in
E. coli, 304
Nocardia, 531
Streptomyces, 161–163, 539, 609, 610
resistance of *Methylococcus,* 315
Streptovaricins, 146, 149, 151, 153
Sulphatase activity, relationship to
cephalosporin synthesis, 269, 270

Sulphide, affect on cephalosporin production, 455–457, 463
Suppressiveness,
of nonkiller yeast strains, 335
of petite mutants, 61, 62
Suppressor mutations, 47, 412
in *Streptomyces* and actinophage, 595ff
ochre suppressors, 12
Suppressor-sensitive mutations, 595ff
Synergism, in arginine metabolism, 401–404
Syzigites megalocarpus, 506

T

Temperature-sensitive mutants,
of actinophage, 597, 600, 601
of cultured cells, 81
of *E. coli*, 21, 295
of killer yeast, 334, 335
of *Streptomyces*, 518, 596
of transducing phage, 297
Tetracycline (TCN), 157ff
effect of mutations on synthesis, 156–161, 174–176
Tetracycline-resistance plasmid, pSC101, 53, 54, 299
Tetrad analysis,
of bakers yeast, 350, 351, 353
of brewers yeast, 346–349, 352, 353
of commercial yeast strains, 339ff
of flocculation, 343–347
Thigmotropism, 503–505
Threonine, production of, 445, 446
Tolypomycins, 149, 150, 153
Transcription,
and bacterial sporulation, 46, 421–424
and gene expression, 30–34, 38, 42, 292, 378–379, 584
Transducing phage, 36, 49–51, 296–298, 378, 379
Translation,
and bacterial sporulation, 424–433
and gene expression, 38, 378, 379, 584
Translocations,
in *Aspergillus*, 209
in parasexual crosses, 245
Triethylenemelamine (TEM), 258
Triethyltin, 62

Tripeptide,
in gramicidin S biosynthesis, 120
in penicillin and cephalosporin biosynthesis, 131ff, 264, 265, 269, 452, 453
Trisporic acids, 499–505
structures of, 500
Trophase, 210
Tryptophan, production of, 440
Tyrosinase, 535
genes controlling synthesis of, 542–550
incorporation of glycine into, 541
induction and assay, 537
regulation of, 541, 542
Tyrosine, production of, 438–440

U

Ultrastructure, of *Streptomyces*, 163–171, 562, 588, 592
Ultraviolet light, 61
advantages of as a mutagen, 12, 13, 258
and mitotic recombination, 246
in conjunction with ethyleneimine, 275, 281
in conjunction with *N*-methyl-*N'*-nitro-*N*-nitrosoguanidine, 258
mechanism of mutagenesis by 8, 316
mutation of
actinophage by, 597
Aspergillus and *Penicillium* by, 202, 203, 208, 215, 231
Cephalosporium by, 254, 255, 258–261
E. coli by, 304
Methylococcus by, 315–321
Nocardia by, 531
φX174 by, 12
Streptomyces by, 161, 162, 489, 490, 522, 523, 536, 555
Ultraviolet light sensitivity, of *Cephalosporium* spores, 268
Urocanase, 25, 26

V

Valine,
and arginine metabolism, 404, 405

Valine—*continued*
 involvement in antibiotic biosynthesis,
  130, 131, 133, 135, 210, 264, 268,
  285, 452
Variance(s),
 changes in during selection, 108, 109
 effect of gene action on, 105
 effect of sexual *vs.* parasexual crossing
  on, 107
 environmental, 99, 106, 109, 234, 238,
  239
 genetic, 99, 101, 106, 109, 234, 238, 239
 in quantitative genetics, 96, 97
 phenotypic, 109
Variation,
 due to instability, 244
 in *Cephalosporium,*
  induced, 258
  spontaneous, 256, 258
 in selfs and outcrosses, 234, 235
 of penicillin titres in *Aspergillus,* 232,
  233
Venturicidins, 64. 477
Vibrio, 49
Viruses,
 immunodiffusion   assay   of   titre,
  325, 326, 328, 329
 of *Agaricus,* 330–332
 of industrial fungi, 323ff
 of *Penicillium,* 324–330
 Sendai, 74, 75, 81

X

Xenopus laevis, and expression of genes in
  E. coli, 54, 299
X-irradiation, *see* Ionizing radiation
Xylitol, as a growth-limiting substrate for
  mutant selection, 18

Y

Yeast, *see Saccharomyces cerevisiae* and *S.
  lipolytcia*
"Yeastlike" appearance, of *Mucor,* 507

Z

Zygophores, 499, 500, 502–506
Zygorhynchus, 505

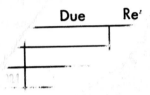